THE RULE BOOK

Other St. Martin's Press books by the Diagram Group

COMPARISONS
HANDTOOLS: THE ENCYCLOPEDIA OF THE FINE, DECORATIVE AND APPLIED ARTS
THE SPORTS FAN'S ULTIMATE BOOK OF SPORTS COMPARISONS
WEAPONS: AN INTERNATIONAL ENCYCLOPEDIA FROM 5000BC to 2000AD

THE DIAGRAM GROUP

THE RULE BOOK

THE AUTHORITATIVE, UP-TO-DATE, ILLUSTRATED GUIDE TO THE REGULATIONS, HISTORY, AND OBJECT OF ALL MAJOR SPORTS

ST. MARTIN'S PRESS
NEW YORK

The Diagram Group

Managing Editor	Ruth Midgley
Editors	Susan Bosanko; David Harding
Contributors	John Bishop; Ruth Cavin; Jan Dalley; David Heidenstam; Carolina Rowley; Caroline Tomalin; Laurence Urdang Associates Ltd; Elizabeth Wilhide
Designer	Debra Lee
Art Editors	Mark Evans; Richard Hummerstone
Artists	Russell Barnett; Sheila Galbraith; Sean Gilbert; Ashley Haddock; Brian Hewson; Elly King; Susan Kinsey; Pavel Kostal; Steven Leverington; Kathleen McDougall; Sean MacGarry; Janos Marffy; Eitetsu Nozawa; Joseph Robinson ; Graham Rosewarne; Max Rutherford; Jerry Wathiss
Art Assistants	Neil Copleston; Jane Robertson

Library of Congress Cataloging in Publication Data
Main entry under title:

The Rule book.

Includes index.
1. Sports—Rules. 2. Sports facilities—Handbooks, manuals, etc. I. Diagram Group.
GV731.R75 1983   796   82-61824
ISBN 0-312-69576-4
ISBN 0-312-00677-2 (pbk.)

FOREWORD

The aim of **The Rule Book** is to provide the reader with an easily accessible and up-to-date reference to the rules and regulations of the world's major sports. Every sports enthusiast – whether on or beside the field of play, or sitting at home watching the television – will find that his or her enjoyment of any sport is greatly enhanced by a better understanding of the current rules of play. Why was that a foul? When am I offside? How does the scoring system work? I've never tried that sport – what will it involve?

In its style of presentation **The Rule Book** follows the now familiar Diagram Group practice of using detailed, explanatory illustrations and diagrams in close conjunction with clear, concise text. This technique is particularly useful for presenting and explaining the intricacies and complexities of sports rules.

During the preparation of this new book the Diagram Group have also had the advantage of being able to draw upon the very considerable experience gained during the preparation of their earlier book **Rules of the Game,** which has appeared in 12 languages and sold more than one million copies since its publication in 1974. **The Rule Book,** with its 150,000 words and 5000 illustrations, is the Diagram Group's biggest sports book to date.

The Rule Book includes more than 50 Olympic and other major sports. For each sport there is a brief historical introduction and synopsis, as well as sections on such features as the playing area and equipment, players and officials, duration and scoring, starting and playing procedures, and major fouls and penalties. The guidelines adopted for **The Rule Book** have been the international rules and laws of the various sports.

Without the cooperation and very considerable assistance of the many sports governing bodies who have supplied rule books, answered queries, and checked the text and illustrations for accuracy, this book could never have been completed. With their help, it is hoped that the Diagram Group has been able, once again, to provide the sports enthusiast with a truly invaluable work of reference.

SPORTS BODIES AND CONSULTANTS

National Archery Association (USA)
Grand National Archery Society (UK)
International Badminton Federation
National Baseball Congress (USA)
American Association of College Baseball Coaches
British Amateur Baseball and Softball Federation
Fédération Internationale de Basketball Amateur
Dr Edward S. Steitz (basketball)
British Bobsleigh Association
Wing Commander Mike Freeman (bobsleigh)
Amateur Boxing Association (UK)
British Boxing Board of Control
British Canoe Union
Test and County Cricket Board (UK)
British Cycling Federation
Jenny MacArthur (equestrianism)
Fédération Internationale d'Escrime (fencing)
Amateur Fencing Association (UK)
National Football League (USA)
National Football League of Australia
Canadian Amateur Football Association
Canadian Football League
The Rugby Football League (UK)
Rugby Football Union (UK)
British Amateur Gymnastics Association
Nik Stuart (gymnastics)
US Handball Association (court handball)
British Handball Association (team handball)
Hockey Rules Board (UK, field hockey)
British Ice Hockey Association
International Judo Federation
British Judo Association
English Lacrosse Union
All England Women's Lacrosse Association
Fédération Internationale de Luge de Course
Christopher Dyason (luge)
Union Internationale du Pentathlon Moderne et Biathlon
National Paddle Ball Association (USA)

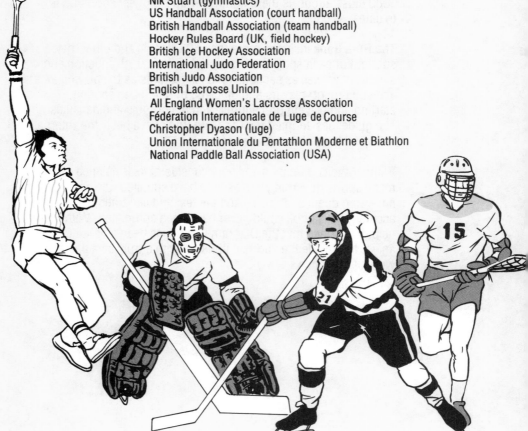

US Polo Association
The Hurlingham Polo Association (UK)
Billiard Congress of America (pool)
American Amateur Racquetball Association
Amateur Rowing Association (UK)
Union Internationale de Tir (shooting)
National Rifle Association of America
International Skating Union
Canadian Figure Skating Association
National Skating Association of Great Britain
Fédération Internationale de Ski
National Ski Federation of Great Britain
Colonel John Moore (biathlon)
The Billiards and Snooker Control Council (UK)
The Football Association (UK, soccer)
Amateur Softball Association of America
US Squash Rackets Association
The Squash Rackets Association (UK)
Fédération Internationale de Natation Amateur (swimming sports)
Amateur Swimming Association (UK, swimming sports)
International Table Tennis Federation
English Table Tennis Association
US Tennis Association
The Lawn Tennis Association (UK)
American Bowling Congress (tenpin bowling)
British Tenpin Bowling Association
Amateur Athletics Association (UK)
D.R. Littlewood (track and field athletics)
United States Volleyball Association
Canadian Volleyball Association
English Volleyball Association
International Weightlifting Federation
British Amateur Weight Lifters' Association
Commonwealth Weightlifting Federation
Fédération Internationale de Lutte Amateur (wrestling)
British Amateur Wrestling Association
Royal Yachting Association (UK)

CONTENTS

Explanation of symbols

a) A flag symbol indicates that a sport is to be included in the 1984 Olympic program.

b) One colored player symbol on its own indicates that a sport is for individuals or that only one player competes at any time.

c) Two or more colored player symbols indicate the maximum number of players per side or team that are permitted to play at any time: it does not include substitutes.

d) Colored and white player symbols together indicate the minimum (colored) and the normal maximum (colored and white) number of participants per side or team.

Measurements in this book are given either in metric or in US customary/imperial units according to the current practice of the governing bodies of the sports concerned.

ARCHERY (TARGET)

HISTORY
The modern bow used for competition target archery is a descendant of the longbow of medieval Europe, and competitive target archery today has survived broadly unchanged since the days of Robin Hood. Target archery was included in the Olympic Games of 1900, 1904, 1908 and 1920, but was then dropped until 1972, when it was reintroduced in response to a great upsurge in the sport's popularity. The international governing body for the sport is the Fédération Internationale de Tir à l'Arc (FITA), formed in 1931.

SYNOPSIS
Target archery competitions at all levels of the sport consist of shooting a specified number of arrows over a series of prescribed distances at targets of approved design. Target faces are marked with concentric circles, and points are scored according to the position of the arrow shafts in the target. Competition details vary according to the sex, age, and proficiency of the competitors. At Olympic Games and world championships, competitors shoot two FITA rounds, comprising a total of 288 arrows from four different distances.

RANGE AND TARGETS
The range is divided into lanes at least 5m wide, with one to three (usually two) targets per lane. Men (**A**) and women (**B**) are separated by a clear lane.

For major tournaments, there is a permanent shooting line (**1**), with a waiting line (**2**) at least 5m behind it. Also marked are target lines for the different shooting distances (90m, 70m, 50m, and 30m for men; 70m, 60m, 50m, and 30m for women), measured from a point vertically beneath the gold of each target back to the shooting line.

In club shooting, the target line is usually permanent and the shooting line and waiting line moved up for each distance.

Buttresses, on which the target faces are mounted, may be either round or square, with a maximum dimension of 124cm in any direction.

Buttresses are set up at an angle of about 15° to the vertical. When mounted on the buttress, the center of the gold is to be 130cm above ground level.

Each buttress is pegged securely to the ground, and carries a number 30cm square.

130cm   15°

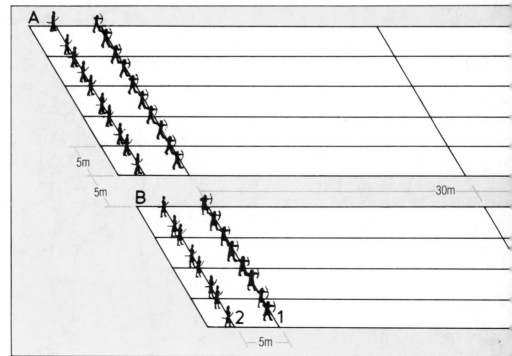

A

5m

5m

B

30m

2 1

5m

Target faces There are two standard circular FITA target faces of 122cm and 80cm diameters. The larger target face is used at 90m, 70m, and 60m distances, the smaller target face at 50m and 30m.

Target faces are divided into 10 concentric scoring zones of equal width: 6.1cm on the 122cm target face, and 4cm on the 80cm target face.

They are also divided into five concentric color zones, which give scores as follows:

white (outer) 1 point; white (inner) 2 points;
black (outer) 3 points; black (inner) 4 points;
blue (outer) 5 points; blue (inner) 6 points;
red (outer) 7 points; red (inner) 8 points;
gold (outer) 9 points; gold (inner) 10 points.

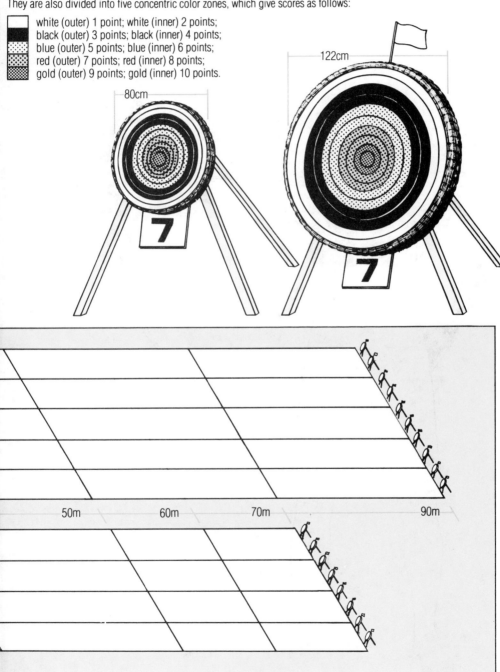

© DIAGRAM

EQUIPMENT

The bow Any form of bow is allowed provided it conforms to the accepted principle and meaning of the word as used in target archery. For example, it must have a handle (grip) (**a**), riser (**b**), and two flexible limbs (**c**) each ending in a tip (**d**) with a string nock (**e**). A single bowstring (**f**) is to be attached directly between the two string nocks only. One lip or nose mark (**g**) is allowed on the string.

Also permitted are an arrowrest, which may be adjustable, and any moveable pressure button, pressure point, or arrowplate and draw check indicator provided they are not electric or electronic and do not offer any additional aid in aiming.

Either a bowsight or a single bowmark is permitted; alternatively the archer may place a "point of aim" mark on the range. All are subject to specific regulations.

Certain attachments, including lenses, prisms, rearsights, and mechanical releases are forbidden. Torque flight compensators and stabilizers (**h**) are permitted subject to specific regulations.

Arrows must conform to the accepted principle and meaning of the word arrow as used in target archery, and must not cause undue damage to targets.

An arrow consists of a nock (**A**), shaft (**B**), and arrow head (point) (**C**) with fletching (**D**) and, if desired, cresting (**E**).

Each archer's arrows must be marked with his name, initials, or insignia, and all arrows used for the same end must be similarly fletched and crested.

Other equipment On the drawing hand, a glove (**1**), or shooting tab (**2**), finger stalls or tips, or tape may be used for protection.

On the bow hand an ordinary glove or mitten may be worn.

Field glasses, telescopes, and other visual aids may be used for spotting arrows.

Correcting eyeglasses and sunglasses may be worn as necessary, but must not be modified to assist in aiming.

Permitted accessories include a bracer (**3**),   (**4**), dress shield (**5**), and a ground or belt quiver (**6**).

Foot markers must not protrude more than 1cm above the ground.

Dress Normal clothing is worn.

Competitors must wear their target numbers on their backs.

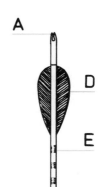

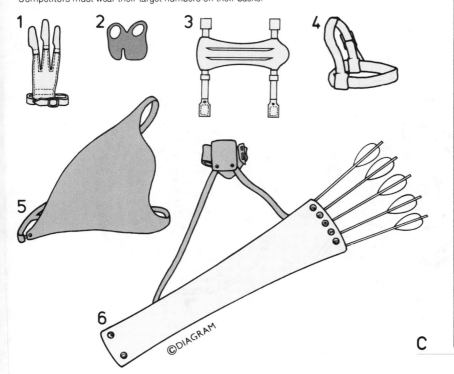

©DIAGRAM

13

ARCHERY (TARGET) 3

COMPETITORS AND OFFICIALS

Competitors Archers compete as individuals and as teams. World championships and Olympic Games are for individuals only. National teams comprise three archers.

Officials These may include: an organizing committee; a director of shooting (or field captain) and his deputy; a scores committee; scorers (one per target); and a technical commission of at least five members.

TOURNAMENT RULES

Form of tournament A complete tournament is either one or two FITA rounds (two at world championships and Olympic Games). A FITA round consists of 144 arrows (36 at each of four distances). Distances shot are:

men: 90m, 70m, 50m, 30m;

women: 70m, 60m, 50m, 30m.

A single round may be shot over one or two days. Distances are shot in order from the longest to the shortest. If shot over two days, the two longest distances are shot on the first day.

Starting A draw is used to allocate archers to targets. There is a maximum of four (preferably three) archers to each target.

Under the control of the field captain, each competitor begins each day with six sighting arrows, which are not scored.

The shooting then divides into ends of three arrows from each archer.

Shooting Except for the disabled, shooting is from an unsupported standing position, with a foot on each side of the shooting line.

The bow is held in one hand by its handle (grip) while the fingers of the other hand draw, hold back, and release the string.

Archers shoot in turn, usually one archer per target. The target group member who shoots first changes with each end.

During an end an archer shoots three arrows consecutively, then returns behind the waiting line while other members of the group shoot.

Each archer has a maximum of 2½ minutes for these three arrows, from the moment he steps up to the shooting line. A warning signal is given after two minutes. Twenty seconds is allowed between archers. Time signaling is by whistle blasts in conjunction with colored lights, striped plates, or digital clocks. Any arrow shot outside the allotted time for an end forfeits the highest scoring arrow of that end.

a

b

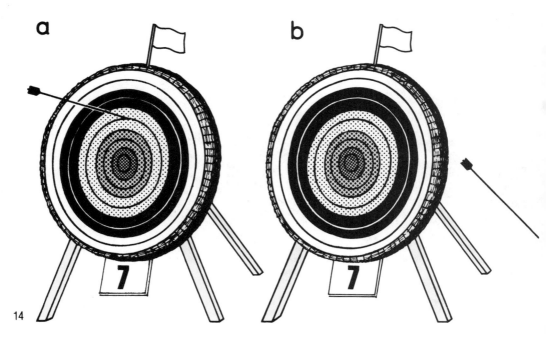

While on the shooting line archers may not receive any information, unless it is necessary for making essential changes in their equipment.

An arrow is not regarded as being shot (and may be retrieved and then shot) if the archer can touch it with his bow without moving his feet from their position at the shooting line.

Scoring At 90m, 70m, and 60m distances, scoring is after every second end (in world championships, regional championships, and Olympic Games) or after each end. At 50m and 30m distances scoring is always after each end.

Archers call their own scores, with other archers in the group verifying.

No archer may touch the arrows or the target face until the scores have been verified.

Scores are determined by the position of the arrow shaft on the target face.

An arrow touching two colors or a dividing line scores the higher value (**a**).

An arrow passing through the target (**b**), an arrow rebounding from the target, or an arrow rebounding from another arrow, will only score if their marks on the target face or arrow can be identified.

An arrow embedded in another arrow scores the same as that arrow (**c**).

An arrow deflected from another arrow scores as it lies in the target (**d**).

Arrows that hit the wrong target or hit their target after rebounding from the ground do not score.

An archer who has shot too many arrows scores only the three (or six) lowest in value; repeating this offense may result in disqualification.

After arrows have been drawn from the target, all holes are marked.

Result Competitions are won by the archer with the highest total score after the prescribed rounds have been completed.

Ties (individuals) If the score total is tied, the winner is the archer with the greatest number of scoring hits. If a tie persists, the winner is the archer with most golds, and then the most hits scoring nine points. If a tie still persists the archers are declared equal.

Ties (teams) In team competitions ties are decided in favor of the tying team that contains the archer with the highest individual score; then, if the tie persists, in favor of the tying team containing the archer with the second highest individual score. If the tie still persists, the tying teams are declared equal.

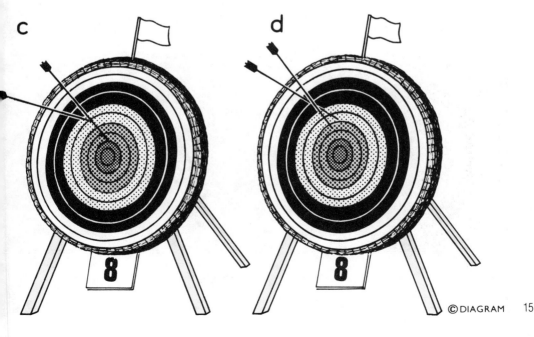

BADMINTON

HISTORY

Badminton takes its name from the home of an English duke, the Duke of Beaufort. Based on a children's game known as battledore and shuttlecock, the game that later came to be known as badminton is believed to have been developed by adults at a house party at Badminton, Gloucestershire, in about 1870. The new game is known to have been popular among British Army officers in India in the 1870s and to have developed a following in England. The Badminton Association of England was formed in 1893 and produced a standard set of rules. Rules given here are those of the international governing body, the International Badminton Federation (IBF), which was founded in 1934. Official world championships for men and for women were first held in 1977, and are to take place every two years.

SYNOPSIS

Badminton is a game for two players (singles) or four players (doubles) played with rackets and a shuttlecock on a court divided by a net. The object is to score points by striking the shuttle so that it lands inside the court on the opponent's side of the net. It is a relatively simple game to learn for recreation, but competition play is extremely fast and requires high levels of skill and fitness.

COURT AND EQUIPMENT

The court Illustrated here is a court marked out for doubles or singles play; courts for singles play only may be marked out where there is insufficient space for doubles.
A standard badminton court is 44ft long and 20ft wide. Lines, 1½in wide and included within the overall dimensions of the court, are marked in white, yellow, or some other easily distinguishable color.
Court markings are as follows: back boundary line and long service line for singles (**a**), long service line for doubles (**b**), side line for doubles (**c**), side line for singles (**d**), center line (**e**), short service line (**f**). Right service courts (**g**) and left service courts (**h**) are bounded by the long and short service lines, side lines, and center lines.
Long service lines for doubles are 2ft 6in in front of the back lines. Short service lines are 15ft 6in in front of the back lines and 13ft apart. Side lines for singles are 1ft 6in inside the side lines for doubles.

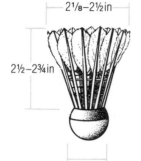

2¹⁄₈–2½in

2½–2¾in

1–1¹⁄₈in

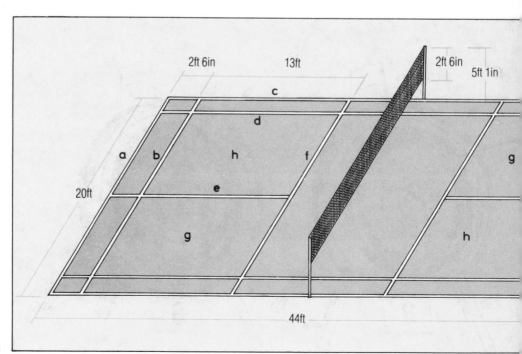

The net is stretched across the center of the court. It is 2ft 6in deep and made of dark-colored, natural cord or artificial fiber with a mesh size of $5/8-3/4$in.

It is supported by a cord or cable, which is threaded through doubled white tape at the top of the net and strained over and flush with the top of two posts. The top of the net must be 5ft above the floor at the center and 5ft 1in above the floor at the posts.

The posts must be 5ft 1in high and firm enough to keep the net taut. Where possible they should be positioned on the side boundary lines. If the posts are positioned outside the court area, a thin post or strip of material at least 1½in wide should be fixed to the boundary line and rise vertically to the upper edge of the net.

Racket There are no rules governing the type of racket to be used for badminton. A typical modern badminton racket is illustrated here.

Shuttle A standard shuttle has from 14 to 16 feathers fixed in a cork base, and weighs 73–85 grains (4.74–5.50g). The cork is 1–1⅛in in diameter. The feathers measure 2½–2¾in from their tips to the top of the cork base. They must have a spread of 2⅛–2½in at the top and must be firmly fastened with thread or some other material. Provided there is no substantial variation in performance, modified shuttles (eg made of nylon or plastic) are allowed subject to the approval of national organizations involved.

Dress For international matches, clothing should be predominantly white or of a color approved by the players' national organization.

PLAYERS AND OFFICIALS

Players The game is played by two players (singles) or four players (doubles). The player or pair with the right to serve are termed the "in" side; the opposition is the "out" side.

Officials Games are supervised by an umpire, who may be assisted by linesmen and a service judge. The umpire's decision is final on all points of fact, but he must accept as fact all line decisions by the linesmen, and service decisions by the service judge. If a tournament has an overall referee, a player may appeal to him on points of law only.

DURATION AND SCORING

Duration Play is continuous from the delivery of the first service until the match is completed, except that an interval of up to five minutes is permitted between the second and third games in international matches and in countries where climatic conditions make this desirable.

The umpire has the right to suspend play at any time in response to conditions outside the control of the players. Under no circumstances may play be suspended to allow a player to recover his strength or breath, or to receive instruction or advice.

Scoring A match generally consists of the best of three games, although a one-game match may be played by prior arrangement.

In doubles and men's singles, the usual game consists of 15 points, with the option of "setting" (see below) the game at 13 or 14 points. In a one-game match, the game may consist of 21 points, with the option of setting at 19 or 20 points. In women's singles, a game consists of 11 points, with the option of setting at 9 or 10 points.

Only the serving side can score: 1 point is scored when the receiving side commits a fault.

Setting is a procedure whereby a new deciding score is established when both sides have equal scores just short of the original points total required.

In a 15-point game, setting may be to 5 at 13-all, or to 3 at 14-all. In a 21-point game, setting may be to 5 at 19-all or to 3 at 20-all. In an 11-point game, setting may be to 3 at 9-all or to 2 at 10-all.

The option to set the game belongs to the side that first reached the appropriate number of points. Claims to set must be made before the next service after the specified equal scores are reached. Rejection of the option to set at the first opportunity does not prohibit a side from setting if a second opportunity arises.

After a game has been set, the score is called "love all." Play then proceeds normally until one side reaches the new total required—5, 3, or 2 points as specified above.

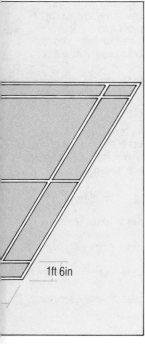

1ft 6in

BADMINTON 2

RULES OF PLAY

Choice of ends and service is determined by a toss. The winner of the toss has the option of serving first, receiving first, or of choosing ends. The side losing the toss is then given the choice of any alternative remaining.

Change of ends Players change ends after each game, and during the third game when the leading side's score reaches 6 points in an 11-point game, 8 points in a 15-point game, and 11 points in a 21-point game.

If players fail to change ends at the appropriate time, they should do so as soon as the mistake is noticed. Any score stands.

Service order (singles) A player retains the right to serve until he commits a fault. The service then passes to his opponent.

The service court from which a service is made is always determined by the serving player's score. If his score is 0 or an even number, he serves from his right service court (**A**). If his score is an odd number, he serves from his left service court (**B**). A service must send the shuttle into the service court diagonally opposite the one from which the service is made.

Service order (doubles) At the start of a doubles game, pairs decide which of them will serve or receive first.

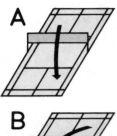

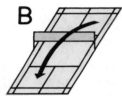

Players must always serve into the service court diagonally opposite. Service order and changing of service courts is determined as follows.

1) The first player to serve (**a**) serves from his right service court to the player who is to receive first (**b**).

2) If the serving pair wins the first point, the first server (**a**) then serves from his left service court to the second player of the receiving pair (**c**). As long as the serving pair continues to score, player (**a**) retains the service and serves from alternating courts to each opponent in turn.

3) When the first pair to serve fails to score from a rally, service passes to the opponent in the right service court (**b**). He serves to the player who was diagonally opposite him in the previous rally—player (**d**) in the example illustrated.

4) If the serving pair scores a point, player (**b**) then serves from his left service court to the opponent who did not receive in the previous rally—player (**a**) in our example. As long as the serving pair continues to score, player (**b**) retains the service, serving from alternate courts to each opponent in turn.

5) If the serving pair fails to score from a rally, the service passes to the serving player's partner (**c**). Player (**c**) serves from the service court that was not used in the previous rally and serves to the opponent who did not receive in that rally—player (**d**) in the example illustrated. Player (**c**) retains the service until a point is lost, serving from alternate courts to each opponent in turn.

6) Service then passes to player (**d**), the partner of the first player to serve. His first service is from the court that was not used in the previous rally and is to the opponent who did not last receive. As long as the serving pair scores, player (**c**) continues to serve from alternate courts to each opponent in turn.

After player (**d**) loses the service it reverts to player (**a**). Starting by serving from the service court not used in the previous rally and to the player who did not last receive, player (**a**) then serves from alternate courts and to each player in turn until his side fails to score. Thereafter service passes from player to player in accordance with the order and procedures described above.

Winning a game gives a pair the right to serve first in the next game; either winner may serve first and either loser may be first to receive.

Error in service order If a player serves out of turn or from the wrong service court and his side wins the rally, a let may be allowed.

If a service is received by a player who stood ready to receive it in the wrong service court and his side wins the rally, a let may be allowed.

A let must be agreed to or ordered by the referee before the next service is made; otherwise the error stands and the players' positions are not corrected.

If in any of the above cases the offending player loses the rally, the mistake stands and the players' positions are not corrected.

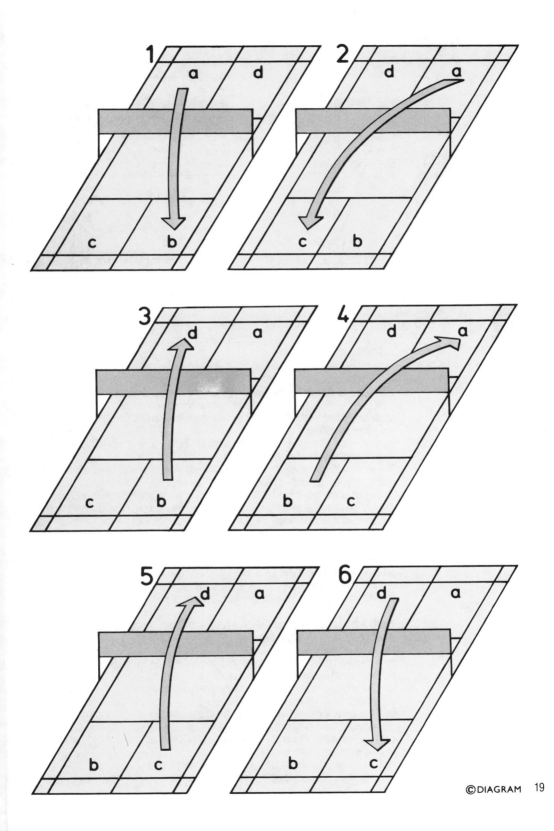

BADMINTON 3

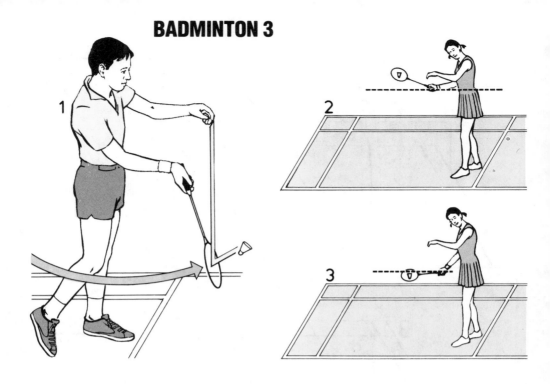

Service and return For the service (**1**), both the server and the receiver must be completely within (and not on the lines of) their correct service courts, and must keep some part of both of their feet in contact with the ground until the shuttle is delivered (struck by the racket).

Partners of the server and receiver may adopt any position, provided that they do not unsight or otherwise obstruct an opponent.

The server may not serve until the receiver is ready. A receiver who makes any attempt to return a service cannot then claim that he was not ready for it. If the server misses the shuttle while attempting to serve, it is not a fault and he may attempt a new service action. After the service is delivered, the server and the receiver are permitted to adopt any positions on their own side of the net, regardless of any boundary lines.

Only the player served to is permitted to receive a service; if the shuttle touches the proper receiver's partner, the serving pair gains a point.

Provided the service is good, the receiver must make a good return. (For prohibited actions, see Faults and Lets.) Any return must be made before the shuttle touches the ground. After the service and initial return, either player of a pair may make a return. Play continues with the shuttle being sent from one side of the net to the other until there is a fault or a let.

Fault A fault made by a player of the serving side causes the right to serve to pass to the other side. A fault made by a player of the receiving side gives a point to the serving side. Faults occur as follows.

a) If, in serving, the shuttle is struck when above the server's waist (**2**), or if the initial point of contact with the shuttle is not on the base of the shuttle.

b) If, in serving, the whole of the head of the racket is not completely below the whole of the server's hand holding the racket (**3**).

c) If the feet of the server are not within the appropriate service court and partly on the ground when the service is delivered.

d) If the feet of the receiver are not within the appropriate service court and partly on the ground when the service is delivered.

e) If, in serving, the shuttle lands outside the correct service court.

f) If any player seeks to obtain an unfair advantage by deliberately delaying making a service or getting ready to receive service.

g) If, once a service has started (when server and receiver are in position and the server has made his first forward movement with his racket), any player makes a preliminary feint or otherwise intentionally balks his opponent.

h) If, in service or in play, the shuttle falls outside the boundaries of the court (**4, 5**).

i) If the shuttle passes through or under the net (**6**). (It is not a fault if the shuttle touches the net before passing over it, or if the shuttle passes outside one of the posts and then lands within the court beyond the net.)

j) If the shuttle touches the roof or side walls, or the person or dress of a player (**7**).

k) If a player's initial contact with the shuttle in play is not on his own side of the net (**8**). (It is not a fault if a player's racket follows the shuttle over the net in the course of a stroke.)

l) If, when the shuttle is in play, a player touches the net or a post with his racket, person, or dress.

m) If the shuttle is caught and held on the racket and then slung during a stroke.

n) If the shuttle is hit twice in succession by the same player.

o) If the shuttle is hit successively by a player and his partner (**9**).

p) If, in play, a player strikes the shuttle (except to make a good return) or is struck by it, whether or not he is inside the court boundaries.

q) If a player obstructs an opponent. (It is counted as obstruction if a player's racket or person invades the opponent's court, except during the follow-through of a stroke. It is also obstruction if, when his opponent has a chance of striking the shuttle in a downward direction quite near the net, a player raises his racket near the net on the chance that the shuttle will rebound from it; a player may, however, hold up his racket to protect his face, provided that he does not thereby balk his opponent.)

Lets If a let occurs, play since the last service is not counted. The server who served at the start of the discounted rally makes another service, except when the let is due to an error in service order.

A let may be declared:

a) in some situations where there has been an error in serving order;

b) if, during a service or rally, the shuttle lodges in or on the net after first passing over it;

c) if the receiver is faulted for moving before the service or for being in the wrong service court and the server is faulted at the same time for a service infringement.

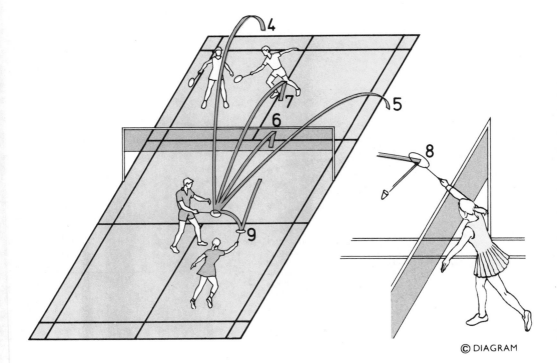

© DIAGRAM

BASEBALL

HISTORY

Developed from rounders, a British children's game, baseball was imported to the American colonies in the eighteenth century, where it was known as town ball and by other names. Gradually, the infield evolved to its present diamond shape, flat plates replaced the upright posts used as bases, field positions were established, and baseball became the 18-player, nine-inning game it is today. The first professional baseball game in the United States between organized clubs took place on June 19, 1846, in Hoboken, New Jersey. Known as ''America's national game,'' baseball is played throughout North and Central America, in Japan and other countries in the Far East, and in Europe.

SYNOPSIS

Baseball is played between two teams of nine players each. In nine periods called innings, teams alternate in batting and fielding. The object is for batters to reach first base by one or another means and advance around the bases to home base (commonly, home plate) without being put out, thereby scoring a run. A team remains at bat in any one inning until three players have been legally put out, when the teams change positions. At the end of nine innings (with certain exceptions) the team with more runs has won.

PLAYING AREA AND EQUIPMENT

The playing area consists of an infield (**1**) and an outfield (**2**). These two areas, including boundary lines, are fair territory; any other area is foul territory.

The infield is a 90ft square (the ''diamond''), with a base at each corner: home base (**a**),

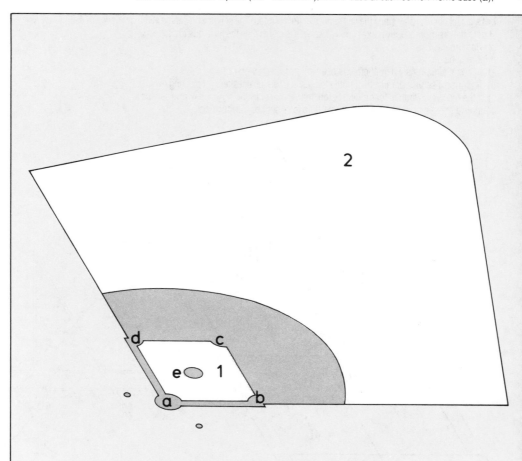

first base (**b**), second base (**c**), and third base (**d**). The pitcher's plate (**e**) is positioned 60ft 6in from the rear point of home base; it is set in an 18ft diameter circle, on the flattened top of a low mound, 10in higher than home base.

The outfield is the area between the two foul lines (**f**) formed by extending two sides of the square. It is not of uniform size from one ballfield to another. However, there must be at least 250ft from home base to the nearest obstruction in fair territory. For professional play, there must be 325ft or more along the foul lines and at least 400ft to center field. It is recommended that there be at least 60ft from home base to any boundary beyond the playing area.

Most of the playing area is covered with natural or artificial turf; other areas are bare earth. Marked in white on the field are the foul lines (**f**), the 3ft first base lines (**g**), and lines around the batter's boxes (**h**), the catcher's box (**i**), the coaches' boxes (**j**), and the next batter's boxes (**k**).

Home plate (A) is a 17in square of whitened rubber with two corners cut off to form a pentagon of the dimensions shown. The point opposite the longest side is placed at the intersection of the lines from first and third base.

Other bases (B) are marked by white canvas bags, 15in square, 3-5in thick, and filled with soft material. Bags at first and third base are placed entirely within the infield; the bag at second base is centered on the base.

The pitcher's plate (C) – commonly "the rubber" – is a rectangular slab of whitened rubber 24in long by 6in wide.

Players' benches, one for each team, must not be less than 25ft from the base lines.

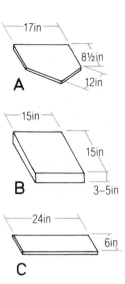

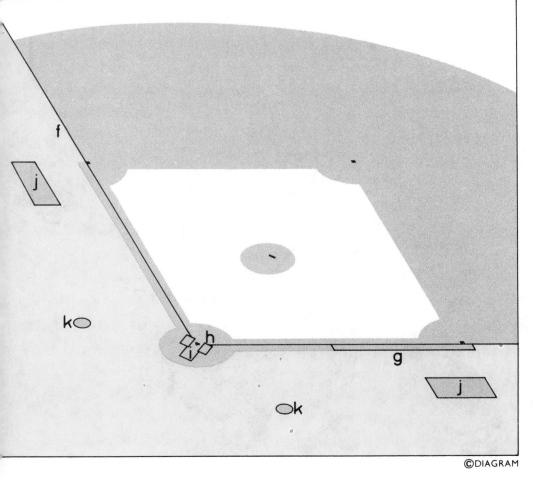

©DIAGRAM

BASEBALL 2

2¾in

42in

9–9¼in

The bat may be up to 42in long, and up to 2¾in in diameter at its thickest part. It should be smooth and rounded, and, for professional play, made from a single piece of wood, or of laminated wood whose grain is parallel to the length of the bat. Aluminum bats are not permitted for professional play.

The handle section may be covered with tape, or treated with pine tar or other materials to improve the grip, providing that such materials do not extend more than 18in from the end. Cupped bats, whose thicker ends are concave rather than convex, are permitted providing that the indentation in the end of the bat conforms to specific regulations. Colored bats may be used only with special permission.

The ball is made of yarn wound around a cork, rubber, or similar core, and covered with tightly stitched white horsehide or cowhide. It must weigh 5–5¼oz, and have a circumference of 9–9¼in.

Players may not damage or discolor the ball by rubbing it with sandpaper or other prohibited substances.

A supply of replacement balls must be available at all times during the game. A new ball may be put into play:
a) when the ball has been batted out of the playing field or into a spectator area;
b) when the existing ball has become discolored or otherwise unfit for further use:
c) at the request of the pitcher.

Dress All members of a team must wear shirts, pants, and socks that are identical in color, trim, and style. Sleeve lengths may vary from player to player, but the sleeves of each individual player should be the same on both arms. Exposed undershirts must be of a uniform solid color.

All players must wear identifying numbers at least 6in high on the backs of their shirts. Glass buttons, polished metal, and patterns imitating or suggesting a baseball are prohibited on players' uniforms.

Shoes may be fitted with shoe plates or toe plates, but pointed spikes are prohibited. Certain protective equipment may be worn by the fielders, providing it conforms with specific dimensions and specifications. A catcher (**A**) may wear a leather mitt, protective chest pad, protective mask, and knee and shin pads. The first baseman may wear a leather mitt or glove; other fielders may wear a leather glove. The pitcher may wear a glove which must be of uniform color all over, and may not be white or gray.

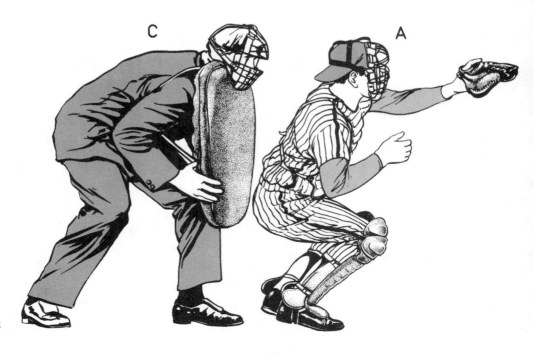

C   A

When batting, a player (**B**) must wear a protective helmet; helmets resembling ordinary caps, but made of hard plastic, are gradually being replaced by a more effective type of helmet that covers the temples and the ears.

PLAYERS AND OFFICIALS

Players A team consists of nine players, and a number of substitutes.
Fielding positions are as listed and shown in the diagram.
Each team's batting order must be handed to the umpire before the beginning of the game, and that order must then be followed except when a substitution is made. The player to pitch to the first batter should be indicated with the batting order.

Substitutions may be made at any time during the game when the ball is dead. Substituting players must bat in the same position as the player being replaced. Once removed from the game, a player may not reenter it. If approved by the league involved, a player (the "designated hitter") may be named in the batting order to bat for the pitcher each time it is the pitcher's turn to bat. The pitcher continues to pitch unless replaced by a substitute, for whom the designated hitter also bats. The designated hitter takes no other part in the game. He may be replaced by a substitute designated hitter, but once replaced may not reenter the game in any capacity. No multiple substitutions may be made that will alter the batting rotation of the designated hitter.

Officials The game is controlled by up to four umpires. The umpire-in-chief is also the plate umpire (**C**), and stands behind the catcher to judge all decisions on pitching and batting. The other umpires are responsible for making decisions on the bases. An official scorer is responsible for recording the progress of the game.

Team officials The manager is responsible for the administration of the team and its conduct. He is assisted by uniformed coaches, who direct the actions of the batter and base runners from their positions in the coaches' boxes.

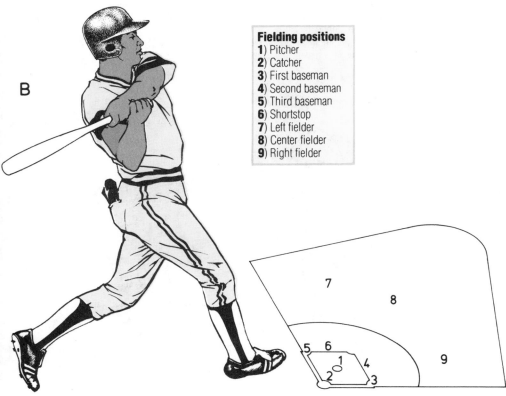

B

Fielding positions
1) Pitcher
2) Catcher
3) First baseman
4) Second baseman
5) Third baseman
6) Shortstop
7) Left fielder
8) Center fielder
9) Right fielder

BASEBALL 3

DURATION

Duration A regulation game normally consists of nine innings. Each inning is in two parts: the "top," or first part, when the visiting team bats, and the "bottom," when the home team bats. A half-inning ends when three members of the batting team have been legally put out (three "outs").

If the home team is leading after 8½ innings, the bottom of the ninth is not played. The game may also end during the bottom of the ninth if the home team scores a winning run in their half of the inning.

If the score of a game is tied at the end of nine innings, play continues for any number of innings necessary to break the tie.

Called game A game in which, for any reason, the umpire-in-chief stops play (a "called game") is considered a regulation game if:

a) five innings have been completed; or

b) the home team is leading in four or four-and-a-fraction innings, and the visiting team have completed five innings; or

c) the home team scores one or more runs in its half of the fifth inning to make the score a tie.

If the game is called before these conditions are met, it is considered a no game.

If a game that has gone on long enough to be a regulation game is called when the score is tied, it is considered a tie game and must be replayed.

Suspended game A game may be suspended if it is interrupted by lack of light, weather, or other external circumstances, and has progressed far enough to be considered a regulation game. It is then resumed at some later date at the exact point of suspension.

Time is the announcement by an umpire of a legal interruption during play, during which the ball is considered dead. Time may be called:

a) because of weather or light conditions;

b) because of an accident to a player or umpire;

c) at a manager's request, for a substitution or player consultation;

d) when a fielder falls out of the playing area after catching a batted ball that goes high in the air in flight (a fly ball);

e) when an umpire ejects a player;

f) for any other reason at the discretion of the umpire.

A

RULES OF PLAY

Starting play Players from the home team take up their fielding positions, and the first batter from the visiting team takes his place in the batter's box.

The game begins on the umpire's call of "Play"; the ball then becomes alive and in play, and only becomes dead when the umpire calls "Time," or for other legal cause.

When the ball is put into play, all fielders except the catcher and the pitcher may place themselves anywhere within fair territory. The pitcher should take up his legal position on the mound. The catcher should stand or crouch directly behind home plate; he may leave his position at any time to field a ball, except that if the pitcher is giving an intentional base on balls, the catcher must not leave his box until the ball has left the pitcher's hand.

Fielding A fielder tags a base when he touches that base with his body when holding the ball securely in his hand or glove (**A**). He tags a runner when he touches that runner with the ball, or with his hand or glove holding the ball (**B**).

A fielder makes a catch when he gains secure possession of the ball in flight with his hand or glove, providing that he does not use any other part of his uniform in his attempt to gain possession. He must hold the ball long enough to prove that he has complete control of it, and that his release of it is voluntary.

A fielder who handles a batted ball that rolls or bounces on the ground in fair territory may choose to throw the ball at first base in an attempt to put out the batter-runner, or may throw it to another base in order to put out a preceding runner.

A fielder who is not in possession of the ball, and who is not attempting to field the ball may not impede the progress of any runner.

A fielder may not touch the ball with any part of his uniform detached from its proper place on his person, or throw his glove or any part of his uniform at the ball.

B

BASEBALL 4

Pitching positions There are two legal pitching positions – the windup position and the set position. Either may be used at any time.

A) In the windup position the pitcher holds the ball with both hands in front of his body and stands facing the batter. The pitcher's pivot foot should be on, or in front of and touching but not off the end of, the rubber. His other foot is free, and with it he may take one step backward and one step forward during his delivery of the ball. He may not lift his pivot foot from the ground. Any movement from the full windup position that is associated with the pitcher's actual pitch commits him to completing the pitch without stopping or changing.

B) Before taking up the set position, the player may stretch (**1**). He should next hold the ball with both hands in front of his body, and stand facing the batter. The whole of the pitcher's pivot foot should be on, or in front of and touching but not off the end of, the rubber. His other foot should be in front of the pitcher's plate. He must then come to a complete stop (**2**). From the set position the pitcher may deliver the ball to the batter, step backward off the rubber with his pivot foot, or throw to a base. After coming to a stop, any natural motion associated with delivering the ball to the batter commits the pitcher to an unaltered and uninterrupted pitch.

Pitching At the beginning of each half-inning, or when a relief pitcher enters the game, the pitcher may take up to eight practice pitches. In an emergency, such as injury to a preceding pitcher, the umpire may decide how many practice pitches to allow.

The pitcher may throw to a base at any time before his natural pitching motion commits him to deliver the ball to the batter, providing that he steps directly toward the base before making the throw.

A

B1

B2

If the pitcher steps backward off the rubber (**C**), and thus removes his pivot foot from contact with the pitching plate, he becomes an infielder and any throws he makes are governed by the rules governing fielders' throws.

A pitcher may apply rosin to his hands from the officially supplied rosin bag; he may not apply the rosin to any other part of his person, uniform, or glove.

A pitcher may not:

a) deface the ball in any way;

b) affect the surface of the ball by rubbing it with a foreign substance, spitting on it, or rubbing it on his person or clothing (**D**) except that he may rub the ball between his bare hands;

c) put his hands to his mouth while in the 18ft circle surrounding the rubber, except that he may receive permission to blow on his hands in cold weather;

d) carry any foreign substance;

e) delay the game by throwing the ball to fielders other than the catcher when the batter is in position, except in an attempt to catch a runner off base;

f) wait more than 20sec after receiving the ball from the catcher before making the next pitch when there is no-one on a base;

g) intentionally direct the ball at the batter's body.

Balk If a runner or runners are on base, it is a balk (an illegal act by the pitcher entitling all runners to advance one base) if the pitcher while touching the pitching plate:

a) makes a motion naturally associated with his pitching motion, but does not deliver the ball;

b) feints a throw to first base but does not make the throw;

c) does not step toward a base before throwing to that base;

d) throws, or feints a throw, toward an unoccupied base, except for the purpose of making a play;

e) makes a quick or other illegal pitch;

f) pitches without facing the batter;

g) unnecessarily delays the game;

h) does not have the ball;

i) comes to a legal pitching position and removes a hand from the ball except when actually pitching or throwing to a base;

j) accidentally or intentionally drops the ball;

k) in giving an intentional base on balls, pitches when the catcher is out of his box;

l) pitches from the set position without coming to a stop.

It is also a balk if the pitcher makes any movement normally associated with his pitch, or otherwise feints a pitch, when he is not in contact with the pitching plate, and when a runner or runners are on base.

BASEBALL 5

Batting Players must bat in the order they appear on their team's batting list.

The batter must take up his position with both feet inside the batting box, and may not step out of the box after the pitcher has begun his windup or come to the set position.

The batter may or may not choose to strike at a delivered pitch. Every pitch delivered by the pitcher will be judged by the umpire to be a ball or a strike.

The batter will be charged with a strike if the pitcher makes a legal pitch and:

a) the ball is within the area over home plate between the batter's knees and his armpits (the "strike zone") and the batter does not swing (**A**);

b) the batter swings at any pitch and misses;

c) the ball is sent into foul territory by the batter when the count on him is less than two strikes;

d) the ball is bunted (met with the bat and tapped slowly within the infield, rather than swung at) foul;

e) the ball touches the batter as he strikes at it;

f) the ball touches the batter in flight in the strike zone;

g) the ball is touched by the bat and goes directly to the catcher's hands and is legally caught (a "foul tip").

The batter will be credited with a ball if the pitched ball does not enter the strike zone and is not swung at by the batter (**B**). If the batter elects to swing at such a pitch, and hits it, the ball is played like any batted ball.

A batter completes his time at bat when he becomes a runner or when he is put out.

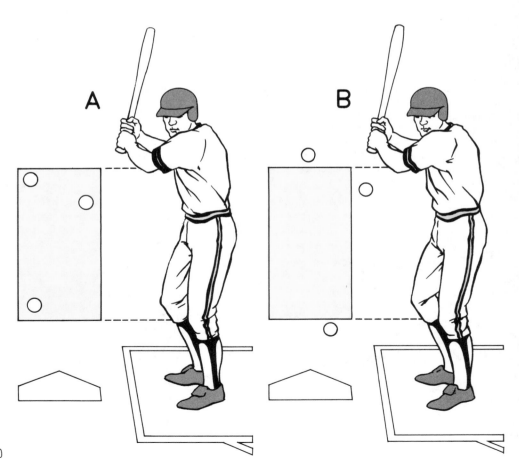

Batter-runner The batter becomes a runner and advances to first base or succeeding bases, and base runners advance on his action as necessary when:

a) he hits a ball into fair territory (a "fair ball");

b) the catcher fails to catch the third strike when no runner is on first base, or when there is a runner on first base with two out;

c) a fair ball has passed a fielder other than the pitcher, or has been touched by a fielder including the pitcher, and then touches an umpire or runner in fair territory.

The batter becomes a runner and may advance to first base without the possibility of being put out when:

a) the umpire has called four balls;

b) he is touched by a pitched ball that is not within the strike zone, which he is not attempting to hit, and which he has endeavored to avoid;

c) he is interfered with by the catcher or another fielder;

d) a ball batted into fair territory touches an umpire, or a runner in fair territory, before it touches a fielder.

The batter becomes a runner and he and any other runners are entitled to two bases when a fair ball passes or bounds into the stands, shrubbery, or some other obstruction that makes it impossible for the fielders to retrieve it.

The batter is entitled to a home run if he hits a fair ball over a fence or into the stands at a distance of 250ft or more from home base. If the ball passes out of the field less than 250ft from home base, he is entitled to two bases only.

Batter put out A batter is put out when:

a) a fielder makes a legal catch of his fair or foul fly ball;

b) a third strike is legally caught by the catcher (**1**);

c) a third strike is not caught by the catcher and first base is occupied before two players are out;

d) he bunts the ball into foul territory on his third strike (**2**);

e) he attempts to hit a third strike but is touched by the ball;

f) he runs more than 3ft outside a direct line between bases to avoid a tag;

g) he hits the ball so it can be caught in the infield with ordinary effort when there are fewer than two out and there are runners on first and second, or on first, second, and third bases (infield fly rule);

h) he hits a fair ball, and hits it a second time in fair territory, or touches the ball before it touches a fielder;

i) he hits a foul ball, and intentionally deflects the course of the ball while running to first base;

j) he is tagged before touching first base, or first base is tagged before he reaches it, after a third strike or after he has hit a fair ball;

k) he or a preceding runner breaches the rules.

© DIAGRAM

BASEBALL 6

Running A runner is entitled to an unoccupied base when he touches it before he is put out. He may remain on the base until put out, or until required to vacate it for a succeeding runner who is entitled to it ("forced") (**A**).

The runner must touch the bases in order when advancing, or in reverse order when required to retreat (except if the ball is dead, when he may return directly to his original base).

If two runners touch a base and are tagged, the preceding runner is entitled to the base, and the following runner is put out.

A runner other than the batter-runner may advance one base without the possibility of being put out when:

a) there is a balk;

b) the batter's advance without liability to be put out forces the runner to vacate his base;

c) a fielder catches a fly ball and falls into a bench, stand, or other spectator area;

d) he is attempting to steal a base (ie gain a base without the help of a hit, walk, or error) (**B**) and at that time the batter is interfered with by the catcher or another fielder.

All runners, including the batter-runner, may advance, without risk of being put out:

a) to home base, when a fair ball goes out of the field on the fly;

b) to home base, if a fair ball that would have gone out of the field on the fly is deflected by a fielder throwing any part of his uniform at it;

c) three bases, if a fielder deliberately throws any part of his uniform (including his glove) at a fair ball and so touches the ball;

d) two bases, if a fielder deliberately throws part of his uniform (including his glove) at a thrown ball and so touches the ball;

e) two bases, if a fair ball goes, or is deflected into, an irretrievable position;

f) two bases, if a wild throw by a fielder goes directly into the stands or a bench, or over or through a field fence or backstop;

g) one base, if a wild pitch or throw to base by the pitcher goes into a stand or bench, or over or through a field fence or backstop;

h) one base, if the batter becomes a runner on the third strike or the fourth ball, and the pitch passes the catcher and lodges in the umpire's equipment;

i) at least one base, if a fielder who is not in possession of the ball nor in the act of fielding the ball, obstructs the progress of the runner.

Runner put out A runner is out when:

a) he runs more than 3ft off the direct line between bases in order to avoid a tag, unless he does so to avoid interfering with a fielder about to field a batted ball;

b) he leaves the baseline after touching first base, and is obviously not intending to touch the next base;

c) he interferes with a fielder attempting to field a batted ball, or intentionally interferes with a thrown ball;

d) he is tagged while the ball is in play when he is off his base, except that a batter may not be tagged after overrunning or oversliding first base if he returns to it at once;

e) he is forced to advance when a batter becomes a runner, and is unable to reach the next base before he or the base are tagged by a fielder, except that if the following batter-runner

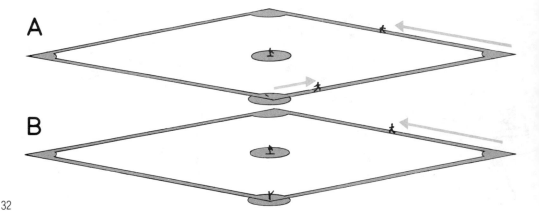

is put out, the force is no longer in effect, and the fielder must tag the runner and not the base for a putout;
f) he is touched by the ball in fair territory before it has touched or passed an infielder, except when he is touched by an infield fly when he is touching his base;
g) he passes a preceding runner before that runner is out;
h) he attempts to score when the batter has interfered with the play at home base, except that if two players are already out, the interference puts the batter out;
i) he runs the bases in reverse order or otherwise attempts to confuse the game.
A runner may be out on an appeal by a fielder to the umpire before the next pitch when:
a) he or his original base is tagged after a fly ball has been caught and before he is able to retouch that base;
b) he fails to touch each base in order when advancing or returning to a base before he or the missed base is tagged;
c) he overruns or overslides first base, fails to return to the base immediately, and he or the base is tagged;
d) he fails to touch home base, makes no attempt to return to touch it, and he or the base is tagged.

SCORING

Scoring statistics Games are decided by the number or runs scored; the team with more runs at the end of the game is the winner. Other scoring statistics are related to the records of the teams or the individual players, but do not affect the final outcome of the game.

Runs A run is scored each time a batter becomes a runner and legally advances to and touches all of the bases in turn before three outs have been made.

A base hit occurs when a batter reaches first base or a succeeding base on a fair ball.

A stolen base is when a base runner safely advances a base unaided by another action.

A base on balls ("walk") is awarded to a batter who has received four pitched balls that were outside the strike zone during his time at bat. He may advance to and touch first base without liability to be put out.

Batting average A player's batting average is the number of times he has hit safely in relation to the number of times he has batted. He is not charged with a time at bat if he:
a) is awarded a base on balls;
b) is hit by a pitched ball;
c) is awarded first base because of interference or obstruction by a fielder;
d) hits a sacrifice.

Runs batted in ("RBI") are runs scored because of the batter's action, and are credited to the batter.

A putout is an action credited to a fielder who is directly responsible for putting out a batter or runner by catching a fly ball, line drive, or thrown ball, or by tagging a runner off the base to which he is entitled.

An assist is an action credited to a fielder that results in a putout by a teammate.

A double play occurs when two baserunners (possibly including the batter) are put out in a single play. In a triple play, three baserunners are put out in a single play.

An error is a misplay that allows a runner to advance a base, or to avoid being put out against expectations. Any fielder may be charged with an error.
A passed ball is a catcher's error, and occurs when he is unable to catch or hold an ordinary pitched ball.
A wild pitch is a pitcher's error, and occurs when his pitch goes so far off target that the catcher cannot stop or control it, and the runner or runners are able to advance.

An earned run is a run for which a pitcher is charged. He is not charged for runs scored:
a) by a runner or runners who would have been put out if it were not for an error by one of the pitcher's teammates;
b) by a player whom a preceding pitcher allowed to reach base.

The earned run average (ERA) is the ratio of earned runs charged against a pitcher to the number of innings pitched.

A winning pitcher is one who has pitched at least five innings, and whose team is in the lead if and when he is replaced, and remains in the lead for the rest of the game.

A losing pitcher is one whose team is behind when he is replaced, and thereafter fails to tie or gain the lead.

BASKETBALL

HISTORY
Although basketball is similar in some respects to ancient games played by the Olmecs and Aztecs in Mexico, the game as we understand it today was invented in 1891 by James Naismith, a Canadian clergyman teaching in the USA. Basketball rapidly won and continues to enjoy great popularity among participants and spectators in the USA and in other parts of the world. The international governing body is the Fédération Internationale de Basketball Amateur (FIBA), formed in 1932. Basketball was added to the main Olympic program in 1936.

SYNOPSIS
Basketball is a very fast, no-contact game for two teams of five players and five (or occasionally seven) substitutes. The object is to score more points than the opposing team in the allotted time. The ball may be passed, thrown, batted, tapped, rolled, or dribbled, but may not be carried or kicked deliberately. Points are scored by throwing the ball into the appropriate basket: two for a field goal and one for a goal from a free throw. FIBA rules are here described first. Rules in the USA differ in some important respects (see pp. 46–47).

COURT AND EQUIPMENT
The court is a rectangle on a hard surface (not grass). The standard size is 26m long and 14m wide.

The ceiling must be at least 7m high. Lighting must be uniform and not hinder players shooting for a goal.

The court is bounded by side lines (**a**) and end lines (**b**), and is divided by a center line (**c**) that extends 15cm beyond each side line.

A circle (**d**) with a radius of 1.80m is marked in the center of the court.

Free throw lines (**e**) 3.60m long, with their midpoints opposite the midpoints of the end lines, are drawn parallel to the end lines and 5.80m in front of them.

Restricted areas (**f**) are bounded by lines that join the ends of the free throw lines to points 3m from the midpoints of the end lines.

Free throw lanes comprise the restricted areas together with semicircles (**g**) with a radius of 1.80m and centered on the midpoints of the free throw lines.

Similar semicircles (**h**) are marked by a broken line within the restricted areas.

Spaces along the free throw lanes, to be used during free throws, are indicated by lines at right angles to and outside the side lines of the free throw lanes. The first space (**i**) is 1.80m from the end line and is 85cm wide. The second space (**j**), also 85cm wide, is adjacent to the first.

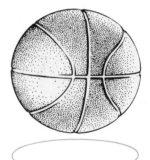

75–78cm

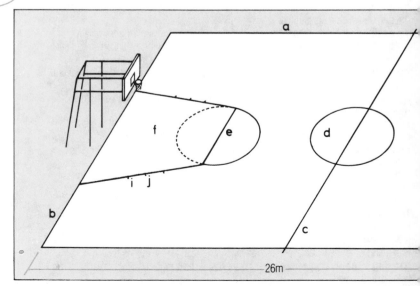

26m

Backboards, to which the baskets are fixed, are positioned at each end of the court. Backboards are made of 3cm-thick hardwood or of a single piece of equally rigid transparent material. They measure 1.80m horizontally and 1.20m vertically.

Markings, usually black on white or white on transparent, consist of an outer border 5cm wide and an inner rectangle 59cm by 45cm measured to the outer edges of its 5cm-wide lines. The top edge of its lower line is to be level with the ring.

The backboards are rigidly mounted at each end of the court at right angles to the floor, parallel to, centered on and 1.20m in front of the end lines, and with their lower edges 2.75m above the floor.

The supports are bright in color, at least 40cm from the end lines, and padded to prevent injuries.

Baskets consist of orange-painted iron rings and white cord nets.

The rings have an inside diameter of 45cm and are rigidly attached to the backboard so they are in a horizontal plane 3.05m above the floor, 15cm away from the backboard at its nearest point, and equidistant from the backboard's vertical sides.

Nets, suspended from the rings, are 40cm long and hold the ball briefly as it drops through.

The ball is spherical and has a leather, rubber, or synthetic case, with a rubber bladder. Its circumference is 75–78cm and its weight 600–650g. When inflated and dropped onto a solid wooden floor from a height of about 1.80m (measured to the bottom of the ball), it should bounce to a height of about 1.20–1.40m (measured to the top of the ball).

Technical equipment, provided by the home team, consists of:
a) at least two stopwatches, including the "game watch" and the "time-out watch";
b) a device for administering the 30-second rule;
c) an official scoresheet;
d) a scoreboard;
e) markers, numbered 1–4 in black, 5 in red, to show the number of fouls per player;
f) two red flags to serve as team foul markers (displayed on the scorer's table after a team's eighth player foul).

Dress Players wear shirts and shorts with basketball boots or shoes. Shirts must have numbers that are at least 10cm high on the front and 20cm high on the back. Only numbers 4–15 are used. Players in the same team may not wear duplicate numbers. Players are not permitted to wear any object that could injure others.

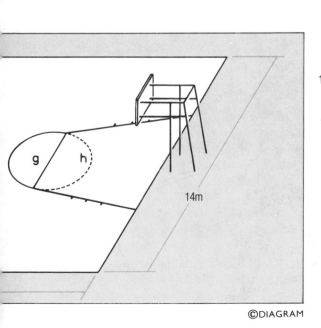

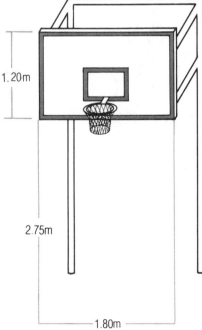

©DIAGRAM

BASKETBALL 2

PLAYERS AND OFFICIALS
Players Teams consist of five players on the court during play and five (or occasionally seven) substitutes.
Substitutions are permitted in accordance with the rules.
Coaches Teams have a coach, whose duties include informing the scorer of the names and numbers of the players and captain, and making requests for substitutions and charged time-outs.
The team captain may act as coach.
Officials are the referee and umpire, assisted by the scorer, timekeeper, and 30-second operator. The referee and the umpire divide the court between them, exchanging places after each foul and after each jump ball decision. They use whistles and hand signals to make and explain decisions.

DURATION AND SCORING
Duration A game consists of two halves of 20 minutes each, with an interval normally of 10 minutes. If the score is tied, play continues for as many extra 5-minute periods as necessary. Teams toss for baskets for the first extra period, then change for the others.
Scoring A goal is scored when a live ball enters a basket from above and stays in or passes through. Goals from the field count two points, from free throws one point.

STARTING PROCEDURES
Starting Visitors choose ends; on a neutral court the teams toss up. The teams change ends at half time. Each team must begin with five players on court. The game starts with a jump ball at the center.
Center jump A jump ball at the center starts each half or extra period.
The referee throws the ball up in the center circle, and the two opponents taking part jump to tap the ball away. The jumpers must stand in the half of the circle nearer to their own baskets, with one foot near the center line. The ball is thrown up at right angles to the side line to a height greater than either player can reach by jumping and so that it drops between them.
Each player may tap the ball twice after it has reached its highest point and then cannot tap it again until it touches the ground, a basket, a backboard, or another player. The jumpers must remain in position until the ball is tapped. Other players must be outside the circle, and must not interfere with the jumpers.
Any violation of the jump ball rules is penalized if the opponents do not gain an advantage from it. The throw is repeated if it is a bad one or if both teams violate the rules.

Jump ball In addition to provisions for a jump ball at the center, a jump ball also occurs in the following instances.

a) If there is doubt as to which of two opponents put the ball out of bounds, there is a jump ball between them in the nearest circle.

b) If the ball lodges on the basket supports, it is put into play by a jump ball between any two opponents on the nearest free throw line. (Except that other rules apply if this situation arises during a free throw after a technical foul by a coach or substitute.)

c) If the ball accidentally enters the basket from below, the ball becomes dead and is put into play by a jump ball at the nearest free throw line. (If a player deliberately causes the ball to enter a basket from below, it is a violation and play is resumed by a throw in from the nearest point on the side line.)

Restart after a field goal After a field goal the game is restarted by a throw in from the end line.

A player from the team against which the goal is scored takes the throw in. Once a member of the team has the ball at his disposal he has 5 seconds in which to make the throw in. The scoring team must not handle the ball, or a technical foul is awarded against it. Allowance is made for accidental handling.

After a last free throw for goal If the free throw was for a technical foul by a coach or substitute, and whether or not the throw was successful, play is restarted by a throw in from out of bounds at mid-court by any player of the free thrower's team.

Otherwise, if the throw was successful, the game is restarted by a throw in from behind the end line by any opponent of the free thrower. If the throw was unsuccessful and the ball rebounded from the ring, play continues from the rebound.

TIMING RULES

Timing the game The game watch is started for each half or extra period when the ball is first tapped by a player.

The game watch is stopped after the expiry of time for each period. Play ends as soon as the timekeeper signals the end of playing time, except:

a) time is allowed for free throws following a foul committed simultaneously with or just before the timekeeper's signal;

b) a goal counts if the ball was in the air for the shot before time expired.

Ball into play The ball goes into play:

a) when the official enters the circle to administer a jump ball;

b) when the official enters the free throw lane to administer a free throw;

c) when the ball is at the disposal of a player in position for a throw in from out of bounds.

Live ball The ball becomes alive:

a) when, after reaching its highest point in a jump ball, it is tapped by a player;

b) when the official places it at the disposal of a free thrower;

c) when on a throw in from out of bounds it touches a player in court.

Dead ball The ball becomes dead in the following circumstances:

a) when a goal is made;

b) when a violation occurs;

c) when a foul occurs while the ball is alive or in play;

d) when held ball occurs;

e) when the ball lodges on the basket support;

f) when it is apparent that the ball will not go into the basket either on a free throw for a technical foul by a coach or substitute, or on a free throw that is to be followed by another free throw;

g) when the official's whistle is blown while the ball is alive or in play;

h) when the 30-second operator's signal is sounded while the ball is alive;

i) when time expires for a half or extra period.

But the ball does not become dead and any goal made is scored:

1) if the ball is in flight on a free throw or a shot for goal when (c), (g), (h) or (i) occurs;

2) if an opponent fouls while the ball is still in the control of a player who finishes his shot with a continuous motion that started before the foul occurs;

3) if a jump ball violation is ignored.

BASKETBALL 3

Time-out The game watch stops when an official signals a violation, a foul, a held ball, unusual delay in getting a dead ball into play, the end of a 30-second period, suspension of play for an injury, or when a field goal is scored against the team of a coach who has requested a charged time-out.

Charged time-out Each team is allowed two charged time-outs per half, each of 1 minute. They may not be saved up for a subsequent half. One charged time-out is allowed for each extra period of play.

The request for a time-out is made by the coach to the scorer, who stops the game watch as soon as the ball is dead.

A coach may also be granted a charged time-out if the opposing team scores a field goal after he has requested a time-out.

A charged time-out cannot be granted from the moment the ball is in play for the first or only free throw until the ball becomes dead after being alive again after the free throw or throws.

No time-out is charged if an injured player is ready to play at once or is substituted as soon as possible, or if a disqualified player or a player who has committed his fifth foul is replaced within 1 minute, or if an official permits a delay.

Time-out for injury The officials may order a time-out for injury. Except when an immediate stop is needed to protect the injured player, they must first wait for the team in possession to complete its play.

If the injured player cannot continue to play at once, he must be substituted within 1 minute or as soon as possible. If free throws have been awarded to the injured player, the time-out is charged and free throws are taken by the substitute.

If an injured player is not substituted in accordance with the provisions of this article, his team is charged with a time-out except in cases where the team has to continue with fewer than five players. If the team has no charged time-outs remaining, a technical foul is charged against the coach.

Time-in is the restarting of the game watch after a time-out. The game is resumed with:
a) a throw in by a member of the team that had control of the ball;
b) a jump ball if neither team had control of the ball;
c) a free throw.

The game watch is restarted when the ball is tapped in a jump ball, or when the ball touches a player on court after a throw in or an unsuccessful free throw.

Three-second rule No player may remain more than 3 seconds in the restricted area between his opponents' end line and free throw line (the line included) while his team has control of the ball (including throw ins).

This rule does not apply when the team is no longer in control of the ball, including when it is in the air on a shot for goal, is rebounding from the backboard, or is dead. Allowance may be made for a player who dribbles in to throw for a goal.

Five-second rule Held ball is called if a closely guarded player fails to shoot, pass, roll, or dribble the ball within 5 seconds.

Ten-second rule A team that has control of a live ball in its back court must move it into its front court within 10 seconds.

A player in his front court may not cause the ball to go into his back court. This restriction applies at all times except:
a) when a player gains control of the ball directly from a center jump ball;
b) at a throw in from the midpoint of the side line following a technical foul by a coach or substitute;
c) at a throw in from the midpoint of the side line after a player has been fouled in the act of shooting, and the team captain has exercised his right of option.

Thirty-second rule A team must try for a goal within 30 seconds of gaining control. A new 30-second period begins if the ball goes out of play; the opponents gain the ball if it was purposely sent out. The 30-second clock continues if the ball touches an opponent but the first team keeps control.

PLAYERS' RULES

Playing the ball The ball may be passed, thrown, batted, tapped, rolled, or dribbled, but it may not be carried or kicked deliberately.

Control of the ball A player has control if holding or dribbling a live ball.
A team is in control if one of its members has control or the ball is being passed between them. Team control ends with a dead ball, loss of possession to the opponents, or on a shot for goal when the ball is no longer in contact with the shooter's hand.

Player out of bounds A player is out of bounds if he touches the floor on or beyond the boundary lines (**A**).

Ball out of bounds The ball is out of bounds when it touches the floor or any person or object on or beyond the boundary lines, including the rear of the backboard or its supports. It is a violation to cause the ball to go out of bounds. If the ball is out of bounds because of touching something other than a player, it is caused to go out by the last person to touch it before it goes out. If it is out of bounds because of touching a player who is out of bounds then that player puts it out of bounds, except when a player deliberately throws or taps the ball onto an opponent to make it go out of bounds.

Progressing with the ball Subject to the rules given here, a player is permitted to move with the ball by pivoting on one foot – which he must keep stationary on the floor—while he steps once or more than once in any direction with the other foot (**B**).
A player who receives the ball while standing still may use either foot as the pivot foot.
A player who receives the ball while progressing or on completion of a dribble may come to a stop or dispose of the ball using a two-count rhythm. If either foot is on the floor when he receives the ball, the first count (one) occurs as he receives the ball. If both feet are off the floor when the ball is received (**C**), the first count (**1**) occurs as either foot touches the floor or as both feet touch the floor simultaneously. The second count (**2**) occurs when, after the first count, either or both of the player's feet again touch the floor.
If a player makes a legal stop he may then use only the rear foot as pivot, unless both feet are together with neither foot in front of the other.
A player who receives the ball while standing still or comes to a legal stop while holding the ball may lift his pivot foot or jump, but must pass or shoot before one or both feet touch the floor again. If he is going to dribble he must release the ball before lifting his pivot foot.

©DIAGRAM

BASKETBALL 4

Dribbling A dribble occurs when a player with control of the ball gives impetus to it by throwing, tapping or rolling it, allows it to bounce on the floor, and then touches it again before it touches another player(**A**). The player may take any number of steps when the ball is not in contact with his hand.

The dribble is completed when the player touches the ball with both hands at once, or lets it rest in one or both hands.

A player is entitled to a dribble each time he gains control of the ball, but it is a violation to make a second, consecutive dribble. After completing a dribble a player must lose and then regain control of the ball before he dribbles again. He loses control when the ball leaves his hand(s) on a shot or pass, or when an opponent causes him to lose possession. A player who throws the ball against a backboard and touches it before it touches another player commits a second dribble violation unless the official considers he made a shot.

It is not a dribble if a player makes successive tries for goal, fumbles, attempts to gain control of the ball by tapping it away from other players striving for it, bats it from the control of another player, blocks a pass and recovers the ball, or tosses the ball from hand(s) to hand(s) and permits it to come to rest before touching the floor.

Held ball occurs when two or more opposing players are both firmly holding the ball (**B**) or when a closely guarded player takes more than 5 seconds to shoot, pass, roll, or dribble. Officials should not call a held ball too hastily. A player lying on the floor in possession of the ball must have a chance to play it, unless he is in danger of injury.

After a held ball, play resumes with a jump ball between involved players at the nearest circle; if several players were involved in the held ball, the jump ball is between two players of similar height.

Shooting A player is in the act of shooting if, in the judgment of an official, he starts an attempt to score by throwing, tapping, or dunking (forcing or attempting to force the ball downward into the basket). The act of shooting continues until the ball leaves the player's hand(s)(**C**). A player who taps the ball toward a basket directly from a jump ball is not in the act of shooting.

Interference with the ball Rules differ according to whether a player is attacking or defending a basket.

1) In attack, a player in the restricted area must not touch the ball in its downward flight above the level of the ring, whether during a try for a goal or a pass, until the ball has touched the ring. No point can be scored. The opponents throw in from the side line at the place nearest where the violation occurred.

2) In defense, a player must not touch a falling ball above ring level (**D**) during an opponent's throw for a goal until the ball touches the ring or will obviously miss. This applies only to a throw for a goal. If such a violation occurs the ball becomes dead. The thrower gets one point if it occurs during a free throw, two if it occurs during a shot for goal from the field.

The game is restarted as if a goal had been scored and no violation had taken place.

Interference with a basket No player is allowed to touch a basket or its backboard while the ball is in or on the basket (**E**). Resulting procedures depend on whether the offending player was in attack or defense, and are the same as if the player had interfered with the ball.

Substitutes must report to the scorer and be ready to play at once. The scorer signals the substitute's entry when the ball is dead; the substitute waits for the official's signal before entering the court. He gives the official his name or number and that of the player to be replaced (except at the beginning of the second half).

A time-out is charged if more than 20 seconds is taken to replace any number of players. A player involved in a jump ball may not be replaced. After a violation the offending team may field substitutes only if their opponents do so.

A substitution is not permitted from the moment the ball is in play for the first or only free throw until the ball becomes dead after being alive again after the free throw or throws.

After a successful last free throw only the thrower may be replaced and the request must be made before the ball went into play for the first or only free throw; in such a situation the opponents are allowed one substitution provided they request it before the ball goes into play before the last free throw.

D

E

©DIAGRAM

BASKETBALL 5

VIOLATIONS AND FOULS

Violation This is an infraction of the rules that does not involve personal contact with an opponent or unsportsmanlike conduct.

When a violation is called the ball becomes dead, and if a goal is made it is not counted. The ball is awarded to a nearby opponent for a throw in from the side line nearest where the violation occurred.

Foul This is an infraction of the rules that involves personal contact with an opponent or unsportsmanlike conduct.

When a foul by a player is called the official indicates to the scorer the number of the offender, who must at once face the scorer and raise his hand (failure to do so, after being warned once, is a technical foul). The scorer then records the foul against the offender.

If the fouled player was not in the act of shooting, his team is awarded a throw in from the side line nearest where the foul occurred.

If the fouled player was in the act of shooting and scores, the goal counts and an additional free throw is awarded. (Note that the goal counts even if the ball leaves the player's hands after the whistle blows, provided the whistle did not affect the shot.)

If the fouled player was shooting but misses, the official takes the ball to the free throw line and puts it at the disposal of the free thrower (except when play is to be resumed by a jump ball, as after a double foul). The free thrower is awarded two free throws, but if either or both are unsuccessful, he is given one additional free throw. A team that is awarded two free throws has the option of either taking the free throws or of putting the ball into play from the midpoint of the side line, being entitled to pass to a player in any part of the court. (This option is not available to a team awarded possession of the ball as well as one or two free throws.)

If a player commits a foul while his team has control of the ball, the foul is charged to the offender and the ball is awarded to an opponent for a throw in from the nearest point on the side line.

Further fouls committed when the ball is dead after a foul are considered as occurring at the time the ball became dead from the first foul. Any number of fouls may therefore be called at the same time.

Personal foul This is a player foul involving contact with an opponent whether the ball is in play, alive, or dead.

Some personal contact is inevitable, and officials need not impose penalties where contact is incidental when trying to play the ball and where the contacted player is not put at a disadvantage.

It is a personal foul if a player:
a) blocks the progress of an opponent not in control of the ball (**1**);
b) holds, pushes, charges, or trips any opponent;

c) impedes the progress of any opponent by extending his arm, shoulder, hip or knee, or by bending his body into an abnormal position (**2**);

d) uses rough tactics;

e) contacts an opponent as a result of guarding from the rear (in this instance the fact that the defending player is trying to play the ball is not justification for personal contact)(**3**);

f) contacts an opponent with his hands (except when contact is only with the opponent's hand or hands on the ball and is incidental to playing the ball).

A player making a dribble commits a personal foul if he charges into or contacts a player in his path, or attempts to dribble between opponents or between an opponent and the boundary line, unless there is a reasonable chance of avoiding contact. But if there is no contact until after the dribbler has his head and shoulders past an opponent, responsibility for subsequent contact is the opponent's.

If a dribbler has established a straight line path, he may not be forced out of it but if an opponent establishes a legal guarding position in that path, the dribbler must avoid contact by stopping or changing direction.

A player who screens (prevents an opponent not in control of the ball from reaching a desired position) is held responsible for any contact occurring because he took up a position so near an opponent, or took up a position in the opponent's path so quickly, that the opponent was unable to avoid pushing or charging him.

(Penalties for personal fouls are given on pp. 44 – 45.)

Technical foul by a player It is a technical foul for a player to disregard an admonition from an official, to be disrespectful to an official, or to use unsportsmanlike tactics such as offensive language, baiting an opponent, or delaying the game.

Unintentional technical infractions not affecting the game and administrative infractions are not technical fouls unless repeated after a warning.

Any play that continues before a technical foul is discovered is valid, but a penalty is given on discovery.

Each technical foul is recorded and the penalty is two free throws to the opponents, to be taken by a player chosen by the captain.

Technical fouls by others It is a technical foul if a coach, assistant coach, substitute, or team follower:

enters the court to attend an injured man without official permission;

leaves his place to follow the action from the boundary line without permission; or

disrespectfully addresses officials, assistants, or opponents.

The coach may address his team in a charged time-out if he does not enter the court and the players do not leave it (unless permission is granted). Substitutes may listen if outside the court area.

Each foul is recorded against the coach and the penalty is one free throw to the opponents, to be taken by a player chosen by the captain. During the free throw players do not line up along the free throw lanes. Whether or not a goal is scored, any member of the free thrower's team next puts the ball into play from the midpoint of the side line.

A flagrant infraction, or the charging of three technical fouls against a coach, results in his disqualification and replacement by the assistant coach or the captain.

Technical fouls during an interval These are charged against the offending player or substitute, or against the coach if the foul is by the coach, assistant coach or team follower. The penalty is two free throws followed by a jump ball at the center.

Intentional foul This is a personal foul that an official considers was deliberate. A player commits an intentional foul if he deliberately disregards the ball and makes personal contact with a player who has control of the ball (**4**). A player in control of the ball may also commit an intentional foul if he deliberately contacts an opponent. A player who repeatedly commits intentional fouls may be disqualified.

Disqualifying foul A flagrant infraction of the personal foul or technical foul rules makes a player liable to immediate disqualification in addition to the usual penalties.

Double foul This occurs when two opponents commit fouls against each other at approximately the same time. A personal foul is charged against each of them. Play resumes with a jump ball between them at the nearest circle, except when a valid goal was scored at the same time, in which case there is a throw in from the end line.

©DIAGRAM

BASKETBALL 6

Multiple foul This occurs when two or more teammates commit personal fouls against the same opponent at approximately the same time. A personal foul is recorded against each offender and two free throws are awarded to the offended player.

If the offended player was in the act of shooting when fouled, a goal counts if scored and one additional free throw is awarded.

Double and multiple foul When these occur at the same time, the double foul is dealt with first (being charged to each offender) and then the multiple foul. The game is restarted as if the double foul had not occurred.

Special situations The following principles are applied when fouls occur at approximately the same time.

a) Each foul is charged.

b) Simultaneous fouls by both teams involving similar penalties result in no free throws – the game is restarted with a jump ball at the nearest circle, or the center if in doubt.

c) Penalties that are not compensated by similar penalties against the other team are maintained, but no team may receive more than two free throws and possession of the ball.

Five fouls by a player A player who has committed five fouls, either personal or technical, must automatically leave the game.

Eight fouls by a team After a team has committed eight player fouls, either personal or technical, in a half (with extra periods counted as part of the second half), all subsequent player fouls are penalized by two free throws. Exceptions are:

a) when a player fouled in the act of shooting managed to score;

b) when the penalty is a throw in from the side line because a foul was committed by a player whose team had control of the ball;

c) when the three for two rule is brought into operation.

PENALTIES

A

Throw in (A) A throw in from out of bounds is the penalty imposed for a violation and for some types of foul.

Except when a throw in from the midpoint of the side line is specified, the throw in is from the point on the side line nearest where the ball left the court or the violation or foul was committed. Whenever the throw in is awarded to a team member in his front court, the ball must be handed to him by an official.

The player nominated to take the throw in must release the ball within 5 seconds of having it placed at his disposal. He may throw, roll, or bounce the ball to another player within the court. He must not step on the side line or the court while releasing the ball, and must not touch it in the court before it has first touched another player. Failure to take the free throw in the prescribed manner is a violation.

While the throw in is being taken, no other player may have any part of his body over the boundary line before the ball has been thrown across the line. If the out of bounds territory free from obstruction at a throw in is less than 1m, no player of either team may be within 1m of the player throwing in.

Free throw This is an unhindered throw for goal from a position directly behind the free throw line. One point is scored if the ball legally enters the basket.

A player earns the right to one free throw each time he scores a field goal. Also, free throws are awarded to the opposing team as penalties for personal and technical fouls.

If a player taking a free throw directs the ball toward the wrong basket, the try is annulled and another try granted at the correct basket.

Free throw after a personal foul (B) After a personal foul on a player in the act of shooting, free throws are to be taken by the player who was fouled. If he is about to be replaced by a substitute, he must take any free throws first (unless he is injured). If the wrong player takes a free throw, any goal made is not scored and the ball is given to the opponents for a throw in.

The free thrower stands directly behind the free throw line and must not touch the floor on or across the free throw line until the ball touches the ring or obviously will not do so. Meanwhile other players may take up positions as follows: two opponents of the free thrower occupy the two spaces along the outside of the free throw lane that are nearest the basket; other players lining up outside the free throw lane take alternate positions by team; other players may take up any other position except along the free throw lane next to the end line.

Players must not disturb the free thrower, touch the free throw lane, move position until the ball touches the ring or it is apparent it will not touch it, or touch the ball or the basket while the ball is on or within it.

After the ball is placed at his disposal the free thrower must throw within 5 seconds and in such a way that the ball enters the basket or touches the ring before it is touched by a player. He must not touch the ball or the basket while the ball is on its way to the basket or is on or within it.

Free throw after a technical foul Basically the procedure is the same as after a personal foul except that any member of the offended team may take the throw and players do not line up outside the free throw lane. After the throw, whatever its outcome, the ball is put into play by a throw in by any member of the free thrower's team from out of bounds at midcourt.

Free throw violations If the violation is by the free thrower only, no point can be scored. Play is resumed as follows. If the free throw was awarded for a player foul, play resumes with a throw in by the opposing team from the side line opposite the free throw line. If the free throw was for a technical foul charged against the coach, the throw in is by the free thrower's team from the side line opposite the center circle.

If a teammate of the free thrower touches the ball or the basket during the free throw, no point is scored and the violation is penalized as above. If both teams committed this offense, no point is scored and there is a jump ball on the free throw line. If only an opponent touched the ball or the basket, one point is scored and play resumes as if a successful throw had been made.

If a player of either team touches the free throw lane or disconcerts the thrower and a goal is still made, the goal counts and the violation is disregarded. If no goal was made, action depends on who committed the offense. If it was a team member of the free thrower, action is as for an offense by the free thrower (but if the ball misses the ring and goes out of bounds or falls within bounds, it is returned to play by a throw in by the opponents from opposite the free throw line). If the offense was by the free thrower's opponents only, the free thrower takes another free throw. If the offense was committed by both teams, there is a jump ball on the free throw line. (Out of bounds and jump ball provisions apply only to a violation during the last free throw.)

Ball into play after a missed free throw If the free throw was for a foul by a player, the ball continues in play after the last free throw. But if the ball misses the ring, it is a violation and there is a throw in by the opponents from out of bounds opposite the free throw line. If the free throw was for a technical foul charged against the coach, there is a throw in by the free thrower's team from out of bounds at mid-court.

45

©DIAGRAM

BASKETBALL 7

NORTH AMERICAN BASKETBALL

Rule differences Here we summarize the major differences between US and FIBA rules. US rules referred to are those of the National Basketball Association (NBA) for the professional game, and the National Collegiate Athletic Association (NCAA) for the amateur game.

Court The FIBA court is described on p. 34 . The NCAA court (**A**) and NBA court (**B**) are 94ft long and 50ft wide; court markings and dimensions are as shown below.

Ball The NCAA uses a basketball with a circumference of 29½–30in; NBA players must use an officially approved NBA ball.

Technical equipment The NBA requires a 24-second clock in place of the 30-second clock used by FIBA; no such equipment is required under NCAA rules.

Own basket In the USA this is the basket at which a team is shooting; under FIBA rules it is the basket it is defending.

Dunking is permitted at any time under FIBA and NBA rules. Under NCAA rules, dunking is permitted during the game, but not during the warmup or intermissions.

Held ball The FIBA five-second rule does not apply in NBA and NCAA games.

Pivot foot In the USA, a player who stops on the count of one may pivot on either foot.

Duration NBA games consist of four 12-minute periods, with a 15-minute interval at half time. NCAA games, like FIBA games, are in two 20-minute halves.

Time-outs FIBA rules for time-outs are described on p. 38 .

Under NCAA rules, five one-minute time-outs are allowed per game, plus one additional time-out for each overtime period. Time-outs may be accumulated and used as required, including in overtime periods.

Under NBA rules, seven 90-second time-outs are allowed during regular play. Each team is limited to a maximum of four time-outs in the fourth period, and a maximum of three in the last two minutes of regular play, during which the clock is stopped whenever a field goal is scored. Teams must take at least one time-out per period. Each team is allowed two time-outs in overtime periods, regardless of the number previously taken.

Under NBA rules, players as well as coaches may request time-outs.

Scoring In NBA games, a field goal from behind the 3pt line (**a**) scores three points. Otherwise, NBA, NCAA, and FIBA scoring is similar.

Try for goal Under NBA rules, a team must try for goal within 24sec of gaining control of the ball; teams are allowed 30sec under FIBA rules. NCAA rules give no such time limit.

Substitutes under NBA rules may enter the game after the first of two or more free throws, whether made or missed. Under NCAA rules, substitutes may enter the game after any successful free throw. Under NBA rules, a player who is designated to throw the ball in may only be substituted if a time-out has been called by one of the teams.

Starting procedure NCAA and FIBA starting procedures are the same.

In NBA games, a jump ball is held at the start of the first period and of any overtime period. At the start of the second and third periods, the ball is thrown in from their opponents' end line by the team that lost the "tap" (first jump ball). The team that won the tap throws the ball in from their opponents' end line at the start of the fourth period. NBA teams do not change ends for the first overtime period.

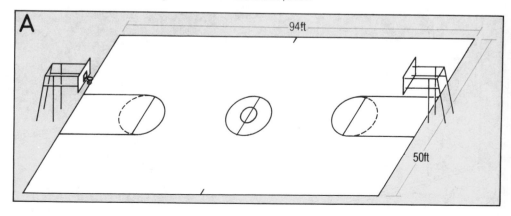

Interference with ball In the USA, players may not touch the ball when it is touching the ring (**b**), basket, or the cylindrical space above the basket with the ring as its base.

Technical fouls Under FIBA rules, two free throws are awarded for a technical foul by a player, and one for a foul by a coach or substitute; the reverse is the case under NCAA and NBA rules. However, two free throws are awarded under NCAA rules for a flagrant technical foul by a player, and under NBA rules for certain specific technical fouls.

Double fouls After a double foul in an NCAA game, the ball is next put into play by the team entitled to the throw-in at the out-of-bounds spot nearest to where the double foul took place.

In an NBA game, if the double foul occurs on the ball, a jump ball is held at the nearest circle between the players involved in the foul. If the double foul occurred off the ball, the team that was in possession at the time of the foul takes the throw-in.

Disqualification FIBA players are disqualified after committing five personal or technical fouls; NCAA players after committing five personal fouls; and NBA players after committing six personal fouls.

Free throws Under FIBA rules, a team captain has the option of taking the ball out-of-bounds at midcourt when two free throws are awarded; this rule does not apply in NCAA and NBA games. Players in FIBA games have five seconds in which to take a free throw; players in NCAA and NBA games have 10 seconds.

Free throws awarded Under NBA rules, two free throws are awarded for all fouls in excess of four in each period of regular play, or three in each overtime period. A team committing fewer than four team fouls in the first 10 minutes of each period of regular play, or fewer than three in the first three minutes of any overtime period, may incur one team foul without penalty during the last two minutes of each regular quarter or overtime period. Under NCAA rules, two free throws to score one goal are awarded for all fouls except player control fouls after a team has committed six personal fouls in a half.

Under both NCAA and NBA rules, two free throws are awarded if a player is fouled in the act of shooting and the goal is missed; FIBA rules also award an additional free throw if one of these two free throws is missed (three throws to score two points).

Free throw violations Under NCAA and NBA rules, no point can be scored if the thrower or his teammates touch the court in the lane. Under FIBA rules, there can be no score only if the thrower commits the violation.

Under NCAA rules, a violation occurs if the free thrower steps into or breaks the plane of the free throw lane before the ball has touched the ring or the backboard.

Throw-in Under NBA and NCAA rules, a throw-in for a violation is taken at the nearest out-of-bounds spot. Under FIBA rules, the throw-in is always from out-of-bounds at the side line.

Under NBA and FIBA rules, a player may not throw the ball into the back court if the throw-in was awarded at an out-of-bounds spot adjacent to the front-court area. Under NCAA rules, the ball may be passed into either the front or the back court.

b

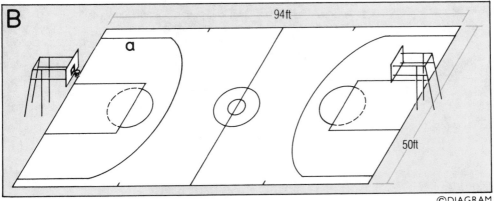

B

94ft

a

50ft

©DIAGRAM

BOBSLEIGH RACING

HISTORY

Bobsleigh racing originated in Switzerland in 1890, supposedly the invention of a group of Englishmen who added runners to their toboggans in order to go faster. Races were originally held on a winding road running from St Moritz to Celerina, but the new sport became so popular that a special banked track was built alongside the road. The first organized competition was held in 1898.

With the formation of the Fédération Internationale de Bobsleigh et Toboganning in 1923, bobsleigh became an internationally recognized sport and was included in the first Winter Olympics at Châmonix, France, in 1924. The first American bobrun was built in 1931 near Lake Placid for the 1932 Olympic Games.

SYNOPSIS

Teams of two or four members in bobsleighs compete by attempting to finish a course in the fastest possible time. The specially built track is a downhill run of ice with steep curves. Teamwork keeps the bobsleigh from crashing into walls of ice or from leaving the track.

TEAMS AND OFFICIALS

Teams There are events for two-man bobsleigh and four-man bobsleigh. One team member acts as the driver.

The same team members, with the same captain, must normally run all the heats of a race. A team member other than the driver may if injured be replaced by a substitute at the discretion of the jury.

All teams must train on the course before competing, as a thorough knowledge of the run is essential for speed and safety. Training must take place for a minimum of four days but not on the morning of a race, or, except in certain circumstances, on the day before a race. Teams can be disqualified for insufficient training.

Officials for a bobsleigh event form an organizing committee consisting of race directors, starters, finishing judges, and timekeepers. The committee supervises the state of the track and installations. A jury with three members decides on any protests related to the actual competition. The president of the jury has final jurisdiction in any dispute.

COURSE AND EQUIPMENT

The course For championship events the course must be at least 1500m long and have a gradient of between 8% and 15%. It must have at least 15 banked curves, designed so that the radii of the curves make it impossible for a bob to exceed a force of 4G during a period of 3 seconds. The highest part of the curve must be concave. The walls at the corners may be as high as 6m (**A**). The straight sections have horizontal bottoms, not more than 1.40m wide; the side walls, at right angles to the bottom of the run, must be a minimum of 50cm high, at least high enough to keep the bobs on course (**B**).

Before the starting line, which is marked by a piece of timber, there is an area at least 15m long with a maximum gradient of 2%. After the finishing line, there must be an area in which a bobsleigh should be able to halt without using brakes; some cushioning should also be provided in the braking area.

Permanent courses have stone or concrete foundations on which wet snow and water freeze in wintry conditions. On some courses, electric equipment is used to keep critical places frozen. Awnings must also be provided to shield the course if necessary from rain, snow, or sun. Runs with artificial icing must be at least 1200m long.

Control stations at critical points on the course are connected by telephone to the control tower. These ensure that the run is clear before each heat and keep the spectators informed, over loudspeakers, of a bobsleigh's progress.

No members of the public are allowed on the run. A safety service must be provided at certain points on the course.

Timing Automatic electric timing equipment is compulsory for championships and international races. Two stopwatches are also used for timing in case of breakdown of the automatic timing system. All timing is to two decimal places of a second.

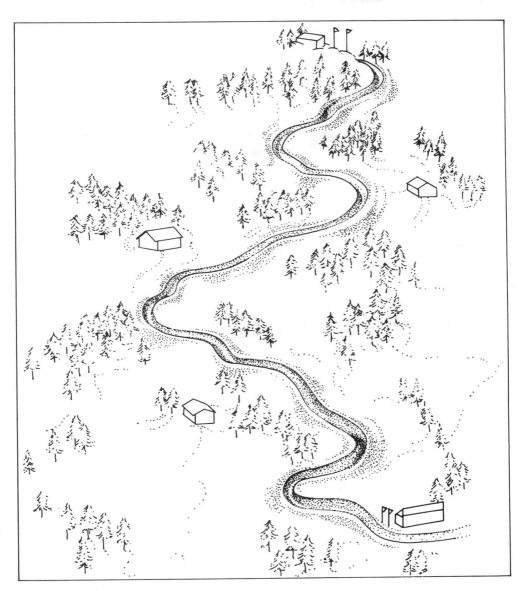

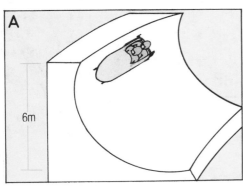

A

6m

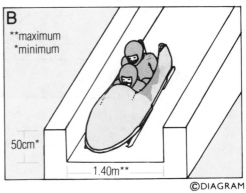

B

**maximum
*minimum

50cm*

1.40m**

©DIAGRAM

BOBSLEIGH RACING 2

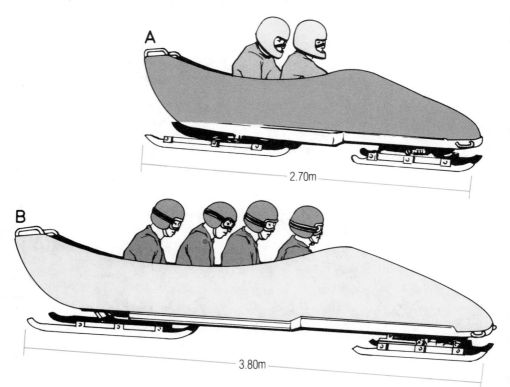

A

2.70m

B

3.80m

Bobsleighs are made of steel and aluminum. They are fitted with streamlined cowls and rigid handles on the sides for push starts. The cowls must be at least 65cm in height, measured from the bottom of the bobsleigh to the upper edge of the cowl.

The bobs must have four steel runners. The rear tips of the runners must be rounded and raised 2.5cm. The two rear runners are attached to the rear axle, which is fixed to the frame of the bob. The two front runners are attached to the front axle and used to steer the bob; a mechanical pulley system connects the runners to two steering ropes fitted with handgrips. Between the rear runners is a "rake" type of brake made of hardened steel. The brake is only used in emergencies, as its serrated edge damages the surface of the run and can make it dangerous.

The maximum length of a two-man bob (**A**) is 2.70m with a front width of 90cm, and a rear width of 80cm. The runners must be at least 8mm thick, with a radius of at least 4mm.

The maximum length of a four-man bob (**B**) is 3.80m with a front width of 90cm and a rear width of 80cm. The runners must be at least 12mm thick, with a radius of at least 6mm.

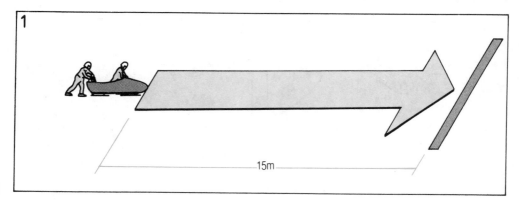

1

15m

The combined weight of the bob and team must not exceed 390kg for a two-man bob, or 630kg for a four-man bob. If the permitted weight is not reached, ballast may be added to the bob, but it must be firmly secured.

A team must use the same bob for all heats of a race unless the bob is damaged, in which case it may be replaced with another of a similar type.

Dress All team members must wear crash helmets and elbow pads for both official training and races. Goggles may be worn. Shoes may be fitted with spikes to aid in pushing the bob; the size and arrangement of the spikes is governed by specific regulations.

THE RACE

Heats Events consist of four runs, or heats, for each team. The winner is the team with the lowest aggregate of times.

Running order for heats is determined by a draw.

The start The teams must line up in their running order, keeping the starting line clear. A team not in position when its starting number is called is disqualified unless the delay is caused by circumstances beyond its control.

The bob must be placed 15m behind the starting line (**1**). After the starter has given the signal, the team has 60 seconds to start. Timing begins as soon as the front of the bob's runners crosses the starting line.

The team may push the bob for whatever distance they wish, but must not accept any outside help. No bob or team member may cross the starting beam backwards.

False start If there is a false start for which no member of the team is responsible, the run is allowed to continue. The team will be told that their heat is not valid and will begin again as soon as they return to the start of the course.

Leaving the bob Team members may get off the bob to push it, but even if they fall off or leave the track, they must not have any outside help to get back on the run. All team members must cross the finish line on the bob (**2**).

PENALTIES

Fines are imposed for losing part of the ballast, part of the bobsleigh, or part of the equipment during a race. Fines are also given for damaging the run by leaving braking traces in the curves.

Disqualification Other offenses are punishable by disqualification, which may be for any period, up to life. The entire team is liable to be disqualified if any member:

a) does not wear a crash helmet or elbow pads during training or races;

b) is considered either physically or psychologically unfit to compete by the jury and a doctor;

c) warms the runners before the start, other than by hand friction, or applies any substance to the runners;

d) uses any mechanical means to propel the bob;

e) carries any advertising not conforming to the regulations of the governing body;

f) accepts any outside help during a race;

g) trains on a course outside authorized hours;

h) refuses to abide by the decisions of the jury.

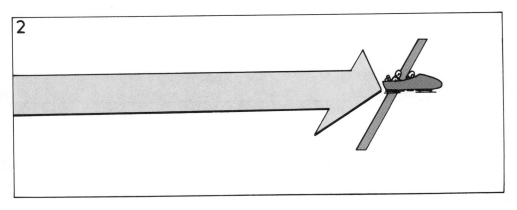

BOXING

HISTORY
Boxing was first included in the ancient Olympic Games in c. 686BC.
The modern sport has its origins in the bare-knuckle prize-fights of eighteenth and nineteenth century Britain. The rules of amateur boxing as included in the modern Olympics, and of the many professional boxing organizations, are all based on the Marquess of Queensberry's rules, first drafted in c.1867. The sport spread to the USA and to mainland Europe early in the twentieth century.

SYNOPSIS
Two fighters of similar weight contest a bout of limited duration, using only their gloved hands to hit each other on the front and sides of the head and on certain areas of the upper body. Bouts are won by a knockout, by forcing the opponent to retire, or by the accumulation of points.

COMPETITION AREA AND EQUIPMENT
The ring is a raised area surrounded by ropes. The ropes enclose an area a maximum of 20ft square, and a minimum for amateur fights of 12ft square, or for professional fights of 16ft square. There must be at least 1ft 6in of floor space beyond the ropes, and the corner posts must be padded.

For amateur fights three ropes at heights of 1ft 3.7in, 2ft 7.5in, and 4ft 3in above the canvas are specified.

The floor covering is of canvas over an underlayer of felt, rubber, or similar substance ½–¾in thick.

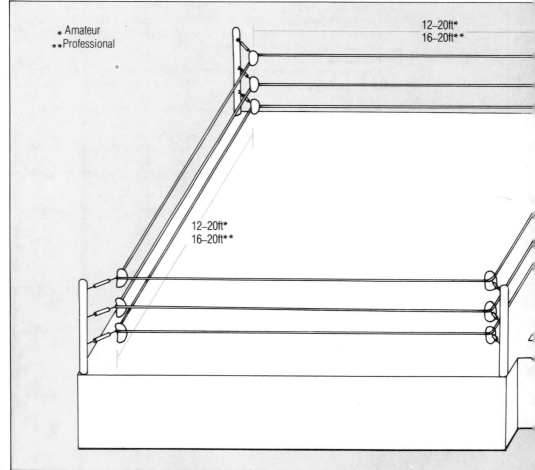

* Amateur
** Professional

12–20ft*
16–20ft**

12–20ft*
16–20ft**

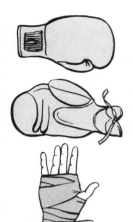

Dress Professionals wear light boots and shorts. Amateurs wear light boots, shorts, and an undervest. The belt (an imaginary line between the top of the hips and the navel) must be clearly shown by a contrast in color. A groin protector is worn under the shorts, and a gumshield in the mouth.

Gloves normally weigh 8oz except for professional light middleweight and below, when they weigh 6oz.

Tape is wrapped around the hands inside the gloves. For amateurs, this may be a soft surgical bandage up to 8ft 4in long by 2in wide, or not more than 6ft 6in of Velpeau type bandage. The bandage may not cover the knuckles. Adhesive plaster is not permitted, except for a 3in by 1in strip to secure the end of the bandage at each wrist.

Professionals of all weights may use up to 18ft of 2in-wide soft bandage and/or 9ft of 1in-wide zinc oxide plaster tape for middleweight class and below or up to 11ft for light heavyweights and heavyweights.

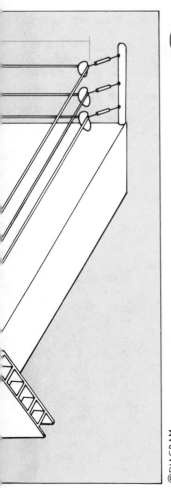

©DIAGRAM

BOXING 2

COMPETITORS AND OFFICIALS

Competitors are matched by weight. The weight categories of the International Amateur Boxing Association (IABA) and World Boxing Council (WBC) are shown in the table. Competitors are weighed at the weigh-in on the day of the fight, and are medically examined to establish their fitness to fight and to check for contagious diseases.

Each amateur boxer is allowed one second and one assistant second, who may only assist him in the intervals between rounds.

Professional boxers may have up to four seconds.

Officials In amateur bouts there is a referee who officiates inside the ring but does not mark a score card, five judges (or three in minor fights) around the edge of the ring, and a timekeeper.

In professional bouts the referee acts as one of the three judges, except in the United Kingdom where he is the sole scorer.

PROCEDURE

The bout The two boxers are called to the center of the ring by the referee and shake hands with each other. They then return to their respective corners until a bell is sounded to mark the start of the first round.

Amateur bouts consist of three rounds of three minutes each. The intervals between rounds are of one minute's duration.

In major professional championship contests there are normally fifteen rounds of three minutes each; in professional bouts of ten rounds or fewer the rounds may be of two minutes each. Intervals are of one minute's duration.

The end of each round is signaled by a bell, and the boxers retire to their respective corners where they may sit down and be attended by their seconds.

At a knock-down the standing boxer must withdraw to the farther neutral corner while the referee makes the count. If the boxer who is down does not get up before the count of ten, his opponent is declared the winner by a count-out and the bout ends. In amateur and some professional contests a count of eight is mandatory.

At the referee's order "Break!" both boxers must take one step back before starting to box again.

The referee calls "Stop!" to interrupt boxing, and "Box!" to restart it.

In professional contests the boxers shake hands again at the beginning of the final round. The referee raises the hand of the winner when the result is announced. Amateurs then shake hands again.

Weight categories	Amateur (IABA)	Professional (WBC)
Light flyweight	48kg (106lb)	49kg (108lb)
Flyweight	51kg (112lb)	51kg (112lb)
Bantamweight	54kg (119lb)	53.5kg (118lb)
Super bantamweight	—	55kg (121lb)
Featherweight	57kg (126lb)	57kg (126lb)
Junior lightweight	—	59kg (130lb)
Lightweight	60kg (132lb)	61kg (134.5lb)
Light (junior) welterweight	63.5kg (140lb)	63.5kg (140lb)
Welterweight	67kg (148lb)	66.5kg (147lb)
Light middleweight	71kg (156.5lb)	70kg (154lb)
Middleweight	75kg (165lb)	72.5kg (160lb)
Light heavyweight	81kg (179lb)	79kg (174lb)
Cruiserweight		88.45kg (195lb)
Heavyweight	91kg (201 lb)	88.45+kg (195+lb)
Super-heavyweight	91+kg (201+lb)	

FOULS AND PENALTIES

Fouls The following are the most important actions that are prohibited under both amateur and professional rules:

a) hitting below the belt (**1**);

b) hitting on the back of the head (**2**) or neck, or on the kidney area (**3**);

c) striking with the head (**4**), shoulder, elbow, forearm, or with any part of the gloved hand other than the knuckle area (**5**);

d) hitting while pivoting (the "pivot blow");

e) holding the opponent (**6**);

f) hitting the opponent when he is down or rising;

g) hitting while breaking;

h) disobeying the referee, eg not breaking when ordered.

Penalties The referee may disqualify a boxer without warning for an offense. In amateur events it is more usual first to caution an offender at a suitable moment, or to stop the fight to issue a formal warning. The third such warning results in immediate mandatory disqualification.

SCORING

Count-outs A count-out ends the bout in immediate victory for the boxer who knocked his opponent out.

A technical count-out occurs when the referee stops a bout because he considers that one boxer is not fit to continue.

Points systems Points are awarded by the referee or judges at the end of each round according to the proportion of hits made by each boxer; in professional bouts the quality of a boxer's defense and style are also reflected in the points.

In order to count, a hit must be made cleanly with the knuckle part of either glove on the front or sides of the opponent's head or of his body above the belt.

At the end of a round a maximum number of points (20 in amateur events) is awarded to the boxer who is judged to have been the more skilful, and proportionately fewer to the other.

The points awarded for each round to each boxer are added at the end of the bout, provided the bout was not ended before the full time limit by a count-out, stoppage, retirement, or disqualification. The winner is the boxer with the greater aggregate of points.

When contestants are otherwise equal, marks are given to the one who does more leading or who displays the better style. Drawn decisions are permitted in professional boxing.

If a tie persists in an amateur event, victory is awarded to the boxer who displayed the better defense.

1

2

3

4

5

6

© DIAGRAM

55

CANOEING

HISTORY

Canoes were the first true boats to be built by early man, and examples have been found dating back to the Stone Age. The two families of modern canoes, the kayaks and the Canadian canoes, owe their respective origins to the closed Eskimo sealskin kayak and the open North American Indian birchbark canoe. Organized recreational canoeing began in the late nineteenth century, and canoe racing on a flat-water course was first included in the Olympic Games in 1936. Slalom and wildwater racing grew in popularity in the 1940s and 1950s, but to date canoe slalom has been included only once in the Olympic Games, in 1972. The international governing body for all forms of canoe racing is the International Canoe Federation, formed in 1924.

SYNOPSIS

Both kayaks and Canadian canoes compete in the following races: canoe races, held over flat-water regatta courses; slaloms, where competitors must negotiate slalom gates while racing through turbulent water containing natural hazards; wildwater races, over longer rough-water courses without slalom gates; and marathon races, over long-distance courses where the water is not subject to prescribed standards.

COMPETITORS AND OFFICIALS

Competitors in international events must be authorized by their national federation.

Officials include: starters, timekeepers, and finishing line judges; raft or boat officials responsible for scrutinizing canoes and equipment; aligners, 15m judges, and turning point umpires (in canoe races); gate judges (in slalom races); and safety officers, responsible for rescuing competitors who have capsized (especially in slalom and wildwater races).

EQUIPMENT

Nomenclature Kayaks are referred to by the letter K followed by the number of paddlers – K1, K2, K4; Canadian canoes by C followed by the number of paddlers – C1, C2.

Canoe racing Canoes must conform to the measurements given in the table. All types of construction materials are permitted, providing that the canoe's size and shape conform to specific regulations. All canoes must carry a vertical numberplate indicating the lane in which they are racing.

Steering rudders are permitted on kayaks, but not on Canadian canoes.

Canadian canoes may be entirely open. Any covering on a C1 may not extend more than 150cm from the stem and 75cm from the stern; on a C2, the length of the opening may not be less than 295cm.

Marathon racing canoes must conform to the measurements and specifications for racing canoes, and to the buoyancy specifications for slalom and wildwater canoes. Additionally, marathon canoes may be fitted with bailing systems; removable spray decks are permitted on Canadian canoes.

Canoes conforming to the specifications for wildwater racing are also permitted in marathon races.

Slalom canoes must conform to the measurements given in the table.

All slalom canoes must be made unsinkable, and should float level with the surface when filled with water. The canoes must also be fitted with safety handles at the bow and the stern. Competitors must be able to free themselves immediately from their canoes at all times.

Steering rudders are prohibited on both kayaks and Canadian canoes.

Wildwater canoes must conform to the measurements given in the table. In all other respects they should conform to the standards for slalom canoes.

Paddles Kayaks may be propelled only by double-bladed paddles (**a**), and Canadian canoes by single-bladed paddles (**b**).

Dress At international events, competitors' dress must be approved by their national federation. All competitors must wear a clearly visible starting number.

Competitors in slalom and wildwater races must wear lifejackets (with a buoyancy of 6kg) and safety helmets; competitors in marathon races may be required to wear similar safety equipment.

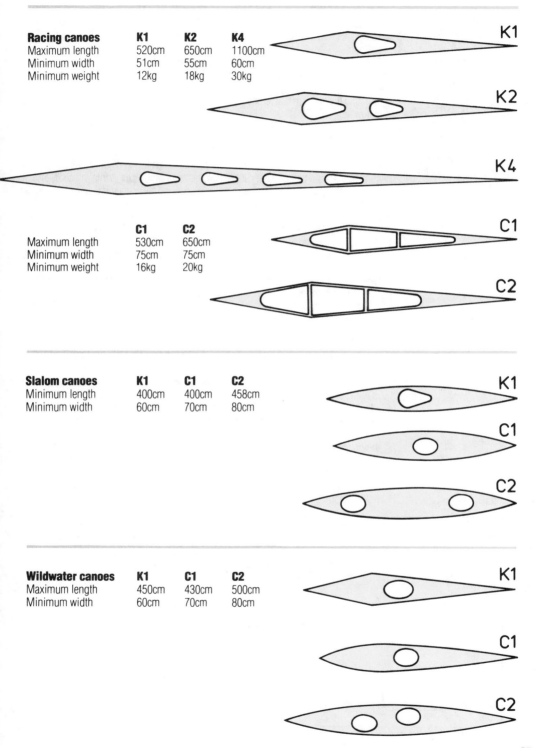

Racing canoes

	K1	K2	K4
Maximum length	520cm	650cm	1100cm
Minimum width	51cm	55cm	60cm
Minimum weight	12kg	18kg	30kg

	C1	C2
Maximum length	530cm	650cm
Minimum width	75cm	75cm
Minimum weight	16kg	20kg

Slalom canoes

	K1	C1	C2
Minimum length	400cm	400cm	458cm
Minimum width	60cm	70cm	80cm

Wildwater canoes

	K1	C1	C2
Maximum length	450cm	430cm	500cm
Minimum width	60cm	70cm	80cm

CANOEING 2

CANOE RACING

Events At international level, men race K1, K2, K4, C1, and C2 over 500m, 1000m, and 10,000m. Women race K1, K2, and K4 over 500m and 6000m. Olympic events are listed in the table.

The course should be clearly marked by flags mounted on buoys.

The starting and finishing lines, which should be at right angles to the course, are marked by red flags. The starting line should allow a clear width of 5m for each canoe (**A**); the finishing line should be at least 45m wide. A line 15m from the start should be marked with yellow flags.

For championships, the water should be at least 2m deep over the whole course.

For races up to 1000m, the course should be straight and in one direction. In championships, the racing lanes should be 9m wide.

For races over 1000m, turning points are permitted; they should have a radius of at least 40m, and should be marked by at least six red and yellow flags. A minimum distance of 1000m should be allowed between the starting line and the first turning point, between the centers of subsequent turning points, and between the last turning point and the finishing line.

In championships, the 10,000m course should have a minimum distance of 1500m between the starting line and the first turning point, and between the centers of subsequent turning points. The distance from the last turning point to the finishing line should be at least 1000m.

Heats may be held for races up to and including 1000m. Heats and finals must be held over the same course, and no heat may include more than nine canoes. Allocation to heats and lanes is decided by lot.

Depending on the total number of entries, the first three or four canoes to cross the finishing line in each heat go forward to the next round. The remaining canoes take part in repechage heats, giving them another chance to qualify for the higher rounds.

For championships, intervals between rounds must be at least 1hr for 500m races, and at least 1½hr for 1000m races.

Heats are not held for races over 1000m, but canoes may be started at intervals if the water is not wide enough to permit a simultaneous start.

Start (**A**) Starting positions are decided by lot, drawn separately for each heat.

The aligner should notify the starter when all competing canoes are level and stationary, with their bows on the starting line. In championships, canoes are held by officials so that their sterns touch the starting dock or pontoon until the signal is given.

The starter gives the signal by the word "Ready" followed by a shot or the word "Go." It is a false start if a competitor or crew begin paddling after the "Ready" and before the shot or "Go." Any competitor or crew making two false starts is disqualified, whether or not they were responsible for them.

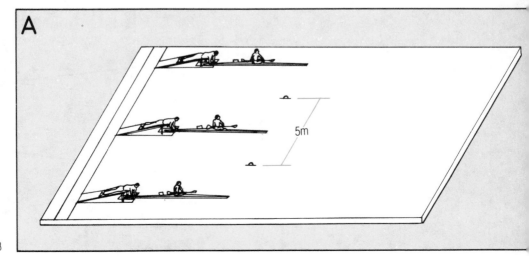

A

5m

If a competitor breaks his paddle between the starting line and the 15m line, the canoes are recalled, and a new start is held after the broken paddle has been replaced.

Race procedure In races up to and including 1000m, competitors must remain in their own lanes for the whole length of the race. Canoes must be kept at least 5m apart, and no competitor may derive any benefit from hanging in another's wake.

In races over 1000m, competitors may leave their lanes providing that they do not impede other competitors. Over the last 1000m of the course (signaled by a bell) they must return to their lanes and remain at least 5m apart.

Turning points in a race must be taken in a counterclockwise direction (**B**). When making a turn, competitors should follow the course marked by the buoys as closely as possible; touching a turning point buoy results in disqualification only if it results in an advantage for the touching canoe. If more than one canoe rounds the turning point at the same time, the competitor on the outside course (**a**) must give room to the competitor on the inside course (**b**) if the inside competitor has the bow of his canoe level with:
a) the front edge of the outer canoe's cockpit in K1 races (as illustrated);
b) the fore cockpit of the outer canoe in K2 and K4 races;
c) the body of the competitor in the outer canoe in C1 races;
d) the body of the foremost competitor in the outer canoe in C2 races.

An overtaking canoe must keep clear of the canoe being overtaken at all times; however, the canoe being overtaken may not alter course to cause difficulties to the overtaking canoe.

Finish A canoe is considered to have finished the course when its bow crosses the finishing line. In championships, photofinish equipment is used to decide placings; two or more competitors crossing the finishing line simultaneously share the placing.

All boats qualifying for the next round, or the first four boats in a final, are checked after the race to ensure that they conform with ICF regulations.

Disqualification Competitors may be disqualified for:
a) making two false starts;
b) arriving late at the start;
c) using a canoe that does not conform with ICF regulations;
d) receiving outside help during the race, or being accompanied by another boat along the course;
e) not taking part in a heat as instructed;
f) capsizing, unless the competitor or crew are able to right the canoe and get in it again without outside help;
g) causing a collision, or being responsible for damage to the canoe or paddle of another competitor;
h) any other breaches of the racing regulations.

A competitor withdrawing from one race without valid reason is disqualified from all other events in the same meeting.

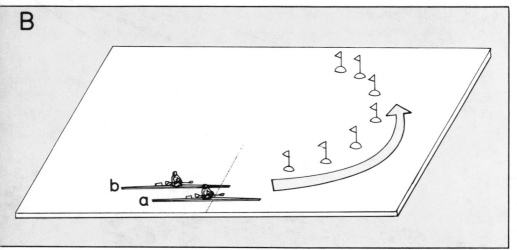

B

© DIAGRAM

CANOEING 3

MARATHON RACES

Events Men race in K1, K2, C1, and C2; women in K1 and K2; mixed pairs in K2 and C2.

Courses The minimum racing distance is 15km for women, and 20km for men. Races may be held on river courses without obstacles; on river courses with obstacles such as rocks, weirs, and shallows; on lakes, estuaries, or the open sea; or on any combination of these. Obligatory or optional portages (where the competitor leaves the water and transports his boat overland) may also be included.

Races may include one or more stages, and be run over one or several days; results are based on the total racing time.

The starting and finishing lines are marked by red flags at the points where the lines intersect the outer edges of the course. Any turning points on the course must be taken in a counterclockwise direction, unless otherwise indicated.

The start should preferably be a stationary start, as used in canoe racing. If circumstances make this impossible, permitted alternative procedures are:

a) Le Mans start, with the canoes lined up on the bank in an order determined by lot, and the competitors racing for their boats on the signal;

b) grid start, with positions determined by lot but with national teams equally represented in each rank of the grid;

c) rolling start, where canoes are allowed to drift toward the starting line in order to cross it on the signal;

d) interval start, with competitors starting at timed intervals either singly or in groups.

These procedures are also used for restarting a race following an overnight halt. If, however, two or more stages of a race are run on the same day, competitors start the second and subsequent stages in their order of arrival from the previous stage, and at the same time intervals.

Portage Official compulsory and optional portages are marked by red and yellow flags at the beginning and end of the section; there must be enough space to allow at least four canoes to be portaged at the same time. Competitors must land within the 100m of bank before the first flag, and relaunch within the 100m after the second flag. They may not land or relaunch on the bank between the flags marking the portage.

Competitors may make portages at other points along the course providing that this does not shorten the distance raced. On these portages they should follow the route of the river, keeping as close to it as possible.

Competitors encountering shallow water may disembark in the river and drag their canoe into deeper water.

Assistance Competitors may not take pace from, or receive assistance from, boats not competing in the race. They may receive assistance from bank support crews; this may include first aid, provision of food, drink, and clothing, replacement or repair of paddles or faulty equipment, and assistance in emptying and righting a capsized canoe.

Competitors may repair damaged boats, but may not replace or exchange them; each competitor must use the same canoe throughout the race.

Finish A canoe is considered to have finished the race when its bow crosses the finishing line. Two or more canoes crossing the line simultaneously share the placing.

Disqualification Competitors may be disqualified for:

a) making two false starts;

b) using a canoe that does not conform with ICF regulations;

c) being accompanied by another boat along the course;

d) causing a collision, or being responsible for damage to the canoe or paddle of another competitor;

e) any other breaches of the marathon racing regulations.

SLALOM

Events In the individual events, men compete in K1, C1, and C2; women in K1; mixed pairs in C2.

There are team events for teams of three canoes in each of the above categories.

A competitor may take part in one individual event and one team event only; however, his individual category may be different from his team category.

The course may not be more than 800m long, measured through all the gates from the starting line to the finishing line. World championship courses must be at least 700m long.

There should be 25–30 gates, including at least four reverse gates. For team races, one gate should be designated a team gate. The last gate on the course should be at least 25m from the finishing line.

The current velocity must be at least 2m/sec.

The course should include natural and artificial obstacles, and must be navigable throughout its entire length. It should provide the same conditions for both left- and right-handed C1 paddlers.

Gates Each gate consists of two round poles, 2m long and 35–50mm in diameter, suspended so that the lower end of the poles is at least 10cm above the surface of the water. It must not be possible for the poles to be put into motion by the water.

Gates should be 1.2–3.5m wide, measured between the poles.

All gates should be numbered in the order in which they are to be negotiated. Reverse and team gates should be clearly designated by the letters "R" and "T" respectively.

Numbers and letters should be at least 20cm high, and painted in black on yellow panels. A diagonal red line should be painted on the reverse of the panels, ie on the side of the panel opposite the direction of correct negotiation.

The gate pole that will be to the competitor's right should be painted with green and white rings; the pole that will be to the competitor's left with red and white rings.

The team gate should be so placed on the course that the arrival of a team at the gate avoids contact with any subsequent gates.

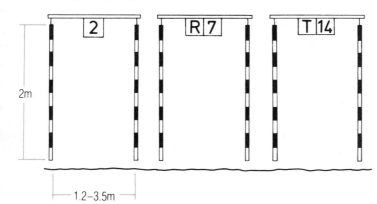

2m

1.2–3.5m

©DIAGRAM

CANOEING 4

Training At least one hour before official training begins, a non-competitor capable of negotiating the course should make a demonstration run.

Each competitor is allowed one run over the course during official training.

Starting order Competitors are divided into start groups on the basis of their national federations' results in previous world championships. The slower groups race before the faster groups, with a separate draw for the individual starting order in each group.

Start In individual events, competitors start at one minute intervals. In team events, teams start at two minute intervals, with the canoes of each team starting one after the other.

All starts must be directly upstream or downstream. Each boat is held at the starting line by an official until the starting signal is given.

A competitor's starting time is taken when his body (or the body of the first paddler in a C2) crosses the starting line. In team events, the time is taken when the body of the paddler in the first canoe crosses the starting line.

Race procedure Each competitor in each category makes two runs over the course, the better of which is counted in the final score. In the team events, the competition may be over one run only. Substitutions may be made for individual members of a team between the first and second run in a team event, providing that only one canoe of the three is so substituted.

A competitor who is overtaken by another competitor must give way when signaled to do so by an official. A competitor who is hindered by another competitor may repeat his run at the discretion of the officials.

If a competitor loses or breaks his paddle in an individual event, he may make use of an extra paddle carried in his canoe; he may not be given a paddle by anyone else. However, in team events, a spare paddle may be borrowed from another member of the team.

Competitors may make Eskimo rolls during their runs. In team runs, members of a team may assist each other to Eskimo roll.

Negotiation of gates All gates must be negotiated in numerical order. Forward gates must be negotiated bow first (**A**), and reverse gates stern first (**B**). In the team events, the team gate must be negotiated by all three canoes in a team within 15 seconds.

Negotiation of a gate begins when the trunk or head of the competitor (or of one of the two competitors in a C2) crosses the line between the poles, or when the canoe, paddle, or competitor's body touches a pole of the gate.

Negotiation of a gate ends when the body of the competitor (or of both competitors in a C2) has crossed the line between the poles and the canoe has left the line between the poles either down the course or sideways.

For the team gate, the time begins when the negotiation is begun by the first canoe in the team, and ends when the third canoe in the team has completed its negotiation.

Penalties Competitors are penalized for errors made at gates. Gate judges use yellow disks marked with the figures 5,10, or 50 to signal the number of penalties incurred, and a red disk to signal elimination or disqualification.

A competitor who negotiates the gate in the correct direction without touching either pole with his body, paddle, or canoe incurs no penalty points. Correct negotiation of the gate but with a touch on one pole (**1**) incurs 5 penalty points; with touches on both poles (**2**), 10 penalty points. Repeated touching of the same pole is only penalized once.

A competitor incurs a 50 point penalty if he:

a) negotiates a gate in a different direction from that shown on the course map;

b) negotiates a gate so that the green and white pole is to his left, and the red and white pole is to his right;

c) intentionally pushes a gate to allow his negotiation of it (**3**);

d) touches either or both poles of a gate, or performs an Eskimo roll in a gate, when failing to negotiate the gate in the correct direction;

e) omits a gate, when the penalty is signaled only after negotiation of a subsequent gate has been completed;

f) makes repeated attempts to negotiate a gate after his body has already crossed the line between the poles, except that he may make an unlimited number of attempts at a gate until his body has crossed that line.

In team events, a 50 point penalty is incurred if a team fails to negotiate the team gate within 15 seconds.

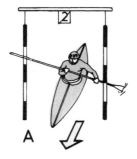

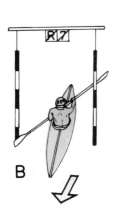

Direction of negotiation

Finish A competitor has completed his run, and his finishing time is recorded, when his body (or the body of the first paddler in a C2) has crossed the finishing line. A team has completed its run when the body of the competitor in the third canoe has crossed the finishing line.

A competitor who crosses the finishing line upside down (ie with his body completely under water) is eliminated for that run.

Scoring A competitor's score is calculated by adding the number of penalty points incurred to the time of his run in seconds.

A team's score is calculated by totaling the number of penalty points incurred by each of the three canoes, any penalty incurred at the team gate, and the time of the team's run in seconds.

The competitor or team with the lowest score for the better of their two runs is the winner. If two or more competitors or teams obtain the same score, the order is decided by the scores on their other runs.

Disqualification A competitor may be disqualified for:

a) using a canoe that does not conform with ICF regulations;

b) receiving outside assistance during a run;

c) intentionally negotiating gates after capsizing his canoe;

d) any other breaches of the racing regulations.

A competitor may be eliminated from a specific run over the course for:

a) capsizing (except that an Eskimo roll is not considered a capsize);

b) leaving his canoe;

c) being late at the start;

d) crossing the finishing line upside down.

WILDWATER RACES

Events Individual and team categories are as for slalom races.

The course must be at least 3km long, and must be navigable throughout; portages are not allowed. Part of the course must be of at least Grade III difficulty, with fast-flowing water, large rapids, high regular waves, and boulders. Gates may be used to indicate the correct channel in dangerous stretches.

Start In the individual events, competitors start at 30 second intervals. Teams in the team event start at one minute intervals.

Race procedure Competitors are allowed only one run over the course. Otherwise, with the exception of those rules specifically relating to negotiating the gates, rules for slalom races apply.

Result The winner is the competitor or team completing the course in the fastest time.

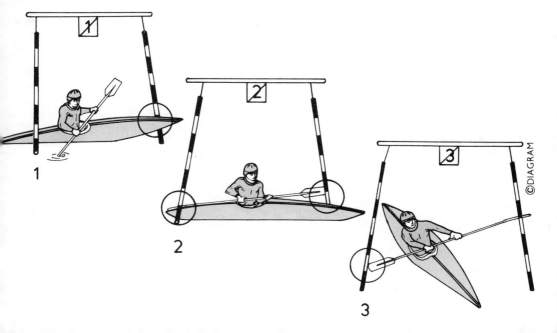

1

2

3

©DIAGRAM

CRICKET

HISTORY

Cricket originated in England as a simple bat and ball game five or six hundred years ago. By the mid-sixteenth century it was known as cricket, and by 1700 it was played to a set of recognized rules. The earliest known written rules date from 1744. The Marylebone Cricket Club was formed in 1787, and has remained ever since the recognized world authority of the game. Cricket spread to the former British colonies, and by the middle of the nineteeth century it was played in Australia, South Africa, the West Indies, New Zealand, India, and Pakistan. The first international match—Test Match—was played in Melbourne in 1877, and the famous Ashes series was begun soon afterward.

SYNOPSIS

Cricket is a ball game played between two teams of eleven players. It is played on a pitch with two wickets placed 22yd apart. Each team bats, or takes an innings, in turn, with two batsmen on the field at any time. The object of the fielding team is to dismiss the batsmen; the object of the batting side is to score runs. A match consists of one or two innings of each side, and the winning team is the one that scores the greater number of runs.

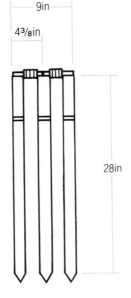

PLAYING AREA AND EQUIPMENT

The pitch is bounded at either end by lines known as bowling creases (**a**), which are 22yd apart. It extends 5ft in width on either side of an unmarked line joining the center of the wickets. The bowling creases are 8ft 8in long.

Parallel to the bowling creases and 4ft in front of them are the popping creases (**b**). These are marked for at least 6ft on either side of the center of the wickets but are considered to extend indefinitely.

The return creases (**c**) run at right angles to the bowling creases, at either end. The return crease joins the popping crease at its forward extension and must be marked to at least 4ft behind the wicket, although it is considered to extend indefinitely.

The inside edge of each line marks the crease.

The pitch is usually of grass, although approved artificial surfaces may be used. The grass must be level and cut short. In first-class cricket, regulations govern the rolling, mowing, watering, and covering of the turf.

The pitch stands in the center of a much larger playing area enclosed by a boundary marked by a line, fence, or rope.

Sightscreens are sometimes erected on or inside the boundary.

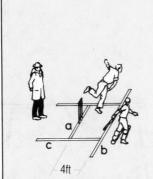

The wickets stand on the bowling creases at each end of the pitch. Each is composed of three vertical wood stumps with two horizontal wood bails resting on top. Each wicket is 9in wide. The stumps must be equal in size and wide enough to stop the ball passing between them. They are 28in high, and have grooves in their tops for the bails to rest in. The bails are 4³/₈in long, and must not project more than ½in above the top of the stumps.

The bat must not exceed 38in in overall length. It usually has a rubber grip; the blade must be made of wood and must not be more than 4¼in wide.

The ball is red leather with a stitched seam. The weight must be 5½–5¾oz, and the circumference 8¹³/₁₆–9in. Smaller and lighter balls may be used by juniors or women. Each innings usually starts with a new ball, and in matches lasting three days or more the fielding side may demand a new ball after a certain number of overs. If a ball is lost or becomes unfit for use during a game, a ball in similar condition should be substituted.

Dress Players wear white or cream shirts and pants, with a sweater if necessary, and a peaked cap or protective helmet. Batsmen and wicket keeper wear white pads to guard the lower leg, and gloves. Players also wear abdomen protectors. Cricket boots may be spiked or have rubber soles.

PLAYERS AND OFFICIALS

Players There are 11 players on each side, one of whom is the captain. The captains nominate their players before the toss, and may not change them afterward except with the agreement of the opposing captain.

Officials The game is controlled by two umpires. They stand at either end of the pitch: one behind the stumps at the bowler's end; the other at the striker's end, level with the wicket and usually on the leg side. The umpires change positions after each over as the bowling end changes, and they change ends after each team has had one innings. The umpires signal to a scorer, who records details of play.

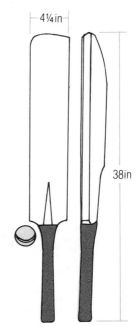

4¼in

38in

8¹³/₁₆–9in

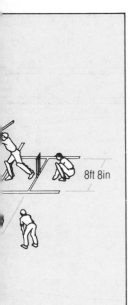

8ft 8in

©DIAGRAM

65

CRICKET 2

DURATION AND SCORING

Duration varies with the standard of the match. There may be a limited playing time, or a specified number of overs. In both cases play ends before time if a result is obtained. Matches consist of one or two innings per team. An innings is complete either: when 10 of a team's batsmen have been dismissed; when the batting captain "declares" (voluntarily ends the innings); or after a specified number of overs.

Test match (international) cricket is played over five six-hour playing days, and first-class cricket over three or four days. At other levels, two-day, one-day, and afternoon cricket matches are played.

Intervals are allowed for meals (usually 40 minutes for lunch and 20 for tea) and between innings (10 minutes). Meal intervals are by agreement, but if an innings ends or there is a stoppage within a few minutes of the interval time, the interval may be taken immediately. The umpires decide whether conditions are fit for play to start, resume, or continue. If the umpires decide to stop play but both teams wish to continue in the prevailing conditions, they may do so. In the case of bad light, only the batting team has the option of deciding that play should continue.

Runs Scoring is in runs. A run is scored when both batsmen, after the ball has been hit or at any time when the ball is in play, pass each other and touch the ground beyond the opposite popping crease with any part of their body or bat (**A**).

If one or both batsmen run short (fail to reach the popping crease when turning for another run) the first run is not scored, but the second counts. If batsmen deliberately run short, the umpire signals "dead ball" and all runs scored off that ball are canceled.

After running, batsmen remain at the wicket reached on the last run. This may involve a different batsmen facing the bowler.

Boundaries Runs are also scored when the ball crosses the boundary. Normally only the boundary score counts, not the runs made between the wickets. However, completed runs shall count if they exceed the boundary allowance at the moment when the ball crosses the boundary. After a boundary, the batsmen resume their original positions.

If the ball touches (**B**) or runs along (**C**) the ground before crossing the boundary, it counts four runs.

If the ball crosses the boundary without first touching the ground (**D**), six runs are scored, even if the ball has been touched by a fielding player.

If a fielding player carrying the ball touches the ground on or over the boundary with any part of his body, a boundary is scored. If a fielding player catches the ball and then carries it over the boundary, six runs are scored.

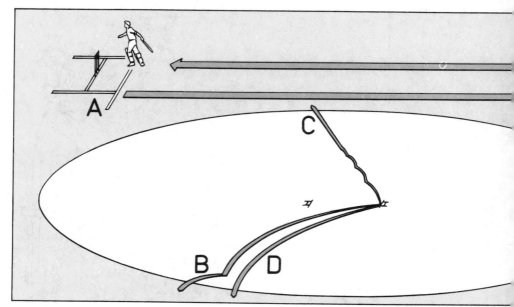

If the ball crosses the boundary from an overthrow or other fielding action, the boundary allowance is scored in addition to the runs made.

If a ball hits a sightscreen that is inside or partly inside the boundary, four runs are scored—the ball must clear it completely to score six.

Extras are runs scored without hitting the ball. They can be scored from a wide ball, a no ball, a bye, a leg bye, or a fielding offense.

If a "lost ball" is called six runs are scored; if more than six runs have been made before the call, all completed runs count. The run in progress also counts if the batsmen have crossed at the instant of the call.

Result In a two-innings match, the team that scores the highest total of runs is the winner. In a one-innings match the same applies, but if there is time remaining the captains may agree to continue the match. If a result is not achieved in this continuation, the first innings result stands.

If the scores are equal when the innings are complete, the match is a tie. If any innings is incomplete, the match is a draw.

In limited-over cricket, the match is won by the team that scores more runs in the specified number of overs. A limited-over match can be tied, but can only be a draw if poor conditions stop play.

The result of a match is expressed as a win by the number of runs by which one team beats the other, or as a win by the number of wickets still to fall if the last side to bat exceeds the other's total of runs.

Runs are credited to the personal score of the striking batsmen, unless they are runs made from extras and scored as such. Dismissals of batsmen are credited to the bowler, except those by run out, handled the ball, hit the ball twice, obstructing the field, or timed out.

RULES OF PLAY

Starting play The choice of batting (taking an innings) or fielding goes to the captain who wins the toss of a coin before the match.

The umpire calls "play" at the start of a day or after an interval or interruption.

Batting The first batsman (the striker) faces the bowler's ball and guards his wicket by standing with one foot inside his popping crease. His partner stands opposite, at the bowler's end, within his ground. A batsman is within his ground if some part of his body or the bat in his hand is grounded behind the popping crease. The batsmen's object is to make runs, and to guard their wickets.

Each team takes its innings in turn. In a two-innings match, the teams take their innings alternately unless one side is forced to "follow on" (take its second innings immediately after its first). A team batting second may be asked to follow on by the opposing captain if it scores:

200 fewer than the opposition in a match of five days or more;

150 fewer in a three- or four-day match;

100 fewer in a two-day match;

75 fewer in a one-day match.

Fielding At the start of play, all members of the fielding side take up positions on the field. The wicket keeper is positioned behind the striking batsman. He must stay wholly behind the stumps until the ball touches the bat or the striker's body, or passes the wicket, or until the batsman attempts a run. If he infringes this rule, the umpire will call a no ball. The wicket keeper must not interfere with the batsman's playing of the ball.

Nine fieldsmen take up various positions in the field, according to whether the batsman is right- or left-handed, the technique of the bowler, and other considerations. These positions are decided by the captain, and he may move his players after each ball. However, no more than two fielders may be behind the popping crease on the leg side at the moment of bowling. Until the ball has hit or passed the bat or batsman, no fielder other than the bowler may stand in or have any part of his body extended over the pitch (the area 22yd by 10ft). If these positional rules are broken, the umpire will call a no ball.

A fielder may stop the ball with any part of his body, but if he uses any other means (eg his cap) the batting side is awarded five runs. These are in addition to any runs made (including the run in progress if the batsmen have crossed).

©DIAGRAM

CRICKET 3

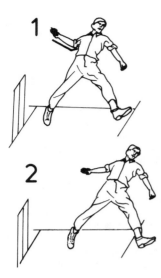

Bowling The bowler bowls the ball from one end to the batsman defending the opposite wicket. He may bowl overarm or underarm, over or round the wicket, and from either hand, but the batsman must be informed.

Bowling is in "overs" of six or eight balls. (The number is agreed beforehand and is consistent throughout the game.) A no ball or a wide ball is not counted in the over. Overs are delivered from alternate ends. A bowler must bowl a complete over unless he is injured or suspended. A bowler may change ends as often as he wishes, but he may not bowl two overs in succession in one innings.

The umpire calls "over" after the sixth or eighth ball, once he sees that both sides no longer regard the ball as in play. If an umpire miscounts an over, his count stands.

No ball A no ball is called if:

a) the bowler throws (**1**) instead of bowling the ball (for a fair ball the arm must be straightened well before the ball leaves the hand);

b) in his delivery stride the bowler does not ground his back foot within the return crease or its forward extension, or does not have some part of his front foot grounded or raised behind the popping crease (**2**);

c) the bowler throws the ball at the striker's wicket to try to run him out;

d) the bowler changes his delivery without informing the umpire or batsman;

e) a fielder or wicket keeper breaks a positioning rule.

Either umpire may call and signal "no ball" immediately on delivery.

The receiving batsman can hit a no ball and can make runs from it. He can be dismissed only by being run out, handling the ball, hitting the ball twice, or obstructing the field.

A penalty of one run is scored to the batting team for a no ball if no runs are made otherwise. This run is scored even if the batsman is dismissed.

Wide ball A wide is called if the bowler sends the ball so high over (**a**) or so wide of (**b**) the wicket that it goes out of the striker's reach when he is standing in the normal guard position.

Runs can be made from a wide ball, but if the striker hits the ball the umpire revokes the call of wide. The umpire signals the wide as soon as the ball passes the striker's wicket.

A penalty run is scored for a wide if no other runs are made, and this is scored even if the batsman is dismissed.

Batsmen may be stumped, run out, out handling the ball, out obstructing the field, or out hit wicket.

A bye is a run taken when the ball has not touched the bat or any part of the batsman's body (**c**).

A leg bye is a run taken when the ball touches but is not deliberately deflected by a part of the batsman's body except his hands (**d**).

Leg byes are scored only if the batsman tried to hit the ball with his bat, or tried to avoid being hit by the ball.

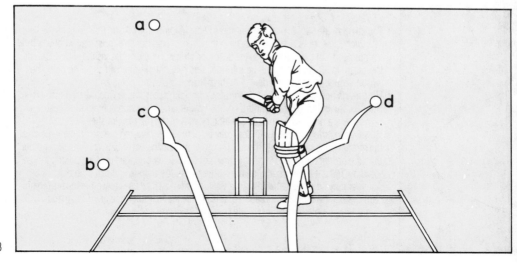

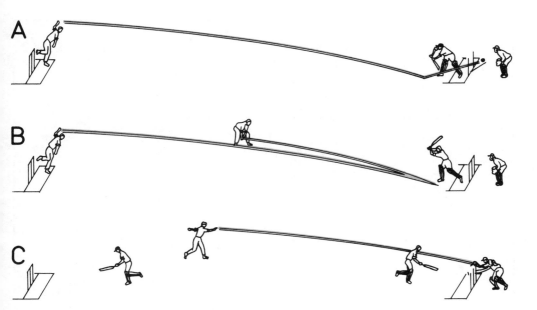

Dismissing the batsman The umpire will not decide that a batsman is out unless the other team makes an appeal of "How's that?" The appeal must be made before the bowler begins his run up or bowling action for the next ball. The umpire at the bowler's wicket usually answers the appeal first, unless the other umpire was in a better position to see the action. The umpires may consult with each other. If there is any doubt after consultation, the decision will be in favor of the batsman. A batsman may be out in various ways.

Bowled A batsman is out bowled when the ball delivered by the bowler puts down the striker's wicket (**A**). (The wicket is down if either bail is completely removed from the top of the stumps.) The striker is out bowled even if the ball touches his bat or body before hitting the wicket, or if he breaks the wicket by hitting or kicking the ball onto it.

Caught A batsman is out caught when a fielder within the playing area catches the ball after it has come off the striker's bat or gloves and before it touches the ground (**B**). The catch is considered fair if:
the ball is hugged to a fielder's body or lodges in his clothing or the wicket keeper's pads, but not if it lodges in a protective helmet;
the ball is caught after it has touched a person on the field, but not if it has touched a protective helmet;
the ball is caught off an obstruction within and not part of the boundary;
the hand holding the ball touches the ground but the ball does not.
If the striker is caught, no runs are scored.

Run out A batsman is run out if he is out of his ground to make a run, or for another reason while the ball is in play, and his wicket is broken by the opposing side (**C**).
If a wicket is put down while batsmen are running and they have crossed, the player running toward the broken wicket is out. If they have not crossed, the player running from it is out. If a batsman stays in or returns to his ground and the other batsman joins him there, the latter is out if the empty wicket is put down.
If a no ball is called, a batsman can be run out only if he tries to make a run.
The run on which a player is run out is not scored, but other runs still count.

Leg before wicket (LBW) A batsman is out LBW if any part of his body, equipment, or dress intercepts a ball that would have hit the wicket (**D**), provided that:
the ball has not previously touched his bat or a hand holding the bat;
the ball pitched or would have pitched in a straight line between the wickets;
the point of impact is in a straight line between the wickets, even if above the bails.
Provided the other conditions are met, a player who makes no genuine attempt to play the ball can be out LBW even if the ball is stopped outside the line of the offside stump.

©DIAGRAM

69

CRICKET 4

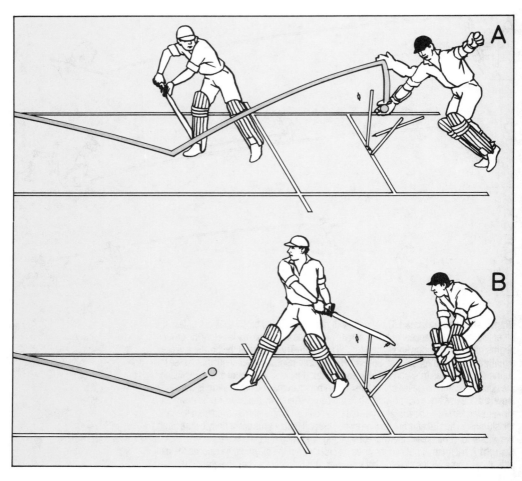

Stumped The striker is out stumped if the wicket keeper, without the intervention of another fielder, puts down the striker's wicket while the striker, in receiving a ball, is out of his ground for any reason other than to attempt a run (**A**).

The wicket keeper cannot go in front of the wicket to stump the striker unless the ball has hit the bat or batsman's body.

The striker can be stumped if the ball rebounds from the wicket keeper's body, or is thrown or kicked onto the wicket by the wicket keeper.

Hit wicket A batsman is out if he breaks his wicket with his body or equipment while playing a shot (**B**) or setting off for a first run.

Handled the ball A batsman is out if, without the opponents' consent, he touches the ball in play with his hand not holding the bat.

Hit the ball twice A striker is out if he hits or stops the ball with his bat or any part of his body, and then deliberately hits the ball again, except if he is guarding his wicket. A batsman can be out under this rule if he uses his bat or body to return the ball to fielders. Even if the ball is legally hit twice, no runs can be scored except if there is an overthrow or a penalty.

Obstructing the field A batsman is out if he deliberately obstructs the opponents or prevents a catch being made.

Timed out A batsman is timed out if he deliberately takes more than two minutes to enter the field of play, timed from the moment the previous wicket falls.

Retiring A batsman may retire or voluntarily end his innings at any time, but may not resume his innings without the consent of the opposing captain.

Substitution Substitutes may replace fielding players who are ill or injured after the nomination of teams. If a substitution is made for any other reason, the opposing captain must give his consent. A substitute may field, but may not bat or bowl. The opposing captain has the right to object to a substitute acting as wicket keeper. The umpire's permission must be obtained if a substitution is made after an interval.

A player may return to the match and bat, bowl, or field even if a substitute has previously replaced him. If a fielder returns after more than 15 minutes out of the game, he may not bowl until he has been back in the game for at least as long as he was out.

A batsman may leave the field because of illness or injury, after informing the umpires. He can resume his innings at the fall of a wicket.

If a batsman is injured but continues to bat, a substitute runner may be allowed to make his runs for him. The runner should if possible be a member of the batting side who has already batted in that innings. The runner wears similar gloves and pads to the batsman. The batsman is out if his runner is run out or handles the ball or obstructs the field. If the batsman moves out of his ground he can be stumped or run out at the wicket keeper's end regardless of the positions of the runner and the other batsman, and in this case no runs will be scored.

Dead ball The ball becomes dead when:
it settles in the hands of the wicket keeper or the bowler;
it crosses the boundary;
a batsman is out;
it lodges in the clothing of a batsman or an umpire, or in the protective helmet of a fielding player;
a penalty is awarded for a lost ball or a fielding infringement;
the umpire calls "over" or "time";
there is a serious injury;
there is a case of unfair play;
the umpire is satisfied that the striker is not ready to receive the ball;
the bowler accidentally drops the ball or does not deliver it for some reason;
the umpire leaves his normal position;
one or both bails fall from the striker's wicket before delivery;
the umpire disallows a leg bye.
The ball is no longer dead when the bowler starts his run up or bowling action.
The ball is not dead when:
it hits an umpire;
an unsuccessful appeal is made;
a wicket is broken but a batsman is not out;
the umpire calls "no ball" or "wide."

Unfair play The umpires will intervene if:
players lift the seam of the ball to get a better grip;
bowlers use wax or resin to polish the ball, although they may dry it with a towel or sawdust or remove mud from it;
the fielding side distracts the striker while he is receiving the ball;
the fielding side deliberately obstructs a run;
any player damages the pitch to help the bowler;
bowlers bowl short fast deliveries in an attempt to intimidate the striker, or bowl fast high full pitches deliberately;
batsmen try to "steal" runs during a bowler's run up;
any player wastes time deliberately.

Ending play When one hour of playing time is left, the next over counts as the first of a minimum of 20 six-ball or 15 eight-ball overs, unless a result is reached earlier and there are no interruptions to play.

If there is an interval or interruption during the last hour, the minimum number of overs is reduced in proportion to the length of the stoppage.

The last over before an interval or close of play will be started if the umpire arrives in position at the bowler's end before time is called.

The last over before an interval or close of play will be completed unless a batsmen is out or retires within two minutes of the interval. The final over of a match will be completed at the captains' request even if a wicket falls after time.

CYCLE RACING

HISTORY

The first organized cycle race was held in Paris in 1868, soon after the introduction of the pedal-driven bicycle. The new sport rapidly became popular in many parts of the world, with cyclists competing in increasingly longer races on public roads, or on the many purpose-built cycling tracks constructed during the 1880s and 1890s. Cycling has been included in the Olympic Games since 1896; the first Tour de France was held in 1903. The international governing body for the sport, The Union Cycliste Internationale (UCI) was formed in 1900.

SYNOPSIS

Cycle racing is broadly divided into road and track racing. Both categories include a variety of different events over distances ranging from a few hundred meters to several thousand kilometers. Olympic events are listed in the table.

COMPETITORS AND OFFICIALS

Competitors must be licensed by their national federation.

Officials include a chief referee, assistant referee, starters, scorers, and timekeepers.

DRESS AND EQUIPMENT

Dress Competitors must wear a racing jersey that covers the shoulders, and black shorts reaching approximately to mid-thigh.

National and international champions, and race leaders in stage races, may be permitted to wear special jerseys indicating their status.

Protective helmets of rigid molded material or woven padded straps must be worn.

Bicycles must conform to specified dimensions and be without streamlining. They may be propelled only by human force. For road racing (**A**), bicycles should have a free wheel and one working brake for each wheel. Track racing bicycles (**B**) may not have free wheels, brakes, or similar accessories.

Olympic events

Track events:
1000m sprint
1000m individual time trial
4000m individual pursuit
4000m team pursuit
Road events:
100km team trial
individual road race (c.200km)

A

ROAD RACES

Course The course must not cross itself, and may be from place to place, around a circuit, out and back, or any combination of these. All races must be held in conformity with the laws of the country in which they are run, and with regard to local traffic regulations. Control points, feeding stations, and repair pits should be set up at suitable intervals.

Procedure Starts are at the drop of a flag or a pistol shot, and may be made either standing or rolling (with the riders on the move before crossing the starting line). Riders may be given a short untimed distance in which to settle down, or to clear a built-up area. Riders are permitted to carry refreshments with them, but glass containers are prohibited and their use may lead to disqualification.

Competitors may not receive outside assistance, but members of the same team are permitted to exchange refreshments or equipment. Pacing is allowed between members of the same team who are competing as a team.

Riders may be penalized for pushing, deliberately hampering other riders, leaving the prescribed course, and other rule infringements. Penalties, which depend on the severity of the offense, include time penalties, fines, reprimands, and disqualification.

Individual road races may be held over any prescribed distance. Starts may be massed starts, or staggered handicap starts. The winner is the rider who is first to complete the course.

Time trials Competitors race against the clock and aim to cover a set distance in the fastest possible time. In English-speaking countries the usual distance for individual events is 25 miles; major team events are held over 100km. In individual events, riders start at one-minute intervals; in team events teams start at two-minute intervals. Riders in individual events may not take pace from other riders; teams may not take pace from other teams.

The Olympic team time trial is for teams of four; the times of the fastest three team members are used to determine the winners.

Stage races are sequences of races, including road races, criteriums, and time trials. The overall winner is the competitor with the lowest cumulative time for all the stages. The best known stage race is the Tour de France, in which competitors cover approximately 4000km in 21 one-day stages.

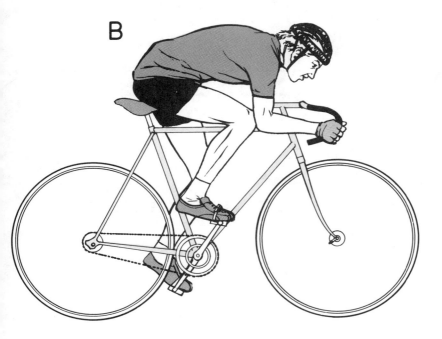

B

CYCLE RACING 2

TRACK RACING

The track should be a symmetrical circuit with banked corners, and preferably less than 500m long. The surface may be of wood, asphalt, shale, concrete, or cinders.

Track markings include starting (**a**) and finishing (**b**) lines, 200m line for sprint races (**c**), pursuit finishing lines, and numbered markers indicating the distance from the finishing line. A red line, the sprinter's line, is marked around the track 90cm from its inside edge; no overtaking is allowed inside this line if the rider ahead is on or inside the line.

Sprints (**A**) are races between two or more riders, held over three laps of a track of 333.33m or less, or two laps of a larger track.

The race is run on a heats basis, with the winner of each heat going forward to the next round. In championship events runners-up take part in repechage heats, giving them another chance to qualify for the higher rounds.

Timing is only over the last 200m of the last lap; earlier laps are generally devoted to maneuvering for position. The winner is the first cyclist over the finish line, whether or not he had the fastest time.

Individual pursuit (**B**) Two riders start on opposite sides of the track and race over a specified distance. If one rider does not catch the other (by overtaking and drawing even), the rider with the faster time for the complete distance is the winner. Women race over 3000m, amateur men over 4000m, and professional men over 5000m.

Team pusuit is similar to individual pursuit, but is contested by two teams of four riders. Victory is decided on the times of the first three riders of each team.

Time trials (**C**) Riders race against the clock and aim to cover a set distance, usually 1km, in the fastest possible time. Each rider makes a standing start from exactly the same point, and is alone on the track during his trial.

Points races (**D**) are massed start races with rolling starts, in which sprints for points are held on certain previously designated laps. Riders gain points for winning sprints, and for gaining laps on other riders. The rider with the greatest number of points at the end of the race is the winner.

Madison races (**E**) are points races for teams of two or three riders, run on a relay basis. No more than two members of the team may be on the track at the same time. Relays are effected by the outgoing rider touching his incoming partner.

Motor pacing (**F**) Track events of over 10km may be motor-paced races, in which each rider is preceded by a motorcyclist who sets the pace.

Motorcycles must be between 500cc and 1000cc. Each machine must carry a roller, 60cm wide and 3.5cm in diameter, supported on a frame projecting behind the rear wheels, to prevent the following rider from getting too close to the pacer.

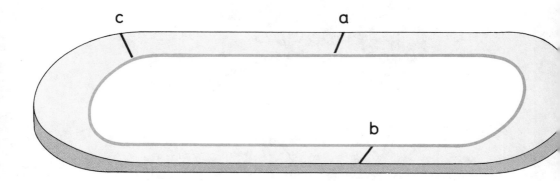

A

B

C

D

E

F

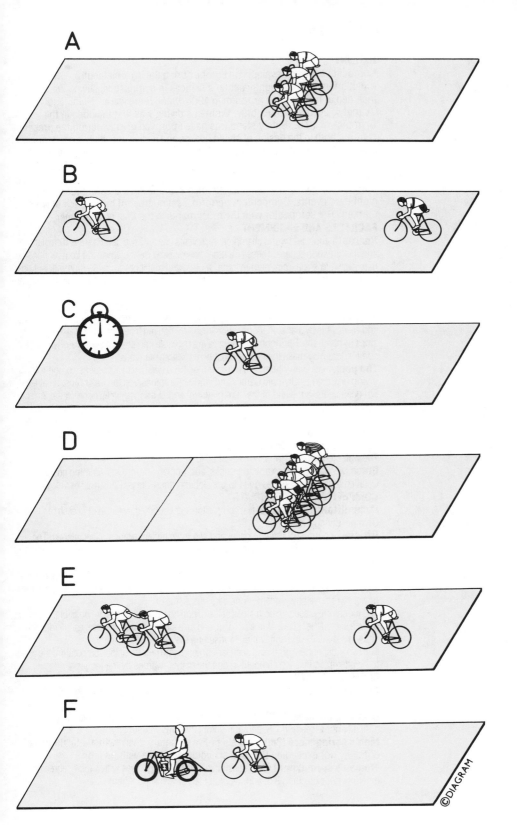

DIVING

HISTORY

Competitive diving developed in Europe during the late nineteenth century, being much influenced by slightly earlier advances in gymnastics. Diving was first included in the Olympic program in 1904, when there were ''plain'' and ''variety'' events for men only. Women's diving was first included in the Olympics of 1912. Safety standards have improved greatly during the present century, both in the design of diving boards and in dive specifications. Diving is governed by the same international governing body as swimming – the Fédération Internationale de Natation Amateur (FINA), founded in 1908.

SYNOPSIS

Competitive diving is separated into men's and women's springboard and highboard events. Competitors perform a set number of dives, each of which is marked. The competitor with the most marks in the final is the winner.

FACILITIES AND EQUIPMENT

Boards Olympic and world championship events use only two boards – the 10m platform and the 3m springboard. These and other boards used in less advanced competitions are here drawn to scale; minimum lengths, widths, and distances from the plummet (a line vertical to the diving end of the board) to the pool edge are listed in the table. Heights are measured to the surface of the water. Other regulations govern such factors as the height of the ceiling and the minimum permitted distance between boards.

All boards must be covered with an approved non-slip material. Platforms must be rigid, and accessible by stairs. Platforms more than 1m high must be surrounded at the back and sides by handrails. Springboards must have a movable fulcrum that can be easily adjusted; competitors may make their own adjustments, within set limits.

The pool must everywhere be a minimum of 1.8m deep, with a deeper area under the diving boards. For Olympic Games and world championships the water must be at least 5m deep beneath the end of the 10m platform, and at least 4m deep beneath the 3m springboard.

Natural and artificial illumination must meet specific requirements, and must not cause glare. Mechanical agitation of the water's surface beneath the boards must be provided to help divers judge the distance of the water.

The water temperature must be at least 26°C.

Dress Men must wear swimming trunks, and women one-piece swimming costumes. Detailed regulations are designed to prevent immodest dress. Caps may be worn.

COMPETITORS AND OFFICIALS

Competitors A maximum of two competitors per country may take part in each of the four Olympic diving events.

Officials comprise a judging panel and two independent groups of secretaries. The judging panel consists of a referee and seven (compulsory for Olympic Games and world championships) or five judges.

The referee manages the competition and makes sure that the rules are obeyed. He gives a signal, preferably a whistle, for each competitor to begin his dive. The referee also has the power to remove any judge he considers unsatisfactory.

The judges are placed on both sides of the diving board, or, if this is not possible, together on one side of the board. After each dive, and on a signal from the referee, each judge must show his mark clearly and without consulting the other judges.

The two independent groups of secretaries record the minutes of the competition, the dives to be attempted by each competitor, and the marks awarded by the judges.

OLYMPIC EVENTS

Men's highboard (10m) consists of four voluntary dives with a total degree of difficulty not exceeding 7.6 (see Selection of dives, p. 78), and six voluntary dives without limit.

Women's highboard (10m) consists of four voluntary dives with a total degree of difficulty not exceeding 7.6, and four voluntary dives without limit.

Men's springboard (3m) consists of five voluntary dives with a total degree of difficulty not exceeding 9.5, and six voluntary dives without limit.

Women's springboard (3m) consists of five voluntary dives with a total degree of difficulty not exceeding 9.5, and five voluntary dives without limit.

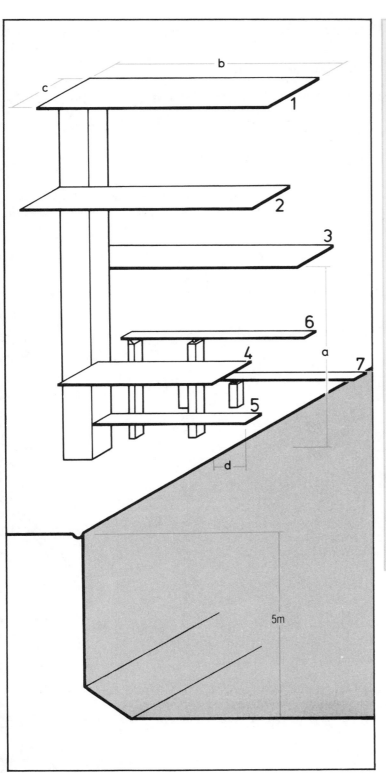

a
Height
1	10m	Platform*
2	7.5m	Platform
3	5m	Platform
4	3m	Platform
5	1m	Platform
6	3m	Springboard*
7	1m	Springboard

b
Length
1	6m
2	6m
3	6m
4	4m
5	4m
6	4.8m
7	4.8m

c
Width
1	2m
2	1.5m
3	1.5m
4	1.5m
5	60cm
6	50cm
7	50cm

d
To pool edge
1	1.5m
2	1.5m
3	1.25m
4	1.25m
5	75cm
6	1.5m
7	1.5m

*Used in Olympic Games and world championships

DIVING 2

PROCEDURES

Selection of dives Divers must restrict their selection of dives to those included in the official FINA handbook. This handbook gives details of all permitted dives, divides them into groups, and indicates their official degree of difficulty. A dive's degree of difficulty is taken into account for scoring purposes.

Each event has two sections: dives with limit, in which divers must select dives that do not exceed an overall maximum degree of difficulty, and dives without limit. Divers are not permitted to perform the same dive in each of the two sections.

Within each section, each dive shall be selected from a different group:

a) forward dives, with the body facing the water;
b) backward dives, with the body facing the board;
c) reverse dives, with the body facing the water;
d) inward dives, with the body facing the board;
e) twist dives, in which the body changes direction in the air;
f) armstand dives, which are permitted only in platform events.

At least 24 hours before the competition, each competitor must give the secretaries the

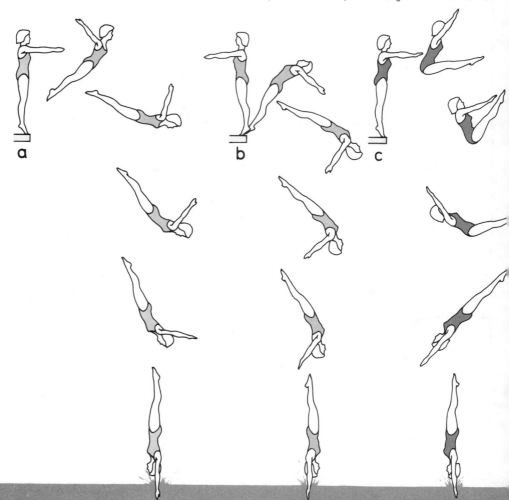

a   b   c

following written information about each of his dives: its official number; whether execution is to be straight, piked, with tuck, or free (see p. 81); the height of the board; the dive's official degree of difficulty.

Competition organization There is a preliminary round followed by a final round. The 12 divers with the highest scores in the preliminary round go forward into the final; if there is a tie for twelfth place, all tied competitors go into the final. Divers perform all of their selected dives in each round.

Separate sessions are held for each group of divers. Diving order among competitors is determined by lot in the preliminary round; in the finals, divers perform in reverse order of their scores in the preliminary round.

Before each dive, the referee or official announcer calls out the name of the competitor and the dive that he is about to attempt. The number of the dive to be performed and the manner of its execution may be displayed on an indicator board. The diver should be allowed sufficient time to prepare for and execute his dive; failure to dive within one minute of receiving a warning from the referee results in no score for the dive.

d

e

f

©DIAGRAM

DIVING 3

EXECUTION OF DIVES

Parts of a dive A dive is composed of the starting position, takeoff, flight through the air, and entry into the water. A dive begins when the starting position is assumed and ends when the entire body is under the water.

Start and takeoff The four starting positions are forward standing, forward running, armstand, and backward. Any starting position must be free and unaffected.

Forward dives from the springboard may be performed with either a standing or a running start, at the option of the diver. When scoring a standing dive, judges take into account the height and standard of execution that might be expected from a running dive.

For a forward standing dive the starting position is assumed when the diver stands at the front end of the board. The diver's body should be straight, his head erect, and his arms either straight in front of the body, out to the sides, above the head, or in any sideways position. A dive should not be restarted after the start of the armswing (after the arms leave the starting position). The diver must not bounce on the board before the takeoff.

For a forward running dive the starting position is assumed when the competitor is ready to take the first step of his run. The run must be smooth, straight, and without hesitation or interruption. It must consist of at least four steps, including the takeoff. In a running dive from the springboard, the takeoff must be from both feet simultaneously; from the platform, the takeoff may be from one foot.

For a backward dive, the starting position is as for a forward standing dive except that the diver faces the board. Lifting both feet slightly off the board while preparing for takeoff is not penalized as a bounce but as an involuntary action.

For an armstand dive, the starting position is assumed when both feet are off the platform. The diver must attain a steady balance in the straight position; failure to attain this at the first attempt leads to penalty.

Takeoffs should be bold, reasonably high, and confident. Points are deducted if the diver touches the end of the board after takeoff.

Flight Divers are penalized for diving to the side of the direct line of flight. During the flight, the body may be straight, piked, with tuck, or in a free position.

1) In the straight position, the body should not be bent at the knees or at the hips. The feet should be together and the toes pointed.

2) In the pike position, the body should be bent at the hips. The legs must be straight at the knees. The feet should be together and the toes pointed.

3) In the tuck position, the body should be compact, bent at the knees and at the hips. The knees and feet should be together, the hands on the lower legs, and the toes pointed.

In the free position, the body can be held in any position, but the legs should be together and the toes pointed.

In flying somersault dives, a straight position should be held for approximately half a somersault. Except where the dive specifications state otherwise, the straight position should be assumed from the takeoff.

A twist must be within 90° of whatever was specified. In straight dives with one half or full twist, the twisting should not be done from the board. In pike dives with twist, the twist should not be started until there has been a marked pike position. In somersault dives with twist, the twist may be performed at any time.

Entry The diver should enter the water in a vertical or nearly vertical position, with the body straight, the feet together, and the toes pointed.

In headfirst entries, the arms should be stretched beyond the head in a line with the body, with the hands close together (**a**).

In feetfirst entries, the arms should be close to the body and not bent at the elbows (**b**).

SCORING

Judging principles Judges consider each dive for its run, takeoff, flight, and entry. They must consider only the technique and execution of the dive. The difficulty of the dive and the approach to the starting position are not taken into consideration.

Marking Unless the referee declares a failed dive, judges mark each dive in points and half-points from 0 to 10. For certain faults, FINA has established set deductions or the maximum number of points that can be awarded.

Failed dives A failed dive, scoring 0 points, is declared by the referee if:

a) the diver takes more than one minute to prepare for a dive after he has received a warning from the referee;

b) the diver receives any assistance during the course of his dive;

c) the dive is other than that announced;

d) the diver refuses to execute a dive;

e) the diver takes off from only one foot in a springboard dive;

f) the diver bounces at the end of the board in a standing dive;

g) the diver interrupts his run during a running dive;

h) the diver makes more than one jump before takeoff;

i) the diver is unsuccessful in his second attempt to gain balance in an armstand dive;

j) a second restart is unsuccessful in a running or standing dive;

k) a twist is greater or less than that announced by 90°.

Deductions FINA rules specify whether deductions are to be made by the referee or by the judges. The number of points to be deducted or the maximum number of points that can be awarded is specified for the following faults:

a) clearly making a position, either wholly or partly, different from that announced;

b) holding the arms beyond the head in a feetfirst entry;

c) taking fewer than four steps in a running dive;

d) making a second attempt to achieve a balanced position in an armstand dive;

e) restarting in a standing or running dive;

f) not assuming the correct starting position;

g) having an unsteady balance in an armstand;

h) having the arms in an incorrect position upon entry into the water.

Result To find the score for each dive, the secretaries take the judges' marks, cancel the highest and lowest (one only if two or more judges give the same score), total the remainder, and then multiply this figure by the official degree of difficulty for the dive. The winner of a competition is the diver with the highest total number of points in the final round. If two or more divers have the same total, equal placings are given.

EQUESTRIANISM

HISTORY

Modern competitive equestrianism is divided into three main events: dressage (**A**), show jumping (**B**), and the three-day event (**C**).

Dressage has its origins in the riding academies of renaissance Europe, where the skills of horses and riders were perfected.

Interest in competitive show jumping probably resulted from the challenge of clearing obstacles when out hunting. The late nineteenth century saw the introduction of ''leaping'' classes at some horse shows, and these have evolved into the various types of contest known today.

Three-day eventing derives directly from cavalry endurance tests in the late nineteenth century, and is still known in some countries as ''the military.''

Although some horseback riding events were included in the 1900 Olympics, it was not until 1912 that equestrianism became a regular feature of the Games. The international governing body of equestrian sports, the Fédération Equestre Internationale (FEI), was founded in 1921.

GENERAL RULES

Introduction In addition to the specific regulations for the various equestrian sports included in this section (dressage, p. 84 ; show jumping p. 92 ; three-day event, p. 100), there are a number of general rules applicable to horses and riders taking part at international level in all sports under the jurisdiction of the FEI.

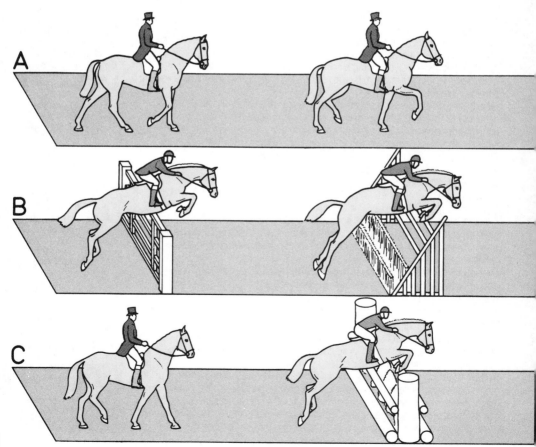

Horses must be registered with a National Federation, which keeps a record of any change of ownership as well as other information.

Horses are in one of three categories – Competition, International Competition, or International Champion horses – according to the major competitions in which they have competed or been placed. A horse that has reached a higher category cannot then return to a lower one.

Some events are restricted to Competition horses, or to Competition and International Competition horses. Championships, Official International competitions, and Regional and Olympic Games are open to all categories of horses.

In Olympic Games, horses must have riders of the same nationality as the owner.

Riders in international competitions must be officially entered by their National Federation, and must be in possession of either an amateur or a professional license from that National Federation, according to their status.

Only amateurs may take part in Championship and Official International competitions for dressage and three-day event, and in dressage, show jumping, and three-day event competitions at Olympic Games. National teams for Official International jumping competitions and Championships may include professionals.

All juniors under 18 are classified as amateurs.

Riders in Senior competitions should be over 18 years of age.

There are separate competitions for Juniors, aged 14 to 18, and for Young Riders aged 16 to 21. Riders under 18 may not take part in both Junior and Young Riders' events in the same discipline in the same year. Riders aged from 18 to 21 may not take part in both Young Riders' and Senior events in the same year in the same discipline.

EQUESTRIANISM (DRESSAGE 1)

SYNOPSIS

Dressage competitions test the harmonious development of a horse's physique and ability, requiring it to be supple, calm, confident, attentive, and keen, and to achieve perfect understanding with its rider. Competitors carry out official tests incorporating a variety of paces, movements, and figures, for which they are awarded marks and penalties by a panel of judges.

ARENA AND EQUIPMENT

The arena must be a completely flat and level rectangle measuring 60m long by 20m wide. A sand surface is specified for Olympic Games.

The arena must be enclosed by a low fence, about 30cm high, with an easily removable section in the middle of one of the short sides (point **A**) so that competitors can easily enter and leave the arena.

There must be at least 20m between the arena and any area for spectators. Indoor arenas should, if possible, be at least 2m from any wall.

Compulsory markings on the arena surface are the center line and three points on it (**D, X, G**). The center line, which runs the entire length of the arena, is marked by rolling or raking if the surface is sand, and by mowing if the surface is grass. Points along the center line may be marked by rolling, raking, or mowing 2m lines straight across it.

Points near the sides of the arena are indicated by lettered markers positioned about 50cm outside the fence, and ideally also by special markers on the fence itself.

Two other points on the arena (**I, L**) are used in dressage tests and are indicated on our diagram; these points need not be marked on the arena surface, being easily located with reference to other markers.

A practice arena with the same dimensions as the competition arena must be provided; competitors may not use the competition arena except when actually competing.

Dress At major events civilians wear a black jacket or dark coat with top hat or bowler hat respectively, white breeches, hunting stock, black boots, and spurs. Service dress is also permitted. A whip may be carried only by ladies riding side saddle.

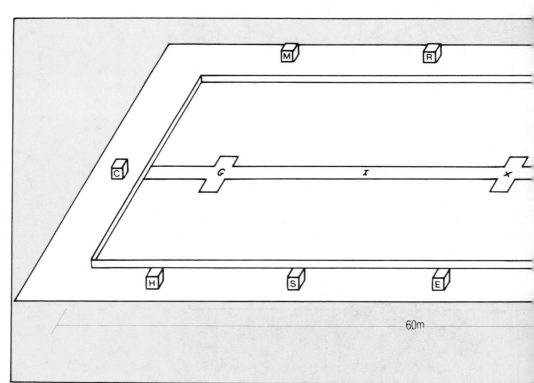

60m

Saddlery An English saddle and double bridle are compulsory. Boots, bandages, blinkers, martingales, and any kind of gadgets such as special reins are prohibited.

HORSES, RIDERS, OFFICIALS

Horses must conform with general rules for equestrian events (see p. 83). They must be at least six years old.

Participation or placing in more advanced competitions affects a horse's eligibility for less advanced competitions. At the same meeting a horse may take part in no more than two competitions (excluding a Grand Prix Special), and these competitions must be of consecutive standard.

The number of horses that may be entered by any rider is at the discretion of the organizing committee (except for a Grand Prix when only one horse is allowed).

At an official international competition or championship, a horse will be disqualified if it is schooled during the four days preceding the first competition, or at any time during the entire event, by any mounted person other than the rider competing on it or another competitor from the same team.

Riders All competitions are open to men and women. Riders may compete as individuals or as team members. For major competitions teams consist of three riders, all of whose scores count for the final classification.

Officials At major international events there must be a ground jury of five judges, including the president.

Three judges, with the president in the center, stand 5m behind the fence on the short side of the arena opposite the entrance. The other two judges stand 5–10m behind the fence in the center of each long side of the arena.

Each judge must be assisted by a secretary, and the president must also have an assistant to ring the bell, to inform him of competitors' errors, and to record times.

Official scorers are responsible for calculating the final classification.

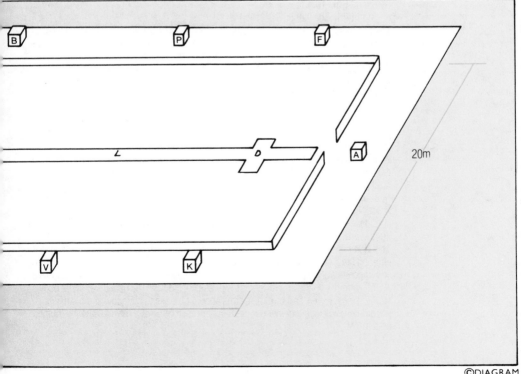

EQUESTRIANISM (DRESSAGE 2)

TESTS

Official tests for horses at different stages of training in dressage are drawn up and published by the FEI. Official tests used at international events are:

a) Prix St Georges, a test of medium standard;
b) Intermediate Competition no.1, a test of relatively advanced standard;
c) Intermediate Competition no.2, a test of advanced standard;
d) Grand Prix, a test of the highest standard;
e) Grand Prix Special, a test of the same standard as the Grand Prix, but slightly shorter and more concentrated, and limited to the 12 (or sometimes 18) best-placed competitors in an initial Grand Prix.

Content of tests All tests include a variety of paces, movements, figures, and transitions, which must be performed at specified points in the arena; in some cases the number of steps to be taken is also specified.

Tests are divided into numbered sections for scoring purposes, and there are also collective points for overall impression.

PROCEDURE

Starting order for each competition is determined by a separate draw.

Execution of the test Competitors must at their turn enter the arena within 90 seconds of the starting bell.

All official tests must be executed completely from memory. If a test requires a particular action to be carried out at a certain point in the arena, it must be executed when the rider's body is over that point.

If a competitor departs from the test as laid down in the test sheet, the president may order the bell to be sounded to warn him. If necessary, the president will indicate where in the arena the competitor should resume the test and with what movement.

TIME

Time allowed The time allowed for different international tests is:

a) Prix St Georges, 9min 30sec;
b) Intermediate Competition no.1, 10min;
c) Intermediate Competition no.2, 11min 30sec;
d) Grand Prix, 10min;
e) Grand Prix Special, 8min 45sec.

Timing begins at the moment when the horse moves forward after the competitor salutes the judges at the start of the test. It ends when the competitor salutes the judges after the final halt. The clock is not stopped for errors or falls.

A competitor who fails to complete a test within the time allowed is permitted to continue; time penalties will be imposed (see p. 91).

GENERAL IMPRESSION

The horse should at all times give the impression of doing of its own accord all that is required of it. During the execution of the test, the judges will assess, and award collective marks for, the freedom and regularity of the horse's paces, its impulsion, and its submission.

When assessing impulsion, the judges will consider the horse's desire to move forward, the elasticity of its steps, the suppleness of its back, and the engagement of its hindquarters.

Although the horse must immediately obey the rider's aids, there must be no impression of subservience. Submission is assessed with reference to the horse's attention and confidence, the lightness and ease of its movements, its acceptance of the bridle, and the lightness of its forequarters.

The rider must take his horse through all the movements of the test without any apparent effort on his own part. Only by adopting the correct riding position can all aids be correctly and imperceptibly given. This requires the rider to be well balanced, with his loins and hips supple, and his thighs and lower legs well stretched down. The upper part of his body should be easy, free, and erect. His arms should be close to his body, and his hands should be low, close together but not touching each other or the horse, and the thumbs uppermost.

PACES

The walk (A) is a marching pace in which the horse's four feet follow each other in well marked "four time."

Four different walks are recognized for dressage: collected, medium, extended, and free. For the collected walk the horse takes higher, shorter steps than in the medium walk, which requires strides of moderate extension. In the extended walk the horse should cover as much ground as possible. The free walk is a relaxed pace in which the horse is allowed complete freedom of the head and neck.

The trot (B) is a two-time pace on alternate diagonals (near fore and off hind and vice versa) separated by a moment of suspension. The trot should always be entered without hesitation, and steps should be free, active, and regular. Recognized trots for dressage are: collected, working, medium, and extended. The working trot is easier to perform than the collected trot, which it replaces at lower levels of competition.

Except where a test states otherwise, all work at the trot is with the riders "sitting."

The canter (C) is a three-time pace. For example in the canter with the right leg leading, the sequence is left hind, left diagonal (simultaneously left fore and right hind), right fore, followed by a period of suspension with all four legs in the air.

Recognized canters are: collected, working, medium, and extended. The working canter replaces the collected canter at lower levels of competition.

The counter canter or "false" canter is a movement in which the horse is made to lead with the fore leg other than the one that would be more natural. For example, when making a circle to the left, the horse is made to canter with its right leg leading.

Change of leg at the canter In a simple change of leg the horse is brought back into a walk for two or at the most three steps, and is then restarted into a canter with the other leg leading.

In a flying change of leg or change of leg in the air, the change is executed in close connection with the suspension that follows each stride of the canter.

Transitions All changes of pace and speed should be quickly but smoothly made. The same is true of transitions between passage and piaffer (p. 88).

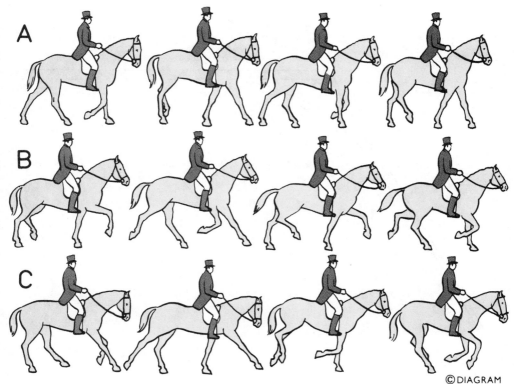

©DIAGRAM

EQUESTRIANISM (DRESSAGE 3)

MOVEMENTS

The halt The horse should stand attentive, still, and straight, with its weight evenly distributed over all four legs. The transition from any pace to the halt should be made progressively in a smooth, precise movement.

The half-halt is an almost imperceptible action intended to increase the attention and balance of the horse before the execution of several movements, or transitions to lesser or higher paces.

The rein back is a backward walk in which the legs are raised and set down almost simultaneously by diagonal pairs. If after a rein back, the horse is required to move into a trot or canter it should do so at once with no halt or intermediate step.

The passage is a measured, very collected, very elevated, and very cadenced trot. Each diagonal pair of feet is raised and returned to the ground alternately, gaining little ground, and with an even rhythm and a prolonged suspension.

The piaffer is a very collected, cadenced, elevated, and majestic trot on the spot. Each diagonal pair of feet is raised and returned to the ground alternately, with an even rhythm and a slightly prolonged suspension.

Changes of direction The horse should adjust the bend of its body to the curvature of the line followed, remaining supple and following the indications of the rider without any resistance or change of pace, rhythm, or speed.

When changing direction at right angles, for example when riding corners, the horse should describe a quarter circle approximately 6m in diameter at collected or working paces (**A**), and approximately 10m in diameter at medium and extended paces (**B**).

When changing direction in the form of a counter-change of hand, the horse must move obliquely either to the quarter line, the center line, or the opposite long side of the arena, and then return on an oblique line to the line being followed at the start of the movement.

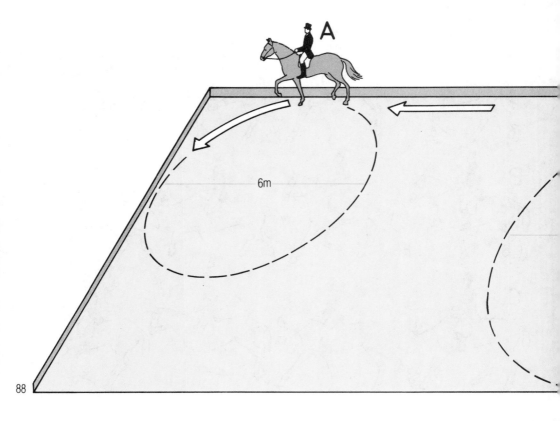

LATERAL MOVEMENTS

General points In all lateral movements, also known as work on two tracks, the horse moves with its forequarters and hindquarters on two different tracks.

Lateral movements include: leg-yielding; shoulder-in; travers; renvers; half-pass. In leg-yielding the horse should be bent only at the poll. In all other lateral movements it should be bent uniformly from the poll to the tail.

In descriptions of lateral movements, the side to which the horse should be bent is the inside and the opposite side is the outside.

Leg-yielding The horse is quite straight except for a slight bend at the poll. Its inside legs pass and cross in front of its outside legs, and it looks away from the direction in which it is moving. Leg-yielding can be performed "along the wall" (**a**), in which case the horse should be at an angle of about 35° to the direction in which it is moving. It can also be performed "on the diagonal" (**b**). In this case the horse should be as near as possible parallel to the long sides of the arena but with its forequarters slightly in advance of its hindquarters.

Shoulder-in (c) The horse is slightly bent around the inside leg of the rider. Its inside legs pass and cross in front of its outside legs, and it looks away from the direction in which it is moving. The shoulder-in is performed "along the wall" at an angle of about 30° to the direction in which the horse is moving.

Travers (d) The horse is slightly bent around the inside leg of the rider. Its outside legs pass and cross in front of its inside legs, and it looks in the direction in which it is moving. The travers is performed "along the wall" or, preferably, along the center line. The horse's head is parallel and close to the wall or line, and its body is at an angle of about 30° to the direction in which the horse is moving.

Renvers (e) This is the inverse movement to the travers. It resembles the travers except that the horse has its tail instead of its head to the wall.

Half-pass (f) This is a variation of the travers, executed "on the diagonal" instead of "along the wall." The horse should be as near as possible parallel to the long sides of the arena, although the forequarters should be slightly in advance of the hindquarters.

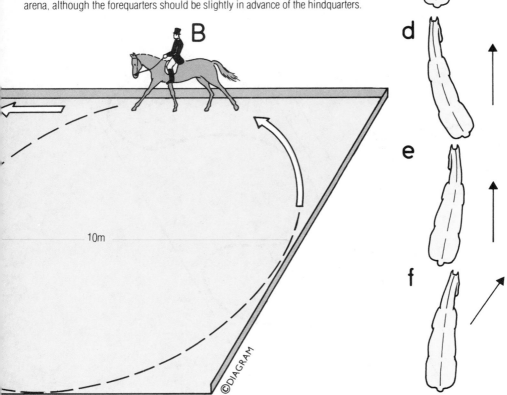

89

EQUESTRIANISM (DRESSAGE 4)

FIGURES

The volte (a) is a circle with a diameter of 6m.

The circle (b) has a stated diameter in excess of 6m.

The figure of eight (c) consists of two exact voltes or circles of equal size (as prescribed), joined at the center of the eight. The horse should be kept straight for an instant before changing direction at the center of the figure.

The pirouette (d) is a small circle on two tracks, with a radius equal to the length of the horse. The forelegs and outside hindleg move around the inside hind foot, which forms the pivot and should return to the same spot, or slightly in front of it, each time it leaves the ground.

The half-pirouette is a half-circle executed in a similar manner to a pirouette.

The serpentine (e) is a series of loops across the width of the arena. It starts from the middle of one short side of the arena, and ends at the middle of the opposite side. The long sides of the arena are approached at the quarter, half, and three quarter distances.

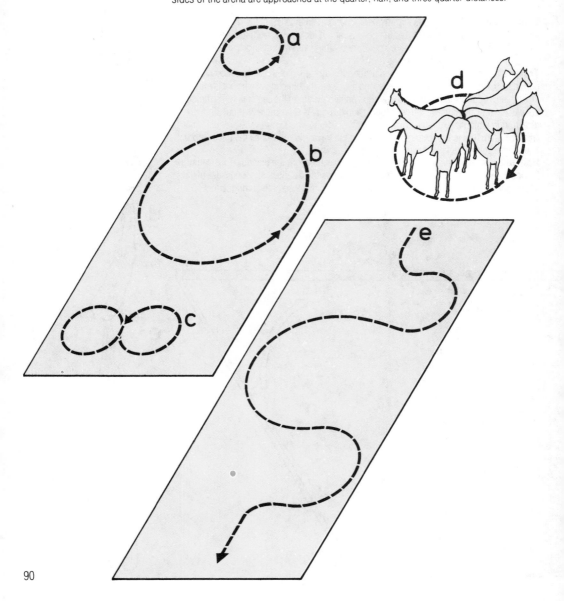

ELIMINATION AND PENALTIES

Elimination Competitors are eliminated:

a) if a forbidden article of saddlery is worn;

b) for carrying a whip (ladies riding side saddle excepted);

c) for starting the test early, or for failing to start within 90 seconds of the signal;

d) if the horse leaves the arena completely, with all four feet, at any time after first entering the arena for the test and before leaving it when the test is completed;

e) for marked lameness of the horse;

f) for a fourth error (see Penalties).

Penalties are incurred for "errors of the course" (eg, taking the wrong turn, or omitting a movement), and for "errors of the test" (eg, rising instead of sitting at the trot, or failing to take the reins in one hand at the salute). Penalties are imposed even if an error is corrected. The scale of penalties is as follows:

a) for a first error, 2 points;

b) for a second error, 4 points;

c) for a third error, 8 points;

d) for a fourth error, elimination.

A competitor eliminated for a fourth error is, however, permitted to continue to the end of the test; marks will be awarded in the normal way but the competitor will be excluded from the classification.

Time penalties Competitors are penalized ½ point for each second or part of a second by which their test time exceeds the time allowed.

SCORING

Marking Tests are divided for scoring purposes into separate sections containing one or more paces, movements, figures, and transitions. Each section is given a mark from 0–10 by each judge. A mark of 0 means that a competitor performed almost nothing of the required movement: a mark of 10 indicates an excellent performance.

Each judge also awards collective marks from 0–10 for each of the following: paces; impulsion; submission; and the position and aids of the rider.

Result A competitor's score from each judge is calculated by totaling the marks awarded for the different sections of the test and the collective marks, and then subtracting penalties as appropriate.

Coefficients, fixed by the FEI, may be used to adjust collective marks and also the marks for certain difficult and/or infrequently repeated movements.

Individual placings are determined by adding together the scores from all five judges. In the case of a tie in any test other than a Grand Prix Special, equal placings are given. In the case of a tie for first, second and/or third places in a Grand Prix Special, a ride-off is held, using the same test and the same order of starting. In the case of a tie for lower placings in a Grand Prix Special, equal placings are given.

Team placings are determined by adding the scores of each team member. In the case of a tie, the winning team is the one whose lowest classified member has the best result.

EQUESTRIANISM (SHOW JUMPING 1)

SYNOPSIS

There are a large number of different jumping competitions, in all of which the rider's skill, and the horse's jumping ability and sometimes speed are tested over a course of obstacles. Certain defined errors are penalized, and the winner is the individual or team with the lowest number of faults, the fastest time, or the highest number of points, depending on the type of competition.

ARENA AND OBSTACLES

The arena should have a minimum area of 2500sq.m for major indoor events. It must be completely enclosed, and all entrances and exits must be shut when a horse is competing. After a competition begins, competitors may not enter the arena on foot, or, except in special circumstances, exercise their horses or jump any obstacle in the arena except as part of the competition. Exercise areas and practice jumps are usually provided elsewhere.

Courses of obstacles vary according to the type and standard of competition (see p. 94). In all cases the length in meters from the starting line (**a**) to the finishing line (**b**) must not exceed the number of obstacles multiplied by 60. The starting line must always be no less than 6m and no more than 25m from the first obstacle, and the finishing line must be no less than 15m (10m indoors) and no more than 25m from the last obstacle.

Red and white flags are used to mark the starting and finishing lines and also all obstacles and compulsory turning points. Riders must always pass the flags so that red flags are to their right and white flags to their left.

No alteration to the course for any round or jump-off is permitted once a competition has started, except in a few special circumstances. If an event is interrupted by bad weather, it must be resumed using the same course and obstacles.

Plan of the course A detailed plan of the course is posted before the competition begins. It shows the starting and finishing lines, the length of the course, the position, number, and type of all obstacles, the track to be followed, compulsory turning points, the time allowed and the time limit if any, and the table of penalties.

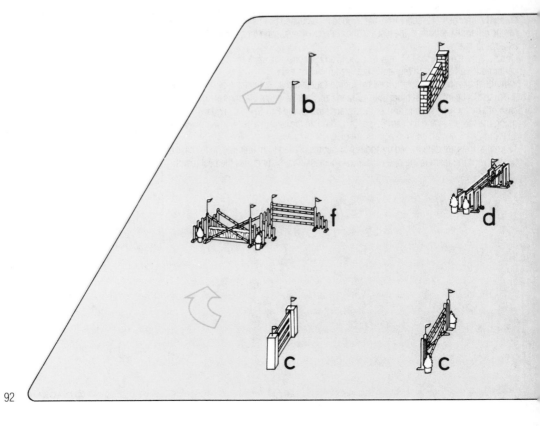

Obstacles (general rules) Obstacles must match their surroundings and be varied and generally attractive. They must not be unsporting or cause unpleasant surprises. Obstacles and parts of obstacles must be capable of being knocked down; they must not be so heavy as to cause horses to fall, nor so light as to be knocked down too easily.

Each obstacle is numbered in the order in which it is to be jumped; the elements of a combination jump all have the same number but a different letter (eg 3A,3B,3C).

Described below and illustrated in our arena are the basic types of obstacle used in show jumping competitions. Maximum dimensions for different types of obstacle are given in the rules for particular competitions (see p. 94).

Straight obstacles (c) have all their elements in the same vertical plane on their take-off side. Examples are walls, posts and rails, single rails, and gates.

Spread obstacles (d) require horses to jump width as well as height. Examples are triple bars, double oxer, and hog's back.

A water jump (e) must not have any obstacle in front, beyond, or in the water.

There may be a guard rail or hedge about 50cm high on the take-off side; this is counted in the measurement of the total spread but there is no penalty for displacing it.

The jump's limits must be clearly marked on the landing side, and on the take-off side if there is no guard rail or hedge, by a white strip of wood or rubber about 5cm wide.

Combinations (f) of obstacles are made up of two, three, or more obstacles to be jumped separately and consecutively. They include banks, slopes, ramps, and sunken roads as well as combinations of fences.

Combinations are classified as open, closed, or partially open and partially closed. A horse can leave a closed combination, such as a sheep pen, only by jumping.

Faults incurred at each part of a combination are added together. If there is a refusal, run-out, or fall at an open combination, the entire combination must be retaken on penalty of elimination. Failure of a horse, with its rider mounted, to leave a closed combination by the correct side within 60sec of entering it also results in elimination.

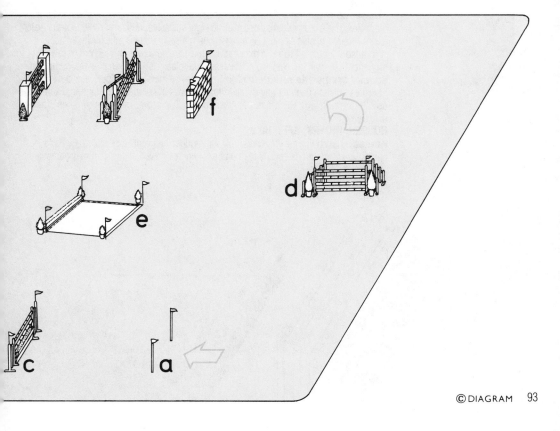

EQUESTRIANISM (SHOW JUMPING 2)

COMPETITIONS

Normal and Grand Prix These are the most common forms of individual and team competitions. There may be one or two rounds, over the same or different courses. The number and type of obstacles are decided by the organizers. Obstacles must not exceed 1.70m in height (**a**) or 2.20m in spread (**b**). The water jump must not exceed 5m wide (**c**).

Nations Cup This is the official international team jumping competition. It consists of two rounds over the same course on the same day. Teams consist of four riders, but only the scores of the best three in each round are counted in the final classification. There must be 13 or 14 obstacles. Straight obstacles must be 1.30–1.60m high (**a**); spread obstacles must have a spread of 1.50–2.20m (**b**); a water jump must be at least 4m wide (**c**).

World Championship This consists of three competitions and one final, each on a different day. Course specifications differ at each stage. There are team and individual classifications.

A team may have three or four riders. The total scores of a team's three best-placed competitors in each of the first two rounds are counted in the team classification.

The individual classification is determined by the final, in which only the four riders with the best scores at the end of the third round are entitled to participate. The final consists of four rounds; each competitor rides his own horse for one round and the horses of each of his rivals for the others.

Olympic Games This is a two-round competition, with individual and team classifications.

All competitors take part in Round A; the best 20 individuals and eight teams go forward into Round B. Scores for both rounds are counted for the final classification.

The course for Round A has 12 to 15 obstacles; straight obstacles are 1.30–1.60m high (**a**), spreads must be 1.50–2.20m (**b**), and the water at the water jump at least 4.5m wide (**c**). The course for Round B has a maximum of 10 obstacles; straight obstacles are 1.40–1.70m high (**a**), spreads must not exceed 2m (**b**), and the water jump (**c**) is as for Round A.

Puissance These competitions test a horse's ability to jump a small number of large obstacles. There is an initial course of six to eight obstacles, with no combinations or water jump. Straight obstacles must be at least 1.40m high. If there is a tie for first place, compulsory jumps off (up to a maximum of four) are held over shorter, progressively higher courses with at least two obstacles. Equal placings are given after four jumps off.

Special competitions Organizers are free to devise their own competitions, but special FEI rules must be used for any of the following types of competition: Hunting; Fault and out; Six bars; Relays; Hit and hurry; Accumulator; Top score; Take your own line; Knock out; Derby.

HORSES, RIDERS, OFFICIALS

Horses must conform with general rules for equestrian events (see p. 83). Rules for particular competitions specify the number of horses on which any rider may compete.

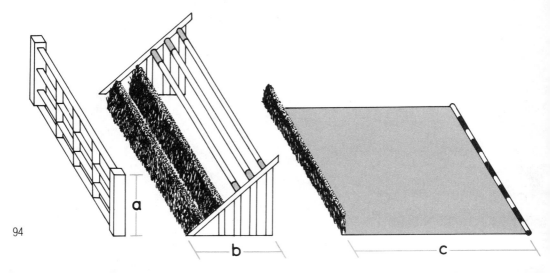

Riders There are competitions for individuals and for teams. At international level, competition rules specify teams of three, four, five, or six riders.

Officials Competitions are controlled by a ground jury consisting of a president and at least one other judge. Rules for particular events state the numbers of judges needed. Other officials are the clerk of the course, clerk of the scales, timekeeper, technical delegate, veterinary delegate, and arena and collecting ring stewards. Courses for major competitions must be built by a recognized course designer.

DRESS AND EQUIPMENT

Dress Civilians should wear riding club or hunting uniform, a red or black coat, white breeches (or fawn for women), a hunting cap or top hat (or bowler for women), and black boots. A hunting stock is recommended for international events; otherwise a tie and white shirt must be worn. Members of a uniformed service should wear its uniform.

Saddlery There are no restrictions on saddles and bridles, but blinkers and hoods are not allowed. Only an unrestricted running martingale may be used. Reins must be attached to the bit or bits but gags or hackamores are permitted. Whips must not exceed 75cm in length or be weighted at the end; no substitute for a whip may be carried.

Weight Minimum weights for riders with their saddles are:
a) for men or women riding astride, 75kg; for women riding side saddle, no minimum;
b) for juniors in adult competitions, 70kg; for juniors in other competitions, no minimum.
Competitors are weighed each time they leave the arena; failure to meet minimum weight requirements results in elimination.

PROCEDURE

Walking the course Before the start of a competition, riders are permitted to inspect the course and fences on foot.

Starting order is determined by a draw; the same order is kept throughout an event.

The round When his number is called, the competitor enters the arena already mounted. He crosses the starting line only after the starting signal, which is usually a bell. He must follow the correct track as given on the course plan, attempting to jump each obstacle in turn. If an obstacle is knocked down on a refusal, the rider must wait for it to be rebuilt before retaking it and going on. At the end of the course, having crossed the finishing line, the rider must leave the arena still mounted and go at once to be weighed.

TIME AND SPEED

Timing Automatic timing equipment is required at major international competitions; stopwatches are also used. Timing is to tenths or hundredths of a second.

Time allowed This is calculated with reference to course lengths and to official speed limits for different types of competition, for example:
for normal competitions, 325–400m/min indoors and 350–400m/min outdoors;
for Nations Cup competitions, 375m/min indoors and 400m/min outdoors;
for World Championships and Olympic Games 400m/min.
Penalties for exceeding the time allowed vary according to the marking system in use.

Time limit In all types of competition, the time limit is twice the time allowed. Riders are eliminated for exceeding the time limit.

Timing of a round is from when the rider crosses the starting line to when he crosses the finishing line; in both cases he must be mounted and going in the proper direction.
The clock is stopped to allow obstacles to be rebuilt, but is not stopped for falls by horse or rider, for deviations from the course, or for saddlery to be adjusted.
During interrupted time, riders may move about freely and are not penalized for disobediences; penalties for falls, and elimination rules continue to apply.

Time penalties If a competitor as a result of a disobedience knocks down any part of an obstacle, the clock will be stopped for it to be rebuilt and time penalties are imposed. Penalties, which are added to the time for the round, are: six seconds for a single obstacle or the first part of a combination, eight seconds for the second part of a combination, and 10 seconds for the third part. Similar penalties apply if the knock down is followed by a refusal or run out at the next part of a combination.
If a knock down is followed by a fall the clock is stopped only if the obstacle is not rebuilt by the time the rider has remounted.

MISTAKES SUBJECT TO PENALTY

Obstacles knocked down (1) An obstacle is considered knocked down if it or any part of it falls, even if the falling part is stopped in its fall by another part of the obstacle, or if one end is still in position. If all the poles of the obstacle are in the same vertical plane, only knocking down the top element is penalized.

Only one mistake is counted if more than one element of a straight or spread fence falls. A mistake is counted if a dislodged obstacle starts falling before the finishing line is crossed, even if it reaches the ground after the line is crossed.

Any part of a knocked down obstacle that stops a rider jumping another obstacle must be removed before the rider goes on; time for this is deducted from the time for the round.

Water jump fault It is a fault if any of the horse's feet touches the water or a white strip marking the jump's limits. Displacing a water jump barrier is not penalized.

Falls A rider is considered to have fallen if he is separated from his horse, which has not fallen, so that he touches the ground, or needs to remount or vault into the saddle, or needs help to get back into the saddle. A horse is considered to have fallen when its quarters and shoulders have touched the ground.

Any fall after crossing the starting line and before crossing the finishing line is penalized. A fall is penalized in addition to another mistake occurring at the same time.

A loose horse is subject to further penalty after a fall only if it jumps out of a closed combination or leaves the arena.

After a fall, the rider must resume his round within 60sec, either from the place of the fall or from a point no nearer the finishing line.

Disobedience The following are penalized as disobediences:
a) a rectified deviation from the course;
b) a refusal, run-out, or resistance;
c) circling, except to get back into position after a run-out or refusal;
d) crossing the track first taken between any two consecutive obstacles, except when specifically allowed to do so by the course plan;
e) crossing back over the extended line of the previous obstacle, if this is in the same direction as the next obstacle to be jumped;

f) if any part of a horse passes an obstacle or the finishing line after approaching it sideways, by zigzagging, or by turning sharply toward it.

Deviation A deviation from the course occurs when a competitor:

a) does not follow the plan of the course;

b) passes the wrong side of a flag;

c) jumps obstacles in the wrong order;

d) jumps an obstacle outside the course or misses a jump.

To correct a deviation, the competitor must return to the course at the point where the error was made; a corrected deviation is penalized as a disobedience.

Refusal (2) It is counted as a refusal if a horse halts in front of an obstacle to be jumped, whether or not the obstacle is knocked down or displaced.

It is not a refusal if a horse stops at an obstacle without knocking it down or reining back, and then immediately makes a standing jump.

It is a refusal if the stop is prolonged or if the horse steps back even a single pace, voluntarily or not, or if it takes more room to jump.

If a horse slides through an obstacle, the officiating judge will decide at once whether this should be counted as a refusal or as an obstacle knocked down.

Resistance A horse is considered to offer resistance if at any time and for any reason it halts (whether or not it moves back), turns around, rears, etc.

Running out A horse is considered to have run out if:

a) it is not fully under its rider's control and avoids an obstacle it should have jumped;

b) it jumps an obstacle outside the flags marking the obstacle's limits.

Unauthorized assistance During a round, a rider is permitted to receive no assistance (solicited or not) other than:

a) having his hat or eyeglasses handed back to him;

b) help after a fall, such as having his horse brought back to him, being helped to readjust his saddlery, or being helped to remount.

EQUESTRIANISM (SHOW JUMPING 4)

ELIMINATION AND DISQUALIFICATION

Discretionary elimination The jury has discretionary powers to eliminate riders who:
a) fail to enter the arena when called;
b) enter or leave the arena dismounted;
c) enter the arena on foot after the start of the competition;
d) wear incorrect dress;
e) fail to stop when signaled by the bell to do so;
f) resume after a fall from a point nearer the finishing line than where the fall occurred;
g) accept any unauthorized assistance;
h) jump in the wrong direction an obstacle in the exercise area;
i) jump a modified obstacle in the exercise area.

Automatic elimination Competitors are automatically eliminated if they:
a) jump an obstacle in the arena before the start of the course;
b) start before the signal and jump the first obstacle of the course;
c) jump the first obstacle of the course without first crossing the starting line;
d) fail to cross the starting line within 60 seconds of the starting signal;
e) show an obstacle to a horse before starting or after a refusal;
f) have more than 60 seconds of continuous resistance from their horse during a round;
g) fail to jump an obstacle within 60 seconds, even after a fall;
h) jump an obstacle without first correcting a deviation from the course;
i) jump during the course an obstacle that is not part of the course;
j) omit any obstacle that is in the course;
k) jump an obstacle in the wrong order;
l) jump an obstacle in the wrong direction;
m) exceed the time limit for the round;
n) jump a knocked-down obstacle before it is rebuilt;
o) resume after an interruption before the signal to do so;
p) jump a practice jump in the main arena more than twice, or jump it in the wrong direction;
q) fail to jump all parts of a combination (**1**) after a refusal, run-out, or fall;
r) fail to jump each element of a combination separately;
s) fail to jump out of a closed combination in the correct direction (**2**), or interfere with it;
t) have a loose horse that jumps out of a closed combination;
u) have a third disobedience during the whole round;
v) accept any unauthorized assistance during a round;
w) fail to cross the finishing line mounted before leaving the arena;
x) leave the arena or have a horse that leaves the arena before finishing a round;
y) fail to meet minimum weight requirements at the weigh-in after a round;
z) dismount before being given permission by the official in charge of weighing.

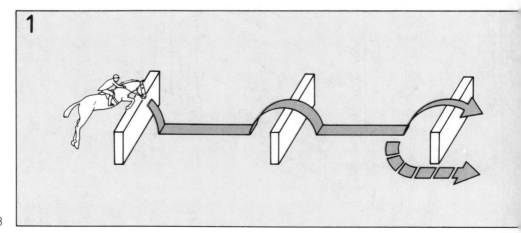

Disqualification may be for the competition in progress, for an entire event, or for a period of time. A rider (and his horse) may be disqualified for:
a) exercising a horse in the arena, except when this is specifically allowed;
b) jumping an obstacle that is part of a competition in which he is to compete;
c) jumping an obstacle that is part of a subsequent course, or showing such an obstacle to his horse;
d) giving up before or during a jump off without jury permission or adequate reason;
e) getting himself deliberately eliminated in a jump off;
f) rapping a horse (using training methods that give pain).

SCORING
Scoring systems The FEI publishes official tables for scoring competitions. Here we give information on two of these: Table A and Table C. Most competitions use Table A.
Table A This system gives a penalty score expressed in "faults." Scoring is as follows:
a) for knocking down an obstacle, or for having one or more feet in the water jump, 4 faults;
b) for a fall by horse or rider or both, 8 faults (which are added to any other faults incurred at the same time);
c) for a first disobedience, 3 faults; for a second disobedience in a round, 6 faults; for a third disobedience in a round, elimination;
d) for a disobedience plus knocking down an obstacle, 3 or 6 faults (depending whether it is the first or second disobedience) plus 6, 8, or 10 seconds (see Time penalties, p. 95);
e) for actions listed in the rules as being penalized by it, elimination;
f) for exceeding the time allowed, ¼ fault for each commenced second.
A competitor's faults are added together to give his final score. Depending on the rules for particular competitions, competitors' round times may be used to determine placings where competitors have an equal number of faults. In cases of equality for first place, competition rules may call for one or more compulsory jumps off.
Table C Under this system, penalties are scored in seconds and added to the time for the round. The number of penalty seconds for each jumping mistake (ranging from 3–17sec) depends on the length of the course and the number of obstacles to be jumped; an official table is published in the FEI handbook.
Jump off Rules for some competitions provide for jumps off to determine placings among competitors tying for first place after earlier rounds.
Jumps off may be against the clock or not, depending on particular competition rules. No new obstacle may be introduced for a jump off, and obstacles may not be changed in shape or nature. Except when competition rules state otherwise the number of obstacles may be reduced. Only if competitors taking part in the jump off had no faults in the previous round may the height and/or spread of obstacles be increased.
Most competitions specify a maximum of two jumps off, after which tied competitors are given equal placings.

© DIAGRAM

EQUESTRIANISM (THREE-DAY EVENT 1)

SYNOPSIS
The three-day event consists of three distinct equestrian competitions – dressage (**1**), endurance (**2**), and show jumping (**3**). The different competitions are held on consecutive days, and each competitor must ride the same horse throughout. The event is designed to test the harmonious development, speed, endurance, obedience, and jumping ability of the horse, and requires excellent understanding between horse and rider.

GENERAL RULES
Event categories Major international three-day events are categorized as follows.
a) At a CCI (Concours Complet International) there may be an individual and a team classification, but only the individual classification is recognized by the FEI. An FEI technical delegate may be appointed.
b) At a CCIO (Concours Complet International Officiel) there must be official FEI individual and team classifications. Each nation may enter only one team, and there must be at least three teams competing. An FEI technical delegate must be appointed to approve the course and conditions.
(All the laws described here as relating to CCIOs also refer to Olympic events.)
Competition ratio Courses and conditions are arranged so that the relative influence of the event's three competitions is as close as possible to the ratio: dressage 3: endurance 12: jumping 1. A multiplying factor is used to adjust the relative influence of the dressage; the factor to be used, which must be between 0.5 and 1.5, is fixed by the technical delegate (at CCIOs) or the ground jury (at CCIs) after an inspection of the endurance course and before the start of the dressage competition.
Horses must conform with general rules for equestrian events (see p. 83), and must be at least six years old. At CCIOs horses must be ridden by competitors of the same nationality as their owners.
A competitor must ride the same horse in all three stages of the event. If competitors are allowed to enter more than one horse, the horse nominated for the team classification must always be ridden first.
Horses are inspected for fitness before the dressage competition, between phases C and D of the endurance competition, and before the jumping competition. Any horse that is found to be unfit at an inspection is eliminated without right of appeal.
Riders may compete as an individual or as a member of a team. A team usually consists of four members, but only the best three results are considered for the final classification. If a team of three is allowed to enter, all three competitors must complete the event and all three results are counted.
Officials A ground jury of three members judges the dressage and show jumping, and supervises all arrangements for the judging and timing of the endurance competition. The ground jury and a veterinary official check that horses are fit to participate.
At CCOs without an FEI technical delegate, the ground jury is also responsible for approving the endurance course.

Dress requirements are different for the three competitions.

For the dressage competition, civilians must wear hunting dress or a riding club uniform, white shirt and tie, white or fawn breeches, a hunting cap or top hat, gloves, and black boots. Service members must wear service uniform with regulation headgear. Normal blunt spurs are compulsory for all competitors.

For the endurance competition, lightweight clothing is considered appropriate. Protective headgear secured by a chinstrap is compulsory, as are boots.

For the jumping competition, dress for civilians and service members is as for the dressage except that top hats are not worn, and spurs are optional.

Saddlery For the dressage competition, a double bridle or a snaffle, and an English saddle are compulsory. Martingales, blinkers, bandages, and any kind of gadgets (such as bearing, side, running, or balancing reins) are all forbidden.

For the endurance and jumping competitions, saddlery is optional except that blinkers and hoods are forbidden. Only running unrestricted martingales are permitted. Any rein must be attached to the bit or bits but gags and hackamores are allowed.

Whips may not be weighted, and must not exceed 75cm in length.

Weight There is no minimum weight for the dressage competition. For the endurance and show jumping competitions, a minimum weight of 75kg must be carried.

Riders are weighed at the start and finish of the endurance competition and at the end of the jumping. If necessary riders are weighed with saddlery and equipment carried by the horse. The bridle may be included only in finish weights. Whips must not be weighed. Failure to be weighed in front of the official steward or dismounting before he gives the order results in elimination, as does failure to reach the minimum weight.

Schooling During the three days preceding the dressage competition and for the entire duration of the event, a horse may be schooled only by its normal competitor or by a team member or individual competitor from the same country. A groom is also permitted to school a horse but not when mounted.

Starting order The order of starting is determined by a draw. Starting order within a team is decided by the team captain.

Starting order is the same for all three competitions, except that where there is no team classification the organizing committee may order that competitors start in the jumping competition in the reverse order of their classification after the endurance competition.

Elimination from one competition means elimination from the entire event.

Scoring and results Scoring of all three competitions is in penalty marks. Event classifications are obtained by adding together the penalty marks from each competition. The individual winner is the competitor with fewest penalty marks. In the case of a tie, the winner is the competitor with the best cross-country result. If there is still a tie, the best steeplechase result decides. In the final resort, a tie is broken in favor of the competitor whose cross-country time was closest to the optimum time.

The winning team is the team with fewest penalty marks after adding together the penalties incurred by its three best-placed riders. In the case of a tie, the event is won by the team whose third competitor had the best result.

3

©DIAGRAM

EQUESTRIANISM (THREE-DAY EVENT 2)

DRESSAGE: DAY 1

The aim is to test the harmonious development of the horse's physique, and the degree of understanding between horse and rider.

The test used at CCIOs and at CCIs must be the official three-day event dressage test approved by the FEI. It is less difficult than tests used in comparable dressage competitions, and excludes the more difficult paces, movements, and figures. Included in the three-day event dressage test are working, medium, and extended paces, circles, serpentines, changes of rein, a rein back, half passes, and halts (see pp. 87–90).

Rules are generally as for other dressage competitions (see pp. 84–91), with certain specific exceptions.

Marking is generally as for other dressage competitions (see p. 91). Each judge's marks are multiplied by a coefficient of 0.6 before any penalties for errors are deducted. Marks from each judge are then added together and the average mark found. This mark is then deducted from the maximum obtainable in order to give a result expressed in penalties. This penalty score is then multiplied by a previously decided multiplying factor to give the dressage results the correct relative influence on the result of the event as a whole.

Dressage result The competition is won by the competitor with the lowest penalty score. In the event of equality of scores, equal placings are given.

ENDURANCE: DAY 2

The aim of the endurance competition is to test the stamina, speed, and jumping ability of the horse, and also the ability of the rider to use his horse well across country.

Phases The endurance competition consists of four independently timed phases:
A) Roads and tracks; **B**) Steeplechase; **C**) Roads and tracks; **D**) Cross-country.
Competitors proceed directly from one phase to the next, except for a compulsory 10-minute halt between phases C and D.
Phases A and C are normally carried out at the trot or slow canter, phases B and D at the gallop.

Distances and speeds for the four phases are fixed by the competition organizers according to the standard of the competition and within the following limits.
Phases A and C should together have a total distance of 10–16km (at CCIs) or 16–20km (at CCIOs) to be carried out at a speed of 220m/min.
Phase B should be 2880–3450m long to be carried out at 640–690m/min (at CCIs) or 3450m, 3795m, or 4140m long to be carried out at 690m/min (at CCIOs).
Phase D should be 5200–7410m long to be carried out at 520–570m/min (at CCIs) or 7400–8000m long to be carried out at 570m/min (at CCIOs).

The course A map or plan of the course is given in advance to each competitor.
All courses are marked with yellow flags or signs bearing the letter of the phase. These show the general direction to be followed; competitors are not required to pass close to them.

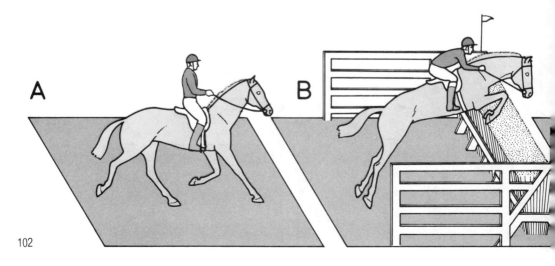

Red and white flags indicate all compulsory sections, obstacles, compulsory changes of direction, and the start and finish of each phase. Competitors must always pass with red flags to their right, and white flags to their left.

Obstacles in phases B and D are numbered in the order in which they are to be jumped; combination obstacles are given a different letter for each element, eg 3A,3B,3C.

Roads and tracks sections are marked at 1km intervals with numbered posts showing the distance in kilometers from the start of that phase.

Appropriate signs indicate the start and finish of each phase. The finishing line of phase A must be close to the start of phase B. The finish of phase B must also be marked as the start of phase C.

Obstacles There are an average of three obstacles to every kilometer in phase B, and four to every kilometer in phase D. The last obstacle in phase D must be 50–150m from the finishing line.

The number of obstacles formed of several elements must not exceed 10% of the total. No more than 50% of all obstacles may be of maximum height.

For phase B, obstacles must be of the type usually found in steeplechases. The maximum height for the fixed and solid part of an obstacle is 1m; the maximum overall height for a brush obstacle is 1.40m. The maximum spread for obstacles with spread only is 3.50m, or 4m for a water jump. The maximum spread for obstacles with both height and spread is 1.80m at the highest point and 2.80m at the base (at CCIs), or 2m at the highest point and 3m at the base (at CCIOs).

For phase D, the cross-country, obstacles must be fixed, imposing in shape, and left as near as possible in their natural state. Where necessary, natural obstacles should be reinforced so that they stay in the same state throughout the competition. Artificial obstacles must not demand acrobatic feats of jumping, nor give unpleasant surprises. Obstacles in which a horse could be trapped in the event of a fall must be built so that they can quickly be dismantled and rebuilt.

Cross-country obstacles must conform with the following dimension requirements. The maximum height for the fixed and solid part of an obstacle is 1.20m; the maximum height for a guard rail or hedge designed to aid jumping is 50cm. Maximum dimensions for obstacles with spread only or with both spread and height are the same as for phase B. The maximum drop on the landing side of an obstacle is 2m, and not more than two obstacles may have a drop exceeding 1.60m. At obstacles where a horse must jump into or out of water, the water must be no deeper than 50cm, the bottom must be firm, and the length of the water crossing must be at least 6m.

Each steeplechase and cross-country obstacle is within a penalty zone (see p. 104).

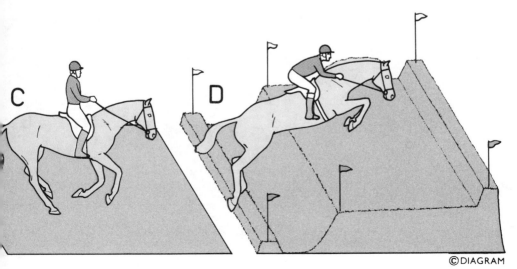

©DIAGRAM

EQUESTRIANISM (THREE-DAY EVENT 3)

Timing Competitors are penalized for exceeding the optimum time for any phase. The optimum time is calculated by dividing the set distance by the set speed.

Each phase is independently timed. Individual starting times are based on optimum times for the various phases. Timing is from the instant the starter gives the starting signal until the instant when the mounted horse reaches the finishing line. Timing is in seconds, with parts of a second counting as a whole second.

Gaining time in one phase does not compensate for loss of time in another. Similarly, exceeding the time in one phase does not affect the timing of the next phase, even though it is started late.

Competitors who finish phase A in less than the optimum time must wait for their official starting times for phase B; other competitors proceed directly to phase B. At the end of phase B, all competitors go straight on to phase C. At the end of phase C, competitors who have gained any time are given an extended break and start phase D at their official times. Competitors who are late finishing phase C must have a full 10 minutes' break before starting phase D.

Time penalties For each second or part of a second over the optimum time and up to the time limit for a phase, competitors are penalized as follows:

phases A and C, 1 penalty: phase B, 0.8 penalty; phase D, 0.4 penalty.

Time limit Competitors are eliminated from the entire competition for exceeding the time limit for any phase. Time limits are calculated as follows:

phases A and C, one fifth more than the optimum time:

phase B, twice the optimum time;

phase D, a time calculated on the basis of a speed of 225m/min.

Faults in the penalty zone Penalty zones extend 10m in front (**a**), 20m beyond (**b**), and 10m to either side (**c**) of obstacles or combinations of obstacles. They are marked with chalk, sawdust, or pegs, or in any other way that does not obstruct competitors. Competitors are penalized as follows:

a) for a first disobedience (phases B and D), 20 penalties;

b) for a second disobedience at the same obstacle (phases B and D), 40 penalties;

c) for a third disobedience at the same obstacle (phases B and D), elimination;

d) for a first fall by horse or rider or both (phases B and D), 60 penalties;

e) for a second fall by horse or rider or both (phase B), elimination;

f) for a second fall by horse or rider or both (phase D), 60 penalties;

g) for a third fall by horse or rider or both (phase D), elimination;

h) for dismounting within the penalty zone, the penalty is as for a fall;

i) for leaving the penalty zone without having jumped all its obstacles, 20 penalties.

A competitor who is penalized for a disobedience or fall is not penalized for leaving the penalty zone to renegotiate an obstacle. A competitor who is penalized for leaving the penalty zone without having jumped an obstacle is not penalized for a disobedience.

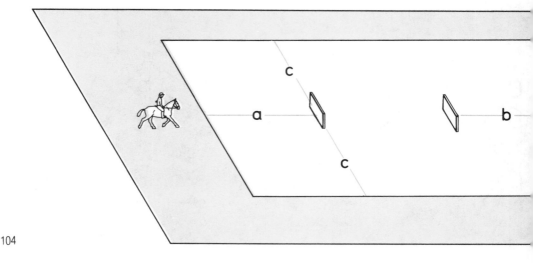

Elimination Competitors are eliminated for the following:
a) exceeding the time limit for a phase (see above);
b) cumulative disobediences or falls in the penalty zone (see above);
c) an uncorrected error of the course;
d) omission of an obstacle or a red and white flag;
e) jumping an obstacle in the wrong order, or retaking an obstacle already jumped;
f) arriving late at a starting point, or starting before the signal;
g) moving or altering a flag;
h) riding a horse on any part of the course except when actually competing;
i) any act of cruelty, such as excessive use of whip or spurs, or excessive pressing of an exhausted horse;
j) rapping a horse before, during, or after a competition, or at any time during the event;
k) wilfully obstructing a competitor who is overtaking;
l) receiving unauthorized assistance;
m) failure to be weighed as required, or failure to carry sufficient weight.

Endurance result The classification for the endurance competition is determined by adding all penalties incurred in the four phases.

JUMPING: DAY 3

The aim of the jumping competition is to test whether the horses have retained the suppleness, energy, and obedience needed to remain in use the day after a severe test of endurance; it is not an ordinary show jumping competition.

The course is designed in accordance with the overall standard of the event. It also depends on the intended influence of the jumping competition on the final result.
Course lengths are 700–800m (at CCIs) or 750–900m (at CCIOs). Tracks are irregular, with direction changes to test the horses' handiness. There are no compulsory passages, and no acrobatic feats of jumping or turning are required.

Obstacles There are 10 to 12 standard show jumping obstacles, with one double and/or one triple (giving a maximum of 15 efforts in all).
No obstacle may exceed 1.20m in height. The maximum spread for obstacles with spread only is 3m (at CCIs) or 3.50m (at CCIOs). The maximum spread for obstacles with height and spread is 1.80m at the highest point and 2.80m at the base (at CCIs), or 2m at the highest point and 3m at the base (at CCIOs).

Time and speed The time allowed for a round is based on a speed of 350–400m/min (at CCIs) or 400m/min (at CCIOs).
Exceeding the time allowed results in ¼ penalty for each excess second or part of a second. Exceeding the time limit (twice the time allowed) results in elimination.

Faults at obstacles Competitors are penalized as follows:
a) for knocking down an obstacle, or for a foot in the water jump or on the marking strip, 5 penalties;
b) for a first disobedience, 10 penalties; for a second disobedience in the whole round, 20 penalties; for a third disobedience in the whole round, elimination;
c) for a fall by horse or rider or both, 30 penalties;
d) for jumping an obstacle in the wrong order, elimination;
e) for an uncorrected deviation from the course, elimination.

Jumping result The classification for the jumping competition is determined by adding penalties incurred for faults at obstacles to penalties for exceeding the time allowed.

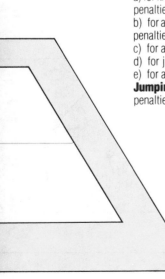

FENCING

HISTORY

The modern sport of fencing is directly descended from the historic role of swordsmanship in combat and dueling. It is based on the skilful use of the sword according to established rules, conventions, and movements which, with many of the fencing terms, date from the introduction of the light court sword in France in the seventeenth century. Fencing has featured in the Olympic Games since 1896. The world governing body for the sport, the Fédération Internationale d'Escrime (FIE), was founded in 1913, and its rules were adopted for Olympic events in the following year. World championships take place annually except in Olympic years.

SYNOPSIS

Two opponents engage in a friendly combat called an ''assault'' if there is no scoring, or a ''bout'' if the score is kept. They use one of three types of weapon – foil, épée, or saber – and attempt to score hits on their opponent's target area. Procedures and target areas differ according to the weapon being used. The fencer against whom the greater number of hits is scored – up to a specified maximum or within a given time – loses the bout.

COMPETITION AREA AND EQUIPMENT

The piste The fencing area must be flat and evenly lit, giving equal advantage to both fencers. Permitted surfaces include wood, cork, plastic, linoleum, metallic mesh, or a metal-based compound.

The piste must be 1.8–2m wide and at least 14m long. At each end of the piste there should be a continuous extension 1.5–2m long.

The piste is crossed by:

a) the center line;

b) on guard lines, 2m each side of the center line;

c) warning lines for épée and saber, 3m from the on guard lines and 5m from the center;

d) warning lines for foil, 4m from the on guard lines and 6m from the center;

e) rear limit for all weapons, 7m from the center.

Electric judging equipment is always used in official foil and épée competitions. An indicator, positioned opposite the center line, registers hits by means of lights and sound signals. Red lights indicate target hits by one fencer, green lights indicate target hits by his opponent, and white lights indicate non-target hits by both fencers. For épée events, the time interval between hits is also recorded.

A wire, connected to the indicator by a spring-loaded drum positioned at the end of the piste, passes under the fencer's jacket and is connected, via the hilt, to the tip of the foil or épée. When a hit is registered with sufficient force a circuit is completed and the appropriate light shows.

The piste and parts of the weapon other than the tip must be earthed so as not to register any contact if hit.

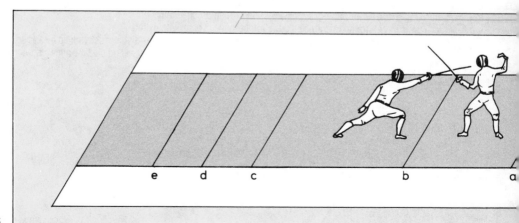

e   d   c   b   a

Dress All clothing and equipment must give freedom of movement combined with maximum protection. Clothing must be white, of strong material, not so smooth that a weapon point will glance off it, and without buckles or openings in which a weapon might be caught up.

Jackets and collars must be completely fastened up. The jacket sleeve on the sword arm must be lined so that there is a double thickness of material down to the elbow and under the armpit.

For épée a jacket covering the whole of the front of the trunk must be worn (**1**). This type of jacket may also be used for foil, as may the shorter jacket (**2**), which is always used for saber fencing. Short jackets are cut horizontally at the waist, and the lower edge must overlap the breeches or pants by at least 10cm when the fencer is in the on guard position.

A protective undergarment called a plastron (**3**) is compulsory for all fencers. Women must wear rigid breast protectors under their jackets.

A metallic overjacket (**4**) covering the valid target area is compulsory in foil competitions in which electric judging equipment is used.

Breeches must be fastened below the knees, and must be worn with white socks that cover the remainder of the legs. If long pants are worn, these must be fastened at the ankles.

A glove (**5**) must be worn on the hand holding the sword. Gloves may be slightly padded and must have a gauntlet fully covering approximately half of the forearm.

The mask (**6**) must conform to detailed specifications, and for foil must be insulated inside and out.

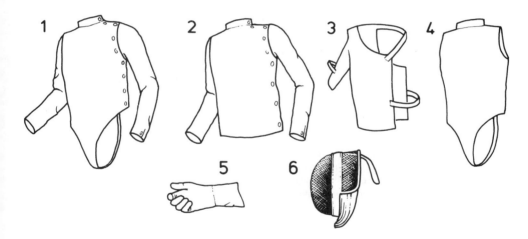

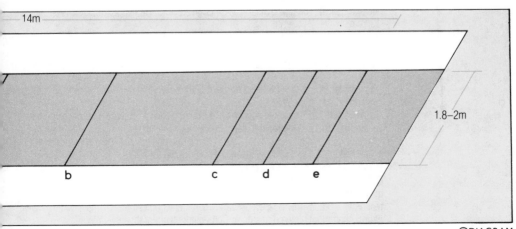

©DIAGRAM

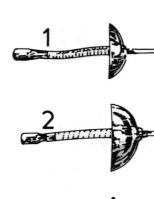

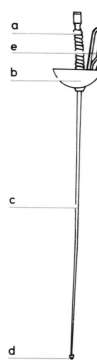

Weapons (general rules) All weapons are subject to official scrutiny, and it is the responsibility of each competitor to ensure that his own weapons conform to precise regulations, some of which are described here. No weapon must be constructed in such a way that it might normally injure either the user or his opponent.

All weapons – foil, épée, and saber – have a hilt (**a**), a guard (**b**), and a flexible steel blade (**c**) with a button (**d**) at its tip. For foil and épée, a martingale (**e**) – a strap holding the sword to the hand – is compulsory if the weapon is not otherwise secured by an attachment or the body wire.

Foil (1) This is a light sword that was developed for fencing practice in the eighteenth century. It must weigh less than 500g.

The total length must not exceed 110cm (90cm maximum for the blade and 20cm for the hilt and guard). The guard must pass through a cylindrical gauge 12cm in diameter.

Blade flexibility must be within the range 5.9–9.5cm if the blade is fixed horizontally 70cm from the tip of the button and a 200g weight is suspended 3cm from the button tip.

The point must either be covered, or fitted with an electric point. In electric foil a hit must register only when the pressure on the point exceeds 500g.

Epée (2) This is the traditional dueling sword, heavier than the foil and with a wider and deeper guard. It must weigh less than 770g.

The total length must not exceed 110cm (90cm maximum for the blade and 20cm for the hilt and guard). The guard must pass through a cylindrical gauge with a diameter of 13.5cm.

Blade flexibility must be 4.5–7cm (measurement as for foil).

In electric épée a hit must register only when the pressure on the point exceeds 750g.

Saber (3) The fencing saber is a light version of the cavalry sword. It must weigh less than 500g.

The total length must not exceed 105cm (88cm maximum for the blade and 17cm for the hilt and guard). If the blade is curved, the curve must be continuous, with a deflection of less than 4cm, and not in the direction of the cutting edge. The guard must pass through a rectangular gauge 15×14cm in section.

Blade flexibility must be 7–12cm if the blade is fixed horizontally 70cm from the tip of the blade and a 200g weight is suspended 1cm from the tip.

COMPETITORS AND OFFICIALS

Competitors For team events in Olympic Games and world championships each country may enter up to 18 competitors (four fencers per event, plus one man and one woman reserve). For each individual event countries may enter up to three (Olympic Games) or five (world championships) competitors. Competitors fence at their own risk.

Officials Bouts are controlled by a president, with the assistance of a number of judges and/or electric judging equipment.

In foil and épée competitions there may be two judges in addition to the electric equipment.

In saber events there must be four judges, positioned two at either side of the piste. The president and judges together comprise the jury.

Other officials in fencing competitions are scorers, timekeepers, and electric equipment supervisors.

COMPETITION PROCEDURES

Duration and scoring A bout lasts until an agreed number of hits is made or until an agreed time limit is reached. Most bouts are fenced for five hits within a time limit of six minutes. There may also be bouts for four hits (five minutes), eight hits (eight minutes), or 10 hits (10 minutes).

If fewer than the agreed number of hits is scored within the time limit, the winner is the competitor with the greater number of hits.

In foil and saber events if both fencers have equal scores a deciding hit is fought. In épée a tie counts as a defeat for both fencers.

The president issues a warning one minute before the end of the bout. The timekeeper calls "Halt" when time is up.

The assault The first fencer called stands to the right of the president. To start, the two competitors face each other behind their respective on guard lines. The president then orders "On guard," asks the competitors if they are ready, and orders "Play."

If the president wishes to stop the bout (for example if a fencer is disarmed, if the fencers pass each other on the piste, or if an offense is committed), he does so by calling "Halt." If necessary, he will reposition the fencers before restarting the bout with the call "Play."

After a valid hit the contest is resumed with both fencers behind their on guard lines. If a hit is invalid, play continues at the spot where fencing was halted.

In saber contests, the fencers change ends after one fencer has scored half the possible number of hits.

Target area To be valid a hit must be made on the opponent's target area, which differs for each of the three weapons.

A) In foil the target area is limited to the whole of the trunk, both front and back.

B) In épée the target area is the whole of the opponent's body.

C) In saber the target area comprises any part of the body above the line of the hips.

Use of the weapon In fencing with foil (**1**) and épée (**2**), only the point of the weapon may be used for scoring hits. In events for saber (**3**), hits may be scored with all parts of the cutting edge, the side or back edge, or the point.

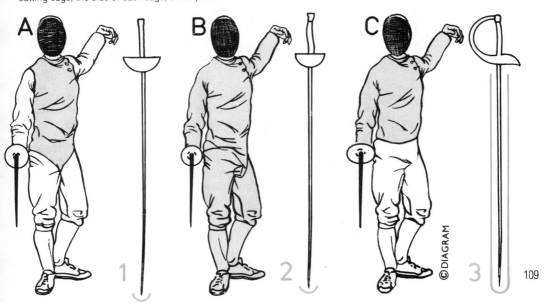

© DIAGRAM

FENCING 3

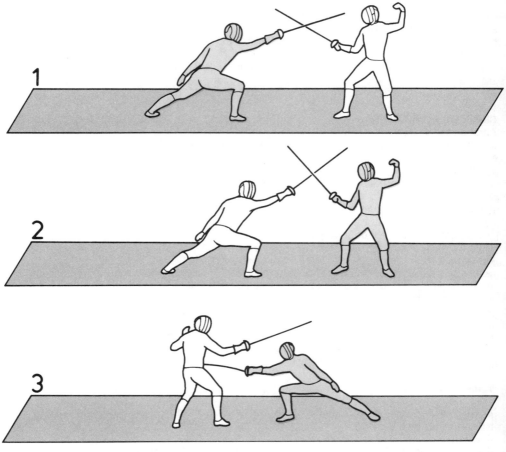

The fencing phrase In foil and saber fencing a hit is valid only if the correct "phrase"(sequence and priority of movements) has been followed. Embodying the principle that a fencer who is being attacked must defend himself before making a counter-attack, the correct fencing phrase comprises: attack; parry; riposte; counter-riposte.

The attack (**1**) is the initial offensive action made by the fencer extending his arm and continuously threatening the target. A running attack, or "flèche," is permitted with all types of weapon.

If the attacker misses or is parried, the right of way reverts to his opponent. The parry (**2**) is made by deflecting the attacker's sword with the blade or guard of the defender's sword. The defender may make a "stop-hit," provided that the hit reaches the attacker's target before the final movement of the attack has begun. Alternatively, he can parry, or counter-parry and riposte (**3**).

A counter-riposte is the next offensive action made by the fencer who attacked first. Other rules and conventions apply to different situations in attack and defense, and variations depend on speed of movement and the line and complexity of each attack.

In épée fencing there is no "phrase" or priority of movements. The bout is fought, according to conventions and rules, more on the lines of a duel, with the whole body including the arm as the target and with unique importance given to the interval of time between hits.

Judging of hits Hits are awarded by the president, aided by electric equipment and judges as applicable to the different events.

When a hit is signaled by a judge or by the electric judging equipment, the president briefly reconstructs the movements in the last phrase and decides on the hit's validity.

In foil and épée competitions the president may only award a hit if it has been properly registered by the electric apparatus, except in the case of a penalty.

In saber events hits with the blade edge ("cuts") or with the point must be clear and distinct.

In all types of competition, a hit is valid only if the fencer is standing on the piste. Hits made when the fencers are in the act of passing each other are valid, but hits made after the fencers have passed are invalid.

Hits that land off-target in foil and saber may be judged as valid if the fencer who was hit adopted an extreme position to avoid being hit on the target area.

In épée events if both fencers make hits within 1/25sec of each other a double hit is recorded, which counts against both.

In foil and saber there can be no double hit. If both fencers register hits at the same time, it is either counted as "simultaneous action" and both are annulled, or it is judged to have been the result of a break in convention by one of the fencers, in which case the president decides who is the offender and awards the hit to his opponent.

Offenses The following offenses are subject to penalty, in most cases after a warning:
a) crossing the lateral boundaries or rear limit of the piste;
b) initiating a hit before the call "Play" or after the call "Halt";
c) having equipment that does not conform to the rules;
d) irregular use of the unarmed arm or hand (**A**);
e) taking hold of the electric equipment with the unarmed hand;
f) in épée events, allowing the tip of the weapon to drag along the metallic piste;
g) in foil or saber events, intentional corps-à-corps (fencing so close that swords cannot be wielded correctly) (**B**);
h) turning the back on an opponent;
i) removing the mask before the president gives his decision on the bout;
j) in foil, bringing an uninsulated part of the weapon into contact with the metallic overjacket;
k) making a flèche (running) attack that jostles the opponent;
l) deliberately making a hit on some surface other than the opponent;
m) in saber, deliberately hitting the opponent off target;
n) acts of violence;
o) leaving the piste without permission;
p) seeking to favor, or collusion with, an opponent;
q) disturbing the maintenance of order;
r) doping offenses;
s) failure to appear when called;
t) unsportsmanlike conduct.

Penalties Offenses can be penalized by:
a) loss of ground on the piste (1m at foil, and 2m at épée and saber);
b) refusal to award a hit actually made, or annulment of the next hit yet to be made;
c) awarding a hit that has not actually been made;
d) exclusion from the competition, or from the entire meeting;
e) temporary or permanent suspension;
f) disqualification;
g) expulsion from the competition venue.

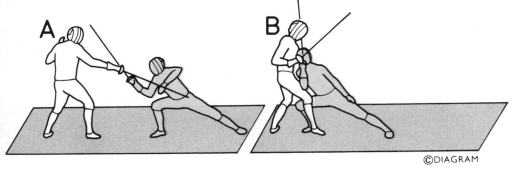

©DIAGRAM

FOOTBALL (AMERICAN)

HISTORY

American football began in the Ivy League universities in the nineteenth century. Originally based on the rules of soccer (p. 324) and rugby union football (p. 146), the evolution of the current rules began in 1880 with the introduction of the scrimmage. At that time, the game was renowned for its violence, and many injuries occurred, some fatal. The rules were gradually amended to reduce brutal play and to increase mobility. These modified rules made the game more popular, and by the end of World War I it was played throughout the USA. The first professional game is believed to have been held in 1895. The National Collegiate Athletic Association (NCAA), which governs the amateur game, was founded in 1910. The governing body for the professional game, the National Football League (NFL), was founded in 1922. NFL rules are summarized here, with major NCAA differences given on p. 123.

SYNOPSIS

In American football two teams with 11 players on the field attempt to score points by putting the ball behind their opponents' goal line in various approved ways. The game is won by the team scoring more points in the allotted time.

PLAYING AREA AND EQUIPMENT

The field is 360ft long and 160ft wide, bounded by the inside edge of end lines (**a**) and side lines (**b**), and surrounded by a 6ft wide white border. Goal lines (**c**), 8in wide, are marked in white 10yd inside and parallel to the end lines.

The areas bounded by the end lines, goal lines, and side lines are termed end zones (**d**). The area bounded by the goal lines and side lines is termed the field of play. The areas between the side lines and inbounds lines (see below) are termed side zones.

Marked by 4in wide white lines within the field of play are:

e) yard lines, at 5yd intervals and parallel to the goal lines;
f) inbounds lines, intersecting each yard line, 70ft 9in from the side lines;
g) lines at 1yd intervals, from goal line to goal line, in line with the inbounds lines;
h) lines at 1yd intervals by the side lines;
i) numbers indicating yard lines in multiples of 10, marked 12yd from the side lines, 2yd long, and supplemented by direction arrows;
j) lines parallel to and 2yd from the middle of each goal line.

The intersections of goal lines and side lines, and of end lines and side lines, must be marked with pylons mounted on flexible shafts.

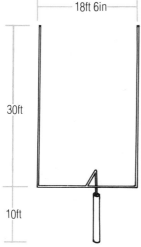

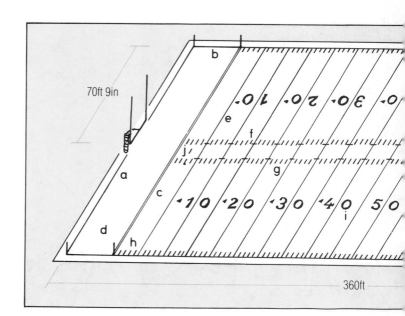

Goal posts must be the single-standard type and bright gold in color. The top of the 18ft 6in long crossbar must be 10ft above the ground. The uprights must be 3–4in in diameter and extend 30ft above the crossbar.

The goal is the vertical plane extending indefinitely above the crossbar and between the outer edges of the uprights. Goal posts are offset behind the center of the end lines so that the goal itself is above the end line.

The ball is a spheroid, 11–11¼in long, with a short circumference of 21¼–21½in, and a long circumference of 28–28½in. It consists of an inflated rubber bladder enclosed in a leather casing, and must weigh 14–15oz. Only approved balls may be used.

Dress Players must wear uniform jerseys, pants, head protectors, and stockings. Other compulsory items of equipment are protective shoulder pads, hip pads, thigh pads, and knee pads. Jerseys must carry identification numbers at least 8×4in on the front and back. Chinstraps on helmets must be kept fastened during play. Shoes of approved design are compulsory (except that barefoot kicking is permitted).

All items of equipment that might cause injury are prohibited.

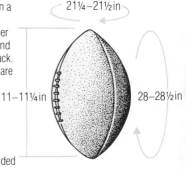

21¼–21½in

11–11¼in   28–28½in

PLAYERS AND OFFICIALS

Players Each team consists of 11 players and a number of substitutes. One or more players from each team are designated as captains, and only they are permitted to communicate with officials.

Substitution Substitutes may enter the field at any time when the ball is dead, provided the players they are replacing have first left the field via their own end line.

A player must be withdrawn and replaced by a substitute if he is disqualified, suspended, requires treatment lasting more than two minutes for injury, or takes more than three minutes to repair legal equipment.

Officials There are normally seven game officials: referee, umpire, linesman, line judge, back judge, side judge, and field judge. The referee has overall control of the game and is the final authority in disputes concerning the score or the number of a down. All officials have the power to stop the game for any foul; there is no territorial division in this respect.

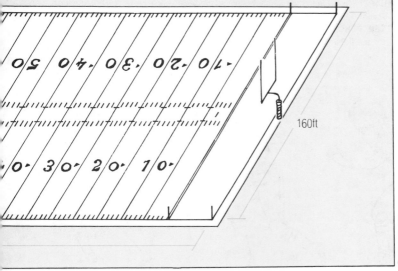

160ft

© DIAGRAM

113

FOOTBALL (AMERICAN) 2

DURATION AND SCORING

Duration There is 60 minutes' actual playing time divided into four periods of 15 minutes each. There is an intermission of two minutes between the first and second, and the third and fourth periods. A 15 minute intermission separates the second and third periods and divides the game into two halves.

Each team is permitted three charged team time-outs during each half. Team time-outs are normally for 1min 30sec.

Extra time The following "sudden death" method of determining a winner is used in NFL games in which there is a tie at the end of regulation playing time. In preseason and regular season league games, an intermission of three minutes is followed by one extra period of up to 15 minutes; play ends as soon as one team scores. In playoff games, further extra periods of up to 15 minutes are separated by two minute intermissions.

Scoring Each team aims to score the greater number of points, and so win the game. Points are scored in the following ways:

a) a touchdown (6 points) is made when an offensive player carrying a live ball advances from the field of play so that the ball breaks the plane of his opponents' goal line, or when any player inbounds behind his opponents' goal line catches or recovers a loose ball;

b) a field goal (3 points) is scored when an offensive player makes a place kick or drop kick from scrimmage, or a free kick after a fair catch, and causes the ball to pass entirely through the goal without first touching either the ground or any player of the offensive team;

c) a safety (2 points) is awarded to the opposing team if a defending team sends the ball into its own end zone and the ball becomes dead in its possession in the end zone or goes out of bounds behind the goal line, or if a team commits an offense that would otherwise require a penalty to be enforced behind its own goal line;

d) a try-for-point or try (1 point) succeeds when, during the scrimmage down awarded after a touchdown, and provided that the snap was inbounds and at least 2yd from the opponents' goal line, a player kicks a field goal (try-kick) or there is no kick and the try results in what would ordinarily be a touchdown or safety.

DEFINITIONS

Offensive and defensive teams The team that is in possession of the ball is the offensive team; the other team is then the defensive team.

Possession A player is in possession when he has held the ball long enough to control it when his second foot has clearly touched the ground inbounds.

Team possession occurs when one of its players has possession of a live ball, and persists during a loose ball after such player possession.

Live ball The ball becomes live after it is legally free kicked (p. 117) or snapped (p. 118), and remains live until the end of the down (p. 119).

Runner The runner is an offensive player in possession of a live ball, ie holding the ball or carrying it in any direction.

A touchback is a situation in which a ball is dead on or behind a team's own goal line, provided the impetus came from an opponent and it is not a touchdown.

1   2   3

Recovery and interception A live ball is recovered when a player gains possession after the ball strikes the ground.

For an interception, a player must catch an opponent's pass or fumble before the ball strikes the ground.

Player out of bounds A player is out of bounds when he touches a boundary line, or touches anything other than a player on or outside such a line.

Ball out of bounds The ball is out of bounds when:

a) a loose ball touches a boundary line or anything on or outside such a line;

b) a ball in player possession touches a boundary line or anything other than a player on or outside such a line;

c) a runner is out of bounds.

STARTING PROCEDURES

Choice of privileges The referee tosses a coin, and the captain of the visiting team normally calls. The winner of the toss may choose to kick off or receive the kick off, or may select which end his team will defend first. The other captain normally chooses first from the same options for the second half of the game.

Change of ends Teams change ends before the second and fourth periods.

Start of periods At the start of the first and third periods, play begins with a kick off (see p. 116).

At the start of the second and fourth periods, play resumes at a point exactly corresponding to where it ended in the other half of the field; the ball is put into play as though there had been no interruption.

PLAYING THE BALL

Modes of play Players may hold the ball and run with it (**1**), bat or punch the ball (**2**), kick the ball in certain ways described below, or throw the ball (**3**).

Batting or punching Players are permitted to bat or punch the ball except in the following cases. A player may not bat or punch:

a) a loose ball in any direction if it is in either end zone;

b) a loose ball toward the opponents' goal line if it is within the field of play but not within the end zone;

c) a ball in player possession, nor may he attempt to do this;

d) a pass in flight forward toward the opponents' goal line, unless he is a defensive player, or an offensive player preventing the defense from intercepting such a pass.

Kicking the ball Only the following types of kick are permitted:

a) a punt (**4**), in which the kicker drops the ball and kicks it as it falls;

b) a drop kick (**5**), in which the kicker drops the ball and kicks it as or immediately after it touches the ground;

c) a place kick (**6**), in which the ball is kicked from a fixed position on the ground (or from a tee at kick offs), and for which the ball may be held by a teammate.

BLOCKING AND TACKLING

Blocking involves using the body to obstruct an opponent. A block may be either a pass block or a run block (see below).

A player of either team may block at any time provided this does not involve illegal interference, unnecessary roughness, or an illegal cut (block below the waist).

During a down in which there is a free kick or a kick from scrimmage. players of the receiving team may block below the waist only offensive players lined up within 2yd of the tackle at or behind the line of scrimmage.

Pass blocking (A) is obstructing an opponent by using the body above the knees. During a legal block. the hands must be inside the blocker's elbows and can be thrust forward to contact an opponent provided the contact is inside the opponent's frame (ie that part of his body below the neck presented to the blocker).

The blocker may not use his hands or arms to push from behind, hang onto, or encircle an opponent in any way that restricts his movement as play develops.

The blocker is permitted to use his arms in an up and down action to prevent the opponent from grasping his jersey or arms and to prevent legal contact to his head.

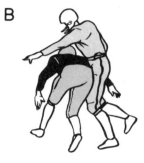

Run blocking (B) is an aggressive action by a blocker in order to obstruct an opponent from the ball carrier.

During a legal block, contact may be made with any part of the body. Hands, with the arms extended, may not be used to contact an opponent.

The blocker may not use his hands, arms, or legs to grasp. trip. hang onto. or encircle an opponent in order to gain advantage.

As the play develops, a blocker is permitted to work for and maintain position on an opponent provided he does not push from behind, clip illegally, or make an illegal crackback block.

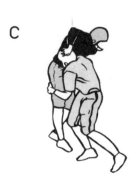

Tackling (C) involves using the hands or arms in an attempt to hold an opponent or throw him to the ground.

A defensive player may not tackle or hold any opponent other than a runner. except:
a) to defend or protect himself against an obstructing opponent;
b) to push or pull an obstructing opponent out of his way on the line of scrimmage;
c) in an actual attempt to get at or tackle a runner;
d) to push or pull an obstructing opponent out of the way in an actual legal attempt to recover a loose ball;
e) during a legal block on an opponent who is not an eligible pass receiver;
f) when legally blocking an eligible pass receiver above the waist (or below the waist if the eligible pass receiver is within 2yd of the tackle).

Physical interference Offensive players may not:
a) assist the runner except by individually blocking opponents for him;
b) push the runner or lift him to his feet;
c) use interlocking interference (ie encircling each others' bodies to any degree with their hands or arms).

Offensive players may not push or throw their bodies against a teammate:
a) if this assists the runner;
b) in order to help the teammate obstruct an opponent or recover a loose ball:
c) to trip an opponent;
d) in charging, falling, or using their hands into the back above the waist of an opponent.

FREE KICKS AND FAIR CATCH

A kick off is a type of free kick and is used to start play:
a) at the start of the first and third periods of a game;
b) after a try-for-point;
c) after a successful field goal.

A kick off is taken from the offensive 35yd line. Rules are as for other free kicks. except that a tee may be used for a place kick and that a punt is not permitted.

A free kick other than a kick off is used to put the ball into play:

a) after a safety:

b) after a fair catch;

c) when a free kick has to be retaken.

A free kick may be a drop kick, place kick, or punt. It may be made from any point on or behind the offensive (kicking) team's free kick line and between the inbounds lines. Initial free kick lines (plus or minus any distance adjustments required because of a penalty imposed before the free kick) are:

a) the offensive 20yd line after a safety; or

b) the yard line through the mark of the catch after a fair catch.

At the moment that a free kick is taken all players of the offensive team must be inbounds and behind the ball, except that a player may be beyond the ball to hold it for a place kick, and that the kicker may be in front of the ball provided that his kicking foot is behind it. During any free kick all members of the defensive (receiving) team must be inbounds and behind the line that is 10yd in advance of the offensive team's free kick line.

A free kick will be penalized as short if the ball fails to reach or cross the defensive team's free kick line, except when the kicked ball is first touched by a defensive player or goes out of bounds.

The offensive team may not direct a free kick out of bounds between the goal lines, except that if the defensive team is last to touch the ball before it goes out of bounds, the offensive team is not penalized and the defensive team puts the ball into play at the inbounds spot.

No player of the offensive team may touch or recover a free kick before:

a) the ball has been in the possession of a defensive player if the offensive player has been out of bounds during the free kick; or

b) the ball has crossed the defensive team's free kick line or, before doing so, has been touched by a defensive player.

If a free kick (legal or illegal) is recovered by the offensive team, the ball becomes dead. If the recovery by the offensive team is legal, the ball is next put into play by the offensive team at the spot of recovery. However, if the offensive team's recovery (legal or illegal) unduly advances the ball, that team is penalized for delaying the game.

If the defensive team recovers the ball after a free kick it is permitted to advance.

If a free kick is simultaneously recovered by two opposing players, the ball is awarded to the defensive team.

A fair catch is an unhindered catch made by any member of the receivers (ie the opponents when a kick is made), provided he has signaled his intention of attempting the catch by raising one hand at full arm's length above his head (**D**). A fair catch may be made from a free kick, scrimmage kick (p. 120), or return kick (p. 120) that has crossed the offensive team's scrimmage line, even if the kick is muffed (ie touched in an unsuccessful attempt to gain possession).

D

The mark of the catch is the spot where the ball was caught following a fair catch signal, or the spot of the ball following a penalty for fair catch interference.

A player who signals for a fair catch may not block or otherwise initiate contact with one of the kickers until the ball has touched a player.

If a player has signaled for a fair catch, the ball becomes dead when caught by any receiver, even if the fair catch signal was invalid. However, any receiver may recover the ball and advance after a fair catch signal if the kicked ball in flight touches a member of the kicking team or if it touches the ground. If no signal was made, the ball is put into play by the receivers at the spot where the ball was caught.

A player may not tackle, block, or make contact with a player of the opposing team who has made a fair catch and come to a legal stop.

It is fair catch interference if, when a receiver could reach the kick in flight, any member of the kicking team interferes with the receiver, his path to the ball, or the ball.

The captain of the team awarded a fair catch must choose to put the ball into play with a snap or a free kick; his first choice is irrevocable.

DOWN AND SCRIMMAGE

A down, or play, is a period of action beginning when the ball is put into play by a free kick (p. 117) or a snap (see below, Scrimmage down) and ending when the ball is next dead.

Series of downs An offensive team is awarded a series of four consecutive scrimmage downs (ie downs beginning with a snap) in which to advance the ball to the necessary line (ie to the line 10yd in advance of the spot of the snap that starts the series, or to the goal line if this is nearer).

A new series of downs is awarded to the offensive team if:

a) during a given series, the ball is declared dead in possession of the offense while it is on, above, or across the necessary line, except if the ball is placed there by a penalty, or there is a touchback for the offense;

b) the ball is dead in the field of play in the offensive team's possession after having been in the defensive team's possession in the same down;

c) a foul is made by the defense, unless prior to or during a play from scrimmage, or when an impetus by them results in a touchback for the offensive team;

d) the offensive team recovers a scrimmage kick anywhere in the field of play after it has first been touched beyond the line by the defensive team.

Measurement of any distance gained is always to the forward part of the ball in its position when declared dead in the field of play; the ball must not be rotated.

If the offensive team fails to advance the ball to the necessary line during a series, the ball is awarded to the defense for a new series starting either where the ball became dead at the end of the fourth down, or where it is placed because of a penalty or a touchback for the defensive team. However, the ball is not awarded to the defense if a fourth down results in either a safety or touchback for the offense.

Scrimmage down This is a down that starts with a specific form of backward pass known as a snap. Typical player positions are illustrated (**A**).

The line of scrimmage (**a, b**) for each team is a yard line passing through the end of the ball nearest the team's own goal line; the area between the two lines of scrimmage is termed the neutral zone (**c**).

Before the snap takes place, no defensive player may enter the neutral zone or touch the ball or the snapper. At the snap, no player of either team may be out of bounds.

The offensive team must have seven or more players on its line (ie on or not more than 1ft behind its line of scrimmage) for the snap. Line players other than the snapper must have no part of their body within the neutral zone; the snapper must have no part of his body beyond the opponent's line of scrimmage.

Players on the line must have both hands, or both feet, or a hand and the opposite foot on

Scrimmage positions
Offense
1) Center (snapper)
2) Guard
3) Tackle
4) End
5) Quarterback
6) Back
Defense
7) Defense tackle
8) Defense end
9) Line backer
10) Defense back

A

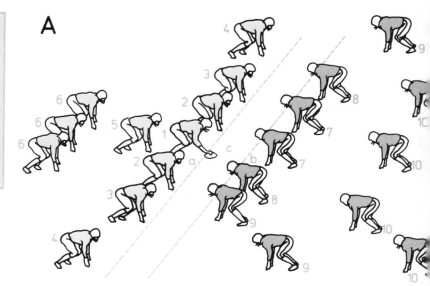

the ground, and their shoulders facing the opponents' goal line. They may lock legs only with the snapper; otherwise both feet and hands must be outside those of the next player. An offensive center, guard, or tackle may be anywhere on his line at the snap, but may be behind it only if he has informed the referee of his change of position. Offensive players who are not on the line, with the exception of the snap receiver, must be at least 1yd behind the line when the snap is made.

At the snap, all offensive players must be stationary in their positions, except the snapper may move just his head immediately before the snap, and one backfield player may be moving parallel to or backward from the line of scrimmage.

Any offensive player on the line may make the snap, which must start with the ball on the ground, with its long axis horizontal and at right angles to the line. The impulse must be given by one quick and continuous movement of the snapper's hand(s), and the ball must actually leave or be taken from his hands during this motion (**B**).

The snapper may not:

a) move his feet from the start of the snap until the ball has left his hands;

b) slide his hands along the ball before grasping it;

c) grasp the ball with two hands and then lift his hand(s) without simultaneously passing;

d) make quick plays if the referee has not had time to assume his normal stance.

The snap must be to a player who was not on the line at the snap, unless the ball first strikes the ground. If the ball first strikes the ground, or is first touched or caught by an eligible backfield receiver, play continues in accordance with the rules for a backward pass (see p. 121).

Dead ball An official declares "Dead ball" and a down ends when:

a) a runner is out of bounds, cries "Down," or falls to the ground and makes no effort to advance;

b) a runner's forward progress ends through being held or otherwise restrained;

c) a runner is contacted by a defensive player and so caused to touch the ground with any part of his body except his hands or feet;

d) an opponent takes a ball (hand in hand) that is in possession of a runner who is down on the ground;

e) any forward pass is incomplete (p. 120);

f) a backward pass that has struck the ground is recovered by an opponent, except when the defense recovers the ball after the offense muffs a snap in flight;

g) any legal kick touches the receivers' goal posts or cross bar unless it later scores a goal from the field;

h) any scrimmage or return kick (p. 120) causes the ball to cross the receivers' goal line and the ball is lying loose in the end zone or no attempt is made to run it out;

i) any legal kick or a short free kick is recovered by the kickers, except when kicked and recovered behind the line of scrimmage, or illegally touched or recovered within 5yd of the opponents' goal line and then carried over that line;

j) the defensive team gains possession during a try, or a try-kick is no longer in play;

k) a touchdown, field goal, safety, try, or touchback has been made;

l) a fair catch is made;

m) any official signals dead ball or sounds his whistle, even inadvertently;

n) a fourth down fumble by an offensive player is recovered by a teammate;

o) a loose ball comes to rest within the field of play and no player attempts to recover it (in which case any legal kick is awarded to the receivers and any other ball to the team last in possession).

Snap to restart play Play is restarted by a snap at inbounds by the team entitled to possession when:

a) a runner or a loose ball is out of bounds between the goal lines;

b) the ball is dead in a side zone, or is placed there as the result of an enforcement;

c) the mark of a fair catch is in a side zone.

The snap is held at the previous spot (ie the spot where the ball was last put into play) if a forward pass or free kick goes out of bounds, or if an incompletion or a foul by the defense occurs in a side zone during a try.

After a touchdown, the touchback team next snaps from any point on its 20yd line between the inbounds lines and the forward point of the ball.

Scrimmage and return kicks A scrimmage kick is a kick (punt, drop kick, or place kick) made before team possession changes during a scrimmage down; it may be made either behind or beyond the scrimmage line.

A return kick is a kick made after team possession changes during a scrimmage down; either team may make a return kick from anywhere.

During a kick from scrimmage, only the end men as eligible receivers may go beyond the line before the ball is kicked.

A kicker (ie member of the kicking team) may not touch the ball after a scrimmage or return kick until it has been first touched by an opponent, except that there is no such restriction on a kicker behind the line touching a kick made behind the line.

If a kick from behind the line is touched in the immediate vicinity of the neutral zone or behind the kicker's line by a receiver (ie opponent of the kicker), such touching does not make a kicker eligible to recover the kick beyond the line.

If any kick is recovered by the receivers they may advance, except in some cases when there is a fair catch. If a kick is recovered simultaneously by two eligible opponents, or is lying on the field of play and no player is trying to recover it, the ball is awarded to the receivers. If the kickers recover a kick the ball is dead, except when the kickers behind the line recover a kick that was made behind the line, in which case they may advance.

PASSES AND FUMBLE

A pass The runner may pass the ball by handling, throwing, shoving, or pushing it. Provided that a teammate takes the ball, these actions constitute a pass even if the ball does not leave the runner's hand(s).

A forward pass is a pass that moves forward toward the opponents' goal line, or is handled, regardless of the direction in which the ball is moving, by a player who is in advance of a teammate from whose hands he takes or receives it (except that it is not a forward pass if the ball is handed forward to an eligible pass receiver behind his line, or if the receiver fails to gain possession).

The offensive team is allowed one forward pass from behind the line during each play from scrimmage (provided that the ball does not cross the line and return behind it before the pass is made).

Any other forward pass by either team is illegal. If an illegal pass is intercepted, the receivers may advance the ball and decline the penalty.

Players eligible to touch or catch a forward pass from behind the line are:
a) all defensive players;
b) offensive players at the ends of the line (**1**), excluding centers, guards, or tackles;
c) offensive players legally at least 1yd behind the line at the snap (**2**), excluding T-formation quarterbacks not in the position of a backfield player.

An eligible receiver becomes ineligible if he goes out of bounds before or during a pass. All offensive players become eligible once the forward pass has been touched by an eligible receiver.

Complete and incomplete pass A forward pass thrown from behind the line is complete and may be advanced if it is:

a) caught by an eligible offensive player before any illegal touching by a teammate;

b) caught by any offensive player after being first touched by an eligible player;

c) intercepted by a defensive player with both feet inbounds before and after the interception.

Any illegal or legal forward pass is incomplete and the ball immediately becomes dead if the pass:

a) strikes the ground or goes out of bounds;

b) is illegal and is caught by the offensive team;

c) is caught by any offensive player after it has touched an ineligible offensive player before any touching by any eligible receiver;

d) touches a goal post or crossbar.

A forward pass from behind the line must not be intentionally thrown to the ground, out of bounds, or into any player behind the line in order to escape loss of yardage from being downed behind the line.

If there is a foul by the defensive team from the start of the snap until a legal forward pass ends, the foul is not offset by an incompletion by the offensive team.

Pass interference There must be no pass interference beyond the line of scrimmage when a forward pass is thrown from behind the line, whether or not it crosses the line. For the offensive team the restriction on pass interference begins with the snap; for the defensive team it begins when the ball leaves the passer's hands.

It is pass interference by the offensive team if, before the ball leaves the passer's hands, an ineligible offensive player does any of the following:

a) advances beyond his line (determined by his initial line charge while in contact with an opponent);

b) loses his contact after the initial charge and continues to advance or move laterally;

c) moves laterally or forward beyond the line.

It is not offensive pass interference when ineligible forward pass receivers:

a) voluntarily retreat behind their line;

b) are forced behind their line;

c) move laterally behind their line without advancing beyond it until the ball leaves the passer's hands;

d) have legally crossed their line in blocking an opponent.

It is pass interference by players of either team if any player movement beyond the offensive line hinders the progress of an eligible opponent in his attempt to reach a pass. except any incidental movement or contact occurring when two or more eligible players make a simultaneous and bona fide attempt to catch or bat the ball.

A backward pass is any pass that is not a forward pass. A runner may make a backward pass at any time.

An offensive player may advance either after catching a backward pass in flight or after recovering the pass after the ball has touched the ground.

A defensive player may advance only after catching a backward pass in flight. If a defensive player recovers a backward pass after the ball has touched the ground, the ball becomes dead and the recovering team snaps at the spot of recovery.

If a snap in flight is muffed by an eligible receiver after the ball touches the ground, it is a backward pass. But if a snap in flight is muffed by an eligible receiver behind the line, the muff is treated as a fumble if the ball then touches the ground.

A fumble is any act, other than a pass or legal kick, that results in loss of player possession. The term fumble always implies possession.

Any player of either team may recover and advance a fumble before or after it strikes the ground, except during a fourth down, when specific rules limit its recovery and advance. The fourth down fumble rule does not apply in the last two minutes of a half.

If the runner intentionally fumbles forward it is treated as a forward pass.

FOULS AND PENALTIES

Personal fouls Players must not:

a) strike with their fists;

b) strike an opponent's head, face, or neck with the side, back, or heel of the hand, with clasped hands, or with the wrist, forearm, or elbow (**1**);

c) strike an opponent above the shoulders with the palm of the hand (except that a defensive player may make such an action to ward off or push an opponent during an actual attempt to get at the ball, or to ward off an opponent on the line provided he does not do so more than once against the same opponent during any one action);

d) when blocking, strike an opponent below the shoulders with the forearm or elbows because of turning at the waist, pivoting, or any other unnecessary action;

e) kick or knee an opponent (**2**);

f) grasp an opponent's face mask (**3**);

g) use helmets to butt, spear, or ram an opponent, or for any other unnecessary action;

h) when on defense, run into or rough a kicker kicking from behind his line (unless the contact is incidental to and after he touches the kick in flight, or is caused by the kicker's own actions, or occurs during a kick or after a run behind or beyond the line, or during a quick kick, or after the kicker recovers a loose ball on the ground);

i) run into an opponent after the ball has left his hand for a legal forward pass;

j) run or dive into, or throw the body against or on, a ball carrier who falls or slips to the ground untouched and makes no attempt to advance;

k) run or dive into, or throw the body against or on any player who is obviously not involved in the play;

l) tackle or in any other way contact a runner who is out of bounds;

m) throw a runner to the ground after the ball is dead;

n) pile on a player other than a runner, or on a runner after the ball is dead (ie fall upon him while he is prostrate);

o) clip an opponent (ie approach him from behind and then throw the body across the back of his leg (**4**), or charge or fall into his back below the waist), except that such action is permitted against a runner during close line play (ie between the original positions of the offensive tackles and 3yd on either side of each line of scrimmage);

p) make an illegal block, including a crackback block (ie when an offensive player, who is more than 2yd outside an offensive tackle at or after a snap,blocks an opponent anywhere or contacts an opponent below the waist if the blocker is moving in toward the ball and the contact occurs within 5yd to either side of the line of scrimmage);

q) crawl when a runner (ie attempt to advance after being touched by an opponent when any part of the body other than the hands and feet has touched the ground);

r) act unnecessarily roughly in any way not specifically referred to in the rules;

s) interfere with play by any act that is obviously unfair;

t) act in an unsportsmanlike manner;

u) unless a captain, address an official about an interpretation of the rules, or attempt to exercise any of a captain's privileges except in an emergency.

Penalties Infringements by players or team officials are penalized by one or a combination of the following:

a) loss of down, meaning that the down in which the offense occurred is charged as a completed down in the current series;

b) down to be replayed;

c) loss of yards, when the team concedes 5yd, 10yd, 15yd, depending on the offense;

d) loss of team possession;

e) award of points to the opponents;

f) withdrawal, suspension, or disqualification of an offender, with substitution permitted;

g) time penalty;

h) time-out to be charged.

Enforcement of penalties is usually at one of the following:

a) the spot of the foul;

b) the previous spot, ie where the ball was last put into play;

c) the spot where an act (snap, fumble, free kick, etc) connected with a given foul occurred, or where the penalty is to be enforced;

d) the succeeding spot, ie where the ball would next be put in play if no distance penalty were to be enforced.

If the enforcement of a distance penalty would place the ball more than half the distance to the offender's goal line, the penalty awarded is half the distance from that spot to the goal line.

If a team commits two fouls at the same time, only one penalty is enforced; the captain of the offended team may in most circumstances choose which. Similarly, the offended captain may in most circumstances choose to decline any penalty.

COLLEGE FOOTBALL

Rule differences between college (NCAA) and professional (NFL) football are summarized here.

The field for the college game has the same overall dimensions as that for the professional game, but the inbounds lines are only 53ft 4in in from the side lines, and the goal line is the equivalent of the end line on the professional field.

Goal posts under NCAA rules must be 23ft 4in wide and must extend at least 10ft above the 10ft high cross bar.

The ball prescribed by NCAA rules has similar dimensions to that prescribed under NFL rules, except that the short circumference must be 21–21¼in.

Officials NCAA rules require four, five, or six officials; there is no side judge.

Scoring Under college rules, a try-for-point resulting in a touchdown scores 2 points.

Rules of play NCAA rules that differ significantly from NFL rules include the following:
a) the ball becomes dead in all circumstances when any part of a runner's body except his hand or foot touches the ground;
b) for a catch to be complete, a defensive player must first touch the ground inbounds on landing with the ball in his possession;
c) the ball is dead if a fumble is recovered by an opponent;
d) a return kick is an illegal kick.

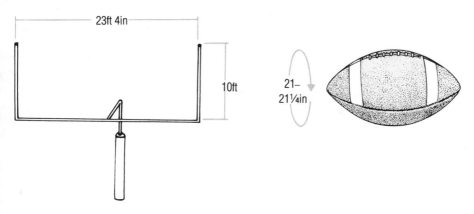

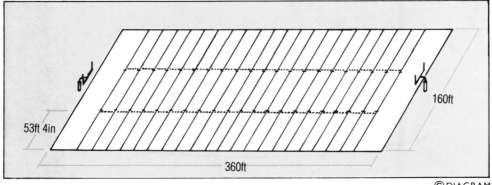

© DIAGRAM

FOOTBALL (AUSTRALIAN)

HISTORY

Australian rules football was developed in the late nineteenth century following the introduction into Australia of Gaelic football, played by Irish gold miners, and rugby football, which was then at an early stage of its development. The Australian game has many individual features, including the oval playing ground – a reminder of the days when Australian football was a winter game for cricketers, who played both games on the same field. The first official set of laws for Australian football were published in 1858. Today, Australian football is easily the most popular football code in Australia, where there are more than 360,000 players of all ages.

SYNOPSIS

This fast and exciting field game is played between two opposing teams, each with 20 players of whom only 18 may play at any one time. The teams try to score goals (six points) or behinds (one point) by putting the ball between posts positioned at the edge of the very large oval playing ground. The ellipsoid ball is mainly moved about by long kicks, although handballing and running when carrying the ball are also permitted. Throwing the ball is prohibited. A player must immediately dispose of the ball when held by an opponent.

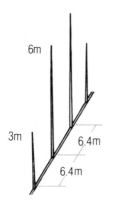

The playing ground is a grass oval 110–155m wide and 135–185m long. It is bounded by a white line called the boundary line (**a**).

Marked in white in the center of the ground is a circle (**b**) with a diameter of 3m and a square (**c**) with sides each measuring 45m.

At each end of the playing ground are two goal posts (**d**), 6.4m apart and at least 6m high. The line between the goal posts is termed the goal line (**e**).

Outside the goal posts, at a distance of 6.4m from them, are posts known as behind posts (**f**), of which the minimum recommended height is 3m. The lines between the goal posts and the behind posts are termed behind lines (**g**).

Marked in white in front of each goal are lines known as kick off lines (**h**): two lines extend from the goal posts at right angles to the goal line, and a third line connects them at their outer edge to form a rectangle with the goal line.

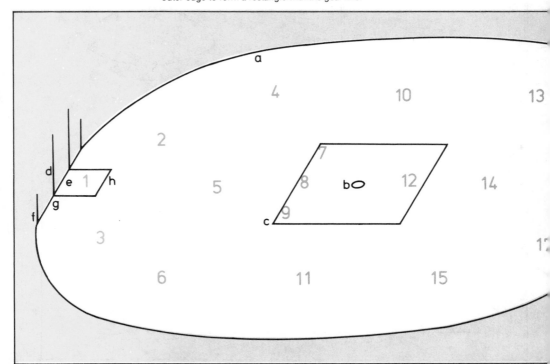

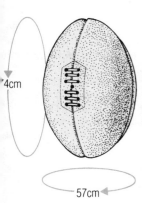

4cm

57cm

The ball, made of hide with a rubber bladder inside, should have a short circumference of 57cm and a long circumference of 74cm, and should weigh 450–500g.

Only with the consent of both captains may a ball be changed during a match.

Dress Players wear jerseys, shorts, socks, and studded boots.

Boots must not have protruding nails or plates.

Also prohibited are finger rings and surgical appliances or guards that might injure other players.

PLAYERS AND OFFICIALS

Teams consist of 20 named players, two of whom are interchangeable substitutes.

Playing positions are shown on the field diagram and listed beside it.

Substitution A player taking part in the match may at any time be replaced by a player not then taking part, provided that procedures for obtaining permission are correctly followed.

A substitute must usually wait until the player he is replacing has left the playing area, and must then enter the playing area at the point where the other player left it.

If a player appears to have been too badly injured to be removed immediately from the playing area, his substitute can enter the playing area as soon as he has the permission of the field umpire. An injured player replaced in this way may take no further part in the match.

Suspension The field umpire can caution offenders and report them to the controlling body, which may suspend them from further matches.

Officials A match is controlled by a field umpire, two goal umpires, two boundary umpires, and two timekeepers. Alternatively two field umpires can share the duties.

DURATION AND SCORING

Duration A game consists of four quarters, each lasting 25 minutes plus any time added on by the official timekeepers. Teams change ends after each quarter.

A maximum of 3 minutes is allowed between the first and second quarters, 15 minutes at half-time, and 5 minutes between the third and fourth quarters.

The timekeepers sound a siren at the end of each quarter. Play ceases when the field umpire blows his whistle to indicate that he has heard the siren.

Time on may be added when there has been an undue delay, for example in getting the ball when it is out of play.

Scoring The team scoring the most points wins; if the score is equal, the game is drawn. Points are scored for goals and behinds.

A goal (6 points) is scored when an attacker kicks the ball over the goal line between the goal posts (the center posts) without it touching either the posts or another player.

A behind (1 point) is scored:

a) when the ball goes between the goal posts without fulfilling all the conditions for a goal to be scored;

b) when the ball touches or passes over a goal post;

c) when the ball passes over a behind line without touching a behind post; or

d) when the ball is kicked or carried over the behind or goal line by a defender.

If a ball touches or passes over a behind post, it is out of play.

Scoring after time is allowed if:

a) the ball was in transit before the first siren;

b) the player was awarded a free kick;

c) the player took a mark (see p. 128) before the siren.

Scoring is not allowed after time if the ball was touched and assisted in transit or if it touched any player below the knee.

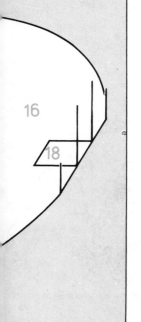

16

18

Playing positions		
1) Full back	**7**) Rover	**13**) Left half forward
2) Left full back	**8**) Follower	**14**) Center half forward
3) Right full back	**9**) Follower	**15**) Right half forward
4) Left half back	**10**) Left center (Wing)	**16**) Left full forward
5) Center half back	**11**) Right center (Wing)	**17**) Right full forward
6) Right half back	**12**) Center	**18**) Full Forward

FOOTBALL (AUSTRALIAN) 2

STARTING PROCEDURES

Start The captains toss for choice of ends.

Center bounce (**A**) At the start of each quarter and after a goal the field umpire blows his whistle and bounces the ball in the center circle. (He may throw the ball in the air if the ground is unsuitable.)

Until the ball touches the ground, no player may enter the center circle and no more than four players per team are allowed inside the center square.

Kick off After a behind, unless a free kick has been given, the defending team kicks the ball from within the kick-off lines.

No opponent is allowed within 10m of those lines. The ball must be kicked clear of the hands and feet, but does not have to be kicked over the kick-off line.

RULES OF PLAY

Bouncing the ball The field umpire bounces the ball at an appropriate spot in the following instances:

a) when there is doubt over which player has taken a mark;

b) when a player claims a mark, the ball having been touched, and retains possession when held by an opponent, provided the field umpire is satisfied that the player has not heard his call "play on";

c) in scrimmages;

d) when the ball has been bounced and has gone over the goal line, behind line, or boundary line, without having been touched by any player;

e) when the goal umpire could not see whether the ball crossed the goal or behind lines;

f) when a player, kicking off from behind, kicks off from outside the kick-off lines.

Out of play The ball is "out of bounds" only when it is completely outside the boundary line; if any part of it is on or above the boundary line it remains in play.

Provided that a free kick has not been awarded, the ball is returned to play by a throw from the point where the ball went out of bounds. The throw is made by the boundary umpire, who throws the ball over his head toward the center of the field. The ball must travel between 10m and 15m at a minimum height of 3m.

If, after a mark or free kick, the player does not put the ball back into play from outside the boundary line, the ball is returned to the field at the point where the original mark or free kick took place.

If a defender, kicking from behind the goal line or behind line, hits a post, time on and another kick are allowed.

A

Playing the ball A player may kick the ball, but may not throw it; he may pass the ball with the hands only by handballing (punching) it.

A player may hold the ball until he is held by an opponent.

Players are allowed to tackle an opponent who has the ball (as permitted by the laws), or to block opponents near the ball but not in possession (known as "shepherding").

Running with the ball A player may run with the ball, but he must bounce or touch it on the ground at least once every 10m.

If, when running with the ball, a player hits it over an opponent's head and catches it, he must bounce or touch it on the ground, or pass it, within 10m.

Handball A player may pass the ball with the hands only by holding the ball in one hand and hitting it with the clenched fist of the other hand (**B**).

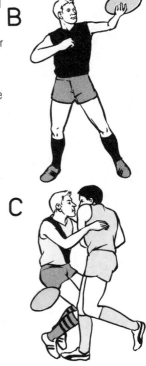

Checking A player with the ball may be tackled with the hip, chest, shoulder, arms, or open hands.

A player without the ball may be pushed in the chest or side in the proper manner in accordance with the laws, providing the ball is within 5m of him (**C**).

Holding the man It is an offense to hold an opponent who is not in possession of the ball (**D**). A player is in possession of the ball if he is holding it, bouncing it, or lying on or over it.

Holding the ball A player in possession of the ball, when held by an opponent firmly enough to stop him or retard his progress (**E**), must dispose of the ball by kicking or handballing it.

Failure to do so within a reasonable time allowed by the field umpire is penalized by a free kick.

If the player in possession is forced to lose the ball (for example, by being swung off balance), play continues.

Substitute kicker Where a player is unable to take a mark or free kick through accident, the field umpire will award the kick to the injured player's nearest teammate.

FOOTBALL (AUSTRALIAN) 3

MARKS

Making a mark A mark is awarded when a player catches and holds the ball directly from the kick of another player at least 10m away (**1**), without the ball having been touched before the mark was made.

A mark is allowed on the goal, behind, or boundary line.

A player who is out of bounds may mark the ball provided he does so before the ball completely passes over the boundary line.

A mark is also awarded if the ball strikes an official but is caught by another player before it touches the ground.

Taking a mark The player who made the mark is allowed an unhindered kick from anywhere behind where he marked.

Only one opponent is allowed to stand at a mark and no other player is allowed within a 10m semicircle behind the mark.

Kicking at goal When a player is kicking at goal from a mark or free kick, the kick must be on a direct line through the mark to the center of the goal line.

Running over a mark If an opponent crosses the mark of a player who successfully kicks for goal from a mark or free kick, the goal is scored.

If, in similar circumstances, the ball is kicked over a behind line, the player has the option of taking another kick from a mark 15m in advance of the first one.

FREE KICKS

Awarding free kicks A free kick is awarded to the nearest opponent of a player who:

a) infringes at a center bounce;

b) unduly interferes with the bouncing of the ball by the field umpire;

c) deliberately interferes with an umpire during the progress of the match;

d) interferes with an opponent when the ball is out of play or is more than 5m away;

e) deliberately holds back or throws an opponent who has kicked or handballed the ball;

f) trips or kicks (or attempts to trip or kick), or slings an opponent (**2**);

g) is guilty of dangerous kicking when not in possession;

h) strikes or attempts to strike an opponent with his hand or arm, or deliberately with his knee;

i) seizes an opponent below the knee or above the neck (including the top of the shoulder) (**3**);

j) charges an opponent;

k) pushes an opponent from behind (**4**), except when legitimately going for a mark;

l) pushes an opponent in the face (**5**);

m) pushes an opponent who is in the air for a mark;

n) infringes the rules on holding the ball;

o) handballs the ball incorrectly;

p) throws or hands the ball to another player while the ball is in play (**6**).

q) infringes rules on running with the ball;

r) deliberately kicks or forces the ball out of bounds without it being touched by another player;

s) when kicking off from a behind, kicks the ball out of bounds without another player touching it;

t) kicks the ball out of bounds without it first touching the ground;

u) interferes with an opponent when the ball is out of bounds;

v) deliberately wastes time.

Taking a free kick A player may take a free kick from any point behind where it was awarded.

No other player may be within 10m and only one opponent is allowed at that distance.

The field umpire will allow play to continue if a free kick would benefit the offending side.

If an opponent deliberately delays a free kick or a mark, it may be advanced a maximum of 15m toward the goal being attacked by the offended team.

If the offending team commits another offense before the free kick is taken, the kick shall be taken where the second offense occurred if that is to the disadvantage of the offending team.

If the offense was against a player who had disposed of the ball, his team may take the kick from:

a) where the ball touched the ground;

b) where the ball was caught;

c) where the ball was marked;

d) where the ball went out of bounds;

e) where the offense occurred.

Scoring from a free kick If an offense by an opponent occurs during a successful kick at goal, the goal will count. If a behind is scored, the player is given the option of another kick.

If an attacker commits an offense during his team's kick for goal, no points may be scored and a free kick is awarded to the opposition.

If a player is fouled immediately after a score and "all clear," another free kick is awarded where the offense occurred. There may then be another score before the ball is bounced in the center circle or kicked off.

4

5

6

©DIAGRAM

FOOTBALL (CANADIAN)

HISTORY
Canadian football, like American football (p. 112), developed from England's rugby union football (p. 146). Rugby was played by Canadian and US college teams in the 1870s, but development of the Canadian game took place more slowly than that of American football. The rules given here are abridged from those of the Canadian Football League, which in 1960 replaced the Canadian Rugby Union as the governing body of the professional game. The amateur game is broadly similar, with a number of minor differences in rules.

SYNOPSIS
Canadian football is a ball game played by two teams of 12 men. The object of the game is to move the ball to the opposing team's goal area and score points in a number of different ways. The team that scores the greater number of points in the allotted time is the winner.

COMPARISON WITH AMERICAN FOOTBALL
Canadian football is now fairly similar to American football. Points of difference between the Canadian and American games include the following: the Canadian field is larger, there is one more player per team, only three downs are allowed to gain 10yd, there are fewer time-outs, there is no fair catch, there is an extra means of scoring (a rouge), and a greater number of distances is used to penalize offenses and to restart play.

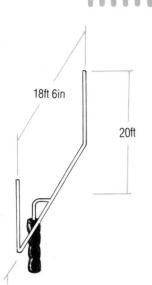

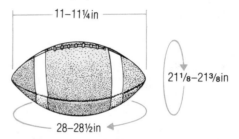

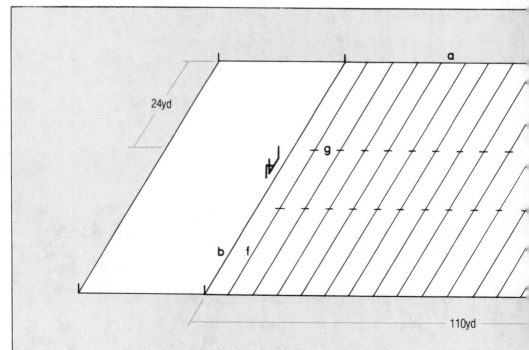

PLAYING AREA AND EQUIPMENT

The field The area termed the field of play is 110yd long by 65yd wide, bounded by the inside edge of side lines (**a**) and goal lines (**b**).

Behind each goal line is an area called the goal area (**c**). This is bounded by the goal line, by extensions of the side lines known as side lines in goal (**d**), and by a line termed the dead line (**e**) that runs parallel to and 25yd behind the goal line.

The field of play is crossed at 5yd intervals by lines (**f**) running parallel to the goal lines. Each of these is crossed by hash marks (**g**), parallel to and 24yd in from the side lines. Flexible markers indicate the intersections of goal lines with side lines, and of dead lines with side lines in goal. It is recommended that markers are also used to indicate the 5yd line before each goal line.

Goal posts are centered on the goal lines. They must be at least 20ft tall, 18ft 6in apart, and joined by a crossbar 10ft high. A wishbone type or single-shaft post may be used if the length and height of the crossbar conform with the above standards, and the base is not more than 6ft behind the goal line.

The ball is made of leather enclosing a rubber bladder. It is 11–11¼in long, with a long circumference of 28–28½in and a short circumference of 21⅛–21⅜in. It weighs14–15oz and is inflated to a pressure of 12½–13½lb.

Dress Players wear a short-sleeved sweater in team colors, with a number on the back, front, and upper arms or shoulders. If a long-sleeved undershirt is worn it must be similar in color to the regular shirt. Shirts must be tucked into uniform pants, which together with team stockings must cover the whole leg.

Protective padding is to be worn under the sweater, pants, and stockings, except that knee pads in the same color as the pants may be worn on the outside provided they overlap both pants and stockings. Any arm padding that is exposed must be in one of the basic team colors.

A helmet with face mask is compulsory, and must not be removed during the game. Players wear lightweight boots. Cleats on the soles must conform to certain specifications. Any equipment that might injure or confuse another player is prohibited.

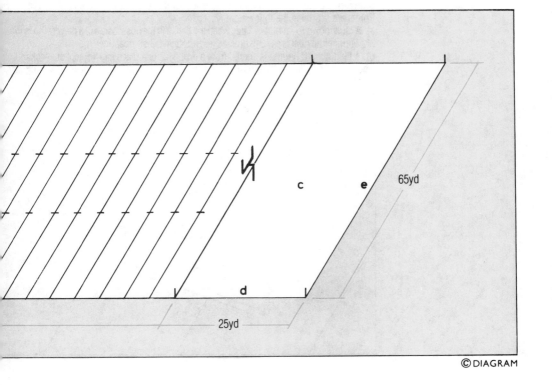

FOOTBALL (CANADIAN) 2

PLAYERS AND OFFICIALS

Players Each team consists of 12 players and a number of substitutes. One of the players on the field is the team captain. Only the captain is allowed to speak to the referee. He is entitled to an explanation of a decision but is not permitted to argue with the referee. He may also request measurements to ascertain whether a first down has been made or what is the distance still required.

Substitution A substitute may enter the game at any time when the ball is dead. Having entered the game to the extent that he can talk to a team mate, a substitute must stay in the game for at least one play.

A player leaving the game must go straight to his team bench.

A team will be penalized if it has more than 12 players on the field following an error in substitution.

Team personnel Substitutes and a maximum of 12 other people—coaches, trainers, doctors, etc—sit on the team bench. Coaches must remain close to their team bench and may not enter the field except with the referee's permission. At an official time-out, only one player can come to the side line to talk to the team coach.

Officials The game is controlled by field officials and side line officials.

There are six field officials: referee, umpire, back judge, field judge, head linesman, and line judge. Field officials have individual functions laid down in the rules and all of them have the power to stop the game for a foul. The referee is the chief official and directs and guides the other officials. Side line officials are: the downsman, three yardsmen, the timekeeper, the scorer, and the communications coordinator.

DURATION AND SCORING

Duration The game consists of 60 minutes' playing time divided into four periods of 15 minutes. A 15-minute rest period at the end of the second period divides the game into two halves.

There may be one 60-second team time-out in the final three minutes of each half, at the request of either team captain.

When a game is tied and a winner is needed, a 20 minutes' overtime game is played, divided into two halves. If there is still no winner, additional overtime games may be played.

Scoring Each team aims to make the greater number of points, and so win the game. Points are scored in the following ways.

a) A touchdown (6 points) is made when the ball is in the possession of a player who is in his opponents' goal area, or who crosses or touches their goal line (**A**).

b) A field goal (3 points) is scored from a drop kick or a place kick (except at a kick off) when the ball goes over the crossbar and between the posts of the opponents' goal without first touching the ground (**B**).

c) A safety touch (2 points) is scored to the opposing team when a team plays the ball into its own goal area and the ball becomes dead in that team's possession or touches or crosses the dead line or side line in goal.

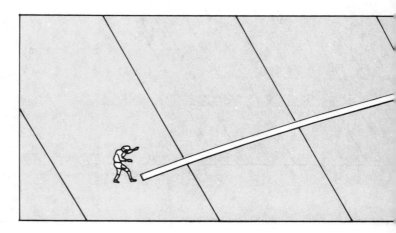

d) A rouge (1 point) is scored when the ball is kicked into the opponents' goal area and becomes dead in their possession, or when the ball touches the ground or an object or player beyond the dead line or a side line in goal.

e) A convert (1 or 2 points). After scoring a touchdown a team can add to its score from a scrimmage play anywhere on or beyond the opponents' 5yd line. Kicking a field goal scores 1 point. Making a touchdown by carrying or passing the ball scores 2 points (an onside-kick play is not permitted).

STARTING PROCEDURES

Choice by captains The visiting captain, or the winner of a toss, can choose to kick off or receive the kick off, or may select which end his team will defend first. The other captain may then choose between the remaining alternatives. At the start of the second half, the order of choosing is reversed.

Change of ends Teams change ends before the second and fourth periods.

Start of periods At the start of the first and third periods (the two halves), the team to kick off does so from between the hash marks on its own 45yd line.

At the start of the second and fourth periods, play resumes at a point exactly corresponding to where it ended in the other half of the field. The ball is put into play in such a way as if there had been no interruption.

Restart after a score Play is resumed in different ways depending on the score made. The ball is always put into play between the hash marks on the appropriate line.

a) After a touchdown, the team scored against may kick off from its own 45yd line or may require the scoring team to kick off from its own (the scorers') 45yd line.

b) After a field goal, the team scored against may kick off or scrimmage the ball as first down at its 35yd line, or may require the scoring team to kick off its own (the scorers') 35yd line.

c) After a safety touch, the team scored against kicks off from its own 35yd line.

d) After a rouge, the team scored against scrimmages as first down on its 35yd line.

Kick off The ball is put into play by a place kick from the appropriate line.

For the place kick the ball may be held by a member of the kicker's team (**C**), placed on the ground, or placed on a tee, provided that the lowest point of the ball is not more than 1in above the ground.

When the ball is kicked, players of the kicking team must be behind the ball, except for a player holding the ball for the kick. All opponents must be at least 10yd away, on their own side of the kick off line.

From the kick off the ball must travel at least 10yd toward the opponents' goal line, unless touched by an opponent.

As soon as the ball is kicked, any member of the other team may interfere with an opponent. Members of the kicking team may interfere with opponents only if a member of the kicking team recovers the ball on the kick off. Any interference must occur within bounds, and all contact with an opponent must be above the waist.

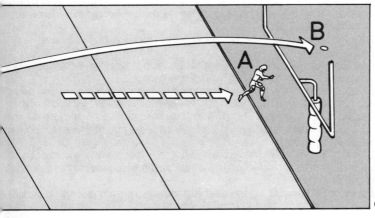

©DIAGRAM

133

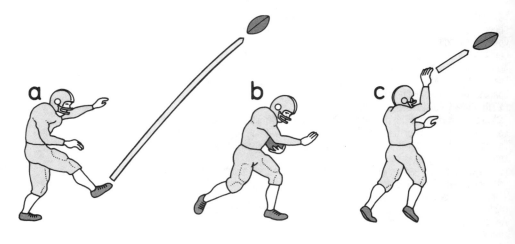

RULES OF PLAY

Playing the ball Players may kick (**a**), strike, carry (**b**), and throw (**c**) the ball, with certain exceptions defined in the rules.

Possession of the ball A player has possession if the ball is firmly held in one or both hands, arms, or legs, or under the body.

When two opposing players have possession, the ball belongs to the player who first gained and has not lost possession.

If both players legally gain possession simultaneously, it belongs to the player whose team previously had possession of the ball.

Dead ball The ball becomes dead when:

a) a field official blows his whistle or signals a score;

b) the ball goes out of bounds;

c) the ball carrier is tackled (grasped or encircled with hands and arms) and held (**1**);

d) the ball carrier touches the ground with a part of the body other than the hands or feet as a result of contact with an opponent (**2**);

e) when a player in possession of the ball in his own goal area intentionally kneels on the ground;

f) when a forward pass is declared incomplete;

g) when a kicked ball hits the post or crossbar of the opponents' goal in flight, without first touching the ground, a player, or an official;

h) when the ball carrier is on the ground and, in the judgment of an official, is not attempting to advance the ball.

Ball out of bounds The ball goes out of bounds when it or a player in possession touches a side line, a side line in goal, or the ground or any object beyond those lines.

A ball carried out of bounds belongs to the carrying team, except on a third down when yards have not been gained.

A ball kicked out of bounds belongs to the opposing team, subject to the penalty applicable on a kick off.

A ball thrown out of bounds by a forward pass remains in possession of the passing team, except on a third down when yards have not been gained.

Unless there is a forward pass, any ball that is fumbled out of bounds or goes out of bounds after touching a player on the field of play is awarded to the team that last touched the ball; the ball is put into play 24yd in from the side line opposite either where the ball went out of play or where the ball was last touched in the field of play, whichever is nearer the possessor's goal line.

Special provisions apply when the ball is fumbled over the opponents' goal line, or is fumbled by a player in his own goal area so that it crosses the goal line and then goes out of bounds in the field of play.

Player out of bounds A player of either team who goes out of bounds, except as a result of body contact, must stay out of the play in progress.

Scrimmage When the ball is dead in the field of play, the team in possession of the ball puts it into play by means of a scrimmage.

One player (the center) places the ball on the ground in front of him. He must be facing the opposing goal and behind the scrimmage line. The scrimmage line is an imaginary line from side line to side line, parallel to the goal lines, and passing through the point of the ball farthest from the attacking team's goal line. The area extending 1yd on either side of the scrimmage line is termed the scrimmage zone.

At least six other players line up with the center. These seven (line) players must be within 1yd of their side of the scrimmage line; the other five (backfield) players must be clearly behind the scrimmage zone.

Line players other than the center must be completely behind the scrimmage line; the center is permitted to have his head, arms, and hands across the line.

Five of the line players must be in an unbroken line, and are ineligible for a pass. The two end line players and the backfield players may receive passes.

The opposing team must stand at least 1yd behind their side of the scrimmage line, and must remain there until the ball is "snapped."

Any deviation from the specified positions is offside. No player may make a movement so as to draw an opponent offside, for example making a quick movement or moving out of position before the ball is snapped.

After adopting their positions, line players must remain motionless for one second before the center snaps the ball. It is not necessary for the center to wait until the opponents are onside, but an offside penalty cannot be claimed against them unless they interfere with the play while still offside.

After the referee's whistle, the offensive team has 20 seconds to call a play, to get into position on the scrimmage line, and for the center to "snap" the ball back between his legs in one continuous action. The ball must leave the center's hands and he may not touch it again until another player has played it.

If the ball is scrimmaged after a score, the scrimmage takes place between the hash marks on the appropriate yard line.

If the ball becomes dead within 24yd of a side line, or goes out of bounds, the following scrimmage will be 24yd in from the side line at the same yardage point.

If the ball becomes dead within 1yd of either goal line, the scrimmage will be 1yd out from the goal line.

If a team scrimmages on or inside its own 15yd line on third down, it may position the ball away from its own goal posts toward the nearest side line, but not closer to it than 24yd.

If a team scrimmages within 5yd of its own goal line, it may move the ball out to the nearest hash mark.

— 1yd — — 1yd —

135

FOOTBALL (CANADIAN) 4

Downs The team in possession of the ball is allowed three downs to gain 10 yd. A down is a period of action starting from the moment when the ball is put into play at a scrimmage and ending when the ball becomes dead.

If a team gains the 10yd, it is allowed another series of three downs. If not, the ball is awarded to the opponents at the place where it became dead.

A down may be repeated if a penalty is given against either team.

The series of three downs must be consecutive, ie the ball must stay in the possession of the same team throughout the series.

A series of downs is interrupted when:
a) the ball is kicked—other than dribbled—across the scrimmage line;
b) the ball is fumbled at a scrimmage play and the opposing team dribbles the ball;
c) the ball passes clearly into the possession of the opponents;
d) the required distance is gained;
e) the ball is kicked out of bounds.

A down is measured to the forward point of the ball after it has been rotated so that its long axis is parallel to the side lines. A touchdown cannot be scored by such rotation.

Passing When passing, the ball may be thrown, handed, knocked, batted, or fumbled. Passes are legitimate or illegitimate as follows.

An onside or lateral pass is one made parallel to or in the direction of the player's own dead line (**A**). Whether or not a pass is onside—and thus a legitimate pass—is determined by the point at which the ball is caught, goes out of bounds, or hits the ground, a player, or an official.

A hand-off pass occurs when the ball is handed, not thrown, to another player behind the scrimmage line (**B**). There is no restriction on the number of hand-off passes in any down, but a line player cannot receive a hand-off pass.

A forward pass is one made in the direction of the opponents' dead line (**C**). Only one forward pass is permitted in any one down. It must be thrown from behind the line of scrimmage to an eligible receiver, and must not touch the ground, goal posts or crossbar, an official, or any other object, or go out of bounds.

Offside With the exception of a legal forward pass, the ball may not be passed toward the opponents' dead line: such a pass is offside (**D**). A pass is also offside if the ball goes out of bounds, or is touched by a player who is offside.

A player is offside if the ball has last been touched by a teammate behind him, except in the case of a hand-off or legal forward pass. A player who is offside is put onside again as soon as the ball touches an opponent.

Interference is when a player blocks, obstructs, screens (interferes without direct contact), or charges an opponent to prevent him getting to the ball, the ball carrier, or the potential ball carrier.

Any player from the team in possession may interfere with an opponent anywhere between the dead lines on a play from scrimmage, except when a forward pass is thrown or the ball is kicked across the scrimmage line.

After a forward pass, offensive players may interfere only with opponents up to 1yd in front of the scrimmage line, until the pass is complete.

On a kicking play from scrimmage an offensive player may interfere with an opponent up to 1yd in front of the scrimmage line. A defending player may interfere with any opponent who has crossed the line of scrimmage, provided that contact is above the waist.

On any play from scrimmage a defensive player may only tackle (grasp or encircle with the hands or arms) the player with the ball, although he may interfere with opponents who are in a position to block him. Otherwise he may not interfere with a potential pass receiver.

FOULS AND PENALTIES

Fouls Players must not:

a) hold, with hands or arms, any opponent other than the ball carrier;

b) tackle an opponent, other than the ball carrier, from the rear (clipping);

c) charge or fall on a player with the ball when the ball is dead (piling);

d) kick an opponent;

e) trip an opponent (**1**);

f) hold hands or lock arms at a scrimmage (**2**);

g) deliberately touch the kicker when he is kicking from scrimmage;

h) contact a defending opponent below the waist in the area up to 2yd beyond the line of scrimmage, having started more than 3yd outside the offensive tackle (crackback blocking);

i) use another player to gain height in an attempt to block a field goal or convert (**3**);

j) strike an opponent with the fist, knee, elbow, or heel of the hand;

k) tackle an opponent out of bounds;

l) contact an opponent in any other unnecessarily rough or unfair manner;

m) abuse opponents, officials, or spectators.

Penalties Infringements are penalized by one or more of the following:

a) loss of a down, meaning that the down during which the offense occurred has used up one of the downs in a series;

b) loss of yards, when the team concedes 5, 10, 15 or 25 yards according to the offense committed (but it cannot also lose a down);

c) option provided, meaning that the non-offending team may accept a penalty, or may decline it to take advantage of position, score, down, time, etc;

d) loss of possession of the ball;

e) award of points to the opponents;

f) automatic award of a first down to the team in possession;

g) disqualification of a player, with substitution permitted.

Teams are liable to be penalized on the field for offenses by their non-playing personnel, who may also be disqualified and told to leave the bench or surrounding field area.

FOOTBALL (RUGBY LEAGUE)

HISTORY

In the late nineteeth century, many rugby clubs in the north of England wished to compensate players for wages lost in taking time off to play in matches. Repeated refusals by the Rugby Football Union to sanction these payments led to the formation of the breakaway Northern Rugby Football Union in August 1895; in 1922 the name was changed to the Rugby Football League. The 13-a-side team was introduced in 1906, and the first international matches were played in the following year. The international governing body for both professionals and amateurs, the Rugby League International Board, was formed in 1948.

SYNOPSIS

Rugby League football is played with an ovoid ball by two teams of 13 players, who may be amateurs or professionals. Players may carry, pass, or kick the ball, and aim to score points in a number of different ways. The team scoring the greater number of points in the allotted time is the winner.

PLAYING AREA AND EQUIPMENT

The playing area consists of the field-of-play and the in-goal areas. The field-of-play is the rectangular area bounded by the goal lines (**a**) and touch lines (**b**). The in-goal areas are the areas behind each goal bounded by the touch-in-goal lines (**c**) and the dead ball line (**d**).

The playing area should not exceed 122m long and 68m wide; the maximum dimensions are also the preferred dimensions. Touch lines should not exceed 100m long; their touch-in-goal extensions should be at least 6m and not more than 11m long.

Lines marking the field of play are:

e) halfway line, a solid line parallel to and equidistant from the goal lines;

f) 22m lines, solid lines parallel to and 22m from the goal lines;

g) 10m lines, broken lines parallel to and 10m from the goal lines, 22m lines, halfway line, and touch lines.

The intersections of touch lines and goal lines are marked by 1.25m high posts with flags.

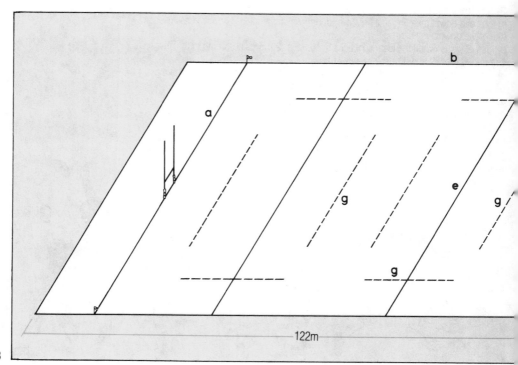

The goal consists of two upright posts joined by a crossbar, and is placed in the middle of the goal line. The crossbar should be 5.5m long, and set 3m above the ground. The uprights should be at least 4m high; the bottom 2m may be padded. For the purpose of judging a kick at goal, the upright posts are assumed to extend indefinitely upward.

The ball is an ovoid, 27–29cm long, with a short circumference of 58–61cm, and a long circumference of 73–75cm. It should weigh 380–440g.

The casing may be of leather or other approved material, and preferably of a light color.

Dress Players wear uniform shorts, shirts, or jerseys, and socks in distinctive colors. Protective clothing may be worn providing that it is not of a rigid construction. Studs on a player's boots may be of metal or other approved material, and should have a minimum diameter of 8mm.

PLAYERS AND OFFICIALS

Players A team consists of not more than 13 players. Up to two substitutes are permitted.

Officials The game is controlled by a referee, assisted by two touch judges.

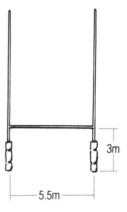

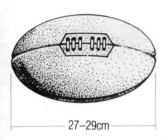

58–61cm

27–29cm

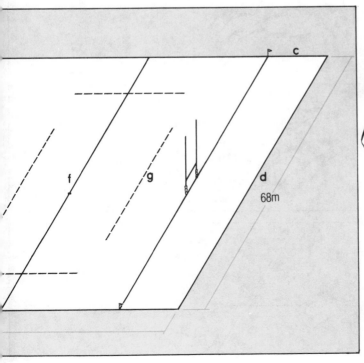

68m

FOOTBALL (RUGBY LEAGUE) 2

DURATION AND SCORING
Duration A match is played in two halves of 40min each, with a five-minute interval at half-time. Playing time lost as a result of injuries or other delays may be added on at the referee's discretion.

Points A team scores three points for a try, two points for a goal scored after a try (conversion goal) or for a goal scored from a penalty kick, and one point for dropped goals scored during play.

Try Providing that the attacking player is within the in-goal area or the field-of-play, a try is scored when:

a) the player grounds the ball in his opponents' in-goal area;

b) opposing players simultaneously ground the ball in the in-goal area;

c) a tackled player's momentum is sufficient to carry him into the in-goal area where he grounds the ball, even if the ball has first touched the ground in the field-of-play (a sliding try).

The ball is grounded when a player holding the ball in his hands or arms brings it into contact with the ground, or, when the ball is already on the ground, touches it with downward pressure with his hands or arms, or falls upon it so that it is anywhere under his body from his waist to his neck.

A try is awarded at the point where the ball was first grounded in the in-goal area, or, for a sliding try, at the place where the ball first crossed the goal line.

A penalty try is awarded at a point between the goal posts if unfair play by the defending team prevents a probable try being scored.

A try is awarded at the point of contact if an attacking player carrying the ball comes into contact with the referee, touch judge, or an encroaching spectator in his opponents' in-goal area.

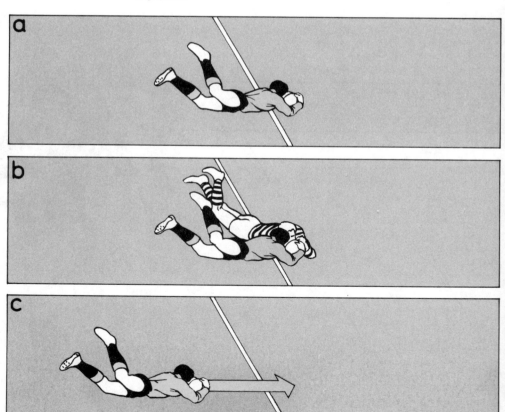

Goal kick after a try A team scoring a try is entitled to a place kick at goal on a line parallel to the touch line through the place where the try was awarded. A place kick is a kick from the ground, where the ball has been placed in position (**1**); the kicker may have another player hold the ball on the ground for him. Until the kick is taken, the kicker's team must be behind the ball, and the opposing team must be outside the field-of-play.

A goal is scored if the whole of the kicked ball passes over the crossbar at any time during its flight (**2**), provided it is not touched by a player. A goal is allowed if the ball passes over the crossbar and is then blown back by the wind.

Other goals A team awarded a penalty kick may elect to attempt a kick at goal, providing that they indicate in advance that this is their intention.

An attacking player may attempt a goal from a drop kick during general play when anywhere on the field-of-play. A drop kick is made by allowing the ball to fall from the kicker's hands to the ground, and kicking it on the rise from its first rebound (**3**).

A goal may not be scored from a kick off, drop-out, play-the-ball, or free kick.

STARTING PROCEDURES

Toss Team captains toss for choice of ends; the team losing the toss kicks off.

Kick off Play is started at the beginning of a match, after half-time, and after points have been scored, by a place kick at the center of the halfway line.

The kicked ball must travel at least 10m forward in the field-of-play. All other players must remain at least 10m away until the kick off has been taken, and may not touch the ball after it has been kicked until it has traveled at least 10m forward.

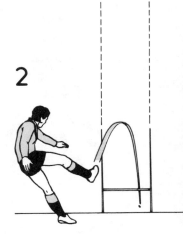

2

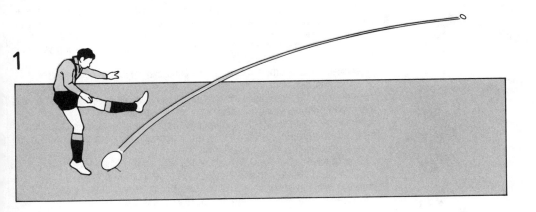

1

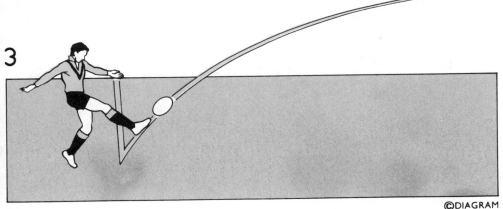

3

©DIAGRAM

A

Mode of play All players who are not offside may at any time run with the ball (**A**), kick the ball in any direction (**B**), or throw or knock (**C**) the ball in any direction other than forward in the direction of the opposing team's goal line.

A player who deliberately knocks the ball forward with his hand or arm (knock-on) or who throws the ball forward (forward pass) is penalized. Play is allowed to continue after an accidental knock-on providing that the player knocking-on kicks the ball before it touches the ground, or any part of the goal.

Any player may at any time tackle an opponent who is holding the ball. A player who is not holding the ball may not be tackled, except that if two players are running side by side near to and toward the ball, one may shoulder charge the other.

A tackle occurs when a player in possession of the ball:

a) is held by at least one opponent so that the ball, or his hand or arm holding the ball, comes into contact with the ground, providing that the hold on him is not broken before he is grounded;

b) is held by at least one opponent so that he can make no further progress and is unable to part with the ball;

c) is lying on the ground, and an opponent places a hand on him;

d) on being held by an opponent, makes it clear that he is succumbing to the tackle and wishes to play-the-ball.

No attempt may be made to move a tackled player from the point where the tackle took place.

B

The play-the-ball (**D**) is used to bring the ball back into play after a tackle, and occurs at the point where the tackle took place. If a tackled player's momentum has caused him to slide along the ground, the tackle is considered to have taken place where his slide ends. The tackled player should be immediately released, and should regain his feet and face his opponents' touch line (**a**). One opponent may take up position immediately opposite the tackled player (**b**), and one player from each team (the acting half-backs) may stand immediately and directly behind their respective teammates (**c,d**). All other players must be at least 5m away until the ball has been dropped to the ground.

The tackled player lifts the ball clear of the ground, and drops or places the ball on the ground in front of his foremost foot. Neither the tackled player nor the player marking him may raise a foot from the ground until the ball has been released; once the ball has touched the ground it may be kicked or heeled in any direction by any player.

A team in possession of the ball is allowed five successive play-the-balls, providing that the ball has not been touched by a member of the opposing team. If the team in possession is tackled a sixth time, play is restarted with a scrum.

C

Ball in touch The ball goes into touch or into touch-in-goal when it or the player in contact with it touches or crosses the touch line or the touch-in-goal line.

If the ball is kicked into touch without first bouncing in the field-of-play ("on the full"), play is restarted by a scrum at the point where the ball was kicked.

If the ball is kicked forward so that it first bounces in the field-of-play before going into touch, play is restarted by a scrum 10m into the field-of-play from the point where the ball crossed the touch line.

A free kick is awarded 10m into the field-of-play from the point where the ball crossed the touch line if the ball goes into touch from a penalty kick without touching any other player.

D

E

Scrum positions
Backs
1) Full back
2) Right wing threequarter
3) Right center threequarter
4) Left center threequarter
5) Left wing threequarter
6) Stand off half
7) Scrum half
Forwards
8) Prop forward
9) Hooker
10) Prop forward
11) Second row forward
12) Second row forward
13) Loose forward

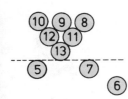

A scrum (**E**) is formed in the field-of-play by players from each team closing up together to allow the ball to be put on the ground between them. The players then attempt to gain possession of the ball with their feet; the ball may not be played with the hand while it is in the scrum.

No fewer than three and not more than six players on each side may assist in the formation of a scrum, and the front row must be made up of not more than three players. Not more than eight players of each team may act as backs. Scrum positions and numbers are usually as illustrated.

Players in the front rows should interlock, leaving a clear tunnel between them at right angles to the touch line. All forwards must pack in with their bodies and legs at right angles to this tunnel, and the upper parts of their bodies horizontal. All players outside the scrum should remain behind their own forwards until the ball has emerged correctly.

The ball is put into the tunnel between the two rows of forwards by the scrum half of the defending team, either by a downward throw from below waist height or by rolling it along the ground. The scrum half should then immediately retire behind his own forwards.

Forwards in the front row may not raise or advance their feet until the ball has been put into the scrum. Once it has touched the ground, the hookers may strike for the ball with either foot; only then may other players in the scrum kick or heel the ball.

A player may not wilfully collapse a scrum, or have any part of his body except his feet in contact with the ground.

Play proceeds when the ball emerges from the scrum between and behind the inner feet of the second row forwards.

A scrum is used to restart play:
a) when a player in possession of the ball is tackled in his opponents' in-goal area before grounding the ball;
b) when the ball goes into touch, except from a penalty kick;
c) when a player accidently knocks-on the ball without kicking it before it touches the ground;
d) after five successive play-the-balls;
e) if a player in the kicker's team infringes the rules during a penalty kick.

A scrum is normally formed at or near the place where the stoppage of play occurred, but must not be formed less than 10m from a touch line or less than 5m from a goal line.

FOOTBALL (RUGBY LEAGUE) 4

22m place kick A place kick at the center of the 22m line is awarded if an attacking player:
a) is the last to touch the ball before it goes out of play across the dead ball or touch-in-goal lines, except after a penalty kick; or
b) accidentally infringes the rules while in the in-goal area.
The kick may be taken in any direction. The kicker's team must remain behind the ball until it is kicked; the opposing team must retire at least 10m.

A drop-out is a drop kick awarded to the defending team.
A drop-out is awarded at the center of the 22m line if the ball is kicked over the dead ball line or the touch-in-goal line from a penalty kick, without being touched by any player other than the kicker.
A drop-out is awarded at the center of the goal line if:
a) a defending player is the last to touch the ball before it goes over the dead ball or touch-in-goal lines;
b) a defending player accidentally infringes the rules while in the in-goal area;
c) a defending player makes a touchdown (grounds the ball in his own in-goal area);
d) a defending player in possession is tackled in the in-goal area;
e) a defending player kicks the ball into touch from his own in-goal area, and the ball goes into touch on the full;
f) the ball, or a defending player carrying the ball, touches an official or spectator in the in-goal area so that play is affected.
The kicked ball must travel at least 10m forward in the field-of-play; it may not be kicked on the full over the touch line, touch-in-goal, or dead ball line. All other players must remain at least 10m away until the drop-out is taken, and may not touch the ball after it has been kicked until it has traveled at least 10m forward.

Offside Unless he is in his own in-goal area, a player is offside if the ball has been kicked, touched, or is being carried by a member of his own team who is behind him.
A player who is offside may not attempt to take any part in the game, or approach within 5m of an opponent who is waiting for the ball. He must immediately retire 5m from any opponent who gains possession of the ball.
A player ceases to be offside when:
a) an opponent moves 5m or more with the ball;
b) an opponent touches the ball without retaining possession of it;
c) a member of his own team in possession of the ball runs in front of him;
d) a member of his own team kicks the ball forward and moves into a position in front of him;
e) he retires behind the point where the ball was last touched by a member of his own team.

FOULS AND PENALTIES

Fouls Players may not:
a) deliberately trip, kick, or strike another player;
b) make a dangerous tackle (**1**);
c) deliberately obstruct an opponent who is not in possession of the ball (**2**);
d) deliberately breach any of the rules of the game.

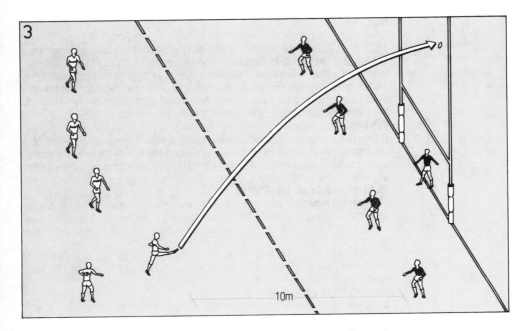

3

10m

Penalties Referees may caution and send off players in breach of the rules, and award penalty kicks, free kicks, 22m place kicks, drop-outs, and penalty tries.

A penalty kick (3) may be awarded against any player who is guilty of a foul.

A team awarded a penalty kick may elect to take a place kick or drop kick at goal, providing that they indicate that this is their intention.

Except when kicking at goal, the ball may be kicked in any direction, and the penalty kick may be a place kick, drop kick, or punt (when the ball is dropped by the player and is kicked before it touches the ground).

The kicker's team must remain behind the ball until it is kicked. The opposing team must retire at least 10m toward their own goal line, and may not attempt to distract the kicker.

Unless otherwise indicated, a penalty kick is awarded at the point where the offense occurred.

A penalty kick is awarded:

a) at the center of the halfway line, for any offense at the kick off;

b) at the center of the 22m line, for any offense at a 22m place kick;

c) at the center of a line drawn parallel to and 10m from the goal line, for any offense at a drop-out awarded at the center of the goal line;

d) 5m from the goal line into the field-of-play opposite the point where the offense occurred, for any offense by a defending player in his own in-goal area, or an attacking player in his opponents' in-goal area;

e) 5m from the touch line into the field-of-play opposite the point where the offense occurred, for any misconduct in touch.

In the case of obstruction, a penalty kick is awarded at one of the following points, depending on which gives the greater advantage to the non-offending team:

a) where the ball next bounces or is caught in the field-of-play;

b) 5m from the touch line opposite the point of entry if the ball goes into touch on the full;

c) 5m from the goal line opposite the point of entry if the ball crosses the goal line on the full.

If the team against whom the penalty kick was awarded commits a further foul, the referee may move the penalty kick 10m toward its goal line.

If a player is fouled when he is touching down for a try, he is awarded a penalty kick at goal. The kick is taken from in front of the goal posts after the attempt to convert the try.

FOOTBALL (RUGBY UNION)

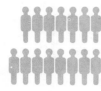

HISTORY

Traditionally, rugby is believed to have begun at Rugby School in England in 1823 when William Webb Ellis disregarded the rules of football and picked up the ball and ran with it. Early rules allowed for matches with up to 300 players that could last up to five days. The game began to assume its modern form in the 1870s, when teams were reduced to 15-a-side, and countries began to set up their national governing bodies. The international governing body for the sport, the International Rugby Football Board (IRFB) was formed in 1886.

SYNOPSIS

Rugby Union football is played with an ovoid ball by two teams of 15 players, all of whom must be amateurs. Players may carry, pass, or kick the ball, and aim to score points in a number of different ways. The team scoring the greater number of points in the allotted time is the winner.

PLAYING AREA AND EQUIPMENT

The playing area consists of the field-of-play and the in-goal areas. The field-of-play is the rectangular area bounded by the goal lines (**a**) and touch lines (**b**). The in-goal areas are the areas behind each goal line bounded by the touch-in-goal lines (**c**) and the dead ball line (**d**).

The playing area should not exceed 144m long and 69m wide; the maximum dimensions are also the preferred dimensions. Touch lines should not exceed 100m long, and their touch-in-goal extensions should not exceed 22m.

Lines marking the field-of-play are:

e) halfway line, a solid line parallel to and equidistant from the goal lines;
f) 10m lines, broken lines parallel to and 10m from the halfway line;
g) 22m lines, solid lines parallel to and 22m from the goal lines;
h) 5m lines, broken lines parallel to and 5m from the touch lines;
i) 15m lines, parallel to and 15m from the touch lines, intersecting the 10m, 22m, and halfway lines, and extending 5m in from each goal line.

The intersections of the halfway, 10m, 22m, goal, and dead ball lines with the touch and touch-in-goal lines are marked with 1.20m high posts with flags.

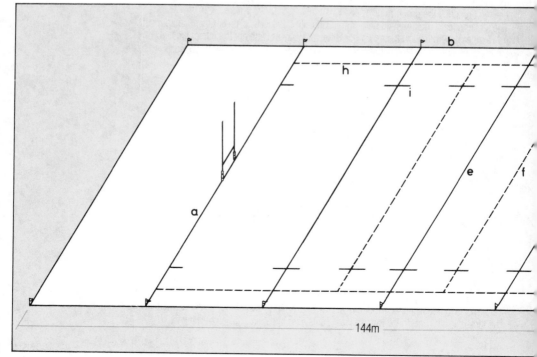

144m

The goal consists of two upright posts joined by a crossbar, and is placed in the middle of the goal line. The crossbar should be 5.6m long, and set 3m above the ground. The uprights should be at least 3.4m high. For the purpose of judging a kick at goal, the upright posts are assumed to extend indefinitely upward.

The ball is an ovoid, 28–30cm long, with a short circumference of 58–62cm, and a long circumference of 76–79cm. It should weigh 400–440g.

The four-panel casing may be of leather or other suitable material, and may be treated to make it resistant to mud and easier to grip. .

Dress Players wear uniform shorts and jerseys or shirts. Soft leather helmets may be worn to protect the head and ears, but shoulder harnesses and other body armor are forbidden. Studs on a player's boots may be of leather, rubber, aluminum, or an approved plastic, and must conform to specific measurements. Players are not permitted to wear boots with a single stud at the toe.

PLAYERS AND OFFICIALS

Players A team consists of not more than 15 players. Substitution may only take place in the case of injury, and not more than two players in a team may be substituted.

Officials The game is controlled by a referee, assisted by two touch judges.

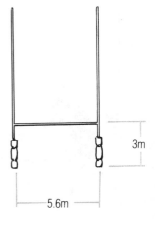

3m

5.6m

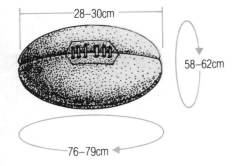

28–30cm

58–62cm

76–79cm

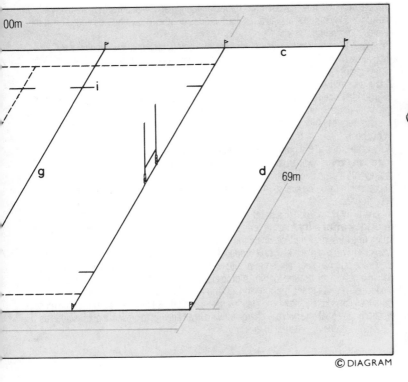

00m

c

i

g

d

69m

DURATION AND SCORING

Duration A match is played in two halves of 40min each, with a five-minute interval at half-time. Playing time lost as a result of injuries or other delays may be added on at the referee's discretion.

Points A team scores four points for a try, two points for a goal scored after a try (conversion), and three points for goals scored from a penalty kick or for dropped goals otherwise obtained.

A try is scored when a player grounds the ball in his opponents' in-goal area (**A**). The ball is grounded when a player holding the ball in his hands or arms brings it into contact with the ground, or, when the ball is already on the ground, touches it with downward pressure with his hands or arms, or falls upon it so that it is anywhere under his body from his waist to his neck.

A try is awarded at the point where the ball was first grounded in the in-goal area.

A penalty try is awarded if foul play by the defending team:

a) prevents a probable try being scored; or

b) prevents a try being scored in a more favorable position than that in which the ball was first grounded.

A penalty try is awarded at a point between the goal posts.

Goal kick after a try A team scoring a try is entitled to a goal kick on a line parallel to the touch line through the place where the try was awarded.

The kick may be a place kick or a drop kick. A place kick (**B**) is a kick from the ground, where the ball has been placed in position; the kicker may choose to have another player hold the ball on the ground for him. A drop kick (**C**) is made by allowing the ball to fall from the kicker's hands to the ground, and kicking it on the rise from its first rebound.

Until the kick is taken, the kicker's team must be behind the ball. The opposing team must be behind the goal line but may charge forward in an attempt to prevent a goal as soon as the kicker begins his attempt to kick.

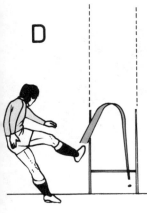

D

A goal is scored when the ball has been kicked over the crossbar and between the goal posts (**D**) without touching the ground or any players of the kicker's team.

A goal is allowed if the ball passes over the crossbar and is then blown back by the wind, or if it hits the crossbar or goalpost and rebounds over the crossbar.

Other goals A team awarded a penalty kick may elect to attempt a kick at goal, providing that they indicate in advance that this is their intention.

An attacking player may attempt a goal from a drop kick during general play when anywhere on the field-of-play.

A goal may not be scored from a kick off, drop-out, or free kick.

STARTING PROCEDURES

Toss Team captains toss a coin for the right to kick off, or for the choice of ends.

Kick off Play is started at the beginning of a match, after half time, or after a goal has been scored by a place kick at the center of the halfway line.

After an unconverted try (ie when no goal has been scored) play is restarted by a drop kick at or behind the center of the halfway line. The kicker's team must be behind the ball when it is kicked. The opposing team must stand on or behind the 10m line, but may charge forward as the kick is taken.

The kicked ball must reach the 10m line unless it is first reached by a member of the opposing team.

LAWS OF PLAY

Playing the ball All players who are not offside may at any time:

1

a) catch (**1**) or pick up the ball and run with it (**2**);

b) throw, kick (**3**), knock, or otherwise propel the ball;

c) pass the ball to any other player (**4**);

d) tackle (**5**), push, or shoulder an opponent holding the ball;

e) fall on the ball, providing it is not emerging from a scrummage or ruck;

f) take part in scrummages, rucks, mauls, or lineouts.

The ball may be passed, thrown, or knocked in any direction except forward in the direction of the opposing team's dead ball line; knock-ons and throw-forwards are penalized.

A player who has not been tackled but who is lying on or near the ball must pass or release the ball immediately.

2

A tackle occurs when one or more players hold a member of the opposing team who is carrying the ball so that:

a) the player carrying the ball is no longer on his feet and is brought into contact with the ground; or

b) the ball comes into contact with the ground.

A tackled player must immediately release and move away from the ball without making any effort to play it. He may not play the ball until he has regained his feet, but he may tackle or attempt to tackle another player in possession of the ball.

A player tackled near his opponent's goal line may still score a try if his momentum is sufficient to carry him into the in-goal area.

3

4   **5**

A

A scrummage (**A**) is formed in the field-of-play by players from each team closing up together to allow the ball to be put on the ground between them. The players then attempt to gain possession of the ball with their feet.

The front row of a scrummage must at all times be made up of three players. Although any number of players may make up the other rows, scrummage positions and numbers are usually as illustrated.

Players in the front row should interlock, leaving a clear tunnel between them. Other players in the scrummage must bind together with at least one arm around a teammate; opponents may be held with one arm to keep the scrummage steady.

The ball is put into the scrummage by the team not responsible for stopping play. The player putting in the ball stands 1m away from the scrummage, midway between the two front rows. He should hold the ball with both hands midway between his knees and ankles, and throw it with a single rapid forward movement so that it first touches the ground just beyond the width of the nearer prop's shoulders. If the ball runs straight through the tunnel it is put in again, unless a free kick or penalty kick has been awarded.

Scrummage positions
Forwards
1) Loose head prop
2) Hooker
3) Tight head prop
4) Lock forward
5) Lock forward
6) Flanker
7) Flanker
8) Number 8
Backs
9) Scrum half
10) Stand off half
11) Left wing threequarter
12) Left center threequarter
13) Right center threequarter
14) Right wing threequarter
15) Full back

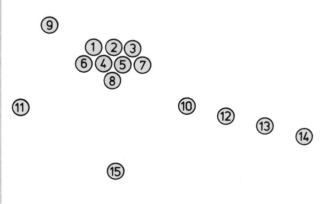

B

Players in the front row may not raise or advance their feet until the ball has touched the ground. They may then use either foot in an attempt to gain possession of the ball, but may not at any time raise both feet off the ground.

Players not in the front row may not play the ball while it is in the tunnel.

Players may not attempt to gain possession of the ball with any part of the body except the foot or lower leg, nor may they take any action that could cause the scrum to collapse.

Play proceeds when the ball comes out of the scrummage otherwise than at either end of the tunnel, providing no rule infringements have occurred.

A scrummage is used to restart play after certain rule infringements, or after certain legitimate actions (eg tackling) which prevent play continuing. It normally takes place at or near the place of stoppage, and parallel to the goal lines. A scrummage is held 5m from the goal line opposite to the place of stoppage after certain stoppages of play in the in-goal area.

A ruck (B) occurs in free play in the field-of-play when one or more players from each team close around the ball when it is on the ground. Players must be on their feet and in physical contact; any player joining the ruck must bind in with at least one arm around the body of a teammate.

Players may not:

a) return the ball into the ruck;

b) handle the ball in the ruck except in an attempt to score a try or touchdown;

c) jump on other players in the ruck or take other action to make the ruck collapse;

d) interfere with the ball when lying on the ground, or take any action other than rolling away from the ball.

A maul occurs in free play in the field-of-play when one or more players from each team close around a player who is carrying the ball.

A maul ends when:

a) the player with the ball frees himself from the maul; or

b) the ball touches the ground; or

c) the ball becomes unplayable and a scrummage is called.

A drop-out is a drop kick awarded to the defending team, taken from anywhere on or behind the 22m line. The kicker's team must be behind the ball until it is kicked; the opposing team may not charge over the 22m line.

Providing that no knock-on, throw-forward, try, or goal has occurred, a drop-out is awarded when an attacking player kicks, carries, or passes the ball so that it travels into his opponents' in-goal area directly, or after being touched by a defender who has not wilfully attempted to intercept it, and there:

a) is grounded by a player from either team; or

b) goes over the touch-in-goal or dead ball lines.

A mark or fair catch occurs when a player who is stationary with both feet on the ground behind his own 22m line (either in the field-of-play or the in-goal area) catches the ball cleanly and cries "Mark." The catch may be from a kick, knock-on, or throw-forward by the opposing team. A player making a fair catch is awarded a free kick.

A touchdown occurs when a player grounds the ball in his own in-goal area. Depending on circumstances, play may be restarted by a scrummage or a drop-out.

151

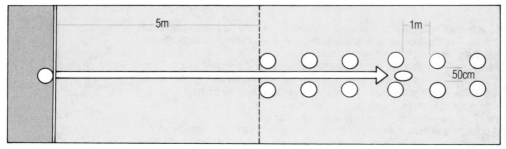

Line-out If the ball or the player carrying it touches or crosses the touch line, the ball is said to be "in touch" and a line-out is used to restart play.

The line-out is taken on a line perpendicular to the touch line (the "line-of-touch"), usually at the point where the ball crossed the touch line. At least two players from each team form separate lines 50cm apart, starting from a point on the 5m line. Members of the same team must be at least 1m apart; the player farthest in toward the field-of-play may not be more than 15m from the touch line.

The ball is thrown in by an opponent of the player who last touched the ball, or by the defending team if there is any doubt as to which player last touched it. The ball is thrown in so that it first touches the ground, or touches or is touched by a player at least 5m from the touch line. The thrower's feet must not cross the touch line.

A line-out begins when the ball leaves the hands of the thrower and ends when:
a) a ruck or maul takes place, and the feet of all the players involved have moved beyond the line-of-touch; or
b) a player carrying the ball leaves the line-out; or
c) the ball has been passed, knocked back, or kicked from the line-outs; or
d) the ball is thrown beyond the farthest player in the line-out; or
e) the ball becomes unplayable.

Before the ball has been thrown, a player in the line-out may not push, charge, shoulder, or bind with any other player, or use another player as a support to help him jump for the ball.

A player may charge another player in an attempt to tackle him or to play the ball only after the ball has touched the ground, or has touched or been touched by a player in the line-out.

Players must remain in the line-out unless jumping for the ball, or moving to catch the ball when it has been passed or knocked back by another member of their team ("peeling off"). They may move into the space between the touch line and the 5m line only when the ball has been thrown beyond them.

Players who are not taking part in the line-out may not move forward and take the ball from the throw-in.

A quick throw-in from touch without waiting for the players to form a line-out is permitted in certain circumstances; many of the rules governing line-outs are then not applicable.

Offside A player is in an offside position in general play if the ball has been kicked, touched, or is being carried by a member of his own team who is behind him. Players are not penalized for being offside in general play unless they play the ball, obstruct an opponent, or approach or remain within 10m of an opponent waiting to play the ball.

At a scrummage, the offside line is a line parallel to the goal line through the back foot of the back player taking part in the scrummage. Players not taking part in the scrummage are offside if they fail to retire behind this line.

The offside line at a ruck or maul is as for a scrummage. A player is offside if he joins the ruck or maul from his opponents' side, or from in front of the ball. He is also offside if he fails to retire behind the offside line when not taking part in, or having taken part in and left the ruck or maul.

A player taking part in a line-out is offside if he:

a) advances in front of the line-of-touch before the ball has touched a player or the ground, except when jumping for the ball; or

b) advances in front of the ball after it has touched the ground or a player, except when tackling or attempting to tackle an opponent; or

c) fails to keep close to the line-out when peeling off; or

d) moves beyond the position of the farthest player before the line-out ends.

The offside line in a line-out is 10m beyond the line-of-touch, and parallel to the goal line (or is the goal line, if that is less than 10m from the line-of-touch). Players not participating in the line-out are offside if they fail to retire behind this line.

FOULS AND PENALTIES

Fouls Players may not:

a) charge an opponent running for the ball, except shoulder to shoulder;

b) when offside, run or stand in front of a member of their own team who is carrying the ball so as to obstruct an opponent attempting to reach that player;

c) deliberately knock or throw the ball into touch (**1**), or over the touch-in-goal or dead ball lines;

d) strike, trip, kick, hack, or trample an opponent;

e) make an early, late, or dangerous tackle;

f) hold, push, charge, or grasp an opponent not holding the ball, except in a scrummage, ruck, or maul;

g) deliberately cause a scrummage or ruck to collapse;

h) molest, obstruct (**2**), or in any other way interfere with an opponent when the ball is out of play;

i) otherwise breach the rules of the game.

Penalties Referees may caution and send off players in breach of the laws, and award penalty kicks, free kicks, penalty tries, and drop-outs.

When a penalty kick or free kick is awarded, the non-offending team has the option of taking a scrummage at the place at which the kick was awarded. When a penalty or free kick is taken, the kicker's team must remain behind the ball until it has been kicked, and the opposing team must retire to or behind a line 10m away, parallel with the goal lines.

©DIAGRAM

GOLF

HISTORY

Evidence of various "club-and-ball" games exists from Roman times and from medieval France and the Netherlands, and some researchers consider these games to have been early forms of golf. However, the modern game comes from Scotland, where four centuries ago it survived legal prohibition enacted because of the threat its popularity posed to the warlike and useful sport of archery. The first set of rules for the game were adopted by the Royal and Ancient Golf Club of St Andrews, Scotland (R&A) in 1754. With the worldwide spread of golf last century, other national governing bodies were formed, of which the United States Golf Association (USGA) is now the most influential. The USGA and the R&A control and revise the code of rules in consultation with other participating countries, particularly in relation to international competitions.

SYNOPSIS

Players, competing individually or in pairs, use a variety of clubs to propel a small ball, with the aim of "holing out" in the smallest possible number of strokes. This consists of hitting the ball into each of 18 holes in succession. Each "hole," or the part of the course between the teeing ground and the relevant hole itself, is surrounded or intersected by obstacles such as sand bunkers, water courses, and rough ground.

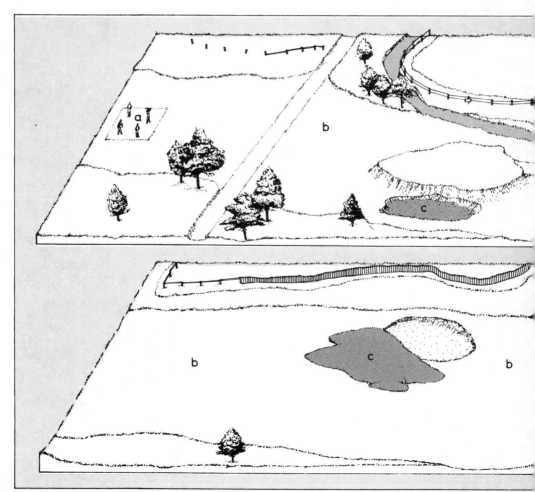

The two basic forms of competition game are match play and stroke play. In match play the side winning the majority of holes wins the match. In stroke play the winner is the player who finishes the course in the fewest strokes.

PLAYING AREA AND EQUIPMENT

The course is the whole area in which play takes place. A standard full course consists of 18 "holes" – meaning the playing area between and including a teeing ground and its putting green where the hole itself is located. Holes vary in length from about 100–600yd. A typical hole includes the following features:

a) the teeing ground, a smooth, level area from which each player makes the first stroke;

b) "through the green," which includes the whole area of the course except the teeing ground and putting green of the hole being played, and excluding all hazards on any part of the course (note that it includes the mown area of each hole commonly called the fairway, as well as the "rough" surrounding it);

c) hazards, such as areas of water, or bunkers (sand traps);

d) the putting green, which is the area of carefully prepared grass in which the hole is located;

e) the hole, 4¼in in diameter and at least 4in deep;

f) the flagstick, a removable pole with a flag, placed centrally in the hole to indicate the latter's position, recommended to be 7ft long.

7ft

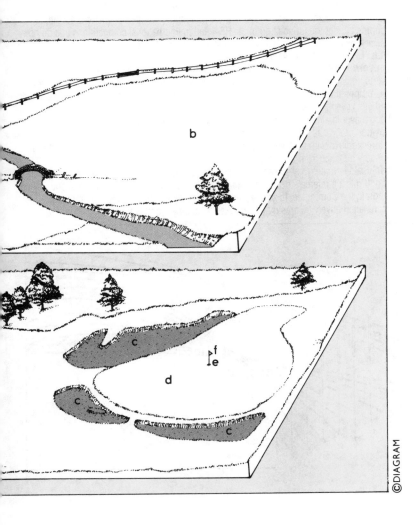

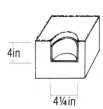

4in

4¼in

©DIAGRAM

GOLF 2

The clubs A maximum of 14 clubs may be used in a round (18 holes) by each player, or partners who share a set. Clubs damaged in the course of play may be replaced, but not by borrowing from any other player.

Clubs may not be "substantially different from the traditional and customary form and make," as judged by the R&A and USGA. There are three basic types:

A) a wood has a head of wood, plastic, or light metal that is relatively broad from front to back, and is used for long shots – the usual woods are numbered from 1 to 4;

B) an iron has a head, usually of steel, that is relatively narrow from front to back, and a shaft that is shorter than that of a wood – irons are numbered from 1 to 10;

C) a putter is a metal or wood club made in a variety of shapes and is used to play the ball on the putting green.

Except for the putter, each club has only one striking face. The striking face may consist partly of grooves or punch marks but may not be shaped or finished so as to cause extra movement of the ball.

The length of the shaft and angle of the face vary according to the kind of shot that the club is designed to play. Steeply angled faces produce sharply lifting shots.

The diagram (below) shows the comparative trajectories of the number 1–4 woods, 2–10 irons, and the sand iron (**a**) and putter (**b**).

The grip must not be shaped to fit the hands.

The ball is made of rubber with a plastic outer surface that is dimpled to improve the accuracy and distance of flight. The maximum permitted weight is 1.62oz. In the USA and in some international competitions, the minimum permitted diameter is 1.68in; in countries under the jurisdiction of the R&A and in international competitions that do not specify the use of a 1.68in diameter ball, the minimum diameter is 1.62in.

PLAYERS AND OFFICIALS

Players The game is played by two, three, or four players competing individually or in teams. In competition golf there are events for men's and women's individual and team championships. There are separate championships for amateur and professional golfers, and open events in which both categories compete.

Each player is allowed one caddie to carry his or her clubs. The caddie may mark the position of the ball and assist in other ways according to the rules.

A forecaddie is one employed by a committee for a competition to indicate the lie of the ball at some distance from the player.

Officials Referees may accompany players to decide questions of fact and the application of golf rules; a referee's decision is final. Official observers may be appointed, and report to the Committee. In stroke play, markers may follow a competitor and record his score; alternatively, scores may be marked by another competitor.

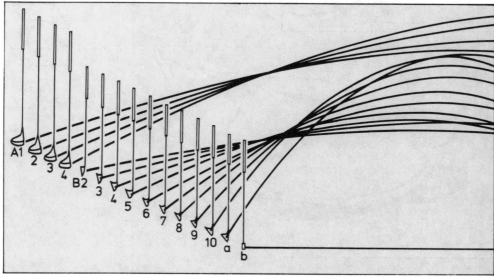

1.62in or 1.68in

DEFINITIONS

Addressing the ball (D) A golfer is said to have addressed the ball when he has taken up his stance and (other than in a hazard) has grounded his club.

Ball in play A ball is in play from the time that it is struck on the teeing ground to the time that it is holed out, except when it is lost, out of bounds, or lifted, or when another ball has been substituted according to the rules.

Casual water is a temporary accumulation of water (ie puddle) that is visible before or after the player takes his stance but is not in a water hazard.

Honor The honor is the right to play first from the teeing ground.

Loose impediments are natural objects on the course, such as leaves, twigs, and (when on the putting green) loose soil or sand, which are not growing or otherwise fixed in place, or stuck to the ball.

Obstructions are artificial objects on the course, including paths or roads, but excluding anything used to define out of bounds or declared officially to be an integral part of the course.

Par is the score that in theory an expert player would take to complete a given hole. It may range from "par 3" to "par 6," and is higher for women than for men.

One stroke under par is a "birdie," two under is an "eagle," and one stroke over par for the hole is a "bogey."

Rub of the green A rub of the green is said to have occurred when an outside agency stops or deflects a ball in motion.

GENERAL RULES AND ETIQUETTE

Waiving of rules Players may not agree to waive any rule or penalty.

Advice and assistance A player may ask for advice from, or give it to, only his partner and their caddies. Advice includes anything which might for instance influence the choice of club, or the way to make a stroke; it does not include information on the rules.

A player may not ask for or accept physical assistance or protection from the weather when making a stroke. It is permissible for someone to indicate the line of play to him, but any mark giving such an indication must be removed before a stroke is made.

Artificial devices, either to assist play or to measure distances, are forbidden.

Practice strokes are forbidden during a round, but practice swings without striking a ball are permitted.

In stroke play a competitor may not practice on the competition course on the same day of a competition, or during it.

Stopping play Players must not stop play because of bad weather unless there is danger from lightning, or unless there are other accepted reasons such as illness.

Damaged ball A ball that is so damaged that its movement is affected may be replaced by another ball (to be placed where the damaged one lay) during play on the hole where the damage occurred. The opponent (in match play) or marker (in stroke play) must agree that the ball is sufficiently damaged and witness its replacement.

Striking the ball The ball must be fairly struck with the head of the club; it may not be pushed, scraped, or scooped. If when making a stroke a player strikes the ball twice, that stroke is counted and a penalty stroke is added as well.

Identifying and cleaning the ball Except in a hazard a player may lift and identify a ball without penalty, and replace it where it lay, in the presence of his opponent (in match play) or marker (in stroke play).

A ball may be cleaned when lifted for identification, or when lifted because it is unplayable or embedded in turf, or when lifted from water or from a green.

Etiquette This is largely a matter of consideration for other players and preservation of the course. No penalties for non-observance are specified.

Competitors should not make a stroke until any players in front are out of range.

Competitors should play without delay, and move off the putting green promptly having holed out.

No-one should do anything that might distract a player who is addressing the ball or making a stroke.

Players should avoid damaging the course, and especially the putting greens. They should repair any damage caused by the club, the ball, or the player himself; this includes releveling the sand in bunkers if it is disturbed.

©DIAGRAM

GOLF 3

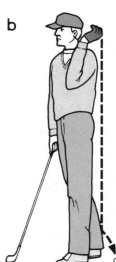

Lifting the ball A ball may be lifted only in accordance with the rules and only by its owner, his partner, or someone authorized by the owner.

If the ball is lifted contrary to the rules before holing out in stroke play, the owner incurs a two stroke penalty and must replace the ball or be disqualified. In match play he automatically loses the hole.

Dropping the ball In order to reposition the ball anywhere except on the putting green, the ball is dropped in the following manner by the player himself.

He must stand erect facing the hole and drop the ball behind him over his shoulder (**a**). If the ball touches the player before it reaches the ground (**b**), it is dropped again without penalty. If it comes to rest against him after first touching the ground, he may play it without penalty even if it moves when he moves.

The ball must be dropped as near as possible to the place where it lay and not nearer the hole. In a hazard, the ball must come to rest within that hazard, unless in circumstances where the rules allow it to be dropped elsewhere.

If a dropped ball rolls into a hazard, or out of bounds, or onto a green, or more than two club lengths from where it first strikes the ground, or ends up closer to the hole than its original position, it must be redropped and no penalty is incurred.

Placing the ball In circumstances where the rules permit the placing of a ball to reposition it, this must be done by the player or his partner.

If a replaced ball fails to remain where it is placed, it can be replaced in the nearest spot where it will rest, but not nearer the hole.

If the original lie of the ball has been altered, it must be placed in the nearest similar lie within two club lengths, and not nearer the hole.

SCORING

Match play In this version the game is played by holes, each hole being won by the side that holes out in the fewest strokes.

A match consists of a stipulated number of holes and is won by the side that is leading by a number of holes greater than the number still to be played. A match can thus be won before the round is completed.

In three-ball matches, each of the three competitors plays two distinct matches simultaneously, one against each of the other two players.

In best-ball matches, one competitor plays against the better ball of two other players, or the best ball of three others.

In four-ball matches, two players play their better ball against the better ball of their opponents.

Stroke play Unless specified otherwise, the same rules apply to stroke play as to match play, but the winner is the player who completes the whole round or rounds (as stipulated for the match) in the fewest strokes.

Each competitor has a marker to record his number of strokes on a scorecard, which both competitor and marker must sign before it is handed in at the end of the round.

In four-ball stroke play, two competitors play as partners, each playing his own ball. The lower of the two partners' scores is counted as the score for the hole.

In bogey, par, or Stableford competitions, competitors play against a fixed score per hole.

Handicaps A player's handicap is based on the number of strokes by which he normally exceeds the rating for the course. The handicapping system allows players of differing skill to compete on level terms.

A man may have a handicap of up to 24 strokes, and a woman of up to 36.

In the USA, but not in all countries, all courses are carefully rated according to a common standard, and a player's handicap remains the same wherever he plays.

In stroke play, a player's full handicap is simply subtracted from his total score.

In match play, strokes are given or taken at predetermined holes.

STARTING PROCEDURE

On the teeing ground Each competitor plays a ball from the first teeing ground. The ball may be played from the ground, from a wooden or plastic tee, or from a "tee" of sand.

A draw decides who plays first. Subsequently the side winning the hole decides who plays first at the next teeing ground; this entitlement is known as the honor.

If a hole is halved (ie each side holes out in the same number of strokes), then the side that last had the honor retains it.

Outside the teeing ground If a competitor plays his first ball from outside the teeing ground in match play, his opponent may require it to be replayed correctly, without penalty. In stroke play the offender is penalized two strokes, the strokes already made do not count, and failure to rectify the mistake can lead to disqualification. It is, however, permissible to stand outside the teeing ground to play a ball within it.

Ball off the tee If the ball falls off the tee before the stroke is made, or is knocked off as the player addresses it, it may be teed again. If a stroke has been made it is counted, but no penalty is incurred.

PROCEDURE THROUGH THE GREEN

Order of play In a threesome or foursome, partners strike alternately from the teeing grounds and play successive strokes alternately.

In match play, when through the green or in a hazard, if a competitor plays when his opponent should have done so, his opponent may require him to abandon the ball and replay in correct order, without penalty. In stroke play a ball played out of turn is in play. In match play, if a player makes his stroke when his partner should have played, his side loses the hole. In stroke play such strokes are canceled, and a two stroke penalty incurred. A ball is then played from the same spot in correct order.

Playing the ball The ball farthest from the hole is played first.

The ball must be played as it lies, except that a ball embedded in its own pitch-mark in a closely mown area through the green may be lifted and dropped without penalty.

Long grass and bushes may be moved only to find and identify a ball, and not to improve the lie. The player is not necessarily entitled to see the ball when playing his stroke.

A player must not try to improve his shot by bending or breaking anything fixed or growing. He may not move or press down loose soil, sand, or cut turf except in the course of taking a stance or making a stroke or moving the club back preparatory to a stroke. Loose impediments may be removed without penalty, except when the impediments and the ball lie in or touch a hazard, or when the ball is moving.

A player must not play a moving ball unless it is in water, or moves after his stroke began.

Hazards When a player's ball lies in or touches a hazard he must not do anything to improve its lie. He may not touch the ground or water in the hazard before making his stroke, or move loose impediments.

In water hazards a player may probe for a lost ball and no penalty is incurred for moving it. A stroke may be made at a ball moving in water but must not be delayed so that the ball will be in a better position.

If a ball lies in or is lost in a water hazard, the player has the option of dropping a ball, with a one stroke penalty, either as near as possible to the point from which the ball was played, or at any distance behind the water hazard.

If a ball lies in or is lost in a lateral water hazard, the player has a choice of dropping a ball from a point two club lengths from the place where it crossed the hazard's edge (but no nearer the hole), from any point behind this, or from where the original shot was played.

Ball lost or out of bounds If a ball is lost (except in a water hazard) or out of bounds, the player must play his next stroke from as near as possible to the place from which he originally played the ball. A penalty stroke is incurred. If the ball was played from the teeing ground it will be played from there again; if from through the green or a hazard it must be dropped; if from a putting green it must be placed.

A competitor may stand out of bounds to play a stroke if the ball is on the course.

Unplayable ball If the ball is unplayable, the player, who is the sole judge, may play again from the original spot, or drop the ball within two club lengths of where it lay, but not nearer the hole. In both cases he incurs a penalty stroke.

Wrong ball If a player plays the wrong ball, except in a hazard, in match play he loses the hole, or in stroke play incurs two penalty strokes.

In a hazard, strokes at the wrong ball are not penalized or counted provided the player then plays the correct ball. If the wrong ball belongs to another player, its owner should play another ball from the same place.

If a player holes out with the wrong ball he must take a two stroke penalty and play the correct ball before playing a stroke from the next teeing ground, or he will be disqualified.

If he plays a ball which has been dropped or placed in the wrong place but otherwise plays correctly, he loses the hole in match play, or incurs a two stroke penalty in stroke play.

GOLF 4

Provisional ball To save time when a ball may have been lost outside a water hazard or may be out of bounds, a competitor may play another ball from as near as possible to the point where the original ball was played. This is known as a provisional ball.

If the original ball was played from the teeing ground, the provisional ball may be played from any point on the teeing ground; if from through the green or a hazard, the provisional ball must be dropped; if from the putting green, it must be placed.

If the original ball is found and is not out of bounds, it comes back into play and the provisional ball is abandoned.

If the original ball is confirmed as lost outside a water hazard or as out of bounds, the provisional ball becomes the ball in play under penalty of stroke and distance (ie as under "Ball lost or out of bounds," see p. 159).

Once the provisional ball has been played from a point nearer the hole than the place where the original ball is likely to be, that ball is deemed to be lost.

Penalties for a breach of these rules are the loss of the hole in match play, or two strokes in stroke play.

PROCEDURE ON THE PUTTING GREEN

General rules When a ball is in motion after a stroke on the putting green, no other ball may be played or touched. If the ball is stopped or deflected by an outside agency the stroke is canceled and must be played again from the same spot.

If a ball hangs over the edge of the hole for more than a few seconds it is deemed at rest. When a ball on the putting green is to be lifted, its position must be marked. Failure to do this incurs a one stroke penalty and the ball must be replaced.

A ball on the wrong putting green must be lifted and dropped outside the green, not nearer the correct hole, and not in a hazard.

The line of the putt must not be prepared, except for the removal of loose impediments. A player must not press anything down with his club, although he may touch the ground with the club in front of the ball when addressing it.

If the line of the putt is obstructed by something that cannot be moved, such as an animal hole or casual water, the player may lift the ball and place it not nearer to the hole.

The line of the putt may be indicated by a partner or caddie but may not be marked or touched.

The player may not test the surface by rolling a ball, or scrape the surface of the green, but he may repair damage caused by the ball's impact.

The flagstick A player may have the flagstick removed, or held up to indicate the hole, before he plays his stroke.

A flagstick is said to be attended when it is held. If the ball strikes the flagstick when it is attended, or the person attending it, the penalty is the loss of the hole in match play, or two strokes in stroke play. This also applies when a ball played from the green strikes an unattended flagstick.

If the flagstick is unattended when a stroke is played, it must not be touched or lifted while the ball is in motion.

If the ball comes to rest against the flagstick while it is in the hole, the player may have the flagstick removed; if the ball then falls into the hole, he is deemed to have holed out with his last stroke.

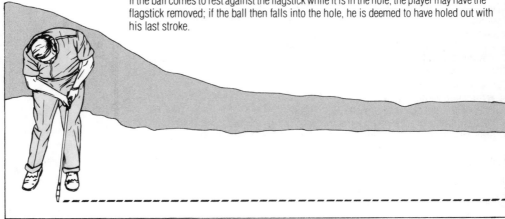

INTERFERENCE

General The term interference covers any deliberate or accidental act that interferes with the ball while in play.

Any other ball that interferes with a player's stroke through the green or in a hazard may be lifted and must be replaced after the stroke is played.

Moving ball If a moving ball is stopped or deflected accidentally by any outside agency (**a**), it must be played where it lies. This is classed as a "rub of the green."

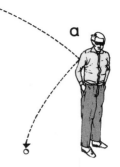

If the ball lodges in anything that is moving, the player must drop a ball (or if on the green, place it) as near as possible to the spot where it became lodged. There is no penalty.

If the ball is stopped or deflected by its owner, his partner, or one of their caddies or a part of their equipment (**b**), the player loses the hole in match play or incurs a two stroke penalty in stroke play.

In match play, if a player's ball is stopped or deflected accidentally by an opponent or his caddie or equipment, there is no penalty. In stroke play in the same situation, with certain exceptions, it is regarded as a rub of the green and the ball is played from the place where it comes to rest.

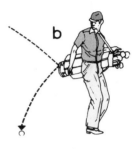

Ball at rest moved If a ball at rest is moved by any outside agency except wind or water, the player must replace it before making his stroke. If he, his partner, or their caddies move the ball on purpose there is a one stroke penalty.

If a player accidentally moves the ball after addressing it, he incurs a penalty stroke.

If a player's ball is moved by an opponent, his caddie, or equipment, in match play the opponent incurs one penalty stroke, and the ball must be replaced before another stroke is played. In a similar situation in stroke play, the ball must be replaced, but no penalty is incurred.

If a player's ball moves an opponent's ball, there is no penalty; the opponent may play the ball as it lies or replace it.

Obstructions Movable obstructions can be removed and if the ball is moved in the process, it can be replaced without penalty.

If the ball is in or near an immovable obstruction including casual water, ground under repair, or animal holes, the player may play the ball as it lies or drop or place it in a new position not nearer to the hole, and incurs no penalty.

On the green The rules differ between match and stroke play.

In match play if an opponent's ball might interfere with the player's putt, the opponent may be required to lift it. If a player's ball knocks an opponent's ball into the hole, the opponent will be deemed to have holed out with his last stroke. If the opponent's ball is knocked clear of the hole, he may replace it.

A player may concede that an opponent would hole out with his next stroke. He may then move the opponent's ball before playing his own stroke.

In stroke play if a competitor's ball might interfere with another competitor's stroke on the green he may be required to lift it.

If a player thinks that his ball could assist a competitor, he may remove it or play first without penalty. When both balls are on the green, if one competitor's ball strikes another's, the former incurs a two stroke penalty. He must play the ball as it lies and the other competitor's ball must be replaced.

©DIAGRAM

GYMNASTICS

HISTORY

Gymnastics formed an important part of the educational system of the ancient Greeks, from whose word "gymnasion" – meaning "a place for excercising naked" – the modern name of the sport derives. The revival of gymnastics in modern times was largely due to the influence of Friedrich Ludwig Jahn (1778–1852), a German who, like the Greeks, saw gymnastics as helping the moral as well as physical development of the young. He is credited with devising three at least of the modern types of apparatus – the rings, the horizontal bar, and the parallel bars. Gymnastics were included in the program of the first modern Olympics in 1896. The international governing body for the sport is the Fédération Internationale de Gymnastique (FIG).

SYNOPSIS

Men and women compete separately, the men on six types of apparatus (including the floor), the women on four. For both sexes a major contest has three parts:
Competition 1 is for teams, with the six members performing a compulsory and an optional exercise on each apparatus;
Competition 2 is the individual all-round championship, for which the top 36 gymnasts from the team event perform an optional exercise on each apparatus;
Competition 3 decides the individual champion on each apparatus, involving the eight (or six in the Olympics) best competitors from the team competition.
In all the competitions, each gymnast's performance is evaluated by a number of judges, whose marks are adjusted mathematically to produce the final mark. Compulsory exercises are fixed for four-year periods after each Olympic Games. The optional exercise may not be a mere repetition of the compulsory exercise.

GENERAL RULES

Dress (men) Men must wear a shirt (jersey) in all events.
In the events performed on the pommel horse, rings, parallel bars, or horizontal bar, men must wear long white pants and footwear (gym shoes and/or socks). The same clothing may be worn for the floor exercise and vault, or else short pants with or without footwear. In Competition 1 the members of a team must wear uniform clothing of the same color, but an individual's choice of long or short pants for the floor exercise and vault is unaffected.
Dress (women) Women wear leotards (with a national emblem in international competitions), the precise cut of which may be varied to suit a particular event provided the general appearance remains essentially unchanged. Securely fastened bandages are

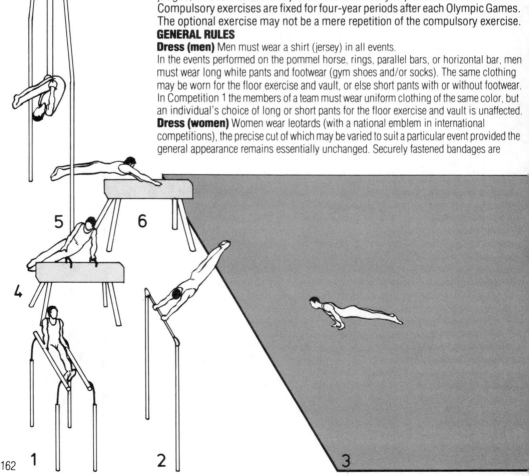

5

6

4

1

2

3

allowed, but padding is prohibited. The wearing of gymnastic slippers and socks is optional. In Competition 1 the members of a team must wear identical leotards.

Competitors Teams in Competition 1 consist of six gymnasts.

Officials In men's competitions there are four judges and a head judge.

In women's competitions there are four judges, and a head judge (two in Competition 3) who is aided by a Scientific Technical Collaborator (STC) and assistants.

In both men's and women's competitions there is also a jury with power over the judges.

Scoring Each competitor's performance on each apparatus is marked on the scale 0–10. Each judge, including the head judge, assesses the gymnast's performance in strict accordance with the standards and points of reference laid down by the FIG. Deductions of whole, half, and one-tenth points may be made.

In some events there is a starting score, with a possible bonus for risk, originality, and virtuosity, which together make up the maximum possible of 10.

Basically gymnasts are penalized for general faults, such as lack of assurance, rhythm, or suppleness, or for faults specific to the apparatus or exercise.

Exercises and movements are officially defined and graded in terms of difficulty into three categories – A, B, and C (C being the most difficult). In the optional exercises, a competitor must include a specified number of A, B, and C elements (also called parts) in order to score the highest possible marks for difficulty.

Bonus points can be earned by the demonstration of risk and originality in the B and C parts selected.

Adjustment of scores Of the scores awarded by the four judges, the highest and lowest are disregarded and the average is taken of the two remaining. If the difference between these two remaining scores exceeds a certain margin (also in women's competitions if their average differs from the head judge's score by such a margin) then the following action is taken. In men's competitions the head judge tries to reduce the difference by discussion with the judges concerned. In women's competitions all four judges are consulted. If this does not produce a remedy then the "base score" is calculated. This is done by adding the average of the two middle judges' scores to the head judge's score (or to the average of both head judges' scores in women's Competition 3) and dividing the resulting figure by two.

Order of events Competitors perform the various events in the order given in the table, although because all types of apparatus are in use simultaneously, different competitors begin at different points on the list.

Men's events
1) Parallel bars
2) Horizontal bar
3) Floor exercise
4) Pommel horse
5) Rings
6) Vault

Women's events
A) Vault
B) Uneven bars
C) Beam
D) Floor exercise

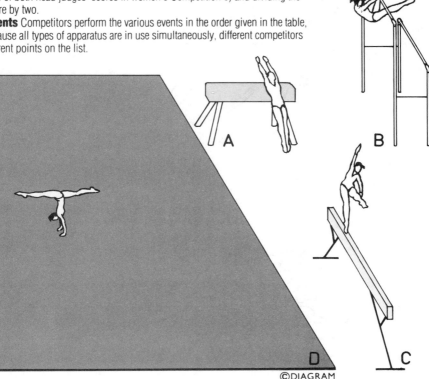

163

©DIAGRAM

GYMNASTICS (PARALLEL BARS, MEN'S)

APPARATUS
The parallel bars consist of two bars of round cross section, 350cm long, set 42cm apart, and supported 160cm above the floor on uprights that are fixed to a broad, stable base.

COMPETITION CONTENT
Compulsory exercise Each competitor first performs the current compulsory exercise as laid down by the FIG. The elements comprising the compulsory exercise are of the same general kind as outlined below for the optional exercise.

Optional exercise Each competitor also performs an optional exercise composed of parts (elements) of his choice, within certain guidelines.

The exercise must include a predominance of swinging and flight parts, in addition to holds of two seconds' duration and demonstrations of strength. It may not include more than three pronounced hold parts.

In all three competitions, B and C grade parts must be included that involve releasing the grip of both hands and regrasping the bars.

A minimum number of swing C parts is specified: one in Competition 2, and two in Competition 3, one of which should be executed through the inverted hang or glide hang.

Examples of movements Illustrated are the opening movements of the 1981–1984 compulsory exercise.

Examples of movements
a) Peach basket to glide.
b) Kip to support.
c) Clips.
d) Elephant lift.
e) Stutz turn.
f) Back roll to handstand.

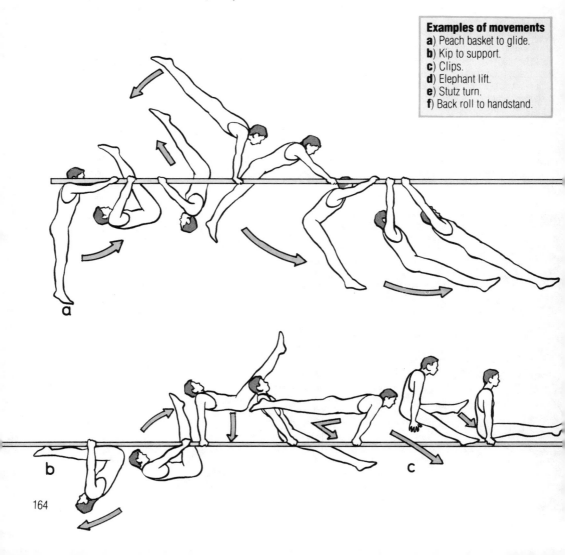

EVALUATION

Compulsory exercise A total of 9.8 points can be awarded for the interpretation of the exercise as laid down in the rules. A further 0.2 points can be awarded as a bonus for special virtuosity. The judges also take into consideration the form and technique of the execution.

Optional exercise The assessment is based on the following aspects, which can attract the maximum points as listed:
a) difficulty (of the parts chosen), 3.4;
b) combination (ie construction), 1.6;
c) execution (technical correctness), 4.4.
Bonus points up to 0.6 may be awarded for risk, originality, and virtuosity, making a total of 10 points.

Deductions The following are examples of the many possible deductions laid down by the FIG:
if no B or C part executed with grip release is included in the optional exercise, 0.3;
if more than three pronounced hold parts are included, up to 0.3;
in Competitions 2 and 3 if no swinging C part is executed through an inverted hang or glide hang: 0.3.

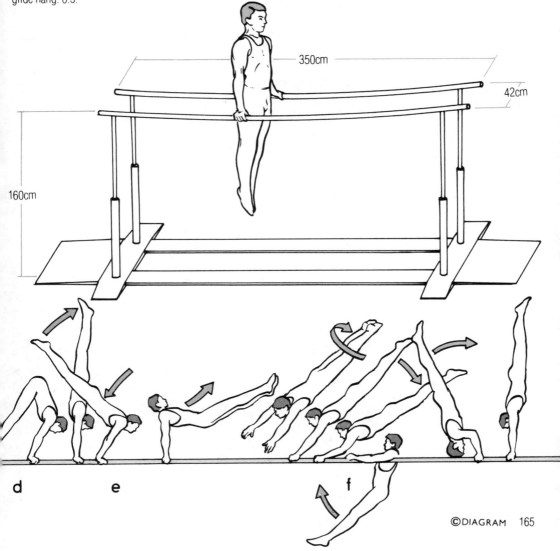

d   e   f

©DIAGRAM   165

GYMNASTICS (HORIZONTAL BAR, MEN'S)

APPARATUS

The horizontal bar (or high bar) is simply a bar 240cm long supported at a height of 255cm above the ground by an upright at each end. For the sake of rigidity the apparatus is also braced with wires.

COMPETITION CONTENT

Compulsory exercise Each competitor first performs the current compulsory exercise as laid down by the FIG. The elements comprising the compulsory exercise are of the same general kind as outlined below for the optional exercise.

Optional exercise Each gymnast also performs an optional exercise composed of parts (elements) chosen, within guidelines, by himself.

The exercise must consist exclusively of swinging parts without stops. It must include:
a) forward and backward giant swings;
b) changes of grip;
c) other variations, such as free hip-circles and twists.

For a maximum score for difficulty, the minimum requirements include exercises in dorsal hang or el-grip hang, and at least one B part that involves releasing the grip of both hands and regrasping the bar.

Examples of movements Illustrated are the opening movements of the 1981–1984 compulsory exercise.

EVALUATION

Compulsory exercise A total of 9.8 points can be awarded for the interpretation of the exercise as laid down in the rules. A further 0.2 points can be awarded as a bonus for special virtuosity. The judges also take into consideration the form and technique of the execution.

Optional exercise The assessment is based on the following aspects, which can attract the maximum points listed:
a) difficulty (of the parts chosen), 3.4;
b) combination (ie construction), 1.6;
c) execution (technical correctness), 4.4.

Bonus points up to 0.6 may be awarded for risk, originality, and virtuosity, making a total of 10 points maximum.

Examples of movements
a) Shoot to handstand with ½ turn.
b) Giant swing to straddle in and out with ½ turn.
c) Kip to handstand.

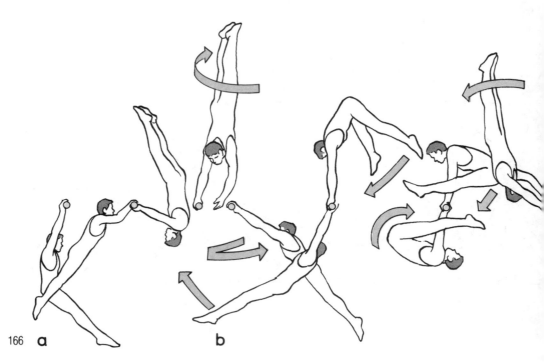

a   **b**

Deductions The following are examples of the many possible deductions laid down by the FIG:

for the inclusion of hold or strength parts, up to 0.2;
for omitting one of the minimum requirements, 0.3;
if the exercise is not concluded with a proper dismount, 0.3 to 0.5.

255 cm

240 cm

C

GYMNASTICS (FLOOR EXERCISES, MEN'S)

FLOOR AREA

The floor is a marked out area 12m square. Competitors must make use of the whole area, but not step outside it.

COMPETITION CONTENT

Compulsory exercise Each competitor first performs the current compulsory exercise as laid down by the FIG. The movements comprising this exercise are of the same general kind as outlined below for the optional exercise. Elements of the exercise are to be performed at given points on the mat; the path of the 1981–1984 compulsory exercise is shown here.

Competitors are given a plan (such as the example illustrated) showing where on the floor the prescribed movements must be performed.

Optional exercise Each gymnast also performs an optional exercise composed of parts (elements) chosen by himself in accordance with certain guidelines.

The exercise must form a harmonious and rhythmic whole, with alternating gymnastic movements, balance parts, parts of strength, kips, jumps, handsprings, and saltos.

There should be a personal touch in the expression of movements, but at the same time they must be technically correct.

The time limit is 1min (± 10sec), with audible signals given at 50sec and 70sec after the commencement.

Examples of movements Illustrated are the opening movements from the 1981–1984 compulsory exercise.

Examples of movements
a) Front somersault ½ turn, piked.
b) Flik flak.
c) Back roll to handstand with ½ turn.
d) Roll down and stand.

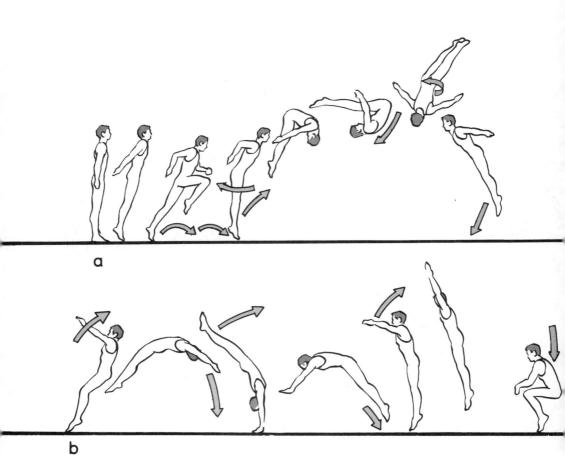

a

b

EVALUATION

Compulsory exercise A total of 9.8 points can be awarded for the interpretation of the exercise as laid down in the rules. A further 0.2 points can be awarded as a bonus for special virtuosity. The judges also take into account the form and technique of the execution.

Optional exercise The assessment is based on the following aspects, which can attract the maximum points shown:
a) difficulty (of the parts chosen), 3.4;
b) combination (ie construction), 1.6;
c) execution (technical correctness), 4.4.
Bonus points up to 0.6 may be awarded for risk, originality, and virtuosity, making a total of 10 points maximum.

Deductions The following are examples of the many possible deductions for errors laid down by the FIG:
if more than three steps (plus a final jump or roundoff) are made before a jump, salto, or handspring, up to 0.3, according to the difficulty of the part that follows;
stepping out of the floor area, 0.1 each time;
for too long or too short a performance: up to two seconds, 0.1; up to five seconds, 0.2; up to nine seconds, 0.3; over nine seconds, 0.5.

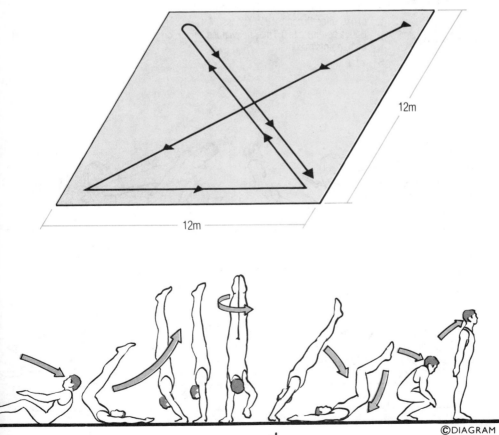

12m

12m

c

d

©DIAGRAM

GYMNASTICS (POMMEL HORSE, MEN'S)

APPARATUS

The pommel horse is similar to a vaulting horse, 110cm high and 163cm long, but with two raised handles near the center. It is anchored firmly to the floor.

COMPETITION CONTENT

Compulsory exercise Each competitor first performs the current compulsory exercise as laid down by the FIG. The elements comprising the compulsory exercise are of the same general kind as outlined below for the optional exercise.

Optional exercise A competitor also performs an optional exercise composed of parts (elements) chosen by himself in accordance with certain guidelines.

All three parts of the horse (as divided by the raised handles) must be used.

The exercise must consist of clean swings performed without stops, and must include:
a) undercuts of one leg;
b) circles of one and both legs;
c) forward and reverse scissors, at least one of which must be executed twice in succession.

Double leg circles must predominate in the performance.

Examples of movements Illustrated are the opening movements from the 1981–1984 compulsory exercise.

EVALUATION

Compulsory exercise A total of 9.8 points can be awarded for the interpretation of the exercise as laid down in the rules. A further 0.2 points can be awarded as a bonus for special virtuosity. The judges also take into account the form and technique of the execution.

Optional exercise The assessment is based on the following aspects, which can attract the maximum points listed:
a) difficulty (of the parts chosen), 3.4;
b) combination (linking of parts), 1.6;
c) execution (technical correctness), 4.4.

Bonus points up to 0.6 may be awarded for risk, originality, and virtuosity, making a total of 10 points maximum.

Examples of movements
a) Direct Stöckli.
b) Flank into circles.
c) Alternate undercuts.

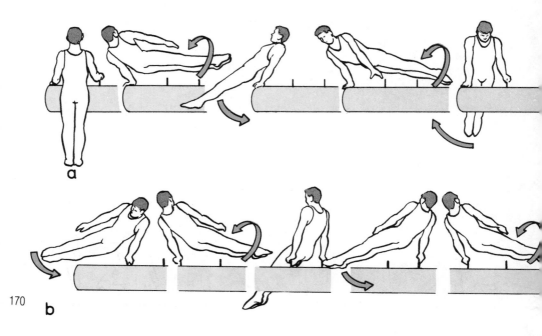

170
b

Deductions The following are examples of the many possible deductions for error laid down by the FIG:

if one part of the horse is not used, 0.3;
if there is a marked tendency to use one part of the horse, up to 0.2;
if there is no scissor part, 0.6;
if there are not two scissors in succession but there is one forward and one reverse scissor, 0.3.

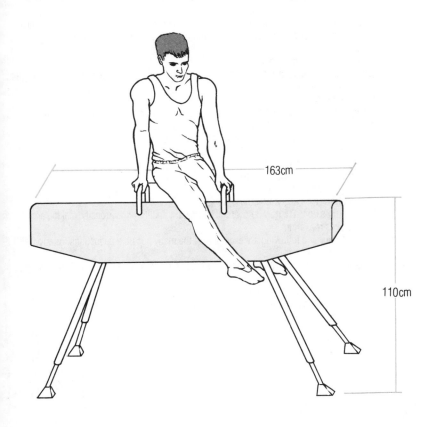

163cm

110cm

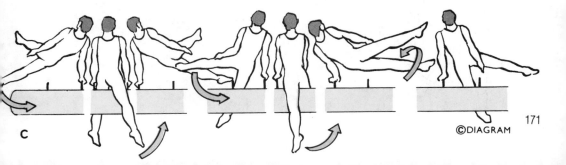

C

©DIAGRAM

GYMNASTICS (RINGS, MEN'S)

APPARATUS

The rings (or stationary rings) consist of two rigid rings 18cm in diameter suspended 250cm from the floor by two wires 50cm apart attached to a frame 550cm high. The frame is braced with wires for rigidity.

COMPETITION CONTENT

Compulsory exercise Each competitor first performs the current compulsory exercise as laid down by the FIG. The elements comprising the compulsory exercise are of the same general kind as outlined below for the optional exercise.

Optional exercise A competitor also performs an optional exercise composed of parts (elements) chosen by himself in accordance with certain guidelines.

The exercise must contain movements alternating between swing, strength, and hold parts, without letting the rings swing back and forth on the frame. There must be:

a) at least two handstands, one executed with strength, and the other with swing from hang, inverted hang, or support;

b) an additional strength part, of a difficulty that matches the total difficulty of the exercise. In Competition 2 one of the C grade parts must be a swing, and in Competition 3 two must be swings.

Hold parts must last for two seconds.

Examples of movements Illustrated are the opening movements from the 1981–1984 compulsory exercise.

EVALUATION

Compulsory exercise A total of 9.8 points can be awarded for the interpretation of the exercise as laid down in the rules. A further 0.2 points can be awarded as a bonus for special virtuosity. Also considered are the form and technique of the execution.

Optional exercise The assessment is based on the following aspects, which can attract the maximum points listed:

a) difficulty (of the parts chosen), 3.4;

b) combination (linking of parts), 1.6;

c) execution (technical correctness), 4.4.

Bonus points up to 0.6 may be awarded for risk, originality, and virtuosity, making a total of 10 points maximum.

Deductions The following are examples of the many possible deductions for error laid down by the FIG:

if the additional strength part does not correspond to the general difficulty of the exercise, up to 0.3;

if swing, strength, and hold parts are not properly distributed, up to 0.2;

if there is no handstand, or if the handstand does not correspond to the general difficulty of the exercise, 0.2 to 0.3.

Examples of movements

a) From hang kip to support.

b) Roll forward to handstand.

c) Giant enlocates to back uprise.

d) Roll back to planche.

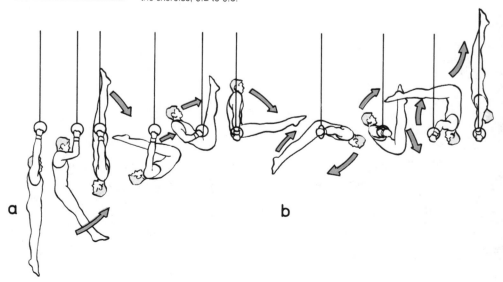

a   b

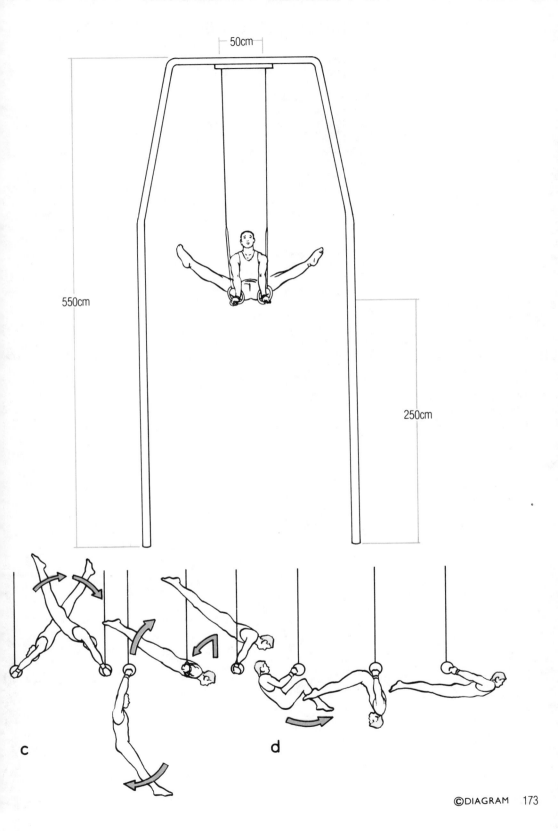

50cm

550cm

250cm

c

d

GYMNASTICS (HORSE VAULT, MEN'S)

APPARATUS

The horse for the men's vault is 163cm long and 135cm high. The springboard is 120cm long and is placed in line with the long axis of the horse.

COMPETITION CONTENT

Competition 1 Each gymnast performs a compulsory and an optional vault. The compulsory vault for 1981–1984 is illustrated and described below.

Competion 2 Each competitor performs an optional vault.

Competition 3 Each competitor performs two different optional vaults, chosen from those rated as C grade for difficulty.

THE VAULT

The run up must not be longer than 25m, measured from a vertical line through the near end of the horse. It is not evaluated for scoring purposes.

The pre-flight is the term used for the initial part of the vault, up to the moment when the hands leave the horse. All vaults must be supported by placing one or both hands on the horse.

The second flight is comprised of the remainder of the vault from the moment when the hands leave the horse.

EVALUATION

General The scoring system is the same for compulsory and optional vaults, with a maximum score of 10 points in both cases.

Base score All vaults have a base score that reflects their level of difficulty. For A grade vaults it is 9.0; for B grade, 9.4; for C grade, 9.8.

Deductions are made from the base score for technical faults in the pre-flight and second flight phases, and for errors in form. Bonus points may be awarded for virtuosity. (Risk and originality have been taken into account in fixing the base score.)

The following are examples of deductions laid down by the FIG:

if the run up exceeds 25m, 0.3;

if the gymnast deviates from the line of the long axis of the horse during the flight phases, up to 0.3;

if the arms are bent when they should be straight, 0.3 to 1.0.

Compulsory vault, 1981–1984

a) Jump with body and arms outstretched.

b) Momentary handstand on near end of horse.

c) Body piked with arms outstretched to the sides.

d) Body straightened with 180° turn to land facing the horse.

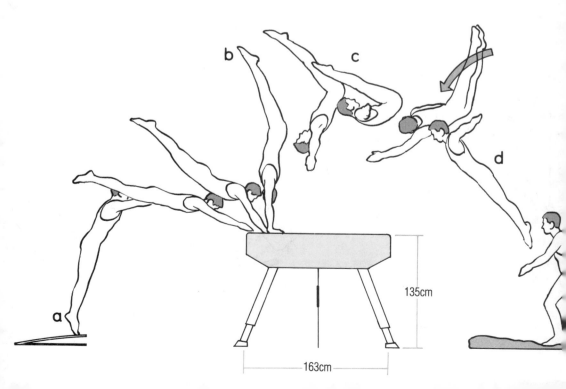

135cm

163cm

GYMNASTICS (HORSE VAULT, WOMEN'S)

APPARATUS

The horse for the women's vault is 163cm long and 120cm high. The springboard is 120cm long and is placed in line with the short axis of the horse.

COMPETITION CONTENT

The compulsory vault specified for 1981–1984 is illustrated and described below.

The optional vault may in no case be the same as the current compulsory vault. The vaults chosen in Competitions 1 and 2 may be the same or different.

All known vaults are graded A, B, or C for difficulty, and also divided into eight groups by type.

In Competition 3, two C grade vaults from groups 1 to 7 must be performed.

In all three competitions the gymnast must display the group number of the vault she is about to perform.

THE VAULT

Phases The vault is divided into four phases for purposes of evaluation: first flight phase; support phase; second flight phase; and landing. The run up is not evaluated.

All vaults must be performed with the support of both hands on the horse.

Number of attempts In both compulsory and optional vaults the gymnast has the right to two attempts, with the better score of the two being counted.

EVALUATION

Scoring Each judge scores the vault by making deductions from a maximum possible of 10 points, disregarding at this stage the value for difficulty.

Deductions The following are examples of the deductions laid down by the FIG:
if an optional vault does not correspond to the number displayed by the gymnast, 0.5;
if the body position is at fault in the first flight phase, up to 0.2;
if the arms remain bent in the support phase, up to 0.5.

Adjustment of scores The head judge calculates the average of the four judges' scores and checks the difficulty value of the vault as laid down by the FIG. The difference between the difficulty value and 10 points is then deducted from the average of the judges' scores to give the final score.

> **Compulsory vault, 1981–1984**
> **a**) Jump with body and arms outstretched.
> **b**) Handspring from horse.
> **c**) In second flight phase turn 360° around the long axis of the body and land with the back to the horse.

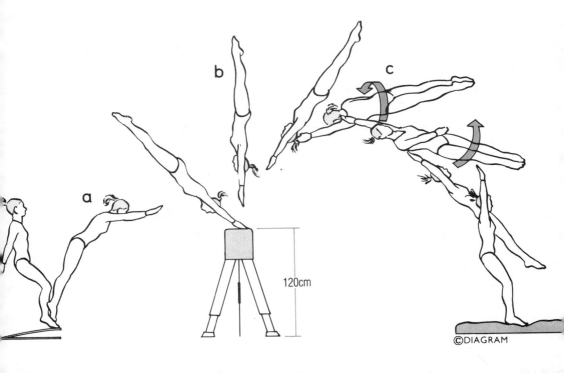

120cm

©DIAGRAM

GYMNASTICS (UNEVEN BARS, WOMEN'S)

APPARATUS

The uneven bars (or asymmetrical bars) are two horizontal bars 350cm long arranged parallel to one another but at different heights. The lower bar is 150cm above the floor and the upper bar 230cm above the floor. Each is supported by an upright at each end, and the two frames thus formed are placed 43cm apart. Bracing wires are usually added to aid rigidity.

COMPETITION CONTENT

Compulsory exercise Each competitor first performs the current compulsory exercise as laid down by the FIG. The elements comprising the compulsory exercise are of the same general kind as outlined below for the optional exercise.

Optional exercise Each competitor also performs an optional exercise composed of elements chosen by herself within the following guidelines.

The competitor must select her B and C grade parts from at least three of the following groups:

a) upward swings or circular swings;
b) movements from swing to handstand;
c) turns around the longitudinal axis of the body (pirouettes);
d) turns around the short axis (saltos);
e) counter, grip-change, and flight elements;
f) Hecht elements;
g) kips.

In addition she must aim to include:

a) a variety of directional changes;
b) movements under the low bar and over the high bar;
c) movements outside and inside the bars;
d) a number of changes between the bars.

The exercise should be continuous, but two stops for balance or concentration are allowed. Only four consecutive elements may be performed on the same bar; she must then change bar, touch the other bar, or dismount.

If she falls the competitor may resume within 30 seconds.

Examples of movements Illustrated are movements from the 1981–1984 compulsory exercise.

EVALUATION

Compulsory exercise The FIG's text of the exercise currently in use specifies deductions for missing elements and faults of technique. The judges adjust the maximum possible score of 10 points in accordance with those instructions.

Optional exercise The assessment is made on the basis of the following factors, with points being allocated up to the maximum listed:

a) difficulty (value of the elements chosen), 3.0;
b) combinations (construction of the exercise), 2.5;
c) execution and virtuosity, 4.0;
d) bonus points (for originality, risk, or additional C grade elements), 0.5.

The maximum possible score is thus 10 points.

Examples of movements
a) Stoop through straddle cut backward.
b) Cast to handstand with 180° turn.
c) Beat to release high bar, land in handstand on low bar.

Deductions The following are examples of the many possible deductions for error in the women's uneven bars optional exercise:
monotony in rhythm, 0.2;
fewer than 10 elements, 0.2;
dismount not corresponding to the exercise's level of difficulty, 0.2.

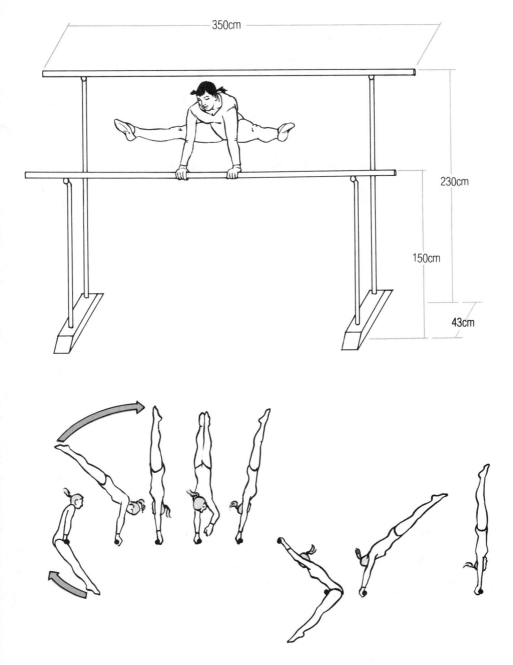

b   c

GYMNASTICS (BEAM, WOMEN'S)

APPARATUS

The beam (or balance beam) is a rigid piece of wood 5m long mounted horizontally so that its 10cm wide top edge is 120cm above the floor.

COMPETITION CONTENT

Compulsory exercise Each competitor first performs the current compulsory exercise as laid down by the FIG. It is permissible to reverse the order of the elements (parts) as long as the specified direction of movement is not reversed. Up to two extra steps to facilitate this are allowed.

Optional exercise Each competitor also performs an optional exercise composed of elements chosen by herself, within the following guidelines.

The exercise is essentially one of balance. It must last not less than 70sec and not more than 90sec. The timing begins when the gymnast's feet leave the floor and ends when they return to the floor. If she falls she may resume within 10sec.

The exercise must make use of the entire length of the beam.

The B and C grade parts must be selected from the following different element groups:
a) acrobatic elements, with and without a flight phase in the forward, backward, or sideways movement;
b) acrobatic strength elements;
c) gymnastic elements, such as turns, leaps, steps, runs, and balance elements in sitting, standing, or lying positions.

High points in the performance should be created by the combination of two or more acrobatic elements, two or more gymnastic elements, or the combination of both of these types of element in a series.

Examples of movements
a) Mount to support on one foot, 180° turn.
b) Flik flak to one foot.
c) Linking element.
d) Bodywave.

5m

10cm

120cm

b

c

Changes between element groups should be harmonious. Rhythm should be varied by means of faster and slower movements. The height of movements above the beam should be varied.

The following special requirements must be included:

a) a series of two or more acrobatic elements, one of which must have a flight phase:

b) a 360° gymnastic turn on one leg:

c) a gymnastic leap of great amplitude:

d) acrobatic elements in two or more directions (forward, backward or sideways).

Examples of movements Illustrated are selected movements from the 1981–1984 compulsory exercise.

EVALUATION

Compulsory exercise The text of the exercise currently in use specifies a time limit for its conclusion, deductions for missing elements, and deductions for other faults. The judges make adjustments to the maximum possible score of 10 points on the basis of those instructions.

Optional exercise The assessment is made on the basis of the following factors, and points are allocated up to the maximum listed:

a) difficulty (value of the elements chosen), 3.0:

b) combinations (construction of the exercise), 2.5:

c) execution and virtuosity: 4.0:

d) bonus points (for originality, risk, or additional C grade parts), 0.5.

The maximum possible score is thus 10 points.

Deductions The following are examples of the many possible deductions for error in the women's beam optional exercise:

monotony of presentation, 0.2:

monotony in direction of movement, 0.2:

omission of an acrobatic series, 0.2:

supporting a leg against the side of the beam, 0.2:

more than three pauses, 0.1 each.

a

d

©DIAGRAM

GYMNASTICS (FLOOR EXERCISES, WOMEN'S)

FLOOR AREA

The floor is a marked out area 12m square. Competitors must make use of the whole area, but must not step outside it.

COMPETITION CONTENT

Compulsory exercise Each competitor first performs the current compulsory exercise as laid down by the FIG. The elements comprising this exercise are of the same general kind as outlined below for the optional exercise. Movements are to be performed at given points on the mat; the path of the 1981–1984 compulsory exercise is shown here.

Optional exercise Each competitor also performs an optional exercise composed of elements chosen by herself within the following guidelines.

The exercise must last not less than 70sec and not more than 90sec. A musical lead in or conclusion of four measures beyond these limits is allowed. Timing begins with the first gymnastic or acrobatic movement.

The musical accompaniment may consist of taped orchestral music (with no singing) or taped or live piano music.

The exercise should express the personality of the gymnast. She should select the B and C grade parts from the following different elements groups:
a) acrobatic elements, with and without a flight phase in the forward, backward, or sideways movement;
b) acrobatic strength elements;
c) gymnastic elements, such as turns, leaps, steps, runs, arm swings, and balance elements in sitting, standing, or lying positions.
High points in the exercise should be created by:
a) acrobatic series with one or more saltos;
b) combined acrobatic and gymnastic series with great amplitude of movement;
c) gymnastic series with great amplitude of height and distance in the movement;
d) harmonious changes between the acrobatic and gymnastic elements;
e) dynamic changes, in harmony with the music, between fast and slow movements.

Examples of movements
a) Tucked walk over.
b) Cartwheel.
c) Linking element.
d) Cartwheel in spin on hands.
e) Straddle down to support.
f) Backward walk over from lunge.

a   b

c   d   e

Versatility and originality must be aimed for in the direction and height of movements. There is a special requirement that two acrobatic series be included, one of which has a salto as the high point, and the other two saltos or one double salto.

Examples of movements Illustrated are selected movements from the 1981–1984 compulsory exercise.

EVALUATION

Compulsory exercise The FIG's text of the exercise currently in use specifies a time limit for its conclusion, and deductions for missing elements and faults in execution. The judges make adjustments to the maximum possible score of 10 points on the basis of those instructions.

Optional exercise The assessment is made on the basis of the following factors, and points are allocated up to the maximum shown:
a) difficulty (value of the elements chosen), 3.0;
b) combinations (construction of the exercise), 2.5;
c) execution and virtuosity, 4.0;
d) bonus points (for originality, risk, or additional C grade parts), 0.5.
The maximum possible score is thus 10 points.

Deductions The following are examples of the many possible deductions for error in the women's floor exercise:
lack of high points (peaks), 0.1;
monotony in presentation, up to 0.2;
elements of exaggeratedly theatrical character, 0.1 each;
stepping outside the floor area, 0.1 each time;
lack of a series with two salto high points or a double salto, 0.2.

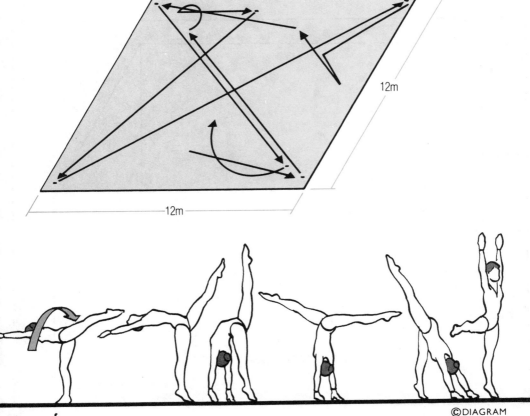

12m

12m

f

HANDBALL (COURT)

HISTORY
The exact origins of court handball are obscure. There is evidence that a game of this type was played by the Romans; it was certainly played in Ireland about a thousand years ago. Irish emigrants took their four-wall game to America in the nineteenth century; the one-wall version was developed soon after.

National and international championships have been staged by a number of organizations and, since the 1960s, attempts have been made to produce a unified set of playing rules. There is still no overall governing body; the rules described here are those of the United States Handball Association.

SYNOPSIS
In court handball, the ball may be struck only with the gloved hands; players score points by hitting shots that their opponents are unable to return. Courts are usually four-wall or one-wall; three-wall courts are less common and are not standardized. The game may be played by two players (singles) or four (doubles); a three-player version ("cut-throat") is usually found only as a practice game. Rules for the four-wall game are described first; rules for the one-wall game differ in some respects (see p. 187).

COURT AND EQUIPMENT
Court Illustrated here is a standard four-wall court, 20ft wide and 40ft long. The front (**a**) and side (**b**) walls should be 20ft high; the back wall (**c**) should be at least 12ft high. The 2in-wide white lines marking the court floor are:

d) short line, parallel to and 20ft from the front wall;

e) service line, parallel to and 15ft from the front wall;

f) service boxes, marked by lines parallel to and 1ft 6in from each side wall;

g) receivers' restraining lines, parallel to and 5ft behind the short line, and extending 6in from the side walls.

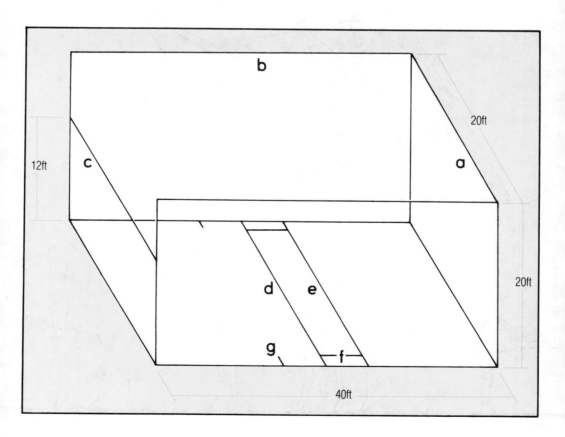

1⁷⁄₈in

The ball should be of rubber or composition, but may be of any color. It should have a diameter of 1⁷⁄₈in, and weigh 2.3oz. When dropped from a height of 70in onto a hardwood floor, it should rebound 46–50in in a temperature of 68°F.

During the game, every effort must be made to keep the ball dry; in tournaments, a new ball must be used for each match. The ball also may be changed during a game at the referee's discretion.

Gloves Court handball may not be played barehanded. The gloves worn must be light-colored, and made of leather or other soft material. They should be snug-fitting, and the fingers may not be removed, webbed, or otherwise connected.

Players may wind surgical gauze, tape, or thin foam rubber around their hands under their gloves to protect their palms. They may not wear metal or any other hard substance under their gloves, nor may they use tape, rubber bands, etc on the outside of their gloves.

Players must change their gloves when they have become sufficiently wet to dampen the ball, or when requested to do so by the referee.

Dress Players may wear shirts, shorts, socks, and shoes of any color that does not affect their opponents' view of the ball. Wet shirts must be changed on the request of the referee.

PLAYERS AND OFFICIALS

Players Each side may consist of one player (singles) or two (doubles).

Officials The referee in charge of the match may be assisted by two linesmen and a scorer.

DURATION AND SCORING

Duration A match consists of two games, plus a tiebreaker if required. Five-minute intervals are allowed between the games and before the tiebreaker.

Both sides must be ready to play within 10 seconds of the end of the previous rally; the server must then serve within the next 10 seconds. Any delays by the serving side are penalized by loss of the service; the serving side is awarded a point for any delays by the receiving side.

Providing that players have not taken up their positions for the next service, either side may request a time-out. Each side is allowed up to three one-minute time-outs in each game, and two one-minute time-outs during the tiebreaker.

At the discretion of the referee, players are allowed equipment time-outs to replace damaged or wet clothing or equipment. If the player wishes to change to dry gloves, he must show his palms to the referee, who may then grant a two-minute time-out. Equipment and glove time-outs are in addition to players' time-outs.

An injured player is allowed up to 15 minutes' rest, after which time he must either continue play or forfeit the match.

Scoring A game is won by the first side to score 21 points. A match consists of two games; if the two sides win one game each, the first side to win 11 points in the tiebreaker wins the match.

Points are awarded only if the side that is serving wins the rally. When the serving side loses a rally, or fails to serve according to the rules, the service passes to the other side.

HANDBALL (COURT) 2

RULES OF PLAY

Service order The player or pair that wins the toss serves first in the opening game. In doubles, when the starting player loses the service, it passes to the opposing pair. Thereafter, both players in each team must serve and lose service before the service passes to the opposition.

The service may be taken only when both serving and receiving sides have been in position for at least one second. It may be taken anywhere within the service zone (the area between the short line and the service line); the server must have both feet on or within the lines of the zone.

The server should bounce the ball once on the floor of the service zone, and hit it once with his hand or fist (**A**). The ball should be served direct onto the front wall; on the rebound it should hit the floor beyond the short line, either with or without touching one of the side walls (**B**).

The server must remain in the service zone until the ball has crossed the short line on the rebound. In doubles, the server's partner must stand with both feet in the service box and his back to the wall while the service is taken. He should remain in the service box until the ball has crossed the short line on the rebound.

The receiving side must stand at least 5ft behind the short line (as indicated by the receivers' restraining lines) until the ball is struck by the server.

Service faults A player who serves two successive faults loses the service. It is a service fault if:

a) the server leaves the service zone before the served ball passes the short line on the rebound;

b) in doubles, the server's partner leaves the service box before the served ball passes the short line;

c) the served ball first hits the floor on or in front of the short line, either with or without touching one of the side walls;

d) the served ball hits two side walls after it has hit the front wall;

e) the served ball hits the ceiling after hitting the front wall, either with or without touching one of the side walls;

f) the served ball rebounds from the front wall and hits the back wall before touching the floor;

g) the served ball goes out of court on the service;

h) in doubles, the served ball rebounds from the front wall, hits the floor, and touches the server's partner while he is in the service box.

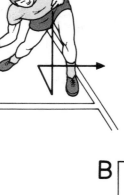

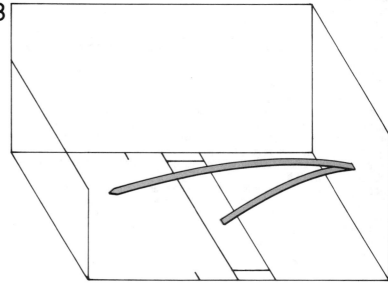

Out serves Certain service errors lead to an immediate loss of service (an "out"). A server loses the service if:

a) once the server and the receiver are ready to play, the server bounces the ball anywhere other than in the service zone;

b) the server fails to strike the ball on the first bounce, or touches it with any part of his body other than his hand or fist;

c) the served ball touches any other part of the court before striking the front wall;

d) in doubles, the served ball touches the server's partner before striking the front wall;

e) on the rebound from the front wall the served ball touches the server;

f) in doubles, the served ball on the rebound from the front wall touches the server's partner while his feet are out of the service box;

g) in doubles, the players serve out of order;

h) the served ball hits the front wall where it joins the floor (the "crotch") – except that a serve into the crotch of the back wall is an ace, as is a three-wall crotch serve;

i) once the server and the receiver are ready to play, the server fails to serve within 10 seconds.

Dead ball service There is no penalty for a dead ball service; the server takes the service again. Any previous service fault is unaffected.

A dead ball service occurs if, on an otherwise legal service:

a) in doubles, the served ball on the rebound from the front wall touches the server's partner while he is still in the service box, but before it hits the floor;

b) the ball passes so close to the server or the server's partner that the receiver's view is obstructed;

c) the ball passes between the server's partner and the side wall;

d) the ball passes through the server's legs on the rebound from the front wall;

e) the ball hits any part of the court that under local rules is a dead ball.

Return of service (C) It is a good return of service if the receiver plays the ball after it has crossed the short line but before it has bounced on the floor, providing that his feet do not touch or cross the short line before he has made contact with the ball. He may also play the ball after it has bounced once on the floor.

The returned ball must not touch the floor before touching the front wall. The player may return the ball so that it strikes the front wall directly (**a**), or after touching one or both side walls (**b**), the back wall (**c**), the ceiling, or any combination of these surfaces.

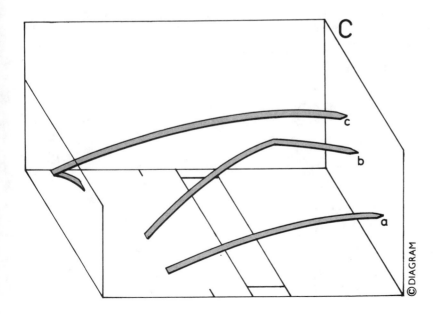

HANDBALL (COURT) 3

Good rally Each legal return after the service is called a rally; the player may strike the ball with either the front or the back of his hand.

It is a good rally if the player volleys the ball, or hits it after it has bounced once on the floor, so that it is returned to the front wall, either with or without touching any part of the court except the floor.

If a player strikes at a ball and misses, he may make further attempts to make a good return before it touches the floor for a second time. In doubles, both members of a side are entitled to attempt to return the ball, and may make one or more attempts to strike it before it touches the floor for a second time.

Bad rally It is a bad rally and results in a point or out against the offender if the player:

a) hits the ball with two hands (**1**);

b) hits the ball with any part of his body other than his hand (**2**);

c) touches the ball more than once;

d) fails to return the ball to the front wall but instead strikes it out of court, except that any ball that is returned to the front wall but goes out of court on the rebound or after the first bounce is considered a dead ball, and the service is replayed.

Touching the ball Except for the player making the return, any player touching the ball before it has bounced twice on the floor is penalized by an out or point against him (unless the ball touches the offender without first bouncing, when it is a dead ball hinder). In doubles, if the offending player is the server's partner, the server loses the service.

Dead ball hinder There is no penalty for a dead ball hinder (obstruction) but the point is replayed. It is a dead ball hinder when:

a) in the referee's opinion, play was affected by an erratic bounce caused by an obstruction on the court or the ball skidding on a wet patch on the floor;

b) body contact with an opponent unsights a player or interferes with his returning the ball;

c) the ball rebounds from the front wall so close to the striker or his partner (including passing between their legs) that their opponents are unsighted, or do not have a fair chance to return the ball;

d) a returned ball, without first bouncing, touches the striker's opponent before returning to the front wall.

Avoidable hinder The penalty for an avoidable hinder is an out or point against the offender, depending on who was serving or receiving. It is an avoidable hinder when:

a) a player does not move out of the way to allow his opponent a shot;

b) a player moves into a position that blocks or crowds his opponent;

c) in doubles, the partner of the player who is striking the ball blocks or crowds a member of the opposing team;

d) a player moves into the path of the ball just after it has been struck by his opponent;

e) a player deliberately moves across his opponent's line of sight just before that opponent is about to strike the ball;

f) a player forcibly pushes an opponent;

g) a player deliberately intimidates or distracts his opponent.

ONE-WALL HANDBALL

Court Illustrated is a standard one-wall court. The wall is 20ft wide and 16ft high; the playing zone on the floor is 20ft wide and 34ft long.
Lines marking the court are:
a) long line, marking the edge of the playing zone parallel to and farthest from the wall;
b) short line, parallel to and 16ft from the wall;
c) service markers, parallel to and equidistant from the long and short lines, and extending 6in inward from the sidelines;
d) sidelines, marking the edges of the playing zone perpendicular to the wall, and extending for 3ft beyond the long line.

Service is as for the four-wall game, with the following exceptions:
a) the service zone is the area bounded by the short line, service markers, and side lines;
b) the server must remain in the service zone, and the receiver must remain behind the service lines, until the served ball has rebounded off the front wall past the short line;
c) in doubles, the server's partner must stand outside the side lines behind the short line until the served ball has passed him;
d) it is a service fault if the served ball rebounds from the wall and first hits the floor beyond the long line;
e) it is an out serve if the served ball rebounds from the wall and first hits the floor outside the side lines.

Other rules are generally as for four-wall handball, except that as play is limited to the front wall and floor of the court, rules relating to other walls and the ceiling do not apply.

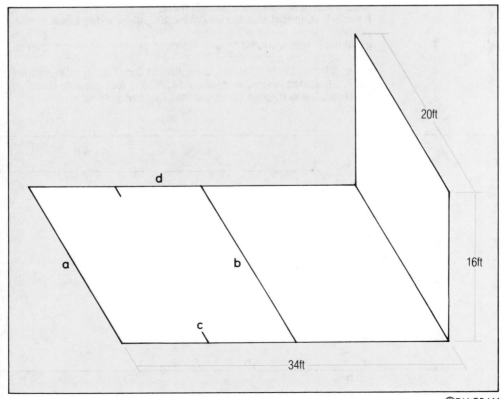

187

HANDBALL (TEAM)

HISTORY
The origins of modern team handball date back to the 1890s, when a version of the game was devised in Germany for the training of gymnasts. The game enjoyed only limited popularity, however, until the 1920s, when it was further developed by the application of adapted soccer rules. The first international governing body for team handball was founded in 1928; the present body, the International Handball Federation, was founded in Copenhagen in 1946. Team handball is played in two main versions: an 11-man outdoor game, also called field handball, and a seven-man game played on a smaller indoor court. The seven-a-side version has been included in the Olympic Games since 1972. The rules of the seven-man game are described here.

SYNOPSIS
Team handball is a fast attacking ball game played, in its most popular version, by two teams of seven players and five substitutes. The object is to score more goals than the opposing team within the time allowed. Players pass or dribble the ball with their hands until a shooting opportunity is created.

PLAYING AREA AND EQUIPMENT
The court The playing area is a rectangle 40m long by 20m wide; if possible, there should also be a safety zone extending 2m beyond each goal line and 1m outside each side line. Court markings are as follows:

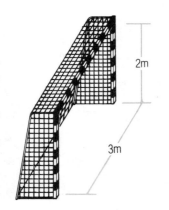

a) goal lines;

b) side lines;

c) center line, dividing the court into two halves;

d) goal area lines, comprising a straight line, 3m long, parallel to and 6m from the goal area line, equidistant from the side lines, and extended at each end to join the goal line by means of two quarter circles with a radius of 6m measured from the back inside corner of the goal posts;

e) free throw lines, also called 9m lines, parallel to and 3m beyond each goal line, and made up of solid lines and spaces each 15cm long;

f) penalty lines, 1m long, parallel to and 7m from each goal line, and equidistant from the side lines;

g) goalkeeper lines, also called 4m lines, 15cm long, parallel to and 4m from each goal line, and equidistant from the side lines;

h) lines defining the entry and exit area for substitutions, 15cm long, at right angles to one side line, protruding into the playing area, and 4.5m either side of the center line.

All lines are 5cm wide, except that the goal line between the goal posts is 8cm wide.

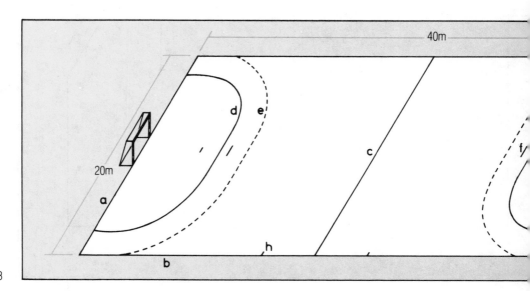

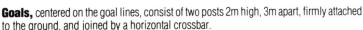

54–56cm* ◄
58–60cm**

*women
**men

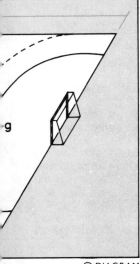

Goals, centered on the goal lines, consist of two posts 2m high, 3m apart, firmly attached to the ground, and joined by a horizontal crossbar.

Posts and crossbars should by 8×8cm in cross-section and should be made of wood, light metal, or synthetic material. They must be painted in contrasting bands of color to stand out from the background. Each rectangle of color should be 20cm long, except at the corners, where two rectangles 28cm long and of the same color should join to give an "L" shape.

Goals must have nets attached in such a way that a ball thrown into them will not rebound out immediately.

The ball must be spherical and uniform in color, made of a solid casing of leather or synthetic material. The surface must not be shiny or slippery.

For women, the ball must have a circumference of 54–56cm and weigh 325–400g.

For men, the ball must have a circumference of 58–60cm and weigh 425–475g.

Dress Team members other than goalkeepers must wear identical uniforms that are easily distinguishable from those of the opposing team. Goalkeepers' uniforms must be easily distinguishable from those of all other players.

Players must wear numbers 10cm high on the fronts of their shirts and 20cm high on their backs. Numbers 1 through 20 are used, with 1, 12 and 16 being reserved for goalkeepers. Captains must wear an armlet approximately 4cm wide and of a color contrasting with their shirts.

All players must wear sports shoes. Any item that might cause injury is prohibited.

PLAYERS AND OFFICIALS

Players Teams consist of 12 players – 10 court players and two goalkeepers.

No more than seven players per team – six court players and one goalkeeper – may be on the court at any time. At least five players, one of whom must be listed as a goalkeeper, must be on the court at the start of a game. Once a game is started, play may continue even if a team has fewer than five players on the court.

Players listed on the scoresheet as goalkeepers may not play in any other position. Court players may play as goalkeepers provided that the scorekeeper is informed and that they change into goalkeeper's uniform; they may later return to being court players.

Substitution Substitutes may enter the game at any time and as often as required. They need not notify the timekeeper provided that the players to be replaced have already left the court. All players must leave and enter the court within the boundaries of their team's substitution area.

Officials Two referees – termed the court referee and the goal line referee according to their positions on the field – have joint responsibility for the conduct of a game. They are assisted by a scorekeeper and a timekeeper.

DURATION AND SCORING

Duration There are two periods of 30 minutes' playing time, with a 10-minute interval between them.

The referees decide if and when the playing time is to be interrupted and when it is to be restarted. Time must be allowed at the end of a period for a free throw or penalty throw awarded immediately before a period is due to end.

If a game is tied at the end of normal playing time but competition rules require there to be a winner, there is a 5-minute interval followed by two 5-minute periods of play with no interval between them. If there is still no winner a further 5-minute interval is followed by two more consecutive 5-minute playing periods. If the tie still persists, the winner is determined by the application of specific competition rules.

Scoring A goal is scored when the entire ball crosses over the goal line between the posts and under the crossbar.

Referees have the power to award a goal if they consider that the ball was prevented from entering the goal by any person or object not authorized to be on the court.

A goal will not be allowed if there is an infringement by any player of the attacking team before or during the scoring of a goal, or if the referee or timekeeper has signaled to interrupt the game before the entire ball has crossed the goal line.

© DIAGRAM

HANDBALL (TEAM) 2

STARTING PROCEDURES

Start Team captains toss for choice of ends or the right to throw-off. Ends and the right to throw-off change for the second period. A new toss is held before extra time.

Throw-off Each period commences with a throw-off by the team entitled to take it. After a goal, play recommences with a throw-off by the team that conceded the goal.

A throw-off must be taken from the center of the court and within 3sec after the referee has blown his whistle. The ball may be thrown in any direction.

When the throw-off is taken, all players must be in their own half of the court, and players of the team not in possession of the ball must be at least 3m away from it.

General rules for throws also apply (see p. 191).

RULES OF PLAY

Playing the ball Court players, and goalkeepers outside their goal areas, may:
a) stop, catch, throw, or strike the ball in any manner and in any direction using hands, fists (**1**), arms, head (**2**), torso, thighs (**3**), or knees;
b) hold the ball for up to 3 sec, either in one or both hands or with the ball held against the ground;
c) take a maximum of three steps with the ball (including lowering a raised foot to the ground, and raising a foot from the ground and returning it to the same spot);
d) while standing or running, tap the ball once toward the ground and catch it again with one or both hands;
e) while standing or running, bounce the ball repeatedly toward the ground with one hand, or roll the ball on the ground repeatedly with one hand, and then catch the ball and pick it up again with one or both hands;
f) move the ball from one hand to the other without losing contact with it;
g) play the ball when sitting, kneeling, or lying on the ground.

Players may not:
a) touch the ball more than once unless it contacts another player, the ground, or part of the goal between touches (although fumbling is not penalized);
b) touch the ball with the foot or any part of the leg below the knee, except when the ball has been thrown at the offender by an opponent;
c) deliberately play the ball over the side lines or the goal line outside the player's own goal;
d) dive for the ball on the ground;
e) keep the ball in team possession if there is no attempt to attack or shoot.

Tackling When approaching an opponent, a player may:
a) use his hands and arms to gain possession of the ball;
b) use his open hand to play the ball from an opponent;
c) use his torso to obstruct an opponent;

A player may not:
a) pull, hit, or use his fist to force the ball out of an opponent's hand or hands;
b) use his arms, hands, or legs to obstruct an opponent;
c) force an opponent into the goal area;
d) hold, push, run into, jump into, hit, or threaten an opponent;
e) endanger an opponent with the ball, or by making a dangerous feint;
f) endanger a goalkeeper.

Goal area rules The goal area, which includes the goal area line, is entered when a player touches the ground within it with any part of his body.

Only the goalkeeper may enter the goal area. A court player who enters the goal area is subject to penalty; an attacker who ends up in the goal area after playing the ball, or any defender, is penalized only if he disadvantages the opponents.

When the ball is inside the goal area it belongs to the goalkeeper. No court player may touch the ball when it is on the ground within the goal area or in the possession of the goalkeeper within the goal area. A court player may, however, play a ball in the air above the goal area.

A ball that enters the goal area and returns to the playing area stays in play.

If the ball comes to rest in the goal area it is put back into play by a goal throw by the goalkeeper. Play continues if the ball is touched by a defender and is then immediately taken up by the goalkeeper or comes to rest in the goal area.

A player is penalized for deliberately playing the ball into his own goal area, unless it returns to the playing area without being touched by the goalkeeper.

Goalkeepers' rules Outside his goal area a goalkeeper is subject to the same playing rules as court players. A goalkeeper is considered to have left his goal area as soon as any part of his body touches the ground outside the goal area.

Special rules for goalkeepers are described here. A goalkeeper may:

a) touch the ball with any part of his body when defending within his goal area;

b) move freely around his own goal area with the ball, subject to no restrictions other than that he must not delay the taking of a throw-in, goal throw, or free throw;

c) leave the goal area without being in possession of the ball and take part in play in the playing area;

d) leave the goal area and play the ball again in the playing area, if in the act of defending the goal he has not succeeded in getting the ball properly under control.

A goalkeeper may not:

a) endanger an opponent;

b) intentionally play the ball over his own goal line after gaining control;

c) leave his goal area with the ball under his control;

d) after a goal throw, touch the ball again outside the goal area unless the ball has first contacted another player;

e) touch the ball on the ground outside the goal area line while he is within his goal area;

f) take the ball into his goal area if it is on the ground outside the goal area line;

g) reenter the goal area from the playing area while in possession of the ball;

h) touch the ball with his feet or legs below the knees when it is moving out toward the playing area or stationary in the goal area;

i) touch or cross the goalkeeper line, or its projection to either side, before the ball has left the thrower's hand during a penalty throw.

THROWS

General rules Before a throw is taken, the ball must rest in the thrower's hand and all players on the court must comply with positioning rules for the different throws.

In cases where the throw is preceded by a whistle signal from the referee, the thrower must throw the ball within 3 sec of the signal.

When taking a throw, the player must actually throw the ball, not hand it to a teammate. Except for goal throws and referee's throws, at least one part of one of the thrower's feet must be in constant contact with the ground. The thrower may not touch the ball again until it has touched another player or the goal.

A goal can be scored direct from any throw.

Throw-in (4) A throw-in is awarded if the whole of the ball crosses the side line, or crosses the goal line outside the goal after last being touched by a defending player other than the goalkeeper.

The throw-in is taken, normally without a whistle signal from the referee, by a player from the team that did not last touch the ball before it crossed the line. It is taken from the place where the ball crossed the side line, or from the end of the side line on the side of the goal where the ball crossed the goal line.

The thrower must have one foot on the side line until the ball has left his hand; he is not allowed to bounce the ball or to put it on the ground and pick it up again.

While the throw-in is being taken, the opponents must stay at least 3m from the thrower, except that they are permitted to stand immediately outside their goal area line even if they are less than 3m from the thrower.

Goal throw A goal throw is awarded when the ball completely crosses the goal line outside the goal after last being touched by the goalkeeper, except that a free throw is awarded if the goalkeeper deliberately plays the ball over his own goal line after gaining control of the ball.

A goal throw is also required if the ball comes to rest in the goal area, except that a free throw from the 9m line is awarded to the attacking team if a defending player deliberately plays the ball into his own goal area.

A goal throw is taken by the goalkeeper, who must throw the ball from the goal area out over the goal area line into the playing area. There is normally no whistle signal.

HANDBALL (TEAM) 3

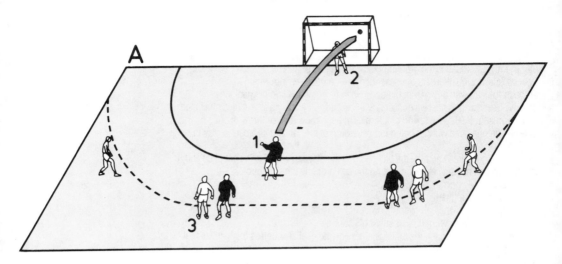

Free throw A free throw is awarded for:
a) illegal substitution (plus a suspension);
b) infringements by the goalkeeper (except where a penalty throw is specified);
c) infringements by court players in the goal area (unless a penalty throw is specified);
d) playing the ball incorrectly;
e) intentionally playing the ball across the goal line or side line;
f) passive play;
g) tackling infringements (plus disqualification in serious cases);
h) taking a throw-off incorrectly;
i) infringements at a throw-in;
j) infringements at a goal throw;
k) infringements at a free throw;
l) infringements at a penalty throw;
m) infringements at a referee's throw;
n) serious or repeated fouls (plus a suspension);
o) unsporting conduct (plus warning or disqualification).
A free throw is also used to restart play if one team has possession of the ball when play is interrupted without there being an infringement; the free throw is awarded to the team that had possession of the ball and is taken from where the ball was when play was interrupted.
A free throw is generally taken from the place where the infringement occurred. However, if the attacking team is awarded a free throw for an infringement by a defending player between the goal area line and the free throw line, the free throw is taken from the nearest point outside the free throw line. There is normally no whistle signal from the referee.
Once the player who is to take the free throw is in position and ready to throw, he is not permitted to bounce the ball or to put it down and pick it up again.
Players of the attacking team must remain outside their opponent's free throw line until the free throw is taken.
While the free throw is being taken, the opponents must stay at least 3m from the thrower, except that they are permitted to stand immediately outside their goal area line if the free throw is being taken on their free throw line.
Penalty throw (A) A penalty throw is awarded when:
a) an infringement in any part of the court interferes with a clear chance of scoring;
b) a court player enters his own goal area to gain an advantage over an attacking player who is in possession of the ball;
c) the ball touches the goalkeeper but does not completely enter the goal after having been deliberately played into the goal area by a teammate of the goalkeeper.
d) a goalkeeper reenters his goal area from the playing area when the ball is in his possession, or takes the ball into his goal area from on the ground outside it.

A penalty throw consists of a shot at goal and is to be taken within three seconds after a whistle signal by the referee. The player taking the throw (**1**) must not touch or cross the penalty throw line before the ball has left his hand. After the throw has been taken, the ball may not be played by any court player until it has touched the goalkeeper or the goal. While the throw is being taken, all players other than the player taking the throw and the defending goalkeeper (**2**) must be outside the free throw line. All players of the defending team (**3**) must be at least 3m from the thrower.

If a player of the attacking team touches or crosses the free throw line before the ball has left the thrower's hand, a free throw is awarded to the defending team.

If a defender crosses the free throw line, or the goalkeeper his goalkeeper's line, before the ball leaves the thrower's hand, the throw must be retaken unless a goal is scored.

Referee's throw (B) Play is restarted by a referee's throw if:
a) play is interrupted because both teams committed infringements simultaneously;
b) the ball touches the ceiling, or anything attached to it, above the court;
c) play is interrupted, without there being an infringement, when neither team has possession of the ball;
d) the end of a playing period is signaled prematurely and the players have already left the court.

The throw is taken by the court referee, who throws the ball vertically up in the air.

The throw is usually taken from where the ball was when play was interrupted. If the ball was between the free throw line and the goal area line the throw is taken from the nearest spot outside the free throw line. If a playing period ended too soon, the throw is taken from the center of the court.

There is usually no whistle signal, except when a playing period ended too soon.

While the throw is being taken, all but one player from each team must stay at least 3m from the referee taking the throw. The two players jumping for the ball at the throw must stand beside the referee, each on the side nearer to his own goal.

Warnings are given for:
a) infringements when tackling (usually only when infringements are repeated);
b) infringements when opponents are taking a throw;
c) unsporting behavior.

Suspensions are given for:
a) failing to put the ball down immediately a free throw is called;
b) faulty substitutions;
c) numerous infringements when tackling;
d) repeated infringements when opponents are taking throws;
e) repeated unsporting behavior.

Suspensions are for a period of two minutes, during which time the player's team must play at reduced strength. Suspended players must remain within the substitution area.

A player who receives his third suspenion is also disqualified.

Disqualifications are given for:
a) receiving a third suspension;
b) entering the court when not entitled to play;
c) assaults outside the playing court;
d) serious infringements when tackling;
e) extreme unsporting behavior, even by a team official.

A disqualified player or team official may take no further part in the game and must leave both the playing area and the substitution area.

The disqualification of a player on the playing court is always accompanied by a two minute suspension period, during which time the team must play at reduced strength. A substitute is permitted on the expiry of the suspension period.

Exclusions are given for assaults against opponents or referees on the playing court. An excluded player may take no further part in the game and must leave both the playing court and the substitution area. His team must play at reduced strength for the rest of the game.

Penalization of goalkeepers If a goalkeeper is suspended, disqualified, or excluded from play his team may replace him on the playing court with its reserve goalkeeper, but a court player must leave the court in his place.

HOCKEY (FIELD)

HISTORY

Evidence of games in which a ball was struck by curved sticks or clubs has survived from ancient Egypt, Greece and Rome as well as from medieval Europe. The modern game of field hockey, however, was broadly shaped in the 19th century and continues its development to the present day. The international governing body for the sport is the Fédération Internationale de Hockey (FIH), founded in 1924. Field hockey has been an Olympic sport for men since 1908 (1924 excepted) and for women since 1980.

SYNOPSIS

Two opposing teams are each allowed up to 11 players on the field of play at any one time. Players use a curved wooden stick to hit a hard, leather-covered white ball about the field of play with the objective of gaining ground as a prelude to scoring goals. As well as dribbling the ball, players use four basic types of shot: the hit, the push, the flick and the scoop. The game is won by the team that scores the greater number of goals in the time allowed.

The field hockey rules described here include a number of important experimental rules, notably affecting the starting and restarting of play. Use of certain experimental rules is currently mandatory, and most of these are expected to be adopted as official rules in September 1983.

PLAYING AREA AND EQUIPMENT

The pitch, usually on grass or artificial turf, measures 100×60yd. The side lines (**a**), goal lines (**b**) and center line (**c**) are marked with solid lines 3in wide. Two 25yd lines (**d**) are marked with broken lines. Lines 2yd long are marked across the center line and the 25yd lines, 5yd in from and parallel to the side lines (**e**).

Marks 12in long and parallel to the goal lines are drawn from each side line 16yd from the goal line (**f**). For corner hits, marks 5yd from each corner are drawn on the goal lines (**g**). For penalty corner hits, marks are drawn in from the goal line 5yd (**h**) and 10yd (**i**) from the outside edge of the nearer goal post. A spot 6in in diameter (**j**) is marked 7yd in front of the center of each goal.

Shooting circles (**k**) are drawn in front of the goals: a line 4yd long, parallel to and 16yd from each goal, is extended to the goal line by quarter circles centered at the goal posts. Flag posts, 4–5ft high, are placed at each corner and also parallel to and at least 1yd outside each end of the center line.

Goals consist of two perpendicular posts 4yd apart and touching the outer edge of the goal line, joined together by a horizontal crossbar 7ft from the ground. Goal posts and

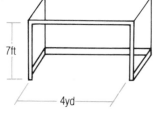

7ft

4yd

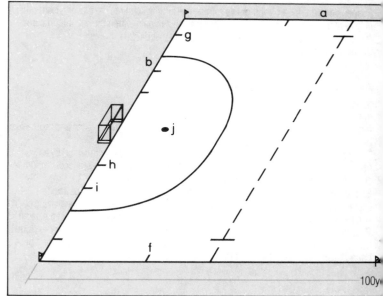

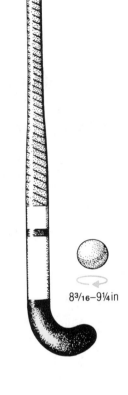

crossbar, painted white, are rectangular in shape, 2in wide and not more than 3in deep. Nets are attached to the goal posts and crossbar and to the ground behind the goal. Sideboards behind the goal posts must be at least 4ft long and no more than 18in high; backboards, also with a maximum height of 18in, must be 4yd long.

The stick has a flat face on its left-hand side; the usual style is illustrated here. The head is of wood, must have rounded edges, and must have no metal fittings, sharp edges or splinters. The stick must be narrow enough (including its binding) to pass through a ring with an interior diameter of 5.10cm. The minimum weight for a stick is 12oz. The maximum weight is 28oz.

The ball is white, and made of cork and twine covered in stitched or seamless leather. It has a circumference of $8^{13}/_{16}$–$9^{1}/_{4}$ in and weighs $5^{1}/_{2}$–$5^{3}/_{4}$oz. A ball of the specified size and weight but of different materials or color may be used by mutual agreement.

Dress Players wear shirts, shorts (or skirts), and socks in team colors, and boots on their feet. The wearing of dangerous objects or boots with metal studs, spikes or nails is prohibited. Goalkeepers wear special clothing: pads, kickers, gauntlet gloves, and masks.

PLAYERS AND OFFICIALS

Teams Each team may have only 11 players, including no more than one goalkeeper, on the field at any time. Each team is permitted to substitute up to two players during the game.

Substitution may take place only with the prior permission of an umpire during any stoppage of play other than for the award of a corner, a penalty corner, or a penalty stroke. No player who has been replaced by a substitute may return to the game and no substitute is permitted for a suspended player during his suspension.

Officials There are two umpires and may also be one or two timekeepers.

DURATION AND SCORING

Duration Unless otherwise agreed before the game, there are two playing periods of 35 minutes separated by a 5-minute interval. In no event may the interval exceed 10 minutes. Extra time may be added to a period for time lost through injury, substitution, or the taking of a penalty stroke. Teams change ends at the interval.

$8^{3}/_{16}$–$9^{1}/_{4}$ in

Scoring A goal is scored when the whole ball has passed over the goal line between the posts and under the crossbar, provided it has been hit by or glanced off the stick of an attacker within the shooting circle (and except as specially provided for in rules governing penalty corners and penalty strokes). It does not matter if the ball is subsequently played by or touches one or more defenders.

If the posts or crossbar are displaced during a game, the umpire decides whether or not a goal is valid.

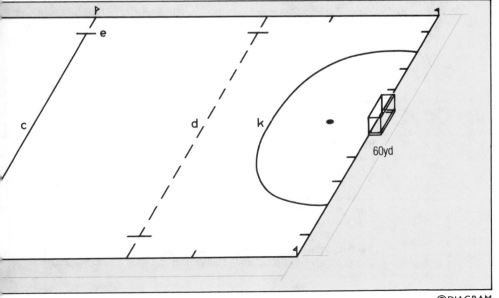

60yd

HOCKEY (FIELD) 2

STARTING PROCEDURES

Start of play Team captains toss for choice of ends or possession of the ball at the start of the game. The loser automatically has the second option.

Pass-back The pass-back has been introduced on a trial basis to replace the center bully at the start of the game, after half time, and after a goal. After half time it is taken by the team that did not pass-back at the start of the first half. After a goal it is taken by the team that conceded the goal.

Pass-backs are taken at the center of the field. All players must be in their own half of the field. The player taking the pass-back must not direct the ball across the center line. No other player may approach within 5yd of the ball while the pass-back is taken.

Bully (A) The bully is retained as a neutral means of restarting play after stoppages resulting from simultaneous fouls by two opponents, injury, etc. If the bully is to be taken within the shooting circle, it must be at least 5yd from the goal line.

To take a bully one player from each team stands squarely facing the side lines, with his own goal line to his right. The ball is placed on the ground between the two players, and each then taps his stick first on the ground on his own side of the ball, then—with the face of the stick—his opponent's stick above the ball. This is done three times, after which one of the players taking part in the bully must strike the ball before it goes into general play. During the bully all other players must stand at least 5yd from the ball and between it and their own goal line.

If there is any infringement, the bully is replayed. For persistent infringements, the umpire may award a free hit to the opposing team or, if the breaches are by a defender in the circle, he may award a penalty corner.

Push-in or hit-in (B) If the whole ball passes completely over the side line, play is restarted by a hit-in (experimental) or push-in by a member of the team that did not send the ball out of play.

The ball must be placed on the side line at the spot where it went out, and then hit-in or pushed-in without undue delay. The player taking the hit-in or push-in is not required to be wholly inside or outside the side line.

While the hit-in or push-in is being taken, all other players must be at least 5 yd from the ball. If they are not, the umpire may order the hit or push to be retaken. For persistent infringements of this type, the umpire may award a free hit.

A player who has taken a hit-in or push-in must not play the ball again, nor approach within playing distance of the ball, until it has been touched or been played by another player. Infringement is penalized by a free hit to the opponents.

Behind There are three methods of restarting play if the ball crosses the goal line without scoring.

a) A free hit from 16yd is awarded to the defending team if the ball was last played by an attacker, or if a defender more than 25yd from the goal line unintentionally sent it over the line. The hit is taken from a spot opposite where the ball crossed the goal line and not more than 16yd from that line.

b) A corner is awarded to the attacking team if the ball was unintentionally sent over the goal line by a defender within his 25yd area. Provisions are as for a penalty corner except that the push or hit is made from a spot on the goal line within 5yd of the corner flag nearer to the point where the ball crossed the goal line.

c) A penalty corner is awarded if a defender intentionally plays the ball over his goal line from any part of the field.

RULES OF PLAY

Playing the ball A player may play the ball only with the flat side of his stick (including the handle above the flat side). Under experimental rules, a player other than a goalkeeper is no longer permitted to stop the ball with his hand or to catch the ball and then immediately release it into play.

Although a player is permitted to tackle from the left, the ball must be played without previous interference with the opponent's stick or person.

A goalkeeper within his own circle is also permitted to kick the ball or to stop it with any part of his body. If the ball becomes lodged in the goalkeeper's pads or the clothing of any player or umpire, play restarts with a bully on the spot where the incident occurred.

Offside A player who is in an offside position may not play or attempt to play the ball, gain any advantage for his team, or influence the play of an opponent.

A player of the same team as the striker or pusher-in is in an offside position if, at the moment when the ball is hit or pushed in, he is in his opponents' half of the field and is nearer to his opponents' goal line than the ball without there being at least two opponents nearer to that line than he is. (For the purposes of this rule, players are deemed to be on the field of play even if they are outside the side line or behind the goal line.)

Fouls A player is not permitted:

a) to play the ball with the rounded side of his stick (**1**);

b) to take part in or interfere with the game unless he has his own stick in his hand;

c) to change his stick temporarily to take part in a free hit, penalty corner, penalty stroke, 16yd hit or corner;

d) to raise his stick in a manner that is dangerous, intimidating, or hampering to another player when approaching, attempting to play, playing, or stopping the ball;

e) to play a ball above the height of his shoulder with any part of his stick (**2**);

f) to hit wildly into an opponent or play or kick the ball in a way that is itself dangerous or is likely to lead to dangerous play;

g) to stop or deflect the ball on the ground or in the air with any part of his body in a way that is to his own or his team's advantage (**3**);

h) to use the foot or leg to support the stick in order to resist an opponent;

i) to hit, hook, hold, strike at, or interfere with an opponent's stick;

j) to charge, kick, shove, trip (**4**), strike at, or handle an opponent or his clothing;

k) to obstruct by running between an opponent and the ball (**5**) or position himself or his stick as an obstruction;

l) to waste time or behave in any other way that the umpire regards as misconduct.

© DIAGRAM

HOCKEY (FIELD) 3

PENALTIES

Free hit A free hit is awarded to the non-offending team for an infringement, and is usually taken where the offense occurred.

If the offense was by an attacker within the circle, the free hit is taken either from any spot within that circle, or from any spot within 16yd of the defenders' goal line on a line drawn through where the offense occurred and parallel to the side line.

If the offense was by an attacker outside the circle but within 16yd of the defenders' goal line, the free hit is taken from any spot within 16yd of the defenders' goal line on a line drawn through where the offense occurred and parallel to the side line.

For the free hit the ball must be stationary. The striker must then either push or hit it. If the striker hits at but misses the ball, the free hit may be taken again.

When the free hit is taken all players of the opposing team must be at least 5yd away from the ball. (If players deliberately try to delay a free hit by standing too close, the umpire may allow the free hit.)

After taking the free hit, the striker may not play the ball nor approach within playing distance until it has been touched or played by any other player.

For an infringement by the defending team within the circle, the penalty is a penalty corner or a penalty stroke to the attacking team. For a deliberate infringement by a defender within his own 25yd area the penalty is a penalty corner.

All other free hit infringements are penalized by a free hit to the opposing team.

Penalty corner (A) A penalty corner is awarded against defenders for:
a) deliberately playing the ball over the goal line;
b) an offense within the circle (unless a penalty stroke is given);
c) a deliberate foul within the 25yd line;

An attacking player pushes the ball along the ground or hits it from a spot on the goal line not less than 10yd from either goal post. He is not required to be either wholly inside or outside the field of play when taking the corner.

All other attackers stand with both sticks and feet outside the circle, in the field of play. Not more than six players of the defending team may stand with both sticks and feet behind their own goal line; other defenders must be beyond the center line.

No player may be within 5yd of the player taking the corner, and until the ball is pushed or hit no attacker may enter the circle and no defender may cross the goal line or center line.

If the player taking the penalty corner hits at but misses the ball, the penalty corner is taken again.

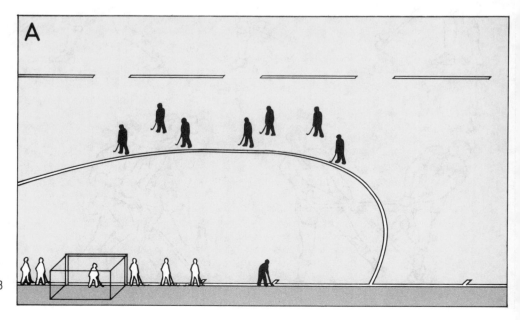

The player taking the penalty corner may not score directly from it. After taking the corner he must not approach within playing distance of the ball until it has been touched or played by any other player.

No shot at goal may be made from a penalty corner or from a deflection until the ball has first been stopped (not necessarily motionless) on the ground by an attacker or has touched the stick or person of a defender.

If an attacker enters the circle or a defender crosses the goal or center line before the penalty corner is taken, the umpire may order it to be retaken. For persistent positioning infringements, he may give a free hit against members of the attacking team or a penalty stroke against defenders. For all other penalty corner infringements, the penalty is a free hit to the defending team.

Penalty stroke (**B**) A penalty stroke is awarded to the opposing team if:
a) a defender deliberately fouls within the circle;
b) a defender in the circle prevents a probable goal by committing an unintentional foul;
c) defenders persistently commit positioning offenses at penalty corners.

The penalty stroke is taken by a member of the attacking team from the penalty spot 7yd in front of the goal. On the umpire's signal, he may make one step forward to push, flick or scoop the ball to any height. He may touch the ball only once after which he is not permitted to approach either the ball or the goalkeeper.

Until the attacker has struck the ball the goalkeeper must not leave the goal line nor move either foot. Nor may he touch the ball with any part of his stick when the ball is above the height of his shoulder.

Until the penalty stroke is taken all other players must be beyond the nearer 25yd line. If the goalkeeper illegally prevents the ball from entering the goal, a goal will be awarded except when the attacker induced the offense (for example by a feint to strike the ball).

If the ball halts inside the circle, lodges in the goalkeeper's pads, is caught by the goalkeeper, or passes outside the circle, the penalty stroke is ended.

Unless a goal is scored or awarded, the game restarts with a free hit by a defender from a spot 16yd in front of the center of the goal line.

If there is an infringement by an attacker during a penalty stroke, play resumes with a 16yd hit. For positioning offenses by defenders the umpire may order the stroke to be retaken.

Warnings and suspensions For rough or dangerous play or for misconduct, in addition to the appropriate penalty, the umpire may warn the offender, or may suspend him either temporarily (for at least 5 minutes) or for the rest of the game. A temporarily suspended player must remain behind his own goal, or such other place as is agreed, until the umpire that suspended him allows him to resume play.

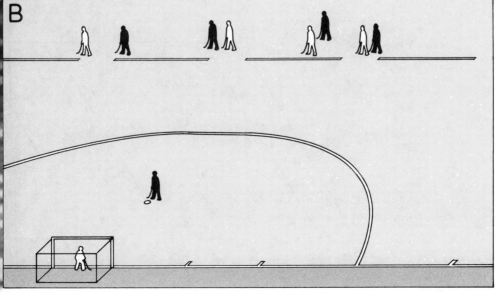

199

HOCKEY (ICE)

HISTORY
Forms of hockey have been played on ice since at least the sixteenth century, but the origins of modern ice hockey can probably be dated to 1860 when British soldiers stationed in Canada are recorded as having introduced the puck. By the 1880s and 1890s hockey was competing with lacrosse to be the national game of Canada. The game spread to the USA and Europe at the turn of the century, and the International Ice Hockey Federation (IIHF) was founded in 1908. Today, ice hockey is played in more than 30 countries, and is especially popular in Eastern Europe, North America, and Scandinavia. It has been an Olympic sport since 1920.

SYNOPSIS
Ice hockey is an extremely fast team game played on an ice rink. Players wearing skates use curved sticks to propel a vulcanized rubber disk, the puck, with the object of scoring more points than their opponents in the time allowed. Points are scored for goals and assists. A team may have no more than six players, including a goalkeeper, on the ice at any time; substitutions are permitted during stoppages and also while play is in progress. The high speed of play and the considerable body contact permitted result in many rule infractions; most penalties involve players being withdrawn from the ice to serve time on a penalty bench.

PLAYING AREA AND EQUIPMENT
The rink for World and European championships must be 56–61m long and 26–30m wide, and have corners rounded in the arc of a circle with a radius of 7–8.5m; different dimensions are permitted for other games.

The playing surface must be white, except for the following markings:

a) goal lines are marked in red across the entire width of the rink 4m from each end;

b) zone lines, 30cm wide, are marked in blue across the width of the rink and divide it into three equal zones (a neutral zone in the center, and two end zones);

c) a center line, 30cm wide, is marked in red across the center of the rink;

d) a goal crease in the form of a rectangle (with side lines 1.22m long marked 30cm outside each goal post) is marked by red lines in front of each goal and is considered to extend vertically to a height of 1.22m;

e) a referee's crease in the form of a semicircle with a 3m radius is marked directly in front of the penalty timekeeper's seat;

f) the center of the rink is marked by a circular blue spot, 30cm in diameter;

g) centered on the center spot is the center circle, with a radius of 4.5m and marked in blue;

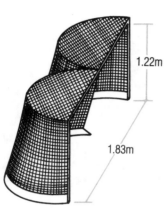

1.22m

1.83m

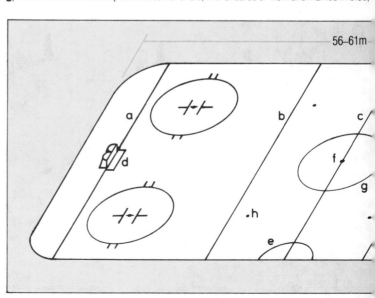

56–61m

h) four red face-off spots, 60cm in diameter, are marked within the neutral zone, with their centers 1.5m from the zone lines and 7m from an imaginary line extended out from the center of the goal;

i) two red face-off spots, 60cm in diameter and with 15cm long lines extending from them, are marked in each end zone, with their centers 6m from the goal line and 7m from an imaginary line extended out from the center of the goal;

j) end zone circles, marked in red and with a radius of 4.5m, are centered on the end zone face-off spots;

k) extending from the outer edge of both sides of the end zone face-off circles are 60cm long red lines, drawn parallel to the goal line and 5.5m and 6.5m away from it;

l) equidistant from the center of each end zone circle and 1.8m apart are two Ts, with lines 7.5cm wide, tops parallel to the goal lines and 2m long, and stems 1m long.

Except where specified otherwise in the rules, all lines must be 5cm wide.

Goals are positioned in the center of the goal lines, and must be fixed firmly.
Goals consist of posts, crossbar, and net, all of which must be of approved design and materials. Posts and crossbar, as well as the exterior surface of other supporting framework for the goal, must be painted red. The surface of the base plate inside the goal and the interior surface of supports other than the goal posts must be painted white. Interior measurements of the goal must be 1.22m high, 1.83m wide, and 0.6–1m deep at its deepest point.

The boards surrounding the rink must be 1.15–1.22m high, and made of either wood or plastic. They must be painted white, except that the goal lines, zone lines, and center lines are all continued up them. Plexiglass or wire screens may be positioned above the boards to protect the spectators.
All doors giving access to the playing surface must swing away from the ice surface.

Players' benches, one for each team, must be placed alongside the neutral zone on the same side of the rink. Each bench must have room for at least 14 persons. Only players in uniform, and not more than six officials per team, may occupy the benches.

Penalty bench One, or preferably two, benches must be provided alongside the neutral zone on the opposite side of the rink to the players' benches.

Signal and timing equipment includes:
a) a siren or other sound device to be used by timekeepers;
b) some form of electrical clock to inform players, officials, and spectators of all necessary time information, including time remaining to be played in any period and time remaining to be served by at least two penalized players per team;
c) electric lights behind the goals (red for a goal, green for the end of a period).

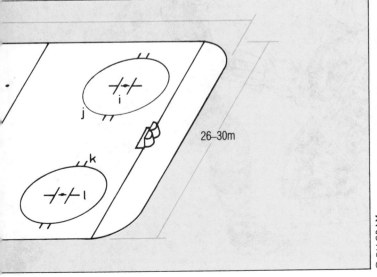

26–30m

© DIAGRAM

HOCKEY (ICE) 2

Sticks must be made of wood or other approved material and be without projections. There are detailed regulations governing the angle between the shaft and the blade. All blade edges must be beveled. Adhesive tape of any color may be wrapped around any part of the stick. No stick may measure more than 147cm from the heel to the end of the shaft. A stick used by players other than a goalkeeper (**a**) must measure no more than 32cm from the heel to the end of the blade; the blade at any point must be 5–7.5cm wide. A goalkeeper's stick (**b**) must measure no more than 39cm from the heel to the end of the blade; the blade must be no wider than 9cm except at the heel where the maximum width is 11.5cm.

The puck must be of vulcanized rubber or other approved material, and primarily black in color. It must be 2.54cm thick and 7.62cm in diameter, and must weigh 156–170g.

Skates Players other than the goalkeeper must wear skates equipped with safety heel tips. Speed skates, fancy skates, or any skates that might cause injury are prohibited.

Dress Players must wear sweaters, pants, stockings, and helmets in their team colors. All players must wear an individual number at least 25cm high on the back of their sweaters; captains must wear a "C" about 8cm high on the front of their sweaters.

Protective equipment other than gloves, headgear, or goalkeepers' leg guards must be worn entirely under the uniform.

All players, including goalkeepers, must wear approved headgear, with the chinstrap properly fastened. Facemasks are compulsory for goalkeepers, and for juniors in matches sanctioned by the IIHF.

The use of pads or protectors that might cause injury to another player is prohibited, as is the use of gloves from which all or part of the palm has been deliberately removed to permit use of the bare hand.

Goalkeepers' equipment, except for skates and stick, must be constructed solely to protect the head or body and must not give undue assistance in keeping goal. Leg guards must not exceed 25cm in width when on the goalkeeper's legs.

a 147cm

32cm

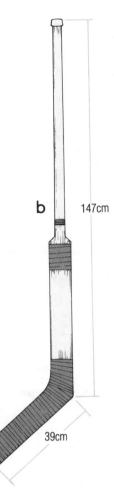

b 147cm

39cm

2.54cm

7.62cm

PLAYERS AND OFFICIALS

Players A maximum of 18 players, plus two goalkeepers, is permitted per team. A team may have no more than six players, including a goalkeeper, on the ice at any time; this maximum is reduced when players are serving penalties that do not allow for substitution.

Before the start of the game, team managers or coaches must indicate to the referee or official scorer the names of all players and goalkeepers eligible to play in the game, the names of the captain and an alternate captain, and the names of the players in the starting line-up.

A team may have only one goalkeeper on the ice at any time; a second goalkeeper must at all times be fully dressed and equipped for play. If any other player is substituted for a goalkeeper, he is not normally given goalkeepers' privileges.

Only the captain, or his alternate if he is not available, may discuss with the referee any questions relating to the interpretation of rules. No goalkeeper, playing coach, or playing manager is allowed to be captain or alternate captain.

Change of players A team is not permitted to change its starting line-up, or its playing line-up on the ice, until the game is actually in progress.

Following a stoppage of play, the visiting team must promptly place a line-up on the ice ready for play, and may then make no further substitutions until play is resumed. Having seen the visitors' line-up the home team is permitted to make any substitutions it wants provided that the game is not thereby delayed.

Players may be changed from the players' bench at any time during play, provided that the player or players leaving the ice are at the players' bench and out of play before any change is made.

A player on the penalty bench, who is to be changed when his penalty expires, must proceed by way of the ice to his own players' bench before any change may be made. Substitution for a goalkeeper is permitted as for other players, except that a goalkeeper replaced during a stoppage of play is not permitted to reenter the game until the next stoppage of play. Substitute goalkeepers are not allowed a warm-up.

Injured players If a player other than a goalkeeper is injured or becomes ill, he may retire from the game and be replaced by a substitute; play must continue without the teams leaving the ice.

If a goalkeeper is injured or becomes ill, he must be ready to resume play at once or be replaced by a substitute goalkeeper. If a team's two goalkeepers are incapacitated and unable to play, the team is given 10 minutes to prepare and dress another player to take over as goalkeeper; this player is then subject to all goalkeepers' rules.

If a penalized player has been injured, he may go immediately to the dressing room; a substitute must replace him on the penalty bench if a minor, major, or match penalty is to be served. A player replaced in these circumstances is not permitted to return to the game until his penalty has expired.

If an injury prevents a player from continuing play or from going to his players' bench, play is stopped at once if the injured player's team had possession of the puck but were not in a scoring position. If the opposing team were in possession of the puck when the injury occurred, play continues until the injured player's team gains possession. Note, however, that play may always be stopped immediately if a referee and/or linesman consider an injury to be sufficiently serious.

Officials For international matches one referee and two linesmen are compulsory; national federations are permitted to use two referees and no linesmen for matches completely under their own jurisdiction.

Other required officials are a game timekeeper, a penalty timekeeper, an official scorer, and two goal judges.

HOCKEY (ICE) 3

DURATION AND SCORING

Duration A game consists of three 20-minute periods of actual playing time, separated by 15-minute intermissions.

If any unusual delay occurs within five minutes of the end of the first or second periods, the referee may order the next intermission to be taken at once and the balance of that playing period to be added to the next one.

Scoring A team scores one point for each goal or assist. The team scoring the greater number of goals in the time allowed wins the game. If the score is equal after the three regular periods, the game is generally a tie (subject to national regulations).

A goal is scored when the puck legally and completely crosses the goal line, between the goal posts and below the crossbar. In certain cases where an offense prevents a player from scoring, a goal is awarded by the referee to the non-offending team.

Assists may be awarded by the referee to players taking part in the play immediately preceding the scoring of a goal. A maximum of two assists may be awarded on any goal, but any player may score only one point at a time.

A goal is scored if the puck:

a) is put into the goal by the stick of an attacking player;

b) is put into the goal in any way by a defending player (no assists given);

c) is kicked by an attacking player and is deflected into the goal by any defender except the goalkeeper (no assists given);

d) is shot by an attacking player and enters the goal after being deflected off a teammate's person.

A goal is not allowed if the puck:

a) is kicked, thrown, or otherwise deliberately directed into the goal by any means other than by a stick;

b) is deflected directly into the goal off an official;

c) enters the goal if an attacking player was standing within or on the lines of the goal crease, or had his stick within the goal crease, before the puck entered the crease (except when the player was caused to enter the goal crease by being physically interfered with by the action of a defending player and did not have sufficient time to leave the crease before the puck entered it).

STARTING PROCEDURES

Choice of ends The home team has the choice of ends at the start, except that if both players' benches are on the same side of the rink the home team begins by defending the goal nearest its own bench. Teams change ends after each period.

Start of play Each period begins with a face-off at the center; a face-off at the center is also held to restart play after a goal. Face-offs at other points are used to restart play after stoppages.

Face-off procedure The referee or linesman (**a**) "faces" the puck by dropping it on the ice between the sticks of the two players facing-off.

The players facing-off (**b, c**) must stand squarely facing their opponents' goal line, about one stick length apart, with their stick blades touching the ice.

At a face-off in an end zone circle, the players taking part must stand within, but not touching the lines of, the T, as shown. Their stick blades must be touching the ice, in contact with the spot.

During a face-off, players other than the two taking part must be outside the circle, at least 4.5m away from the players facing-off, and onside.

If a player who is to face-off fails to position himself promptly and correctly, the referee or linesman may order him out of the face-off; he must be replaced by a team member then on the ice.

If a player who is to face-off fails to position himself promptly and correctly after a warning, the official may face the puck without waiting for him to do so.

If players are in the wrong position at a face-off, the referee or linesman will allow play to continue if the non-offending team gained possession of the puck; otherwise he will order the face-off to be retaken. A second violation by the same team during the same face-off is penalized by a minor penalty to the player committing the second violation.

A player taking part in a face-off must not contact his opponent's body with his own body or stick, except in the course of playing the puck after the face-off ends; a violation of this rule is penalized by a minor penalty to the player or players responsible for the physical contact.

Face-offs after stoppages are located as follows.

If a rule is infringed or a stoppage of play is caused by an attacker in his attacking zone, a face-off is held at the nearest face-off spot in the neutral zone.

If a rule is infringed by players of both teams, a face-off is held where the puck was when play was stopped.

If a stoppage occurs between the end face-off spots and that end of the rink, the puck is faced-off at the end face-off spot on the side where the stoppage occurs, except where the rules specifically state otherwise.

No face-off may be held within 6m of the goal or nearer to the sideboards than the end zone and neutral zone face-off spots.

If the puck is deflected directly into the goal off or by an official, a face-off is held at either of the face-off spots in that end zone.

If the game is stopped for any reason not specifically covered in the rules, a face-off is held where the puck was last played.

Refusing to start play If, when ordered to do so by the referee, a team fails to go on the ice and start play within two minutes, the game is forfeited and the case reported to the proper authorities for further action.

If, when both teams are on the ice, one team fails to start or resume play within 30 seconds of receiving a warning from the referee, the offending team is given a bench minor penalty and the case reported to the proper authorities.

HOCKEY (ICE) 4

A

PLAYING RULES

Puck in motion The puck must be kept in motion at all times.

A team in its own defense area may carry the puck behind its own goal once; otherwise it must advance the puck toward its opponents' goal unless it is prevented from doing so by its opponents' actions. For a first infringement, a warning is given to the team captain, and a face-off is held at either face-off spot adjacent to the goal of the offending team. For a second infringement in the same period by a member of the same team, a minor penalty is imposed on the second offender.

Only if his team has fewer players on the ice than the opposing team, may a player beyond his defense zone pass or carry the puck back into that zone with the purpose of delaying the game. For an infringement, a face-off is held at the nearest end face-off spot in the offending team's defense zone.

Any player who holds, freezes, or plays the puck with his stick, skates, or body along the boards in such a way that a stoppage is caused, is given a minor bench penalty, unless he was actually being checked by an opponent.

Kicking the puck (A) The puck may be kicked in all zones, but a goal may not be scored from a kick by an attacking player. However, if an attacker kicks the puck and it is deflected into the goal by a defender other than the goalkeeper, the goal is allowed.

Handling the puck (B) A player may push the puck along the ice with his hand, or may use his open hand to stop or "bat" a puck in the air. However, if the referee considers that a player uses such actions deliberately to direct the puck to a teammate, a face-off is held at the appropriate face-off spot. Also, if the puck enters the goal after being batted by an attacking player and deflected off any player or goalkeeper, the goal is disallowed.

A minor penalty is incurred if:

a) a goalkeeper holds the puck in his hand(s) for more than three seconds, or in any way that the referee considers causes a stoppage of play;

b) a goalkeeper throws the puck forward toward his opponents' goal and it is first played by a teammate;

c) a goalkeeper deliberately drops the puck into his pads or onto the goal net;

d) a player other than the goalkeeper closes his hand on the puck;

e) a defender other than a goalkeeper uses his hands to pick up the puck from the ice (except that if the puck is within the goal crease at the time of the offense, the non-offending team is awarded a penalty shot).

Puck out of bounds If the puck leaves the playing area or strikes any obstacle above the playing surface other than the boards, glass, or wire, a face-off is held where the puck was shot or deflected, except when the rules specifically state otherwise.

If the puck comes to rest on the top of the boards, it is considered still in play and may be played legally with the hand or stick.

Puck unplayable If the puck is unplayable through being lodged in the goal netting or frozen against the goal between opposing players:

a) a face-off is held at the nearest end zone face-off spot; or

b) if the referee considers that the stoppage was caused by a player of the attacking team, a face-off is held in the neutral zone.

A minor penalty is imposed on a goalkeeper who deliberately drops the puck onto the goal netting to cause a stoppage of play.

Puck out of sight If the referee is unable to see the puck because of a scramble or because a player accidentally falls on top of it, he will stop play at once. Except when the rules specifically state otherwise, play is restarted by a face-off where play was stopped.

Puck striking an official If the puck strikes an official anywhere on the rink, play is stopped only if the puck has entered the goal, in which case a face-off is held at the nearest end zone face-off spot.

Illegal puck If during play another puck appears on the ice, play continues with the legal puck until the play in progress is completed by a change of possession.

Broken stick A player other than the goalkeeper may play without a stick, or with a broken stick if he drops the broken portion. He must not receive a stick thrown onto the ice for him; he must collect a new stick from his team bench.

A goalkeeper may continue to play with a broken stick until a stoppage of play, or until a teammate legally hands him a replacement. He must not receive a stick thrown onto the ice, nor may he go to his team bench to obtain a new stick during a stoppage of play.

A player or goalkeeper is given a minor penalty for an infringement; a bench minor penalty is also given if anyone on the bench throws a stick onto the ice.

Interference by spectators If a player is being interfered with by a spectator, play is stopped and restarted by a face-off where the puck was last played at the time of the stoppage; if the team of the player being interfered with is in possession of the puck, the stoppage is delayed until the end of that play.

If objects are thrown onto the ice and interfere with the progress of the game, play is stopped for their removal and a face-off held where play stopped.

HOCKEY (ICE) 5

Passing (A) The puck may be passed by any player to a teammate in any zone, except that it is a passing violation if a pass from a player in his defense zone (**1**) is received by a player (**2**) who precedes the puck across the center line.

There is no passing violation if, in the situation described above:

a) the puck goes on to cross the goal line and there is an icing violation (see below);

b) the puck touches any player's person, skates, or stick between the passing player's defense zone and the center line.

For a passing violation, play is stopped and restarted by a face-off where the pass originated, or at the nearest face-off spot.

If the linesman makes an error in calling a passing infringement, the puck is faced-off at the center face-off spot.

Icing the puck (B) The puck is "iced" if a player (**1**) hits or deflects the puck from behind the center line to beyond his opponents' goal line, and the puck is then first touched by a defender (**2, 3**) other than the goalkeeper (**4**).

Icing is not called and play continues:

a) if the attacking team has fewer players on the ice than its opponents;

b) if the puck entered the goal (in which case the goal is allowed);

c) if an onside player of the team that hit the puck is the first to touch it;

d) if the puck goes beyond the goal line directly from a face-off;

e) if, before reaching the goal line, the puck passes through any part of the goal crease;

f) if, before reaching the goal line, the puck touches the person, skates, or stick of an opponent other than the goalkeeper;

g) if, before or after crossing the goal line, the puck touches the person, skates, or stick of the defending goalkeeper;

h) if an official considers that an opponent other than the goalkeeper could have played the puck but did not do so (except that the referee will order a face-off at the end zone face-off spot nearest the offending team's goal if he considers that failure to play the puck was deliberate).

Following an icing infringement, play is stopped and the puck is then faced-off at the end face-off spot of the offending team nearest to where they last touched the puck.

If the linesman makes an error in calling an icing infringement, the puck is faced-off at the center face-off spot.

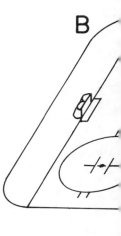

Offside (C) Players of an attacking team (**1**) may not precede the puck into their attacking zone; an attacker is deemed offside only if both his skates are completely within the attacking zone and beyond the blue line when the puck passes completely into that zone.

If an attacking player (**2**) is offside but a member of the defending team (**3**) intercepts the puck at or near the blue line and then passes or carries it into the neutral zone, the "offside" is waived and play continues. If a player is in his attacking zone when an opponent carries or passes the puck back into it, the "offside" is waived.

For an offside violation, play is stopped and restarted by a face-off. If the puck was carried over the blue line at the time of the violation, the face-off is held at the nearest neutral zone face-off spot to where the puck crossed the line. If the puck was hit over the blue line, the face-off is held where the hit was made.

If the linesman considers that a player deliberately caused an off-side play, the face-off is held at the end face-off spot in the offending team's defending zone.

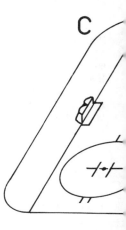

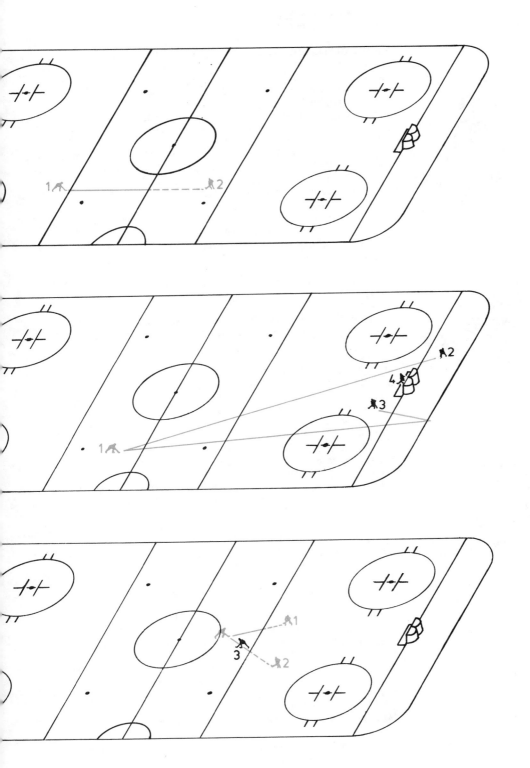

HOCKEY (ICE) 6

FOULS AND PENALTIES

Fouls In addition to prohibitions mentioned in specific playing rules, a player is not permitted:

a) to hold or carry any part of his stick above normal shoulder height (**1**), or to bat the puck above normal shoulder height (high sticks);

b) to throw or shoot his stick or any other object in the direction of the puck;

c) to intefere with or impede the progress of an opponent not in possession of the puck;

d) to impede or seek to impede the progress of an opponent by "hooking" with his stick;

e) to impede or seek to impede the progress of an opponent by "slashing" with his stick;

f) to knock or shoot any abandoned or broken stick, an illegal puck, or any other debris toward an opposing puck carrier in such a way that he might be distracted;

g) deliberately to fall onto the puck or to gather it into his body (unless he is a goalkeeper within his own crease area);

h) deliberately to knock the stick out of an opponent's hand, or to prevent a player who has dropped his stick or any other piece of equipment from regaining possession of it;

i) to check an opponent while having both hands on his stick and no part of the stick on the ice (cross-checking) (**2**);

j) to hold an opponent with his hands or stick or in any other way (**3**);

k) to trip an opponent with his stick, knee, foot, arm, hand, or elbow;

l) to kick or attempt to kick another player;

m) to elbow or knee an opponent;

n) to spear or butt-end, or attempt to spear or butt-end, an opponent with his stick;

o) to cause an opponent to be thrown violently against the boards (board-checking or boarding);

p) to initiate or join in fisticuffs or roughing;

q) to injure deliberately, or to attempt to injure, an opponent or team official;

r) to delay the game unnecessarily;

s) to leave his players' bench or the penalty bench except legally to enter the play, at the end of a period, or on the expiry of a penalty;

t) to challenge or dispute the rulings of, or show disrespect toward, a game official;

u) to interfere physically with a game official;

v) to interfere physically with a spectator.

Types of penalty are as follows: minor penalty; bench minor penalty; major penalty; misconduct penalty; match penalty; and penalty shot.

The severity of the penalty imposed depends upon the offense committed, and in some cases also upon where and when it was committed. Most penalties involve serving time on the penalty bench.

Special rules apply when a goalkeeper is penalized, and where an offense is committed by a player who has two teammates already on the penalty bench.

Calling of penalties If an offense is committed by a player in possession of the puck, the referee will stop play at once and impose the penalty.

If an offense is commited by a player not in possession of the puck, the referee raises his arm to signify a penalty but waits for the end of the play before imposing it.

If the penalty or penalties to be imposed are minor and a goal is scored by the non-offending side while the play is being completed, the first minor penalty is not imposed but all other minor, major, or match penalties are imposed as usual.

Minor penalty For a minor penalty, the offender is ruled off the ice for two minutes, with no substitution permitted.

If the opposing team scores a goal while a team is "short-handed" because one or more players are serving a minor penalty, one such penalty terminates automatically.

Bench minor penalty Rules are as for a minor penalty, except the team manager or coach, through the captain, designates a player other than a goalkeeper to serve it.

Major penalty For his first major penalty in a game, an offender is ruled off the ice for five minutes, with no substitution permitted. For committing a second major penalty in the same game, the player is ruled off the ice for the balance of the playing time but after five minutes may be replaced by a substitute.

Misconduct penalty Depending on the offense, the referee may impose a misconduct penalty, a game misconduct penalty, or a gross misconduct penalty.

For a misconduct penalty, the offender is ruled off the ice for 10 minutes, with immediate substitution permitted. After the penalty expires he must wait on the penalty bench until the next stoppage of play.

For a game misconduct penalty, the offender may take no further part in the game and is sent immediately to the dressing room; immediate substitution is permitted.

For a gross misconduct penalty, the offender is suspended from taking part in any further games until his case is heard by the proper authorities.

Match penalty For a match penalty, the offender may take no further part in the game and is sent immediately to the dressing room; substitution is permitted after five minutes' playing time. After receiving a match penalty, a player is banned from further games until his case is dealt with by the proper authorities.

Penalty shot Depending on the offense committed, a penalty shot is taken either by the player against whom a foul was made, or by a player of the non-offending team selected by the captain from among the players on the ice at the time of the offense.

After announcing who is to take the shot, the referee places the puck on the center face-off spot. The announced player then plays the puck from the center in an attempt to score against the opposing goalkeeper; all other players must withdraw to the sides of the rink and behind the center line while the shot is being taken.

Only a player designated as a goalkeeper or alternate goalkeeper may defend against the penalty shot; a goalkeeper removed from the ice before the offense occurred is permitted to return to the ice before the shot is taken. The goalkeeper must remain in his crease until the player taking the penalty shot has touched the puck; he may attempt to stop the shot in any way except by throwing his stick or another object.

The player taking the shot is allowed to make one circle in his defense zone after taking possession of the puck. He must then proceed to his opponents' goal line and make a single shot at the goal. No goal can be scored by a second shot from a rebound of any kind, and the shot is considered complete as soon as the puck crosses the goal line.

If a goal is scored from a penalty shot, play resumes in the usual way with a face-off at the center. If no goal is scored, the puck is faced-off at either of the end face-off spots in the zone where the shot was taken.

If the goalkeeper throws his stick or another object to defend his goal during a penalty shot, a goal is awarded to the opponents. If the goalkeeper commits any other offense, the referee allows the shot to be completed; if a goal is scored it is counted, if no goal is scored the penalty shot is retaken.

Goalkeepers' penalties A goalkeeper incurs a minor penalty if he leaves the immediate vicinity of his crease during an altercation, or participates in the play in any way when beyond the center line.

If a goalkeeper is given a minor, major, or misconduct penalty, he is permitted to remain on the ice while his time on the penalty bench is served by a teammate, chosen by the team manager or coach from among the players on the ice at the time of the offense.

If a goalkeeper incurs a game misconduct penalty or a match penalty, his place must be taken by the substitute goalkeeper or another member of his team, who is allowed 10 minutes in which to dress in the goalkeeper's full equipment.

Delayed penalties If a player is penalized while two teammates are serving penalties, his penalty time commences only when the penalty time of one of the others ends; the third player must go to the penalty bench at once, but a substitute is permitted for him on the ice until his penalty time begins.

After such substitution has been made, none of the three penalized players may return to the ice on the expiry of their penalties until play has been stopped.

JUDO

HISTORY

Judo was developed in Japan by Dr Jigoro Kano (1860–1938), who in 1882 founded the Kodokan, a club that specialized in teaching a new form of ju-jitsu, which Kano called judo, meaning "the gentle way." Judo was taken to the USA by Yamashita, a pupil of Kano's, in 1902. It did not become popular in Europe until Gunji Koizumi (1885–1965) opened a club—the Budokwai—in London in 1918. The world governing body, the International Judo Federation, was founded in 1951. Judo has been an Olympic sport for men since 1964; the first world championships for women were held in 1980.

SYNOPSIS

A sport of worldwide popularity with over 8 million participants, judo still uses the original Japanese terminology. Two participants *(judoka)*, each wearing judo suits *(judogi)* fight each other on a mat *(tatami)* according to set rules. The participants initially attempt to throw each other; groundwork *(ne-waza)* follows if a throw does not bring outright victory or in any other situation in which one or both contestants attempt to apply joint locks to each other or to hold an opponent to the ground for 30 seconds. Strangleholds and locks can be applied in the standing position or in groundwork. The main difference between judo and ju-jitsu is that Dr Kano introduced into judo the principle of *tskuri-komi*, breaking an opponent's balance before trying to throw him.

COMPETITION AREA AND EQUIPMENT

Competition area This must be a minimum of 14×14m and a maximum of 16×16m, covered by green matting. A central square (**a**), termed the contest area, is bounded by a danger zone (**b**) marked in a different color, usually red, and approximately 1m wide. The contest area and danger zone together must be no less than 9×9m and no more than 10×10m. The safety zone (**c**) outside them must be at least 2.5m wide.

Contests must be fought within the contest area (including the danger zone). Techniques applied when one or both contestants are outside the contest area are not recognized. A contestant is considered to be outside the contest area if:

a) he has even one foot outside the contest area when standing;

b) he has more than half his body outside the contest area during sacrifice throws *(sutemi-wazi)* or groundwork.

However, if one contestant throws his opponent outside the contest area but himself stays within it long enough for the effectiveness of the technique to be clearly apparent, the technique is recognized.

After a call of *"osaekomi"* (holding), the referee will allow a hold to continue providing that at least one contestant has any part of his body touching the contest area.

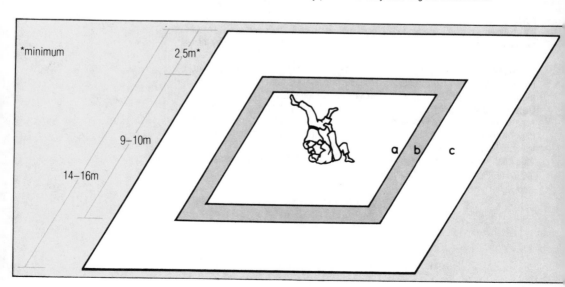

*minimum

2.5m*

9–10m

14–16m

a b c

Dress The costume *(judogi)* must be white or off-white. The jacket must cover the hips and is generally slit about 18cm up each side. It has continuous strengthened lapels about 4cm wide and reinforced stitching at the armpits and below the waistline. Sleeves must be loose and cover more than half the forearm.

Trousers must be loose and cover over half the lower leg.

The belt, colored according to the contestant's proficiency level, fastens the jacket at the waist and is long enough to go twice around the body. It is tied with a large square knot and its ends are about 20–30cm long.

In international contests a red or white tape is tied over the regulation belt to distinguish between contestants; in some tournaments only red or white belts are used.

CONTESTANTS AND OFFICIALS

Grading Participants are graded according to their level of proficiency. There are two groups of grades: *kyu* (pupil) grades and *dan* (degree) grades. Beginners wear a white belt and may then progress to grades denoted by different colored belts (see table).

Weight categories Contestants are divided for most competitions according to weight categories (see table); open contests are now less common than formerly.

Officials Contests are governed by a referee, who generally remains within the contest area and conducts the bouts, and two judges, who assist the referee from their positions at opposite corners of the safety area.

THE CONTEST

Duration Contests shall last for a minimum of 3 minutes and maximum of 20 minutes, to be arranged in advance.

The contest may be temporarily halted on the call of *"matte"* (wait) in the following cases: if the contestants are about to leave the contest area; after a foul; if there is illness or injury; to adjust the costume; or to disentangle unproductive holds.

Start The contestants in the contest area face each other about 4m apart, make a standing bow, and begin when the referee calls *"hajime"* (begin).

Entry into groundwork Contestants begin in a standing position. They may change to groundwork *(ne-waza)* as follows, provided the transitional technique is judged to be continuous:

a) after obtaining some result by a throwing technique;

b) after an opponent falls to the ground or is unbalanced and liable to fall to the ground;

c) after skilfully taking an opponent to the ground by a technique that does not fully qualify as a throwing technique;

d) after obtaining considerable effect with a stranglehold or lock in the standing position.

Grades (international)		Weight categories	
Kyu	**Dan**	**Men**	**Women**
5th: yellow belt	1st-5th: black belt	under 60kg	under 48kg
4th: orange belt	6th-8th: red and white belt	under 65kg	under 52kg
3rd: green belt	9th-11th: red belt	under 71kg	under 56kg
2nd: blue belt	12th: white belt	under 78kg	under 61kg
1st: brown belt		under 86kg	under 66kg
		under 95kg	under 72kg
		over 95kg	over 72kg

©DIAGRAM

4m

JUDO 2

Scoring A contest is judged on the basis of throwing techniques *(nage-waza)* or grappling techniques *(katame-waza)*. The referee may award: *ippon* (a full point); *waza-ari* (almost *ippon*); *yuko* (almost *waza-ari*); *koka* (almost *yuko*). Two *waza-aris* equal *ippon*, but no number of *yukos* or *kokas* ever equals *waza-ari*.

A contestant who scores *ippon* wins outright. Similarly two *waza-aris* or one *waza-ari* plus a penalty of *keikoku* (warning) against the opponent brings outright victory.

If two contestants simultaneously merit *ippon* the contest ends at once in a draw *(hiki-wake)*. A draw is also given if at the end of the contest the contestants have not scored or have equal scores, and are judged equal in attitude and skill.

A superiority win *(yusei-gachi)* is generally given:
a) for a score of *waza-ari* or a penalty of *keikoku* (warning);
b) for a score of *yuko* or a penalty of *chui* (caution);
c) for a score of *koka* or a penalty of *shido* (note);
d) for a recognizable difference in attitude and skill even though scores are equal.

Ippon, is awarded:
a) when a contestant throws his opponent largely on his back with considerable force or speed (**A**);
b) when one contestant holds the other for 30 seconds (**B**) after the referee calls *"osaekomi"* (holding) without a call of *"toketa"* (hold broken);
c) when one contestant says *"maitta"* (I give up);
d) when one contestant indicates that he wishes to give up by tapping his own or his opponent's body or the mat with his hand or foot twice or more;
e) when there is an effective stranglehold or lock.

Waza-ari is awarded:
a) when a throwing technique does not quite merit the score of *ippon* (for example if it lacks sufficient force or speed or if the opponent is not completely on his back);
b) when a hold lasts more than 25 but less than 30 seconds.

Yuko is awarded:
a) when a throwing technique does not quite merit the score of *waza-ari:*
b) for a hold of more than 20 but less than 25 seconds.

Koka is awarded:
a) when a contestant makes an unsuccessful throwing technique but with some force or speed puts his opponent onto his side, thigh(s), stomach, or buttocks;
b) for a hold of more than 10 but less than 20 seconds.

Result At the end of an undecided contest the referee places the competitors in the starting position and calls *"hantei."* The judges then raise a white or red flag to indicate the winner or both flags for a draw. The referee adds his decision and the result is given according to the majority.

INFRINGEMENTS AND PENALTIES

Categories of infringement There are four categories of infringement—slight, moderate, serious, and very serious—and penalties are graded accordingly.

Slight infringements, normally penalized by *shido* (note):
a) avoiding taking hold of an opponent to prevent action in the contest;
b) adopting an excessively defensive attitude (**1**);
c) while in the standing position, continually holding the opponent's collar, lapel or sleeve on the same side with both hands, or his belt or the bottom of his jacket with either or both hands, or continually holding the opponent's sleeve end for a defensive purpose;
d) inserting finger(s) inside the opponent's sleeve or the bottom of his trousers, or grasping the fabric of his sleeve;
e) preventing action by standing continually with the fingers of one or both hands interlocked;
f) disarranging own costume or untying or retying the trouser belt without the referee's permission;
g) from a standing position, taking hold of the opponent's leg, foot, or trouser leg unless simultaneously attempting a throwing technique;
h) winding the end of the belt or jacket around any part of the opponent's body;
i) taking the opponent's costume in the mouth;
j) putting a hand, arm, foot, or leg directly on the opponent's face;

k) while lying on the back, failing to release a hold with the legs around the neck and armpit of the opponent when the opponent stands or gets to his knees in a position from which he could lift up the contestant.

Moderate infringements, normally penalized by *chui* (caution):
a) applying *dojime* (leg scissors) to the opponent's trunk, head, or neck;
b) kicking with the knee or foot the opponent's hand or arm to make him release his grasp;
c) putting a foot or leg in the opponent's belt, collar, or lapel;
d) bending back the opponent's finger(s) to break his grip;
e) pulling down the opponent to start groundwork (**2**);
f) leaving the contest area from a standing position while applying a technique started within the contest area.

Serious infringements, normally penalized by *keikoku* (warning):
a) attempting to apply any technique outside the contest area;
b) intentionally forcing an opponent to go outside the contest area, or going outside the contest area for any reason except while applying a technique started in the contest area or as a result of the opponent's action;
c) attempting to throw an opponent by *kawazu-gake* (a technique involving winding one leg around the opponent's leg and falling backward onto him) (**3**);
d) applying joint locks anywhere except the elbow joint;
e) endangering the opponent's spine or neck or making any other action that might injure or endanger the opponent;
f) lifting off the mat an opponent who is lying on his back in order to drive him back into the mat;

g) sweeping the opponent's supporting leg from the inside when he is applying a sweeping technique (**4**);
h) falling directly to the ground while performing or attempting to perform certain techniques;
i) disregarding the referee;
j) making unnecessary calls or derogatory remarks or gestures;
k) doing anything contrary to the spirit of judo.

Very serious infringements, normally penalized by *hansoku-make* (disqualification):
a) "diving" head first into the mat by bending forward and downward while performing certain techniques;
b) falling back deliberately when an opponent is clinging to the back and when either contestant controls the other's movement (**5**).

Penalties Four types of penalty, corresponding to the four categories of infringement, are treated as follows:
a) if *shido* (note) is announced to one contestant, the other scores *koka*;
b) if *chui* (caution) is announced to one, the other scores *yuko*;
c) if *keikoku* (warning) is announced to one, the other scores *waza-ari*;
d) if *hansoku-make* (disqualification) is announced to one, the other scores *ippon*.
In general, repetition of an infringement results in a penalty in the next highest category. Before awarding *keikoku* or *hansoku-make*, the referee must consult his judges and obtain a majority decision.

LACROSSE (MEN'S)

HISTORY
The original form of lacrosse, known as baggataway, was played by North American Indians as a means of training for war; as many as a thousand players would take part on each side, and games could last for several days. French settlers in Canada christened the game lacrosse, from the resemblance of the playing stick to a bishop's crozier ("la crosse"). The first national governing body was formed in Canada in 1867; touring Canadian exhibition teams were responsible for introducing the game to the rest of the world in the latter part of the nineteenth century. The international governing body for the men's game is the International Lacrosse Federation.

SYNOPSIS
Men's lacrosse is a field game played by two teams of ten players each; the team scoring the greater number of goals in the time allowed is the winner. The players use netted sticks (crosses) to carry, throw, or bat the ball around the field.

PLAYING AREA AND EQUIPMENT
The playing field is a rectangle, 110yd long and 60yd wide, with a flag marker at each corner. The white lines marking the pitch are 2in wide, with the exception of the 4in wide center line. The pitch markings are:

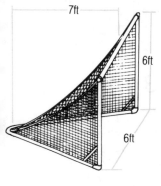

a) end lines;
b) side lines;
c) center line, perpendicular to the side lines and equidistant from the end lines;
d) center, a point on the center line equidistant from the side lines and marked with a cross;
e) wing areas, parallel to the side lines and 20yd from the center of the field, and extending 10yd on each side of the center line;
f) goal lines, 6ft long lines parallel to and 15yd from the end lines, with their midpoints equidistant from the side lines;
g) goal creases, circles with a radius of 9ft centered on the midpoints of the goal lines;
h) goal area lines, parallel to and 20yd from the center line;

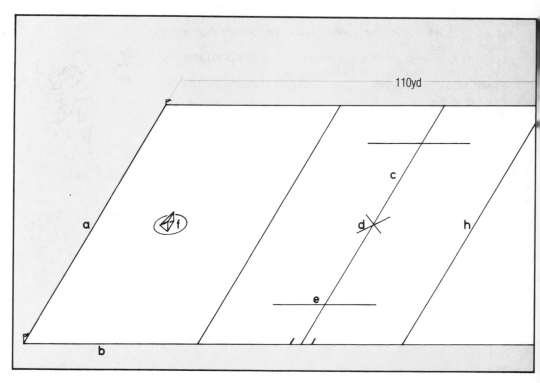

i) special substitution area, marked by two 5ft long lines perpendicular to the side line and extending from points 2yd on each side of the center line.

A timer's table should be placed parallel to and at least 5yd from the side line at the center line.

Team benches should be on either side of and at least 10yd from the timer's table, and parallel to and at least 6yd from the side line. A dotted restraining line, extending the length of the bench area, should be marked parallel to and 5ft outside the side line.

Penalty boxes, with at least two seats for each team, should be placed on either side of the timer's table.

Goal Each goal consists of two 6ft high vertical posts, placed 6ft apart at each end of the goal line, and joined by a top crossbar. The goals are 80yd apart, and 15yd from each end line. The posts should be painted orange.

The pyramid-shaped goal netting should be fastened to the ground at a point 7ft behind the midpoint of the goal line.

The ball should be of white or orange rubber, with a circumference of 7¾–8in, and should weigh 5–5¼oz. When dropped from a height of 72in onto a hardwood floor, it should rebound 45–49in.

Crosse Players other than the goalkeeper should use a crosse 40–72in long; the goalkeeper's crosse may be of any length. The inside measurement of the head should be 4–10in for players other than the goalkeeper, whose crosse may be up to 15in wide.

The crosse should be made of wood, laminated wood, or plastic, the net should be of gut, rawhide, or cord, and should be roughly triangular in shape. Specific regulations govern the shape of the head of the crosse and the construction of the net.

Players may not use crosses that are designed to hold the ball or to make it unreasonably difficult for an opponent to dislodge the ball from the net.

Dress Players wear shorts and numbered jerseys in their team colors; the numbers should be 6in high on the front of the jersey and 8in high on the back. The goalkeeper may wear tracksuit pants.

All players are required to wear protective helmets, faceguards, and gloves; shin and elbow pads are optional. The goalkeeper may also wear chest and thigh protectors.

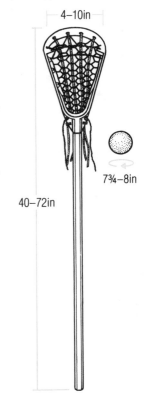

4–10in

7¾–8in

40–72in

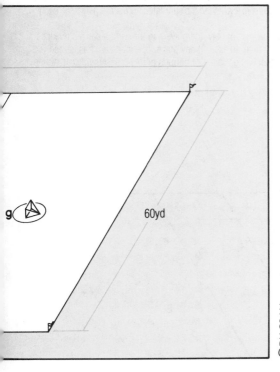

g

60yd

© DIAGRAM

LACROSSE (MEN'S) 2

PLAYERS AND OFFICIALS

Players Each team consists of 10 players: a goalkeeper, three defenders, three midfield players, and three attackers. Each team may also have up to 13 substitutes.

Officials include a referee and an umpire who govern play on the field; a chief bench official who supervises players on the benches or in the substitution area; a timekeeper; two penalty timekeepers; and two scorers.

DURATION AND SCORING

Duration The match is divided into four 25-minute quarters; teams change ends after each quarter. There is a three-minute interval after the first quarter; a 10-minute interval at half-time; and a five-minute interval after the third quarter.

Each team is entitled to two time-outs in each half of the game; each time-out may last up to two minutes. The referee and the umpire may also suspend play at their discretion.

Scoring A goal is scored when the ball has passed over the goal line between the posts and under the crossbar.

A goal is not counted if it is scored:

a) after the playing period has ended, whether or not the whistle has been sounded;

b) after any official has sounded his whistle for any reason;

c) when any part of the body of an attacking player is in the goal crease area;

d) when the attacking team has more than 10 men (including players in the penalty box) on the pitch;

e) when the attacking team or both teams are offside.

The team scoring the greater number of valid goals is the winner. Two or more four-minute periods of extra time may be played to decide a tied game.

STARTING PROCEDURES

Start of match Team captains toss for choice of ends, and play starts with a face-off at the center of the field.

Starting positions (A) One player from each team takes up position at the center of the field for the face-off. Before the whistle is blown for the start of play, each team must confine its goalkeeper and three other players in its defense goal area (the area between the end line and the goal area line around the goal they are defending), three players in its attack goal area, and one player in each of the wing areas. However, a team that is short of players because of penalties may have fewer than the stipulated number of players in each area.

When the whistle is blown for the start of play, the players in the wing areas are released. All other players must remain in their areas until any player of either team has gained possession of the ball, or the ball has gone out of bounds or has crossed either goal line area.

✗   Team 1
◯   Team 2
△   Officials

A

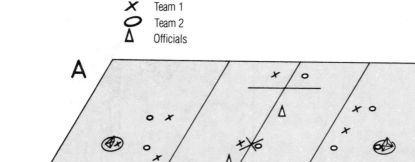

Face-off (B) Play is started at the beginning of each quarter and after each goal has been scored by a face-off at the center.

The two players taking part in the face-off stand either side of the center line, each with his back to the goal his team is defending. Their crosses should be on the ground along the center line, approximately 1in apart. The ball should be placed between the crosses so that it rests on them without touching the ground.

Each facing player should hold his crosse so that his hands are 18in apart on the handle and are not touching the strings; his hands must also rest on the ground. Both his hands and both his feet must be to the left of his crosse's head.

When the whistle is blown for the start of play, each of the facing players may attempt to control the movement of the ball or to gain possession of it by moving his crosse in any manner he chooses.

Face-offs after stoppages must be held at least 20yd away from a goal and at least 20ft from a boundary line. If a face-off is required directly behind a goal, it is held 20ft from the end line.

The crosses of the facing players are placed at right angles to an imaginary line running from the ball to the nearer goal. The defending player stands between his crosse and his own goal, with the attacking player opposite him.

No other player is allowed within 10yd of those facing the ball until the whistle has been sounded for the start of play. The goalkeeper may remain in any part of the goal crease area. Whenever the goalkeeper would be one of the facing players, another member of his team may be substituted for him.

Free play Members of the opposing team must be at least 9ft from any player who has been awarded the ball for any reason.

RULES OF PLAY

Out of bounds (C) A ball in a player's possession goes out of bounds if any part of that player's body or crosse touches the ground on or over a boundary line. The opposing team is awarded a free play at the point where the ball was declared out of bounds.

A loose ball (ie one that is not in a player's possession) goes out of bounds when it touches the ground on or outside a boundary line, or when it touches anything on or outside a boundary line. The ball is put back into play by either a face-off or a free play. If a loose ball goes out of bounds on a face-off, the face-off is taken again at the place where it was first held.

If a loose ball goes out of bounds as the result of a shot or deflected shot at a goal, a free play is awarded to the team whose player was closest to the ball when it went out of bounds. If players from both teams were equidistant from the ball at the point where it went out of bounds, a face-off is held.

Any other loose ball going out of bounds is put back into play by a free play. The free play is awarded to the team other than the team of the player who last touched the ball before it went out of bounds.

219

LACROSSE (MEN'S) 3

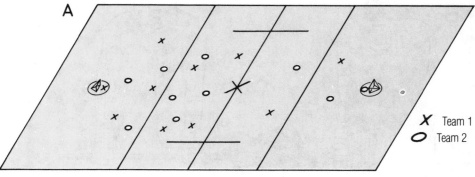

A

X Team 1
O Team 2

Offside (A) A team is considered to be offside if it has fewer than three players in its attacking half of the field, ie between the center line and the end line nearest the goal it is attacking (team 1 in our illustration), or fewer than four players in its defensive half of the field (team 2). However, if four or more players from one team are serving penalties, that team is required to have three players in its attack half of the field and the remainder in the defensive half, and is not considered offside if the number in its defensive half is below four.

If a player realizes that he is about to make his team offside, and runs out of bounds to prevent this, his team is not penalized for failing to have the correct number of players in either zone.

Procedure after offside If only one team is offside, and a goal has not been scored, a penalty for a technical foul is imposed on the offending team.

If both teams are offside, and a goal has not been scored, play is resumed:
a) with the team in possession of the ball at the time of the offense retaining the ball; or
b) with a face-off between the two opponents closest to the ball, in cases where neither team had possession of the ball at the time of the offense.

If the attacking team is offside when a goal is scored, the goal is disallowed; a free play from behind the goal is awarded to the goalkeeper of the defending team.

If the defending team is offside when a goal is scored, the goal is allowed and no additional penalty is imposed.

If both teams are offside when a goal is scored, the goal is disallowed; the two opponents closest to the ball at the time of the offense face the ball at a point directly behind the goal and 20ft from the end line.

Substitution may take place at any time during the match. The player being substituted should leave the field through the substitution area, where his replacement should be waiting. This player may then enter the playing area on either side of the center line, providing that he does not make his team offside. However, substitutions are permitted from other parts of the sideline when a goal has been scored; such substitutions must be completed before the whistle sounds for play to be resumed.

Goal crease area A player is considered to have entered the goal crease area when any part of his body touches the goal crease area.

An attacking player is not allowed in his opponents' goal crease area when the ball is in the attacking half of the field (**B**). But he may reach into the goal crease area with his crosse to play a loose ball (**C**), providing he does not interfere with the goalkeeper.

A defending player may not enter the goal crease area if the ball is already in his possession; he may, however, enter the area when he is not in possession of the ball and receive a pass there.

A player who takes possession of the ball inside the goal crease may not remain there for any longer than is needed for him to step out of the area; nor may any player with the ball in his possession re-enter the goal crease. The goalkeeper is considered to be out of the crease when no part of his body touches the goal crease area, and part of his body is touching an area outside the goal crease.

When the goalkeeper is inside his own goal crease area, he may not be checked, screened, or tackled in any way. If, however, the ball is not inside his crosse, and he extends his crosse outside the goal crease area, it may be checked by an opposing player.

B

C
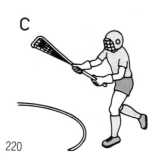

Tackling A player may tackle (bodycheck) an opponent who is in possession of the ball, or who is within 9ft of a loose ball, providing that he does so from the front or side above the knees (**D**). He must keep his arms below the level of his opponent's shoulders, and must keep both hands on his crosse.

A player may check an opponent's crosse with his own if that opponent has possession of the ball, is within 9ft of a loose ball, or is within 9ft of the ball in flight (**E**).

A player may stand in the way of, and facing toward, an approaching opponent so that the opponent is impeded (screened).

Trapped ball If the ball is trapped in a player's crosse for more than four seconds without being dislodged, play is stopped and a face-off is held.

If the ball is trapped in a player's uniform or equipment (other than that of the goalkeeper within his goal crease area), play is stopped immediately and a face-off is held.

If the ball is trapped in a goalkeeper's crosse, uniform, or equipment when he is in his goal crease area, he is awarded a free play at the end line directly behind the goal.

If the ball becomes stuck in any mud inside the goal crease area, a face-off is held 20ft from the end line directly behind the goal.

If the ball becomes stuck in the goal netting, the goalkeeper takes a free play from the end line directly behind the goal.

FOULS AND PENALTIES
Personal fouls It is a personal foul if a player:

a) bodychecks an opponent who is neither in possession of the ball nor within 9ft of a loose ball;

b) deliberately bodychecks an opponent after that opponent has thrown the ball;

c) bodychecks an opponent from the rear, or below the knees (except that it is not a foul if his opponent turns or jumps so as to make a legal check appear illegal);

d) recklessly or viciously swings his crosse at an opponent's crosse;

e) strikes an opponent when attempting to dislodge the ball from his crosse;

f) strikes an opponent on the head with his crosse except when passing or shooting;

g) checks his opponent with the part of his crosse that is between his hands (**F**);

h) trips an opponent (**G**);

i) is unnecessarily rough or violent;

j) uses a trick crosse designed to hold the ball and prevent it being dislodged by an opponent.

It is also a personal foul if a playing or non-playing member of a team (including a coach):

a) argues with an official;

b) uses threatening or obscene language;

c) commits any act considered unsportsmanlike by the officials.

Expulsion fouls It is an expulsion foul if any playing or non-playing member of a team (including a coach) strikes, or attempts to strike, any playing or non-playing member of the opposing team, or any official.

Technical foul Any breach of the rules that is not specifically listed as an expulsion or a personal foul is considered a technical foul. Technical fouls include:

a) a player guarding an opponent who is not in possession of the ball so closely that his freedom of movement is limited;

b) a player holding his opponent or his opponent's crosse;

c) a player other than the goalkeeper touching the ball with his hands;

d) a player lying on a loose ball on the ground or withholding it from play in any manner;

e) a player throwing his crosse;

f) a player taking part in the game without his crosse;

g) a coach or trainer crossing the restraining line, or entering the field while play is in progress;

h) a player or substitute delaying the game for more than 30 seconds;

i) a player failing to remain at least 10yd from a face-off, or at least 9ft from an opponent having a free play;

j) any breach of the offside rule;

k) a player using an illegal crosse other than a trick crosse, or any other illegal equipment.

LACROSSE (MEN'S) 4

Penalties The penalty for a personal foul is suspension from the game for 1–3 minutes depending on the severity of the offense. The non-offending team is normally awarded a free play. However, if the foul takes place before the start of the game, or after the whistle has blown for a goal or the end of a quarter, a face-off is held.

A player who commits five personal fouls is expelled from the game. A substitute is allowed to enter the game at such a time as the expelled player would have been permitted to re-enter if he had not committed five personal fouls.

A player who commits an expulsion foul is suspended from play for the remainder of the game; a substitute is allowed to enter the game after three minutes. The non-offending team is normally awarded a free play. However, if the foul takes place before the start of the game, or after the whistle has blown for a goal or the end of a quarter, a face-off is held. If a non-playing member of a team commits an expulsion foul, the officials select a playing member of the team to serve a three minute suspension.

If a player commits a technical foul during play, he is suspended from the game for 30 seconds only if his team was not in possession of the ball at the time of the offense. If his team was in possession of the ball, or if the ball was not in the possession of either team, the non-offending team is awarded a free play. If the foul occurs before the start of the game, or after the whistle has blown for a goal or the end of the quarter, the offending player is suspended and a face-off is held.

If a goalkeeper commits a technical foul inside the goal crease area, the non-offending team is awarded a free play to be taken from the end line directly behind the goal.

Penalty time may only be served when play is actually in progress; interruptions for time-outs, half-time, etc are not included. However, if a goal is scored against a team that has one or more players serving penalties for technical fouls, those players are released from serving any balance of their penalty time.

Penalty procedure If a foul is committed without a particular member of a team being involved (eg in breaches of the offside rule), or if it is committed by a non-playing member of a team, an official shall select a playing member of the team to serve the penalty. If multiple fouls of this type occur, the official selects additional players from the attacking system of the team to serve the penalties.

If both teams commit simultaneous technical fouls, the fouls are considered to cancel each other out. The team in possession of the ball at the time of the fouls retains possession; if neither team possessed the ball, a face-off is held.

If both teams commit simultaneous fouls that are not both technical fouls, the team incurring the shorter penalty time is awarded the ball. If the penalty times awarded are equal, the team in possession of the ball retains possession; if neither team possessed the ball, a face-off is held.

If a foul occurs in the non-offending team's attacking half of the field, any free play is awarded to the nearest player of that team. The free play is taken at the spot on the field where the ball was when play was suspended for the foul. If, however, this point is within a 20yd radius of the goal, the position for the free play is moved laterally across the field to a point 20yd from the goal. If the player awarded the free play is the goalkeeper, it is taken from the end line directly behind the goal.

If a foul occurs in the non-offending team's defensive half of the field, the free play is awarded to any player of that team who is on its attacking side of the center line.

LACROSSE (WOMEN'S)

HISTORY

Although women's lacrosse shares a common origin with the men's game, it has developed its own distinct character since the first recorded women's match in 1886. The women's game was developed in English girls' schools, and touring English teams have been responsible for introducing the game to the USA and Australia. The international governing body, the International Federation of Women's Lacrosse Associations, was formed in 1973.

SYNOPSIS

Women's lacrosse is a field game played by two teams of 12 players each; the team scoring the greater number of goals in the time allowed is the winner. The players use netted sticks (crosses) to propel the ball around the playing field, which has no side lines or end lines. There are no offside rules, and body contact is forbidden.

EQUIPMENT

The ball should be of rubber, with a circumference of 20–20.3cm, and weigh 135–149g. When dropped from a height of 2.5m onto a concrete floor in a temperature of 68°F, it should rebound 1.3–1.4m.

Crosse All players (including goalkeepers) should use crosses 0.92–1.12m long, with a maximum width of 23cm, and a maximum weight of 567g.

Specific regulations govern the shape of the head of the crosse and the construction of the net.

Dress Goalkeepers may wear leg and body pads, protective helmets, face masks, and gloves. Players other than the goalkeeper may not wear protective clothing, with the exception of close-fitting gloves.

All players must wear composition- or rubber-soled boots or shoes, which may have studs but not spikes.

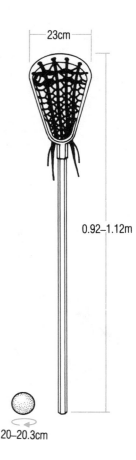

23cm

0.92–1.12m

20–20.3cm

LACROSSE (WOMEN'S) 2

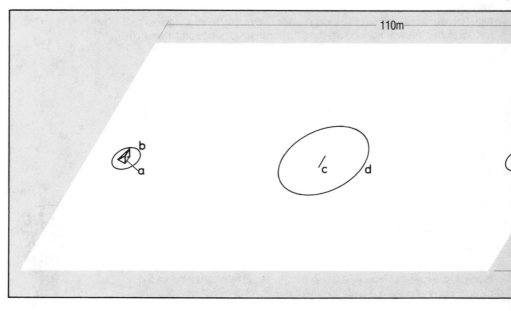

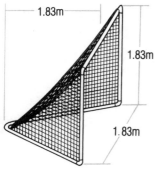

PLAYING AREA

The playing field has no measured boundaries or perimeter lines; for international matches an area 110m long and 60m wide is preferred. Boundaries must be decided before a match by the team captains and the umpire.

The lines marking the pitch are:

a) goal lines, 1.83m long lines parallel to each other and 92m apart;

b) goal circles, with a radius of 2.6m centered on the midpoints of the goal lines;

c) center line, 3m long, parallel to and equidistant from the goal lines;

d) center circle, with a radius of 9m centered on the midpoint of the center lines.

Goal Each goal consists of two 1.83m high vertical posts, placed 1.83m apart at each end of the goal line, and joined by a top crossbar. The posts should be painted white. The pyramid shaped goal netting should be fastened to the ground at a point 1.83m behind the midpoint of the goal line.

PLAYERS AND OFFICIALS

Players Each team consists of 12 players. One substitute is allowed, but she may only replace an injured player who is unable to take any further part in the game.

Officials A center or field umpire is in charge of the game, assisted by two goal umpires, who do not change ends during the game. Alternatively, two umpires may each supervise half the field and one of the goals; they do not change ends during the game.

DURATION AND SCORING

Duration The match is divided into two 25-minute halves, with a 10-minute interval at half-time when the teams change ends. Play may only be suspended for injury, or at the discretion of the umpire.

Scoring A goal is scored when the ball has passed completely over the goal line between the posts and under the crossbar, providing that it has been propelled by the crosse of an attacking player, or the crosse or person of a defending player (own goal).

A goal is not counted if it is scored:

a) by a non-player;

b) off the person of an attacking player;

c) after the whistle has been sounded;

d) when an attacking player has entered the goal circle;

e) by an attacking player who, after shooting, crosses the goal circle with any part of her body or crosse;

f) when a goalkeeper inside her own goal circle is interfered with by an attacking player;

g) with a shot considered dangerous by the umpire.

60m

STARTING PROCEDURES

Start of match Team captains toss for choice of ends, and play starts with a draw on the center line.

Starting positions Apart from those players taking the draw, all other players must have both feet outside the center circle.

Draw Play is started at the beginning of each half, and after each goal has been scored, by a draw on the center line.

One player from each team takes part in the draw; each stands with one foot toeing the center line (**1**). Their crosses should be held back to back, parallel to the center line, and above hip level (**2**). The ball is placed between the crosses; each player should have her crosse between the ball and the goal she is defending.

On the umpire's command "Ready, draw," the players should draw their sticks up and away from each other so that the ball is thrown upward above the heights of their heads. A player may turn her crosse under the ball as the crosses are swept up and away. A left-handed player may swing her stick behind, instead of in front of, her head.

Players are given one warning for an illegal draw. On a second offense:

a) a throw is awarded if both players are responsible;

b) a free position is awarded to the non-offending player if only one player is responsible, and the offending player is placed 4m away at an angle of 45° to the center line on her goal side.

Throw One member of each team takes part in a throw. The two players stand at least 1m apart, each nearer the goal she is defending. The umpire stands 4–8m from the players, with her back to the center of the field, and throws the ball with a short, high throw so that the players takes it as they move in. All other players must be at least 4m away.

A free position takes place at a position indicated by the umpire, which must be at least 8m from the goal circle (unless the free position is to be taken by a goalkeeper within her goal circle.) All other players must be at least 4m away.

The player awarded the free position takes the ball in her crosse, and may run, pass, or shoot when the umpire calls "Play."

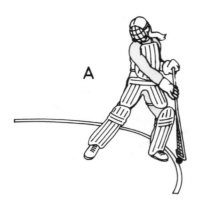

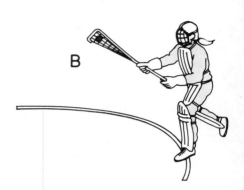

RULES OF PLAY

Stand Whenever the whistle is blown to stop play, all players must remain where they are until the game is restarted ("stand"), unless otherwise directed by the umpire.

Out of bounds If the ball goes outside the agreed boundaries, play is stopped. The player nearest the ball takes it in her crosse and stands 4m inside the agreed boundary, with all other players maintaining their relative positions. Play then restarts.

If two players from opposing teams are equidistant from the ball when it goes out of bounds, a throw is used to restart play.

Play may not be restarted within 8m of a goal circle.

Goal circle area Only one player is allowed in the goal circle at a time; this player should normally be the goalkeeper, or a player deputizing for her. No other player may have any part of her body or her crosse inside the goal circle at any time.

A goalkeeper within her own goal circle may stop the ball with her hand, body, or crosse. If she catches the ball in her hand she must put it in her crosse and continue play. Providing that no part of her body is on the ground outside the circle, she may reach out with her crosse and bring the ball into the circle (**A**). Any ball resting on the goal circle line is considered to be the goalkeeper's.

A goalkeeper who gains possession of the ball when within her own goal circle must pass the ball within 10 seconds. A goalkeeper who gains possession of the ball outside her goal circle may not reenter that circle while she is in possession of the ball (**B**).

Tackling All body contact is forbidden. However, a player may check an approaching opponent by moving into her path so that she is impeded.

A player may check an opponent's crosse with her own providing that the tackle is neither rough nor reckless.

Trapped ball If the ball is trapped in the goalkeeper's pads or clothing when she is within her own goal circle, she should place the ball in her crosse and continue play.

If the ball is trapped in the clothing of any player other than the goalkeeper, a throw is taken.

If the ball is trapped in the goal netting, the goalkeeper takes the ball in her crosse and continues play.

If the ball is trapped in a player's crosse, the crosse should immediately be struck on the ground and the ball dislodged. If the ball cannot be dislodged, a throw is taken where the player caught the ball.

Stoppages If play is stopped because of an accident, outside interference, or any other circumstances unrelated to the ball, the game is restarted by the player who was either in possession of the ball, or closest to it, when the stoppage took place. If two opposing players are equidistant from the ball a throw is taken.

A throw is also taken when:

a) the ball goes into the net off a non-player;

b) the game is restarted after an accident caused by or related to the ball, unless the accident was caused by a foul;

c) play is stopped for any other reason not specified in the rules.

FOULS AND PENALTIES

Fouls It is a foul if a player:

a) checks an opponent's crosse with her own in a rough or reckless manner;

b) checks or tackles an opponent's crosse when she is attempting to gain possession of the ball (**1**);

c) charges, shoulders, backs into, pushes, trips, or otherwise physically obstructs or detains an opponent (**2**);

d) suddenly moves into an opponent's path so that body contact is unavoidable;

e) guards a ground ball with her foot (**3**) or crosse;

f) touches the ball with her hands (other than a goalkeeper in her own goal circle);

g) allows any part of her body to impede, accelerate, or deflect the ball to her team's advantage;

h) propels the ball in a dangerous or uncontrolled manner, or makes a dangerous shot at goal;

i) throws her crosse, or takes part in the game when she is not holding her crosse;

j) guards the goal by positioning herself with one or more other members of her team so that opposing players attempting to shoot are obstructed;

k) has any part of her body or crosse inside the goal circle unless she is deputizing for the goalkeeper.

It is also a foul if the goalkeeper:

a) holds the ball in her crosse for more than 10 seconds when within her own goal circle;

b) draws the ball into the goal circle with her crosse when any part of her body is touching the ground outside the circle;

c) steps back into the circle with the ball, when possession of the ball has been gained outside the circle.

Penalties The penalty for a foul is a free position. If two players from opposing teams foul simultaneously, a throw is taken.

LUGE TOBOGGAN RACING

HISTORY

Tobogganing is recorded in sixteenth century documents as an enjoyable winter recreation, but lugeing as a sport really began in the late nineteenth century, when tourists in the Alps began racing their toboggans on snow covered mountain roads. The first international race was held in 1883; by the end of the century several special toboggan runs had been constructed.

Although the sport rapidly grew in popularity, the first world championships were not held until 1955, and it was not included in the Olympic Games until 1964. The international governing body for lugeing, the Fédération Internationale de Luge de Course (FIL) was founded in 1957. The rules given here are those for racing on artificial courses, as used in the Olympic Games.

SYNOPSIS

Luge toboggan riders adopt an aerodynamically efficient reclining position, as shown on p. 231. Steering is achieved by using shoulder pressure to change the balance of the luge, by leg pressure on the front of the runners, and sometimes with a rein. Competitors make a number of runs down a steep, ice-covered track, attempting to complete each run in the fastest possible time. There are individual ("singles") events for men and for women, and a pairs ("doubles") event for men.

COMPETITORS AND OFFICIALS

Competitors At the Olympic Games, each country may enter three men and three women for the individual events, and two men's doubles pairs. Other races usually permit a greater number of entries from each country.

Officials The race director, starting and finishing officials, timekeepers, and course supervisors are responsible for the smooth running of the races. A three-member jury is responsible for overall control of the event, and technical delegates from the FIL should be present at all major competitions.

COURSE AND EQUIPMENT

The course Artificial luge courses are specially designed and constructed. They may be refrigerated and thus artificially iced, or may simply be brick and earth iced by hand with frozen slush. Olympic events must be held on refrigerated tracks.

Tracks must be a minimum of 1000m long for men's singles events, and a minimum of 700m long for women's singles and for doubles events. The average gradient should be 8–11%.

Each course must include straight sections (**a**), a right-hand bend (**b**), a left-hand bend (**c**), a hairpin bend (**d**), an S-bend (**e**), and a labyrinth (**f**).

Strict safety regulations govern the construction of courses; it must not be possible for toboggans to shoot over the edges or the sides. The radii of the bends should make it impossible to exceed a force of 4.5G (although up to 6.5G is reached on some older courses). The bottoms of the straight sections should be 1.30–1.50m wide; the transition between the bottom and the sides of the course must be molded, with a minimum radius of 10cm.

The whole course must be visible from vantage points or control towers; these, and the start and finish, must all be connected by telephone.

Artificial lighting, where used, must neither blind nor cast shadows. Men's and women's Olympic singles events include one night run under artificial lighting.

The starting area Two starting points are needed so that all classes or events reach a common finishing line. Starting positions should have a horizontal iced surface where competitors can seat themselves on their toboggans. Starting handles or grips are set into the track at the start, from which competitors pull off before leaning back into the aerodynamic reclined position.

Timing equipment Automatic timing equipment is compulsory, providing measurements to thousandths of a second. Additional split-times should be provided by timing lights set at intervals down the track. Forerunners are sent down the track before each heat of a race in order to check the timing equipment.

a

b

c

d

e

f

©DIAGRAM

LUGE TOBOGGAN RACING 2

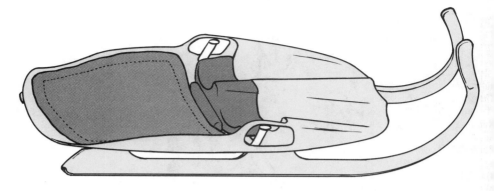

Toboggans have two steel runners bolted to wooden runners that curve up at the front. These are flexibly mounted on two steel cross-members or bridges supporting a fiberglass seat or shell. Riders may not be fixed to their toboggans, except that a crotch strap may be used in doubles events.

Measurements for each part of the equipment must meet detailed specifications, which are updated each year. The weight of a singles toboggan may not exceed 22kg, and that of a doubles toboggan 24kg.

Mechanical braking and steering mechanisms are forbidden, but a hand-held rein may be used.

The steel runners, which are carefully profiled and highly polished, may be waxed before a run, but they may not be heated. Temperature checks on the runners are made before and after each run in a race.

Dress Crash helmets are compulsory for all training and race runs. Goggles may be worn but usually a full-face transparent visor is used. Some competitors use neck-support straps attached to their helmets. Additional protective padding such as elbow and ankle pads may be worn.

For races, skin-tight stretch suits are worn, made of nylon with a plastic coating for maximum aerodynamic efficiency. Special bootees are usually worn for races, or leather sports shoes when training. Gloves are essential and may have short spikes to be used on the start ramp to improve acceleration.

To counteract the weight advantage of heavier competitors, lead-filled weight belts may be worn up to a maximum of 10kg for men and 8kg for women, plus a 4kg clothing allowance over bodyweight. The extra weight allowance is calculated on a sliding scale, with each individual being given a total weight limit before a race. Doubles competitors have no additional weight allowance, but may top up their clothing allowance with lead weights.

PROCEDURE

Training is compulsory; a thorough knowledge of the course is essential for speed and safety. Singles competitors must make at least five training runs before a race; doubles competitors must make at least three. The times achieved in training must be officially announced.

The start Toboggan dimensions and the temperature of the runners are checked by officials before each run of a race. Starting order is determined by a draw, although in some races there is a seeding system to ensure that the best competitors start close together.

A sitting start is compulsory. A starting system involving red and green lights is used. A red light indicates the course is closed. Competitors must start within 30sec of the green light coming on in singles events, and within 45sec in double events.

Only one toboggan is allowed on the track at a time; the starter is notified from the finish when the course is clear.

The race In the Olympic Games, singles events consist of four runs down the track and doubles events of two runs down the track. Other races usually require only three runs for the singles.

Competitors must lie or sit on their toboggans throughout the length of the track unless interrupted by a crash. After a crash, a competitor may push his toboggan if necessary, but may not accept outside help.

The finish Competitors must cross the finishing line in contact with their toboggans. The temperature of the runners is checked, and competitors and toboggans are weighed.

Result The winner is the competitor or pair with the lowest aggregate time for the race runs.

Penalties are either exclusion from the race, or disqualification after the completion of a run or the race. Offenses include:

a) failure to meet technical specification limits on toboggan construction;
b) runner temperature too high;
c) toboggan exceeding the weight permitted;
d) competitor exceeding the weight permitted;
e) failure to complete the required number of training runs;
f) training outside approved training periods;
g) failure to appear at the start when called;
h) failure to start within the time allowed;
i) losing anything other than goggles or visor on the track during a race run;
j) accepting outside help during a race run;
k) leaving the track during a race run;
l) crossing the finishing line not in contact with the toboggan;
m) acting in a dangerous manner during training or during a race.

MODERN PENTATHLON

HISTORY

Modern pentathlon's origins are supposed to lie in the activities of a military dispatch rider traveling through enemy territory. He sets off on horseback, fights his way through with sword and pistol, swims a river, and finally runs to safety across country. The sport was first included in the Olympic Games in 1912, largely at the instigation of their founder, Baron Pierre de Coubertin, who wished the Games to include a test of all-round athletic ability. World championships have been held for men since 1949, and for women since 1981. The international governing body for the sport is the Union Internationale du Pentathlon Moderne et Biathlon (UIPMB), formed in 1948.

SYNOPSIS

The five sports that make up the modern pentathlon are (in order of competition) riding (**1**), fencing (**2**), swimming (**3**), shooting (**4**), and cross-country running (**5**). At Olympic Games and world championships the events are held on five consecutive days. Scoring is on a points basis, reflecting the results obtained in each event; the overall winners are decided by their total scores over the five events.

COMPETITORS AND OFFICIALS

Competitors Modern pentathletes compete as individuals and as teams. National teams consist of three competitors and one reserve.

Officials Each event is judged by qualified officials; the number of officials required varies from sport to sport. At major international competitions there is also a jury of appeal, normally consisting of seven members.

Substitution A competitor injured during the riding event may be replaced in it by a substitute. This substitute, with 0 points from the riding event, then replaces the injured competitor in the remaining four events of the competition. Substitution is not permitted at any later stage.

COMPETITION RULES

Starting A draw is used to determine the starting order of the teams in each event. The individual starting order of the members of a team is decided by the team captain, and submitted in writing before the beginning of the draw.

In all events except fencing the order of starting is the first competitors from each team in the order of the team draw, followed by the second competitors from each team in the order of the team draw, and so on.

Scoring The competition is decided on points, which correspond to the results obtained by each competitor in each event. The competitor or team with the highest total score is the winner.

Only competitors who started in all five events are included in the final classification. A competitor who abandons or who is eliminated in an event scores no points in that event, but may remain in the competition.

1
2

Disqualification A competitor who is disqualified from an event for a deliberate attempt to violate the rules may not compete in the remainder of the competition.

The team to which the disqualified athlete belongs is eliminated from the team competition, but the remaining members of the team may continue to compete as individuals.

Tie In the event of a tie, the winner is the individual or team who gained first place in the greatest number of events. If there is still a tie, the events are valued in the order: cross-country running, shooting, swimming, fencing, riding.

Alternative procedures The cross-country race may be run on a handicap start basis, in which the runners' starting positions are determined by their results in the previous four events. If this procedure is followed, the winner of the cross-country running is also the winner of the whole competition.

A further alternative procedure is a reversed-order start system in the last three events; competitors start in reverse order of their overall placings at the end of the previous event.

RIDING

The event is organized basically according to the rules of the Fédération Equestre Internationale (FEI) for show jumping (see pp. 92–99). The competitors are usually placed in two divisions, with riders starting their rounds at four-minute intervals. Positions are decided by the number of points scored; there is no jump off in the case of equality of points.

The course is 600m long for both men and women, with 15 obstacles including one double and one treble combination.

Competitors are provided with a definitive plan of the course on the day before the riding event. They are then permitted to inspect the course on foot.

Competitors may also inspect the condition of the course immediately before the start of the division in which they are competing.

The obstacles must be strong, heavy, and impressive in appearance. Closed obstacles are not permitted.

Straight fences may not exceed 1.20m in height; spread fences may not exceed 1.10m in height and 1.30m in width; water jumps may not exceed 3m in width.

All obstacles must be numbered consecutively in the order in which they are to be jumped.

The horses are provided by the organizers, who should normally offer one horse for every two riders. There should also be one reserve horse for every eight riders.

The horses must be carefully selected to ensure equality between them. All the horses must be clearly numbered.

The competitors, in their starting list order, draw for the number of the horse they are to ride. The horses start in the same order in both divisions.

Dress and equipment Riders must be correctly dressed according to the regulations of the FEI, and must wear protective headgear fitted with a chinstrap.

Saddlery is provided by the organizers. Competitors may use their own reins, and may also use their own saddles with the permission of the organizers.

MODERN PENTATHLON 2

Practice Competitors may mount 20 minutes before their official starting time, and may then practice in the exercise arena. They are limited to a total of six practice jumps in the exercise arena, and are penalized 200 points for each jump over this number.

Speed and time The speed allowed in international competitions is 350m/min for both men and women.

The time allowed for completing the course is 103sec. The time limit for the course is 206sec; competitors exceeding the time limit are eliminated.

Scoring A clear round in the time allowed scores 1100 points.

Penalty points are deducted as follows:

a) exceeding the time allowed, for each commenced second, 2 points;

b) obstacle knocked down while jumping, 30 points;

c) foot of the horse in the water at the water jump, 30 points;

d) fall of horse or rider or both, 60 points;

e) disobedience (each time), 40 points.

f) When a disobedience results in an obstacle being knocked down, extra penalty points are deducted:

for a single obstacle, or first part of a multiple obstacle, 10 points;

for the second part of a multiple obstacle, 15 points;

for the third part of a multiple obstacle, 20 points.

Elimination The actions that result in a competitor's elimination from the event are similar to those under FEI show jumping rules (see p. 98), with the following exceptions.

a) Competitors are not eliminated for prolonged resistance on the part of their horse; the only penalty is loss of time.

b) Competitors are not eliminated for three refusals at an obstacle. They are, however, eliminated if they do not attempt an obstacle three times before attempting the one following, or if they attempt an obstacle more than three times.

FENCING

The event is organized basically according to the rules of the Fédération Internationale d'Escrime (FIE) for épée fencing (see pp. 106–111).

The area is a standard fencing piste, fitted with electric judging equipment.

One or more reserve pistes must be provided for use as soon as one or more matches are proceeding more slowly than the rest.

Dress and equipment must conform to FIE regulations.

Competitors provide their own épées and body wires, which must be submitted for official inspection two days before the beginning of the fencing event. The inspected equipment is returned to the competitors one hour before the beginning of the event.

Bouts are arranged so that each fencer meets all the other fencers. All these bouts count for scoring points.

Each fencer must compete in at least 20 bouts; a second round is held if there are fewer than 21 competitors.

All bouts are determined by one decisive touch; double hits are not counted.

The time limit for each bout is three minutes; competitors are warned of the time after two minutes.

If there is no decisive touch before the expiry of the time limit both fencers are considered hit, and a defeat is recorded for each of them.

Scoring A competitor who wins 70% of his required total number of bouts scores 1000 points.

Each victory above or below this percentage also gains or loses the fencer a number of points equal to 1100 divided by his required total number of bouts.

In the case of equality of victories, deciding bouts must be held to determine the winner of the event, but these bouts do not affect the number of points scored.

Elimination and withdrawal The results of any bouts fought by a fencer who withdraws or who is eliminated during the event are disregarded.

SWIMMING

The pool must conform to the standards of the Fédération Internationale de Natation Amateur (FINA) (see pp. 350–357).

The race is 300m freestyle for men, and 200m freestyle for women. A competitor may swim any stroke or strokes; FINA regulations referring to stroke definitions do not apply. Competitors swim in heats according to their position on the starting list and the number of lanes available. There are no finals; all results are decided by time.

Scoring For scoring purposes, times recorded are rounded to the nearest half second. Men score 1000 points for completing the race in 3min 54sec, and women for completing it in 2min 40sec. Four points are gained or lost for each half second faster or slower than the set time.

Positions are decided by the actual times recorded without rounding.

SHOOTING

The event is organized basically according to the rules of the Union Internationale de Tir (UIT) for rapid fire pistol shooting (see pp. 274–275).

Pistol and ammunition Competitors provide their own pistols which must be of 5.6mm (.22) caliber and conform to UIT regulations. All pistols must be submitted for official examination, normally during the fencing event. Shooters are penalized by the loss of two target points for every shot fired with an unexamined firearm.

Ammunition must conform to UIT regulations.

Dress Only normal athletic training suits or street sports clothing may be worn. Any clothing that offers the shooter artificial support in the firing position is prohibited.

Range and target The shooting distance is 25m. The target is a standard UIT silhouette target, and there is one target for each firing position.

Course of fire Competitors fire four series of five shots each. They may also fire an optional sighting series of five shots. The targets are exposed for three seconds and concealed for seven seconds. Competitors may fire only one shot on each exposure of the target; competitors who fire more than one shot are eliminated.

Penalties for irregular shots and infringements of the rules vary from loss of points to elimination, depending on the severity of the offense.

Scoring A target score of 194 out of the possible maximum of 200 is worth 1000 competition points.

Competitors gain or lose 22 competition points for each target point above or below 194.

A tie for first place is resolved by:
1) the highest score in the fourth series;
2) the highest score in the third series;
3) the highest score in the second series;
4) the highest number of 10s, 9s, etc in the complete course;
5) determining which competitor's worst shot is closest to the center of the target.

CROSS-COUNTRY RUNNING

Course Men race for 4000m, and women for 2000m. The total climb allowed is 60–100m for men, and 30–50m for women. The course should be laid out across open country, avoiding roads and dangerous obstacles. It must be clearly marked with tapes on both sides along its entire length. The start and finish must be at the same place.

Competitors may inspect the course two hours before the event begins.

Dress Competitors wear normal athletic clothing, clearly marked with their start numbers on their chests and backs.

Procedure Competitors start individually at one-minute intervals, or, in a handicap start, on the basis of their results in the earlier events.

A competitor who starts prematurely must start again; his time is taken from his official starting time. Late starters are also timed from their official starting times.

Scoring For scoring purposes, the times recorded are rounded to the nearest second. Men score 1000 points for completing the race in 14min 15sec, and gain or lose three points for each second slower or faster.

Women score 1000 points for completing the race in 7min 30sec, and gain or lose five points for each second faster or slower.

Positions are decided by the actual times recorded without rounding.

PADDLEBALL

HISTORY
Paddleball was developed from court handball at the University of Michigan during the 1930s. Tennis players there used vacant handball courts to practice their strokes; as many of them were also handball players, they went on to develop a form of handball played with paddles. Members of the armed forces on training programs at the University during World War II were taught paddleball as part of their physical training, and the game spread rapidly throughout the USA.

National tournaments have been staged in the USA since the early 1960s. The rules described here are those of the National Paddle Ball Association (NPA) which was founded in 1966 as the governing body for tournament play.

SYNOPSIS
Paddleball is played on a one-, three-, or four-wall court with a wooden paddle; players score points by hitting shots that their opponents are unable to return.

It may be played by two players (singles), three players ("cut throat"), or four players (doubles).

COURT AND EQUIPMENT
Four-wall court Illustrated (**A**) is a standard four-wall court, 20ft wide and 40ft long. The front (**a**) and side (**b**) walls should be 20ft high, and the back wall (**c**) at least 12ft high. The 1½in-wide red or black lines marking the court are:

d) short line, parallel to and 20ft from the front wall;

e) service line, parallel to and 15ft from the front wall;

f) service boxes, marked by lines parallel to and 1ft 6in from each side wall.

One-wall court A standard one-wall court is shown by the solid lines on illustration (**B**). The wall is 20ft wide and 16ft high, topped with a 4ft high wire fence. The playing zone on the floor is 20ft wide and 34ft long, and should be surrounded by at least 6ft of clear space on every side.

Lines marking the court are:

a) long line, marking the edge of the playing zone parallel to the wall;

b) short line, parallel to and 16ft from the wall;

c) service lines, parallel to and equidistant from the long and short lines, and extending 6in inward from the sidelines;

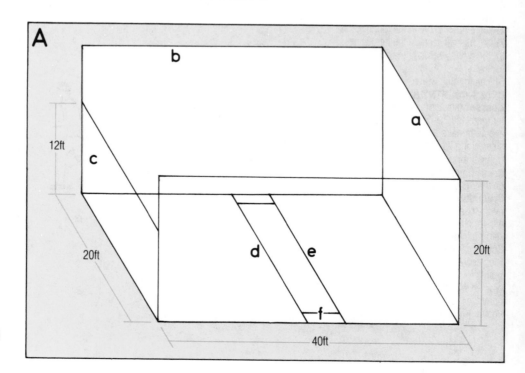

d) sidelines, marking the edges of the playing zone perpendicular to the wall, and extending 3ft beyond the long line.

Three-wall court Dimensions and court markings are as for the one-wall court, with the addition of two side walls – shown by dotted lines on illustration (**B**) – which extend from the top of the front wall along the sidelines to the short line. These walls should be 6ft high at the short line.

Ball The NPA specifies an official brand of ball: the Pennsy Official National Paddleball, made by General Tire-Pennsylvania Athletic Products, Akron, Ohio. When dropped from a height of 6ft it should rebound approximately 3ft 6in.

The paddle should be approximately 16in long and 8in wide. It should be made of wood and weigh approximately 16oz. The leather thong attached to the end of the handle must be worn around the wrist during play.

Dress Players' shirts, shorts, socks, and shoes should be white. For safety, knee and elbow pads (of a soft material), eyeguards, and protective helmets may be worn.

PLAYERS AND OFFICIALS

Players Each side may consist of one player (singles) or two (doubles). In the three-player "cut-throat" game, the two players not serving play against the server.

Officials Play is controlled by a referee, assisted by a scorer.

1⁷⁄₈in

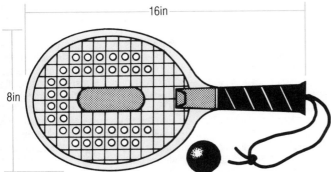

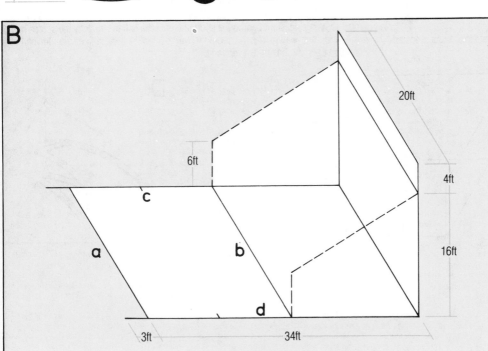

©DIAGRAM

PADDLEBALL 2

DURATION AND SCORING
Duration A match consists of the best of three games. A two-minute interval is allowed between the first two games, and a ten-minute interval between the second and third. Play should be continuous in each game, except that each side may request not more than two 30-second time-outs in each game. Players are penalized for any deliberate delays. An injured player is allowed up to 15 minutes' rest, after which time he must either continue play or forfeit the match.

Scoring A game is won by the first side to score 21 points, and the match by the first side to win two games.

Points are awarded only if the side that is serving wins the rally. When the serving side loses a rally, or fails to serve according to the rules, the service passes to their opponents.

RULES OF PLAY
Service order is determined by the toss of a coin. The player serving first in the first game also serves first in the third game, if any.

In doubles, when the starting player loses the service, it passes to the opposing side. Thereafter, both players in each side must serve and lose service before the service passes to the opposition. The service order established at the beginning of a game must be followed throughout that game.

Service The server may serve from anywhere in the service zone (the area between the short line and the service line); he must have both feet on or within the lines of the zone. The server should bounce the ball once on the floor of the zone and hit it once with his paddle (**A**), serving it directly to the front wall.

In the four-wall game (**B**) the served ball should rebound so that it first hits the floor of the court behind the short line, either with (**1**) or without (**2**) touching one side wall. In the one-wall game (**C**), it should first hit the floor in the area bounded by the short line, the long line, and the side lines; in the three-wall game (**D**), it should first hit the floor in that same area, either with (**1**) or without (**2**) touching one side wall after hitting the front wall. The server must remain in the service zone until the ball has crossed the short line on the rebound. In the four-wall doubles game, the server's partner must stand with both feet in the service box and his back to the wall while the service is taken, and remain there until the ball has crossed the short line on the rebound. In the one- and three-wall doubles games, the server's partner must stand outside the side line between the short line and the long line until the served ball has passed him on the rebound.

The server may not serve until the receiver is ready. In the four-wall game, the receiver must remain at least 5ft behind the short line until the ball is struck by the server; in the one- and three-wall games, he should remain behind the service lines until the ball has crossed the short line on the rebound.

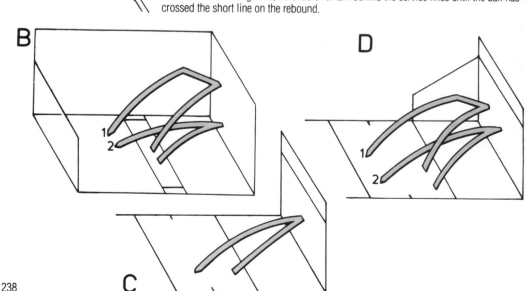

Illegal service (E) A player who serves two illegal services in succession loses the service. A service is illegal if:

a) the server leaves the service zone before the served ball passes the short line on the rebound;

b) in the four-wall doubles game, the server's partner leaves the service box before the served ball passes the short line;

c) in one- and three-wall doubles, the server's partner enters the playing area between the side lines before the served ball has passed him;

d) the served ball first hits the floor in front of the short line (**1**);

e) in the three- and four-wall games, the served ball hits two or more walls after hitting the front wall and before hitting the floor;

f) in the four-wall game, the served ball hits the ceiling after hitting the front wall and before hitting the floor;

g) in the four-wall game, the served ball rebounds from the front wall and hits the back wall before touching the floor (**2**);

h) in the one- and three-wall games, the served ball rebounds from the front wall and first hits the floor beyond the long line but between the side line extensions;

i) in the four-wall game, the served ball goes out of court on the service.

Serve-out serves Certain service errors lead to an immediate loss of service (a "serve-out").

A server loses the service if:

a) he bounces the ball more than twice before striking it when about to serve;

b) he serves by deliberately dropping the ball and hitting it in the air, or attempts to hit it in the air and misses;

c) the ball touches the server's body or clothing when he is serving;

d) the served ball simultaneously strikes the front wall and any other playing surface;

e) the served ball strikes any other playing surface before striking the front wall;

f) in the four-wall game, he bounces the ball and it hits the side wall before he strikes it with his paddle;

g) in the one- and three-wall games, the served ball rebounds from the front wall and goes out of court outside the side lines before hitting the floor;

h) in doubles, the players serve out of order, or the same player takes both turns of service for his side;

i) in the four-wall doubles game, the served ball touches the server's partner when he is out of the service box.

Dead ball service There is no penalty for a dead ball service; the server takes the service again. Any previous service fault is unaffected.

In the four-wall doubles game, a dead ball service occurs if, on an otherwise legal service:

a) the served ball on the rebound from the front wall touches the server's partner while he is still in the service box, but before it hits the floor;

b) the served ball passes between the server's partner and the side wall.

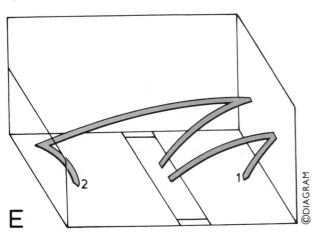

E

PADDLEBALL 3

Return of service (A) It is a legal return of service if the receiver plays the ball after it has crossed the short line but before it has bounced on the floor (**1**), providing that no part of his body crosses the short line before he has made the return. He may also play the ball after it has bounced once on the floor (**2**).

The returned ball must not touch the floor before touching the front wall. In the four-wall game the ball may touch one or both side walls, the ceiling, or the back wall before striking the front wall.

If the returned ball touches the front wall and the floor simultaneously it is not a legal return.

Good volley (B) Each legal return after the service is called a volley; the player may strike the ball with either side of the paddle, and hold the paddle in either one or both hands.

It is a good volley if the player hits the ball, either before or after it has bounced once on the floor, so that it is returned directly to the front wall (**1**). In the four-wall game, the ball may touch any playing surface (**2, 3**) other than the floor before striking the front wall.

If a player strikes at a ball and misses, he may make further attempts to make a good volley before it touches the floor for a second time. In doubles, both members of a side are entitled to attempt to return the ball, and may make one or more attempts to strike it before it touches the floor for a second time.

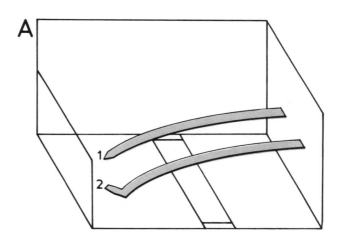

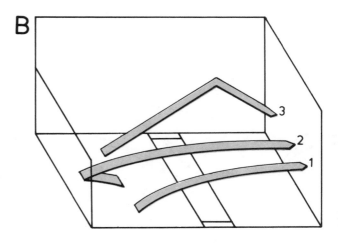

Bad volley It is a bad volley and results in a point or serve-out against the offender if the player:
a) hits the ball with his arm, hand, or any other part of his body;
b) does not have the safety thong of his paddle around his wrist at all times, or switches the paddle from hand to hand during play;
c) touches the ball more than once;
d) fails to return the ball to the front wall but instead strikes it out of court, or returns the ball to the front wall so that it goes out of court on the rebound or on the first bounce on the floor.

Unintentional hinders There is no penalty for an unintentional hinder (obstruction) but the point is replayed. It is an unintentional hinder when:
a) a returned ball rebounding from the front wall touches the striker's opponent before bouncing on the floor;
b) the ball strikes any part of the court that under local rules is a dead ball;
c) body contact or any other accidental interference by an opponent unsights a player or interferes with his returning the ball;
d) the ball rebounds from the front wall so close to the striker or his partner (including passing between their legs) that their opponents are unsighted, or do not have a fair chance to return the ball;
e) the ball breaks during play;
f) any foreign object enters the court, or any outside interference interrupts play.

Intentional hinder (C) The penalty for an intentional hinder is a serve-out or point against the offender, depending on whether he was serving or receiving. It is an intentional hinder when:
a) a player fails to move sufficiently out of the way to allow his opponent a fair shot;
b) a player (**1**) moves into a position that blocks or crowds his opponent (**2**);
c) a player intentionally pushes an opponent during play.

POLO

HISTORY
Polo is generally believed to have been invented in Persia (now Iran). It was certainly played there in the first century AD, and some authorities believe it to be very much older than this. From Persia it spread East to Tibet, India, China, and Japan. It was brought to the West in the nineteenth century from India, where it was popular with British Army officers. The first English rules were drawn up in 1875, and the game soon spread to other European countries, the USA, South America, Australasia, and Africa.

SYNOPSIS
Polo is played between two teams of four players mounted on ponies. Players use long, mallet-headed sticks, which must be held in the right hand only, to hit a ball around a large, outdoor ground. Goals are scored by sending the ball between the opponents' goal posts. Team handicaps as well as goals scored are considered in the final result.

PLAYING AREA AND EQUIPMENT
The ground has a maximum measurement of 300yd long by 200yd wide. It is surrounded by a safety zone extending about 10yd beyond the playing area at the sides and about 30yd at the ends. No one other than officials and players' assistants may enter the safety zone during play.

The goals are at either end of the playing area. They must be at least 250yd apart (usually 300yd). There are two goalposts at least 10ft high, which must be light enough to break easily in a collision. Each goal is 8yd wide, but may be widened to 16yd for extra time if a match is tied.

The playing area is marked with a line (**a**) straight across its width 30yd from each goal. A small cross (**b**) or spot is marked 40yd from each goal, exactly in line with the center of the goal. A broken or solid line (**c**) runs across the width of the playing area 60yd from each goal. In the center of the playing area a "T" (**d**) is marked on the ground.

10ft

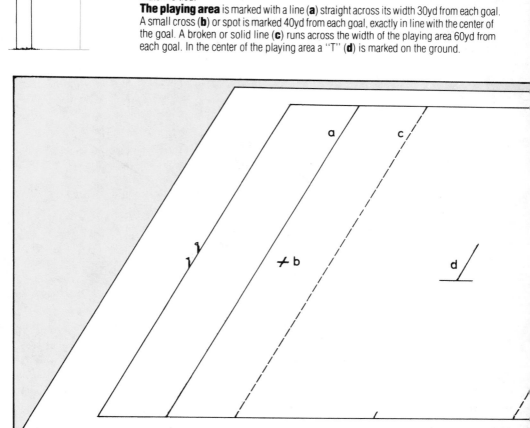

300yd

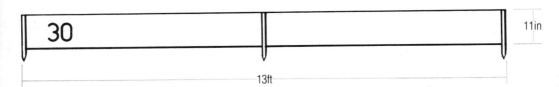

Boards are sometimes placed along each long side of the ground, in order to deflect low balls back into play. They are built in sections 13ft long, so that if they are damaged they can be replaced without interrupting play. The boards have a maximum height of 11in, and are fixed into the ground with iron pegs.

The figures 30, 40, and 60 are painted on the boards beside the appropriate lines; there is also a mark beside the center line. At the 60yd point a line exactly 4yd long is marked on the ground from the boards inward toward the playing area.

If boards are not used, the ground should measure 300yd by 200yd, and there should be flags placed well behind the side lines to indicate the 30, 40, and 60yd points.

Sticks have a solid wooden head, a flexible cane shaft, and a handle fitted with a handgrip. Size and styles vary to suit individual preferences, but a shaft is typically about 51in long and a mallet head about 9in long and about 2in in diameter at the center.

The ball is solid wood or plastic, has a maximum diameter of 3½in, and weighs 4¼–4¾oz.

Dress It is compulsory for players to wear a protective polo helmet or cap, with a chin strap. Distinguishing team colors and numbers 1 to 4 are worn, with breeches, boots, knee pads, and gloves. The upper parts of the boots and the knee pads must not have any protruding buckles or studs. and sharp spurs are not allowed.

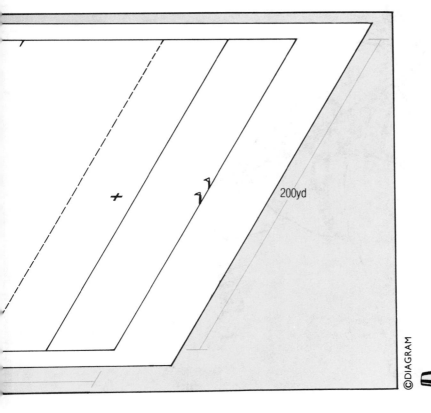

©DIAGRAM

POLO 2

PONIES, PLAYERS, OFFICIALS

Ponies Each player requires several ponies; the same pony is not used in consecutive periods. Ponies may be of any height, with good eyesight and a calm and controllable disposition.

Ponies' legs must always be protected by boots or bandages. Blinkers and any sort of noseband that might restrict vision are not allowed. Shoes that have a rim on the inside only are allowed, but frost nails and screws are forbidden. A calkin (a small projection on the back of the shoe) is permissible on hind shoes, as long as it is not larger than a half inch cube.

Players Each team consists of four players. No player or pony may play for more than one team in a tournament.

Officials There are two mounted umpires on the field of play, and one referee off the field in a central position. Umpires' decisions are final; in the event of a disagreement between two umpires, the referee decides.

In some matches, there may by only one mounted umpire and no referee.

Only the captain of a team has the right to discuss any point with an umpire, and no player may appeal for a foul.

In important matches, two goal judges stand behind each goal and signal with flags when a goal is scored.

There is also an official timekeeper and scorer.

DURATION AND TIMING

Duration In the USA and Europe a match usually lasts 42 minutes, divided into six periods ("chukkers") of seven minutes each. Elsewhere, eight seven-minute periods are usual. Match organizers are permitted to reduce the number or length of periods.

Timing There is a five-minute interval at half-time, and a three-minute interval between other periods. Apart from these intervals play is continuous; time out for changing ponies is permitted only in case of injury.

The timekeeper sounds his bell for play to start at the beginning of each period. On the expiry of time for any period, the timekeeper again sounds his bell. At the end of any period except the last, play continues after the first end bell either until the ball goes out of play or hits a board, a foul is signaled, or the timekeeper sounds a second bell 30 seconds after the first. At the end of the final period, play continues after the first bell as in previous periods only if there is a tied score.

If a tied score is not resolved by the ordinary extension of play, extra periods of the usual length are held after a five-minute interval. Play stops after one team scores a deciding goal.

If a losing team is awarded a penalty within 20 seconds of the expiry of match time, the timekeeper will delay ringing the end bell for 20 seconds from the time that the penalty is taken. Play ends at once, however, if a goal is scored from such a penalty and the regular match time has expired.

If a match cannot be played to a finish because of bad weather or darkness, it should be resumed at exactly the same point as soon as this is convenient.

HANDICAPS AND SCORING

Handicaps Each player has an official handicap expressed in goals from -2 to $+10$ (in many countries beginners start at 0 not at -2). In matches played on a handicap basis, the handicaps of team members are added together to find the team handicap. A team with a higher handicap than another, concedes the difference between their two handicaps divided by six and multiplied by the number of periods to be played. All fractions count as a half goal.

Scoring A match is won by the team with the higher goal score at the end of play. Team handicaps as well as goals scored are taken into account. A goal is scored when the ball passes over the end line between the goal posts or their imaginary extensions.

RULES OF PLAY

Starting play At the start of the game and after a goal, the opposing teams line up facing the umpire in the center of the ground, each on its own side of the "T." The umpire then bowls the ball underarm between the lines of players from a distance of not less than 5yd. The players must remain stationary until the ball has left the umpire's hand.

After every goal except a goal from a penalty, or at half time if no goal has been scored, teams must change ends. After an interval between periods, the game is restarted from where play stopped. If the ball hits the boards at the end of a period, play is restarted as if it had been hit over them.

If a game is stopped for any reason without the ball going out of play (for example, for the replacement of a damaged ball), play restarts at the place where the incident occurred, with a line-up as at the start of play.

Playing the ball A player must play with his stick in his right hand, and uses the side of the mallet head for hitting the ball. A player may not catch or kick the ball or hit it with anything but his stick. He is allowed to block it with any part of his body except his open hand. He must not deliberately carry the ball, and if it becomes lodged in his equipment or against his pony the umpire will stop play.

© DIAGRAM

POLO 3

Out of play When the ball goes over the boards or side lines, it is bowled into the ground by the umpire from just inside the boards or line at the point where it went out. Each team lines up on its own side of an imaginary line parallel to the goal lines, and the ball is bowled between them. Players must not be within 10yd of the boards or side lines, and they must not move until the ball has left the umpire's hand.

When the ball is hit over the back line by the attacking side, it is hit back in by the defenders from the place where it went out, but at least 4yd from the goal posts or boards. The rest of the defending team can position themselves anywhere, but the attacking team must be at least 30yd from the back line. The attacking team should be given enough time to get in place, but the hit in must not be unnecessarily delayed. (Where such a hit is incorrectly taken, the defenders are awarded a hit from the 30yd line opposite where the first hit was or should have been taken.)

If the ball is hit directly over the back line by one of the defending team, or goes over the line after hitting his pony or the boards, the opponents are awarded a penalty hit from the 60yd line, opposite the place where the ball went out provided this was not less than 4yd from a goal post. The defending team must all be at least 30yd away when the ball is hit. If the ball is hit by a defending player and crosses the back line after first hitting any other player, it is hit in as if it had been put out of play by an attacker.

Right of way An officially defined right of way exists at all times during a game. This right of way is considered to extend ahead of the player entitled to it, and in the direction in which he is riding.

The right of way does not depend on who last hit the ball, but depends on the direction in which riders are traveling relative to the line of the ball. (The line of the ball is a theoretical extension of the ball's course at any moment in the game.)

Here we use four diagrams to explain the basic principles determining possession of the right of way among players riding for the ball. (Readers requiring more information on this complex subject are recommended to consult the rule book of their national polo federation.)

1) A player who is following the ball on its exact line to take it on his offside (**a**) has the right of way over any other player, including, as shown in our first diagram, a player (**b**) who is following the ball at an angle to the line of the ball. (In a case where two players are following the exact line of the ball, these two players share the right of way over all others.)

2) If no player is following the exact line of the ball, then the right of way belongs to whichever player is following the ball at the smallest angle to the line of the ball. In our second diagram, the right of way belongs to player (**a**) who is following the ball at a smaller angle to the line of the ball than is player (**b**).

3) If, as shown in our third diagram, one player is riding to meet the ball on the exact line of the ball (**a**), this player has the right of way over any player who is following the ball at an angle to the line of the ball (**b**).

4) In a case where no player is riding on the exact line of the ball, a player who is following the ball (**a**) has the right of way over any player who is riding to meet the ball, even if, as shown in our fourth diagram, the player riding to meet the ball (**b**) is riding at a smaller angle to the line of the ball.

No player other than a player with the right of way may enter or cross the right of way unless he can do so without risking a collision. If there is any risk of a collision, a player without the right of way must give way to a player with the right of way.

No player is permitted to check or pull up on the right of way if this endangers any other player.

Possession of the right of way entitles a player to take the ball on his offside; if he positions himself to take the ball on his nearside and thereby endangers any other player, the right of way passes to the endangered player.

If the line of the ball changes suddenly, by glancing off a player or for any other reason, the right of way will almost inevitably change. The player who had the right of way may continue without obstruction for a short distance along his original course.

If the ball becomes stationary at any time, its line is considered to be in the direction in which it was traveling before it stopped. If a player misses a dead ball when trying to hit it back into play, the line of the ball for the purpose of defining right of way is the same as the direction in which the player was then riding.

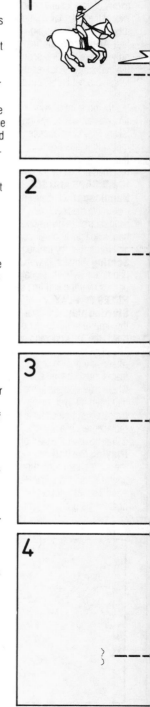

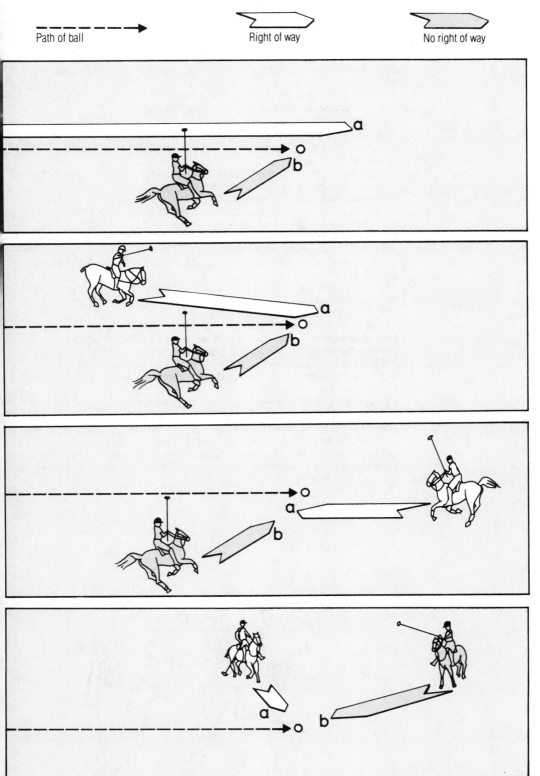

Path of ball

Right of way

No right of way

©DIAGRAM

POLO 4

Riding off or bumping another player riding in the same direction is allowed. However, players must not:

a) bump at angles that may be dangerous to other players or their ponies;

b) strike with the head, hand, forearm, or elbow (although pushing with the upper arm is allowed);

c) try to seize another player, his pony, or his equipment;

d) zigzag in front of another player who is galloping;

e) ride across another pony's legs so as to trip it;

f) ride off an opponent across the right of way;

g) "sandwich" an opponent (where two players of the same team simultaneously ride off an opponent);

h) ride at an opponent so as to intimidate him into pulling up or checking his stroke, even if no foul or cross actually takes place.

Misuse of stick A player will be penalized for:

a) reaching immediately over and across or under and across any part of an opponent's pony (**1**) to strike the ball or hook an opponent's stick;

b) hitting into or among the legs of an opponent's pony (**2**), except if he has the right of way and the opponent rides into his swing;

c) hooking an opponent's stick when he is not on the same side of the opponent's pony as the ball or in a direct line behind;

d) striking or hooking an opponent's stick above the shoulder, or level if the opponent is in the act of striking the ball;

e) deliberately striking his own pony with his stick;

f) using his stick dangerously, or holding it so it interferes with another player or pony.

Loss of headgear The umpire will stop the match to allow a player to replace his headgear, but will do so only when neither team will benefit from the stoppage.

Accident or injury The umpire will stop the match if a pony falls or goes lame, if a pony or player is injured, or if he considers that a pony's equipment has been so damaged as to be a danger to players or ponies.

If a player falls from his pony without injury, the match will not be stopped. While dismounted, the player may not touch the ball or interfere with the game.

When a player is injured, up to 15 minutes are allowed for his recovery. If he is then unable to resume play, the game resumes with a substitute player or, if the injury was a result of a foul by an opponent, the injured player's captain may call for play to continue with three players per team. An injured player who recovers after a substitution has been made is permitted to return to the game in his place.

1

Substitution for players who are unable to play through sickness, accident, or duty is allowed. No player may substitute for another if he has already played for another team in a tournament, unless special circumstances apply and there is no one else available.
If substitution occurs in a handicap match, the handicap of the player with the higher handicap will be counted, regardless of when the substitution is made. A substitute's handicap should not be more than two goals less than that of the player he replaces.

PENALTIES

Penalty goal If the umpire considers that a goal would have been scored but for a dangerous or deliberate foul in the vicinity of the goal, he may award a penalty goal to the fouled team. Ends are not changed after a penalty goal, and the umpire restarts the game by bowling the ball between the ranks of players 10yd from the offending team's goal.

Free hits According to the gravity of the offense, umpires may award penalty hits at appropriate distances.
a) A free hit from 30yd (or 40yd) from the offending team's back line, opposite the middle of the goal, may be awarded. The players of the team taking the free hit must all be behind the ball. The offending team must be behind the back line until the ball has been hit; they may not position themselves between the goalposts, nor ride out from between them when the hit is taken. (When a 30yd or 40yd hit is awarded, the captain of the fouled team may choose instead to take the free hit from the point where the offense occurred.)
b) A free hit from 60yd from the offending team's back line, opposite the middle of the goal, may be awarded. Members of the team taking the hit may position themselves where they like. The offending team must be at least 30yd from the ball.
c) A free hit from the spot where an offense occurred may be awarded by the umpire or chosen by the captain instead of a 30yd or 40yd hit. Members of the team taking the hit may take up any position. Their opponents must be at least 30yd from the ball.
d) A free hit from the center of the ground may also be awarded. Members of the team taking the hit may take up any position. Opponents must be at least 30yd from the ball.

Fouls at free hits If a free hit is not properly carried out, the umpire may:
a) award a penalty goal if the foul prevented a goal from being scored;
b) award a further free hit, regardless of the result of the previous one;
c) award the defending side the right to hit in from the middle of their own goal;
d) bowl the ball into play if there is undue delay in taking a free hit.

Ordering off or disqualification Ponies may be ordered off or disqualified for infringing rules relating to their condition.
Players may be ordered off for using forbidden equipment, or they may be excluded from the game for dangerous and deliberate fouls or for unsportsmanlike conduct. If a player is ordered off, his team must continue with three players or forfeit the match.

2

POOL

HISTORY

Like snooker, pool (or American pocket billiards) is a descendant of billiards. The Spanish introduced a form of billiards into America in the sixteenth century; the British brought English billiards to New England in the early nineteenth century. Pool evolved from these games and their variants; for example, 14.1 continuous pool may have been derived from the game of pyramids, which was also a forerunner of snooker. Today pool in one of its many forms is played by probably more people in the world than any other form of billiards. The Billiard Congress of America (BCA) has been the principal governing body of the game since 1948.

SYNOPSIS

The principal forms of pool played at national and world championship level are eight ball and 14.1 continuous pool; rules for both these versions are described below. Both are played on a pocket billiard table and use 15 colored object balls and one white cue ball.

TABLE AND EQUIPMENT

The table is a smaller version of an English billiard table (see pp. 318–319). It should either be a 4 by 8 table (ie 4ft wide by 8ft long) or a 4½ by 9 table (ie 4ft 6in wide by 9ft long).

The playing area should measure 46in by 92in on the 4 by 8 table, and 50in by 100in on the 4½ by 9 table.

The height of the table bed playing surface should be 29–29½in.

Corner pocket openings should measure 4⅞–5⅛in: side pocket openings should measure 5¾–5⅝in.

Table markings Prior to competition, the following should be marked on the cloth:
a) head spot;
b) center spot;
c) foot spot;
d) the long string, to allow balls to be spotted accurately;
e) the head string, to allow the players and officials easily to determine which balls are behind the head string;
f) the position of the triangle rack, to allow it to be replaced consistently in the same position.

Cue Competitors may use cues of their own choice of length, weight, and design, providing that these conform to accepted competition practice.

Cue rest Mechanical bridges may be used to support the shaft of the cue for strokes, providing that not more than two bridges are used at one time.

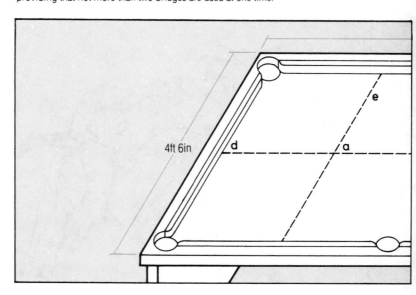

4ft 6in

The balls must be equal in size and weight. A standard ball should be 2¼ in in diameter and weigh 5½–6oz. The object balls are numbered 1–15; numbers 1–8 are in solid colors, numbers 9–15 are striped. The cue ball is white.

Triangle A triangular rack may be used to position the object balls for the start of play.

PLAYERS AND OFFICIALS

Players Eight ball and 14.1 continuous pool may be played by two players or two teams.

Officials include a referee, who is responsible for the conduct of the game, and a marker, who is responsible for keeping the score.

GENERAL RULES

Playing order is determined by drawing lots or by the lag for break (opening shot). The lag for break is similar to "stringing" in snooker (see p.320).

Innings A player's inning (turn at the table) ends when he fails legally to pocket a ball, or commits a foul. Players alternate their innings at the table.

When an inning ends without a foul the incoming player must play the balls as they lie.

A stroke begins when a player touches the ball with his cue, and ends when all the balls have come to rest. Strokes that are not legal are considered fouls, and are penalized accordingly. For a stroke to be legal:

a) only the cue ball may be struck with the cue;

b) the cue ball must be struck with the tip of the cue only;

c) the cue ball must be struck and not pushed;

d) the cue ball must not be struck more than once on the same stroke;

e) the cue ball must not be pocketed;

f) all balls on the table must be motionless at the moment that the cue ball is struck;

g) the player must not intentionally strike the cue ball in such a way that it rises off the bed of the table;

h) the cue ball must not be forced off the table;

i) one of the player's feet must be touching the floor as the cue ball is struck.

Cue ball into play The player with the right to play first may for his first stroke place the cue ball anywhere behind the head string, ie between the head cushion and the head string. The ball is also put into play in the same way after certain fouls (eg pocketing the cue ball). The cue ball remains in hand (not in play), and the player may adjust its position with his hand or his cue until the ball crosses the head string.

It is a foul if, after the cue ball has been set in motion, it is impeded in its progress toward the head string.

2¼in

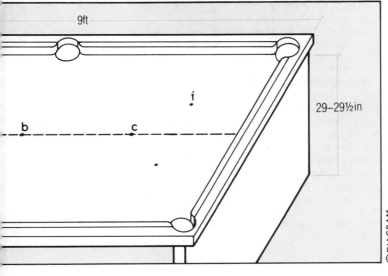

9ft

29–29½in

POOL 2

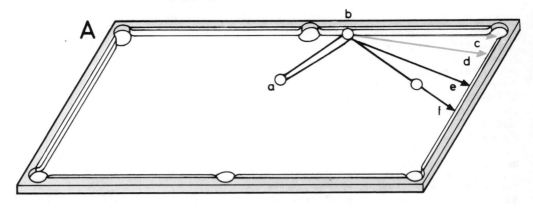

A pocketed ball is one that is sent into a pocket on a legal stroke and remains in that pocket. A ball that rebounds from the pocket onto the table bed is not considered a pocketed ball, and remains in play where it came to rest. A player who pockets more than one ball on a legal scoring shot is credited with the additional ball or balls.

Balls moving spontaneously If a ball falls into a pocket by itself after remaining motionless on the pocket lip for three seconds or more, it is not considered a pocketed ball and should be replaced as close as possible to where it was on the table.

Balls that move spontaneously without falling into a pocket should be allowed to remain in the position that they have assumed. However, an exception is made if a player shoots at an object ball, and that particular ball moves spontaneously in such a way that the cue ball passes over the spot where it had been without being able to hit it. In this case the cue ball and the object ball are replaced in the positions they occupied before the stroke was made. Any other object balls disturbed by the spread are also replaced, and the shot is retaken.

Outside interference Any balls moved because of outside interference should be replaced as near as possible to their original positions before the incident occurred.

Jumped balls After a stroke, a ball that comes to rest anywhere other than on the bed of the table or in a pocket is considered a jumped ball. A ball that bounces off the table equipment (ie the permanent parts of the table, its light fittings, and any chalk resting on the rail) and returns to the bed of the table under its own power is not considered a jumped ball. A ball that touches anything other than the table equipment is always considered a jumped ball, even if it returns to the bed of the table.

Balls touching (A) If the object ball a player nominates for his stroke is touching a cushion ("frozen"), he must cause the cue ball (**a**) to contact the frozen ball (**b**) and then:
c) pocket the frozen ball; or
d) drive the frozen ball to another cushion; or
e) cause the cue ball to contact a cushion; or
f) cause another object ball to contact a cushion.
Failure to accomplish one of these alternatives is considered a foul.
The same alternatives apply if the nominated ball is touching (frozen to) the cue ball.

Locked object balls A referee's assessment of position is required if two or more object balls are locked between the jaws of a pocket with one or more of the balls suspended in air. Suspended balls that in the referee's judgment would fall into the pocket if moved directly downward are considered pocketed; balls that would come to rest on the table bed are not considered pocketed. The balls should then be placed according to the referee's assessment, and play should continue.

Spotting balls A single ball that is to be spotted is placed on the foot spot.
If several balls are to be spotted at the same time they are placed on the long string between the foot spot and the foot rail. They should be spotted in numerical order, with the lowest number on the foot spot. If there is insufficient room for the balls on that part of the long string, they should be spotted on the extension of the long string between the foot and center spots. The balls should again be in numerical order, with the highest number closest to the foot spot.

If balls already on or near the foot spot or the long string interfere with the spotting of balls, the balls that are to be spotted are placed as close as possible to the foot spot without moving the interfering balls. If the interfering balls are object balls, the spotted balls are considered to be frozen to them. If the interfering ball is the cue ball, the balls to be spotted are placed as close as possible to it without being frozen.

14.1 CONTINUOUS POOL

The object is to be first to score a predetermined point total (usually 150).

Balls at start of play (B) The arrangement of the balls at the start of the game (the "rack") is a triangle whose base is parallel with and nearest to the foot of the table. The ball at the apex of the triangle (**a**) should be on the foot spot; the number 1 (**b**) and number 5 (**c**) balls should be placed as shown in the diagram; the remaining balls should be placed at random within the triangle.

B

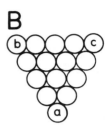

Starting procedure On the first shot of the game (the "opening break shot"), the starting player must either:

a) designate an object ball and a pocket into which it will be pocketed, and accomplish the shot; or

b) cause the cue ball to contact an object ball and then a cushion, plus cause two object balls to contact a cushion.

Failure to accomplish one of these alternatives is a "breaking violation"; the offender incurs a two point penalty. His opponent may then play the balls as they lie on the table ("table in position"), or may have the balls reracked and require the offending player to repeat the opening break. This choice continues until a legal opening break shot has been played, or until the table is accepted in position.

If the starting player pockets the cue ball ("scratches") on an otherwise legal opening break shot, it is considered a foul. He is penalized one point; his opponent then plays with the cue ball in hand behind the head string and with the object balls remaining as they lie.

Playing procedure On all shots other than the opening break shot, the player must cause the cue ball to contact an object ball and then:

a) pocket an object ball; or

b) cause the cue ball or any object ball to contact a cushion.

Failure to accomplish one of these alternatives is considered a foul.

A player may shoot at any ball he chooses, but must announce his choice of ball (the "called ball") and the pocket at which he is aiming (the "called pocket") in advance. He may cause the cue ball to contact other object balls before pocketing the called ball.

A player's turn at the table continues until he fails legally to pocket a called ball on a shot; any illegally pocketed balls are spotted.

Play stops momentarily when 14 balls of a rack have been pocketed. The pocketed balls are reracked (**C**): an empty space is left at the apex of the triangle (**a**). The fifteenth object ball (the "break ball") and the cue ball should if possible remain in position on the table. Specific regulations govern the repositioning of these balls if either or both of them interfere with the placing of the triangle, or if the fifteenth ball is pocketed on the same stroke as the fourteenth ball.

C

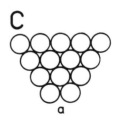

The player at the table then continues his inning, and may shoot at any ball he chooses; he will normally choose to pocket the break ball and use the cue ball to spread the rack.

A safety is a shot in which the player attempts to position the balls in a way that makes it difficult for his opponent to score.

A player may call a safety as an alternative to calling an object ball; his shot must comply with all applicable rules. Any object balls pocketed on a safety are spotted, and are not credited to the player, whose inning ends when the safety has been played.

If, in the referee's opinion, an object ball is within a ball's width of a cushion, a player is permitted only two legal safeties on that ball using that cushion. If he chooses to make his first cue ball contact with that object ball on his third shot, it is considered a frozen ball and must be played accordingly.

If a player has committed a foul on his previous shot, and chooses to play a ball within a ball's width of a cushion, he may play only one safety before the ball is considered frozen.

If he has committed two successive fouls and chooses to play this object ball, it is immediately considered frozen and must be played accordingly; failure to meet the requirements for playing a frozen ball is penalized as a third successive foul.

POOL 3

Jumped object balls are all spotted after the balls have come to rest; the player remains at the table if he has legally pocketed a called ball.

Cue ball in hand If a player has the cue ball in hand behind the head string, and all the object balls on the table are also behind the head string, the object ball nearest the head string may be spotted at his request. If two or more of the object balls are equidistant from the head string, the player may choose which of the two is to be spotted.

Fouls A player is penalized one point for each foul (excluding breaking violations); additional penalties are imposed for special deliberate fouls or for committing three successive fouls.

A player who has committed a foul is recorded as being "on a foul": the foul is cleared from his record if he legally pockets a called ball or plays a legal safety on his next shot. A player who commits two fouls on consecutive strokes ("on two fouls") may clear his record in the same way.

Committing a third successive foul in three consecutive strokes automatically clears the offender's record. He is penalized an additional 15 points (making a total of 18 for the three fouls), the balls are reracked, and he is required to break as at the beginning of the game. Breaking violations do not count toward the three foul limit.

A player commits a special deliberate foul if he in any way interferes with a ball traveling toward a pocket or the rack area. He is penalized an additional 15 points (making a total penalty of 16 for the foul). His opponent may accept the table in position, with the cue ball in hand behind the head string, or may have the balls reracked and require the offender to break as at the beginning of the game.

After a foul in which the cue ball is jumped or scratched, the incoming player has the cue ball in hand behind the head string. If, however, the jump or scratch occurred on a third successive foul, or at the same time as a special deliberate foul, the regulations governing those offenses apply.

The incoming competitor must accept the cue ball and table in position after all fouls except those specified above.

Scoring A player scores one point for each ball legally pocketed.

The point penalties deducted from his score for foul strokes, breaking violations, and other offenses are specified above.

If a player commits a foul on a stroke that has not pocketed a ball, the penalty is deducted from his score at the end of the previous inning. If he commits a foul and pockets a ball on the same stroke, that ball is spotted and is not credited to his score; the penalty for the foul is deducted from his score at the end of the previous inning.

If a player commits a foul or fouls before scoring any points, the penalties are deducted from zero, giving him a negative score.

EIGHT BALL POOL

The object of the game is to be the first player legally to pocket either all the balls numbered from 1–7 followed by the 8 ball, or all the balls numbered from 9–15 followed by the 8 ball.

Options Where alternative forms of a rule exist, they are listed below. Tournament rules should specify which options are to be played.

Balls at the start of play (A) The balls are arranged in a triangular rack with the apex ball (**a**) on the foot spot. The 8 ball (**b**) should be in the center of the rack; the other balls should be placed at random within the triangle.

Starting procedure On the opening break shot the starting player must drive a minimum of four object balls out of the rack onto the cushions (make an "open break"). If he fails to make an open break, his opponent may play the table in position, or may have the balls reracked and shoot the opening break shot himself.

If the 8 ball is pocketed on a legal opening break shot, the player making the break wins the game. (Alternatively, the balls may be reracked and the same player breaks again, without penalty.)

Open table The table is considered open until a player has legally pocketed more balls from one group than the other. The group from which he has pocketed the greater number of balls is then his group; his opponent shoots at the other group.

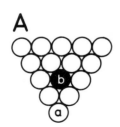
A

254

Playing procedure When playing on an open table, the competitor may shoot at any object ball he chooses. He must cause the cue ball to contact an object ball and then:
a) pocket an object ball; or
b) cause the cue ball or any object ball to contact a cushion.
Failure to accomplish one of these alternatives is considered a foul.
These options also apply when the player's group has been determined; however, his cue ball's first contact must then be with an object ball of his own group, or the shot will be considered a foul.
A player's inning continues until he fails legally to pocket a ball of either group when the table is open, or a ball of his own group when that has been determined.
After all the balls of his group have been pocketed, the player shoots to pocket the 8 ball. The 8 ball may legally be pocketed only if the player causes his cue ball's first contact to be with the 8 ball, and also calls the pocket at which he is aiming.
(Alternatively, the player may be required to pocket the 8 ball into the same pocket as his last group ball – the "last pocket option." He must still call the pocket at which he is aiming. If agreed in advance, the player may call a pocket other than his last group ball's pocket, providing that he causes the cue ball to contact at least three cushions before contacting and pocketing the 8 ball.)

Jumped object balls The player's balls are spotted; his opponent's balls remain off the table. (Alternatively, all jumped balls may remain off the table.)
The player is not penalized if he has played a legal shot at the same time unless the jumped ball is the 8 ball, when he automatically loses the game.

Cue ball in hand If a player has the cue ball in hand behind the head string, and all his object balls are also behind the head string, the object ball of his group nearest the head string may be spotted on the foot spot at his request. This also applies to the 8 ball if it is his next object ball. If two or more of his object balls are equidistant from the head string, the player may choose which of the two is to be spotted.

Fouls do not incur a points penalty. Illegally pocketed balls are spotted only if they are the shooter's; his opponent's balls remain off the table. (Alternatively, all illegally pocketed balls may remain off the table.)

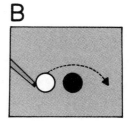

After a foul in which the cue ball is jumped (**B**), or scratched (**C**), the incoming player has the cue ball in hand behind the head string.
After other fouls, the incoming player may accept the table in position, or may play with the cue ball in hand behind the head string. (Alternatively, he may have the cue ball in hand anywhere on the table.)
Additionally, if the 8 ball is the incoming player's legal object ball, he may choose to play with the cue ball in hand behind the head string and the 8 ball spotted on the foot spot.
A player automatically loses the game if he:
a) pockets the 8 ball on an illegal or foul opening break shot;
b) pockets the 8 ball when it is not his legal object ball;
c) pockets the 8 ball on the same stroke as the last ball or balls of his group;
d) pockets the cue ball when the 8 ball is his legal object ball (except when playing the "last pocket option");
e) jumps the 8 ball off the table;
f) pockets the 8 ball in any pocket other than his called pocket;
g) pockets the 8 ball when it is his legal object ball but without calling his pocket;
h) commits three successive fouls.

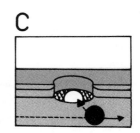

Scoring Individual balls have no points value. A player wins a game if he legally pockets the 8 ball, or if his opponent commits one of the offenses listed above. A match is won by winning the most games.
An optional point system may be used to decide matches; a player receives three points for winning a game, plus one point for each of his opponent's balls remaining on the table. The player with the highest aggregate number of points at the end of the match is then the winner.

RACQUETBALL

HISTORY

As paddleball developed from court handball, so racquetball developed from paddleball when, in the late 1940s and early 1950s, paddleball players decided that the game could be improved by using a strung racquet instead of the standard wooden paddle. The new game was known by various names until the first national American tournament was held in the late 1960s, when the name "racquetball" was adopted. The game's success has been remarkable, with an increase from about half a million players in the early 1970s to well over three million at the beginning of the 1980s. The governing body for the sport is the American Amateur Racquetball Association (AARA).

SYNOPSIS

Racquetball is a court game played with a short-handled racquet and a hollow, pressurized ball; players score points by hitting shots that their opponents are unable to return. The standard game is played on four-wall courts, but because of the links with paddleball and court handball, racquetball rules also allow for play on one- and three-wall courts.

Rules for the four-wall game are described first; rules for the one-wall game differ in some respects (see p. 261). Three-wall courts are less common and are not standardized, and rules are adapted for play on the particular court used.

COURT AND EQUIPMENT

Court Illustrated here is a standard four-wall court, 20ft wide and 40ft long. The front (**a**) and side (**b**) walls should be 20ft high; the back wall (**c**) should be at least 12ft high. The 1½in wide red or white lines marking the court floor are:

d) short line, parallel to and 20ft from the front wall;

e) service line, parallel to and 15ft from the front line;

f) service boxes, marked by lines parallel to and 1ft 6in from each side wall;

g) receiving lines, marked on the side walls 5ft behind the short line, and extending 3–6in upward from the floor.

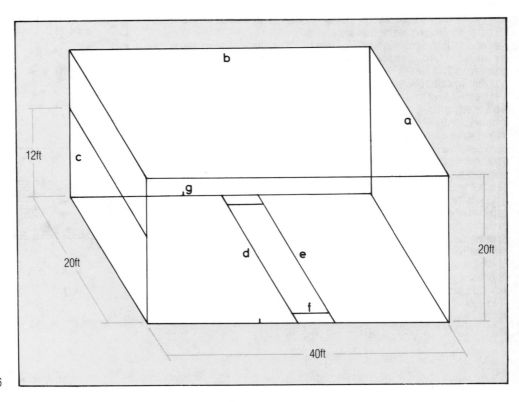

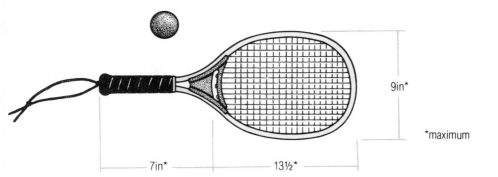

9in*

*maximum

7in*   13½*

The ball is hollow and pressurized; it should be 2¼in in diameter, and weigh approximately 1.4oz. When dropped from a height of 100in, it should rebound 68–72in in a temperature of 76°F.

The referee should select carefully the balls to be used in a match; balls that are not round or that bounce erratically should not be used. At least two acceptable balls should be available before the match begins.

A substitute ball may be put into play at any time during a match, either at the request of a player or at the referee's discretion.

Racquet The maximum length of the racquet head is 13½in, and the maximum width 9in, measured to the outer edges of the rim. The handle may be up to 7in long.

The racquet frame may be of any material; the strings may be of gut, monofilament, nylon, or metal. The thong attached to the end of the handle must be worn around the wrist during play.

Dress Players may wear shirts, shorts, socks, and shoes of any color that does not affect their opponents' view of the ball. Wet shirts must be changed on the request of the referee. Players may also wear a glove on the hand holding the racquet, sweatbands on the wrist and head, and eyeguards or safety glasses.

PLAYERS AND OFFICIALS

Players Each side may consist of one player (singles) or two (doubles). In the three-player "cut-throat" game, the two players who are not serving play against the server.

Officials The referee in charge of the match may be assisted by two linesmen and a scorer.

DURATION AND SCORING

Duration A match consists of two games, plus a tiebreaker if required. Five-minute intervals are allowed between the games and before the tiebreaker.

Both sides must be ready to play within 10 seconds of the end of the previous rally; players are penalized for any deliberate delays.

Providing that the server has not begun his service, either side may request a time-out. Each side is allowed up to three 30-second time-outs in each game, and up to two 30-second time-outs in the tiebreaker. At the discretion of the referee, players are allowed equipment time-outs to replace damaged or wet clothing or equipment. Equipment time-outs are in addition to players' time-outs.

An injured player is allowed up to 15 minutes' rest, after which time he must either continue play or forfeit the match.

Scoring A game is won by the first side to score 21 points. A match consists of two games; if the two sides win one game each, the first side to win 11 points in the tiebreaker wins the match.

Points are awarded only if the side that is serving wins the rally. When the serving side loses a rally, or fails to serve according to the rules, the service passes to the other side.

2¼in

RACQUETBALL 2

RULES OF PLAY

Service order The player or pair that wins the toss serves first in the opening game; the loser of the toss serves first in the second game. The side scoring the highest total number of points in both games combined serves first in the tiebreaker; if both sides score an equal number of points in the first two games a further toss is held to determine the service order in the tiebreaker.

In doubles, when the starting player loses the service, it passes to the opposing side. Thereafter, both players in each team must serve and lose service before the service passes to the opposition. The service order established at the beginning of a game must be followed throughout that game.

The service may only be taken when both serving and receiving sides have signaled their readiness to play. It may be taken anywhere within the service zone (the area between the short line and the service line); the server must have both feet on or within the zone lines. The server should bounce the ball on the floor of the service zone, and hit it once with the head of his racquet (**A**). For a good service (**B**), the ball should be served direct onto the front wall; on the rebound it should hit the floor beyond the short line, either with (**1**) or without (**2**) touching one of the side walls.

The server must remain in the service zone until the ball has crossed the short line on the rebound. In doubles, the server's partner must stand with both feet in the service box and his back to the wall while the service is taken. He should remain in the service box until the ball has crossed the short line on the rebound.

The receiving side must stand at least 5ft behind the short line (as indicated by the receiving lines) until the ball has bounced beyond the short line.

Service faults (**C**) A player who serves two successive faults loses the service. It is a service fault if:

a) the player does not have both feet in the service zone when beginning his service, or leaves the service zone before the served ball passes the short line on the rebound;

b) in doubles, the server's partner leaves the service box before the served ball passes the short line;

c) the served ball first hits the floor on or in front of the short line (**1**), either with or without touching one of the side walls;

d) the served ball hits two side walls after hitting the front wall and before bouncing on the floor;

A

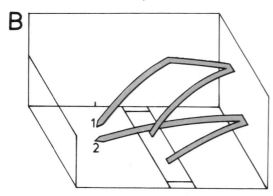

B

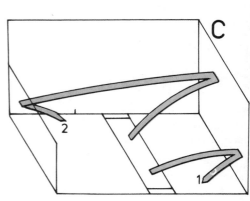

C

e) the served ball hits the ceiling after hitting the front wall, either with or without touching one of the side walls;

f) the served ball rebounds from the front wall and hits the back wall before touching the floor (**2**);

g) the served ball goes out of court on the service;

h) in doubles, the served ball rebounds from the front wall, hits the floor, and touches the server's partner while he is in the service box.

Out serves (D) Certain service errors lead to an immediate loss of service (an "out"). A server loses the service if:

a) the server fails to strike the ball on the first bounce, or touches it with his body or clothing;

b) the served ball touches any other part of the court before striking the front wall (**1**);

c) in doubles, the served ball touches the server's partner before striking the front wall;

d) on the rebound from the front wall the served ball touches the server;

e) in doubles, the served ball on the rebound from the front wall touches the server's partner while any part of his body is out of the service box, or if the server's partner intentionally catches the served ball;

f) in doubles, the players serve out of order;

g) the served ball hits the front wall where it joins the floor (**2**), the ceiling, or a side wall (the "crotch") – except that a serve into the crotch of the back wall (**E**) is an ace, as is a three-wall crotch serve:

h) he hits the ball twice, or hits it with the racquet handle;

i) he makes a fake or balk serve (ie makes a non-continuous movement of the racquet toward the ball as he drops the ball for the purpose of serving).

Dead ball service There is no penalty for a dead ball service; the server takes the service again. Any previous service fault is unaffected.

A dead ball service occurs if, on an otherwise legal service:

a) in doubles, the served ball on the rebound from the front wall touches the server's partner while he is still in the service box, but before it hits the floor;

b) the ball passes so close to the server or the server's partner that the receiver's view is obstructed, or the ball passes between the server's partner and the side wall;

c) the ball bounces erratically because of an obstruction or wet spot on the court;

d) the ball is found to be broken or defective.

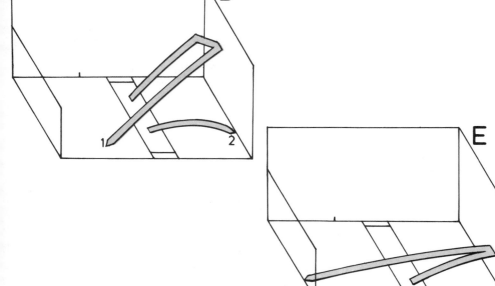

©DIAGRAM

RACQUETBALL 3

Return of service (A) The receiver must stand at least 5ft behind the short line, and may not enter the safety zone between the short line and the receiving lines until the served ball has passed the short line.

It is a good return of service if the receiver plays the ball after it has passed the short line but before it has bounced on the floor (**1**), providing he does not cross the short line with his body or racquet. He may also return the ball when it has crossed the short line and bounced once on the floor (**2**).

The returned ball must strike the front wall either directly, or after touching one or both side walls, the back wall, the ceiling, or any combination of these surfaces. The returned ball must not touch the floor before touching the front wall.

Good rally Each legal return after the service is called a rally; the player may strike the ball with either side of the racquet, and may hold the racquet in either one or both hands.

It is a good rally if the player volleys the ball, or hits it after it has bounced once on the floor, so that it is returned to the front wall, either with or without touching any part of the court except the floor.

If a player strikes at a ball and misses, he may make further attempts to make a good return before it touches the floor for a second time. In doubles, both members of a side are entitled to attempt to return the ball, and may make one or more attempts to strike it before it touches the floor for a second time.

Bad rally It is a bad rally and results in a point or out against the offender if the player:
a) hits the ball with anything other than the head of his racquet;
b) switches his racquet from hand to hand during play;
c) touches the ball more than once;
d) fails to return the ball to the front wall but instead strikes it out of court;
e) deliberately wets the ball;
f) hits his partner with an attempted return.

Touching the ball Except for the player making the return, any player touching the ball before it has bounced twice on the floor is penalized by an out or point against him (unless the ball touches the offender without first bouncing, when it is a dead ball hinder).

Dead ball hinder There is no penalty for a dead ball hinder (obstruction) but the point is replayed. It is a dead ball hinder when:
a) the ball rebounds from the front wall and goes out of court on the rebound or after the first bounce;
b) the ball breaks during play;
c) a returned ball, without first bouncing, touches the striker's opponent before returning to the front wall, excepting a ball that obviously could not have reached the front wall;
d) the ball strikes any part of the court that under local rules is a dead ball;
e) the ball rebounds from the front wall so close to the striker or his partner (including passing between their legs) that their opponents are unsighted, or do not have a fair chance to return the ball;
f) body contact or other accidental interference by an opponent unsights a player or interferes with his returning the ball, unless, in the referee's judgment, the contact was such that it did not severely interrupt the flow of play;

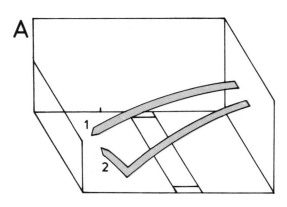

g) any foreign object enters the court, or there is any outside interference, if these occurrences interfere with ensuing play or the players' safety.

Avoidable hinder The penalty for an avoidable hinder is an out or point against the offender, depending on whether he was serving or receiving.

It is an avoidable hinder when:

a) a player does not move out of the way to allow his opponent a shot;

b) a player moves into a position that blocks or crowds his opponent;

c) in doubles, the partner of the player who is striking the ball blocks or crowds a member of the opposing side;

d) a player moves into the path of the ball just after it has been struck by his opponent;

e) a player deliberately unsights an opponent who is just about to strike the ball;

f) a player forcibly pushes an opponent;

g) a player deliberately intimidates or distracts his opponent.

ONE-WALL RACQUETBALL

Court Illustrated (**B**) is a standard one-wall court. The wall is 20ft wide and 16ft high, topped with a 4ft high wire fence. The playing zone on the floor is 20ft wide and 34ft long, and should be surrounded by at least 6ft of clear space on every side.

Lines marking the court are:

a) long line, marking the edge of the playing zone parallel to and farthest from the wall;

b) short line, parallel to and 16ft from the wall;

c) service markers, parallel to and equidistant from the long and short lines, and extending 6in inward from the side lines;

d) side lines, marking the edges of the playing zone perpendicular to the wall.

Rules of play are as for four-wall racquetball with the following exceptions:

a) a player loses the service after one service fault;

b) any serve that lands outside the side lines or the long line is an out;

c) the server must stand either to the left or right of the center of the court and serve to the more open part of the court, or must stand in the center and designate the side to which he is serving;

d) any serve that passes within 18in of the server's body is a fault;

e) in doubles, the server's partner must stand outside the playing zone, either at the serving line or behind the long line.

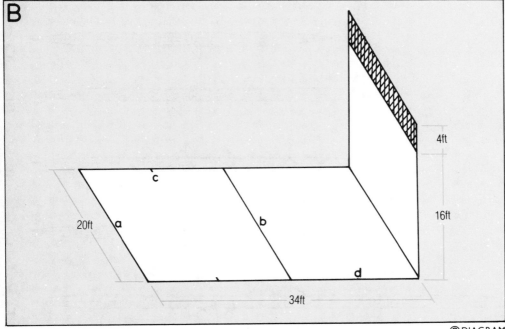

B

20ft

34ft

4ft

16ft

a   b   c   d

ROWING

HISTORY

Although there has probably been competitive rowing wherever oars have been
used to propel boats, the modern sport appears to have its origins in wager
contests between professional boatmen on the rivers of eighteenth century
Europe. Amateur interest grew, especially in Britain and America, in the early
nineteenth century, with the main impetus from schools and universities. The
characteristic features of modern racing boats appeared in the mid nineteenth
century: the smooth shell of the hull and the outrigger (permitting a narrow
boat) in the 1840s and 1850s, and the sliding seat in 1871. Later alterations
have been more by way of refinement than radical change. Since 1892 the
sport has been governed by the Fédération Internationale des Sociétés
d'Aviron (FISA). In 1908 rowing was officially recognized as an Olympic sport.

SYNOPSIS

Rowing events are held on lakes, rivers, tidal water, or on coastal waters (in
which case a different type of boat is used). However, for competition at
international level, a purpose-built dead straight course is now required, which
allows a number of crews to race alongside each other on equal terms. Such
events are of the "regatta" type, a knockout competition ending with a race
between two or more finalists.

On those watercourses that are too narrow for regatta events, competitions may
be of the "head of the river" or processional type, when the boats start at
intervals and the result is decided by their times over the course.

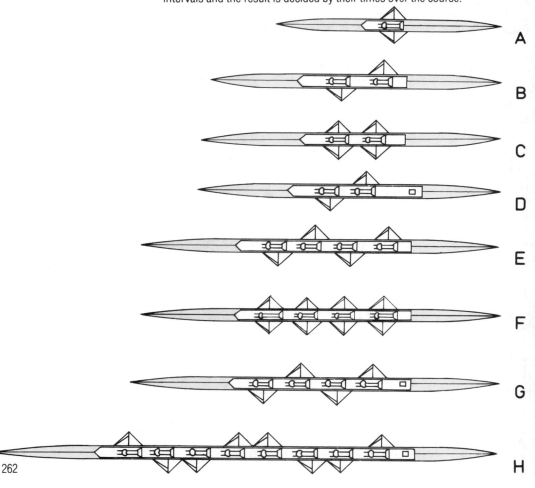

A

B

C

D

E

F

G

H

Technically there is a distinction between rowing and sculling. In the former each oarsman has one oar, and in the latter, two sculls (short, light oars). In some events a coxswain or cox is included in the crew. The cox steers the boat and gives orders to the oarsmen or women.

EQUIPMENT AND COURSE

Boats Construction and design are usually unrestricted. Typical dimensions are given below, for purposes of comparison. Events are confined to boats of the same type. A blunting device must be fitted to the bow: it is usually in the form of a white ball at least 4cm in diameter and made of solid rubber or a similar material.
In sculls there is no provision for a cox, and each oarsman has two short, light sculls (oars). In other boats the outriggers are usually removable so that the arrangement of the oars can be changed. In fours and eights the oars have traditionally been placed alternately, but recently asymmetric arrangements have become common.
Oars (a) are from 12ft to 12ft 8in long and weigh about 8lb. A scull (**b**) is about 9ft 8in to 10ft long and correspondingly lighter. In international competition, both sides of the oar blade are painted with the color of the crew's national association. Blade shape is not laid down, but shorter, wider blades have been popular in recent years.

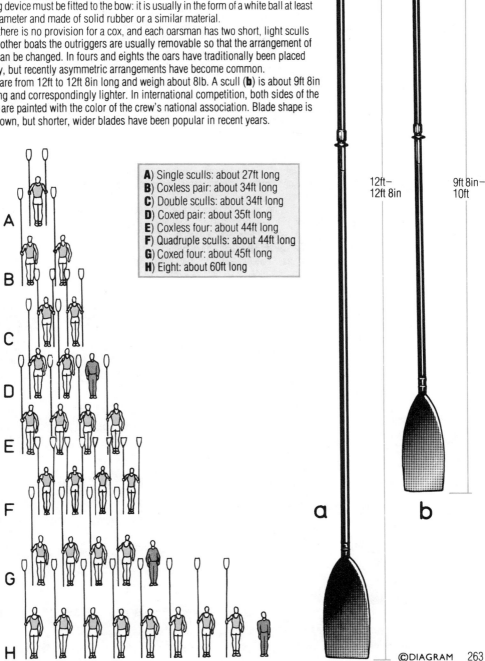

A) Single sculls: about 27ft long
B) Coxless pair: about 34ft long
C) Double sculls: about 34ft long
D) Coxed pair: about 35ft long
E) Coxless four: about 44ft long
F) Quadruple sculls: about 44ft long
G) Coxed four: about 45ft long
H) Eight: about 60ft long

12ft–12ft 8in

9ft 8in–10ft

a

b

263

ROWING 2

Dress Oarsmen and scullers wear undershirts and shorts, which are uniform within a crew. The undershirts bear club or national colors or other insignia. The cox may wear different, warmer clothing.

The course For major international competitions the course should be straight, with no current, and be divided into six lanes.

The standard length of course is 1000m for women and 2000m for men.

Our illustration shows part of a typical layout for the starting area of a modern purpose-bu[ilt] course. (For explanation see below, The start.) The distance to the finish is marked at the start line and every 250m.

COMPETITORS AND OFFICIALS

Competitors Both men and women are divided into age categories, and national federations may place crews in additional categories based on ability.

There is a special lightweight category for men, to qualify for which the average weight of the crew excluding the cox must not exceed 70kg, and no individual may weigh more than 72.5kg.

Coxswains are regarded as members of the crew, and under international rules must be of the same sex as the oarsmen or women. The minimum weight for a cox is 50kg for men and 45kg for women. To reach the minimum, deadweight of up to 5kg may be carried.

Officials A regatta committee is responsible for overall control and organization. A race committee controls the racing.

Supervisors, at embarking and disembarking points, check the composition of crews, the specification of the boats, and the weight of coxswains (or of the whole crew in lightweight events).

Umpires either each control a section of the course or follow the race in a launch. There may also be a separate starter and aligner.

Judges decide the order of finishing, but not necessarily the final results.

RACE PROCEDURE (Regatta events)

The start Crews must be at the start at least two minutes before the race is due to begin. The aligner indicates, by raising a white flag, when all crews are aligned correctly with

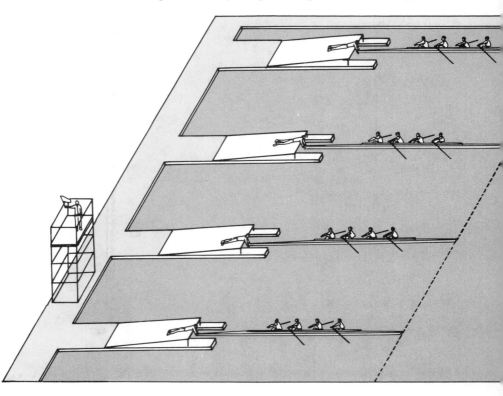

reference to their lanes and start line. To aid alignment the boats may be held by officials in moored stake boats or on platforms (as illustrated).

The starter asks, "Are you ready?" and if there is no objection drops a red flag and orders "Go."

After a false start the boats may be recalled (within 100m of the start) by ringing a bell and waving a red flag.

A crew will be disqualified for causing a second false start in any one race.

The race Each boat must keep within its own lane or the crew may be disqualified.

An umpire may warn a boat about its steering only if it is about to impede or collide with another boat that is on a correct course. If a collision or any interference occurs after a warning, the umpire may disqualify the offending crew or crews. He may order a restart. No instructions or advice may be given to any crew during a race.

The finish A crew has finished when the bows of its boat cross the finish line.

If an oarsman or sculler falls out, the boat can still be placed, but not if the cox falls out.

When all crews have finished, the race umpire raises a white flag if the race was all in order and there are no protests; otherwise he raises a red flag.

The judges decide the finishing order, using photographs if necessary.

HEAD RACES

General rules "Head of the river" or simply "head" races are governed by rules drawn up by the organizing committee, as this form of race is not used for the major international events.

There are no lanes, crews being started at intervals from the same point on the river and timed over the course.

If one boat catches another up, the overtaking boat has right of way.

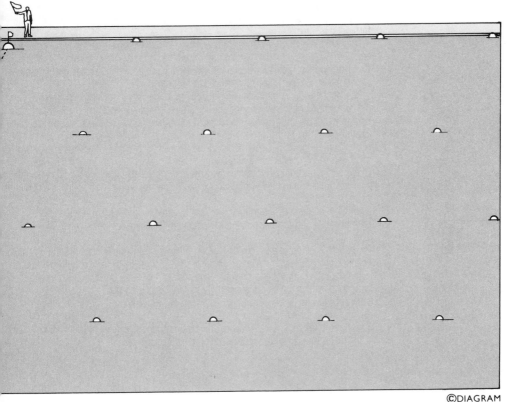

©DIAGRAM

SHOOTING

HISTORY

Civic shooting festivals have been held in some northern European cities, particularly in Germany and Switzerland, since the sixteenth century. The modern worldwide interest in target shooting, however, dates really from the second half of the nineteenth century, when technical advances in rifled firearms greatly improved and facilitated accurate shooting. The International Shooting Union or UIT (Union Internationale de Tir) was formed at Zurich in 1907. The international events described here are governed by the rules of this organization.

SYNOPSIS

Shooting disciplines differ as to the distance, form and behavior of the target, the exact nature of the firearm and ammunition used, the position of the firer, and the timing and number of the shots fired. Some events are designed to test "pure" marksmanship; others simulate hunting or combat in a highly stylized form. Shooting is essentially a sport for the individual, and team matches usually consist of the aggregate of several individuals' scores.

GENERAL RULES

Safety The potential dangers of firearms are obvious, but are eliminated by strict rules so effectively that shooting is in fact far less dangerous than many other sports. The most basic of these rules, applicable to all the events that follow, is that no person may load his firearm except on the firing line and when given the order to do so by the referee. At the end of firing, or on being given the order "cease fire," the breech is opened, inspected, and kept open.

Inspection of firearms, equipment, and clothing may be undertaken by referees and juries at any time, in order to ensure compliance with UIT rules. Firearms must be inspected before each competition. In prone and three-position rifle events the firer's clothing is minutely regulated because of the possibility of gaining unfair advantage from excessive padding or from restrictive and thus supportive garments. It is the competitor's duty to submit any doubtful item for approval. To curb misplaced ingenuity, there is a catch-all rule that forbids any device that is contrary to the spirit of the rules although not expressly forbidden by them.

To prevent the reduction of trigger pressures to unsafe levels, triggers may be tested by applying a weight, with the barrel of the firearm pointing vertically upward.

Contingencies There are special rules in each event, designed to cover every possible contingency, which may be summarized as follows.

Ties in deliberate fire events may be "broken" or resolved by "counting out"; this involves the comparison of scores, shot by shot, in a predetermined sequence (usually working back from the last shot) until a difference is found. In rapid fire and skeet and trap events a "shoot-off" is staged.

A shot hole gauge (left) is used to decide the value of a shot close to the line between two scoring areas. It consists of a plug with a flange 5.6mm in diameter (for the events described in this book), and is necessary because the bullet hole invariably closes slightly after the bullet has passed through. If the flange touches any part of the line, the higher value is awarded.

If a firearm malfunctions through no fault of the firer a reshoot is usually allowed. Infringements of rules may result in a warning, in the deduction of points, or in disqualification.

Protests by the firer or a team official at any alleged irregularity in match conditions must be made immediately to the range officer or jury, and will be dealt with at once. Protests regarding scores must be made within one hour of their entry on the main scoreboard. Further appeals to the jury of appeal may require a monetary deposit.

Competitors In the Olympic Games only two individual competitors are permitted from each nation in each event.

In world championships four individual competitors may be entered by each nation. Their individual scores are added together to produce the team result.

5.6mm

OLYMPIC SHOOTING EVENTS

The following events were included in the 1980 Moscow Olympics, and are described on the pages that follow.

a) Smallbore free rifle (pp. 268-269)
b) Running game target (pp. 270-271)
c) Free pistol (pp. 272-273)
d) Rapid fire pistol (pp. 274-275)
e) Olympic trap (pp. 278-279)
f) Olympic skeet (pp. 280-281)

The following additional events will be included in the 1984 Los Angeles Olympics: air rifle; smallbore standard rifle; and pistol match.

©DIAGRAM

SHOOTING (SMALLBORE FREE RIFLE)

RANGE AND TARGET

The range is 50m long from the firing line (**a**) (where the competitor places his or her foot or elbow) to the targets (**b**). It is usually outdoor, but with firing points protected from wind, rain, and sun. The enclosed firing point for each individual must be not less than 1.25m wide by 2.5m long, and a height of at least 2.2m is advised. Each firing point and its corresponding target is marked with a number.

Flags to indicate the strength and direction of the wind are placed between each individual firing lane, at distances of 10m and 30m (**c**). The flags measure 5×40cm.

The target is of a non-reflecting color and material, with scoring rings of the diameters shown in the table. The lines are 1mm (±0.1mm) wide. The outside diameter of the black aiming mark coincides with the 4 ring. In addition there is an "inner 10" of 1mm diameter in the dead center of the 10 ring, which is used in tie-breaking. The target must present a visible area to the firer of at least 25×25cm.

For practice there may be more than one target printed on a sheet, but for competitions where world records may be established only one is allowed, and a fresh card is exposed for each shot. The optimum height of the center of the target above the level of the firing point is 50cm. The targets may be operated by personnel in a pit, who may also signal the value of the shot to the register keeper.

RIFLE, AMMUNITION, AND DRESS

The rifle must be of 5.6mm (.22in long rifle) caliber, but may be of any form within the following limitations:

it must weigh not more than 8kg including palmrest and buttplate;

the grip for the trigger hand may not be shaped to rest on the non-trigger arm or the sling;

the palmrest may not extend more than 20cm below the axis of the bore;

the buttplate and hook must be within prescribed dimensions.

The sights may be of any kind not containing a lens, but may contain light filters. Correcting eyeglasses may be worn by the firer.

Except when shooting in the standing position, a sling not more than 4cm wide may be worn around the upper part of the non-trigger arm and attached to the forend of the rifle.

The ammunition must be of 5.6mm (.22in long rifle) rimfire caliber, and the bullet must be of lead or a similar soft material.

Dress There are elaborate rules governing the firer's clothing, framed to prevent any unfair advantage afforded by supportive garments. Padding is allowed at the elbows, at the shoulder where the butt is placed, and on the arm where the sling is worn, but the thickness of garments and padding must not exceed 10mm single thickness.

A glove not exceeding 12mm total thickness (front and back together) nor extending more than 5cm above the wrist may be worn on the non-trigger hand.

Scoring rings
(outside diameters)

Ring	Diameter
10 ring	12.40mm (±0.1)
9 ring	29.07mm (±0.2)
8 ring	45.73mm (±0.2)
7 ring	62.40mm (±0.5)
6 ring	79.07mm (±0.5)
5 ring	95.73mm (±0.5)
4 ring	112.40mm (±0.5)
3 ring	129.07mm (±0.5)
2 ring	145.73mm (±0.5)
1 ring	162.40mm (±0.5)

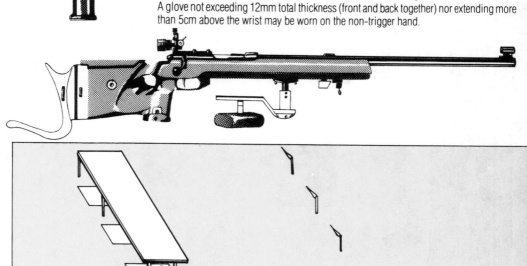

PROCEDURE AND SCORING

Courses of fire There are two events for the smallbore free rifle in the Olympic program: the English match, consisting of 60 shots from the prone position; and the three positions match, consisting of 40 shots prone, 40 standing, and 40 kneeling.

There are time limits for both matches:

if the English match is fired in two series of 30 shots each, then 1hr is allowed for each, including sighting shots; otherwise 1hr 45min is allowed for the whole course, again including sighting shots;

in the three positions match, 1hr 15min is allowed for the prone series, 1hr 45min for the standing, and 1hr 30min for the kneeling, including sighting shots in each case.

The number of sighting shots is unlimited, but none is allowed after the first scoring shot has been fired.

Officials Shooting is conducted under a chief range officer, under whom work several range officers, a register keeper for each firing point, a number of pit officers, and a firearm inspector. Over all these is a jury. There is a separate target control office with its own staff, to supervise the final scoring of targets.

Positions In the standing position (**1**) no sling or any other support is allowed. A palmrest that allows the elbow of the non-trigger arm to be rested on the chest or hip (as shown) may, however, be used.

In the kneeling position (**2**) the point of the elbow may not be more than 10cm over the point of the knee on which it is rested. The kneeling roll may be used as shown, in which case the foot must not be turned at an angle of more than 45 degrees. The buttock and upper leg may not touch the ground.

In the prone shooting position (**3**) the firer may lie on the thin mat provided, with the thicker mat under his elbows. The supporting forearm must form an angle of not less than 30 degrees with the surface of the firing point. Both forearm sleeves must be visibly clear of the firing point or any other support.

A spotting telescope on a stand suited to each position may be used to locate shot holes, but must not be used to support the firer or firearm.

Firing A preparation period of 10 minutes is allowed before the timed shooting period, during which a sighting target is exposed and the firer may adjust his position, spotting scope and sights; 15 minutes is allowed for the changeover between positions.

The firer must inform the register keeper when he is firing sighting shots, and when firing scoring shots. The register keeper informs the firer when the target is ready for the next shot, and once the shot is fired will allow the firer time to spot it before signaling for the target to be lowered.

Coaching is forbidden, and when on the firing line the competitor may speak only to range officials.

A clock should be provided on the range, or else announcements made when 10 and 5 minutes of shooting time remain.

Scoring Official scores are taken from the targets after they have been received at the target control office.

©DIAGRAM

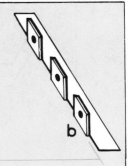

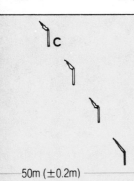

50m (±0.2m)

SHOOTING (RUNNING GAME TARGET)

RANGE AND TARGET

The range is outdoor, but the firing point (**a**) is protected from the weather. Between 50m and 52.5m from the firing line is an opening (**b**) 10m wide flanked by high walls (**c**) that protect the target operators and scorers.

A trolley or similar device is arranged to carry the targets (**d**) horizontally across the opening and is powered by a driving unit, the speed of which can be closely regulated.

A bank behind the target catches the bullets and a low wall in front protects the trolley.

The target is a picture of a wild boar at full stride, with ten concentric scoring rings superimposed on the chest area. Two versions are used, one facing right, one left. The outside diameters of the scoring rings are as given in the table. The lines are 1mm (±0.1mm) wide.

RIFLE AND AMMUNITION

The rifle may be of any kind within the following limitations: it must weigh not more than 5kg; the trigger pressure must be 0.5kg minimum; an adjustable buttplate is allowed, but it must not exceed 150mm in length or 20mm in depth of curvature; the sights may be of any kind, including telescopic. The same rifle and sights must be used for slow and fast runs.

The ammunition must be of 5.6mm (.22in long rifle) caliber. Special high velocity loadings are available and permitted for running game target shooting.

Scoring rings
(outside diameters)

10 ring	60mm (±0.2)
9 ring	94mm (±0.4)
8 ring	128mm (±0.6)
7 ring	162mm (±0.8)
6 ring	196mm (±1.0)
5 ring	230mm (±1.0)
4 ring	264mm (±1.0)
3 ring	298mm (±1.0)
2 ring	332mm (±1.0)
1 ring	366mm (±1.0)

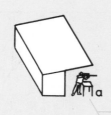

50–52.5m

PROCEDURE AND SCORING

Course of fire The Olympic program consists of two trial runs and 30 shots slow, and two trial runs and 30 shots fast.

In the slow runs, the target crosses the opening in 5sec (±0.2sec). In the fast runs, it crosses in 2.5sec (±0.1sec). Timing commences when the leading edge of the target appears, and ends when the leading edge reaches the far wall.

Runs are in alternate directions, the first always being from right to left. The leading target, facing in the appropriate direction, is the one to be fired at.

Officials The conduct of shooting is under the immediate control of a referee, over whom is a jury, one member of which is present at the firing point.

Scorers examine the targets and signal the position and value of each shot to a register keeper at the firing point, who records the scores.

The technical aspects of the range are looked after by a chief range officer and his assistants.

Positions When ready to fire, the competitor adopts the "ready position" (**1**) until the target appears, when he may raise the rifle to the "standing without support position" (**2**). He must be visibly clear of the table and walls, or any other source of support. A sling may not be used as an aid to steadiness.

Firing The firer stands at the firing point behind a table 80–100cm high on which he places enough ammunition for the series. He adopts the ready position and calls "ready". The target will appear within 4sec, when he raises the rifle, aims and fires one shot. The position and value of the shot is then signaled to him and the register keeper.

This procedure is repeated for the second trial run and the first scoring shot, but thereafter the firer does not call "ready," as the next run will follow automatically after an interval of from 12 to 18sec, during which the value and position of the last shot is signaled.

Scoring is performed by personnel protected by the walls that flank the target opening. The value and position of each shot is signaled to the firer, register keeper and spectators by television in major competitions, and by other means of local devising when television is not available.

Trial shot holes are then covered with a black patch; scoring shot holes are covered with a transparent patch that permits later scrutiny but leaves no doubt as to which is the new shot.

The center ring scores 10, the next 9, and so on until the outer ring, which scores 1. If a shot hole touches a line, or is so close that the scoring gauge (of 5.6mm diameter) touches any part of it, the higher value is given. Doubtful cases may be referred to a classing committee.

1

2

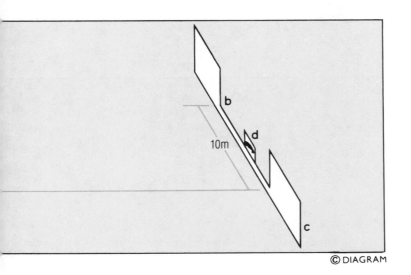

b

10m

d

c

© DIAGRAM

SHOOTING (FREE PISTOL)

RANGE AND TARGET

The range consists of a firing line (**a**) parallel to and at a distance of 50m (±0.2m) from a line of targets (**b**), which may be pit-operated.

The targets are numbered, as also are the corresponding firing points. Each individual firing point measures 1–1.5m wide by 1.5m from front to back, and may be divided from the next by screens that extend 50cm in front of the firing line. The floor is level and the roof is at least 2.2m above it.

Each firing point has a loading table and a chair for the firer, and a chair, desk, telescope, small scoreboard, and a means of communication to the target pit for the register keeper, placed so as not to disturb the competitor.

An automatic target-changing apparatus may replace the pit personnel, and may be controlled by the firer or by the register keeper.

Flags are provided to indicate the behavior of the wind.

The target is printed in black on white, with scoring rings with outside diameters as listed in the table, and is at least 55cm square. The outer limit of the black aiming mark coincides with the outer edge of the 7 ring.

Sighting targets have a diagonal black stripe in the top right hand corner.

The target is fixed so that the dead center is 140cm (±20cm) above the level of the firing point floor.

PISTOL, AMMUNITION, AND EQUIPMENT

The pistol may be of any kind, so long as it is chambered for a 5.6mm (.22in) rimfire cartridge and meets the following requirements:

no part of the pistol may give support beyond the hand, or restrict the movement of the wrist in the firing posture;

optical or mirror sights are not allowed, and any corrective lenses must be worn by the firer.

The ammunition must be of 5.6mm (.22in) rimfire caliber, with a bullet of lead or a similar soft material.

Scoring rings
(outside diameters)
10 ring 50mm (±0.2)
9 ring 100mm (±0.4)
8 ring 150mm (±0.6)
7 ring 200mm (±1.0)
6 ring 250mm (±1.0)
5 ring 300mm (±1.0)
4 ring 350mm (±1.0)
3 ring 400mm (±1.0)
2 ring 450mm (±1.0)
1 ring 500mm (±1.0)

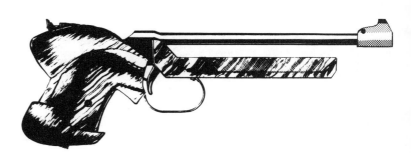

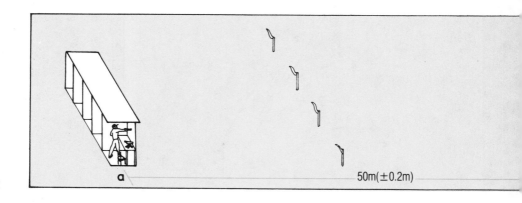

50m(±0.2m)

Equipment The firer may use a telescope on a stand to spot his shots.

Clothing is not specified, but any garment or device that may lend support is forbidden by the general rules.

Wrist watches, bracelets, or similar items are specifically prohibited on the arm used for holding the pistol.

PROCEDURE AND SCORING

Course of fire The free pistol match consists of 60 scoring shots, fired as six series of 10 shots each. Up to 15 sighting shots may be fired, at the beginning of the competition or between any of the 10-shot series. A fresh target is exposed after every five scoring shots. There is an overall time limit of 2hr 30min, including the sighting shots.

Officials There is a register keeper for each individual firing point, a range officer for every group of five to 10 firing points, and a target officer for each corresponding group of targets. There is a chief range officer in charge, but subordinate to a jury. If pit marking is used, there is a marker at each target.

A firearm inspector checks before the competition that the pistols conform to the regulations.

The official scoring of the targets is done at a target control office that has its own staff.

Position The firer must stand without support, within the space of the firing point, and hold and fire the pistol with one hand, and the same hand throughout. The wrist, elbow, and shoulder of the arm used to hold the pistol may not be supported by any part of the pistol, or by any other device. The pistol may be rested between shots within the provisions of the safety rules.

Firing There is a 10min preparation period during which competitors may move onto their allocated firing points, adjust their positions, and try some "dry" shots (ie without ammunition) at a sighting target. There follows a 2min period when warming-up shots may be fired at the backstop, but not at any target.

The 2hr 30min competition period begins with the order "fire," and ends with "cease fire." After each shot, if the pit marking system is in use, the target is lowered, the last shot hole covered with a transparent patch, the value of the hit marked on the target, and the target raised. The value of the shot is then signaled (see Scoring, below).

Coaching is forbidden during the competition.

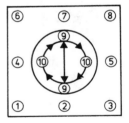

Scoring If pit scoring is used, the UIT suggests a method of signaling the value of each shot after the target is re-raised. A disk on a pole is held over a certain part of the target (as shown in the diagram). This communicates the provisional score to the firer, register keeper, and spectators without the need for a telescope. Other methods of local devising are also permitted if advertised in the program.

In any case, the official score is determined after the targets have been taken in a secure container to the target control office.

b

© DIAGRAM

SHOOTING (RAPID FIRE PISTOL)

RANGE AND TARGET

The range consists of a firing line and a line of targets 25m (±0.1m) away. The firing points are flat, screened off into compartments 1.5m square and with a roof at least 2.2m above the floor. The screens must be at least 1.5m wide by 1.7m high, with the bottom edge not more than 70cm above the floor, the top at least 2m above the floor, and the front edge at least 50cm in front of the firing line. There is a chair and a loading bench for the firer, and a desk, chair, and small scoreboard for the register keeper, placed so as not to inconvenience the competitor.

The target frames all have an apparatus to turn them through 90 degrees (**a**, **b**), and are grouped in fives, each group corresponding with and directly in front of an individual firing point. Within a group the target centers are 75cm (±1.0cm) apart.

The range is divided into sections, each of which consists of two firing points and two corresponding groups of five targets.

The target is a black "silhouette," 160cm high by 45cm wide, with a white border about 1cm wide. It is divided by white lines of about 1mm wide into 10 scoring zones.

The central zone, scoring 10, is 10cm wide and 15cm high, rounded at the top and bottom as illustrated. The width of each subsequent zone is 10cm greater and the height 15cm greater than the zone inside it. The center of the 10 zone is 55cm below the top of the target. The value of all zones but the 10 zone is marked in white numerals 30mm high and 15mm wide, as shown.

PISTOL AND AMMUNITION

The pistol must be of 5.6mm (.22in) caliber and must meet the following requirements:
the axis of the bore must pass above the upper part of the hand in the normal firing position;
the overall size of the pistol must be such that it will fit entirely inside a box of inside dimensions 30×15×5cm;
the grip must not be shaped so as to give support beyond the hand, and if adjustable must conform to the overall size limitations when fully extended;
optical and mirror sights are not allowed;
the weight must not exceed 1260g;
the height from the top of the foresight to the bottom of the barrel (including accessories) must not exceed 40mm.

The speed of firing required in this event clearly demands a revolver or semi-automatic pistol that can discharge five shots in quick succession.

Ammunition Any ammunition of 5.6mm (.22in) caliber having a bullet of lead or a similar soft material is allowed. Most competitors use the 5.6mm (.22in) short cartridge, because of the advantage of its low recoil.

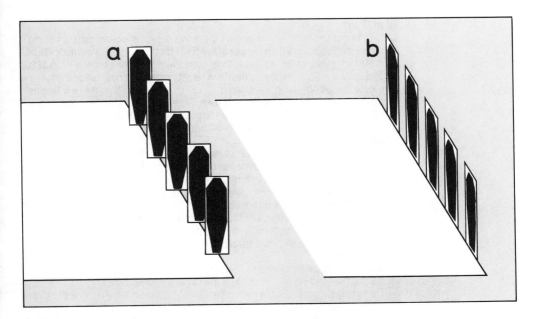

PROCEDURE AND SCORING

Course of fire The match consists of two courses of 30 shots each. Each of these courses is further divided into six series of five shots each, two series being fired within 8 sec, two within 6 sec, and two within 4 sec. One shot is fired at each target in every series.

Officials The range is under the control of a chief range officer, under whom work a range officer and target officer for each section of two groups of five targets. There is a register keeper at each individual firing point who displays the firer's score after each series of five shots, for the benefit of spectators. There is also a second register keeper, a scorer, and a marker, whose duties are explained below. Over all the officials is set a jury.

Position Until the targets appear the firer must wait in the "ready position" (**1**), with the firing arm held downward at an angle of not more than 45 degrees up from the vertical. To fire, he stands without support within the space provided and holds the pistol in one hand (**2**), using the same hand throughout. Watches, etc are forbidden on the firing arm.

1

Firing After competitors have moved onto their allocated firing points there is a three-minute preparation period, during which the targets are exposed and firers may practice "dry" firing (ie without ammunition).

On the order "load," pistols are loaded with five cartridges and firers adopt the "ready" position, to fire one series of five sighting shots in 8, 6, or 4 sec as they choose, beginning with the firer on the left of the section. One shot is fired at each target. After these sighting shots have been patched out, the competition proceeds in the courses described above.

Scoring After each series of five shots, one jury member, the target officer, the second register keeper, the scorer, and the marker all move forward to the targets.

The scorer examines each target and calls out the value of the shot in a loud voice to the register keeper and second register keeper, the former displaying the value on his scoreboard and the latter writing it down on a scorecard. The target officer and jury judge the value of any doubtful shot with a gauge.

2

The marker then places a plug disk in each shot hole, red side showing if the value is 10, otherwise with the white side showing. When the total score of the series has been displayed, the marker removes the plugs and patches out the holes.

After each course of 30 shots, the targets are replaced.

In addition to the normal shot hole gauge of 5.6mm diameter, there is a "skid gauge" with two lines 7mm apart on a clear surface. This is used to determine the value of shots fired while the target is turning. If the elongated shot hole thus formed is not more than 7mm long, it is counted.

275

SHOOTING (CLAY TARGET EVENTS)

HISTORY

Clay target shooting has its origins in the live pigeon shooting matches of the nineteenth century. When the use of live birds for this purpose was made illegal in Britain, glass spheres filled with feathers were used for a time, until in 1880 McCaskey, a Scot, devised a dish-like target made from river silt and pitch, and Ligowsky, an American, invented a "trap" or catapult to fling the new targets through the air, skimming like a frisbee. Skeet shooting was developed in the USA in the 1920s. Some form of clay target shooting has been included in all the modern Olympics except 1896, 1904, and 1928–48.

SYNOPSIS

In clay target shooting, the firer stands in a variety of locations and uses a shotgun to try and break a series of targets launched from various places in differing directions and at differing heights.

There are two Olympic events, known as Olympic trap and Olympic skeet, which are dealt with separately on subsequent pages. They differ chiefly in the layout of the firing points and traps, and thus the behavior of the target. The guns used for trap and skeet are very similar, but skeet guns are generally more open in the bore at the muzzle and thus spread the shot a little more widely.

EQUIPMENT

Guns Any shotgun not exceeding 12-gauge may be used, including semi-automatics (**a**), but the "over-and-under" design (**b**) is that most commonly favored.

The same gun must be used by the firer throughout the competition unless it malfunctions.

Ammunition The unfired cartridge must not exceed 70mm in length. The charge of shot must not weigh more than 32g. The shot must be of lead or lead alloy, but may be plated with another metal.

Special loadings such as tracer or black powder are forbidden.

Targets The "clay" or "bird" is saucer-like, 110mm (±1mm) in diameter, 26mm high and weighs 105g (±5g). It may be black, white, yellow, or orange, or certain combinations of these, selected so as to provide the best contrast against the background on the field in use. The same color is used throughout a championship.

Traps The traps used for major competitions are electrically powered (**c**) and fed automatically with targets, although less sophisticated models (**d**) are not forbidden. They may be activated by a "puller" who presses a switch from behind the firers, or by a microphone system that is triggered by the firer calling "pull," "go," or "los."

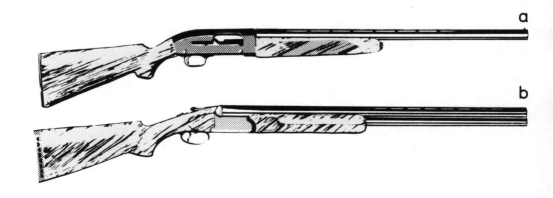

GENERAL RULES

The following provisions apply equally to Olympic trap and Olympic skeet events.

Safety Conventional double barreled guns must be carried "broken" open, and semi-auto guns must have the breech open and the muzzle pointing safely at the sky or ground. Guns may only be loaded on the firing point and after the order "load" has been given, and may not be closed before the next firer on the right is ready to fire.

No-one may try an aim except in a designated safe area or on the firing point when it is otherwise safe to fire, and no-one may try an aim at anyone else's target or at any living creature.

The gun must be opened again before turning away from the firing point and whenever any irregularity interrupts the shooting.

Personnel operating the traps are shielded from both direct fire and ricocheting shot.

Contingencies There are extensive rules that are designed to meet all possible situations resulting from malfunction of guns or traps or from human error or misbehavior. In general these rules are framed so as not to penalize a firer for any mishap that is not his fault, nor to allow any accidental advantage.

Penalties for misconduct consist of the deduction of points from the offender's score, or of disqualification in aggravated cases.

Field In the northern hemisphere the range or field is wherever possible aligned toward the north or northeast, so that the sun is at the firers' backs throughout the day. The stations or firing points usually consist of concrete pathways.

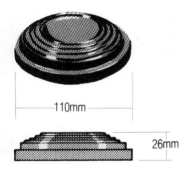

110mm

26mm

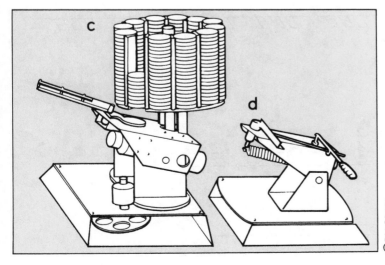

c

d

©DIAGRAM

SHOOTING (OLYMPIC TRAP)

FIELD AND TARGET

The field, or range for Olympic trap shooting consists of a line of five shooting stations or firing points (**a**), numbered from 1 to 5 and each 1m square. There is a sixth waiting point (**b**) to the left rear of station 1, and a return walkway (**c**) connecting stations 1 and 5. At a distance of 15m in front of the line of firing stations is a covered pit or trench (**d**) containing the traps and their operators. Corresponding to each shooting station is a group of three traps in the trench, each of which is set to throw targets in a different prescribed direction.

The targets are thrown so as to travel 75m (±5m) and pass within a height of 1.5-3.5m above the level of the pit roof when 10m forward of the trap.

The direction of the targets from each trap is based on an imaginary line drawn straight ahead of the center trap in a group. Targets from the right trap fall into a segment of 45 degrees to the left of the line (**A**). The center trap throws targets at up to 15 degrees either side of the line (**B**). The left hand trap in each set of three throws the targets into a segment of 45 degrees to the right of the line (**C**).

The distribution of targets in each direction is prescribed in event regulations.

GUN AND AMMUNITION

Gun and ammunition are as prescribed on p. 276, with the added proviso that for Olympic trap events, the pellets or shot must not be more than 2.5mm (+0.1mm) in diameter.

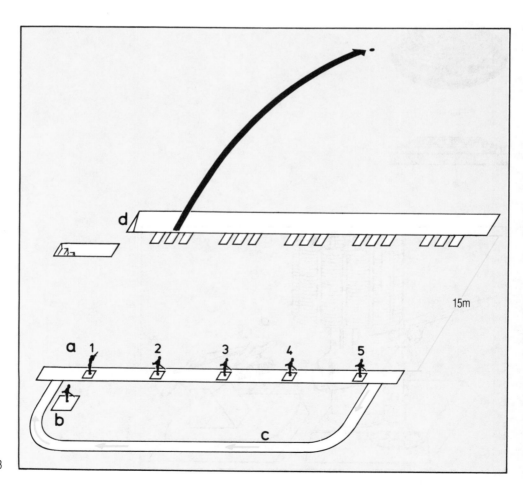

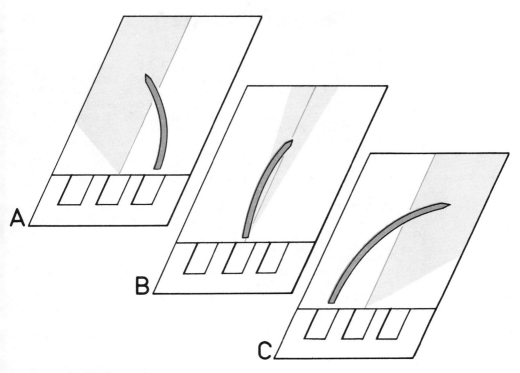

PROCEDURE AND SCORING

Course of fire Competitors fire at 200 targets, in rounds of 25. In a major competition firing is spread over from two to four days.

After 150 targets, the number of competitors may be reduced by eliminating up to 50% of the lowest scorers.

Officials Shooting is under the overall control of a jury, and the immediate supervision of a referee. The referee decides whether a target has been correctly thrown and whether it has been hit. He is helped by three assistant referees, appointed from among the competitors, one of whom stands by the scoreboard to check the recording of scores, and the others stand one each side of the field to observe the targets, signaling if one is "lost" (missed). A scorer positioned near the referee, behind the firers, records each competitor's score on a card. Another scorer posts the scores on a public scoreboard. When the score on the card has been agreed, it is sent to a results office.

Position Competitors fire from an unsupported standing position. The gun may be held at the shoulder in the firing position before the firer calls for the target to be thrown.

Firing Competitors fire in squads of six, one on each shooting station and one at the waiting point near station 1.

The competitor on station 1, having been given the order "load," puts two cartridges into his gun, closes it, and brings it to his shoulder. He calls "pull," "los," or "go." If a microphone-actuated release system is in use the target will be thrown from the trap between 0.1 and 0.2 seconds later. He fires, and if he misses he may fire a second cartridge. He then opens his gun and waits while the competitors on his right take turns to fire. When the person on station 5 has fired, he immediately walks along the return walkway to the waiting point. Competitors on stations 1 to 4 move one station to their right, and the sixth firer steps onto station 1.

This procedure is repeated until each firer has shot at 25 targets, five from each station.

Scoring A target is declared "dead" (ie scored as a hit) if it is thrown and shot at correctly according to the rules and one or more visible pieces are broken off it. It is not sufficient merely to knock dust from it.

A target is "lost" (ie scored as a miss) if it is fired at but missed, or not hit well enough to break off a visible piece, or if the competitor has through his own fault not fired at it.

If a target breaks up on leaving the trap or is otherwise irregularly thrown, the referee calls "no bird" and the target is repeated.

SHOOTING (OLYMPIC SKEET)

FIELD AND TARGET

The field or range consists of seven shooting stations (**1–7**) along an arc of a circle with a radius of 19.2m. Across the open ends of the arc is a notional line (**a**) called the base chord, measuring 36.8m between the front edges of stations 1 and 7. At the center of the base chord is an eighth shooting station (**8**). Stations 1 to 7 measure 91cm square and station 8 is 91×183cm. Behind station 1 is the "high house" (**b**), containing a trap and with an aperture for the target to emerge 3.05m above ground level. Behind station 7 is the "low house" (**c**), with an aperture from which the target emerges 1.07m above the ground. The center of the circle on which stations 1 to 7 lie is known as the target crossing point, and is marked with a stake (**d**). There are two more stakes, known as the shooting boundary markers (**e**), which are placed 40.23m from each throwing house on lines passing through the target crossing point.

The targets are thrown at fixed elevations and directions, so as to pass through an imaginary circle of 91cm diameter, the center of which is 4.57m above the target crossing point.

In calm weather the targets must travel 65–67m.

The targets are presented to the firer in two ways. A "single" is thrown from either house, but the firer will always know from which to expect it. In a "double," one target is thrown simultaneously from each house.

Gun and ammunition are as defined on p. 276, but with the additional provision that the pellets or shot used in Olympic skeet events must not exceed 2.0mm (+0.1mm) in diameter.

The guns used for skeet have a slightly wider boring than those for trap, thus giving a wider pattern of shot.

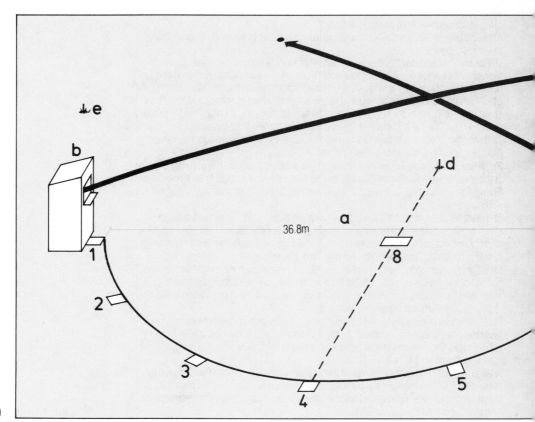

PROCEDURE AND SCORING

Course of fire Competitors fire at 200 targets in eight rounds of 25 each.
Each round of 25 targets is presented to the firer as follows:

Station 1: one single from the high house
        one double
Station 2: one single from the high house
        one single from the low house
        one double
Station 3: as for station 2
Station 4: one single from the high house
        one single from the low house
Station 5: one single from the high house
        one single from the low house
        one double
Station 6: as for station 5
Station 7: one double
Station 8: one single from the low house
        one single from the high house

In the case of the doubles, at stations 1 to 3 the target from the high house must be fired at first; at stations 5 to 7 the target from the low house must be fired at first.

Officials are as for Olympic trap (see p. 279).

Position Competitors fire from an unsupported standing position. Before calling for the target the firer adopts the "ready position" (**A**), with the butt of the gun held against the waistline. A mark 10cm long by 2cm wide is made on the firer's clothing on the side he holds the gun, to assist the referee. The gun may not be brought to the shoulder (**B**) until the target is thrown.

Firing The order of shooting within the squad of six firers is decided by ballot each day. All six take their turn to fire from station 1 at the three targets specified in the course of fire, and then move to station 2, and so on.

When his turn to fire arrives, the firer stands within the boundary of the station and loads. For the first shot from station 1 and for both shots from station 8 he may load with one cartridge only; otherwise he loads with two. At stations 1 and 8 he may try his aim. He then adopts the "ready position" and calls for the target, which may be thrown immediately or up to 3sec later. He must call for the target within 15sec of the preceding firer finishing his turn. If more than one target is to be fired at from the station, the interval between them must not exceed 15sec. When the gun is loaded with two cartridges it may not be opened between shots.

Only one shot may be fired at one single target.

Scoring The definitions of "dead" or hit targets and "lost" or missed targets are as for Olympic trap shooting.

There are additional "no bird" definitions for double targets if:
both barrels go off simultaneously and the first target is hit;
both targets are hit by the first shot (allowed three times only, after which both are "lost");
the firer aims for the first but hits the second (in this case the first target is lost and the second will count only if hit a second time).

SKATING (FIGURE)

HISTORY

There are bone skates in existence that are believed to be 2000 years old. The earliest illustration of the sport is a wood-engraving of the future patron saint of skaters, St Lydwina of Schiedam, who is said to have fallen and broken a rib while skating in 1396. Skating was popular in late seventeenth century England, and in France a hundred years later, when both Marie Antoinette and Napoleon are known to have taken part. The International Skating Union was formed in 1892 by the national associations of six European countries, and still continues to regulate international competition today. The first world championships were held in St Petersburg (Leningrad) in 1896, and the first Olympic figure skating events in London in 1908.

SYNOPSIS

There are three branches of figure skating competition: single skating (**a**), pair skating (**b**), and ice dancing (**c**). In all three events competitors perform compulsory movements and also movements of their own choice.

Marks are awarded for technical merit and artistic impression in single and pair skating, and for composition and presentation in ice dancing. Judges mark each competitor or pair for their performance in each section, and rank them in order of preference. Placings in the different sections (first, second, third, etc.) are adjusted arithmetically to decide the overall winner.

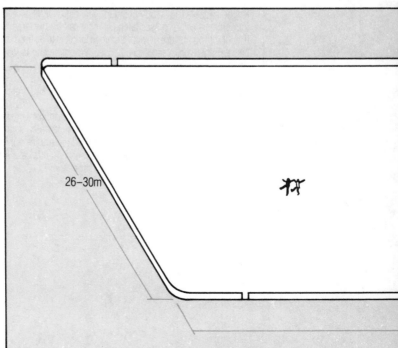

26–30m

SKATING (FIGURE, GENERAL)

GENERAL RULES

Competition area The same rink may be used for all three types of skating, although only a restricted part of it is used for the performance of compulsory figures in single skating. The rink is rectangular and must measure not less than 56×26m and not more than 60×30m.

Music The rink must be provided with a music reproduction system. The music is selected by the competitors.

Dress is required to be modest and dignified, and needs to allow complete freedom of movement.

Skates used for figure skating have a blade about 3mm wide, which must be ground so as to produce a flat to concave bottom edge of uniform width as measured between the two edges.

Officials There is one referee, an assistant referee, a maximum of nine judges, two announcers, two secretaries, and two timekeepers. There is provision for supplementary officials if more are considered necessary.

Restarts If a competitor is interfered with and is not at fault, the referee may allow the program to be restarted after all the other competitors in that skater's group have performed. Any previous score made by the skater who is restarting is disregarded.

Marks In figure skating a scale of marks up to 6 is used, in which the gradings are defined as indicated in the table.

Decimals to one place are allowed as intermediate values.

At the end of a performance every judge simultaneously displays the mark that he or she awards to the skater or pair, by holding up two cards. One card has a black numeral (for whole numbers) and the other a red numeral (for decimals).

Results In order to determine competitors' overall placings in a single skating, pair skating, or ice dancing competition, placings in each section of the contest are multiplied by an "x-factor." The purpose of this is to adjust the comparative importance of the different sections.

The precise x-factors used in each branch of figure skating are given later under the appropriate section headings.

Mark definitions
0 Not skated
1 Very poor
2 Poor
3 Mediocre
4 Good
5 Very good
6 Perfect and faultless

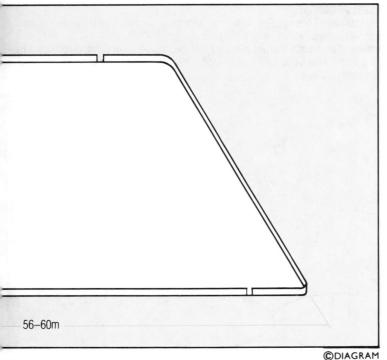

56–60m

3mm

©DIAGRAM

283

SKATING (SINGLE FIGURE)

SYNOPSIS

Major single skating competitions consist of three parts: compulsory figures; a short program that includes compulsory movements; and free skating, also known as the long program.

COMPULSORY FIGURES

General rules In most major championships three compulsory figures must be skated, in order of increasing difficulty. Every figure is generally skated three times on each foot, and there should be no pause between the repetitions.

Types of figure All figures are based on the shape of two or three linked circles. Variations include loops (**a**), threes (**b**), brackets (**c**), rocker (**d**), and counter (**e**), or elaborations or combinations of these. The precise figures to be skated are selected by the ISU from a published list and remain in force for a year.

Procedure Before skating each figure, the competitor indicates the long axis of that figure. He or she must not use the long axis of a previous figure, nor use any painted lines or marks on the ice as a tangent or axis, or to start or locate turns.

Initially the skater stands on the flat of the skates near the intersection of the figure's long and short axes, and must not begin without the referee's permission.

After a figure is finished the skater must change the tracing foot and continue in a straight line in the direction of the short axis.

Style The skater's head should be upright, relaxed, and held naturally. The upper body should be upright but not stiff. The arms should be held gracefully, with the hands not higher than the waist, and the palms parallel with the ice. The skating leg should be flexed and the knee slightly bent. The free leg should be slightly bent at the knee and should be held above the tracing left on the ice, trailing behind but not too close to the skating foot. The motion should be graceful, even, and flowing, with a reasonable speed maintained to the end of the figure.

Marking A mark between 0 and 6 is awarded by each judge for each figure skated by each competitor. The mark is based on the judge's assessment of the skater's style of execution, and on an examination of the tracing left by the skates on the ice.

In case of a failure (eg a fall) in any one of the tracings that constitute a figure, judges use a scale of set deductions to adjust the mark that they would have awarded had the failure not occurred.

SHORT PROGRAM

General rules For single skating the short program consists of the performance of seven specified elements within a time limit of two minutes.

Groups of elements The rules of the ISU list four groups of seven elements each. One of the groups is selected as the one to be used in major competitions during each year, beginning on July 1.

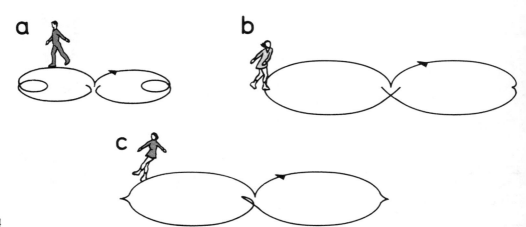

Performance The seven elements may be skated in any order, to music chosen by the competitor, and must be linked by the minimum necessary steps. No additional elements may be added.

Marking Two marks on the scale 0–6 are given for the short program: one for the performance of the required elements and the other for the presentation of the program. In marking the required elements, the jumps, jump combinations, spins, and step sequences are judged according to their difficulty, and fractions of points are deducted for failures and omissions.

In marking the presentation of the program, the aspects considered include: the harmony of the whole composition; conformity with the music and the expression of its character; timing and ease of movement; originality; speed, carriage, and style; utilization of the rink; difficulty of the connecting steps.

FREE SKATING

General rules The free skating part of single skating competitions consists of a balanced program of component movements selected or devised by the competitor, and performed to music of his or her choice. The time limit is 4min maximum for women, and 4½min for men.

Two-footed skating must be kept to a minimum.

Marking Two marks are awarded on the scale 0–6: one for technical merit and the other for artistic impression.

In marking technical merit, special note is taken of the difficulty and variety of the elements chosen, and of the cleanness and sureness of movement.

In marking artistic impression, the aspects considered include: the harmony of the whole composition; conformity with the music and expression of its character; timing and ease of movement; originality; carriage; utilization of the rink.

Movements marred by a fall are not marked.

Prolonged or unnecessary movements on both feet are penalized.

RESULTS

Initial placings The skaters' placings in each section of the competition are determined by a majority decision of the judges (eg a skater placed first by five or more of the nine judges is the winner of the section).

X-factors The skaters' placings in each section are now multiplied by the following x-factors:

compulsory figures 0.6;

short program 0.4;

free skating 1.0.

The comparative importance of each section is thus 30%, 20%, and 50% respectively.

Final placings The skater with the lowest total place value after factoring is the overall winner.

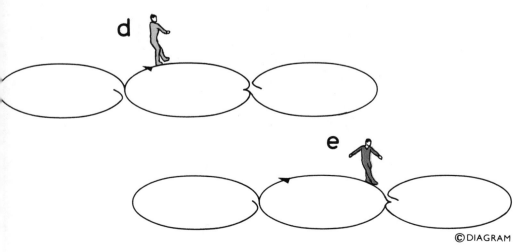

©DIAGRAM

SKATING (PAIR FIGURE)

SYNOPSIS

Major pair skating competitions consist of two parts: the short program, which includes compulsory elements; and free skating, or the long program. The rules resemble those of the equivalent parts of single figure skating, but with additions that concern the cooperation of the two partners.

GENERAL RULES

The pair must consist of a man and a woman. They need not always perform the same movements or stay in contact with each other, but they must give a united, harmonious performance.

Movements Typical pair skating movements include partner-assisted jumps, lifts (see illustration, right), pair spins, and spirals.

The term "mirror skating" is used to describe simultaneous movements performed symmetrically by the pair (**A**), and "shadow skating" to describe those performed in parallel (**B**).

In executing lifts, the legs of the skater being lifted may not be held, nor may any lift continue for more than three revolutions. The simple carrying of a partner and the turning of a partner being carried in a horizontal position are also prohibited.

In rotational movements the partner may not be gripped by the neck, arm, or leg.

SHORT PROGRAM

General rules For pair skating the short program consists of the performance of seven specified elements or movements within a time limit of 2min 15sec.

Four groups of movements are listed in the rules of the ISU, one of which is selected for use in major competitions during each year, beginning on July 1.

The seven elements may be skated in any order, to music of the competitors' choice, and must be linked by the minimum necessary steps.

Marking The system of marking and the criteria of judgment for pair skating short program are the same as for single skating short program (see p. 285).

FREE SKATING

General rules The free skating part of pair skating competitions is governed by rules similar to those that govern single free skating (see p. 285). The maximum time limit for the program is 4½min.

Marking The system and criteria for marking pair free skating are similar to those for single free skating (see p. 285), with the addition that failure to comply with the special rules regarding the execution of lifts, etc will be penalized. Similarly, imperfections in the coordination of the partners' movements will be reflected in the mark for artistic impression.

A   B

RESULTS

Initial placings The pairs' placings in each section of the competition are determined by a majority decision of the judges (eg the pair placed first by five or more of the nine judges is the winner of the section).

X-factors The pairs' placings in each section are then multiplied by the following x-factors:

short program 0.4;

free skating 1.0.

The comparative importance of each section is thus 30% and 70% respectively.

Final placings The pair with the lowest total place value after factoring are the overall winners.

SKATING (ICE DANCING)

SYNOPSIS
Ice dancing competitions consist of three parts: prescribed pattern dances; an original set pattern dance; and free dance. The skaters dance as couples.

PRESCRIBED PATTERN DANCES
General rules Prescribed pattern dances lend themselves to being performed according to a closely predetermined pattern of steps. Certain steps are taken at the same point on the rink by all couples, although some scope is allowed for personal expression.

The dances are performed in strict time to the music, with the couple skating close together and in unison.

Patterns Each prescribed pattern dance is defined in the ISU rules by a diagram or pattern, which consists of an annotated plan of the tracing left on the ice by the skaters. The man's pattern for one dance – the blues – is included here as an example.

Groups of dances Competitors skate one of the following groups of dances:
1) Viennese waltz, Yankee polka, blues;
2) Westminster waltz, paso doble, rhumba;
3) Starlight waltz, kilian, tango romantica;
4) Ravensburger waltz, quickstep, Argentine tango.

Depending on competition rules, the group to be danced is either decided by a draw the previous evening or is specified in the competition announcement.

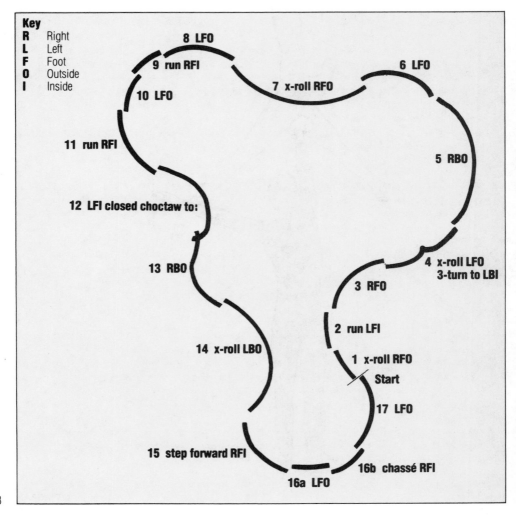

Key
R Right
L Left
F Foot
O Outside
I Inside

8 LFO
9 run RFI
10 LFO
7 x-roll RFO
6 LFO
11 run RFI
5 RBO
12 LFI closed choctaw to:
13 RBO
4 x-roll LFO
3-turn to LBI
3 RFO
2 run LFI
14 x-roll LBO
1 x-roll RFO
Start
17 LFO
15 step forward RFI
16b chassé RFI
16a LFO

Marking Each dance performed by each couple is marked on the scale 0–6.

Of the aspects of the dancing to be assessed, the judges take particular note of whether the skating is strictly in time with the music. At the same time the steps must be in close conformity with the pattern for that dance.

Other aspects noted include movement in unison, carriage, flowing movement, and the uniformity and symmetry of curves.

If either partner skates more than seven introductory steps before the commencement of the prescribed steps, this will be penalized.

ORIGINAL SET PATTERN DANCE

General rules Each couple chooses its own music, tempo, and composition, but the rhythm and bars per minute must be as announced annually by the ISU. The couple must compose their dance from repetitive sequences consisting of either a half or a whole circuit of the rink. The choice of movements, connecting steps, turns and rotations is free, provided they are all in conformity with general ISU rules.

Marking Composition and presentation are separately marked on the scale 0–6.

In assessing the mark for composition, the judges consider: the difficulty, originality, and variety of the dance; placement of the steps and correct repetition of sequences; the cleanness, sureness, and utilization of the ice surface; and correct skating on edges, flow, and continuous skating without interruption.

In assessing presentation, they consider: the correct timing of the music; the couple's movements in rhythm with the music, and the relationship of the skating movements with its character; the correct selection of the music in relation to the rhythm chosen; and the carriage, style, and unison (harmony) of the couple in relation to the music.

If either partner skates more than seven introductory steps before the beginning of the dance proper, this will be penalized.

FREE DANCE

General rules The free dance consists of non-repetitive combinations of either known or new movements, composed into a 4min program that displays the skaters' personal ideas in concept and arrangement. There are a number of rules designed to maintain the distinction betweeen ice dancing and pair skating.

Music Couples choose their own music, which must be dance music with a tempo, rhythm, and character suited to ice dancing. All types of music, including classical, ballet, folk, and contemporary, are allowed providing they meet the requirements.

Vocal music is not allowed, nor may the music have more than three breaks or changes.

Movements All steps and turns are permitted, as are any free skating movements that are appropriate to the music, rhythm, and dance. Feats of strength included for their own sake must be penalized.

Movements that incorporate sitting, standing, or leaning on boots, holding the boots, or lying over the partner's skating leg are not considered to be in character with free skating, and will be penalized.

There are also a number of detailed additional rules designed to maintain the distinction between ice dancing and pair skating. In particular, lifts must not be more than waist-high, and jumps may not exceed a half-revolution.

Marking Two marks are awarded on the scale 0–6, one for technical merit and the other for artistic impression.

In assessing the first, the judges consider the difficulty, originality, and variety of the performance, and the cleanness and sureness of the skating.

In assessing artistic impression they consider the harmonious composition of the whole program and its conformity with the music; the use of the area; easy movement and sureness in time to the music; the flow, carriage, unison, style of the couple, and the expression of the music's character; and the couple's movements in time with the music.

RESULTS

Initial placings are determined as for single and pair figure skating (pp. 285 and 287).

The X-factors are 0.6 for the prescribed pattern dances, 0.4 for the original set pattern dance, and 1.0 for the free dance, giving a comparative importance to each section of 30%, 20%, and 50% respectively.

Final placings The couple with the lowest total place value after factoring are the overall winners.

SKATING (SPEED)

HISTORY

Speed skating is said to date from the twelfth century in Holland, where frozen canals were used as courses. The sport was popular in the USA, Canada, and Scandinavia in the nineteenth century, and the first world championships were held in Amsterdam in 1893. Men's speed skating was included in the first Winter Olympics in 1924, but women's was not included until 1964.

SYNOPSIS

In speed skating two skaters at a time race counterclockwise around a track. Men race over five distances in the Olympics, in the order 500m, 5000m, 1000m, 1500m, and 10,000m.

Women race over four distances in the Olympics, in the order 1500m, 500m 1000m, and 3000m.

Points are awarded according to the skater's time in each event, and the winner over that distance is the skater who achieves the fastest time and thus the lowest number of points. The overall winner is the skater who wins the most races, or in the case of a tie, has the lowest total of points.

TRACK AND EQUIPMENT

The track The standard track is an ice rink with two lanes 4m or preferably 5m wide and between 333⅓m and 400m long (400m for the Olympics). Because of its size it is usually outdoor.

The inner curve at each end is of 25–26m radius. The whole length of one straight is designated as the crossing area, where the skaters change lanes after each circuit.

The lanes are divided, except in the crossing area, either by compacted but not iced snow, or by a painted line and movable blocks of wood, rubber, or other suitable material, placed at intervals. The interval between blocks is 50cm for the first and last 15m of each curve, 1m on the remainder of the curves, and 10m on the non-crossing straight.

All races are skated with the competitors' left hands toward the center of the circuit. Start and finish lines are located on our diagram. A pre-start line is marked 75cm behind each start line. For 5m before the finish lines, each meter is clearly marked.

Dress is not specified, but competitors wear a colored armband: white for the skater who starts in the inner lane, and red for the one starting in the outer lane.

Skates Design of skates is not specified. The type usually preferred has a particularly long and narrow blade reinforced with steel tubing, and a light, low-cut leather shoe.

COMPETITORS AND OFFICIALS

Competitors must take part in every distance event. They are entitled to at least 30 minutes' rest between events.

Officials consist of a referee and assistant, a starter and assistant, a judge, a chief timekeeper and assistants, lap scorers, at least three track stewards, and a crossing controller.

Track features
a) 500m start
b) 1000m finish
c) 10,000m start and 500m, 1500m, 3000m, 5000m, 10,000m finish
d) 1500m start
e) 1000m start
f) 3000m, 5000m start
g) Crossing area

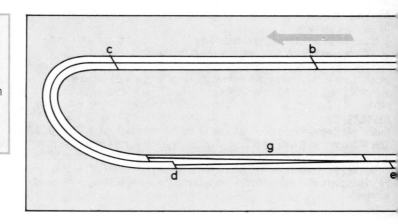

PROCEDURE

Preliminary Rules for determining starting order vary, but the general principle is that the skaters are divided into a number of groups according to ability, as judged from previous competitions, and a draw takes place within each group.

The lane in which each competitor will begin skating is decided either by the draw, or by the skater with the better performance in a preceding distance taking the inner lane.

The start Skaters must stand still in an upright position between the pre-start line and the start line, with their skates not in front of the latter. On the command "Ready," the skaters adopt their starting position; 1–1.5sec later a shot is fired as the signal to start.

Changing lanes Skaters must change lanes in the designated crossing area after each circuit of the track. The only exceptions to this rule are on the first straight of 1000m and 1500m events when these are raced on a standard 400m track. It is an offense to change lanes or to cross the dividing line at all when on a curve or when entering or leaving a curve. When changing lanes, it is the responsibility of the skater who is leaving the inner lane to avoid a collision.

Overtaking A competitor must not impede the other skater when overtaking.

A skater who has been overtaken must remain at least 5m behind his opponent.

Pacemaking is forbidden, whether in front of, beside, or behind the skater being paced.

The finish A competitor reaches the finish when his first skate touches the line.

SCORING AND PENALTIES

Scoring Penalty points are scored on the basis of the time in which the competitor completes the distance, according to the following scales:

in 500m events each second equals one point;

in 1000m events the points are half the number of seconds;

in 1500m events the points are one third the number of seconds:

in 3000m events the points are one sixth the number of seconds;

in 5000m events the points are one tenth the number of seconds;

in 10,000m events the points are one twentieth the number of seconds.

Points totals are calculated to three decimal places; a fourth may be used to decide a tie.

Results The skater who achieves the best time is the winner over that distance, or if two or more have the equal best time all are counted as winners over that distance.

The overall winner is the skater who has skated all the distances and won a majority of them. If several skaters are in this position, or if no-one has a majority of wins, the winner is the one who has skated all the distances and has the lowest number of points.

Penalties The penalties available for punishing offenses are disqualification from the event in question, from all events already skated, from competing in the final distance, or from the whole of the remainder of the competition.

If a competitor is disqualified over any distance he forfeits his eligibility to the championship and his right to compete over the final distance.

Punishable offenses include: deliberate fouls; collisions caused when moving from the inner to the outer lane; causing two false starts; and changing lanes on a curve.

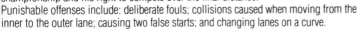

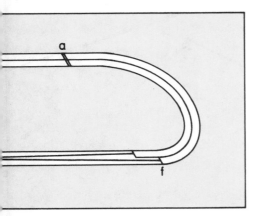

SKIING

HISTORY
Rock drawings in northern Europe show that skis were used as a form of winter transport as early as 3000BC. Organized competitive skiing began in the nineteenth century; the sport was first developed in Norway, where ski jumping was invented in 1840 and where the first cross-country races were held in 1866. Norwegians were also responsible for the introduction of skiing into the USA in 1841. Although skiing was almost unknown in the Alps until the 1880s, the very different snow conditions there rapidly led to the development of downhill and slalom races. The international governing body for skiing, the Fédéderation Internationale de Ski (FIS) was formed in 1924, the year in which the sport was first included in the Olympic Games. The biathlon, which is based on military patrol races, became an Olympic sport in 1960; the governing body is the Union Internationale de Pentathlon Moderne et Biathlon (UIPMB).

SYNOPSIS
Ski races are divided into two basic groups: Alpine skiing, and Nordic skiing. The major Alpine races are the downhill (**A**), slalom (**B**), and giant slalom; combinations of two or more of these events make up the Alpine combined competitions. Nordic skiing includes individual and relay cross-country racing (**C**), and ski jumping (**D**). The Nordic combined event consists of cross-country racing and ski jumping. A combination of cross-country racing and shooting makes up the biathlon.

COMPETITORS AND OFFICIALS
Competitors in international events must be licensed by their national associations.
Officials These may include: an organizing committee; a race committee of at least six members; a jury, chaired by the FIS technical delegate; medical officers; timekeepers; start and finish referees; controllers (for cross-country races); gate judges (for Alpine events); jumping judges, distance recorders and measurers (for ski jumping); range and firing point officials (for biathlon).

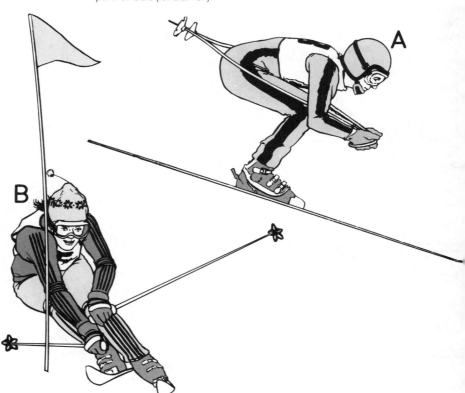

DRESS AND EQUIPMENT

Dress Competitors' clothing and any commercial markings appearing on it should conform to the regulations of the governing body. Downhill skiers must wear crash helmets, and their suits must pass a test for air permeability.

Members of a national team normally wear a uniform in national colors.

In Alpine skiing, goggles may be worn as protection from glare, wind, and snow spray, and to improve visibility in some conditions.

Boots for Alpine skiing should fit to give maximum control over the ski edges and support for the ankles. Alpine boots are stiffer and fit higher than boots used for cross-country skiing, which should be low-cut and flexible.

Skis are made of various materials, usually combining a variety of plastics with metal, fiberglass, and laminated wood. The length and weight of the skis vary with the competition, and the size and preferences of the skier. Any commercial markings must conform to the regulations of the governing body.

Bindings on Alpine skis hold both the toe and heel of the boot firmly to the skis. Skis used for cross-country racing and ski jumping have a special toe binding with cables, leaving the heel free to lift up.

Ski poles should be of a strong, lightweight material, such as aluminum, with steel tips. Handles are usually plastic, and contoured to fit the skier's hand; baskets may be made of plastic, rubber, or metal.

The length and type of stick used varies with the competition, and the skier's size and preference. Downhill skiers usually use bent ski poles, shaped to fit around the body and reduce wind resistance; slalom and giant slalom skiers use straight poles; cross-country skiers use longer poles with asymmetric baskets.

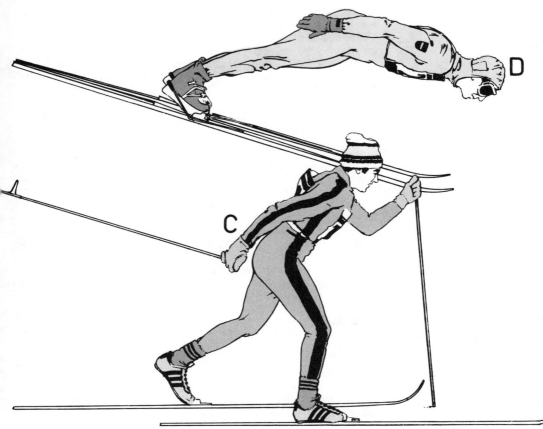

© DIAGRAM

SKIING (ALPINE 1)

COURSE AND TIMING EQUIPMENT (GENERAL)

Courses The lengths, layouts, and steepness of the courses should conform to the particular rules for each event (see pp. 296–301).

The jury must inspect the course before the beginning of official training and ensure that:
a) there is sufficient depth of snow on and beside the course;
b) the surface has been correctly prepared, and that the snow is smooth and compact;
c) all small obstacles that could impede or endanger the skiers have been removed;
d) all gates have been correctly and securely positioned;
e) suitable protection (nets, mattresses, etc) has been provided at all potentially dangerous areas;
f) sufficient medical, rescue, transport, and communications services have been provided.

Starting area Only the starting racer, one trainer, and the starting officials are allowed in the starting area. They should be provided with adequate shelter against the weather. A reserved, roped-off area must be provided for competitors, trainers, and service personnel waiting for the call to start.

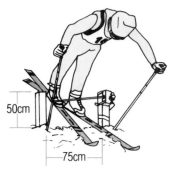

50cm

75cm

The starting gate is marked by two posts 75cm apart, and projecting up to 50cm above the snow. It should be placed so that it is impossible for a racer to start without the gate opening. Competitors must be able to stand relaxed on the starting line, yet quickly reach full speed after starting.

The finishing area must be clearly visible as the competitors approach. The final gates of the course should direct the racers to the finish on a natural line adapted to the terrain. The area must be wide, and there must be a gently sloped outrun with smoothly packed snow. It must be completely fenced in, and snow walls, foam rubber, or other forms of protection should be used to prevent the possibility of skiers colliding with any of the finish structures.

The finishing line is marked by two posts connected by a banner. The posts should be at least 10m apart for slalom and giant slalom, and at least 15m apart for downhill races.

Timing equipment Electric timing apparatus allowing measurements to hundredths of a second is required. At Olympic Games and world championships two independent electrical timing devices should be used.

Supplementary hand timing should also be used at all competitions in case of breakdown of the automatic timing system.

PROCEDURE (GENERAL)

Starting order The jury uses a points list drawn up by the FIS to decide the competitors' starting order. The competitors are divided into three groups as follows.

The first group to race consists of the best 15 competitors present, regardless of nationality. A draw is held to determine their starting order within the group.

The second group consists of all other competitors who have FIS points. These skiers start in the order of their FIS classification.

The third group, which may be further subdivided, consists of competitors without FIS points. A draw is held to determine their starting order.

In exceptional conditions (eg when it is snowing) the jury may alter the starting order. A group of six skiers, chosen by lot from among the last 20% of the starting list, then ski before the first competitor from the first group. All the remaining skiers ski in their starting list order.

In events involving two runs over a course, the starting order for the second run is determined by the results list of the first run. The first five competitors in the first run start the second run in reverse order; all other competitors follow in the order of the results list of the first run.

Forerunners At least three forerunners, who should be able to ski the course at racing speed, should be available during the competition. At least two forerunners must ski the course before all training sessions and before the race itself.

Start Competitors in the downhill and the giant slalom start at one minute intervals; starts in the slalom are at irregular intervals.

On the starter's order, the skier plants his poles in front of the starting line. The racer must start only with the help of his poles; pushing off from the posts is forbidden.

Competitors receive a warning 10 seconds before the start of the race. In races other than the slalom the starter also counts out the last five seconds before giving the order to start. An automatic audible starting signal should be used where possible.

Competitors in the slalom must start within 10 seconds of the starting signal.

Competitors who start more than three seconds early in races with fixed starting intervals are disqualified for a false start. If they cross the starting line more than three seconds after the official starting time, their time is taken as if they had started three seconds after the starting time.

The timing apparatus measures the exact time at which the skier crosses the starting line with his leg below the knee.

The race A competitor must complete the course on his skis, but may finish on only one ski. He must pass through all the gates on the course by crossing the line between the inner poles with both feet.

The finish A competitor has finished the race when both his feet cross the finishing line. With electric timing, the time is taken when a skier crosses the finishing line with any part of his body or equipment. For this time to be valid (eg in the case of a skier falling at the finish), the competitor must immediately cross the line with both feet.

With hand timing, the time is taken when the skier's first foot crosses the finishing line.

Re-runs A skier may appeal for a re-run because of obstructions on the course, failure of the timing equipment, or other similar occurrences outside his control which interfere with his performance.

If a skier's appeal is allowed, the time for the re-run is the one recorded even if it is slower than his original time over the course.

Disqualification A competitor may be disqualified if he:

a) is not ready at the start at the time indicated in races with fixed starting intervals, or within one minute of being called by the starter in the slalom;

b) makes a false start, or otherwise violates the starting regulations;

c) receives any outside assistance when racing;

d) fails to pass through every gate correctly;

e) fails to complete the course on skis, or fails to finish on at least one ski;

f) fails to give way to an overtaking skier, or otherwise interferes with other racers;

g) alters the course in any way;

h) trains on a course closed to competitors;

i) takes a short cut;

j) fails to finish the race by crossing the finishing line with both feet;

k) is not qualified to enter the race, or enters it under false pretences;

l) does not observe the safety regulations;

m) does not wear the official start number, or alters it in any way;

n) makes an unjustified appeal for a re-run;

o) disobeys the rules or instructions relating to training or the running of the race.

SKIING (ALPINE 2)

DOWNHILL

The course is indicated by green direction markers (**a**) on the right-hand side facing downhill, and red markers (**b**) on the left-hand side. Gates (**c**) are used to direct the skier over the course.

The course must not include any sharp, hard ridges, steep ledges, bumps, or convex outward curves. It must be possible to slide down the length of the course without using ski poles.

The width of the course should increase in those sections where the skiers are traveling at increasing speeds. Fast sections, and sections passing through wooded terrain should be at least 30m wide; other sections may be narrower.

Gates consist of two flags; each flag is a rectangular piece of fabric, approximately 1m high and 75cm wide, stretched between two vertical poles. The poles must be solid and splinterproof, and sufficiently high that the lower edge of the fabric remains at least 1m above the surface of the snow.

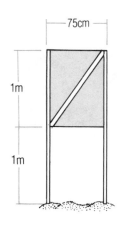

All gates must be at least 8m wide; where possible, the flags marking them should be placed at right angles to the racing line. With the exception of the start and finish, the gates should be numbered in sequence.

Gates should be placed:

a) before dangerous sections of the course so that the skier can approach these sections in control and correctly positioned;

b) on fast sections of the course where it is considered necessary to check the skier's speed;

c) where the course changes suddenly from a steep face to a flat and bumpy section;

d) where the competitors could take dangerous short cuts;

e) on traverses on a steep slope, to ensure that skiers are kept to the upper part of the slope;

f) on bends, to ensure that skiers are kept to the inner part of the curve;

g) to keep skiers away from obstacles;

h) where it is considered necessary to direct skiers to a particular section of the slope.

The men's course is marked by red or luminous orange gates.

For major international competitions, the vertical drop of the course should be 800–1000m (**A**); for other competitions, the drop should be 500–1000m.

At Olympic Games and world championships, the length of the course should be such that the best time recorded should not be less than two minutes.

The women's course should, if possible, be separate from the men's course. It is marked by alternating red and blue gates.

The vertical drop should be 500–700m (**B**). At Olympic Games and world championships the best time recorded should not be less than 1min 40sec.

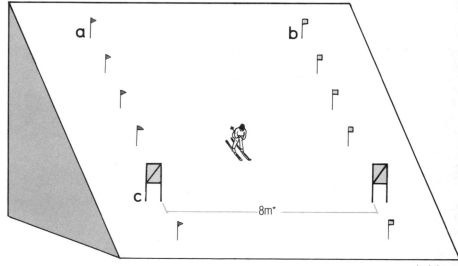

*minimum

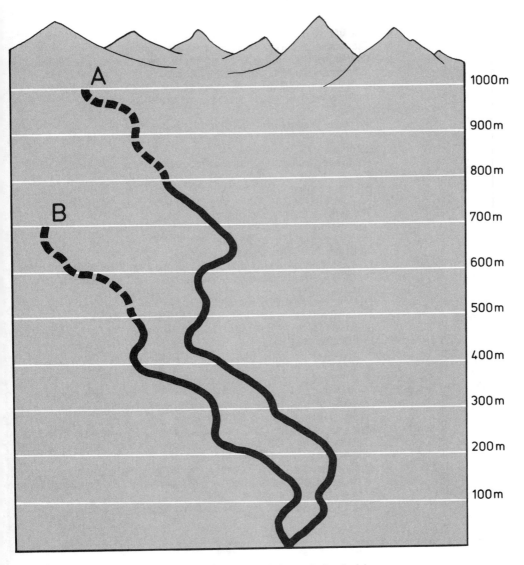

Downhill in two runs Where the topography does not permit the required vertical drop for a single race, the downhill may be organized in two runs. The vertical drop for the course must be at least 450m.

Placings will be decided by the total time for the two runs, which must take place on the same day. The starting order for the second run is decided by the results of the first run (see p. 294).

Training All skiers are required to take part in official training, which is considered part of the competition. During training the course should be completely prepared as for the day of the race.

There must be at least three days of official training, which need not be consecutive. Whenever possible, one training session should take place at the time of day scheduled for the race.

All competitors must complete at least one timed training run. At Olympic Games and world championships times must be taken over the last two days of training; at other competitions times must be taken on at least one of the last two training days.

Result The winner is the skier who completes the course in the prescribed manner in the fastest time.

SKIING (ALPINE 3)

SLALOM

The race is decided by two runs over two different courses.

Course The twisting course, which is defined by gates, should test a wide variety of skiing techniques. It should include turns that allow maximum speed, precision, and neat execution, and should intersperse traverses across the slope with runs down the fall-line. The snow must be as hard as possible, and there must be a prepared practice slope near the start.

The course should be completely prepared at least 1½ hours before the beginning of the race. Competitors may then inspect the course under the supervision of the jury, but may not ski down it.

Width and gradient If the two runs are to be set on the same slope, the course should be at least 40m wide.

At Olympic Games and world championships, the gradient of the slope should normally be 33–45%. It may be below 33% in places, but should reach 52% only over short sections.

The gates consist of two solid, splinterproof poles, 20–32mm in diameter, extending 1.80m above the surface of the snow. The gates must be alternately blue and red, with flags of the same color. All gates should be 4–5m wide; with the exception of the start and finish, they should be numbered in sequence.

Courses should contain open (**a**) and vertical (**b**) gates; at least four hairpin combinations (**c**); and at least two (where possible, three) vertical combinations (**d**) consisting of three to five gates.

Except for vertical combinations and hairpins, the distance between two gates should be 7–15m. Gates in vertical combinations and hairpins should be at least 75cm apart.

Gates should not be set in monotonous combinations, or spoil the fluency of a skier's run by forcing sudden braking.

All difficult combinations of gates should be preceded by at least one gate that allows the competitor to ski the difficult section under control. Difficult sequences of gates should not be set at the beginning and end of the course.

The final gates of the course should be fast, to enable the skier to finish at a good speed. For safety, they should not be too close to the end of the course, but should be placed so as to direct skiers to the center of the finishing line.

Men's course At Olympic Games and world championships, the vertical drop of the course should be 180–220m (**A**); for other international competitions the drop should be 140–200m. It should contain 55–75 gates.

Women's course At Olympic Games and world championships, the vertical drop of the course should be 130–180m (**B**); for other international competitions the drop should be 120–180m. It should contain 45–60 gates.

Result The winner is the competitor with the best aggregate time for the two runs.

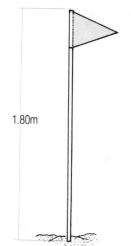

1.80m

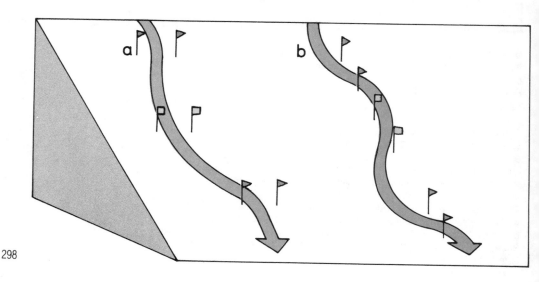

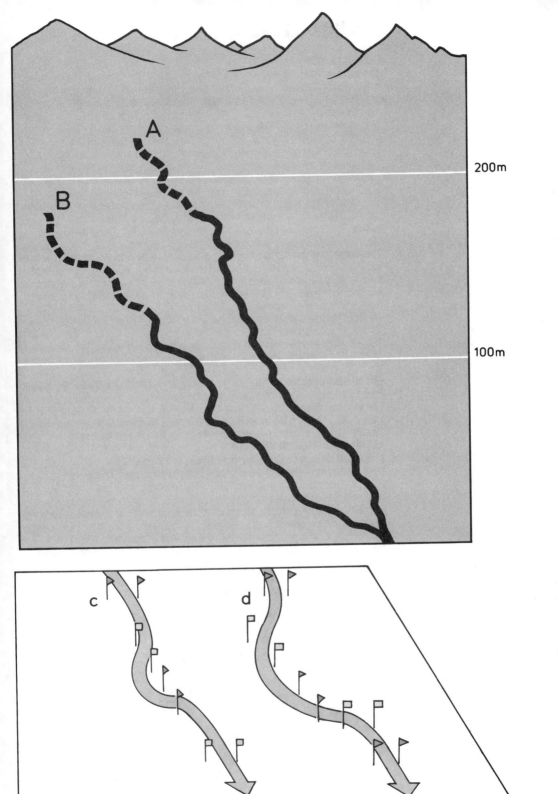

©DIAGRAM

SKIING (ALPINE 4)

GIANT SLALOM
The race is decided by two runs, held when possible on the same day. The second run may be held on the same course as the first, but the gates must be re-set. The two runs should be arranged so that the best times for each are as similar as possible.

The course should be prepared as for a downhill race (see pp. 296–297). The sections where gates are set should be prepared as for a slalom (see pp. 298–299). The ground should be undulating and hilly.

The course should present a variety of long, medium, and small turns, and should allow the skier to choose his own line between the gates. Most of the gates should be single; combinations of gates may be set, but should only be used on uninteresting terrain.

The course should be completely prepared at least one hour before the beginning of the race. Competitors may then inspect the course, but are not permitted to ski through the gates or practice turns parallel to those required by the gates on the course.

Width The course must be at least 30m wide, and should make use of the full width of a hill wherever possible.

The gates consist of two flags; each flag is a rectangular piece of fabric stretched between two vertical poles. The poles must be solid and splinterproof, and sufficiently high that the lower edge of the fabric remains at least 1m above the surface of the snow. The flags marking closed gates (**a**) should be approximately 30cm wide and 50cm high; other flags (**b**) should be at least 75cm wide and 50cm high.

The gates must be alternately red and blue, and the blue flags must carry a distinctive mark (preferably a diagonal white stripe).

All gates must be 4–8m wide; the distance between the nearer poles of two successive gates must not be less than 10m. The flags marking the gates should be set at right angles to the racing line.

The number of gates set is based on the vertical drop of the course: 15% of the vertical drop equals the number of gates plus or minus five gates.

The vertical drop of the course should be 250–400m for men (**A**), and 250–350m for women (**B**). For World Cup races the minimum drop is 300m for both men and women.

Result The winner is the competitor with the best aggregate time for the two runs.

ALPINE COMBINED "KANDAHAR"
The event consists of a downhill race followed by a slalom.

The courses should be set in accordance with the rules for downhill races (see pp. 296–297) and slalom races (see pp. 298–299). The slalom course used must be set especially for the combined competition.

Standard procedure is used to determine the starting order for the downhill (see p.294). The results of the downhill are used to determine the starting order for the slalom, which then follows the standard procedure for the second run of a two-run event.

Result Points are awarded for each race according to official tables: these points are added together to give the final classification.

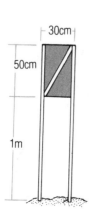

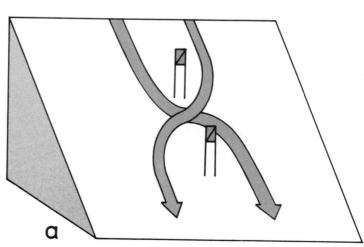

a

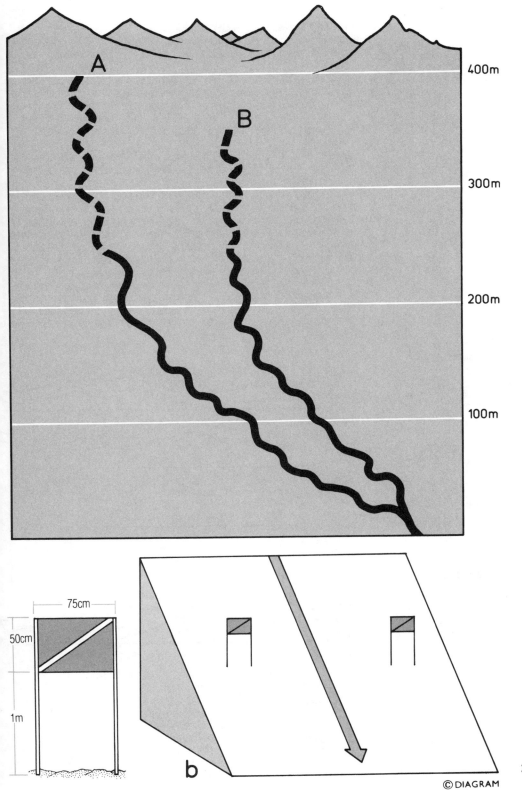

© DIAGRAM

SKIING (NORDIC 1)

COURSE AND TIMING EQUIPMENT (GENERAL)

The course should ideally be one third flat, one third uphill, and one third downhill. It should be laid out as naturally and with as much variety as possible, preferably through woodland. Monotonous flat sections and long unbroken climbs should be avoided.

The skier's rhythm should not be broken by sudden sharp changes of direction, steep climbs, icy bends, or narrow passages. Changes of direction should occur before rather than after downhill sections; it must be possible to negotiate all downhill sections without danger, even when the track is icy. There should be no long downhill runs in the final sections of the course, and the most strenuous climbs should not come in the first two or three kilometers.

The degree of difficulty of the course should relate to the level of the competition, and to the length of the race: the longer distance races should be less arduous than the shorter distance and relay races.

At Olympic Games and world championships, the highest point of the course should not exceed 1650m. The course, or substantial parts of it, should be run at the most twice.

The snow should be prepared to a width of 25m. Tracks for skis and poles must be hard enough to allow skiers to travel at racing speed, and downhill sections must be prepared for skiers traveling at full speed. The course must be freshly prepared after each training session. Patrols should be sent out during the race to ensure that course conditions are the same for all competitors, and to keep the tracks open during poor weather.

Mechanical trackmarkers are used to prepare the tracks, which should be laid out in a way that allows the skier to glide along without breaking his ski bindings. Each track should be 15–18cm wide, and at least 2cm deep. Where double tracking is used the pairs of tracks should be at least 1–1.20m apart, measured from their centers. Mechanical trackmaking

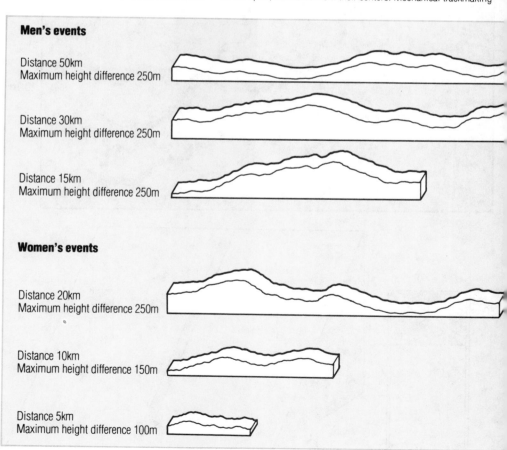

Men's events

Distance 50km
Maximum height difference 250m

Distance 30km
Maximum height difference 250m

Distance 15km
Maximum height difference 250m

Women's events

Distance 20km
Maximum height difference 250m

Distance 10km
Maximum height difference 150m

Distance 5km
Maximum height difference 100m

should not be used at changes of direction, where skiers should be allowed to develop their own tracks. In special cases on downhill sections turns should be prepared without tracks.

Timing equipment Electric timing apparatus that allows measurements to tenths of a second is required. Supplementary hand timing should also be used at all competitions in case of breakdown of the automatic timing system.

In addition to recording the starting and finishing times, one intermediate time should be recorded on all 10km courses, two intermediate times on 15km, 20km, and 30km courses, and at least three intermediate times on 50km courses.

INDIVIDUAL RACES

Course lengths Men race over 15, 30, and 50km courses; women over 5, 10, and 20km.

Height difference The difference in height between the lowest and the highest point of a course may not exceed 100m on women's 5km courses; 150m on women's 10km courses; or 250m on all courses of 15km and above.

The maximum climb is the difference in height of any single climb without a break of at least 200m. It should not exceed 50m on the women's 5km course, 75m on the other women's courses, or 100m on the men's courses.

The total climbs should not exceed:
a) 1000–1500m on men's 50km courses;
b) 750–1000m on men's 30km courses;
c) 450–600m on men's 15km courses;
d) 400–500m on women's 20km courses;
e) 250–300m on women's 10km courses;
f) 150–200m on women's 5km courses;

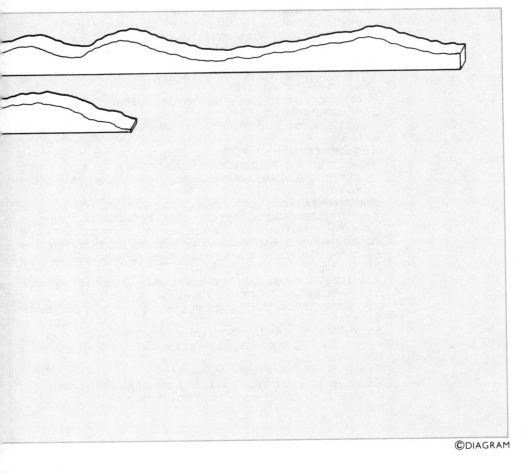

303

SKIING (NORDIC 2)

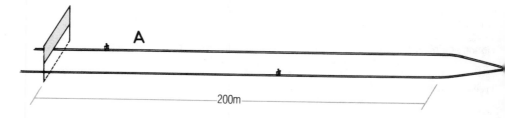

Course markings The markings along the course should be sufficiently clear that the skier is never in any doubt as to the direction of the track.

Boards, arrows, flags, and ribbons are used to mark the course. Each race is indicated by a different color, and in a world championship these are:
a) red on men's 15km courses;
b) red/green on men's 30km courses;
c) orange on men's 50km courses;
d) blue on women's 5km courses;
e) violet on women's 10km courses;
f) violet/red on women's 20km courses.

Kilometer signs should mark the course every kilometer, and all changes of direction must be marked by clearly visible arrows.

The starting and finishing area should be large enough to include the starting and finishing lines and tracks, any necessary equipment, and facilities for the officials and for the care of competitors. It must be fenced off from spectators.

The starting and finishing lines, defined by two vertical poles, should be side by side and on the same level.

The starting line should be accessible only through the special enclosure provided for the official marking of competitors' skis.

For competitions using a double start, two parallel sets of tracks (**A**) should run for at least 200m from the starting line.

The last 100m of the approach to the finishing line should always have two parallel sets of tracks (**B**).

Refreshment stations for competitors should be provided along the course. They must be placed in such a way that skiers can make use of them without loss of time or rhythm. One refreshment station is required on courses of up to 15km; two on courses up to 30km; and four on courses up to 50km.

Starting order At Olympic Games and world championships, each country may have up to four competitors starting in a race. The competitors are divided into four groups, numbered I–IV, which start in numerical order. Only one skier from each country may be included in each group; team captains decide in which of the groups each of their skiers shall compete. The starting order of the individual skiers is determined by a separate draw for each group.

At other international competitions the skiers are divided into three sections, as follows. Section A includes up to 10 competitors from each participating country. These competitors are further subdivided into groups, depending on the total number of skiers in the section.

Section B includes a set number (which should not be more than 20) of competitors from the host country, and the remaining competitors from other countries who were not included in section A.

Section C consists of all the remaining competitors.

The sections start in the order B,A,C. The starting order of the individual skiers is determined by a separate draw for each of sections B and C, and for each group within section A.

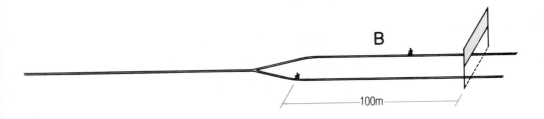

B

100m

Training Competitors must have the opportunity to inspect the course and to train on it when it has been completely prepared for racing. If possible it should be open for training for two days before the day of the race.

Starting procedure To prevent unauthorized changes of skis during the race, all competitors must have both skis marked by an official immediately before the race. At Olympic Games and world championships, the skier's starting number must also be marked on his skis in the appropriate color for the course. Skiers should present themselves in the marking enclosure in good time before their turn to start.

At Olympic Games and world championships, skiers start singly at 30-second intervals. At other international events, single or double starts may be used; mass starts may only be used with the permission of the governing body.

The skier may only come to the starting line from the marking enclosure. Competitors start with both feet behind the starting line, but with their ski poles planted in front of it. Competitors receive a warning 10 seconds before the start of the race. The starter also counts out the last five seconds before giving the order to start. An automatic starting signal should also be used.

With automatic timing apparatus, the skier's exact starting time is accepted if he crosses the starting line between three seconds before and three seconds after the starting signal. If he starts more than three seconds before the signal, it is considered a false start; the skier is recalled and must cross the starting line again, this time outside the starting gate. If the skier starts more than three seconds late, he is considered to have crossed the starting line at his official starting list time.

Race procedure Competitors must follow the marked track, and must pass through all the official control points. They may not receive assistance from pacemakers, and must give way to overtaking skiers at the first demand.

Competitors may scrape and wax their skis during the race, providing they do so without assistance. They may, however, make use of a blowtorch, a scraper, or wax passed to them by another person.

A skier may exchange both his ski poles and one of his skis during the race; the ski may only be exchanged if it is broken or if the binding is damaged.

Finishing procedure Competitors must complete the course wearing at least one marked ski. The finishing time is taken when the skier's first foot crosses the finishing line.

Disqualification A competitor may be disqualified if he:
a) is not qualified to enter the race, or enters it under false pretences;
b) does not follow the marked track, takes a short cut, or does not pass all the control points;
c) receives unauthorized assistance;
d) fails to give way to an overtaking skier, or clearly obstructs another racer;
e) runs part of the course without skis, or finishes with two unmarked skis.

Result The winner is the skier who completes the course in the fastest time.

SKIING (NORDIC 3)

RELAY COURSES

Course length Each section of the relay course is 10km for men and 5km for women.

The course layout is similar to that for other cross-country skiing races (see pp. 302–304). There should be no sharp bends or narrow sections in the first kilometer. With the following exceptions, the height differences, total climbs, etc are as for individual cross-country races (see pp. 302–303):

a) the height difference for the men's course is 200m;

b) the total climb for the men's course should not exceed 300–450m;

c) in world championships, the colors indicating the courses are red/blue for the women's relay and green/orange for the men's relay.

The starting line (A) is an arc of a circle whose radius is 100m. Individual starting places should be 2m apart along this line. Each starting place should have a separate track. If space is limited, the starting positions may be arranged in two or more rows at least 4m behind each other. There should be at least six skiers in the front row.

The starting tracks must run parallel to each other for the first 100m of the course, and converge over the next 100m into at least three separate tracks.

The relay exchange zone (B) is a 30m long roped-off area, situated on flat or smoothly rising ground as close to the starting and finishing area as possible. The last 500m of the course leading to the exchange zone should be double-tracked, direct, and without sharp turns or corners; the last 100m should be clearly marked.

Finishing track The last 200m of the course leading to the finishing line should be double-tracked and without sharp bends or corners; the last 100m should be clearly marked.

RELAY PROCEDURE

Teams At Olympic Games and world championships, a team consists of four men or four women; other competitions may stipulate teams of either three or four skiers. Each member of the team may ski only one section of the relay.

The starting number of each team is determined by a draw. At world championships, teams placed in the previous world championships are drawn first.

Ski marking Separate colors are used to mark the skis of the competitors in each relay section; the same colors are used for the starting numbers worn by the skiers. At world championships, the colors are red for the first section, green for the second, yellow for the third, and blue for the fourth.

The start is a mass start. Skiers in the first relay section should be called to the start one minute before the starting time of the race, and should take up their positions on the starting line according to their starting numbers. The skier with starting number 1 starts on the middle track; skiers with even starting numbers start in numerical order on the tracks to his right, and those with odd starting numbers in numerical order on the tracks to his left. Competitors receive a warning 30 seconds before the start of the race. The starter also calls a warning immediately before giving the starting signal.

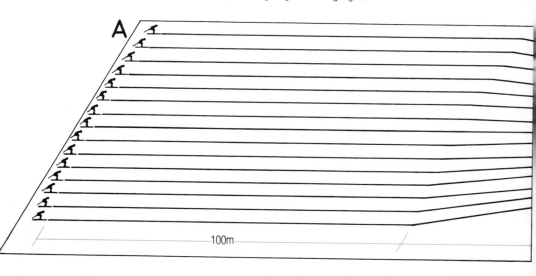

False start Officials should be positioned 100m in front of the starting line, and should bar the way and turn back the competitors if a false start is called. The starter then arranges a new start.

Handover The arriving skier should tap his hand on any part of the next racer's body while both skiers are in the relay exchange zone. The racer taking over may only enter this zone when summoned by an official.

In the case of an incorrect handover both skiers are recalled to the exchange zone, where a correct handover must take place before the skier taking over may start.

Skiers need not give way to other racers in the last 100m of the course leading to the relay exchange zone. Intermediate times for each section of the course are taken when the arriving skier enters the exchange zone; this time is also considered to be the starting time of the racer taking over.

The finish Skiers need not give way to other racers in the last 100m of the course leading to the finishing line. A team's finishing time is taken when the team's last racer crosses the finishing line with his first foot.

Disqualification A team may be disqualified if:
a) the same competitor skis more than one section of the race;
b) a handover is not correctly carried out:
c) a member of the team commits an offense that would lead to disqualification in any other cross-country event (see p. 305). A skier will not, however, be disqualified for failing to give way in the last 100m of the course leading to the relay exchange zone or the finishing line.

Result The winners are the team whose final skier is the first to cross the finishing line. A photo-finish is used to decide the result if two or more skiers cross the finishing line together.

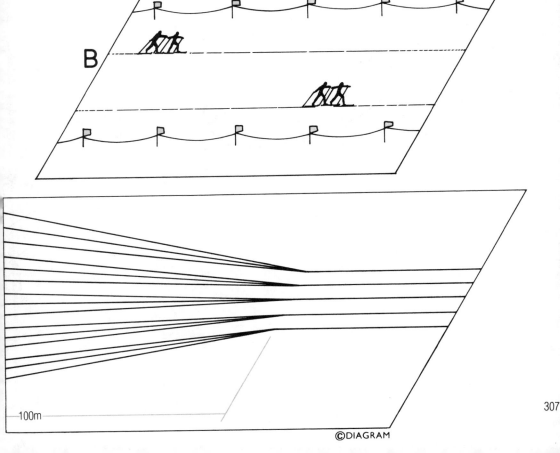

100m

©DIAGRAM

SKIING (NORDIC 4)

JUMPING HILL AND EQUIPMENT

The jumping hill must conform with detailed FIS specifications, and should be tested before training and competitions to ensure that it is in a safe and satisfactory condition. The hill should be smooth and hard from the inrun (**E**) to the outrun (**A**), and conditions must be consistent for all competitors.

The norm point (**P**) marks the start of the competitors' expected landing area: it is marked on the hill by a board, and on the snow on each side of the landing zone by blue lines approximately 2m long.

In most international competitions the norm point should not be more than 90m from the takeoff point (**O**). At Olympic Games and world championships, two jumping hills should be used, with norm points of approximately 70m and of 85–90m respectively. The difference between the norm points of the two hills should be at least 15m.

The table point (**TP**) marks the end of the competitors' expected landing area: it is marked on the hill by a board and green lines. The table point should be approximately halfway between the norm point and the critical point.

The critical point (**K**) marks the maximum safe landing distance, and is marked on the hill by a board and red lines. The distance between the norm point and the critical point should be approximately equal to one quarter of the distance between the takeoff point and the norm point.

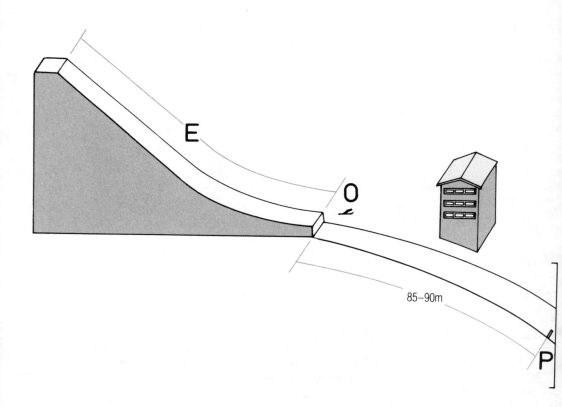

The judges' tower should correspond to FIS specifications. It must be placed so that each judge is able to observe the whole of each jump from the takeoff point to the end of the landing area. The tower should be divided into separate compartments: judges must not be able to see one another's scoresheets.

Distance measuring equipment The automatic distance measuring equipment used should be capable of measuring the distance jumped to an accuracy of ½m.

A supplementary visual distance measuring system should also be used in case of breakdown of the automatic system. Intervals of 1m should be marked out with boards on either side of the landing slope before the competition begins. The distances jumped are then measured to an accuracy of ½m.

Inrun speed and wind speed A hill whose norm point is greater than 80m must have equipment for measuring the speeds of the competitors on the inrun, and the speed of the wind. Instruments for measuring wind speed should normally be placed where the strongest wind is expected.

SKI JUMPING PROCEDURE

Starting order Competitors are divided into four groups, usually on the basis of an FIS classification list. A separate draw is held to determine the starting order within each group.

Training At Olympic Games and world championships, the hill must be open for training at least one week before the date of the competition. At other competitions at least one day's training should be allowed. During training the hill should be completely prepared as for the day of the competition.

Forerunners appointed by the judges must jump the hill before official training and before the competition. Their results should be used to determine the competitors' starting place on the inrun, and the length and inclination of the takeoff. The forerunners should also establish tracks on the inrun for use by the competing skiers; these tracks should not be more than 3cm deep.

Jumping procedure Each competitor has two jumps; an additional jump in a trial round is optional.

Competitors must be ready at the starting place when called, and should start on the starter's signal. A competitor must have finished his jump before the order is given for the next competitor to start.

Competitors may not use ski poles or similar aids to increase their speed on the inrun, nor may they be pushed by another person.

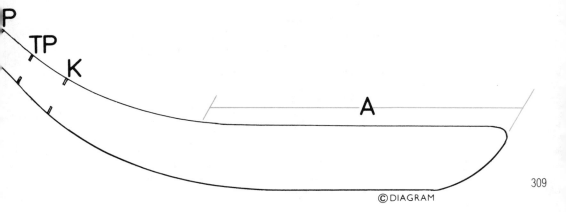

© DIAGRAM

SKIING (NORDIC 5)

EXECUTION OF JUMPS

Parts of a jump A jump consists of the takeoff, the flight, and the landing.

The takeoff (1) should be a powerful action (varying according to the speed and profile of the hill), and made with boldness and precision. The knees must be straightened and the body stretched in a fast, rhythmic, and aggressive movement.

The flight (2) should be calm, steady, and controlled. The body should be stretched out straight at the hips, or only slightly bent; the upper part of the body and the legs must be completely taut.

The skis should be kept horizontal until just before landing, and should be parallel and in the same plane. The skier should lean well forward with an acute angle between his legs and his skis.

The skier should keep his feet together, and his arm movements should be controlled. The skis should be adapted to the gradient of the landing slope only shortly before landing.

The landing (3) should be made with flexible and controlled movements; a hard and stiff landing will be penalized. The skis should be close together; the distance between them should not be more than the width of two skis.

The skier should land with one foot in front of the other, and knees and hips bent in the "telemark" position to counter the force of landing.

After landing the skier should continue to the outrun in a normal downhill skiing position, holding himself as upright as the gradient and the condition of the surface will allow. He should be balanced, and his skis should remain close together.

JUDGING AND SCORING

Distance points are awarded depending on the distance jumped, measured to the nearest ½m. Official tables, varying with the norm point of the hill, are used to convert the distance into points.

Style points The jumping judges are responsible for the award of style points for the jump: the general impression of the entire jump determines the number of points awarded. The ideal jump should be performed with power, boldness, and precision, while giving an impression of calmness, steadiness, and control. The jumper is allowed his own individual style providing that the basic standards of style are met.

Judging begins at the moment of takeoff. Any faults made on takeoff are not penalized, as they will automatically affect the skier's flight through the air and the distance he achieves. A jump is considered to be a standing jump if the skier travels from the landing to the outrun in perfect balance. Provided that the skier has reached the outrun in perfect balance, any fall there is irrelevant. Standing jumps score from 6–20 marks.

A jump is considered to be a fall if the skier touches the snow or his skis with either or both hands in an attempt to maintain his balance before he reaches the outrun. If the fall is caused by circumstances beyond his control, he may be allowed to repeat the jump, or it may be considered a standing jump. If the jumper falls in the outrun because he has lost his balance on landing, the jump is considered a fall. Competitors may be awarded from 0–10 points for a fall; falls in the inrun score 0 points.

Faults Skiers are penalized from ½–10 points for faults occurring during the flight or on landing. Minor faults or faults occurring at the beginning of the flight which are immediately corrected are less severely penalized than faults which occur during the whole flight, or which occur in the last part of the flight and are not corrected.

Faults in the air which are penalized include:
a) bent knees;
b) pronounced bending at the hips;
c) curved or bent back;
d) body insufficiently far forward;
e) unsteadiness;
f) ski points too high or too low;
g) skis crossed vertically or horizontally.

Faults on landing which are penalized include:
a) premature preparation for landing;
b) stiff landing;
c) body too bent on landing;
d) body not far enough forward on landing;
e) landing too low;
f) landing with feet even, instead of in telemark position;
g) unsteadiness.

The total style points score for each jump is reached by eliminating the highest and lowest of the judges' scores, and then totaling the remaining scores.

Result The total points score for each jump is the total of the distance points and the style points. The winner is the competitor with the highest total of points from his two jumps.

SKIING (NORDIC 6)

NORDIC COMBINED
The competition consists of ski jumping and cross-country ski racing.

The jumping hill (1) should be constructed as for ski jumping competitions (see pp. 308–309). It should have a norm point (**P**) of 60–70m; at Olympic Games and world championships, the norm point must be 70m.

The cross-country course (2) is 15km long. The course layout should be similar to that for other cross-country skiing races (see pp. 302–304); it should, however, be less technically difficult. The total climb should not exceed 400–500m, and all course markings should be in green.

Order of events The competition takes place on two consecutive days; the ski jumping should normally take place before the cross-country racing. At Olympic Games and world championships, the ski jumping must take place one day before the racing.

Starting order Separate draws are held for the ski-jumping and the cross-country racing. The competitors are divided into four groups for each event, and each group is drawn separately.

Jumping procedure Each competitor is allowed three jumps, of which the best two count toward his result. Judging is as for other ski jumping events (see pp. 310–311).

Race procedure The cross-country event follows the procedure for other cross-country races (see pp. 305).

Scoring The ski jumping is scored for distance and style as in other ski jumping competitions (see pp. 310–311).

The times in the cross-country race are converted into points according to FIS tables. The skier with the fastest time receives 220 points.

Result The competitor with the highest points total from the two events is the winner.

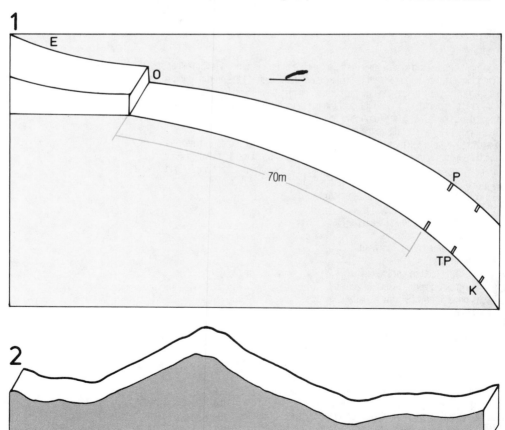

SKIING (BIATHLON 1)

BIATHLON COURSE AND SHOOTING RANGE

The event combines cross-country ski racing (**A**) with smallbore rifle shooting (**B**); the skier carries his unloaded rifle and his ammunition with him while racing. There are three races: the individual biathlon, the sprint, and the relay.

The course layout should be similar to that used for other cross-country skiing races (see pp. 302–304) with the addition of a shooting range. The starting line, shooting range, and finishing line should normally be in the same area.

The last 100m of the course should be as straight as possible, and clearly marked. The last 300m of the course must be double-tracked for races with an individual start, and the last 500m for races with group or mass starts.

At Olympic Games and world championships, the highest point of the course should not exceed 1500m, and the courses or substantial parts of them should be run at most twice. At other competitions the courses or parts of them may be run several times if necessary.

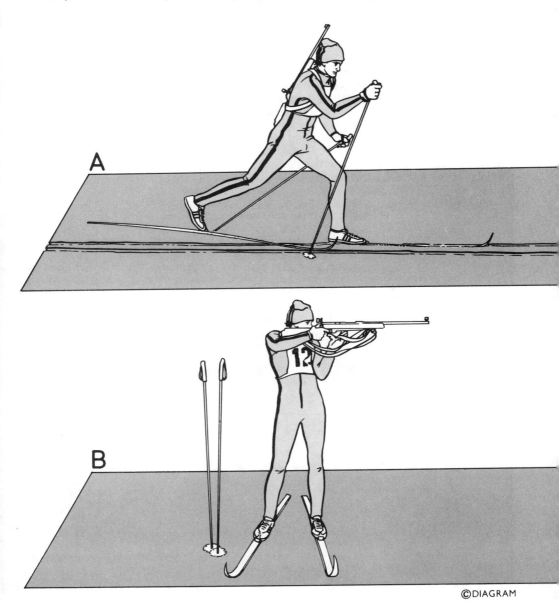

A

B

©DIAGRAM

SKIING (BIATHLON 2)

Timing equipment Electric timing apparatus allowing measurements to tenths of a second should be used. Supplementary hand timing should also be used at all competitions in case of breakdown of the automatic timing equipment.

The shooting range is 50m long from the firing points to the targets. The firing points should be at least 2.5m wide, and numbered along with their corresponding targets.

Targets Mechanical targets which disappear when hit, breakable targets, or electronic target systems may be used.

When a mechanical target system is used, the diameters of the holes in the shield should be 11.5cm for shooting in the standing position, and 4.5cm for shooting in the prone position. The diameter of the black aiming mark should also be 11.5cm. With other systems, the diameter of the aiming mark should be 11cm; the diameters of the targets should be 11cm for standing shooting, and 4cm for prone shooting.

The five targets should be placed next to each other in a horizontal line. The distance between the centers of adjacent targets (**a**) should be 21cm, or 21.5cm if mechanical target systems are used. The centers of the end targets should be at least 15.5cm from the edges of the target board (**b**). The vertical distance from the centers of the targets to the upper and lower edges of the target board should be at least 15.5cm (**c**).

The target board and the background behind the targets must be white. At Olympic Games and world championships, the target system should clearly indicate every hit by showing a white or orange colored surface in place of the black aiming mark.

DRESS AND EQUIPMENT

Dress Competitors are not restricted in their choice of clothing providing that it does not exceed 6mm in thickness.

The rifle should be of 5.6mm (.22 long rifle) caliber, and must not be automatic or semi-automatic. The specifications of the rifle must conform to detailed regulations, which include the following:

a) the trigger resistance must be a minimum of 500g;
b) the sights must not have any magnifying effect;
c) the magazine must not permit the insertion of more than five rounds;
d) loading may not be facilitated by a spring device;
e) there must be no special hand supports.

The number and type of slings on the rifle are not restricted, except that the shooting sling must not be wider than 40mm.

The ammunition must be of 5.6mm (.22 long rifle) rimfire caliber, and the bullets must be of lead or a similar soft material. The muzzle velocity must not exceed 420m/second.

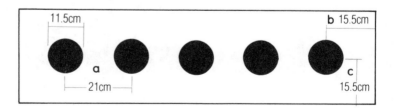

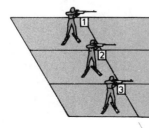

50m

INDIVIDUAL BIATHLON

Course lengths The men's course should be 20km long, with a maximum height difference of 200m, maximum climb of 75m, and total climb of 550–750m. There should be four bouts of shooting between the fourth and eighteenth kilometers of the course, with at least 3km of skiing between any two successive bouts. The first and third bouts of shooting are in the prone position, the second and fourth in the standing position. The women's course should be 10km long, with a maximum height difference of 100m, maximum climb of 50m, and total climb of 200–350m. There should be three bouts of shooting between the second and eighth kilometers of the course, with at least 2km skiing between any two successive bouts. The first and third bouts of shooting are in the prone position, the second in the standing position.

Training Competitors should be allowed at least two training periods on the course and one on the shooting range prior to the start of the competition. They must also have the opportunity to fire sighting shots on the range shortly before the beginning of the race.

Starting order Competitors are divided into four groups; team captains decide in which group each of their skiers shall compete. The starting order for individual skiers is determined by a separate draw for each group.

Starting procedure To prevent unauthorized changes of equipment during the race, all competitors must have their rifles and both skis marked by an official approximately 10 minutes before their official starting time.

Immediately before the start, the competitor must show the starter's assistant that he is carrying the correct amount of ammunition; his ski and rifle markings are also checked. Competitors carrying unmarked equipment or insufficient ammunition are not permitted to start until they have rectified these deficiencies; any time thus lost is added to their overall time for the race.

At Olympic Games and world championships, competitors start singly at one minute intervals. At other competitions, starts may be single or double and at intervals of ½–2min. Starting signals and starting times recorded are as for other cross-country races (see p. 305).

Race procedure is as for other cross-country races (see p. 305).

©DIAGRAM

SKIING (BIATHLON 3)

Shooting procedure On arrival at the firing range, the competitor should go to the firing position allocated to him. He should then load his rifle with five rounds of ammunition, for which he may use a magazine. Competitors may only load their rifles when at the firing position, with the rifle pointing toward the target.

Competitors fire their five shots at the target in their own time; they may remove their skis before shooting if they wish.

When shooting in the prone position, the competitor may support the rifle with his hands only. It should be held against his shoulder and cheek, and must not be rested on the ground. When shooting in the standing position, the competitor should hold the rifle against his shoulder, his cheek, and the part of his chest nearest his shoulder. Any other support is forbidden. However, the use of a shooting sling is permitted in both shooting positions.

If a competitor's weapon is damaged during the race and will not fire, he may exchange it for a reserve rifle at the shooting range with the permission of the range officer.

Competitors may also repair their weapons with the assistance of the competition armorer. Any misfires must be re-shot from the reserve ammunition carried by the competitor. If the competitor loses his ammunition during the course of the race, it may be replaced by his team captain with the permission of the range officer.

Competitors must unload their rifles after each bout of shooting, and remove the empty magazine.

Shooting penalties A one minute penalty is imposed for each target missed. If a competitor continues skiing without firing all five shots at the target, he incurs a two minute penalty for each shot not fired.

Other penalties Competitors incur a one minute penalty for failing to give way at the first request to an overtaking skier, except in the last 100m of the course leading to the finishing line.

Finishing procedure Competitors must complete the course wearing at least one marked ski and carrying the marked rifle. The time is taken when the competitor's first foot crosses the finishing line.

Disqualification In addition to the offenses that lead to disqualification in other cross-country races (see p. 305), a competitor may be disqualified if he:
a) changes his weapon without permission of the range officer;
b) completes the course carrying an unmarked rifle;
c) fires unauthorized sighting shots;
d) makes prohibited alterations (eg changing the trigger pressure) to his rifle after it has been marked;
e) remains in an incorrect shooting position after having been warned;
f) fires more than the set number of shots at the target;
g) allows his rifle to be carried by someone else;
h) receives ammunition outside the firing range;
i) does not unload his rifle after each shooting bout, or loads or unloads it in an unauthorized manner;
j) makes movements with a loaded rifle that might endanger other persons.

Result The running time from start to finish (including the shooting) plus all penalty minutes gives the competitor's total time. The winner is the competitor with the fastest total time.

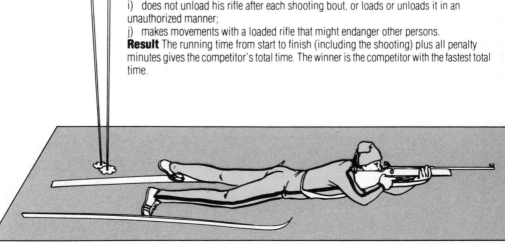

BIATHLON SPRINT

Course lengths The men's course is 10km long, with a maximum height difference of 200m, maximum climb of 75m, and total climb of 300–400m. There are two bouts of shooting, the first prone and the second standing, between approximately 2.5 and 7.5km. The women's course should be 5km long, with a maximum height difference of 100m, maximum climb of 50m, and total climb of 150–200m. There should be two bouts of shooting: prone at approximately 1.5km, and standing at 3.5km. There must be at least 1km of skiing between the two bouts.

Training and procedure are as for the individual biathlon.

Shooting penalties For each target missed, the competitor must ski once around a penalty loop. The penalty loop should be 150m long (plus or minus 5m), round or oval, and laid out on a level piece of ground near the shooting range.

Competitors are themselves responsible for running the correct number of penalty rounds immediately after shooting; failure to do so incurs a 20 second penalty. Competitors who omit penalty rounds after firing from the prone position must run them immediately after firing from the standing position; penalty rounds omitted after firing from the standing position must be run before the competitor passes the finishing line. Every penalty loop omitted incurs a two minute penalty.

If a competitor continues skiing without firing all five shots at the target, he incurs a two minute penalty for each shot not fired.

Other penalties and disqualifications for infringements are as for individual biathlon.

Result The competitor with the fastest time is the winner.

BIATHLON RELAY

Course lengths The men's course is 7.5km long, with a maximum height difference of 200m, maximum climb of 75m, and total climb of 200–300m. There should be two bouts of shooting; prone at approximately 2.5km, and standing at approximately 5km.

The women's course is 5km long; other specifications are as for women's sprint biathlon.

Course layout The course should be laid out with two tracks wherever possible.

The first competitor of each team should have his own individual straight track for at least 100m from the starting line; these tracks should be at least 2m apart. The tracks should then converge into a common track over a further distance of at least 100m.

The relay exchange zone should be a rectangle, 30m long and 10m wide, situated at a place where the competitors arrive at a controlled speed. The last 100m of the course leading to the exchange zone should be as straight as possible, double-tracked, and clearly marked.

Teams At Olympic Games and world championships, a men's team consists of four skiers; other competitions may stipulate teams of either three of four. Women's teams have three skiers. Each member of a team may ski only one lap of the relay.

Race procedure The start is a mass start; the first competitor of each team lines up on the starting line in numerical order from left to right.

Marking of skis and rifles is as for the individual biathlon (see p. 315); starting and handover procedures are as for cross-country relay races (see p. 307).

Shooting procedure Each competitor may shoot eight rounds at the five targets in each shooting position. The first five rounds may be loaded in the magazine; the remaining three rounds must be placed in the container provided at the firing point. If these rounds are required they must be loaded individually into the rifle. Other shooting regulations are as for individual biathlon.

Shooting penalties For each target missed, the competitor must ski once around the penalty loop, as in the sprint biathlon. Competitors who have not hit all five targets and who race on without having fired all eight cartridges incur a two minute penalty for each round not fired. A one minute penalty is imposed on competitors who do not put their spare rounds in the containers provided.

Other penalties Competitors incur a one minute penalty for failing to give way to an overtaking skier at the first request, except in the last 100m of the course leading to either the relay exchange zone or the finishing line.

Disqualification In addition to offenses that may lead to disqualification in the individual or sprint biathlons, teams may be disqualified if the same competitor skis more than one lap of the race, or if a handover is not carried out correctly.

Result The team with the fastest time is the winner.

SNOOKER

HISTORY

Snooker is generally believed to have been invented in 1875 by Colonel Sir Neville Chamberlain, a British Army officer then stationed in Southern India. It is a descendant of English billiards and uses the same table, but whereas billiards is played with only three balls, snooker requires 22. Not until the 1920s and 1930s did snooker begin to challenge the popularity of English billiards; today, snooker is by far the more popular game, largely as a result of commercial sponsorship and television coverage. The world governing body for the amateur game is the Billiards and Snooker Control Council (B&SCC). In 1970, professional players set up their own organization, the World Professional Billiards and Snooker Association (WPBSA).

SYNOPSIS

The game of snooker is played on a pocket billiard table. Fifteen red balls, six differently colored balls, and one white cue ball are used. Points are scored by pocketing balls and by forcing an opponent to give away points through "snookers." It is played by two players, pairs, or teams.

PLAYING AREA AND EQUIPMENT

Table Snooker can be played on any English billiard table. Here we describe the full-size "standard" table.

The table has a sturdy wooden frame, and a perfectly level playing surface comprised of five large slates, with a baize cover that is traditionally green. The playing area must measure 3.50m long by 1.75m wide.

The frame projects above the level of the playing surface to form wooden rails (**a**), on the inner edges of which are baize-covered cushions that protrude into the playing area. The cushions are known as the bottom cushion (**b**), side cushions (**c**), and top cushion (**d**). The height of the cushion rail from the floor must be 85–87.5cm.

The table has six pockets, which must conform to specific regulations. Pockets at the corners are known as bottom pockets (**e**) and top pockets (**f**). Pockets midway along the sides of the table are called center pockets (**g**).

Drawn across the table 70cm from the face of the bottom cushion (⅕ the length of the table) is the balk line (**h**); the space toward the bottom cushion is termed the balk (**i**).

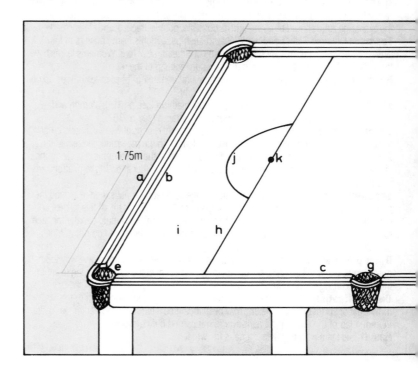

A semicircle known as the "D" (**j**) is drawn within the balk. It is centered on the middle of the balk line and has a radius of 29.2cm (¹/₆ the width of the playing area).

The table is also marked with four spots, which are all midway between the faces of the two side cushions. The balk spot (**k**) is in the middle of the balk line. The center spot (**l**) is equidistant from the faces of the top and bottom cushions. The pyramid spot (**m**) is midway between the center spot and the face of the top cushion. The billiard spot (**n**), which is also known simply as "the spot," is 32cm (¹/₁₁ the length of the playing area) from the face of the top cushion.

Cue Snooker cues must not be less than 91cm long, and must conform to the traditionally accepted shape and form. They are made of wood, and taper as illustrated toward a leather-covered tip. Control over the ball is improved by rubbing the cue tip with chalk.

Cue rests may be used to support the cue for strokes.

Balls Snooker is played with a total of 22 balls, all of which must be equal in size and weight. A standard ball is 52.5mm in diameter. There are 15 red balls (called "reds"); one yellow, one green, one brown, one blue, one pink, and one black ball (called the "colors," or the "pool" balls); and one white ball (the "cue" ball).

The balls are set up in specific positions on the table (see p. 320).

Triangle A triangular rack may be used to position the red balls for the start of play.

Scoreboard The score is recorded on a board showing units, tens, and hundreds.

PLAYERS AND OFFICIALS

Players Games may be played by two players, pairs, or teams. Competition matches are usually for individuals.

Officials consist of a referee and a marker.

The referee is the sole judge of fair play and is responsible for the conduct of the game. Players may appeal to him for decisions but he must not express any opinions or give warnings of likely foul strokes. The referee is allowed to clean a ball at a player's request. The marker keeps the score on the scoreboard and generally assists the referee.

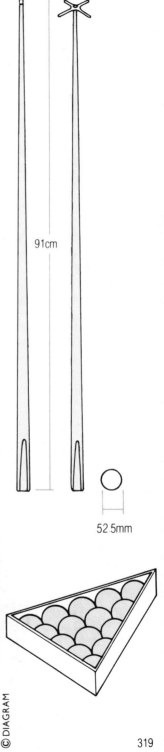

91cm

52.5mm

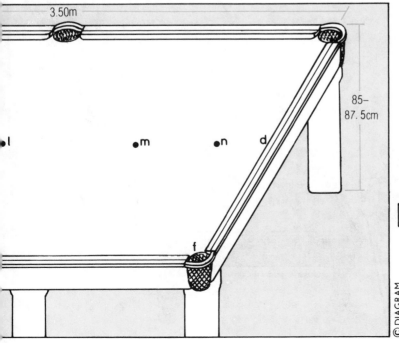

3.50m

85–87.5cm

•l   •m   •n   d

f

© DIAGRAM

319

SNOOKER 2

DURATION AND SCORING

Duration A match consists of a predetermined number of games or "frames." A frame consists of pocketing all the object balls (balls other than the cue ball) according to a set procedure.

Scoring A match is won by winning the most frames, or by scoring the highest aggregate number of points.

Points are scored for correctly pocketing balls, according to the values listed in the table. Points are also scored for foul strokes made by an opponent.

If a match is to be decided by the number of frames won and the score is equal when a frame would normally have ended, players draw lots for the right to play the final black again (with the black respotted and the cue ball played from the "D"). In a match to be decided on aggregate points, the black is played again only if the scores are equal when the final frame would have ended.

RULES OF PLAY

Playing order is determined by drawing lots or by some other convenient method such as "stringing." In stringing, players simultaneously play one ball each from the balk line with the object of making it rebound off the top cushion and come to rest as near as possible to the bottom cushion.

Order of play within a pair or team must remain the same throughout a frame. Turns alternate between sides.

Start of play All the object balls – reds and colors – must be set up in their correct positions:

1) the 15 reds are set up in the form of a triangle, its base parallel with and nearest to the top cushion, and the ball at its apex as near as possible to, but not touching, the pink ball positioned on the pyramid spot;

2) the yellow is positioned on the right-hand corner of the "D" (looking down the table from the balk end);

3) the green is positioned on the left-hand corner of the "D";

4) the brown is positioned on the balk spot;

Value of balls	
Red	1
Yellow	2
Green	3
Brown	4
Blue	5
Pink	6
Black	7

5) the blue is positioned on the center spot;

6) the pink is positioned on the pyramid spot;

7) the black is positioned on the billiard spot;

8) the cue ball may be put into play from anywhere within, or on the lines of, the "D."
It is a player's responsibility to ensure that the balls are correctly positioned before he makes any stroke.

The player with the right to play first may for his first stroke place the cue ball anywhere on or within the lines of the "D" (playing "from hand").

Subsequently, players must begin their turns by playing the cue ball from wherever it came to rest at the end of the preceding player's turn.

A stroke begins when a player touches a ball with his cue, and ends when all the balls have come to rest. For a stroke to be fair:

a) only the white cue ball may be struck with the cue;

b) the cue ball must be struck with the tip of the cue;

c) the cue ball must be struck and not pushed (it is a push stroke if the cue remains in contact with the cue ball after it begins its forward motion, or after the cue ball makes contact with an object ball);

d) the cue ball must not be struck more than once in the same stroke, either before or after contact with another ball;

e) the cue ball may be struck directly at the object ball aimed at, or it may contact the object ball after bouncing off one or more cushions;

f) no ball must be forced off the table;

g) at the moment that the cue ball is struck, one of the player's feet must be touching the floor.

Progression of play Players take turns in attempting to complete the frame by pocketing all the object balls in the correct sequence. A player's turn continues as long as he scores with every stroke (consecutive scoring strokes in any turn are called a "break"). Once a player fails to score with any stroke his turn comes to an end and his opponent takes up play from whatever point in the frame has already been reached.

In the opening stages of a frame (as long as any reds remain on the table), a player must begin his turn by attempting to pocket a red. If he succeeds, the red is left in the pocket and one point is scored. All other balls are left as they lie after his stroke, and the player now nominates any color of his choice. If he succeeds in pocketing the nominated ball with his next stroke, he scores the value of that ball. The pocketed colored ball is then respotted (positioned as for the start of play), but all other balls are left as they lie. Play then continues in this way, with the player alternately pocketing red and colored balls; all red balls are left in the pockets and all colored balls are respotted.

After pocketing the last red ball, the player may pocket any nominated colored ball. This colored ball is respotted after pocketing but the rules of play then change. Colored balls are no longer respotted after pocketing, and they must be pocketed in set order: yellow, green, brown, blue, pink, and black. The frame ends after the black is pocketed, or it ends before this if there is a penalty once the black is the only colored ball remaining on the table.

"On" ball The ball that is next due to be pocketed is termed the "on" ball. If asked to do so by the referee, a player must always state which ball he is "on." A player's cue ball must always strike the "on" ball before it strikes any other ball. A player must always try his best to strike the "on" ball; intentional misses are prohibited.

Respotting balls Illegally pocketed colored balls and colored balls that are legally pocketed while there are reds still on the table must normally be respotted in their starting positions.

If its own spot is covered, a ball should be respotted on the first available spot in descending order of value, starting with the black spot.

If all spots are covered, any ball but the black and pink is placed as near as possible to its own spot, in a position between that spot and the nearest part of the top cushion, and without touching any other ball. The black and pink balls are replaced as close to their own spots as possible, on the centerline of the table, toward the top cushion, and without touching any other ball. Only if all positions toward the top cushion are occupied, should the black or pink ball be respotted below its own spot in the direction of the bottom cushion.

SNOOKER 3

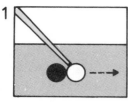

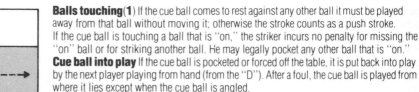

Balls touching(1) If the cue ball comes to rest against any other ball it must be played away from that ball without moving it; otherwise the stroke counts as a push stroke.
If the cue ball is touching a ball that is "on," the striker incurs no penalty for missing the "on" ball or for striking another ball. He may legally pocket any other ball that is "on."

Cue ball into play If the cue ball is pocketed or forced off the table, it is put back into play by the next player playing from hand (from the "D"). After a foul, the cue ball is played from where it lies except when the cue ball is angled.

Cue ball angled (2) The cue ball is "angled" if the striker is prevented by the corner of the cushion from playing it in a straight line toward any ball that is "on." The striker must play the cue ball from where it lies, except that if it is angled after a foul he may choose to play it from hand.

Snookers A player is snookered (**3**) when a ball he must not play obstructs a straight line between the cue ball and the ball that is "on." He must attempt his shot, and will be penalized for missing the "on" ball or for hitting another ball first (**4**).
If a player is due to play a red but is snookered with regard to all reds following an opponent's foul stroke, he may nominate any other ball. This ball then counts as a red, except that it must be respotted if pocketed.
If an opponent's foul stroke snookers a player with regard to a colored ball that is "on," he may nominate any other ball. This ball then counts as the "on" ball, except that if it is legally pocketed it is respotted and the player continues his break on the ball that he was "on" but for the snooker. If as a result of playing the nominated ball the player pockets the "on" ball, he scores that ball and continues his break. If a player pockets both the nominated ball and the "on" ball with the same stroke, the nominated ball is respotted, only the "on" ball is scored, and the player continues his break.

PENALTIES AND FOULS

Penalties After any foul stroke, the striker loses his turn and any score he may have made on that stroke. He also forfeits the appropriate number of penalty points (see under Fouls), which are added on to his opponent's score. His opponent then has the option of playing the balls where they have come to rest, or of asking the offending player to play the stroke.

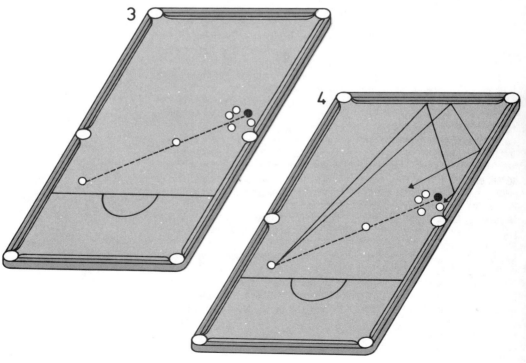

For wilful and persistent misconduct, the offender loses the game and forfeits any points he may have scored or the value of the balls left on the table (counting eight points for each red), whichever is higher. In a competition, he may also be disqualified.

Fouls Foul strokes and their penalty scores are listed below. In all cases the minimum penalty is four points; other scores given apply only if they exceed the minimum.

a) For playing out of turn, the penalty is the value of the ball "on," or of the ball struck, or of the ball pocketed, whichever is highest.

b) For playing before the balls have come to rest, or before they have been spotted, or when they are incorrectly spotted, the penalty is the value of the ball "on," the ball struck, the ball wrongly spotted, or the ball pocketed, whichever is highest.

c) For playing with both feet off the floor, the penalty is the value of the ball "on," the ball struck, the ball wrongly spotted, or the ball pocketed, whichever is highest.

d) For using a dead ball to test whether a ball will pass another or for any other purpose, the penalty is seven points.

e) For playing with a ball other than the cue ball, the penalty is seven points.

f) For striking or touching a ball in play with anything other than the cue tip, the penalty is the value of the ball "on," or of the ball struck or touched, whichever is higher.

g) For a push stroke, the penalty is the value of the ball "on," the ball struck, or the ball pocketed, whichever is highest.

h) For moving an object ball when the cue ball was touching it prior to the stroke, the penalty is the value of the ball "on," or the ball moved, whichever is higher.

i) For playing incorrectly from hand, the penalty is the value of the ball "on," the ball struck, the ball pocketed, or the ball wrongly spotted, whichever is highest.

j) For failing to hit any other ball with the cue ball (a "miss"), the penalty is the value of the ball "on."

k) For causing the cue ball to strike a ball that is not "on," the penalty is the value of the ball struck, or of the ball "on," whichever is higher.

l) For playing at two reds in successive strokes, the penalty is seven points.

m) For a jump shot (making the cue ball jump over any other ball) (**5**), the penalty is the value of the ball "on," struck, or pocketed, whichever is highest.

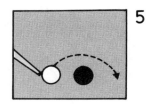

n) For forcing a ball off the table, the penalty is the value of the ball "on," or the ball forced off the table, whichever is higher.

o) For pocketing the cue ball after it has contacted another ball (**6**), the penalty is the value of the ball "on," or the ball struck, whichever is higher.

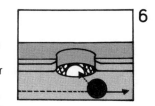

p) For pocketing any ball that is not "on," the penalty is the value of the ball "on," or of the ball pocketed, whichever is higher.

q) For striking simultaneously or pocketing with one stroke two balls other than two reds or the ball "on" and the ball nominated, the penalty is the higher value of the two balls struck or pocketed.

r) For snookering an opponent with the nominated ball after a foul stroke (except when only the pink and black balls remain), the penalty is the value of the ball "on."

AMERICAN SNOOKER

The game adapts the rules of snooker to make play more characteristic of American pocket billiard games. Major variations in the rules are listed below.

a) The table should measure 10×5ft or 12×6ft; corner pocket openings should be 3³/₈–3⁵/₈in; side pocket openings should be 4¹/₁₆in maximum; balls should be 2¹/₁₆–2¹/₈in in diameter and weigh 5–5½oz.

b) The starting player must contact a red ball with the cue ball, pocket a red ball or cause it to contact a cushion, and cause the cue ball to contact a cushion after it has contacted a red ball. Failure to do so is a foul; the opposing player has the choice of playing the table as it lies or requiring the break to be taken again.

c) On all strokes, the player must pocket the "on" ball, or cause the cue ball or an object ball to contact the cushion after the cue ball has struck the "on" ball.

d) All fouls carry a penalty score of seven points.

SOCCER

HISTORY

Soccer (Association football) in something like its present form evolved in England in the mid-19th century, but similar games were played very much earlier, for example in China around 200BC. The Football Association (FA) was formed in England in 1863 to unify soccer rules and in 1871 the FA Challenge Cup was introduced. Professionalism was legalized by the FA in 1885 and three years later the Football League was founded. The game also spread rapidly abroad and in 1904 the Fédération Internationale de Football Association (FIFA), the governing body of international football, was established in Paris. Soccer was first included as an Olympic sport in 1908. The first World Cup competition was organized in 1930. FIFA rules are described here; the rules of the North American Soccer League (NASL) are now very similar following the dropping of the 35yd offside line.

SYNOPSIS

Soccer (Association football) is a ball game played by two teams, each of not more than 11 players (including the goalkeeper but excluding substitutes). The object of the game is to put the ball into the opponents' goal, and the winning team is the one that scores the greater number of goals in the given time.

PLAYING AREA AND EQUIPMENT

The field of play is a rectangle 50–100yd wide and 100–130yd long (70–80yd wide and 100–110yd long for international matches). It is bounded by touchlines (**a**) and goal lines (**b**), which are included in the playing area, and is divided by a halfway line (**c**). No line may exceed 5in in width.

At each end of the field there is an 8yd wide and 8ft high goal (**d**) and a 20×6yd goal area (**e**) enclosed in a 44×18yd penalty area (**f**). The posts and crossbar of the goals must be of an equal width not exceeding 5in. Nets may be attached to the goals and to the ground behind them.

Within each penalty area, 12yd from the mid-point of the goal line, is the penalty mark (**g**). The arc of a circle (**h**), with a radius of 10yd from the penalty mark, is drawn outside the penalty area.

At each corner of the field is a flag on a post that is at least 5ft high and must not have a pointed top (**i**). Centered on each corner flag post and drawn inside the field of play, is a quarter circle (**j**) with a radius of 1yd.

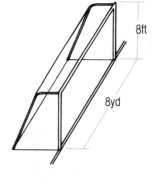

8ft

8yd

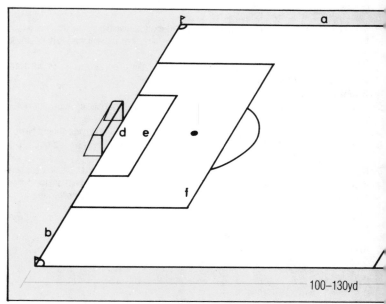

100–130yd

Marked in the center of the field, with a radius of 10yd, is the center circle (**k**).
Flags on either side of the halfway line are optional, but if used must be set back at least 1yd from the touchline.

The ball is spherical with a circumference of 27–28in; its outer casing is leather or another approved material. At the start of a game, it must weigh 14–16oz, and should be inflated to a pressure of 0.6–0.7 atmosphere (9.0–10.5lb/sq.in) at sea level.

Dress The goalkeeper must wear different colors to distinguish him from the other players and the referee. All other players in the team must wear uniform jerseys or shirts, shorts, and socks. A number is usually worn on the back of the jersey.

Footwear (boots or shoes) may be studded or have bars of leather or rubber across the soles. Fitted studs must be of solid leather, rubber, plastic, aluminum, or similar material; they must be rounded and not less than ½in in diameter or more than ¾in long from the mounting. Studs that are molded as part of the sole must be of a soft material; provided that there are at least 10 studs on each sole, the minimum diameter for each stud is ⅜in. Players may not wear anything that might injure another player, particularly faulty studs. Any player wearing dangerous equipment may be expelled from the game until it is replaced.

PLAYERS AND OFFICIALS

Players Each team has a maximum of 11 players, one of whom is the goalkeeper. In competition matches a maximum of two substitutes is permitted; up to five substitutes may be permitted in friendly matches.

Officials A referee controls the game and is assisted by two linesmen.

The referee:

acts as timekeeper and keeps a record of the game;

enforces the laws;

stops the game at injuries, infringements, etc, and restarts it appropriately;

cautions or sends off offenders;

may end the game because of bad weather, interference by spectators, etc.

The linesmen, one on each touchline:

indicate when the ball is out of play, and which team has the right to put the ball into play again with a throw in, corner kick or goal kick;

raise their flags to indicate any infringement (such signals may be acted on or ignored by the referee).

27–28in

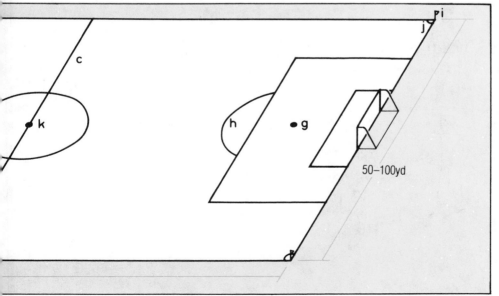

50–100yd

SOCCER 2

DURATION AND SCORING

Duration Unless agreed otherwise, the game is played in two halves of 45 minutes each. The half-time interval may not exceed five minutes, except by consent of the referee. The referee adds on to each period any time lost in that period through injuries, time wasting, etc. Time is also extended to allow a penalty kick to be taken at the end of a period.

Scoring The team scoring the greater number of goals wins. If the number of goals scored is equal the result is a draw, though in some competitions draws are resolved by:

a) replays;

b) periods of extra time (usually two halves of 15 minutes each) immediately after the 90 minutes;

c) a series of kicks from the penalty mark (see below);

d) the toss of a coin or the drawing of lots.

A goal is scored when the whole of the ball has crossed the goal line under the crossbar and between the goal posts, providing that the attacking team has not infringed the laws.

Decision by penalty kicks Players from each team take part in a series of penalty kicks against the opposing goalkeeper. All kicks are at the same goal, chosen by the referee. The referee tosses a coin to decide which team kicks first; the teams then kick alternately. A different player takes each kick; only after all players on the field when time expired have each taken a kick may any player make a second kick.

Each team initially has five kicks, except that the game is decided sooner if one team scores more goals than the other team could possibly exceed with all its remaining kicks.

If there is still no result after five kicks per team, the teams continue to take alternate kicks until one team has scored more goals than the other after an equal number of attempts.

STARTING PROCEDURES

Start The two captains toss a coin and the winner may decide whether to take the option of starting the game (kicking off) or deciding which goal to defend (choice of ends).

Kick off (A) On the referee's whistle a player of the team kicking off shall play the ball from a stationary position on the center spot into the opponents' half of the field. At that moment every player must be in his own half and no opponent may come into the center circle until the ball is in play (when it has traveled its own circumference). The kicker may not play the ball again until it has been touched by another player.

Restart After a goal has been scored play is restarted with a center kick off by a member of the team that did not score.

After the interval the teams change ends and play begins with a kick off by the team that did not start the first half.

If during play the referee stops the game when the ball is in play and there is no reason to award a free kick to either team, the referee shall restart the game by dropping the ball at the place where it was when play was stopped. A player may not play the ball until it has touched the ground.

RULES OF PLAY

Substitution A substitute may replace a player on the field only with the referee's prior permission and only during a stoppage. The substitute must wait until the player he is replacing leaves the field, and must then enter the field at the halfway line. The player who has been replaced may take no further part in the game.

Any other player may change places with the goalkeeper, but only with the referee's prior permission and only during a stoppage.

Playing the ball Except when throwing in, a player other than a goalkeeper is not allowed to play the ball with his hands and arms ; a goalkeeper may play the ball with his hands and arms only when inside his own penalty area.

All players are permitted to use any other part of the body in order to stop, control or pass the ball, move with it, or score.

Out of play The ball is out of play when it completely crosses the boundaries of the pitch, or when the game has been stopped by the referee. Play is restarted by a throw in when the ball has crossed the touchline, or by either a goal kick or a corner kick when it has crossed the goal line.

A throw in (B) is taken along the touchline at the point where the ball went out of play. It is awarded against the team that last touched the ball before it went out of play.

The ball must be thrown into play with both hands, from behind and over the head. The thrower must face the play. As he releases the ball, part of each foot must be on the ground either behind or on the touchline. If these rules are infringed the throw in passes to the opposition.

No goal can be scored from a throw in, and the thrower may not play the ball again until it has been touched by another player.

327

SOCCER 3

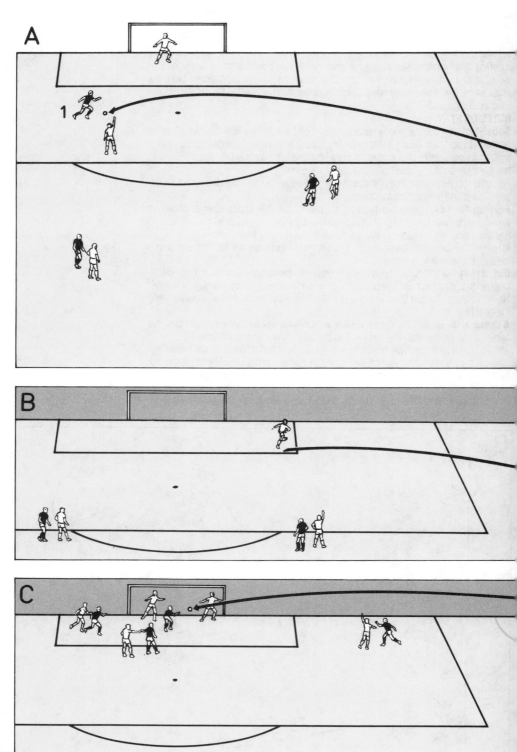

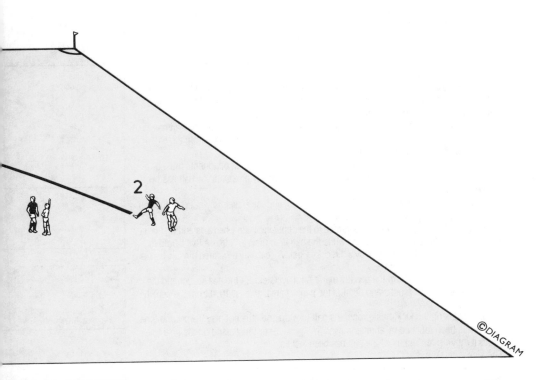

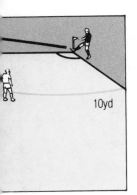

10yd

Offside (**A**) An attacking player (**1**) is offside if, when the ball is being played by one of his own team (**2**), he is nearer the opponents' goal line than at least two opponents and the ball, except when:
he is in his own half of the field of play; or
he receives the ball direct from a goal kick, a corner kick, or a throw in, or when the referee drops the ball.
A player shall not be penalized for being offside unless in the referee's opinion:
he is interfering with play or with an opponent; or
he is seeking to gain an advantage by being in an offside position.

A goal kick (**B**) is awarded to the defending team when the ball crosses its goal line (without passing between the goal posts) after having been last touched by an opponent. The kick may be taken by any player of the defending side, including the goalkeeper. The ball is placed within the half of the goal area nearer the point where it crossed the goal line. The kick must send the ball out of the penalty area and the kicker may not touch the ball again until it has been played by another player. All opponents must retreat outside the penalty area until the kick has been taken and the ball has passed outside the penalty area. No goal can be scored directly from a goal kick.

A corner kick (**C**) is awarded to the attacking team if the ball crosses the goal line (without passing between the goal posts), having been last played by one of the defending team.
It is taken from the corner circle nearest where the ball left the pitch. The flag must not be moved to help the kicker. Opponents must remain 10yd away until the kick has been taken (until the ball has traveled its own circumference).
A goal can be scored direct from a corner kick, but the kicker must not play the ball a second time until it has been touched by another player.

SOCCER 4

Free kick (A) A free kick is awarded to a team for an offense by an opponent. Depending on the offense committed, the referee may award:

an indirect free kick (**1**), from which a goal cannot be scored until the ball has touched another player after the kicker;

a direct free kick (**2**), from which the player taking the free kick can score without the ball first touching another player.

A free kick is usually taken at the spot where the offense occurred, except that for an offense committed by a player in his opponents' goal area the free kick may be taken anywhere within the half of the goal area in which the offense occurred.

When a player is taking a free kick outside his own penalty area and until the ball has traveled its own circumference, all opponents must remain at least 10yd from the ball or must stand on the goal line between the goal posts.

When a player is taking a free kick inside his own penalty area, all opponents must be at least 10yd from the ball and must remain outside the penalty area until the ball has been kicked outside it.

The ball must be stationary when a free kick is taken, and the kicker may not play the ball again until another player has touched it.

Penalty kick (B) A penalty kick is awarded to the opposing team when a defending player within his own penalty area commits, while the ball is in play, an offense that would in other circumstances be penalized by a direct free kick. A goal may be scored directly from a penalty kick.

A penalty kick is taken from the penalty mark. All players except the goalkeeper and the player taking the kick must stand outside the penalty area, at least 10yd from the penalty mark.

The player taking the kick must propel the ball forward and may not play it a second time until it has been touched by another player. The goalkeeper must stand on the goal line, without moving his feet, until the ball has been kicked.

The kick is retaken if:

the defending team breaks the law and a goal has not been scored;

the attacking team, with the exception of the kicker, infringes and a goal has been scored;

there are infringements by players of both teams.

(See p. 326 for details of the use of penalty kicks for deciding draws.)

FOULS AND MISCONDUCT

Penalized by an indirect free kick An indirect free kick to the opponents is awarded for the following offenses:

a) for dangerous play;

b) for charging fairly, ie with the shoulder, but when the ball is not within playing distance;

c) for intentionally obstructing an opponent while not attempting to play the ball, in order to prevent him reaching it;

d) for charging the goalkeeper—unless the goalkeeper is holding the ball, obstructing an opponent, or has gone outside his goal area;

e) when a goalkeeper takes more than four steps while holding the ball, throwing it in the air and catching it, or bouncing it, without releasing it to another player; or when he wastes time;

f) for offside;

g) when a player taking a kick off, throw in, goal kick, corner kick, free kick, or penalty kick plays the ball a second time before another player has touched it.

Penalized by a direct free kick The following offenses, if deliberately committed, are penalized by a direct free kick (or a penalty kick in certain circumstances):

a) tripping an opponent;

b) holding an opponent;

c) playing the ball with a hand or arm (except for the goalkeeper in his penalty area);

d) kicking or attempting to kick an opponent;

e) jumping at an opponent;

f) charging an opponent in a violent or dangerous manner;

g) charging an opponent from behind (unless the opponent is guilty of obstruction);

h) striking, attempting to strike, or spitting at an opponent;

i) pushing an opponent.

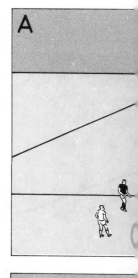

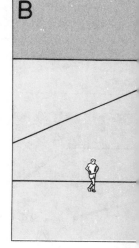

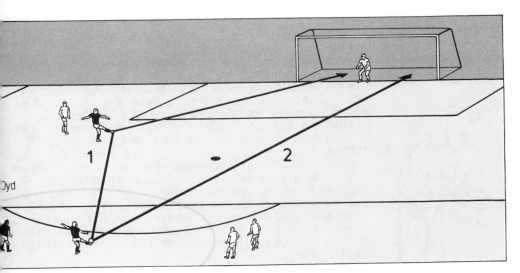

©DIAGRAM

Penalized by cautioning The referee will caution a player who:

a) enters or leaves the game without the referee's permission;

b) continually breaks the laws;

c) shows dissent from any of the referee's decisions;

d) is guilty of ungentlemanly conduct (including leaning on the shoulders of a teammate to gain height to head the ball).

If the referee stops the game to caution a player, play is resumed with an indirect free kick to the opposing team (except when the cautioned player has committed an offense for which a more serious penalty is specified in the laws).

Penalized by sending off The referee has the power to send a player off the field for the rest of the game if he:

a) commits acts of violence or serious foul play;

b) uses foul or abusive language;

c) continues to break the laws after a caution.

If the referee stops play to send off a player without a separate breach of the laws having been committed, play is resumed by an indirect free kick.

SOFTBALL

HISTORY

Softball began in the late nineteenth century as an indoor version of baseball requiring a much smaller playing area than the parent game. It soon became popular in parks and playgrounds, and was known by a wide variety of names – kitten ball, mush ball, and diamond ball – and had an equally wide variety of rules. The first standardized set of rules was produced in 1923.

Softball (which has become the most popular participation sport in the USA) began to develop as an international sport in the late 1940s. The international governing body, the International Softball Federation, was formed in 1952; the first world championship for women was held in 1965, and for men in 1966.

SYNOPSIS

Softball is a stick-and-ball game played between two teams of nine or ten players on a pitch having four bases in a diamond pattern. Each team bats in turn. The object of the fielding team is to dismiss the batters, that of the batting side to score runs by making circuits of the bases. A team's turn at bat (half-inning) ends when it has had three "outs." A full match consists of seven innings, and the winning team is the one scoring the greater number of runs. Rules for the main form (fast pitch) are given first, followed by the main differences for the slow pitch game (p. 341).

PLAYING AREA AND EQUIPMENT

The playing area consists of an infield (**1**) and an outfield (**2**). These two areas, including boundary lines, are fair territory; any other area is foul territory.

The infield is a 60ft square (the "diamond"), with a base at each corner: home base (**a**), first base (**b**), second base (**c**), and third base (**d**). The distance from the pitcher's plate (**e**) to the rear point of home base is 46ft for men and 40ft for women. The plate is at the center of a 16ft diameter circle; the top of the plate is level with the ground.

The outfield is in the shape of a quarter-circle, and is the area between the two foul lines (**f**), formed by extending two sides of the diamond. The distance from home base to the boundary fence should be 225ft for men, and 200ft for women. Two foul poles mark the

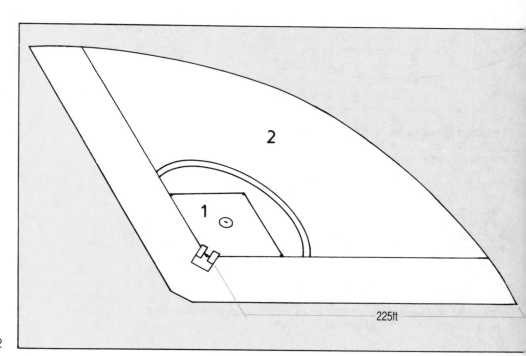

2

1

225ft

intersection of the foul lines and the boundary fence. The backstop should be 25–30ft behind home base.

Also marked on the playing field are the 3ft first base line (**g**), the batter's boxes (**h**) measuring 7ft by 3ft, the catcher's box (**i**), coaches' boxes (**j**), and the next batter's on deck circles (**k**).

Home plate (**A**) is a pentagon made of rubber or other suitable material. It should be 17in wide across the edge facing the pitcher, 8½in long on the sides parallel to the inside lines of the batter's boxes, and 12in long on the sides of the point facing the catcher.

Other bases (**B**) are marked by 15in square bags made of canvas or other suitable material; they may not be more than 5in thick. Bags at first and third base are placed entirely within the infield; the bag at second base is centered on the base. All bags are fastened to the ground.

The pitcher's plate (**C**) is a rectangular slab of wood or rubber, 24in long and 6in wide.

Players' benches, one for each team, must not be less than 25ft from the base lines.

The bat may be made of a single piece of wood, or of laminated wood, plastic, bamboo, or metal. Metal bats may be angular; all other bats should be smooth and rounded, with a diameter of 2¼in at their widest part. The maximum permitted weight is 38oz.

Bats may be up to 34in long overall, including a safety grip which should be 10–15in long. The safety grip should be made of cork, tape, or composition.

It is illegal to use a metal bat with a wooden handle, or a baseball bat that has been shaved down to softball size.

The ball is made of kapok, a mixture of cork and rubber, or other approved material. The outer cover is of horsehide, cowhide, or synthetic material, with smooth seams. The standard ball has a weight of 6¼–7oz and a circumference of 11⅞–12⅛in.

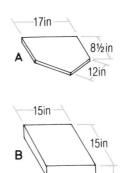

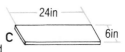

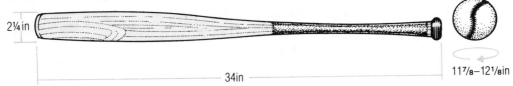

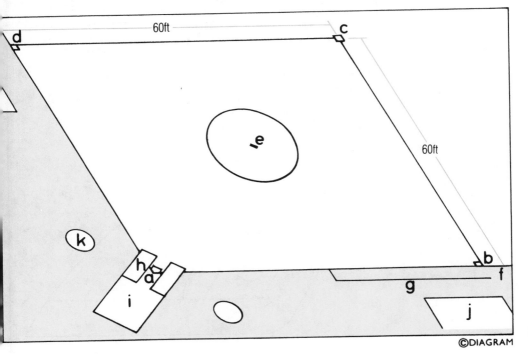

SOFTBALL 2

Dress Players' uniforms are similar to those for baseball, and must be alike for all team members, with 6in high identifying numbers on the shirt back. Umpires' uniforms are blue.

Male players must wear caps; for female players caps, visors, and headbands are optional, but all team members must wear the same. Helmets are permitted for the batting side and for catchers.

In the fast pitch game masks must be worn by catchers and plate umpires; women catchers must wear a body protector. Softball gloves of specified dimensions may be worn by all players, but catching mitts only by the catcher and first baseman. Shoes may have spikes up to ¾in long.

PLAYERS AND OFFICIALS

Players In fast pitch a team has nine players. An additional player, known as a "designated hitter," may substitute for a designated team member on his turn to bat, if this is declared beforehand and applied from the start. The designated hitter must remain in the same position in the batting order for the entire game.

Fielding positions are as listed and shown in the diagram.

Substitutes There is no rule limiting the number of substitutes. A substitute may replace any player at any time, except that a pitcher may not be replaced until the first batter facing him has completed his turn, or the team has been retired, or the pitcher for some reason has been ordered to be removed from the game. A replaced player may not return to the game, except that each of the original starting players may return once, providing they take the same place in the batting order.

A designated hitter may not act as a normal substitute, and may himself be replaced only by someone who has not yet played in the game. Once replaced, he may not return.

Officials The plate umpire stands behind the catcher to judge all decisions on pitching and batting, and also generally controls the game. The base umpire is responsible for making decisions on play at the bases, and also assists the plate umpire in his decisions. An official scorer is responsible for recording the progress of the game.

DURATION AND SCORING

Duration A game consists of seven innings but the seventh need not be completed if the second batting team has already exceeded its opponents' final score.

A tied game continues with further innings until one team leads at the end of an inning (or, again, until a second batting team has passed its opponents' score).

A game terminated by the umpire (eg, for rain) counts as finished if five or more complete innings have been played, or if the second batting team has scored more in four or more innings than the other team in five or more. (If scores are equal, it is a tie.)

Scoring A run is scored by a team each time one of its players completes a circuit of the bases, having touched each in turn.

A "home run" is awarded, and the batter and all runners on bases advance to home plate without risk of being put out, when a legally batted ball:

a) leaves the outfield between the foul poles and lands behind a fence or in a stand beyond the prescribed fence distance from home plate; or

Fielding positions
1) Pitcher
2) Catcher
3) First baseman
4) Second baseman
5) Third baseman
6) Shortstop
7) Left fielder
8) Center fielder
9) Right fielder

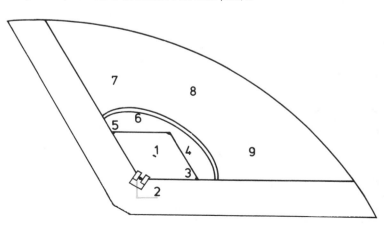

b) hits a foul pole on the fly above fence height.

If the ground is smaller than normal and the fence or stand is not at the required distance, a "two-base hit" is awarded instead. The batter and all the runners advance, without risk, two bases toward home plate.

No score A following runner may not score a run when a preceding runner is the third player out in an inning. A run cannot be scored when the third out in an inning is:

a) the batter being put out before reaching first base;

b) a baserunner being forced out by the batter becoming a baserunner;

c) a baserunner leaving a base before the pitcher has released the ball.

Result The winning team is the one scoring the most runs in a finished game. The scores are those at the end of the last complete inning except when the second team to bat wins or (in a terminated game) ties without the last inning being completed, in which case the score is that at the end of play. The score when a game is forfeited for certain breaches of the rules is 7–0 against the offending team.

RULES OF PLAY

Starting play Teams toss a coin to decide which team bats first.

The game begins on the umpire's call of "Play ball": the ball then becomes alive and in play. The ball becomes dead when it goes outside the established limits of the playing area, when the umpire calls "Time," or for other legal cause.

A minute is allowed for up to five warmup pitches at the start of each half-inning, and when one pitcher replaces another.

Pitching action The pitcher stands with both feet touching the pitcher's plate and within its length, with his shoulders in line with first and third bases, and holding the ball in one hand (**1**). On the catcher's signal he holds the ball in both hands for 1–10sec before delivery. He then removes one hand from the ball and "winds up" to pitch.

He makes the actual pitch underhand, simultaneously taking one step forward (**2**). His release of the ball and follow-through must be forward, past the straight line of the body. His hand on release must be below his hips and his wrist not farther out from his body than his elbow. His rear foot must stay on the plate until his front foot touches the ground.

Any windup may be used, as long as it involves only one forward movement of the arm and ends with the immediate release of the ball. (In a "windmill pitch," one revolution of the arm is allowed.)

A no pitch occurs if the pitcher pitches:

a) during a suspension of play;

b) before the batter is in position;

c) when the batter is still off balance after a previous pitch;

d) when a runner is called out for leaving base too soon;

e) when a runner has not yet retouched base after a foul ball.

It is also a no pitch if an opposing team member calls time in an attempt to make the pitcher commit an illegal pitch. In all cases, the ball is dead, and all subsequent action on that pitch is canceled.

An illegal pitch occurs if:

a) the pitching action is incorrect;

b) the pitcher throws to base without first stepping back from the pitcher's plate;

c) the pitcher drops, rolls, or bounces the ball to stop the batter striking it;

d) the pitcher uses tape or other substances on the ball, pitching hand, or fingers, or wears a sweatband on the pitching wrist or forearm;

e) the catcher is out of position when the pitch is released;

In all cases, the ball is dead, a ball is credited to the batter (see Batting, p. 336), and runners may advance one base without risk.

A wild pitch is any pitch so high, low, or wide that the catcher cannot or does not stop or control it with ordinary effort.

A passed ball is a legally delivered ball that should have been controlled by the catcher with ordinary effort.

Delay If the bases are empty and the batter not running, the catcher must return the ball directly to the pitcher, and he must pitch again within 20sec. If catcher or pitcher act incorrectly, a ball is awarded to the batter.

SOFTBALL 3

Batting order Players bat in the order given in the scoresheets, substitutes in the order of the players they replace. Even if a player's turn at bat ends with him out, he bats again on his turn in the inning. The sequence also carries over unbroken from one inning to the next. (If a player's turn at bat has not ended when his team's half-inning ends, he is first to bat in their next half-inning.)

Batting procedure The batter must stand within the lines of one of the batter's boxes to receive each pitch.

The "strike zone," at which the pitcher aims, is the space above home plate between the top of the batter's knees and his armpits, in his natural batting stance (**A**).

Each legal pitch the batter receives is judged by the umpire to be either a "strike" or a "ball" (see below). A batter is allowed only three strikes on his turn; on the third, if not out, he must run to first base or beyond. He must also run as soon as he hits a fair ball (see below). But if he receives four "balls" before having to leave home plate, he is allowed to advance to first base without risk.

A player's turn at bat ends when he is out or has advanced to first base or beyond. He is then followed by the next batter in order. A team's half-inning at bat ends when it has had three players out while batting or running.

A strike is called by the umpire for each ball pitched into the strike zone (before touching the ground) that the batter misses or at which he does not swing (**B**), and for each foul tip (see Batted balls).

In these cases the ball is in play, and runners may advance at risk of being put out.

A strike is also called, but the ball is dead, and runners must return to their last bases, if:

a) a pitch is struck at and missed and touches the batter;

b) a batter hits the ball against himself;

c) a pitch hits the batter inside the strike zone;

d) a foul ball (see below) is not legally caught on the fly, and the batter has fewer than two strikes.

A ball is called by the umpire for each pitch that misses the strike zone and is not struck at by the batter (**C**), and for each pitch that is not struck at which touches the ground on or before home plate. In these cases the ball is still in play, and runners may advance at risk of being put out.

A ball is also called for each illegal pitch, in which case the ball is dead, and runners may advance one base without risk.

A ball is also called, the ball is dead, and runners may not advance:

a) if the catcher fails to return the ball directly to the pitcher as required;

b) if the pitcher fails to pitch within 20sec;

c) for each excessive warm-up pitch.

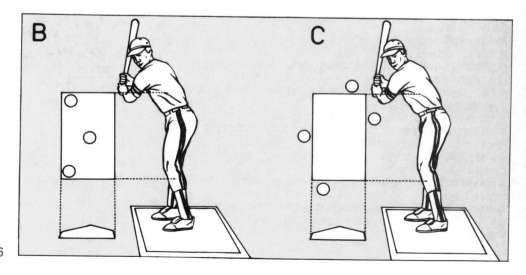

Batted balls The rules recognize certain types of batted ball.

A "fly ball" is a batted ball that has not yet touched the ground or any object other than a fielder.

A "line drive" is a fly ball that is batted sharply and directly into the playing field.

A "bunt" is a legally tapped ball not swung at but intentionally met with the bat and tapped slowly within the infield (**D**).

A "foul tip" is a batted ball that goes not higher than the batter's head and is directly caught by the catcher.

An "infield fly" (as judged and called by the umpire) is a fair fly ball (not including a line drive or attempted bunt) that can be caught by an infielder with normal effort, when first and second, or first, second, and third bases are occupied and before two outs.

A "fair ball" is one that:

a) settles on or is touched on fair ground before first or third base;

b) bounds past first or third base on or over fair ground;

c) touches first, second, or third base;

d) touches a player or umpire while over fair ground;

e) first touches ground on fair ground beyond first or third bases;

f) passes from fair ground over the far boundary fence or hits a foul pole on the fly for a home run or two-base hit.

A batted ball that first hits foul territory and then rolls into fair territory without touching any foreign object, player, or umpire, is considered a fair ball. Except when a home run or a ruled dead ball two base hit is scored, a fair ball is in play, and runners may advance. Other balls are foul balls, and usually the ball is dead and counts as a strike (as long as it does not take the batter's total above two strikes; if it does it is ignored and pitched again). But a foul tip or any other foul ball legally caught on the fly is in play.

Batter put out The batter is out, but the ball remains live and runners may advance at risk of being put out if:

a) a fly ball (other than a foul tip) is legally caught;

b) a third strike (including a foul tip) is caught by the catcher;

c) the batter misses a third strike and the ball touches him;

d) on a third strike, there are fewer than two outs and first base is occupied;

e) the batter hits an infield fly, whether or not the ball is caught (the "infield fly rule").

The batter is also out, but the ball is dead and runners may not advance if:

a) he is not properly in position within 20sec of a "Play ball" call;

b) he uses or enters the box with an illegal or altered bat;

c) he crosses from one box to the other when the pitcher is ready to pitch;

d) he hinders the catcher from fielding or catching the ball (unless a runner is in fact put out, when the interference is ignored);

e) he hits a fair ball twice in fair territory;

f) he hits an "illegally batted ball" (see below);

g) a runner intentionally interferes with a fielder trying to catch a thrown ball or throw it to complete a play, in which case the runner is also out;

h) with any bases occupied (other than third only) and fewer than two outs, a fielder, for an attempted double play, deliberately drops a fair fly ball, there having been no infield fly call. The batter may also be put out when running, before reaching first base (see Running, p.339).

An illegally batted ball occurs if:

a) a batter's entire foot is completely out of the box on the ground when he hits the ball;

b) any part of his foot is touching home plate;

c) he uses an illegal bat.

On deck batter The batter waiting to bat next stands in the on deck circle near his bench. He may leave it to direct runners advancing from third base to home plate, but must not interfere with fielding.

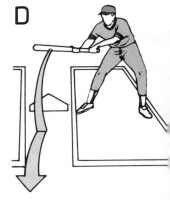

D

SOFTBALL 4

A

B

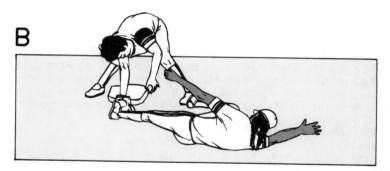

Fielding A fielder legally touches ("tags") a base when he touches that base with his body while holding the ball securely in his hand or glove (**A**). He legally touches ("tags") a runner when he touches that runner with the ball, or with his hand or glove holding the ball (**B**).

A catch of a fly ball is not completed until the ball is grasped by the fielder's hand or glove, and is held long enough to prove he has complete control. If a ball has hit anything other than the fielder or another fielder, it is not a caught fly ball.

An overthrow is a throw between fielders, trying to put out a runner not on base, that goes into foul territory.

A blocked ball is a batted or thrown ball that is touched, stopped, or handled by a person other than a player, team official, or game official, or which touches anything not part of the official playing area or equipment.

A double play is when two batting team players (**1,2**) are put out by continuous action.

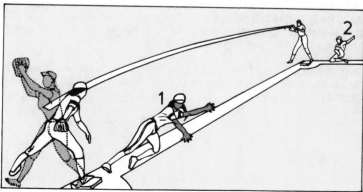

Running Runners must touch the bases in the correct order, including those they were awarded by the umpire. A base left too soon on a caught fly ball must be retouched before advancing to an awarded base.

If a runner must return to bases while the ball is in play, he must touch them in reverse order. A runner may not return to touch a missed base or one left illegally after:

a) the ball has become dead;

b) a following runner has scored;

c) he has returned to his team bench.

Two runners may not occupy the same base simultaneously, and the runner who first legally occupied it is entitled to it. The other runner may be put out by being tagged with the ball. When a base is dislodged on a play, a runner need not follow it if it is unreasonably out of position.

The batter becomes a runner, with the ball in play and liability to be put out, as soon as he hits a fair ball, or when the catcher fails to field a third strike before it touches the ground, and there are two outs or first base is unoccupied.

If four balls have been called, he also becomes a runner and the ball is in play, but he advances to first base without risk (a "base on balls").

The batter is also awarded first base, but the ball is dead and runners may not advance unless forced:

a) if a fair ball hits an umpire or runner on fair ground before passing any infielder;

b) if a fielder interferes with the batter striking at a pitch (unless the batting team chooses the result of play as it stood);

c) if a pitch, not struck at and not called as a strike, hits the batter while he is in the box (unless he made no attempt to avoid it, in which case it is a ball or strike).

Runner advancing A runner on a base may advance at risk while the ball is in play when:

a) the ball leaves the pitcher's hand on a pitch, or if the pitcher drops it in his windup or backswing;

b) the ball is batted into fair territory and not blocked;

c) the ball is thrown into fair or foul territory and not blocked;

d) a legally caught fly ball (fair or foul) is first touched;

e) a fair ball strikes an umpire or runner after passing an infielder (excluding the pitcher) or after touching an infielder (including the pitcher).

A runner may also advance without risk if:

a) forced to leave a base because the batter is awarded a base;

b) obstructed by a fielder from reaching the next base or returning to the last one (unless the fielder is fielding a batted ball or has the ball ready to touch the runner);

c) a pitch goes into or past the backstop;

d) a pitcher makes an illegal pitch;

e) a fielder uses a detached cap, mask, glove, etc, to stop the ball;

f) a ball in play is overthrown or blocked;

g) a home run or a ruled dead ball two-base hit is scored;

h) a live ball is carried by a fielder into dead ball territory.

In all these cases the ball is dead, except if a batter is awarded a base on balls, or if an obstructed runner was not having a play made against him. According to circumstances, an obstructed runner or runners are awarded any base they would have made had they not been obstructed; it they attempt to go farther they do so at the risk of being put out.

A runner loses such exemption from risk in certain circumstances, in particular if he fails to touch the base awarded before attempting the next while the ball is in play.

A runner must return to his base, and the ball is dead, if:

a) a foul ball is not caught or is illegally caught;

b) an illegally batted ball occurs;

c) a batter or runner is called out for interference;

d) the plate umpire or his clothing interferes with the catcher's throw and the baserunner is not thrown out;

e) the batter is touched by a pitched ball that is swung at and missed;

f) a batter is hit by any pitched ball, unless forced;

g) a caught fair fly ball, including a line drive or bunt, is intentionally dropped by a fielder with fewer than two outs and a runner on first base.

SOFTBALL 5

Batter out Once he has started running toward first base, a batter is out if:

a) after hitting a fair ball, or after the catcher has dropped a third strike, he or first base is legally tagged before he reaches first base;

b) he runs outside the 3ft line and so interferes with a fielder throwing to first base;

c) he interferes with a fielder trying to field a batted ball or a dropped third strike;

d) he intentionally interferes with a thrown ball or a play at home plate (if he is attempting to prevent a double play, the runner nearest home base is also out).

Runner out A runner is out, but the ball stays in play if:

a) while not touching a base, he is touched with the ball in the hand of a fielder;

b) he runs more than 3ft wide from the direct line between bases to avoid being so touched;

c) he is forced to advance and a fielder tags him or the base;

d) he fails to return to touch the base last occupied after a suspension of play;

e) he passes a preceding runner who is not out.

A runner may be out on appeal from a fielder to an umpire before the next pitch, with the ball remaining in play, if the runner:

a) advances between bases before a caught fly ball has touched a fielder, providing a fielder tags the runner or the base;

b) fails to touch a base in order, and he or the base is tagged while he is off base;

c) legally overruns first base, fails to return to it immediately or tries for second base, and is legally touched while off base;

d) misses home plate, makes no attempt to return to it, and the base is legally touched by a fielder.

The runner is out, the ball is dead, and other runners must return to the last bases touched if:

a) the runner interferes with a fielder trying to field a batted ball;

b) the runner intentionally interferes with a thrown ball (if he is attempting to prevent a double play, the next runner is also out);

c) the runner interferes with a fielder trying to field a foul fly ball (the batter is also out);

d) the runner, while off his base, is struck by a fair batted ball in fair territory before it passes an infielder other than the pitcher;

e) the runner intentionally kicks a ball an infielder has missed;

f) anyone other than another runner physically helps him while the ball is in play;

g) in certain cases, the batter or members of the batting team deliberately try to interfere with play or confuse the fielding side.

The runner is also out, the ball is dead, and "no pitch" is given, if he fails to keep contact with his base until a legal pitch has been released.

If a runner is legally off base after a pitch or the end of a batter's turn, and the ball returns to the pitcher within his 16ft circle, then the runner must immediately return to his last base or try to advance to the next, or be called out.

Not out A runner is not out if:

a) he is touched with a ball not securely held by a fielder;

b) he runs wide between bases to avoid interfering with a fielder;

c) he runs wide when the fielder in the direct line does not have the ball;

d) he overruns first base after touching it and returns directly to it;

e) he dislodges a base by sliding into it, and so loses contact;

f) he is unintentionally touched by a fair batted ball that has passed an infielder other than the pitcher, and the umpire judges that no other infielder had a chance to play it;

g) he is unintentionally touched by a batted ball when touching his base;

h) he is hit by a fair batted ball after it has been in contact with any fielder, including the pitcher;

i) more than one fielder tries to field a batted ball and the runner comes into contact with one who, in the umpire's judgment, was not entitled to field it;

j) a fielder makes a play on him while using illegal gloves;

k) he is not given enough time to return to base, in which case he may advance as if he had left it legally.

SLOW PITCH SOFTBALL

Playing area The diamond has baselines 65ft long for men, and 60ft long for women. The pitching distance is 46ft for both men and women. The fence distance is 275ft for men, and 250ft for women.

Players Teams have ten players. The additional fielding position is called "short fielder."

Pitching action (A) The pitcher should stand with one foot (the "pivot foot") in contact with the pitching plate, and the other either on, in front, or behind the plate; both feet must be within the length of the plate.

The pitcher must come to a complete stop facing the batter, with his shoulders in line with first and third bases, and the ball held in one or both hands in front of his body. This position must be held for 1–10sec. The pitcher may not begin to pitch until the catcher is ready and the umpire has given the signal. The catcher must remain in his box until the ball is batted or reaches home plate.

The pitch begins when the pitcher begins his windup. His pivot foot must remain in contact with the plate until the ball has left his hand. No step need be taken on the pitch, but any step that is taken must be forward, within the length of the plate, and simultaneous with the release of the ball.

The ball must be delivered to the batter with an underarm motion, with the hand below the hip, and released at a moderate speed. The umpire is the sole judge of the speed of the pitch, and may send off a pitcher who delivers the ball too fast. The pitched ball must travel in an arc that reaches its highest point 6–12ft above the ground (see illustration below). It is a no pitch if the ball slips from the pitcher's hand during the windup or backswing.

Batting (B) The strike zone extends from the batter's knees to his highest shoulder in his natural batting stance. A ball is called by the umpire if a pitched ball hits the batter outside the strike zone.

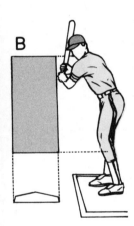

A strike is called by the umpire for each foul ball not legally caught, even when the batter has already been charged with two strikes. The ball is dead after a strike or ball is called, and the runners may not advance.

A base on balls may be awarded at the request of the pitcher, who may ask the umpire to award the batter first base without pitching, or when four pitched balls have been called ball by the umpire. The ball is dead, and other baserunners may only advance if forced. The batter is out if:

a) a third strike is called against him;
b) he bunts or chops (strikes downward so that the ball bounces high into the air) the ball.

Runners may only leave their bases when a pitched ball has reached home plate or has been hit by the batter. Should a pitched ball reach home plate and not be hit by the batter, all runners must return to their bases. A runner who fails to keep contact with his base until the ball has reached home plate is put out.

If a pitch is an illegal pitch, the ball is dead, a ball is awarded the batter, and the runners may not advance, except that if the batter swings at an illegal pitch it becomes legal.

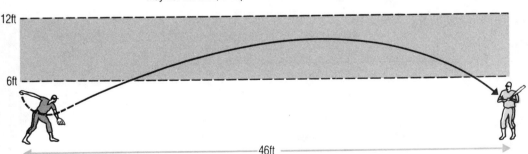

SQUASH

HISTORY

Squash (properly, squash rackets) began at Harrow School in England in the early nineteeth century as a variant of the much older game of rackets. The game spread rapidly throughout the world. By the beginning of World War I national governing bodies had been set up in the USA, Canada, and South Africa; between the wars the British Army built courts in India, Pakistan, and Egypt. The real boom in the popularity of squash began in the 1960s, as more and more people realized its usefulness as a way of keeping fit. The introduction of glass walls at the back of the court made television coverage possible, and so brought the game to a wider audience than had previously been possible. The international governing body for the sport, the International Squash Rackets Federation (ISRF) was founded in 1967.

SYNOPSIS

Squash is a racket and ball game played in an enclosed court; players score points by hitting shots that their opponents are unable to return. Singles play is the more usual form of the game, but doubles is also popular in North America. ISRF rules are here described first. Rules in the USA differ in some important respects (see pp. 347 – 349).

COURT AND EQUIPMENT

Court Illustrated here is a standard international singles court, 9.75m long and 6.4m wide. The court should be a minimum of 6.4m high at a point 3.5m from the front wall. The walls, of concrete/plaster construction, should be completely smooth and painted white; the rear wall may be made of glass. The floor should be of light colored hardwood planks laid parallel to the side walls. Red lines, 5cm wide, mark the court.

A strip of resonating material (**a**), known as the "telltale," the "board," or the "tin," should run along the foot of the front wall of the court. It should be 48cm high, 1.25–2.5cm thick, and make a distinctive sound when hit.

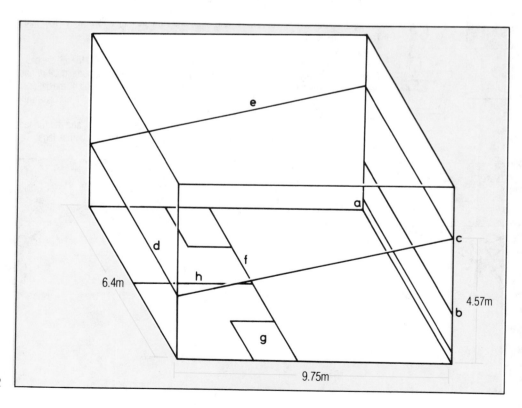

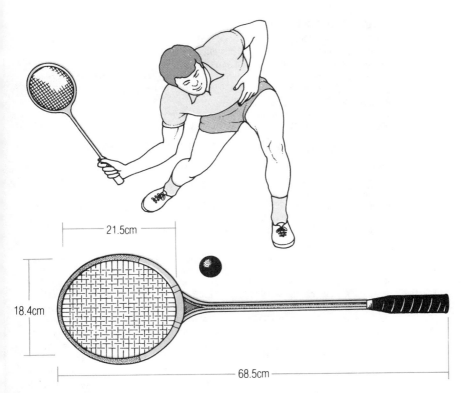

39.5–
41.5mm

Other court markings are as follows:

b) cut line, marked on the front wall 1.83m above the floor;

c) front-wall line, 4.57m above the floor;

d) back-wall line, marked on the back wall 2.13m above the floor;

e) side-wall line, joining the front-wall line to the back-wall line;

f) short line, marked on the floor 5.49m from the front wall;

g) service boxes, 1.6m square;

h) half-court line, marked on the floor between the short line and the back wall, and equidistant from the two side walls.

The area above the front-wall, side-wall, and back-wall lines is out of play, as is the telltale.

The racket must have a wooden-framed head; the handle shaft may be of wood, cane, metal, or glass fiber.

The overall length of the racket must not exceed 68.5cm. The strung area should be a maximum of 21.5cm long and 18.4cm wide, measured inside the framework of the head.

The ball should be of rubber or composition, with a matt finish. It should have a diameter of 39.5–41.5mm, and weigh 23.3–24.6g. The rebound of the ball and its deformation under pressure should conform to specific regulations.

The ball may not artificially be chilled or heated before a match; it may be warmed up to playing condition only by a knock-up by the players on court.

At any time when the ball is not in actual play, a new ball may be substituted by mutual consent of the players, or at the referee's discretion.

Between games the ball must always remain in full view on the floor of the court.

Dress should be white or of a light pastel color. Shoes should be predominantly light, and should have soles that will not mark the court.

PLAYERS AND OFFICIALS

Players The player with the right to serve is termed "hand-in"; the player receiving is termed "hand-out."

Officials Play is controlled by a referee, with the help of a marker to keep the score.

SQUASH 2

DURATION AND SCORING
Duration Play is continuous from the delivery of the first service until the match is completed, except for an interval of one minute between games, and of two minutes between the fourth and fifth games of a five game match.

The referee has the right to suspend play at any time in response to conditions outside the control of the players. When a new ball is necessary, play may be suspended to allow a knock-up to bring it to playing condition.

Under no circumstances may play be suspended or delayed to allow a player to recover his strength or breath.

Scoring A match consists of the best of either three or five games.

The player who first wins 9 points wins the game. However, when the score reaches 8-all for the first time, the player who is hand-out may choose to continue the game to 10 points. In this case the player who first scores two more points wins the game.

Points can only be scored by the player who is serving (hand-in). When a player fails to make a good return, or fails to serve according to the rules, he loses a stroke. When the player who is hand-in wins a stroke, he scores a point; when the player who is hand-out wins a stroke he takes over the service.

RULES OF PLAY
Knock-up Players may knock-up together for a maximum of five minutes immediately before the start of the match.

If the players choose to knock-up separately, the first player is allowed 3½ minutes and the second 2½ minutes. The order of the knock-up is determined by a spin of the racket.

Service order The right to serve first is determined by a spin of the racket. A player retains the right to serve until he loses a stroke, when the service passes to his opponent.

At the beginning of each game, and after each change of service, the server has the choice of service box. He then uses alternate service boxes until he loses the service. However, if he serves a fault, or the rally ends in a let, he should serve again from the same box.

A player who serves from the wrong box is not penalized, and his service is counted as if from the correct box. However, if the player receiving service objects before attempting to strike the ball, the service must be retaken from the correct box.

Service The server, with at least one foot within the service box, should drop or throw the ball into the air and strike it before it touches the walls or the floor (**A**). If he makes no attempt to strike the ball before it touches the walls or the floor, he may take the service again without being penalized.

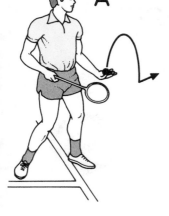

The ball must be served direct onto the front wall of the court between the cut line and the front-wall line; unless volleyed by the hand-out, it must rebound into the back quarter of the court floor opposite the server's box (**B**).

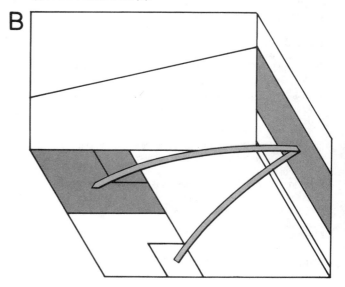

B

Service faults A service is a fault if:

a) when striking the ball, the server does not have at least one foot in contact with the floor within and not touching the lines marking the service box;

b) the ball is served onto or below the cut line;

c) on the rebound, the ball first touches the floor on or outside the lines marking the back quarter opposite the server's box.

A player who serves one fault serves again.

If the hand-out chooses to return a service that is a fault, that service is then considered good, and the ball remains in play.

Loss of service A player loses the service to his opponent ("serves his hand-out") if, on the service:

a) he serves two consecutive faults;

b) the ball touches the walls or floor before he strikes it;

c) he attempts to strike the ball and fails;

d) he strikes the ball more than once;

e) the ball is served onto or below the tin;

f) the ball strikes any other part of the court before striking the front wall;

g) the ball rebounds from the front wall and, before it has bounced twice on the floor or has been struck by the hand-out, touches the server or anything he wears or carries.

Rally After a good service, the players hit the ball alternately until one of them fails to make a good return, or the ball otherwise goes out of play.

Good return It is a good return if, before the ball has bounced twice on the floor, the player hits it so that it strikes the front wall above the telltale and below the front wall line, and bounces back without hitting any out of play area. The ball may strike the side or back walls (or both) before or after being hit by the player.

If a player strikes at the ball and misses, he may make further attempts to make a good return.

Bad returns (C) It is a bad return and the striker loses the stroke if:

a) the ball bounces twice on the floor before he hits it (**1**);

b) he hits the ball twice;

c) after he has hit the ball, it bounces on the floor on its way to the front wall (**2**);

d) the ball hits the tin (**3**);

e) the ball hits any out of play area;

f) the ball touches his body or clothing.

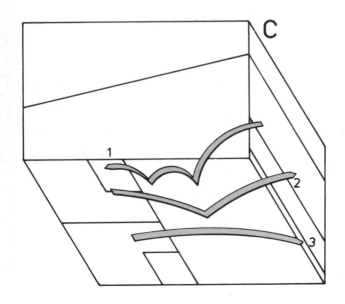

SQUASH 3

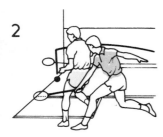

Let When a let is given, play stops, and the server takes the service again from the same service box; the service or rally during which the let was given does not count. A player who wishes to claim a let appeals by calling "Let, please"; this immediately ends the rally. A let is always allowed:
a) if the player receiving service is not ready, and does not attempt to take the service;
b) if the ball breaks during play;
c) if the ball goes out of court on its first bounce on an otherwise good return;
d) in certain cases, for interference or when a ball hits a player.
A let may be allowed at the referee's discretion if:
a) the ball hits any article lying in the court;
b) the striker does not play the ball for fear of injuring his opponent;
c) the striker, when playing the ball, touches his opponent;
d) a player loses a rally because he is distracted by his opponent;
e) the referee is unable to decide upon an appeal.

Ball hitting opponent The ball is considered to have hit a player if it touches him, his racket, or anything he wears or carries.
If the ball hits his opponent before the player can hit it, the opponent loses the stroke. However, if the player's position prevented his opponent from getting out of the way, obscured his opponent's vision, or gave his opponent reason to suppose that the player was able to hit the ball, a let is given.
If, after the player has attempted to hit the ball and failed, the ball hits his opponent, a let is given only if the player would otherwise have made a good return. If the player could not have made a good return, he loses the stroke.
If the ball hits his opponent after the player has hit it:
a) the striker wins the stroke if the ball would otherwise have made a good return and struck the front wall without touching any other wall;
b) the striker wins the stroke if, in the referee's opinion, the opponent has intercepted a winning stroke;
c) the striker loses the stroke if he could not have made a good return;
d) a let is given if the striker would have made a good return but did not hit the ball on his first attempt;
e) a let is given if the striker would have made a good return but turned to follow the ball around before hitting it, or allowed it to pass behind his body;
f) a let is given if the striker would have made a good return but the ball would have touched another wall before touching the front wall (**1**).

Interference After playing the ball, a player must make every effort:
a) to get out of his opponent's way;
b) to allow his opponent a clear view of the ball;
c) not to interfere with his opponent's attempts to play the ball;
d) not to delay his opponent with an excessive racket swing;
e) not to prevent his opponent playing the ball directly onto the front wall or to the side walls close to the front wall.
If any such interference occurs (**2**), and a player has not made every effort to avoid causing it, his opponent is awarded the stroke. A let is given if the player has made every effort to avoid causing interference, unless he prevented his opponent from making a winning return, when the referee will award the opponent the stroke.
If, as a result of interference, a player refrains from playing a ball which, if played, would in the referee's opinion have won the rally, the referee will award that player the stroke.
If either player makes unnecessary physical contact with his opponent, the referee may stop the game and award a stroke accordingly.

NORTH AMERICAN SQUASH

On these pages we summarize the rules of the United States Squash Racquets Association (USSRA) that differ from ISRF rules. Unless otherwise specified, rules apply to both singles and doubles play.

COURT AND EQUIPMENT

Singles court Illustrated here is a standard North American singles court, 32ft long and 18ft 6in wide. The ceiling should be at least 18ft high.

The walls and floor are of white-painted wood; the back wall may be of glass. Red lines mark the court: those marking the out of bounds lines are 1½in wide, others are 1in wide. The telltale (**a**) should be 17in high and painted white.

Out of bounds lines should be marked:

b) 16ft above the floor on the front wall;

c) 16ft above the floor on the side walls for a distance of 22ft from the front wall;

d) 12ft above the floor on the side walls for the remaining 10ft to the back wall;

e) 6ft 6in above the floor on the back wall.

Other court markings are as follows:

f) service line, marked on the front wall 6ft 6in above the floor;

g) service court line, marked on the floor 10ft from the back wall;

h) service boxes, each a quarter of a circle whose radius is 4ft 6in;

i) half-court line, marked on the floor between the service court line and the back wall, and equidistant from the two side walls.

The doubles court is similar to the singles court, but the dimensions are as follows:

1) floor, 45ft long and 25ft wide;

2) front playing wall, 20ft high;

3) side playing walls, 20ft high for a distance of 31ft from the front wall;

4) side playing walls, 15ft high for the remaining 14ft to the back wall;

5) back playing wall, 7ft high;

6) service line, 8ft 2in high;

7) service court line, 15ft from the back wall;

8) service boxes, with a radius of 4ft 6in;

9) half-court line, marked on the floor between the service court line and the back wall, and equidistant from the two side walls.

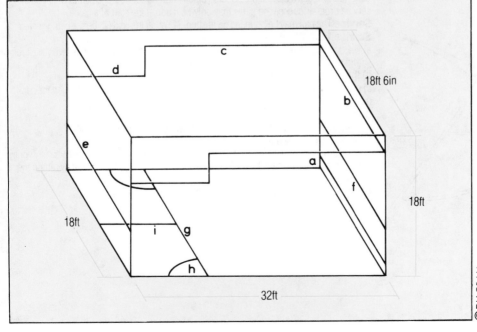

SQUASH 4

Racket The overall length of the racket must not exceed 27in. The diameter of the outside of the circular head should not exceed 9in.

Ball The singles ball should have a diameter of 1.56–1.62in, and weigh 0.68–0.73oz. The doubles ball should have the same diameter, but should weigh 0.76–0.81oz. The rebound of the balls and their deformation under pressure should conform to specific regulations.

DURATION AND SCORING

Duration Players are allowed an interval of up to two minutes between games, and of up to five minutes between the third and fourth games of a match. The referee may penalize any player who is late on the court after an interval.

The referee may suspend play once during the match for a period of up to five minutes for the benefit of a player suffering from cramp or pulled muscles.

Scoring A match consists of the best of five games.

Both the server and the player receiving service can score points. The player who first scores 15 points wins the game, unless it has been "set" at an earlier stage.

Setting If the score reaches 13-all, the player who first scored 13 points must announce one of the following options before the next service:

"no set" – the game remains at 15 points;

"set 3" – the game is played to 16 points;

"set 5" – the game is played to 18 points.

If the score reaches 14-all without first having reached 13-all, the player who first scored 14 points must announce one of the following options before the next service:

"no set" – the game remains at 15 points;

"set 3" – the game is played to 17 points.

Once established, the set cannot be altered.

RULES OF PLAY

Doubles service order The pair to serve first is determined by a spin of the racket. The player serving first (who remains the first server for his side throughout the game) has the choice of service boxes, and then uses alternate boxes until he loses the service. The service then passes to the other pair, who may choose to serve from either box. The first server for that pair then serves from alternate sides until he loses the service, when it passes to his partner, who must continue the service side sequence. When he loses the service, it returns to the opponents.

The first service a pair receives establishes the order of receiving, and the player must continue to receive service on that side of the court throughout the game. Changes in service order and receiving sides may only be made at the start of a game.

Service The ball may be bounced on the floor (**1**) or off the wall (**2**) before being served.

Service faults A service is a fault if:

a) when striking the ball, the server does not have at least one foot in contact with the floor within and not touching the lines marking the service box;

b) the ball is served onto or below the service line;

c) on the rebound, the ball first touches the floor on or outside the lines marking the back quarter outside the server's box;

d) the server strikes the ball more than once;

e) the ball strikes any other part of the court before striking the front wall;

f) the ball strikes any out-of-play area;

A service that is a fault must not be played by the receiver. However, the receiver may volley any service that has legally hit the front wall, and has not yet become a fault by hitting the floor outside the correct service court.

Loss of service A player continues to serve until he loses a point.

Let When a let is given, play stops, and the server takes the service again; he is entitled to two service attempts even if he has already served a fault on the same point.

If the player would otherwise have made a good return, a let is allowed:

a) if the ball breaks during play;

b) if, after bouncing once on the floor, the ball goes out of play by striking on or above the back wall out-of-bounds line;

c) the striker does not play the ball for fear of injuring his opponent;

d) when, because of the position of the striker, his opponent is unable to avoid being touched by the ball;

e) when the striker, as or before he hits the ball, is touched by his opponent or anything he wears or carries (**3**);

f) in certain cases, for interference or when a ball hits a player.

A player who requests a let because he considers the ball has broken must complete the point being played before making his request. In let situations caused by players, appeals for a let must be made as or before the stroke is played.

The referee may call a let at any time because of outside interference with the game, or if he considers a player is about to be injured.

An appeal for a let automatically includes an appeal for a let point.

A let point is awarded to a player if:

a) an obstruction by his opponent prevents him from attempting a winning shot;

b) for any reason (apart from being trapped or in immediate danger of injury), his opponent fails to make his best effort to avoid causing an obstruction, and so prevents the player from attempting a shot;

c) his opponent has caused repeated lets, none of which individually constitutes a let point.

If a let point is awarded, the point is not replayed, but is awarded to the obstructed player.

Ball touching player The ball is considered to have touched a player if it touches him or anything he wears or carries, except his racket when he is about to play a shot.

If the ball in play touches either player after hitting the front wall but before being returned, the player so touched loses the point. However, if the player's contact with the ball was as a result of his opponent's position or obstruction, a let or let point will be awarded.

If the ball in play touches the last player to strike it before it hits the front wall, that player loses the point, unless he was unable to avoid the contact because of his opponent's position, when a let is given.

If, after the player has attempted to hit the ball and failed, the ball touches his opponent, a let is given only if the player would otherwise have made a good return. If the player could not have made a good return he loses the point.

If the ball in play hits his opponent after the player has hit it but before it hits the front wall:

a) the striker loses the point if he could not have made a good return;

b) a let is given if the striker would otherwise have made a good return but the ball would have touched another wall before touching the front wall;

c) a let is given if the ball has hit a wall other than the front wall before hitting the opponent;

d) a let is given if the striker would otherwise have made a good return but turned around to follow the ball before hitting it;

e) a let is given if the striker would otherwise have made a good return but did not hit the ball on his first attempt;

f) in singles play, the striker wins the point if the ball would otherwise have made a good return and struck the front wall without touching any other wall;

g) in doubles play, a let is given if the ball would otherwise have made a good return and struck the front wall without touching any other wall.

3

SWIMMING

HISTORY
Swimming formed an important part of the training for soldiers in many ancient civilizations, but during the Middle Ages it became uncommon because of a fear that outdoor swimming helped spread disease. Modern competitive swimming began in the second half of the nineteeth century, first in Britain, where the organization that later became the Amateur Swimming Association was formed in 1869, and then elsewhere. The present world governing body for the sport, the Fédération Internationale de Natation Amateur (FINA), was formed in 1908. Swimming has been an Olympic sport for men since 1896 and for women since 1912; today it is the second largest sport in the Olympic program.

SYNOPSIS
Swimming is both an individual and a team water sport. Participants compete in races, and the first swimmer or relay team to cover a predetermined distance using a specified swimming stroke or strokes is the winner. Team placings are determined by the awarding of points for individual placings. There are events in each of the following four swimming strokes—breaststroke, butterfly, backstroke, and freestyle—as well as individual medleys and medley relays.

POOL AND EQUIPMENT
The pool For Olympic Games, world championships, regional games, and all international competitions the pool must be 50m long and at least 21m wide. For Olympic Games and world championships it must have an overall depth of 1.8m.

The pool is divided into eight lanes, numbered 1 through 8 from right to left when looking down the pool from the starting end. Each lane, bounded by lane ropes extending the full length of the pool, is 2.5m wide and there is a space at least 50cm wide outside lanes 1 and 8.

Lane ropes (**a**) are made up of colored floats, which must be of a distinctive color for a distance of 5m from each end of the pool. Dark line markings on the floor of the pool indicate the center of each lane for most of its distance, terminating in lines running across the pool 2m from each end wall. Lane centers are also marked by target lines on the end walls.

Starting platforms must be used for races other than backstroke races. They are covered in non-slip material, bear the lane number on all four sides, and have a platform surface at least 50cm square and 50–75cm above the water surface. A maximum platform slope of 10° is permitted.

Handgrips are provided for backstroke starts. Backstroke turn indicators (**b**) in the form of flagged ropes 1.8m above the water surface and 5m from the end walls are provided to inform backstroke swimmers that they are approaching a turn.

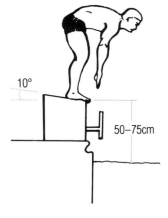

10°

50–75cm

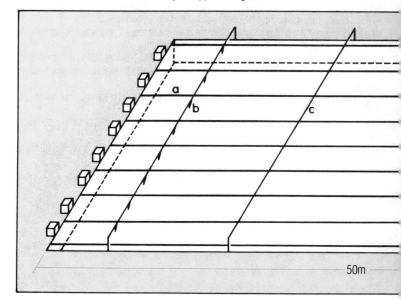

a

b

c

50m

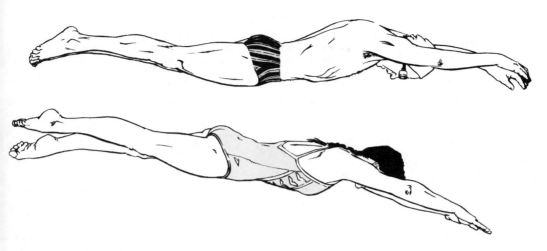

A false start rope (**c**) is suspended across the pool 15m in front of the starting end. In the event of a false start, the rope is dropped down into the water by a quick-release mechanism.

The minimum water temperature for competitions is 24°C.

Timing equipment

Electronic equipment is used to record competitors' race times and to judge finishing order. Official timing is to two decimal places of a second.

Equipment for each lane is independently connected, and is activated by the starter. Finishing times are registered automatically by means of electronic touch pads, which must have a brightly colored, non-slip surface and be at least 2.4m wide and 90cm deep (30cm above and 60cm below the water surface).

In case of a breakdown of the electronic timing equipment, times are also recorded by official timekeepers using stopwatches.

Dress Men must wear swimming trunks, and women one-piece swimming costumes with no open work except at the back. All costumes must be non-transparent. Detailed regulations concerning the cut of costumes are designed to prevent immodest dress. Caps and goggles may be worn if desired. Aids to buoyancy or performance, such as fins, are prohibited.

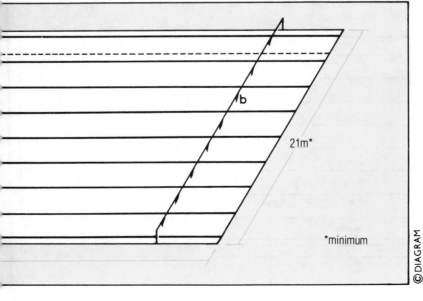

21m*

*minimum

© DIAGRAM

SWIMMING 2

Olympic events
100m freestyle
200m freestyle
400m freestyle
800m freestyle
1500m freestyle
100m breaststroke
200m breaststroke
100m butterfly
200m butterfly
100m backstroke
200m backstroke
200m individual medley
400m individual medley
4×100m freestyle relay
4×200m freestyle relay
4×100m medley relay

COMPETITORS AND OFFICIALS

Competitors Individual and relay events are listed in the table. Except when specified otherwise, there are events for men and for women. In international competitions, team placings are determined by the awarding of points for placings in the various events.

Officials Minimum international requirements are a referee, a starter, a chief timekeeper, three timekeepers per lane plus two reserve timekeepers, a chief judge, three finishing judges per lane, two inspectors of turns per lane (one at each end), two judges of strokes, a clerk of the course, a recorder, and an announcer.

a) The referee has overall control of the officials and competitors. He ensures that all rules are obeyed, and adjudicates in all protests related to the actual competition. The referee's decision is final in any case where the judges' decisions and the recorded times do not agree.

b) The starter controls the competitors until the race has begun. He supervises the start, decides whether the start is a fair one, and has the power to recall any swimmer at any time after the start.

c) The chief timekeeper assigns the timekeepers to their lanes, and examines the results that they record.

d) Timekeepers use stopwatches to time competitors swimming in the lane to which they have been assigned. Results are recorded on cards for examination by the chief timekeeper.

e) The chief judge assigns all judges and inspectors of turns to their lanes, and collects and examines the results that they record.

f) Finish judges report on the order of finish. If required, they may act as inspectors of turns and observe take-offs in relay events.

g) Inspectors of turns ensure that rules concerning turns and relay take-offs are complied with, reporting infringements to the chief judge. They also record the number of lengths completed by each competitor, and keep competitors informed of the number of lengths still to be swum by showing numbered "lap cards" at each turn.

h) Judges of strokes ensure that the rules of the swimming stroke designated for the event are being observed. They report any violation to the referee.

i) The clerk of the course assembles and prepares the competitors before a race.

j) The recorder keeps a complete record of the race results.

THE RACE

Starting stations (A) for all events are decided by assigning the competitor with the fastest entry time the center lane, or, where there are an even number of lanes, the lane to the right of the center. The other swimmers are then placed alternately left and right of the fastest swimmer, so that the slowest swimmers are in the two outside lanes. If the entry times are a true indication of form, the swimmers will fan out into a spearhead formation during the race.

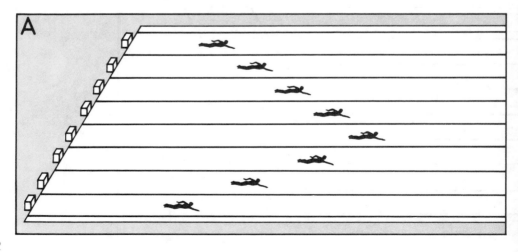

B

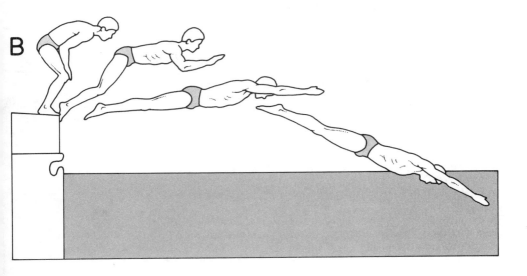

C

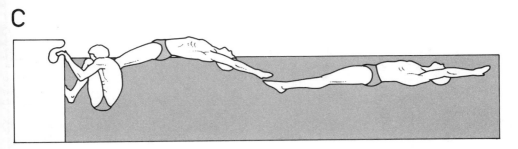

The start (B) Except in backstroke races, competitors start with a dive from the starting platforms. At the referee's signal, the swimmers must step up onto the back of their starting platform. Then, on the command "Take your marks" from the starter, they must step forward to the front of their platform and assume a starting position. When all the swimmers are stationary, the starter gives the signal for the race to begin. The signal may be a shot, whistle, or the command "Go."

Backstroke start (C) Swimmers line up in the water, facing the starting end, with their hands on the starting grips. Their feet must be under the surface of the water and not curled over the starting edge or the gutter.

False start After a false start, the swimmers are recalled by the lowering of the false start rope onto the water. Up to two false starts are allowed before the starter gives a warning to the competitors that the next swimmer to break before the signal will be disqualified. If the starting signal sounds before the disqualification is announced, the race continues and any disqualifications are declared after the finish.

Disqualification of a competitor for misconduct at the start does not constitute a false start.

General rules Competitors must swim the whole length of the course and finish in the lane in which they started. Rules relating to specific strokes or events must be observed as appropriate.

Competitors can be disqualified for general misconduct, for interfering with or obstructing another competitor, for walking (although not for standing) on the bottom of the pool, for taking a step or stride from the bottom of the pool when turning, or for failing to touch the wall at a turn or the end of a race.

SWIMMING 3

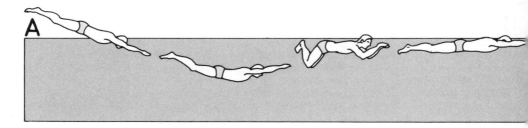

A

Breaststroke (A) The body must be kept on the breast with both shoulders parallel to the water surface.

The hands must be pushed forward together from the breast and then brought back on or under the surface of the water. All arm movements must be simultaneous and no alternating movement is permitted.

In the leg kick the feet must be turned out in the backward movement. All leg movements must be simultaneous and no alternating movement is permitted. The kick cannot be a dolphin kick.

Part of the head must break the surface of the water throughout the race, except at the start and at each turn when the swimmer may take one arm stroke and one leg kick while wholly submerged before returning to the surface.

At turns, the touch must be simultaneous with both hands, although it may be uneven. At the finish, both hands must touch at the same time and at the same level (either below, at, or above the water level).

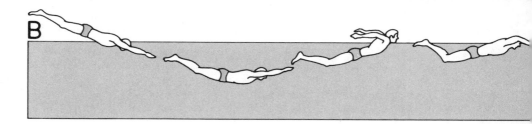

B

Butterfly (B) The arms are brought forward at the same time to enter the water at some point in front of the shoulders and are then pulled backward under the water. No alternating movement of the arms is permitted.

The body must be kept on the breast. From the beginning of the first arm stroke after the start and on a turn, both shoulders must be parallel to the surface of the water.

All movements of the feet must be simultaneous. Up and down movements in the vertical plane are permitted. Although the legs and feet do not need to be in the same horizontal plane, no alternating movement during the kick is allowed.

At the start and at turns, one or more leg kicks and one arm pull under the water are permitted, which must bring the swimmer to the surface.

The touch at a turn or at the finish must be made with both hands at the same time and at the same level.

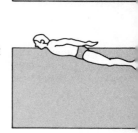

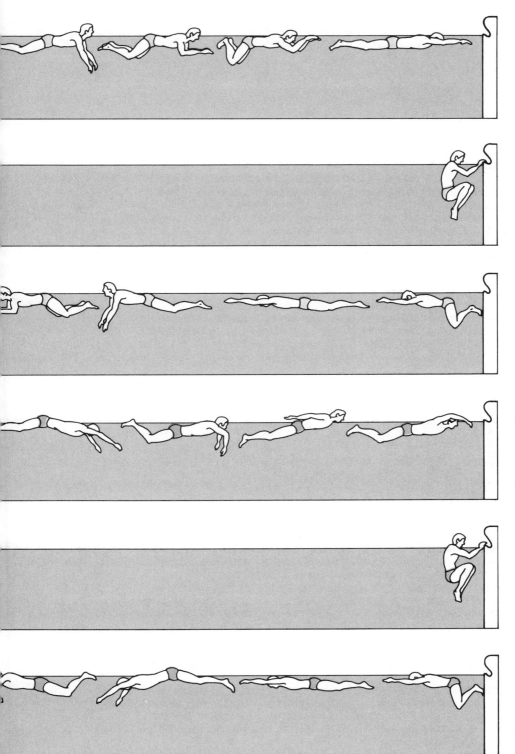

©DIAGRAM

A

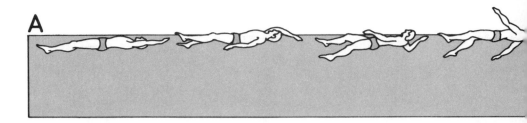

Backstroke (A) Competitors must swim on their backs throughout the race.
A somersault turn may be used, but any swimmer turning beyond the vertical before he touches the end of the pool will be disqualified. After the turn, the swimmer must have returned to a position on his back before his feet have left the wall.
A swimmer will also be disqualified for leaving his position on the back before his head, shoulder, foremost hand, or arm touches the finish line.

Freestyle In freestyle events competitors may swim in any style they choose. In medley relay or individual medley events, freestyle means any stroke other than butterfly, breaststroke, or backstroke.
At the turn and at the finish, the swimmer may touch the wall with any part of his body. The stroke generally chosen for freestyle is the front crawl.

Front crawl (B) The main characteristics of this stroke are the following: each arm is alternately brought over and then into the water while the legs perform an alternating kicking action. The swimmer generally breathes by turning his head to one side as he raises that arm out of the water.

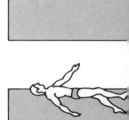

B

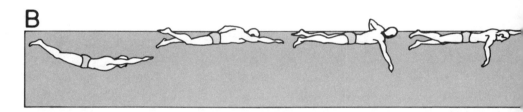

Medley events In individual medleys, competitors swim an equal distance in each of four different strokes. The sequence is butterfly, backstroke, breaststroke, and freestyle. In medley relays, each swimmer swims one stroke for the set distance. The order is backstroke, breaststroke, butterfly, and freestyle.

Relay events Before leaving the starting platform, second and subsequent swimmers must wait until their preceding teammate touches the end wall. If a competitor dives too soon, his team will be disqualified unless he returns to the starting point on the wall (it is not necessary to return to the starting platform).
A relay team will also be disqualified if any team member, other than the swimmer designated to swim a particular length, enters the water before every competitor has finished the race.

Result Performances are timed to $1/100$sec, and placings are awarded accordingly.
If competitors have equal times to $1/100$sec in a heat or semifinal and a decision is needed as to who will go into the next round, a swim-off between these competitors will be held.
If competitors have equal times to $1/100$sec in a final, they will be given the same placing.

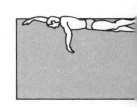

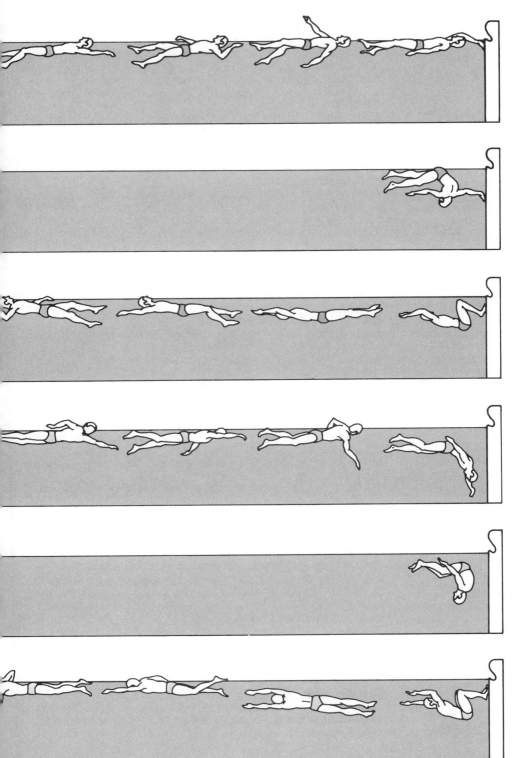

©DIAGRAM

SYNCHRONIZED SWIMMING

HISTORY
Synchronized or ornamental swimming became a popular entertainment in the United States in the 1930s, but did not develop as an organized competitive sport until the 1950s. It was recognized by FINA, the international governing body for swimming sports, in 1952. All competitors are female. The first world championships were held in 1973. Synchronized swimming is to be included in the Olympic Games for the first time in 1984, when there will be a duet event.

SYNOPSIS
Synchronized swimming is a type of water display in which competitors are judged on their performance of officially approved swimming movements. Competitors receive marks for performing a set of compulsory figures, and for a swimming routine performed to a musical accompaniment. There are competitions for solos, duets, and teams.

POOL AND EQUIPMENT
Pool For national and international competitions the pool area must be at least 12m square; for compulsory figures it must be at least 3m deep, and for routines at least 1.7m deep. The water must be clear enough for the bottom of the pool to be visible. The minimum permitted water temperature is 24°C.

Equipment Competition organizers are responsible for providing suitable equipment for the reproduction of competitors' musical accompaniments. This must include underwater speakers conforming to national safety standards.

Dress For the compulsory figures, competitors must wear a dark costume and a white cap. For routines, any costume may be worn provided it conforms to the current concept of what is appropriate.

COMPETITORS AND OFFICIALS
Competitors For world and area championships each country may enter only one solo, one duet, and one team; more entries may be permitted in other competitions. Swimmers may take part in solo, duet, and team events at the same meeting. For major championships a team must consist of eight members; at other levels, a team must have a minimum of four and a maximum of eight members.

Officials The minimum international requirements are:
a) a chief referee, who has full control over competitions, assigns and instructs other officials, signals competitors to start, imposes penalties, and approves marks;
b) one, two, or three panels of five or seven judges, who mark competitors' performances;
c) an assistant referee attached to each panel of judges for the compulsory figures;
d) three scorers for each panel of judges, whose duties are to record the judges' marks and to compute and record competitors' final scores;
e) a clerk of the course, with assistants for the compulsory figures, who ensure that competitors are in the correct starting place at the required time;
f) a controller of music, who is responsible for presenting the music for each routine;
g) two timekeepers, or one timekeeper with two watches, who time deckwork and overall times of routines so that time penalties can be imposed if necessary.

ORGANIZATION OF COMPETITIONS
Content of competitions Each competition consists of two sections:
1) a figures section, in which each competitor performs six compulsory figures;
2) a routines section, in which competitors (solos, duets, or teams) perform a routine, made up of any officially listed figures, strokes, and/or parts of them, and performed to music of the competitors' choosing.

Rounds In the figures section there is only one round, except that swimmers may have to reswim the figures to break a tie in the final result (see p. 360).
In the routines section a preliminary round is held to find eight finalists (those with the highest combined scores for figures and routines). The final consists of a repeat of the routines swum in the first round.

Swimming order The figures section precedes the routines section.
Swimming order for figures and for preliminary rounds of routines is determined by lot. In routines finals, swimmers perform in the reverse order of their scores in the preliminary round of routines.

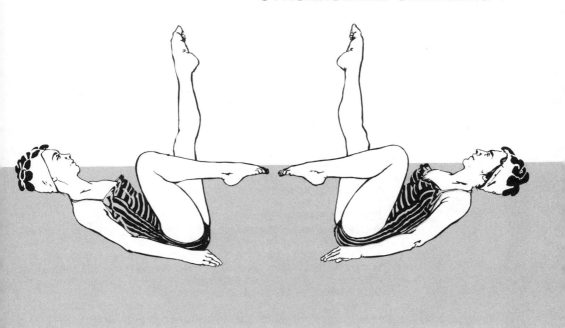

COMPULSORY FIGURES SECTION

Selection of figures FINA publishes full details of the figures to be performed in synchronized swimming competitions. Out of a total of approximately 100 approved figures, FINA makes a selection every four years of six groups of compulsory figures to be used in competitions until the next selection. Each group consists of six figures.
All figures have an official degree of difficulty and this is taken into account when the groups are fixed: three figures in each group have a difficulty of 1.7 or less and three have a difficulty of 1.8 or more. (Examples of figures are described on pp. 360–361.)
Between 18 and 30 hours before a competition begins, the organizers select by lot which group of figures is to be swum.
Judging When there are two panels of judges, one panel judges the first three figures and the other panel judges the remaining three.
When there are three panels of judges, the first judges the first two figures, the second judges the third and fourth figures, and the third judges the last two figures.
During the figures the judges look to see that each part of the figure is clearly defined and in uniform motion and that the performance is slow, high, and controlled. FINA definitions give the exact body positions and transitional movements required, but do not explain the sculling techniques by which movements are attained.

ROUTINES SECTION

Routines There are competitions for solos, duets, and teams. In each case the choice of music and choreography of the routine is completely free.
Alternate swimmers are not permitted in solo competitions, one alternate is allowed for duets, and two alternates are allowed for teams.
Routines must be performed within set time limits, or penalty points are deducted. Time limits are: 3¼–3¾min for solos; 3¾–4¼min for duets; 4¾–5¼min for teams. In each case a maximum of 20sec is permitted for deckwork (movements on the pool side).
Routines may start on the deck or in the water. They must end in the water.
Competitors must not use the bottom of the pool during the execution of any figure.
Judging Judges look for the following points in routines:
a) the correct execution of strokes, figures, and their parts;
b) the variety, difficulty, and pool pattern of the routine;
c) the interpretation of the music and the manner of presentation;
d) the synchronization of the swimmers, with the music and with each other.

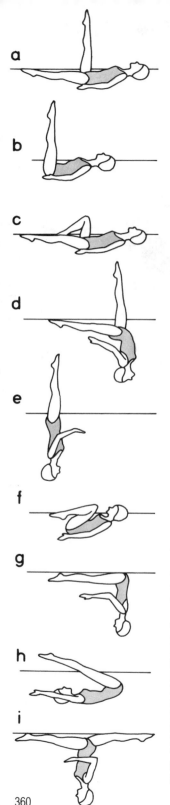

a

b

c

d

e

f

g

h

i

SYNCHRONIZED SWIMMING 2

EXECUTION OF FIGURES

Positions and movements Most figures are executed in a stationary position, although some allow a certain degree of backward or forward movement.

Incorporated in the various figures are a number of basic positions and movements, all of which are described in detail in the FINA handbook. A selection of basic positions is illustrated here: ballet leg (**a**); ballet leg double (**b**); bent knee (**c**); knight or castle (**d**); vertical (**e**); tuck (**f**); front pike (**g**); back pike (**h**); split (**i**).

Examples of figures Here we use illustration sequences, based on those published by FINA, to give an impression of five selected figures (but note that in competitions it is always the FINA written descriptions that carry most weight):

A) ballet leg single (degree of difficulty 1.5);
B) catalina (degree of difficulty 1.9);
C) dolphin bent knee (degree of difficulty 1.5);
D) barracuda back pike somersault (degree of difficulty 1.9);
E) walkover, front (degree of difficulty 1.5).

SCORING AND PENALTIES

Scoring of compulsory figures After performing each figure, competitors are awarded a mark by each judge. These marks are in points and half-points from 0 to 10. The scorers then cancel two of the judges' marks (the highest and lowest awarded), total the remaining three or five marks, divide this figure by the number of judges whose marks are being taken into consideration, and finally multiply the total by the official degree of difficulty for the figure. Any penalties are deducted at this time.

A solo competitor's final score for the figure competition is obtained by adding the scores for each of the six figures. For duets and teams, the overall figure score is obtained by averaging each individual's final score for the six figures.

Compulsory figures penalties A two-point penalty is deducted from the final score for a figure if:

a) a competitor performs the wrong figure but is then allowed to perform the correct one;
b) a competitor stops voluntarily and asks to do the figure again.

A repetition of these errors results in no score being awarded for the figure.

Scoring of routines At the end of each routine, each judge awards a mark from 0 to 10, using tenths of points. The scorers then cancel two marks (the highest and the lowest), total the remaining marks, multiply this figure by 10, and then divide it by the number of judges minus two. Any penalties are deducted at this point. In team competitions, in preliminary and final rounds, teams receive an additional half point for each competitor more than four in the team.

Routines penalties A one point penalty is deducted from the final score for a routine if competitors:

a) exceed the time limit of 20sec for deck movements;
b) deviate from the time limit for a routine;
c) deliberately use the bottom of the pool when executing a figure during a routine;
d) make a new start during deck movements, except when this is caused by circumstances outside the competitors' control.

If one or more competitors leave the water before a routine is completed, the routine is disqualified unless the departure is caused by circumstances outside the competitors' control.

Final result Synchronized swimming competitions are won by the solo, duet, or team with the highest total when scores for compulsory figures and routines are added.

If an alternate swimmer is used in a duet or team competition after the compulsory figures have been swum, the figures scores of the listed swimmer and the alternate swimmer are compared and the lower of these scores is counted for the final total.

In the case of a tie when scores for compulsory figures and routines are added together, the winner is the solo, duet or team with the highest figures score.

In the case of a tie in a competition, final placings are determined by:

1) the sum of the total scores of the best solo and/or duet and/or team; then
2) the highest award for a figure; then
3) the highest score in a reswim of the six compulsory figures by all tied competitors.

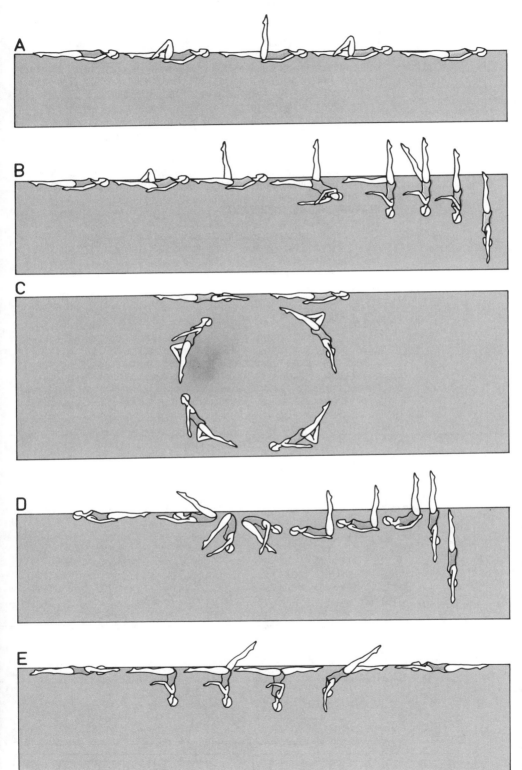

©DIAGRAM

TABLE TENNIS

HISTORY
Following its invention in England in the late 19th century, table tennis—then known by the onomatopoeic trade name of Ping-Pong—acquired worldwide popularity as an entertaining after-dinner pastime. The craze proved shortlived, however, and the game was little played between 1904 and 1922. New interest in the activity, and improvements in racket design, led a group of Englishmen in the 1920s to unify the rules and to adopt the name of table tennis. The first international championships were held in 1926, the year in which the International Table Tennis Federation (ITTF) was founded.

SYNOPSIS
Table tennis is an indoor ball game for two players (singles) or four (doubles). The players use rackets to hit a small resilient hollow ball backward and forward across a table divided by a low net. The object is to win points by making shots that an opponent is unable to return.

PLAYING AREA AND EQUIPMENT
Table The game is played on a rectangular table top 2.74m long, 1.525m wide, and 76cm above the floor. The playing surface may be of any material but must give a uniform bounce of 22–25cm when a standard ball is dropped from 30.5cm above it.

The surface must be dark-colored, preferably green, and matt, with white marking lines. A white line, 2cm wide, marks the edges of the playing surface (**a**). For doubles, the playing surface is divided into halves by a white line, 3mm wide, termed the center line (**b**).

The top edges of the table but not the sides of the table top are considered part of the playing surface.

The net, 1.83m long and 15.25cm high along its whole length, divides the playing surface into two equal "courts." The net is suspended by a cord attached at each end to an upright post 15.25cm high and 15.25cm outside the side line.

The ends of the net should be as close as possible to the support posts, and the bottom of the net, along its whole length, should be as close as possible to the playing surface.

Playing area For international matches the playing space must be at least 14m long, 7m wide, and 4m high. Dark surrounds, about 75cm high, separate each playing area.

37.2–38.2mm

Racket A racket may be any size, weight, or shape.

The blade must be of wood, continuous, of even thickness, flat, and rigid.

Adhesive layers within the blade may be reinforced with various fibrous materials, but 85% of the blade by thickness must be of natural wood.

Each side of the blade must be matt and of a uniform dark color, but the two sides need not be of the same color.

Sides of the blade may be completely uncovered, or may be covered with:

a) plain pimpled rubber, with pimples outward, of a total thickness not exceeding 2mm;

b) a sandwich of cellular rubber surfaced with plain pimpled rubber, with pimples inward or outward, of a total thickness not exceeding 4mm, of which the pimpled layer must not exceed 2mm.

Pimples must be evenly spaced on the rubber surface, between 10 and 50 to the sq. cm.

A side of the blade not intended for striking the ball must be of a dark color but is exempted from covering rules; using such a side for striking the ball is penalized by a lost point.

Ball The ball must be made of celluloid or a similar plastic, colored white or yellow, with a matt surface. It must be between 37.2mm and 38.2mm in diameter. It must weigh between 2.40g and 2.53g.

Dress Players must not wear white clothing, but white edging, subject to detailed regulations for major events, is permitted. Match clothes generally consist of a dark shirt and shorts (or skirt) of uniform color, and flat-soled shoes.

PLAYERS AND OFFICIALS

Players There are events for men's and women's singles and doubles, for mixed doubles, and for men's and women's teams.

Officials A referee has overall control of a competition and he decides any question of rule interpretation; he may disqualify a player for misconduct.

An umpire controls play in an individual match, often in conjunction with an assistant umpire with specific responsibilities of his own.

RULES OF PLAY

Choice of ends and service The choice of ends and the right to serve or receive is decided by tossing a coin. If the winner of the toss decides to serve or receive first, the loser has the choice of ends, and vice versa. The winner of the toss may require the loser to choose first.

In doubles, the pair with the right to serve first in any game decides which of them will do so. The pair to receive in the first game of the match then decides which of them will receive first; in later games the first receiver is determined by which player is serving (see Change of service, p. 366).

Change of ends Players or pairs change ends after each game until the end of the match. They also change ends in the last game when the first player or pair scores 10 points.

If the players are playing from the wrong ends they must change ends as soon as the error is discovered, but all points scored since the error are counted.

Definitions The period when the ball is in play is termed a "rally."

The player who first strikes the ball in a rally is termed the "server," the second is the "receiver."

The hand carrying the racket is the "racket hand," the other hand is the "free hand."

"Struck" means hit with the racket or the racket hand below the wrist.

The ball is regarded as passing "over or around" the net if it passes under the projection of the net and its supports outside the table.

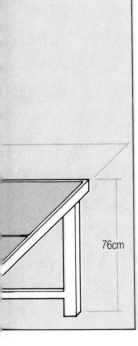

76cm

©DIAGRAM

TABLE TENNIS 2

Order of play (**A**) In singles the server must first make a good service, the receiver must make a good return, and then server and receiver must make good returns alternately.
In doubles the order of play is as follows:
the server (**1**) must make a good service;
the receiver (**2**) must make a good return;
the server's partner (**3**) must make a good return;
the receiver's partner (**4**) must make a good return;
and so on in this sequence.

A good service (**B**) The ball is placed on the palm of the free hand, which must be stationary, open and flat, with the fingers together and the thumb free.
Keeping the free hand above the level of the playing surface, the ball is then thrown, by hand only and without imparting spin, so that it rises within 45° of the vertical. (The ball goes into play when, about to be thrown for service, it ceases to be stationary on the palm of the hand.)
On descent, the ball is struck to touch the server's court first and then, passing directly over or around the net, to touch the receiver's court.
At the moment of striking, the racket must be behind the end of the table or an imaginary continuation of it.
In doubles the ball must first touch the server's right hand court (or the center line) and then the diagonally opposite court (or the center line).

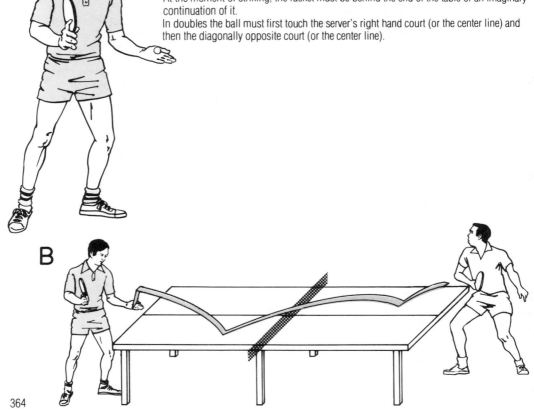

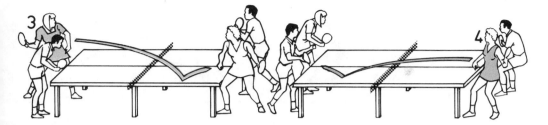

A good return (C) For a good return the ball must normally be struck so that it passes directly over or around the net and then touches the opponent's court (**a**).

A return is, however, also considered to be good if:

the ball, in passing over or around the net, touches the net or its supports;

the ball bounces in such a way as to return to the side of the net where it was last hit and is then hit directly to touch the opponent's court.

A return is not considered good if:

the ball is allowed to bounce twice before the return is made (**b**);

the ball is volleyed – struck before it touches the playing surface of that player's court and is still in play (**c**);

the ball is struck so it touches the striker's court before passing over or around the net (**d**);

the ball passes over or around the net but fails to touch the opponent's court (**e**).

The ball becomes out of play once it has touched any object other than the net, net supports, playing surface, racket, or racket hand below the wrist, or when the rally is otherwise ended.

A stroke made with the hand alone, the racket having being dropped, also puts the ball out of play, as does striking the ball with a racket blade surface that does not comply with covering regulations.

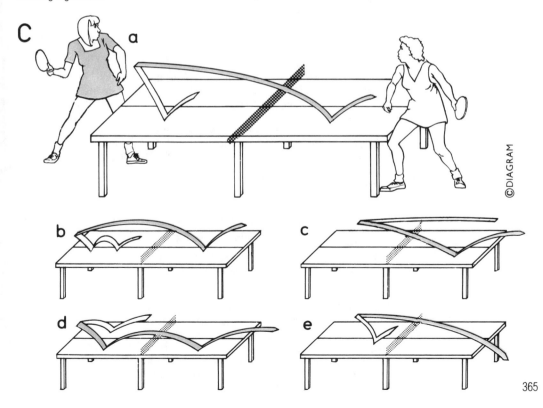

©DIAGRAM

Change of service With certain exceptions (see below), the service in singles and doubles passes from one player to another after every five points scored.
The service sequence in doubles is:
1) the player chosen to serve first from one pair (**a**) serves to the player of the other pair who has been chosen to receive first (**b**);
2) player (**b**) then serves to the partner of player (**a**), player (**c**);
3) player (**c**) then serves to the fourth player, player (**d**);
4) player (**d**) then serves to player (**a**), after which the entire sequence is repeated.
From the score of 20 all, or under the expedite system, the order of serving and receiving is unchanged, but each player serves for only one point in succession until the game ends.
The player or pair who served first in one game receives first in the next game.
In games after the first game in a doubles match, the first player chosen to serve must serve first to the player who served to him in the immediately preceding game. (In effect this means that each player now serves to the partner of the player to whom he served in the game before.)
In the last game of a doubles match the receiving pair changes its order of receiving when the first pair scores 10.
Any error in serving or receiving order must be corrected as soon as it is noticed; all points scored since the error are counted.
SCORING
A match consists of one game, the best of three, or the best of five games.
Play must be continuous throughout except that any player may claim up to five minutes' rest between the third and fourth games of a match, and not more than one minute between any other successive games of a match.
A game is won by the player or pair first scoring 21 points unless both score 20 points, when the winner is the first to score two points more than the opposition.
Points are scored by a player when his opponent:
fails to make a good service;
strikes the ball out of sequence in a doubles game (even if by mistake);
touches the playing surface with his free hand when the ball is in play.
A player also scores when:

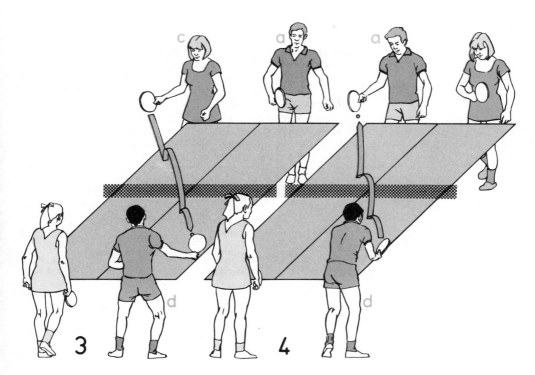

anything his opponent wears or carries comes into contact with the ball in play before it has passed over the opponent's end line or side lines while not having touched the playing surface on that side;

his opponent (or his racket or something he wears or carries) touches the net or its supports or moves the playing surface while the ball is in play.

Under the expedite system a receiver also scores after making 13 good returns.

A let is a rally from which no point is scored. It occurs when:

a) the ball touches the net or its supports in service, provided the service is otherwise good or has been volleyed by the receiver or his partner;

b) a service is delivered when the receiver or his partner, in the umpire's opinion, is not ready to play;

c) in the umpire's opinion, a player fails to make a good service or return through a disturbance beyond his control;

d) in the umpire's opinion, a disturbance in the conditions of play is likely to affect the outcome of a rally;

e) a rally is interrupted to correct a mistake in playing order or ends;

f) a rally is interrupted to apply the expedite system;

g) a rally is interrupted to warn a player that his service is in doubt.

The expedite system must be introduced if a game is unfinished 15 minutes after the start. It may be introduced at an earlier time if both players or pairs agree. Having once been introduced it applies to all points in the game in progress and to all further games in the match.

If the ball is in play at the end of the 15-minute period, the umpire interrupts the rally with a call of "let." Play then resumes with a service by the player who served in the interrupted rally.

If the 15-minute period expires when the ball is not in play, play resumes with a service by the player who received in the previous rally.

The return strokes of the receiving player or pair are then counted out loud, from 1 to 13, by an official other than the umpire. If the rally has not been decided when 13 such returns have been made, the point goes to the receiving player or pair.

TENNIS

HISTORY

Tennis, or lawn tennis, developed in Britain in the nineteenth century from real or royal tennis, a game known since medieval times. There is considerable dispute as to who invented the modern game and several versions were known in the 1870s. In 1880 the Marylebone Cricket Club (governing body for real tennis) and the All-England Croquet Club (founder of the Wimbledon tennis championships) published a standard set of rules broadly similar to those used today. The present world governing body for tennis is The International Tennis Federation (ITF), founded in 1912 as the International Lawn Tennis Federation (ILTF). Tennis was an Olympic sport from 1896–1924, and is to return as a demonstration sport in the Olympics of 1984 and as a regular Olympic sport from 1988. The four most important tournaments today are: the All-England (Wimbledon),French, US, and Australian championships.

SYNOPSIS

Tennis is played with a racket and ball on a court divided by a net. It can be played by two people (singles) or four people (doubles). The object is to propel the ball over the net in such a way that it bounces in court and beats any attempt by an opponent to return it.

COURT AND EQUIPMENT

The court may be on grass, or have a variety of other surfaces including asphalt, clay, porous concrete, or a synthetic composition.

It comprises a rectangle 78ft long and 36ft wide and has markings for doubles and singles versions of the game. It is marked out with white lines that are included within the limits of the court. Except where the rules specify otherwise, lines are 1–2in wide.

The base lines (**a**), which may be 4in wide, and the doubles side lines (**b**) bound the ends and sides of the court. The singles side lines (**c**), 4ft 6in inside the doubles side lines, mark the side boundaries for the singles game and also the side service limits for doubles. Service lines (**d**), parallel to the net and 21ft from it, are drawn across the court between the singles side lines. A center service line (**e**), which must be 2in wide, divides the area between the service lines into service courts, termed left (**f**) and right (**g**) service courts. A center mark (**h**), which must be 2in wide and 4in long is drawn within the court area at right angles to the center of the base line.

The net is suspended from a cord or metal cable held over two posts, which must be 3ft 6in tall, no more than 6in square or 6in in diameter, and positioned 3ft outside the center of the doubles side lines. The side limits of the singles court may be indicated at the

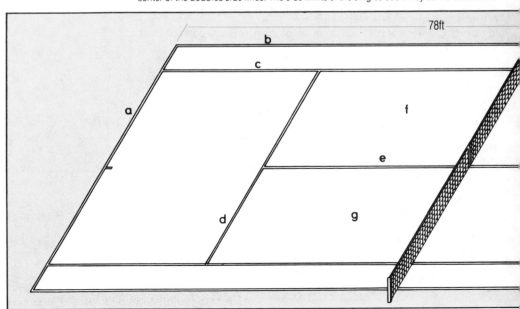

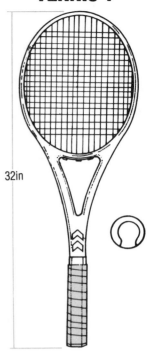

net by vertical sticks. The net must be 3ft high at the center, where it is kept taut by a white strap that must be no more than 2in wide.

The net must fill the entire area between the posts and must be of a sufficiently fine mesh to prevent the ball passing through. A white band at the top of the net covers the cord or cable and must extend 2–2½in down on each side of the net.

The racket must be not more than 32in long and 12½in wide; maximum dimensions for the strung hitting surface are 15½in long and 11½in wide. The hitting surface must consist of crossed strings connected to the frame and alternately interlaced or bonded where they cross; the stringing pattern must be generally uniform and in particular not less dense in the center. The racket may have no device enabling a player to change its shape materially. Attachments or protrusions are limited to those used solely and specifically to limit or prevent wear or tear or vibration, or to distribute weight, and must be reasonable in size and placement for such purposes.

Balls are now usually yellow, but may be white. The outer surface must be uniform, and if there are any seams they must be stitchless.

Balls must be 2½–2⅝in in diameter, and must weigh 2–2¹/₁₆oz. They must bounce between 4ft 5in and 4ft 10in when dropped 8ft 4in onto a concrete base. There are also detailed deformation regulations.

Dress Men wear shirts and shorts. Women wear short dresses, or tops with skirts and shorts. On their feet, players wear white rubber-soled shoes.

PLAYERS AND OFFICIALS

Players Some tournaments are for amateurs or professionals only, others are open to both. Events are men's singles, men's doubles, women's singles, women's doubles, and mixed doubles.

Officials Except in the most important tournaments, there is usually only one umpire, who sits on a high chair to one side of the net. Players assist him by calling whether balls fall in or out of court. Top-class matches now often use a six-umpire system, with:

1) a stationary chair umpire, who can overrule decisions by the other umpires;
2) two stationary base-line umpires;
3) two moving "center to side" line umpires;
4) a "jump" service-line umpire.

If a referee has been appointed, appeals can be made to him over umpires' decisions on matters of law. In such cases the referee's decision is final. If, as in some team matches, a referee is on court, he has the power to change any umpire's decision and to instruct an umpire to order a let.

32in

2½–2⅝in

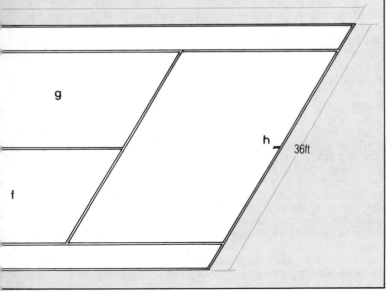

g

h

36ft

f

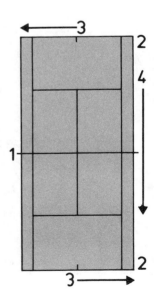

©DIAGRAM

TENNIS 2

RULES OF PLAY

Duration A match lasts a maximum of five sets for men (although three is more common except in major tournaments), and three for women or mixed doubles. In a five-set match, play ends when one player or pair has won three sets. In a three-set match, play ends when one side has won two sets. (See also Scoring, p. 374.)

Play is continuous from the first service until the end of the match, except that after the third set in men's matches and the second set in women's matches players are entitled to a rest of up to 10 minutes (or up to 45 minutes in Equatorial countries).

A maximum of 30 seconds is allowed after the end of one point and before the next service, except that when changing ends this maximum is increased to 1min 30sec.

If the chair umpire considers factors outside the control of the players are interfering with play, he may suspend play for as long as he considers necessary.

Play may never be suspended to allow a player to recover his strength or breath, or to receive advice.

Choice of ends and service is decided by tossing a coin or spinning a racket. Calls when a racket is spun are either "Rough" or "Smooth" (referring to which side of the racket stringing is uppermost), or alternatively "Up" or "Down" (referring to printing on the end of the racket handle).

The player winning the toss may choose, or require his opponent to choose:

a) the right to serve or receive first, in which case the other player chooses ends; or

b) the end at which he wishes to start play, in which case the other player chooses to serve or receive first.

Change of ends Players change ends at the end of the first, third, and every alternate game in a set.

Players change ends at the end of a set only if the total number of games in that set is an odd number. If the number is even the change is after the first game of the new set.

If a mistake in ends is made, players must take up their correct position as soon as the mistake is discovered; any score stands.

Coaching Players are not permitted to receive coaching or advice during a match, except that in team competitions players may while changing ends (other than during a tiebreak) receive instructions from a team captain sitting on the court.

Change of balls If balls are to be changed after an agreed number of games and the change does not take place, balls should then be changed when the player or pair who should have served with the new balls is next due to serve.

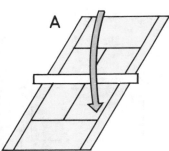

A

Serving order (singles) A player retains the right to serve for an entire game, after which it passes to his opponent.

For the first point in a game, the server must serve from behind his right-hand court (**A**). For subsequent points in the game he serves alternately from the left (**B**) and the right. A service must always direct the ball into the diagonally opposite service court.

Service order (doubles) As in singles, players serve for an entire game at a time and must serve into the diagonally opposite service court.

At the start of each set, players within each pair decide which of them is to serve and which of them is to receive first.

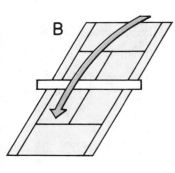

B

1) For the first game, the first server of the pair with the right to serve (**a**) serves for alternate points from behind his right and left courts, serving to each of his opponents (**x,y**) in turn.

2) For the second game, the two pairs change ends. The first server of the second pair (**x**) then serves for.alternate points from behind his right and left courts, serving to each of his opponents (**a,b**) in turn.

3) For the third game, the second server of the first pair (**b**) serves for alternate points from behind his right and left courts, serving to each of his opponents in turn, starting with whichever player received first in the first game (**x**).

4) For the fourth game, the two pairs again change ends. The second server of the second pair (**y**) then serves for alternate points from behind his right and left courts, serving to each of his opponents in turn, starting with whichever player received first in the second game (**a**).

For subsequent games in the set, service passes from player to player in accordance with the sequence outlined above for the first four games.

Error in service order If a player serves out of turn and the error is noticed while a game is in progress, the score stands as it is but the player who should have been serving must take over at once.

If an error in service order is noticed after a game has been completed, the score stands and the service order remains as altered.

A fault served before an error in service order is noticed is to be ignored.

If a server serves from behind his wrong court, all play stands but the server must resume serving from the correct station as soon as the mistake is discovered.

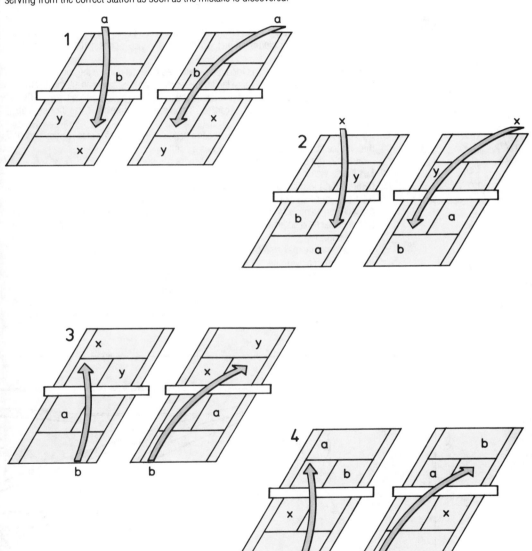

TENNIS 3

1

The service (**1**) Immediately before serving, the server must stand with both feet motionless behind the base line and within imaginary continuations of the center mark and the appropriate side line.

For the service he must throw the ball into the air and then strike it with the racket before it hits the ground. Throughout delivery of the service he must not change his position by walking or running, nor touch with either foot any area other than that behind the base line within the imaginary continuations of the center mark and side line. Delivery of the service is considered to be completed at the moment the racket strikes the ball.

For a good service the ball must cross the net without bouncing, and pitch into the service court diagonally opposite (**2**). The lines bounding that court are part of its area.

If after a correct delivery the ball clears the net and then touches the receiver, or anything that he wears or carries, before hitting the ground, the service is considered good and the server wins the point.

Service fault If the service is incorrectly delivered or lands outside the correct service court, a fault is recorded. It is also a fault if the server misses the ball in an attempt to strike it, or if the ball after being served and before touching the ground touches the server's partner or anything that he wears or carries, or a permanent fixture other than the net, strap, or band.

If a fault is recorded, a second service is permitted from the same side of the center mark. If this service is also a fault, the server loses a point.

A fault may not be claimed once the next service has been delivered.

Let If a service is correctly delivered but the ball then touches the net, strap, or band (**3**) before falling into the correct service court, a "let" is called.

A let on service also occurs if the ball is served before the receiver is ready, except that if the receiver attempts to play the ball he is judged to have been ready for it. (If the receiver signifies that he is not ready he cannot then claim a fault if the ball lands outside the correct service court.)

The chair umpire may also call a let at any time: if it is necessary to provide for an interruption in play; if there is insufficient evidence for a point to be awarded; or if a player's stroke is hindered either by the involuntary action of an opponent or by anything else outside his control other than a permanent court fixture.

If a let is called solely with regard to a service, then that one service (first or second) is to be replayed. If a let is called under any other circumstances, then that point is to be replayed.

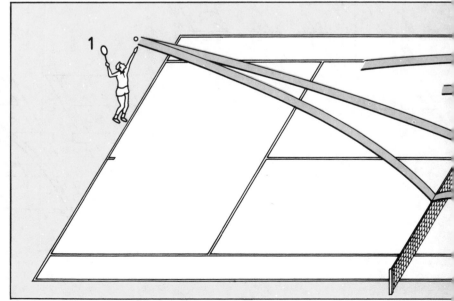

1

Ball in play The ball is in play from the moment the racket strikes the ball in service until the point being played is decided. Each such period of play is termed a "rally."

Returning the ball In singles, the players must strike the ball alternately. In doubles, the ball must be struck alternately by a player from each pair; partners must not strike the ball consecutively.

Before returning the ball after a service, the receiver must wait until it bounces once. All subsequent returns in a rally may be made either before the ball bounces (a "volley") (**4**) or after the ball has bounced once (**5**).

If the ball bounces outside the court area and is then returned, the point is awarded against the player who sent it out. If the ball would have bounced outside the court area but is volleyed before it does so, the fact that it would have gone out is ignored.

If the ball in play touches a permanent fixture – other than the net or related fixtures – after it has hit the ground, the striker wins the point. If it touches the fixture before hitting the ground, the striker's opponent wins the point.

If during a return the ball touches the net or fixtures related to it and then passes over them to land within the limits of the court, the return counts as good.

It is also a good return if a player returns the ball outside a post or singles stick, either above or below the top of the net, even though it touches the post or singles stick, provided that it hits the ground within the correct court.

Provided that a player strikes the ball on his own side of the net, it does not matter if his racket passes over the net during the follow through to the stroke.

If the ball in play lands in the correct area but then rebounds or is blown back over the net, the player who is next due to strike it may reach over the net to play the ball, provided that neither he nor his dress or racket touches the net, any fixture related to the net, or the ground within his opponent's court.

A player is permitted to return a ball that strikes another ball lying in his court.

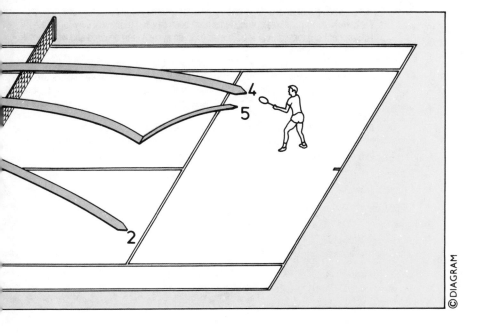

TENNIS 4

SCORING

Points A player scores a point if:

a) when serving, he correctly delivers the ball in a service that is not a let and the ball then touches his opponent, or anything that his opponent wears or carries, before it touches the ground;

b) when receiving, his opponent serves two consecutive faults (a "double" fault);

c) his opponent fails to hit a correctly served or returned ball before it bounces twice;

d) his opponent fails to return the ball directly into the correct court (it must not first hit the ground or an object outside the correct court or a fixture other than the net and related fixtures);

e) his opponent volleys the ball and fails to make a good return even if he is standing outside the court limits;

f) his opponent volleys the ball before it has passed the net;

g) his opponent in playing the ball deliberately carries or catches it on his racket, or deliberately touches it with his racket more than once;

h) his opponent throws his racket and hits the ball with it;

i) the ball in play touches his opponent or anything that his opponent is wearing or carrying other than his racket in his hand or hands;

j) while the ball is in play, his opponent or his opponent's racket (in his hand or not) or anything that his opponent is wearing or carrying touches the net or its related fixtures or the court not on his own side of the net;

k) he is hindered while making a stroke by a deliberate action from his opponent.

Game A game is made up of points, and is scored as follows.

Each player or pair begins a game with no score ("love"). The first point that a side wins is scored as 15. If the other side then scores a point it is called "15-all." A side's second point brings its score to 30, a third point brings it to 40, and a fourth point wins the game unless there is a "deuce," which is called at 40-all.

After deuce, the next point won is scored as "advantage" to the side that won it. If the side with the advantage then wins the next point, it wins the game. However, if the opposing side wins the next point the score returns to deuce; the game then continues until one side wins two consecutive points after a deuce.

Set and match A match is the best of three or of five sets (see Duration, p. 370). A set is won by a player or pair who wins six games with a lead of at least two games over the opposing player or pair.

If one side wins six games but does not have a two-game lead, players continue playing more games either until such a lead is obtained or until the introduction of a tiebreak.

Tiebreak Various tiebreak procedures have been devised to prevent very long sets. Tournament organizers decide beforehand which system is to be used and when it is to come into operation.

All tournaments sanctioned by the ITF or the United States Tennis Association (USTA) use the "7-of-12" tiebreak described here, which operates when the score reaches six-all in a set. It is not usual for a tiebreak to be used in the third set of a three-set match or in a fifth set of a five-set match, unless otherwise decided and announced in advance of the match.

After the introduction of a tiebreak, the winner of each rally scores one point. The set is won by the first player to score seven points with a two-point lead. If the score reaches six-all, play continues until one side establishes a two-point lead.

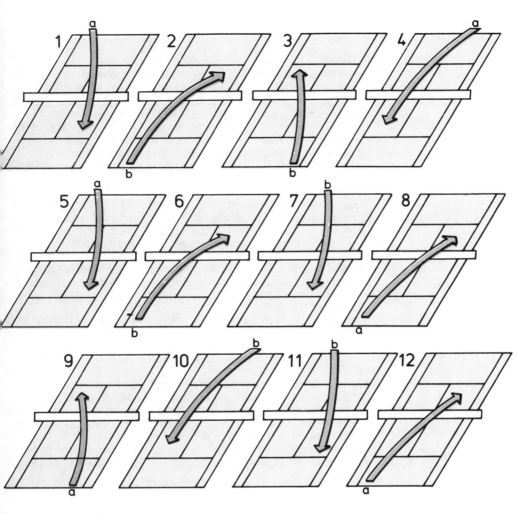

Service during tiebreak Order of service during a singles tiebreak is as follows. For the first point, player (**a**) serves from behind his right court. For the second point, player (**b**) serves from behind his left court. For the third point, player (**b**) serves from the right. The fourth and fifth points are served for by player (**a**), from the left and from the right. The sixth point is served for by player (**b**) from the left.

After the sixth point the players change ends. Player (**b**) then serves from the right for the seventh point. Player (**a**) serves for the eighth (left) and ninth (right) points. Player (**b**) serves for the tenth (left) and eleventh (right) points. Player (**a**) serves from the left for the twelfth point.

If the score is equal at six-all, players again change ends and the order of service is as from the beginning of the tiebreak.

In a doubles tiebreak the order of service is basically similar, with partners following the sequence of their serving turns. Except for the first server, players serve twice consecutively, first from the left and then from the right.

Penalty points In some tournaments the umpire is empowered to impose point penalties for time violations or for unsportsmanlike conduct (visible or audible obscenity or profanity, abuse of equipment. abuse of an official). For a first offense the player receives a warning, for a second offense he loses the next point in the game, for a third offense he loses the game in progress or the next game if play is not in progress, for a fourth offense he loses the match.

Financial penalties may be imposed for unsportsmanlike conduct by professionals.

TENPIN BOWLING

HISTORY
Target games involving throwing a ball at a target of pins or skittles have a long history dating back to ancient Egypt. Much later, European settlers took skittles games to North America, and it was in the USA in the nineteenth century that the modern competitive sport of tenpin bowling developed. Centers were built in many US cities during the course of the century, but not until after the formation of the American Bowling Congress (ABC) in 1895 was there any standardization of rules and equipment. Tenpin bowling remained an essentially US sport until the middle of the present century, when it began to acquire popularity elsewhere. Since 1961 the ABC has been affiliated to the Fédération Internationale des Quilleurs (FIQ), an international organization covering several different bowling games.

SYNOPSIS
Tenpin bowling may be played by individuals or on a team basis. Players roll a heavy ball along a lane with the aim of knocking down ten pins that are positioned in a triangle at the end of the lane. Points are scored for pins knocked down, and the winner is the player or team that scores most points.

PLAYING AREA AND EQUIPMENT
The lane is made of wood or approved synthetic substances. It measures 60ft (plus or minus ½in) from the foul line (**a**) at one end to the center of the number 1 pin spot (**b**). The total length of the lane, from the foul line to the pit behind the pins, is 62ft 10³/₁₆in. The width of the lane is 41–42in.

Gutters (**c**) run along both sides of the lane. They are 9–9½in wide; the total width of the lane and the gutters must be 60–60¼in. The gutters must be 3½–3¾in deep at the pit. The approach (**d**) must be clear and level for a minimum of 15ft, leading up to the foul line. The foul line is marked by a line ³/₈–1in wide. Some establishments have automatic foul judging apparatus.

Markings to help aim are permitted at set points along the approach and lane.

Pin spots are marked on the pin deck (**e**) at the far end of the lane. Each spot is 2¼in in diameter. The spots are spaced 12in apart to form a triangle with the number 1 pin in the center at the front. The other pin spots and the pins standing on them are known by the numbers shown in the diagram (opposite page).

The pit is immediately behind the pin deck. On either side are raised side partitions or kickbacks, 17–24in higher than the level of the pin deck. At the back of the pit is the rear cushion.

The pins are made of wood or synthetic material. They must be 15in high, conform to detailed circumference specifications, and weigh not more than 3lb 10oz. The pins are placed on the pin spots, usually by a mechanical pinsetting device.

Balls are made of a non-metallic composition material. They must be solid and have a smooth surface. There are finger holes for gripping. Balls must not exceed 27in in circumference and 16lb in weight.

60ft

Dress Approved team uniforms are compulsory at international tournaments.
Competitors must not wear shoes that might damage or mark the floor surface.

COMPETITORS AND OFFICIALS

Competitors There are men's and women's events for individuals, doubles, and teams.
ABC team championships are for teams of five. World championships, under FIQ rules,
have events for teams of three and five.

Officials Tournament organizers appoint official scorers.
In establishments without automatic foul judging equipment, a foul judge is required to
watch whether competitors cross the foul line.

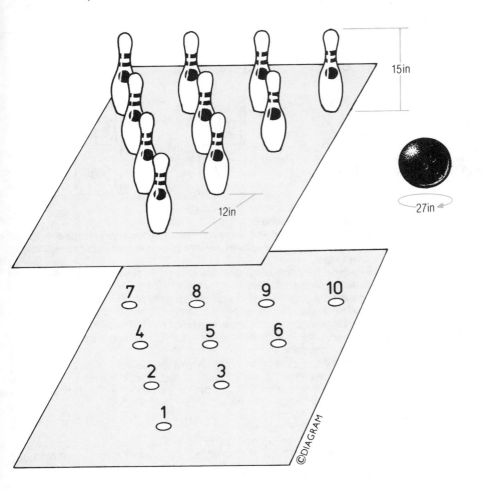

15in

12in

27in

7 8 9 10
4 5 6
2 3
1

©DIAGRAM

b
e

41–42in

TENPIN BOWLING 2

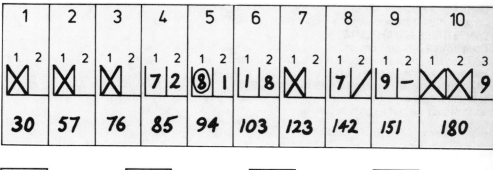

1	2	3	4	5	6	7	8	9	10
X	X	X	7 2	⑧ 1	1 8	X	7 /	9 –	X X 9
30	57	76	85	94	103	123	142	151	180

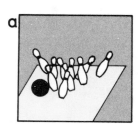

a   1   X   30

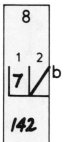

8   7 / b   142

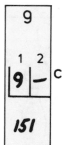

9   9 – c   151

d   5   ⑧ 1   94

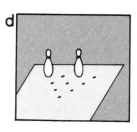

DURATION AND SCORING

Duration A game consists of 10 frames. Each player bowls twice in a frame, except that:
a) in any but the last frame he bowls only once if he knocks down all the pins with his first ball (a strike);
b) in the last frame he bowls a total of three balls if all the pins are down after he has bowled his first or second ball.

Scoring One point is scored for every pin legally bowled down; bonuses are scored for knocking down all the pins (a strike or a spare).

We illustrate a typical scoresheet, with sections for each of the 10 frames. Within each section are small boxes in which the score for each ball is indicated. Below these boxes is a space for the running total.

A strike is scored when a player knocks down all the pins with the first ball of a frame (**a**). A strike scores 10 points, plus the score from the next two balls bowled.

A strike is indicated on the scoresheet by a cross in the left-hand small box (**a**); the score for the frame is written in after the next two balls have been bowled.

If a player bowls two strikes in succession it is called a double. Three strikes in succession are called a triple or a turkey.

To achieve the maximum score of 300 for a game, a player must knock all the pins down 12 times (with the first ball in all 10 frames, and then with the two extra balls in frame 10).

A spare is scored when the player does not bowl down all the pins with the first ball of a frame, but when his second ball either knocks down all the pins or knocks down any pins that remained standing after his first ball. A spare scores 10 points plus the score from the next ball bowled.

A spare is indicated on the scoresheet by a diagonal line in the right-hand small box for that frame (**b**).

An error is committed if any pins remain standing after the second ball of a frame, provided that the pins left standing after the first ball did not constitute a split.

An error is indicated on the scoresheet by a dash in that frame's right-hand small box (**c**).

A split occurs when, after the first ball has been delivered, the headpin (number 1) has been knocked down and at least one pin is down either between or just ahead of two or more pins that remain standing (**d**).

A split may be indicated on the scoresheet with any symbol; most usually an 0 is drawn around the number entered in that frame's left-hand small box (**d**).

378

RULES OF PLAY

Bowling Players take turns to bowl, bowling one or two complete frames at each turn depending on competition rules.

Games are played on two adjacent lanes, alternating frame by frame.

Balls must be delivered entirely manually; an underarm action is used. A ball is judged delivered once it leaves the bowler's possession and crosses the foul line.

Fouls No part of the bowler may touch or cross the foul line (**e**), even after he has sent the ball down the lane. The foul judge or automatic foul-detecting device will signal a foul if the line is touched or crossed, or if the player touches any part of the lane, building, or equipment.

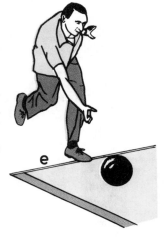

A foul is counted as a ball bowled, but any pins that are knocked down are not scored. If a player fouls when delivering the first ball of a frame, the pins are reset before the second ball. If all the pins are then knocked down, it counts as a spare. If they are not, it counts as an error. If a foul is committed on the second ball of a frame, only the pins knocked down by a legally delivered first ball are scored.

Wrong lane If a lane error in singles play is noticed after only one player has bowled on the wrong lane, a dead ball is declared and the player must bowl from the correct lane. If the error is noticed only after another player has bowled, the scores stand and the correct lanes must be used for subsequent frames.

If a lane error in doubles or team play is noticed after only one player or both lead players from two teams have played, the ball is declared dead and players must rebowl on the correct lanes. If the error is noticed at a later stage, the game is completed without adjustment and the correct lanes are used for subsequent games.

Dead ball If a dead ball is declared, the last ball does not count, the pins are respotted, and the player must bowl again with the cause of the dead ball removed.

A dead ball is declared if:

a) immediately after a player has delivered a ball, attention is called to the fact that one or more pins were missing from the setup;

b) a human pinsetter removes or interferes with a pin or pins before the ball reaches them or they stop moving;

c) a player bowls out of turn;

d) a player bowls on the wrong lane (in some circumstances only, see above);

e) there is any interference to a player during the delivery of a ball, and the player immediately asks for a rebowl;

f) any pins are moved or knocked down as the player is delivering the ball and before the ball reaches them;

g) the ball comes into contact with any foreign obstacle.

Dead wood Any pin that remains lying on the lane, in the gutters, or leaning against the side partitions is termed dead wood. All dead wood must be removed before a delivery.

Legal pinfall Any ball that is not declared a dead ball counts as a ball bowled. A pinfall is legal and points are scored even if:

a) pins are knocked down by another pin rebounding in play from the rear cushion, side partition, or sweep bar;

b) it is discovered after a ball is delivered that the pins were not properly set although not missing.

Illegal pinfall A ball counts as a ball bowled but the pinfall is illegal and no score is made if:

a) a foul is committed during the delivery;

b) pins are knocked down by a ball that leaves the lane before reaching the pins;

c) a ball rebounds from the rear cushion;

d) pins rebound after hitting a human pinsetter;

e) pins are bowled off the lane but then rebound and remain standing on the lane;

f) a standing pin falls when touched by mechanical pinsetting equipment, by a human pinsetter, or when dead wood is removed.

TRACK AND FIELD ATHLETICS

HISTORY

Many of the events staged in a modern athletics meeting would be recognizable to the ancient Greek participants in the original series of Olympic Games, or the other regularly staged contests between the men of the city states. In addition to the simple running races, the Greeks at various times held events for throwing the javelin and the discus, and for long jumping.

Competitive running remained popular at a local level in many societies, but the modern revival of athletics meetings at all levels up to international began in the schools and universities of nineteenth century Britain, before spreading to the USA and mainland Europe. The great landmark of this revival was the first of the modern Olympic games, held at Athens in 1896. Despite the addition of so many other sports to the program, athletics continues to be regarded as the essential core of the Olympics. The international governing body for the sport, the International Amateur Athletic Federation, was formed in 1912.

SYNOPSIS

Athletic events are divided into two broad categories – track and field. Track events include the running, hurdling, and walking races; the field events embrace the various throwing and jumping contests. The variety of competitions provides opportunities for men and women of differing physiques, and offers spectators a spectacle of great variety and interest.

The heptathlon and decathlon programs call for a combination of skills from each participant, as they comprise a whole range of events.

GENERAL RULES

Dress Clothing must be clean, non-transparent even when wet, and designed and worn so as not to cause offense.

Competitors must wear a number as given in the program. The number must be worn both on the front and the back in all events except the high jump and pole vault, when it may be displayed either on the front or the back.

Footwear Competitors may compete in bare feet or wearing one or two shoes.

Styles of footwear vary between events, but all are governed by certain general rules. A maximum of six spikes in the sole and two in the heel is specified for all events except

Track races

Sprints (**a**)
100m
200m
400m
Middle distance
800m
1500m
Long distance
3000m**
5000m*
10,000m*
Relays (**b**)
4 × 100m
4 × 400m
Hurdles (**c**)
100m**
110m*
400m
Steeplechase (**d**)
3000m*

Road races

Marathon (**e**)
Walks (**f**)
20km*
50km*

*Men only
**Women only

high jump and javelin, when four spikes may be worn in the heel. In these events the spikes may project up to 12mm from the sole or heel if an all-weather synthetic surface is in use.
In other events on such a surface the spikes may not project more than 9mm.
The sole may not exceed 13mm in thickness, and the heel may not exceed the thickness of the sole by more than 13mm for walking events or 6mm for all others.
The sole and/or heel may be formed with integral ridges or protruberances provided the total thickness at any point does not exceed the above limits.

Assistance Except as provided for in the rules of the marathon or long distance walking events, no competitor may receive any assistance, including advice or information, from any person.
No official or other person may indicate any intermediate timing to a competitor without the prior approval of the referee.

Doping The use of certain prohibited substances, which might artificially improve an athlete's physical and/or mental condition and thus his or her athletic performance, is strictly forbidden.
Refusal to submit to a doping test when formally required to do so by the responsible officials will result in disqualification.

Timing Fully automatic electric timekeeping is used for the Olympic Games and other major meetings; otherwise manual timekeeping by personnel with stopwatches may be used.
Times are taken from the flash of the starter's pistol to the moment when the competitor's torso reaches the finish line.
For all hand-timed races held on the track, the competitors' times are returned to one tenth of a second.
Fully automatic electric timing is to one hundredth of a second for all races up to 10,000m inclusive. For longer races up to 20km, timing is to one-tenth of a second.
Fractions of a unit of time are rounded up to the next whole unit, as specified above for the event in question.
Any electric timekeeping system used must be fully automatic.

Olympic events Events to be included in the 1984 Olympic program are listed in the tables.

Throwing events
Javelin (**g**)
Discus (**h**)
Hammer (**i**)*
Shot (**j**)
Jumping events
Long jump (**k**)
Triple jump (**l**)*
High jump (**m**)
Pole vault (**n**)*
Combined events
Heptathlon**
Decathlon*

*Men only
**Women only

TRACK AND FIELD ATHLETICS 2

COMPETITION AREAS

Arena The illustration shows the layout of a typical modern arena intended for track and field athletics, with a running track encircling the special areas for the jumping and throwing events.

Any stadium used for major international events now has a synthetic, all-weather surface to the track and run-up areas; cinder tracks may still be used for lesser meetings.

The maximum permitted inclination of the track and run-up areas is 1 in 100 in the lateral direction and 1 in 1000 downward in the direction of running.

Running track The straight stretch in the foreground of our diagram is used for 100m sprints and 100m and 110m hurdle events, and is divided into lanes 1.22m wide.

The circuit is used for events of 200m distance and over. It also is divided into lanes 1.22m wide for use in 200m, 400m, and 800m races. In these events, staggered start positions are needed to equalize the distance run by competitors in each lane.

Races of 1500m to 10,000m distance are run on the circuit but not in lanes; curved start lines are used to remove any advantage in being at the inside end of the start line.

All races are run with the competitor's left hand toward the center of the circuit.

Start lines and finish line		**Other features**	
a) 10,000m	**f)** 5000m	**1)** water jump for steeplechase	**5)** triple jump
b) 800m	**g)** 200m	**2)** pole vault	**6)** javelin
c) 400m	**h)** 110m hurdles	**3)** long jump	**7)** shot put
d) 1500m	**i)** 100m sprint and hurdles	**4)** hammer and discus	**8)** high jump
e) 3000m steeplechase	**j)** finish line for all races		

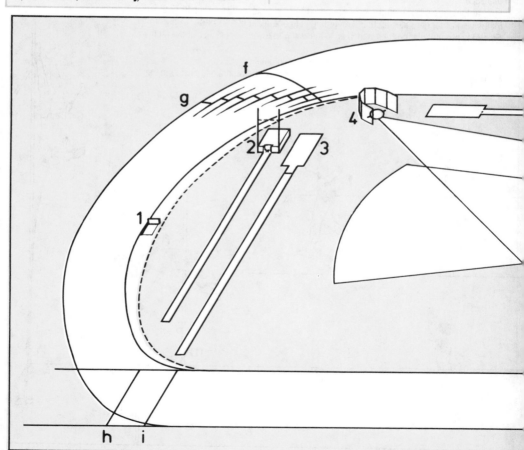

COMBINED EVENTS

Events The combined events are the decathlon for men, and the heptathlon for women. The decathlon consists of 10 events, held in the order listed in the table. Competition takes place over two days, with five events held on each day.

The heptathlon, which replaces the pentathlon, consists of seven events held over two days in the order listed in the table. Four events are held on the first day, and three on the second.

The order of competition is drawn before each event. Competitors are allowed at least 30 minutes between the end of one event and the beginning of the next.

Rules IAAF rules for individual events apply, except that competitors:

a) are allowed only three trials in the jumping and throwing events;

b) are disqualified after three false starts in any one of the track events.

A competitor who retires from any one event is considered to have withdrawn from the whole competition.

Scoring Points are scored for achieving set times, heights, and throwing distances, and are awarded on the basis of IAAF scoring tables. The competitor with the most points is the winner.

In a tie, the competitor with most points in the majority of events wins. If the tie remains, the competitor with the most points in any one event is the winner.

Decathlon
100m
Long jump
Shot put
High jump
400m
110m hurdles
Discus
Pole vault
Javelin
1500m

Heptathlon
100m hurdles
Shot put
High jump
200m
Long jump
Javelin
800m

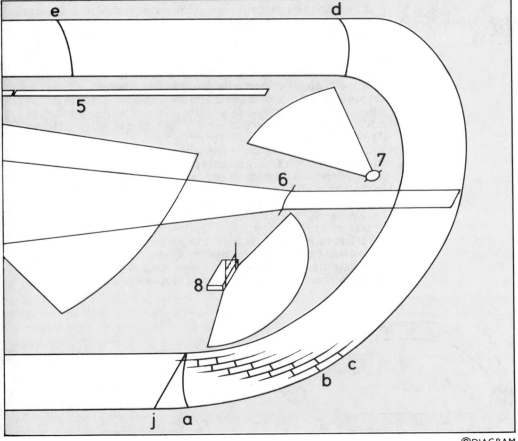

383

TRACK (RUNNING EVENTS)

SYNOPSIS

The essence of all individual running events is that the first competitor to reach the finish line is the winner. The rules for the races over the various distances, however, differ as to the part of the track used, and the allowance or prohibition of starting blocks.

Relay races are team running events. Each team member carries a baton for one set portion of the course and then hands it to the next member.

GENERAL RULES

Starting blocks may be used in the 100m, 200m, and 400m sprints, and by the first runner of each team in the 4×100m and 4×400m relays. The blocks are used to assist a smooth and powerful start.

The apparatus consists of a central rack along which two blocks can be attached at any point. The blocks themselves are adjustable for angle, but once adjusted they must be rigid. They must be without springs or any other device for giving artificial assistance.

Heats It may be necessary to hold preliminary heats to reduce the number of competitors who will take part in the final to the number of lanes available. The number of competitors who go through from each heat, and the number of rounds required depend on the number of entries. The heats are arranged so that the acknowledged best runners will normally reach the final. Only in circumstances approved by the referee may a competitor take part in a heat other than that in which his or her name appears in the program.

The start The location of the start lines for the various races is given on p .382.

In the events where starting blocks are required the orders given by the starter are "On your marks" and "Set," and the postures assumed by the competitors are as shown at (**1a**) and (**1b**) respectively. Both hands must be touching the ground.

In other races only "On your marks" is given, and the posture assumed is as shown at (**2**). The signal for starting is the firing of a pistol or similar device upward into the air. The pistol is not fired until all competitors are steady in the correct position.

False starts It is a false start if a competitor either fails after a reasonable time to comply with the order "Set," or starts before the pistol is fired.

The runners are recalled by a second pistol shot and the offender warned. Disqualification follows a second offense, or a third in the heptathlon or decathlon.

Use of lanes In the 100m, 200m, and 400m events, competitors must keep to their allocated lanes from start to finish. In the 800m (**3**), runners must stay in their lanes from the start (**a**) until they reach the curved line of denouement (**b**) at the beginning of the back straight. They may then maneuver for position at the inside edge of the track.

384

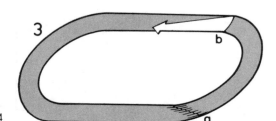

10m

The 1500m, 5000m, and 10,000m events are not run in lanes.
(For use of lanes in relays, see below.)

Finish (4) Competitors are placed in the order in which any part of their torso (as distinct from the head, neck, arms, legs, hands, or feet) reaches the vertical plane of the edge of the finish line that is nearer to the start. Thus (**a**) beats (**b**) in our illustration.

Ties In a tie for first place in a final, the referee decides whether it is practicable for those tying to run again.
If a tie in a heat affects qualification for the next round, the tying competitors run again only if it is impracticable for both to qualify.
All other tied results stand.

RELAY RACES

Teams consists of four runners, each of whom may run only one stage in the race.
Under IAAF rules, six athletes may be nominated for the relay team, and any four of those nominated may run in any round. Team members may run in any order.

The baton is a smooth hollow tube made of one piece of rigid material, 280–300mm long and 120–130mm in circumference. It must weigh not less than 50g. If dropped, it must be recovered by the runner who dropped it.

Starting and lanes In both the 4×100m and 4×400m relays the runner of the first stage must use starting blocks, and the starting procedure followed is as detailed above. The 4×100m relay is run entirely in lanes. The 4×400m is run in lanes until the end of the first bend of the second lap (ie the lap of the second runner in each team).

The takeover (5) The baton must be handed over to the next runner within the takeover zone. The takeover zone is marked by lines placed 10m before (**a**) and 10m after (**c**) the scratch line (**b**). The runner about to receive the baton must not start running more than 10m before the takeover zone.
In the stages of the 4×400m not in lanes, competitors must return to their own lanes for the takeover unless they can use the inside position without causing an obstruction.
After handing over the baton, competitors should remain in their lanes or zones until the course is clear.
Teams will be disqualified for deliberately causing an obstruction or for pushing or giving any other assistance at a takeover.

280–300mm

120–130mm

5

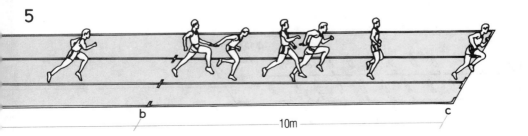

b

c

10m

TRACK (HURDLES)

SYNOPSIS

Hurdle events are sprints in which the competitor must also jump over a series of ten barriers or hurdles.

The Olympic program includes 110m and 400m hurdles for men, and 100m hurdles for women.

In addition the decathlon includes a 110m hurdles race and the heptathlon a 100m hurdles.

EQUIPMENT

The hurdles (A) are of metal with the top bar of wood. They are designed so that a force of 3.6–4kg applied to the center of the top edge is required to make them topple forward. Adjustable weights are fitted to the base so that the balance of the hurdle can be regulated. The height of the hurdles for each event is as follows:

1) 0.840m for 100m (women);
2) 1.067m for 110m (men);
3) 0.914m for 400m (men).

Location of hurdles The positioning of the ten hurdles on the track varies in each event. In the 100m event (**1**) the first hurdle is 13m from the start line, the interval between the hurdles is 8.5m, and there is a gap of 10.5m between the last hurdle and the finish line. In the 110m event (**2**) the first hurdle is 13.72m from the start line, the hurdles are 9.14m apart, and the last one is 14.02m from the finish line.

In the 400m event (**3**) the first hurdle is 45m from the start line (**a**), the hurdles are 35m apart, and the last one is 40m from the finish line (**b**).

SPECIAL RULES

Disqualification A hurdler will be disqualified for trailing a foot or leg alongside any hurdle, deliberately knocking down any hurdle with hand or foot, or jumping any hurdle not in his or her own lane.

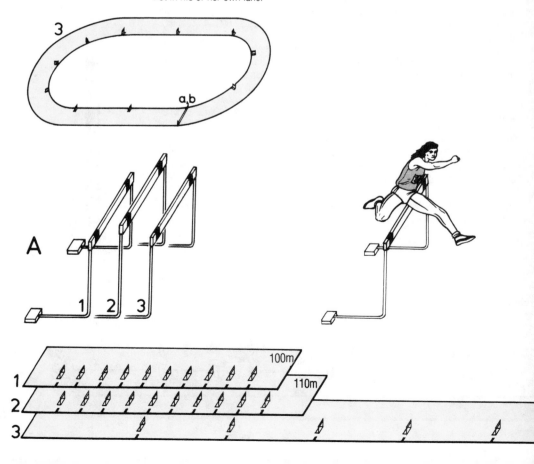

TRACK (STEEPLECHASE)

SYNOPSIS
The Olympic steeplechase is a men's event run over 3000m. It includes 28 hurdle jumps and seven water jumps. Competitors may jump, vault, or step on any of the hurdles. It is not run in lanes.

EQUIPMENT
The hurdles (B) for steeplechase are much heavier and more stable than those for other hurdle events. The top bar is 127mm square in section, strong enough for competitors to step on, and a minimum of 3.96m long. The top edge is 0.914m above the track. The base projects on both sides and is 1.2–1.4m wide. Each hurdle weighs 80–100kg.

The water jump (C) is a permanent feature, usually positioned inside the running circuit on a special curved section of track. It has a fixed hurdle 0.914m high, beyond which is the water jump, 3.66m square (inclusive of the hurdle). The water is 0.7m deep at the end nearer to the hurdle; the bottom slopes upward in the direction of running and is covered at the farther end with matting at least 2.5m long and about 25mm thick.

Location of hurdles (4) The start (**a**), finish (**b**), movable hurdles (**c,d,e,f**), and water jump (**g**) are positioned as shown on the diagram. Movable hurdles are placed so that 0.3m of the top bar overhangs the inside edge of the track; the hurdles thus lie across the inner three lines of the track. Two hurdles (**e,f**) are put in position after the runners have passed those points on the first lap. The runners negotiate the water jump for the first time on the second lap.

SPECIAL RULES
Disqualification A steeplechaser will be disqualified if he steps to either side of a jump, fails to go over or through the water, or trails a foot or leg alongside any hurdle.

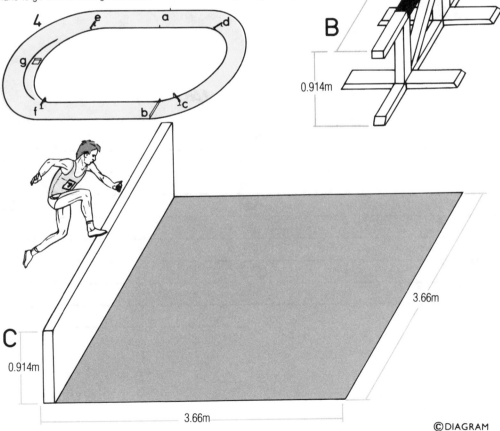

3.96m

B

0.914m

C

0.914m

3.66m

3.66m

©DIAGRAM

400m

ROAD RACES (MARATHON)

SYNOPSIS
The marathon is an individual running event 42.195km long. The start and finish are usually in the arena, but the rest of the race is run on metaled roads.

SPECIAL RULES
The course must be marked, and the distance in miles and kilometers displayed on the route. If circumstances require, the course may be on a bicycle path or footpath alongside the road, but must never be on soft ground or grass.

Refreshment stations are provided by the organizers at intervals of 5km throughout the route. The refreshments may be those provided by the organizers or the athlete's own, and will be made available at the stations nominated by the competitor. The refreshments will be placed so that they are easily accessible, or may be put into the runner's hands.

Sponging points are placed midway between refreshment stations and offer water only.

Disqualification A competitor who takes refreshment other than at the official points is liable to disqualification.

Medical A competitor must retire from the race immediately if ordered to do so by an official member of the medical staff.

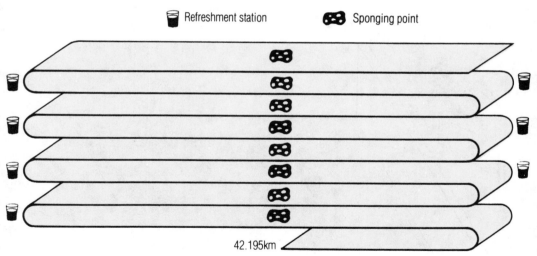

Refreshment station   Sponging point

42.195km

ROAD RACES (WALKS)

SYNOPSIS
In walking events competitors must maintain unbroken contact with the ground. The events currently included in the Olympic program are the 20km and 50km road walks, although at other meetings races may be held over shorter and longer distances and on a track.

SPECIAL RULES
Walking action To comply with the official definition of walking, the competitor's advancing foot must make contact with the ground before his rear foot leaves the ground. During the time in which the foot is on the ground, that leg must be momentarily straightened, including the moment when the leg is vertical.

The course For 20km races, at major meetings a circuit of between 1500m and 3000m is specified.

For races of more than 20km, refreshment stations are provided at intervals of 5km, where competitors may take their own refreshments or those supplied by the organizers. For races of 10km and over, sponging points may be provided at suitable intervals, depending on the weather conditions. At these points, water only is available.

Disqualification If a competitor's style of movement is in danger of failing to comply with the rules he may be cautioned once, when a white flag will be raised. A second offense results in disqualification, and a red flag is shown.

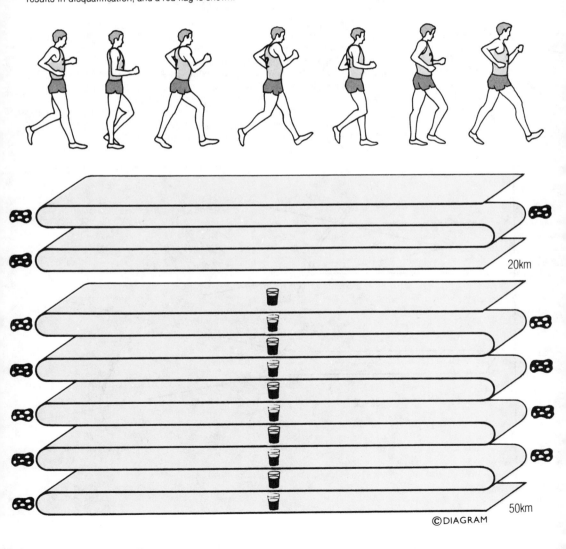

20km

50km

©DIAGRAM

FIELD (JAVELIN)

SYNOPSIS

The javelin is thrown from behind a curved line and must fall within a marked sector. If there are eight or fewer competitors, each one has six trials. If there are more than eight they have three trials, and the best eight then have three more. The competitor achieving the longest throw in his or her six trials is the winner.

COMPETITION AREA

The runway is 4m wide and between 30m and 36.5m long, and is marked out by white lines 50mm wide. The front edge (the throwing arc) is an arc of a circle with a radius of 8m, is 70mm wide, and may consist of a strip of wood or metal sunk flush with the ground, or a painted white line. From each end of the throwing arc, at right angles to the edge of the runway, is extended a line 70mm wide and 1.5m long.

The sector into which the javelin is thrown is bounded by two lines diverging from a point 8m behind the arc (ie the center of the circle of which the arc is a part), and each passing through one end of the arc.

Marks may be made on the sector lines at premeasured distances from the throwing arc, in order to facilitate the measurement of throws.

EQUIPMENT

The javelin consists of three parts: a shaft of wood or metal, a sharply pointed head, and a cord grip. It must have no mobile parts that might change its center of gravity or throwing characteristics during the throw.

The cord grip is placed at the center of gravity of the javelin, must be of uniform thickness, and must not increase the circumference of the shaft by more than 25mm (this implies the use of cord not more than 4mm thick).

Men use a longer and heavier javelin than women.

The men's javelin (**1**) weighs not less than 800g, is 2.6–2.7m long, and of 25–30mm diameter at the thickest point. The metal head is 250–330mm long, and its tip is 0.9–1.1m from the center of gravity. The grip is 150–160mm long.

The women's javelin (**2**) weighs not less than 600g, is 2.2–2.3m long, and of 20–25mm diameter at the thickest point. The metal head is 250–330mm long, and its tip is 0.8–0.95m from the center of gravity. The grip is 140–150mm long.

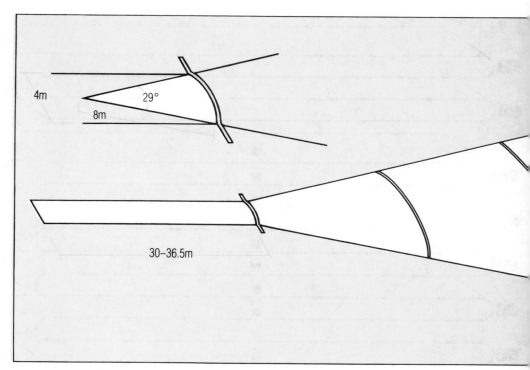

4m

29°

8m

30–36.5m

At major meetings such as Olympic Games, only javelins provided by the organizers may be used.

The hands Gloves are not permitted, but resin or a similar substance may be used to improve the grip. Tape may only be used to cover an open wound.

PROCEDURE

Preliminary Competitors draw lots to decide the order in which they take their trials. If practicable, each competitor may have up to two practice throws, on the competition area and under the judges' supervision, before the contest begins. Thereafter no-one may use the competition area for practice.

The run-up Markers may be placed alongside but not on the runway to help competitors judge their approach.

The throw The javelin must be held at the grip and thrown over the shoulder or upper part of the arm. It may not be slung or hurled, and in landing, the tip of the metal head must strike the ground before any other part of the javelin.

At no point between preparing to throw and releasing the javelin may the competitor turn his or her back toward the throwing arc.

The competitor may not leave the runway until the javelin has touched the ground, and must then leave it in a standing position from behind the line of the throwing arc and its extensions on either side.

Foul throws A throw is declared a foul and disallowed if the competitor touches, with any part of his or her body, the strip that marks the throwing arc or its extension lines or the ground beyond. It is also a foul if the javelin falls outside the sector lines, or fails to land point first. If the javelin breaks during a throw that is not a foul, it is not counted as one of the competitor's trials.

SCORING

Measurement Each throw is measured immediately, from the nearest mark made on the ground by the head of the javelin, to the inside edge of the throwing arc, on a line from the mark toward the center of the circle of which the arc is part.

Results Each competitor is credited with the best of all his or her throws, the winner being the one whose best is longer than anyone else's.

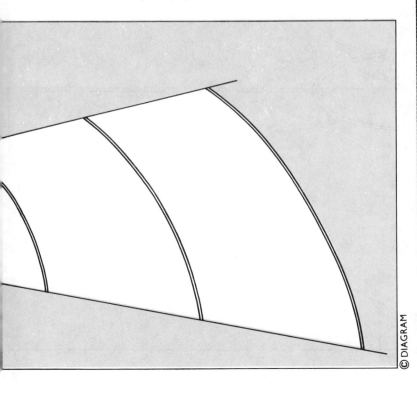

1

2

2 2–2.3m

2.6–2.7m

© DIAGRAM

FIELD (DISCUS)

SYNOPSIS

The discus is thrown from within a circle and must land in a marked-out sector of ground. If there are eight or fewer competitors, each one has six trials. If there are more than eight they have three trials, and the best eight then have three more. The competitor achieving the best throw in his or her six trials wins the event.

COMPETITION AREA

The circle is of 2.495–2.505m inside diameter, marked out by a metal band at least 6mm wide, sunk level with the surface of the ground outside it, and painted white.

The surface is of concrete, asphalt, or other firm, non-slip material, and is 14–26mm below the top edge of the metal band.

White lines, 50mm wide, are marked directly opposite each other on each side of the circle. These lines should extend at least 0.75m from the outside edge of the circle.

The sector into which the discus is thrown is defined by two lines 50mm wide diverging as from the center of the throwing circle at an angle of 40°, and the ends of which are marked by flags.

Safety cage To prevent any danger to spectators or officials from a mis-thrown discus, the throwing circle is surrounded on three sides by netting at least 4m high. The cage must be strong enough to stop a 2kg discus moving at up to 25m/sec. The opening at the mouth of the cage is 6m wide.

The competition areas for discus and hammer throwing can be superimposed so that only one safety cage is needed in the arena.

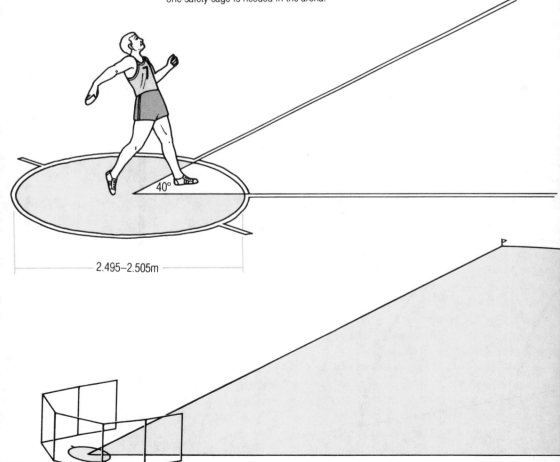

40°

2.495–2.505m

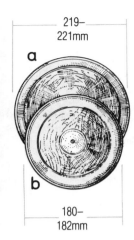

219–
221mm

a

b

180–
182mm

EQUIPMENT

The discus is of wood or other suitable material, with a rounded rim of metal. Both sides are exactly the same, with no sharp edges, indentations, or projections. The flat area in the center may be plain or with a metal disk let in, and is 50–57mm in diameter.

The men's discus (**a**) weighs at least 2kg and has an outside diameter of 219–221mm. It is 44–46mm thick at the flat center area.

The women's discus (**b**) weighs at least 1kg and is 180–182mm in diameter. It is 37–39mm thick at the center.

In both men's and women's types the rim is 12mm thick at 6mm from the outside edge.

In major meetings such as Olympic Games, only discuses provided by the organizers may be used.

The hands Gloves are not permitted, but resin or a similar substance may be used to improve the grip.

Tape may only be used to cover an open wound.

PROCEDURE

Preliminary Competitors draw lots to decide the order in which they take their trials.

If practicable, each competitor may have up to two practice throws, on the competition area and under the judges' supervision, before the competition begins. Thereafter no-one may use the competition area for practice.

The throw The competitor must begin from a stationary position, standing within the circle. The method of holding and throwing the discus is not stipulated, but our illustration shows the most usual hold.

The competitor must remain in the circle until the discus has landed, and must then leave it so that his first contact with the ground is behind the white lines outside the circle.

Competitors may interrupt a throw without it being counted as a trial, provided that the throw is then taken without unreasonable delay, and was not already a foul throw.

Foul throws A throw is declared a foul and disallowed if, after stepping into the circle and beginning a throw, the competitor touches with any part of his or her body the top of the metal band that marks the circle or the ground outside it before the discus has landed.

For the throw to be valid, the discus must land so that its point of impact is within the inner edges of the lines that mark out the sector.

SCORING

Measurement Each throw is measured immediately, from the nearest impression left on the ground by the discus, to the inside edge of the circle, on a line from the impression toward the center of the circle.

Flags are placed just outside the lines marking the sector, to indicate each competitor's longest throw in the current competition.

Results Each competitor is credited with the best of his or her throws, and the winner is the one whose best is longer than anyone else's.

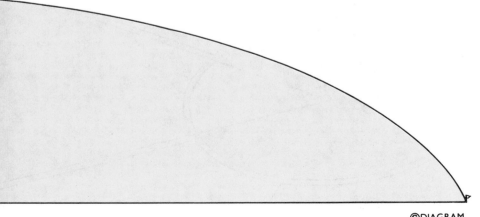

FIELD (HAMMER)

SYNOPSIS

The hammer is swung round and released from within a circle and must land within a marked sector. If there are eight or fewer competitors, each one has six trials. If there are more than eight they have three trials, and the best eight then have three more. The competitor achieving the longest throw in his six trials is the winner.

COMPETITION AREA

The circle is of 2.13–2.14m inside diameter, marked out by an iron band at least 6mm wide, sunk level with the surface of the ground outside, and painted white. The surface is of concrete, asphalt or other firm, non-slip material, and is 14–26mm below the top edge of the iron band.

White lines, 50mm wide, are marked directly opposite each other on each side of the circle. These lines should extend at least 0.75m from the outside edge of the circle.

The sector into which the hammer is thrown is defined by two lines 50mm wide diverging as from the center of the throwing circle at an angle of 40°. The length of the lines is not stipulated, but the ends are each marked with a flag.

Safety cage To prevent danger to bystanders, the throwing circle is enclosed at the sides and rear by netting at least 5m high. The cage (see p. 392 for illustration) must be capable of stopping a regulation hammer traveling at a speed of up to 29m/sec.

The opening at the mouth of the cage is 6m wide, but an additional panel of netting 2m wide and at least 5.5m high is placed on the left for right-handed throwers or on the right for left-handers.

EQUIPMENT

The hammer consists of a metal head joined by a wire to a grip.

The head is spherical and made of any metal not softer than brass, or of a shell of such metal filled with a solid material such as lead. It must measure 110–130mm in diameter and the center of gravity must be within 6mm of the center. It is attached by a swivel to a single piece of spring steel wire not less than 3mm in diameter, looped at the farther end for attachment to the grip. The grip must be rigid, and usually takes the form of a rough triangle with sides approximately 11cm long.

Neither the wire nor the grip may stretch appreciably during throwing.

The complete hammer must weigh at least 7.26kg, and measure 1.175–1.215m long from the inside of the grip to the far side of the head.

At major meetings such as Olympic Games, only hammers provided by the organizers may be used.

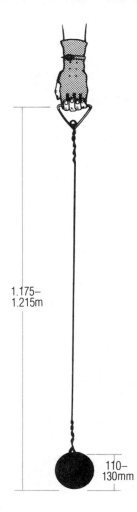

1.175–1.215m

110–130mm

2.13–2.14m

40°

Gloves Smooth gloves that leave the tips of the fingers exposed are permitted. It is usual for a right-hander to wear one glove on his left hand, or a left-hander one on his right. Tape may not be applied to the hands except to cover an open wound, but resin or a similar substance may be used to improve the grip.

PROCEDURE

Preliminary Competitors draw lots to decide the order in which they take their trials. Each competitor may have up to two practice throws on the competition area, if practicable, in the order of the draw, under the supervision of the judges. After the beginning of the contest, no-one may use the competition area for practice.

The throw The competitor begins in a stationary position within the circle. The head of the hammer may be on the ground either inside or outside the circle (**1**), and may touch the ground again during the preliminary swings or turns.

The competitor must remain in the circle until the hammer has landed, and must then leave it so that his first contact with the ground is behind the white lines outside the circle.

Competitors may interrupt a throw without it being counted as a trial, provided that the throw is then taken without unreasonable delay, that the hammer did not touch the ground during the preliminary swings, and that the throw was not already a foul.

Foul throws A throw is declared a foul and disallowed if:

a) after beginning a throw the competitor touches with any part of his body either the top edge of the circle or the ground outside it (**2**); or

b) the competitor improperly releases the hammer; or

c) the hammer lands so that its initial point of impact is outside the sector lines.

If the hammer breaks during a throw or while in the air, the attempt will not count as one of the competitor's trials, nor will it be counted as a foul if he loses his balance and steps outside the circle as a result.

SCORING

Measurement Each throw is measured immediately, from the nearest mark on the ground left by the fall of the head of the hammer, along a line toward the center of the throwing circle, to the circle's inside edge.

A marker showing the length of each competitor's best throw is placed just outside one of the lines marking out the throwing sector.

Results Each competitor is credited with the best of all his throws, the winner being the one whose best is longer than anyone else's.

A tie for first place is decided by the second best throws of the competitors concerned.

395

FIELD (SHOT)

SYNOPSIS

The shot is put, or projected with a pushing action, from within a circle and must land in a marked-out sector. If there are eight or fewer competitors, each one has six trials. If there are more than eight they have three trials, and the best eight then have three more. The competitor achieving the longest put in his or her six trials is the winner.

COMPETITION AREA

The circle is of 2.13–2.14m inside diameter, marked out by a metal band at least 6mm wide sunk level with the surface of the ground outside it, and painted white.

The surface is of concrete, asphalt, or other firm, non-slip material, and is 14–26mm below the top edge of the metal band.

White lines, 50mm wide, are marked directly opposite each other on each side of the circle. These lines should extend at least 0.75m from the outside edge of the circle.

The sector into which the shot is put is bounded by two lines 50mm wide that diverge at 40° from the center of the circle, and the ends of which are marked by flags.

The stop board is a curved piece of wood or similar material fixed to the ground at the front edge of the circle so that its near edge and the inside edge of the circle are coincident. It is painted white.

The board is 1.21–1.23m long on the inside, 112–116mm wide, and the top is 98–102mm above the surface of the circle.

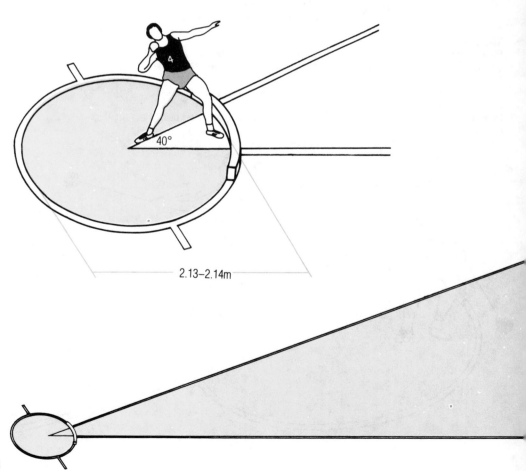

40°

2.13–2.14m

EQUIPMENT

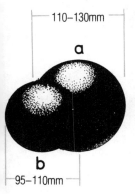

110–130mm

a

b

95–110mm

The shot is a smooth sphere of any metal not softer than brass, or a shell of such metal filled with lead or a similar substance.

The shot used by men (**a**) is 110–130mm in diameter and weighs at least 7.26kg.

The shot used by women (**b**) is 95–110mm in diameter and weighs at least 4kg.

At major meetings such as Olympic Games, only the shot provided by the organizers may be used.

The hands Gloves may not be worn, but resin or a similar substance may be applied to the hands to improve the grip. Tape may only be used to cover an open wound.

PROCEDURE

Preliminary Competitors draw lots to decide the order in which they take their trials. Each competitor may have up to two practice puts, if practicable, in the order of the draw, on the competition area and under the supervision of the judges. After the beginning of the competition proper, no-one may use the competition area for practice.

The put The competitor must begin in a stationary position, standing within the circle, and with the shot held at the shoulder and either touching or very close to the chin. The shot must not be dropped below this position or brought behind the line of the shoulders at any point during the put.

The competitor must remain in the circle until the shot has landed, and must then leave it so that his first contact with the ground is behind the white lines outside the circle.

The competitor may interrupt the put once and lay the shot down, without it being counted as one of his or her trials, provided the put was not already a foul one.

Foul puts A put is declared a foul and disallowed if, after stepping into the circle and beginning the put, the competitor touches with any part of his body the ground outside the circle (**A**), or the top of the iron band or of the stop board (**B**).

For the put to be valid, the shot must land so that its point of impact is within the inner edge of the lines that mark out the sector.

SCORING

Measurement Each put is measured immediately, from the nearest impression left on the ground by the shot, to the inside edge of the circle, on a line from the impression toward the center of the circle.

Results Each competitor is credited with the best of his or her throws, the winner being the one whose best is longer than anyone else's.

A tie for first place is decided by the second best puts of the competitors concerned.

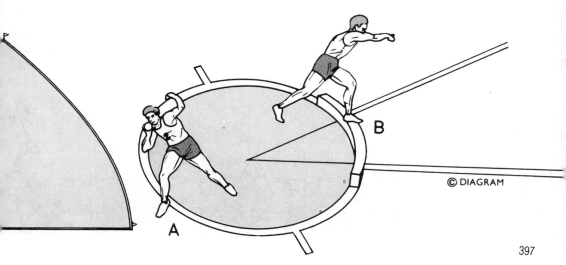

B

© DIAGRAM

A

FIELD (LONG/TRIPLE JUMP)

SYNOPSIS

In both long jump and triple jump competitors run along a runway and leap from a takeoff board into a sand-filled landing area. If there are eight or fewer competitors, each one has six trials. If there are more than eight they have three trials, and the best eight then have three more. The competitor with the longest jump in his six trials is the winner.

LONG JUMP

The runway (1) is at least 1.22m wide, and at least 40m long. However, a minimum length of 45m is recommended where possible.

The takeoff board (2) is a substantial piece of timber or other suitable material sunk flush with the surface of the runway, on which the competitor last steps in making a leap. It measures 1.21–1.22m from side to side, 198–202mm from front to back, and may be up to 100mm thick. It is painted white. The front edge should be not less than 1m from the near edge of the landing area. The competitor's toe must not be placed forward of the front edge of the board (**A**).

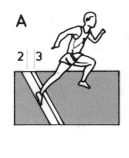

The indicator board (3) is placed immediately beyond the takeoff board, and reveals whether the competitor's toe was placed unlawfully over the front edge. It is usually covered with plasticine, but sand or soft earth is also permitted.

The surface of the layer of plasticine, which is at least 3mm thick, slopes upward at 30° to a height of 7mm above the surface of the takeoff board. The indicator board measures 98–102mm from front to back.

The impression left by a competitor stepping on the plasticine is erased before the next competitor jumps.

The landing area (4) is a pit filled with sand to the same level as the runway. It is at least 2.75m wide, and the distance between the front edge of the takeoff board and the far end of the landing area should be at least 10m.

The sand is dampened before a competition, and raked level with the surface of the takeoff board before every jump.

Preliminary Competitors draw lots to decide the order in which they take their trials. Once a competition has begun, no-one may use the runway for practice purposes.

Run-up There is no limit to the length of run-up. Markers provided by the organizers may be placed alongside but not on the runway by competitors to help them judge their approach.

Failures A jump is counted as a failure if the competitor:
a) touches the indicator board in front of the takeoff board, with any part of the body, so as to leave an impression on the plasticine;
b) takes off from outside the takeoff board to left or right, even if from behind the front edge;
c) while landing touches the ground outside the landing area at a point nearer to the takeoff board than the mark in the sand left by his landing;
d) walks back through the sand after a completed jump;
e) uses any sort of somersault, or weights or grips of any kind.

Measurements of the distance jumped are made from the nearest edge of any break made in the sand by any part of the competitor's body (including the limbs) to the front edge of the takeoff board, and at right angles to it (**B**).

B

TRIPLE JUMP

General The rules for triple jump are mostly the same as for long jump. The exceptions concern the layout of the competition area and the actions of the competitor.

Competition area There is an additional length of at least 13m of runway (**5**) beyond the takeoff board, before the landing area.

Jumping action (C) The competitor makes a hop, a step, and a jump, in that order. For the hop he must land on the same foot with which he took off. In the step he lands on the other foot, from which he immediately takes off again for the jump.

Failures If in any of the three stages the "sleeping" leg touches the ground, the attempt is counted as a failure.

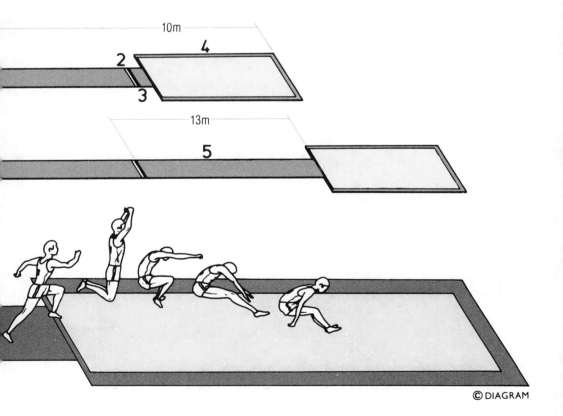

© DIAGRAM

FIELD (HIGH JUMP)

SYNOPSIS

Competitors aim to jump in an approved fashion so as to clear a light crossbar that rests on rigid uprights, and land on the cushioned area beyond. The crossbar is raised after each round, and competitors remain in the contest until eliminated by three consecutive failures.

EQUIPMENT

Runway and takeoff area A typical layout is shown in our illustration. The length of the runway is unlimited, but should be at least 20m at Olympic and other major championships.

Uprights The uprights must be rigid and be placed not less than 4m or more than 4.04m apart. They must extend at least 100mm higher than the maximum height to which the crossbar can be raised.

The supports on the uprights, on which the crossbar rests, must be flat and rectangular, 40mm wide by 60mm long, and may not be covered with any material that increases friction with the crossbar. The supports must be placed on the inside of the uprights, ie each pointing toward the other upright.

Crossbar The crossbar may be of wood, metal or other suitable material. It may be of triangular section with sides of 30mm, or circular, 25–30mm in diameter, with squared ends. It is between 3.98m and 4m long and weighs not more than 2kg.

When in place, there must be a gap of at least 10mm between the ends of the crossbar and the uprights. The crossbar must rest so that, if touched by a competitor, it falls easily forward or backward to the ground.

Height of the crossbar Measurements are made perpendicularly from the ground to the lowest part of the upper side of the bar. New height settings are measured before jumping begins, and are checked after a jump when it seems a record has been established.

Landing area The landing area is deeply padded and should measure at least 5m from side to side and 3m from front to back.

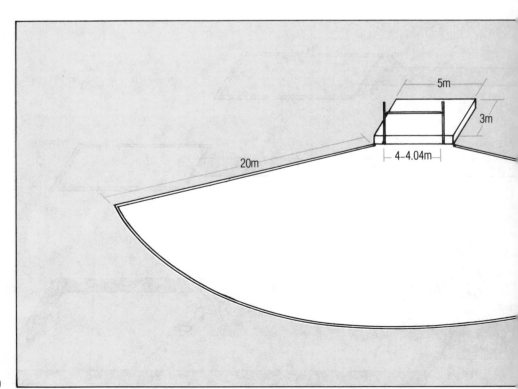

PROCEDURE

Preliminary Competitors draw lots to decide the order in which they take their trials. Before the competition begins, the judges announce the starting height and the heights to which the bar will be raised after each round.

A competitor may commence jumping at any height offered and may attempt or omit any subsequent height.

Run-up The length of run-up is unlimited. Markers provided by the organizers may be placed on the ground to assist run-up and takeoff, and a handkerchief may be placed on the bar as an aid to sighting.

SCORING

Failures An attempt is counted a failure if the competitor knocks off the bar (**A**), or touches the ground or landing area beyond the plane of the uprights with any part of the body (**B**) before clearing the bar. The latter case applies even if he did not make a jump.

Elimination A competitor is eliminated after a third consecutive failure, irrespective of the height at which the failures occur.

Rounds continue at successively greater heights until only one competitor remains uneliminated. He or she may then choose to attempt increased heights.

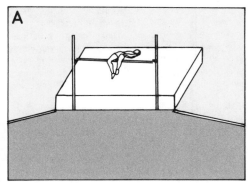

©DIAGRAM

FIELD (POLE VAULT)

SYNOPSIS
Competitors use a flexible pole to help them vault over a crossbar supported on two uprights. The crossbar is raised after each round, and competitors remain in the contest until eliminated by three consecutive failures.

EQUIPMENT
Runway and box There is no maximum length for the runway, but the minimum is 40m, and a length of not less than 45m is recommended.

At the end of the runway is the box into which the end of the pole is placed during the vault. The box is made of metal, or wood lined on the bottom with metal, and is sunk flush with the ground. The dimensions are as shown in the illustration. The angle between the bottom and the stopboard is 105°, and between the bottom and the sides about 120°.

The uprights must be rigid. Competitors may have them moved forward or back, but they may never be more than 0.6m from the line of the top of the stopboard. If moved, the height of the crossbar must be rechecked.

The supports for the crossbar must be smooth, with a uniform diameter not exceeding 13mm. They must not extend more than 75mm from the uprights, and must allow the crossbar to fall easily toward the landing area if it is touched by the competitor or his pole.

The crossbar is between 4.48m and 4.52m long and must weigh not more than 2.5kg. It may be of triangular section with sides of 30mm, or circular, 25–30mm in diameter, with a flat surface at each end where it rests on the supports. It may be made of wood, metal, or other suitable material.

Height of the crossbar Measurements are made perpendicularly from the ground to the lowest part of the upper side of the bar. New height settings are measured before vaulting begins, or when the uprights have been moved, and are checked after a vault when it appears a record has been established.

Landing area The padded landing area must be not less than 5m square, and usually has extensions about 1.3m long projecting forward of the uprights on either side of the box.

The pole may be any length or diameter, and made of any material or combination of materials, provided the surface is smooth. In practice, fiberglass poles are used in all top competitions.

A binding of not more than two layers of adhesive tape, uniform in thickness, may be used to aid the competitor's grip. In addition the bottom 0.3m may be bound to protect it from damage in the box. Competitors may use their own poles. Resin may be used on the hands instead of or as well as tape on the pole.

0.3m

45m

PROCEDURE

Preliminary Competitors draw lots to determine the order in which they take their trials. Before the competition begins, the judges announce the starting height and the heights to which the crossbar will be raised for each new round.

Competitors may begin vaulting at any of the heights offered, and may attempt or omit any subsequent height.

Run-up There is no limit on the length of run-up. Markers provided by the organizers may be placed beside, but not on, the runway to assist the competitor in gauging his approach.

SCORING

Failures A vault is counted as a failure if the competitor:

a) knocks off the crossbar (**1**);

b) leaves the ground for a vault and fails to clear the crossbar;

c) having left the ground places the lower hand above the upper, or moves the upper hand higher up the pole;

d) before taking off, touches the ground or landing area beyond the vertical plane of the top of the stopboard, with the pole or any part of the body (**2**).

An attempted vault during which the pole breaks is not counted as a failure.

Elimination A competitor is eliminated after his third consecutive failure, irrespective of the height at which they occur.

Rounds continue at successively greater heights until only one competitor remains uneliminated. The winner may continue to attempt increased heights.

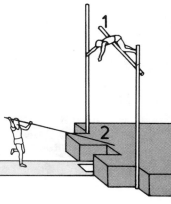

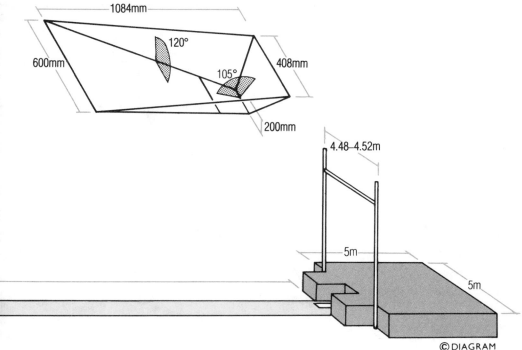

© DIAGRAM

VOLLEYBALL

HISTORY
Volleyball was devised in 1895 by William G. Morgan, the physical fitness instructor of the Young Men's Christian Association in Holyoke, Mass. The first US national tournament was held in New York in 1922. The game spread to the Far East through American missionary schools and reached Western Europe with the arrival of American troops in World War I. In 1947 the Fédération Internationale de Volleyball (FIVB) was founded in Paris. World championships, sponsored by the FIVB, began in 1949; women's teams began to participate in 1952. Both men's and women's volleyball teams first featured in the Olympic Games in 1964.

SYNOPSIS
Volleyball is a team ball game played between two teams of six players. The object of the game is to use any part of the body above the waist to send the ball over a net within the boundaries of the court so that the opposing team is unable to return it or prevent it from hitting the ground. Points are scored for successful actions by a serving team, and these points make up a set. The winning team is the one that wins the most sets in a match—usually three out of five.

PLAYING AREA AND EQUIPMENT
The playing area is a hard court, indoors or outdoors, that measures 18m long and 9m wide, with a net across the center. An unobstructed area of 3m must surround an open-air court on all sides; indoors this space must be a minimum of 2m. In the Olympic Games and the final rounds of world championships, this space must be extended to 8m behind the end lines and 5m beyond the side lines. Above the court there must be 9m of free space measured from the ground; for the Olympics and final world championship rounds this should be 12.5m.

The boundary lines (**a**) around the court are 5cm wide and are included in the court's dimensions. A center line (**b**) under the net divides the court into two equal squares. In each half the attack line (**c**) is drawn across the court 3m from the center line. The attack line and the center line enclose the attack area (**d**), which extends indefinitely beyond the side lines. In the back right-hand corner of each half of the court, the 3m-wide service area (**e**) extends beyond the back line to a minimum of 2m, and is marked by two 15cm parallel lines at right angles to the back line.

65–67cm

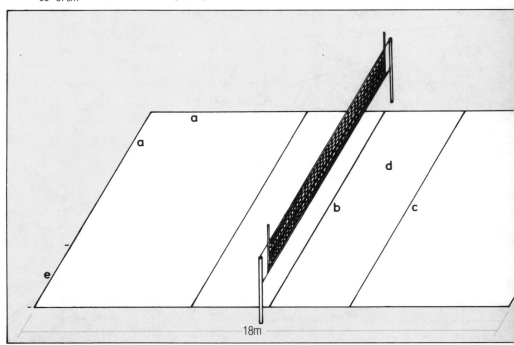

18m

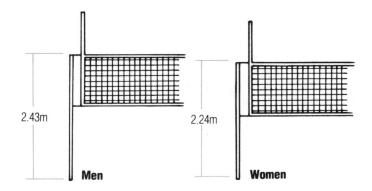

2.43m   **Men**

2.24m   **Women**

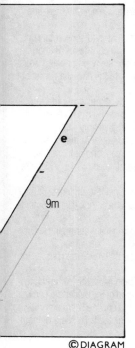

e

9m

The net is stretched across the center of the court at a height of 2.43m for men and 2.24m for women. The net is 9.5m long and 1m deep, made of 10cm square mesh, with 5cm white bands along the top edge and vertically down each side, over the side lines. Over each side marker, multicolored vertical antennas project 80cm above the top of the net.

Temperature Competitive volleyball should not be played when the temperature is below 10°C.

The ball must be spherical, with a circumference of 65–67cm and weighing 260–280g, and it must be uniform in color. It is made of a leather casing enclosing a bladder of rubber or similar material.

Dress Players wear jerseys and shorts in team colors, with numbers on the front and back of their jerseys. Numbered track suits are allowed in cold weather. In international matches the team captain wears a contrasting badge on the left side of the chest. Shoes must be light, pliable, and without heels. Players may obtain the referee's permission to play barefoot. Headgear and any articles that could cause injury are forbidden.

PLAYERS AND OFFICIALS

Players Each team is composed of six players and a maximum of six substitutes. Each team has a captain. The team captain is the only player allowed to speak to officials.

Team coaches and managers are positioned at the side of the court, facing the referee. Together with the team captain, they are responsible for team discipline. Requests for time-outs or substitutions may be made by the team captain or the coach. At time-outs the coach may speak to players but may not enter the court; he may not speak to players during a substitution.

Officials The game is controlled by a first referee, a second referee (umpire), a scorer, and two or four linesmen.

The first referee sits above one end of the net. He has overall control of the game, with power to settle all questions and penalize teams for bad conduct. He blows a whistle at the beginning and end of each point, and to stop play if a fault is committed.

The second referee faces the first referee at the other end of the net. He blows a whistle for center line and attack area infringements. He also authorizes and records time-outs and substitutions, checks rotation and position of players, and takes possession of the ball at time-outs.

The scorer is also placed opposite the first referee. He records the score, substitutions, time-outs, and changes of end, and informs players and officials of these.

Two linesmen must stand at diagonally opposite corners of the court, at the side away from the service area. The linesmen raise flags to signal infringements.

SCORING

A match is won by the team that wins most sets – usually three out of five.

A set is won when one team reaches a score of 15 points with a lead of at least two points. If a set is tied at 14, it continues until one team gains a two-point lead.

Points can only be scored by the serving team. If the team that did not serve in a rally fails to return the ball correctly over the net, a fault is committed and a point is awarded to the serving team. If a fault is committed by the serving team, a "side out" (loss of service) is called.

405

©DIAGRAM

VOLLEYBALL 2

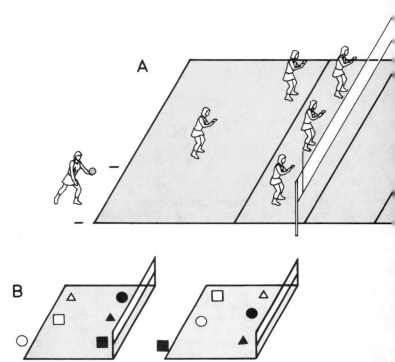

A

C

RULES OF PLAY

Starting procedure The two captains toss a coin for choice of ends or the right to serve.

Position of players for service (A) When the ball is served the players of both teams must be standing in two rows of three—the front-line players at the net, the back-line players behind them anywhere on the court.

When there is a change of service (**B**), the players of the team that is to serve rotate one position clockwise before serving. Players must serve in the correct order of rotation, otherwise the team loses the service and all points scored while the wrong person was serving. The players' order of rotation must remain constant until the end of a game, but the line-up can then be changed if the scorer is informed.

The serve (C) The server stands in the service area at the back of the court. After the referee's whistle the server has five seconds to put the ball into play. He can hit the ball with his open or closed hand or any part of his arm. But he must hit it cleanly with one hand only, after first clearly releasing or throwing the ball from either hand. At the moment of impact the server must be within the service area, although he can land outside it after hitting the ball. The ball must pass over the net between the antennas or their indefinite extensions, to go into the opponents' court.

A fault is committed if the ball goes under the net, or touches the net, the antennas, or their indefinite extensions, a player of the serving team, or any other object, or if it lands outside the opponents' court.

Members of the serving team must not try to distract the opposing team during the service or form groups to "screen" the server's action.

The same player continues to serve until his team commits a fault. Service then passes to the other team.

Starting second and subsequent games At the start of each game the teams change ends, and service goes to the team that was not serving at the end of the preceding game. In the deciding game of a match, a coin is tossed at the start to choose service or playing end. In a deciding game the teams also change ends when one reaches a score of eight points, but service remains unchanged.

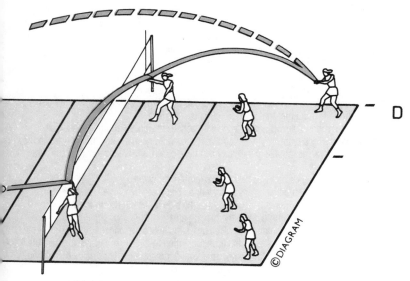

D

Playing the ball after service (D) The ball may be hit with any part of the body above and including the waist, as long as the hit is clean and the ball is not held, lifted, or carried in any way.

Each team may touch the ball up to three times, not counting "blocking" contact, before returning it over the net. Except in blocking, the same player may not hit the ball twice in succession, and if two teammates play the ball simultaneously it counts as two touches. If a player touches or is touched by the ball in any way, he is assumed to have played the ball. The ball may be played while a player is in contact with a teammate, as long as he is not used as a prop.

Once the ball is in play after service, players may move freely on their side of the net. Putting a foot or feet completely across the center line while the ball is in play is a fault. It is not a fault if a player's hand or hands cross the net after an attack, or if they cross the vertical plane below the net, as long as no interference to opponents is caused.

Front-line players may make any kind of attack hit (ie a hit that directs the ball into the opponents' court) provided the ball at the time of contact is partially or totally within their playing space.

Back-line players with both feet behind the attack line at the time of takeoff may make any kind of attack hit; back-line players within the front zone may make an attack hit only after the ball is below the level of the top of the net.

The ball should go completely over the net between the antennas or their indefinite extensions. If the ball hits the net inside the antennas, it is still considered in play unless another rule is infringed.

When either referee blows his whistle, the ball is dead. If it touches the ground or any object outside the court, it is out of play. The ball must clear the lines completely to be out of court. If the ball touches the antennas or the net outside them, it is out.

Blocking (E) Front-line players may block the ball after a third contact by the opponents by making contact with it before, as, or immediately after it crosses the net. Back-line players are not permitted to participate in a block.

After blocking, a team has the right to three more contacts with the ball before returning it. A player who has touched the ball during a block can play the ball again immediately—this counts as the first of the three contacts allowed. If the ball touches more than one blocking teammate, this counts as one touch even if the contacts are not simultaneous.

Blockers may reach over the net inside the antennas, but they must not interfere with the opposing team by trying to touch the ball before the opponents' action in sending the ball toward the blockers' side is complete.

If two opponents touch the ball above the net simultaneously, the team that does not receive the ball as it falls is considered to have made the last touch.

When the ball returns after contact with the opponents' block, the attacking team has the usual right to three more contacts to return it.

E

VOLLEYBALL 3

Time-out Each team may take two 30-second time-outs in each game, but only when the ball is dead. They can be taken consecutively, or a time-out may be followed by a substitution or a substitution by a time-out.

The captain or head coach may request a time-out; if it is not clear whether a time-out or a substitution is requested, it will be assumed that a time-out is wanted.

No player may leave the court during a time-out, but players can receive advice from one coach, who may not enter the court.

Requests for more than two time-outs will be penalized with a warning, then a fault.

Substitution Each team may make up to six substitutions in a game, but only when the ball is dead and at the request of the captain or head coach, and when recognized by either referee.

Substitutes must report to the scorer before joining the game.

Play must resume immediately; any delay will be penalized by a time-out.

When not in the game, substitutes must sit at the side of the court with the coaches, although they may warm up outside the playing area.

A player who starts a game may be replaced by a substitute once, and may then re-enter the game once, provided that he takes his former position in the serving order. A substitute may be replaced only by the player whose place he originally took. Thus no more than two players can participate in any one position in the serving order.

If a player is injured and no substitute is available in accordance with the rules above, the player can be replaced in the following order of priority:

1) by any substitute who has not been in the game;

2) by the player who was in the injured player's position;

3) by any other substitute.

In cases of injury when no substitute is legally available, the referee has the power to grant a special time-out of up to three minutes.

If a player is disqualified, and a legal substitution cannot be made, the team loses the game by default.

Substitution rules may differ in senior division and NAGWS competitions.

Interruptions of play The only stoppages allowed other than time-outs are intervals between games: two minutes for the first three intervals and five minutes between the fourth and fifth games. This includes time to change ends and inform the scorer of new line-ups. If bad weather etc interrupts a match and it is resumed on the same court within four hours, the points scored in the interrupted game remain and play continues normally. If the match is resumed on another court within four hours, the interrupted game will be replayed but the results of completed games stand. If the delay is greater than four hours the whole match must be replayed.

Faults A team loses the service (side-out) or the opponents gain a point if:

a) the ball touches the ground;

b) a team plays the ball more than three times in succession;

c) the ball is held or pushed;

d) the ball touches a player below the waist;

e) a player touches the ball twice consecutively (except when blocking);

f) a team is out of position at the service;

g) a player touches the net (**1**) or antennas (unless the ball knocks the net against him);

h) a player deliberately touches an opponent across the vertical plane of the net (**2**);

i) any part of a player's body touches the opponents' court during play (**3**) (except that it is not a fault if a player touches the opponents' court with his foot, provided part of his foot does not cross the center line);

j) a player reaches over the net or touches the ball above the opponents' court (**4**) (except when blocking);

k) a player reaches under the net and touches the ball while it is in play by the opposite team;

l) a back-line player in the attack area hits the ball from above net height;

m) the ball does not pass completely over the net between the antennas or their indefinite extensions;

n) the ball lands or touches an object outside the court;

o) the ball is returned with the use of a teammate as a support (**5**);
p) a player receives a personal penalty;
q) coaching is disruptive;
r) the game is persistently delayed;
s) a substitute joins the game illegally;
t) a team requests a third time-out after a warning;
u) a team extends a second time-out beyond 30 seconds;
v) a team delays a substitution after taking two time-outs;
w) players leave the court during a time-out or other stoppage without the referee's permission;
x) a player intimidates or makes any distracting noise or gesture toward an opponent;
y) a block or serve is illegal.

When a fault is committed during the same play by two opponents, only the first will be penalized. If the faults are simultaneous, the referee will direct a play-over.

Persistent misconduct by players, coaches or substitutes will lead to disqualification for the rest of the game or match.

WATER POLO

HISTORY

Early forms of water polo—including one in which the players rode on barrels painted to look like horses—were played in Britain in the 1870s. Water polo in something like its present form, however, was first given official recognition in Britain in 1885. The game soon spread to other countries, and was included in the Olympic Games of 1900. A softball version of water polo with more emphasis on retaining possession of the ball was popular in the USA until the 1930s. Other countries, however, have always favored the use of a fully inflated ball and a consequent emphasis on passing skills. International water polo is now governed by Fédération Internationale de Natation Amateur (FINA) rules.

SYNOPSIS

Water polo is a team game played in a swimming pool by two teams of up to 13-a-side, only seven of whom may be in the water at the same time. A large, inflated ball resembling a soccer ball is propelled around the playing area. Players other than the goalkeeper may only use one hand to propel the ball and are not allowed to punch it. A team scores by putting the ball into its opponents' goal.

PLAYING AREA AND EQUIPMENT

68–71cm

Playing area The maximum dimensions are 30m long (between goal lines) by 20m wide. For matches played by women, the maximum dimensions are 25m long by 17m wide. The minimum depth of the pool is 1m, or 1.80m in Olympic, world championship, and international matches.

Lines must be distinct, and suggested colors are: (**a**) goal line (at least 30cm from the end of the field of play), white; (**b**) half-distance line, white; (**c**) 2m line (2m from the goal line), red; (**d**) 4m line (4m from the goal line), yellow. A visible colored sign must be placed on the end of the field of play, 2m from the corner at the same side as the goal judge. There must be enough space for referees to walk from end to end along the edge of the pool. Space must also be provided for goal judges at the goal lines.

Goals must be rigid, perpendicular, painted white, and fixed firmly. The goal posts must be 3m apart. The underside of the crossbar must be 90cm above the water surface when the water is 1.50m or more deep and 2.40m from the bottom of the pool when the water is less than 1.50m deep. The goal space is enclosed by a net.

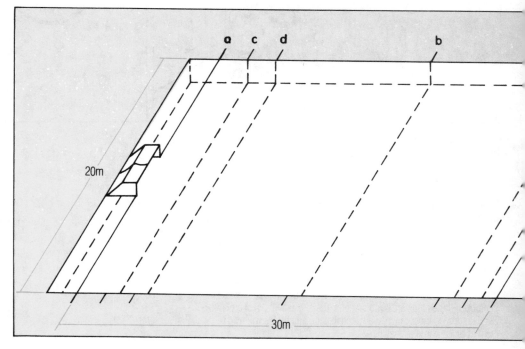

The ball must be round and fully inflated. It must be completely waterproof and not covered with grease or any similar substance. Its circumference must be 68–71cm and its weight 400–450g.

Caps One team must wear dark blue caps, the other white. Goalkeepers wear red caps. All caps must be tied under the chin. Caps fitted with malleable ear protectors are compulsory for Olympic Games and world championships. If a player loses his cap, he must replace it at the next stoppage. Caps are numbered on both sides—the goalkeeper wearing number 1 and the other players 2 to 13.

Dress Players wear trunks with separate drawers or slips underneath. No dangerous articles may be worn. Grease or oil must not be used on the body.

PLAYERS AND OFFICIALS

Players A team comprises 13 players, of whom six are substitutes. Seven players are allowed in the water at any one time, one of whom is the goalkeeper.

Officials The game is controlled by between four and eight officials. For Olympic Games and world championships, officials comprise two referees, two goal judges, timekeepers, and secretaries.

Referees have absolute control over the game. A referee signals with a whistle and two flags (one blue, one white) on a single stick (**1**). He stops and starts the game, decides fouls, goals, and throws. He does not declare a foul if the offending team would benefit from the stoppage. He has the power to order any player out of the water.

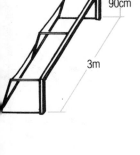

90cm

3m

Goal judges are positioned at each end of the pool, on the opposite side to a referee and directly level with the goal line. They each have a white flag (**2**) to signal goal throws, and a red flag (**3**) to signal corner throws or the improper reentry of an excluded player. Both flags are used to indicate a goal.

Timekeepers use stopwatches to record the time the ball is actually in play, the time a player is excluded, and the periods of continuous possession of the ball by each team. They use a whistle to indicate the end of a period.

Secretaries record the score and major fouls. They signal with a red flag when any player is awarded a third personal fault. They also control players' periods of exclusion by signaling when an excluded player may reenter the water.

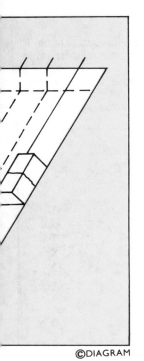

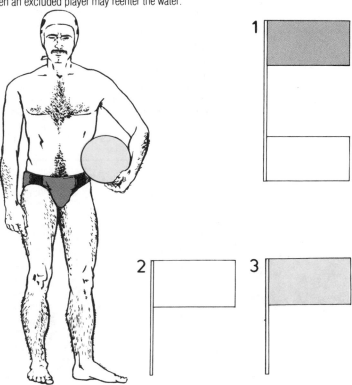

1

2

3

411

© DIAGRAM

WATER POLO 2

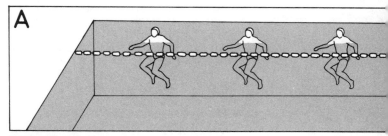

DURATION AND SCORING

Duration Play lasts for four periods of seven minutes' actual playing time. There is a two-minute interval between periods for changing ends.

For an accident or an injury the referee may suspend the play for up to three minutes.

If there is a tie and a winner is required, there is a five-minute break, then two periods of three minutes' actual play with a one-minute interval between. This pattern is continued until a decision is reached.

Scoring A goal is scored when the ball completely crosses the goal line between the posts and under the crossbar, providing it has not been punched and at least two players have touched it after a start or restart (not including a goalkeeper's attempt to stop a shot). The ball may be dribbled into goal.

The team scoring more goals is the winner.

STARTING PROCEDURES

Start of play (A) At the start of each playing period, players take up position behind their own goal lines, about 1m apart and at least 1m from either goal post. Only two players are allowed between the posts. The referee then blows his whistle and throws the ball into the center of the pool.

Restarting play After a goal, players may take up any position in their own half. After the referee whistles, the team that conceded the goal restarts play by one player passing the ball to a teammate, who must be behind the half-distance line when he receives the ball. After a stoppage for illness, injury, or other unforeseen reason, play resumes with a free throw from the point where the ball was last in play, taken by the team that last had possession.

RULES OF PLAY

Playing the ball (B) Players are allowed to dribble with the ball (**a**), seize the ball (**b**), lift the ball out of the water, remain stationary with the ball, pass or shoot the ball (**c**), and play the ball when it is in the air.

Leaving the water Players may only leave the water at an interval, when injured, or with the referee's permission. A player with cramp must leave the pool as quickly as possible; the game proceeds as soon as he has left the water but no substitute is permitted.

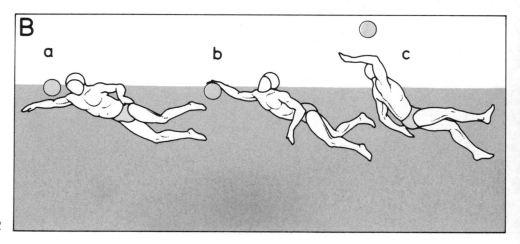

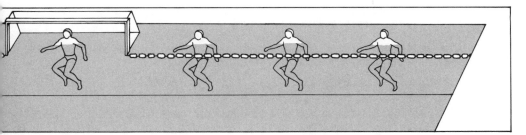

Substitution Except in case of injury or accident, a substitute may only enter the game during the interval between periods of play, after a goal has been scored, before extra time, or after a teammate has been excluded from the rest of the game for disrespect, wearing oil, or committing a third personal fault.

With the referee's permission, a player retiring from the game as a result of injury or accident may be immediately replaced by a substitute. A player replaced in this way is not permitted to reenter the game at any time.

Out of play The ball goes out of play when:
a) it is sent out at either side of the pool (**1**);
b) it rebounds from the side of the pool above the water level (**2**);
c) it strikes or lodges in an overhead obstruction;
d) it completely crosses the goal line outside the goal posts.

In cases a) and b), the ball is returned to play by an opposing player, who takes a free throw from where the ball went out. If the ball went out between the goal line and the 2m line, the free throw is from the 2m line.

In case c), the referee must stop the game and throw the ball into the water under the obstruction; the ball must not be played until it has touched the water.

In case d), there is a corner throw if a defender puts the ball out over his own goal line, or a goal throw if the ball is sent out of play by an attacker.

A corner throw (C) is taken by an attacker from the 2m mark on the side of the pool where the ball went out. Only the defending goalkeeper may be in the 2m area when the throw is taken. At least two players other than the defending goalkeeper must touch the ball before a goal can be scored.

A goal throw is taken by the defending goalkeeper. It may be taken from any place within the 2m area and must not go beyond the opponents' 4m line.

A neutral throw is taken by the referee when one or more players of each team have committed a foul at the same time. The ball is thrown into the water as near as possible to where the incident occurred and in such a way that both teams have an equal chance of gaining possession. At least two players other than the defending goalkeeper must touch the ball before a goal can be scored.

1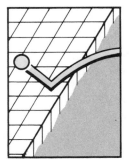

2

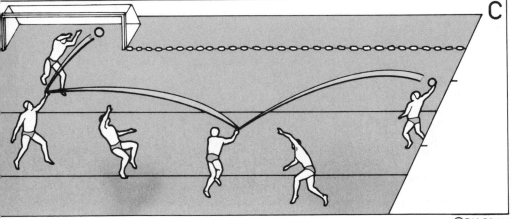

C

©DIAGRAM

WATER POLO 3

FOULS

Types of foul Offenses are classified as:
a) ordinary fouls (penalized by a free throw to the other team);
b) major fouls (penalized by personal faults, periods of exclusion, and penalty throws).

Ordinary fouls It is an ordinary foul for any player to:
a) advance beyond the goal line before the referee's signal to start or restart the game;
b) take or hold the ball under water when tackled (**1**);
c) assist a player at any time;
d) hold onto or push off from the goal posts or their fixtures at any time;
e) hold onto or push off from the sides or ends of the pool during actual play;
f) hold onto the rails except at the start or a restart;
g) splash water in an opponent's face (**2**);
h) touch the ball before it reaches the water from a referee's throw;
i) push or push off from an opponent;
j) deliberately impede, for example by swimming on the shoulders, back, or legs of, an opponent unless he is holding the ball (dribbling does not count as holding the ball);
k) be within 2m of the opposing goal line unless behind the line of the ball;
l) waste time (including having possession for more than 35 seconds without shooting);
m) delay unduly when taking a free throw;
n) take a penalty throw incorrectly.

It is an ordinary foul for any player other than a goalkeeper in his 4m area to:
a) take an active part in the game when standing on the floor of the pool;
b) walk on the floor of the pool when play is in progress;
c) jump from the floor of the pool to play the ball (**3**), or tackle an opponent;
d) touch the ball with both hands at the same time (**4**);
e) punch the ball.

It is an ordinary foul for a goalkeeper to:
a) throw the ball over his opponents' 4m line;
b) go or touch the ball outside his own half.

Major fouls It is a major foul for any player to:
a) illegally stop a goal inside the 4m area, eg by pulling down the goal (**5**);
b) kick or strike an opponent (**6**), or attempt to do so;
c) commit any brutal act;
d) hold, sink, or pull back an opponent not holding the ball;
e) interfere with the taking of a free throw, goal throw, corner throw, or penalty throw;
f) disobey or show disrespect for the referee;
g) be guilty of misconduct (foul language, violence, etc);
h) reenter the water improperly when an excluded player or substitute;
i) persist in committing an ordinary foul.

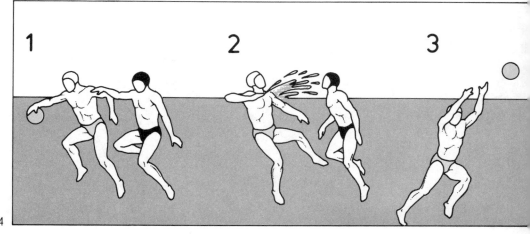

PENALTIES

Free throw The penalty for committing an ordinary foul is the award of a free throw to the opposing team, to be taken by any one of its players.

The free throw must be taken without delay. The player may either throw the ball or drop it into the water and dribble it before passing, but the throw must be made in such a way that the other players can see the ball leave the thrower's hand.

At least two players other than the defending goalkeeper must touch the ball before a goal can be scored.

Any free throw awarded for a foul in the 2m area must be taken from the 2m line opposite the point where the foul occurred. Other free throws are taken from where the offense occurred.

An improperly taken free throw must be retaken.

Personal fault A personal fault is recorded against any player who commits a major foul anywhere within the field of play. This penalty is accompanied by a period of exclusion from the water for the offending player, or by a penalty throw to the opposing team.

The usual period of exclusion is either for 45 seconds or until a goal has been scored, whichever is the sooner. After the player has left the water, play resumes with a free throw to the opponents. The penalty period starts as soon as the throw is taken. After the period is over, the excluded player, or his substitute, must enter the water within 2m of the corner of the field of play on the side of the goal judge.

A player will be excluded for the rest of the game in the following cases:

a) if he commits any brutal act or causes serious injury by deliberately striking an opponent (no substitution permitted);

b) if he fails to obey or is disrespectful toward the referee (substitute permitted after 45 seconds or a goal, whichever is the sooner);

c) if he commits three major fouls (substitute permitted at once if a penalty throw is awarded, otherwise after 45 seconds or a goal).

Penalty throw The following major fouls are penalized by a penalty throw to the opponents:

a) kicking or striking an opponent, or trying to do so, when inside the opponents' 4m area;

b) committing a brutal act inside the opponents' 4m area;

c) committing a foul inside the 4m area and so preventing a probable goal;

d) entering the water incorrectly after a period of exclusion or as a substitute if this offense occurs during the last minute of a game or period of extra play.

Any player except the goalkeeper may take the penalty throw from any point along the 4m line. He must throw directly at goal. All players except the defending goalkeeper must leave the 4m area, and no player may encroach within 2m of the thrower. The goalkeeper must remain on his goal line.

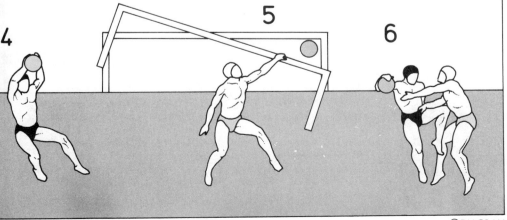

415

WEIGHTLIFTING

HISTORY

There are numerous records through the ages of trials of strength involving lifting, but weightlifting in its present form using barbells began in Western Europe in the 19th century, with professional strongmen appearing in music halls and circuses. The first world championships were held in London in 1891. Weightlifting was included in the Olympic Games of 1896–1904 but it was then left out until 1920, the year that an international governing body for weightlifting – the Fédération Internationale Halterophile et Culturiste (FIHC) – was formed. This body was later renamed the International Weightlifting Federation (IWF), and is based in Budapest, Hungary. There are no official women's events.

SYNOPSIS

Competitors attempt to lift a weighted bar by two different methods: the snatch, and the clean and jerk (or jerk). For each type of lift, each competitor normally makes a maximum of three attempts to lift the bar. There are individual and team classifications for the snatch and for the clean and jerk, and also for the total weight of the competitors' best performances in the two types of lift.

PLATFORM AND EQUIPMENT

Platform This must be 4m square, 5–15cm high, made of any solid material, covered with any non-slippery material, and with a colored edge.

Any lift must be completed on the platform; if a lifter steps off it during a lift, it is a "no lift."

Dress Lifters must wear a full-length costume of the style illustrated. A short-sleeved, collarless T-shirt or vest may be worn under the costume. A belt, if worn, must be over the costume and must not exceed 12cm at its widest. Heels on boots must be of normal shape and not widened.

Bandages Gauze or medical crepe bandages may be worn on the wrist and knee. Such bandages must not exceed 10cm in width on the wrist and 30cm on the knee; their length is not limited. Alternatively, leather wrist straps and elastic knee caps may be worn.

Bandages and adhesive plasters are allowed on the inner and outer surface of the hand; they must not, however, be fastened to the wrist or to the barbell. Plasters are permitted on the fingers, but must not cover the third joint.

Bandages are not permitted on the elbows, around the body, on the thighs or on the shins; medical plasters may be applied on the advice of the doctor on duty, who must at once inform the chief referee and president of the jury.

Weights Only disk barbells may be used. The barbell consists of a bar, disks, and collars. The bar is 220cm long—measuring 131cm between the inside collars—and has a diameter of 2.8cm. It weighs 20kg.

Disks, covered with rubber or plastic, bear clear indication of their weight and are distinctively colored (see table); 50kg disks are used only if there is no other way of loading all the weight on the bar. The largest disks have a diameter of 45cm.

220cm

131cm

45cm

Technical equipment The following equipment is used:
scales to weigh the competitors;
an electrical timing clock to check that lifts are made in the time allowed;
referee light system to indicate "good lifts" (white lights) and "no lifts" (red lights);
scoreboard and recordboard.

COMPETITORS AND OFFICIALS

Competitors There are two classes of lifter: junior (age limit 20) and senior.
Lifters are further divided into ten categories according to bodyweight. Maximum bodyweights for each category are as given in the table.

In major championships, ten competitors and three reserves (two reserves in the Olympics) are allowed from each country. Competitors are spread over the weight categories, with a maximum of two in any one category. Any competitor may compete in only one category.

Officials International competitions require: three referees, one of whom is the chief referee; an international jury; a competition secretary; a technical controller; and a doctor on duty.

COMPETITION PROCEDURES

Drawing of lots Each competitor or his representative must draw a start number 15 minutes before the beginning of weighing in. This number is used to determine the order of weighing in and the order of lifting.

Weighing in The weighing in of each bodyweight begins 2 hours before that contest begins and lasts for 1 hour. The procedure is controlled by the referees.

Any competitor who is too light or too heavy for the category to be contested has 1 hour in which to make the weight. A competitor who is too heavy may in some circumstances move into the next higher category.

Weights attempted A competitor is normally allowed three attempts each for the snatch and for the clean and jerk. An extra attempt at the same weight is permitted if the jury disagrees with the referees' verdict of a "no lift." A fourth attempt may also be permitted to try for a record.

Before lifting begins, each competitor must inform the officials of the weights he intends to attempt assuming he is successful at each attempt. Selections can, however, be changed as the competition proceeds, provided that the officials are informed before the competitor is called to the platform.

The weight of the barbell is increased progressively during the competition. In general, the bar's weight is increased 5kg at a time, but a lifter can request an increase of 2.5kg over the last weight if he is making his final attempt. Increases as small as 0.5kg are permitted when making a record attempt.

A competitor who succeeds at any weight progresses to a higher weight for his next attempt. If he fails at any weight, he repeats that weight at his next attempt; it is not possible to go back to a lower weight.

Bodyweight categories
(maximum weights)
52kg
56kg
60kg
67.5kg
75kg
82.5kg
90kg
100kg
110kg
110kg +

Disk weights and colors
a 50kg green
b 25kg red
c 20kg blue
d 15kg yellow
e 10kg white
f 5kg
g 2.5kg
h 1.25kg
i 0.5kg
j 0.25kg

©DIAGRAM

WEIGHTLIFTING 2

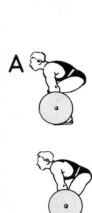

Lifting order The bodyweight categories are competed in sequence, from the lightest to the heaviest.

The order of the competitors within any category is determined as follows:

a) the lifter who stated the lowest weight for his first lift, lifts first;

b) if several competitors stated the same weight for their first lift, the order is determined by their drawn start number;

c) the weight of the barbell is then increased progressively and competitors take their turns as it reaches the weights chosen for their attempts;

d) if several competitors selected the same weight for an attempt, a first lift takes precedence over a second or third lift, and a second lift takes precedence over a third, otherwise, order is determined by the competitors' start numbers.

Announcement of lifts An appointed speaker announces the name of each lifter called to the platform, the country that the lifter represents, the weight on the barbell, and the number of his attempt.

Timing of lifts A total of 2 minutes is normally allowed to lifters from the calling of their name to the beginning of their attempt; there is a warning signal after 1 minute. This time limit is increased to 3 minutes if a lifter is making two lifts in succession.

If a lifter fails to lift the barbell from the platform within the time allowed, that particular attempt is eliminated.

THE LIFTS

General rules All lifts must be made with two hands. A lifter may use the technique known as hooking, in which the last joint of the thumb is covered at the moment of gripping with the fingers of the same hand.

In all lifts, the referee will count as a "no lift" any unfinished attempt in which the bar reaches knee height.

The lifter may replace the bar only after the chief referee's signal. He must then lower the bar in front of his body and must not let it drop either deliberately or accidentally. He may release his grip only after the barbell passes waist level.

When snatching or cleaning in the "squat" position, the lifter may help his recovery by swinging-rocking movements of his body.

A lifter who uses grease, oil, water, or any similar lubricant will be ordered to remove it; the jury will decide whether or not the clock is to be stopped for this.

The snatch (A) The bar is placed horizontally in front of the lifter's legs.

The lifter must grip the bar, palms down, and pull it in a single movement from the ground to the full extent of both arms above his head, while at the same time either "splitting" or bending his legs. The bar must pass with a continuous movement along the lifter's body, of which no part but the feet may touch the ground during the lift.

After fully extending his arms above his head, the lifter is allowed unlimited time to adjust his position (the "recovery"). He must then become motionless, with his arms and legs extended and his feet on the same line parallel to the plane of his trunk and the barbell. He must hold this position until the referee's signal to put the barbell down; this signal will be given as soon as the referee considers him to be motionless.

When lowering the barbell, the lifter must not turn over his wrists until the barbell has passed the top of his head.

The clean and jerk The two parts of this lift are here described under separate headings.

The clean (B) The bar is placed horizontally in front of the lifter's legs.

The lifter must grip the bar, palms down, and bring it in a single movement to his shoulders, while at the same time either "splitting" or bending his legs. During this continuous movement, the bar may slide along the lifter's thighs and lap but must not touch his chest before the final position.

In the final position the bar may rest either: on the collarbones; on the fully bent arms; or on the chest above the nipples. The lifter then has unlimited time to make a recovery, returning his feet to the same line parallel to the plane of his trunk and the barbell, and straightening his legs.

After the clean and before the jerk, the lifter is permitted to withdraw his thumbs or to "unhook" his fingers and thumbs, to lower the bar if it is placed too high and is impeding breathing or causing pain, or to change the width of his grip.

The jerk (C) The lifter must bend his legs and then must extend them while extending his arms to full stretch vertically. He is then allowed unlimited time to make a recovery, bringing his feet to the same line to remain motionless with arms and legs extended. As soon as he is motionless, the referee will signal him to put the barbell down.

No lifts A lift is invalid and the referees declare a "no lift" if the lifter makes any of the following incorrect movements (except where stated otherwise these apply both to the snatch and to the clean and jerk):

a) pulling from the "hang";
b) touching the ground with any part of the body other than the feet;
c) extending the arms unevenly or incompletely at the finish of the lift;
d) pausing while extending the arms;
e) finishing with a press-out;
f) bending and extending the arms during a recovery;
g) touching the area outside the platform with any part of the body;
h) replacing the bar on the platform before the referee's signal;
i) dropping the bar after the referee's signal to replace it;
j) failing to finish with the feet and the barbell in line and parallel to the plane of the trunk;
k) in the snatch, pausing during the lifting of the bar;
l) in the snatch, touching the head with the bar while finishing the lift;
m) in the clean, placing the bar on the chest before turning over the elbows;
n) in the clean, touching the thighs or knees with the elbows or upper arms;
o) in the jerk, failing to complete any apparent jerking effort (this includes lowering the body or bending the knees).

JUDGING AND SCORING

Judging The three referees decide whether a lift has been performed correctly. They announce their decision (usually by lights) after the lifter has replaced the barbell on the platform. If the majority approves the lift (white lights) it is a "good lift"; otherwise (red lights) it is a "no lift."

Scoring The snatch and the clean and jerk are won by the competitors lifting the heaviest weights in these lifts. There is also a combined winner—the competitor lifting the heaviest combined weight in the snatch and the clean and jerk.

If a tie occurs, the lighter competitor is ranked first. If the tied lifters weigh the same, both before and after the competition, they are classified as equal.

A lifter who makes a valid lift in only the snatch or the clean and jerk is eligible for a placing in whichever of these he succeeded, but is not eligible for a placing in the total. Points for his placing in the one type of lift count toward the team classification.

In major international championships, team classifications are determined by the following points system. In each bodyweight category, lifters score as follows for placings in the snatch, in the clean and jerk, and in the combined total: 12 points for first, 9 for second, 8 for third, 7 for fourth, 6 for fifth, 5 for sixth, 4 for seventh, 3 for eighth, 2 for ninth, and 1 for tenth.

If countries tie for a place, the one with most first places is classified first. If they have the same number of first places they are classified by the number of second places, and so on.

B

C

419

WRESTLING

HISTORY

Wrestling is one of the most basic forms of competition between individuals, and it can be traced back through ancient Greece, Egypt, Mesopotamia, and India, until it disappears in prehistory. The sport is now governed by the Fédération Internationale de Lutte Amateur (FILA), and two styles are currently included in the Olympic program – Greco-Roman and Freestyle.

SYNOPSIS

A competitor fights an opponent of similar weight, attempting to overcome him by applying certain permissible "holds." Some holds bring immediate victory, while others earn points according to a fixed scale, the accumulated total of which determines the winner at the end of the bout.

In Greco-Roman style wrestling there are restrictions on the use of the legs that do not apply in Freestyle.

COMPETITION AREA AND EQUIPMENT

Competition area The main feature of this is the mat, which is circular and 9m in diameter. There is a "passivity zone" (**a**) which is a red band 1m wide inside the circumference of the mat. The "central wrestling surface" (**b**) is the area 7m in diameter within the red band. There is an inner red band (**c**) 0.1m wide enclosing a circle 1m in diameter. A "protection surface" (**d**) or safety area surrounds the mat and must be 1.2–1.5m wide.

The mat may be covered in clean, disinfected canvas, or may be of a modern material with an integral surface. The mat and safety area are now usually made in one piece, and must in any case be of the same thickness.

To improve visibility the mat may be raised not more than 1.1m above the ground. In this case there must be a clear level space at least 2m wide outside the passivity zone, or else there must be a 45° ramp sloping to the ground on all sides.

Two opposite corners (**e**, **f**) are colored to correspond with the competitors' costumes: one red and one blue.

Weight categories
1: up to 48kg
2: up to 52kg
3: up to 57kg
4: up to 62kg
5: up to 68kg
6: up to 74kg
7: up to 82kg
8: up to 90kg
9: up to 100kg
10: over 100kg

Dress Competitors must wear a jock strap and a one-piece costume over it. The costume must cling to the body and extend to the middle of the thigh. One competitor wears a red costume and the other blue.

Suitable sports shoes that close firmly round the ankle and are without a heel or any metal part must be worn. There must be no rigid ends to the laces.

Reinforced headwear or ear-protectors are not allowed. Anything worn on the head must be made of an elastic fabric.

Light knee pads are allowed, but bandages on the wrists, arms, or ankles may only be worn in the case of injury and on a doctor's prescription.

Nothing, such as jewelry, that might cause injury to the other competitor may be worn. No grease or sticky matter may be applied to the body, nor may a competitor arrive at the mat already perspiring.

At the time of the weigh-in competitors must either be closely shaven or have a beard of several months' growth.

Competitors must have a handkerchief.

COMPETITORS AND OFFICIALS

Competitors' weight categories FILA weight categories, as used in the Olympics, are listed in the table.

Officials There are three officials: the referee, the judge, and the mat chairman. No two may be of the same nationality, nor may any of them officiate at bouts when a fellow countryman is competing. All three work together to evaluate play, but the mat chairman exercises overall control. The referee works on the mat and the other two observe from the side.

There is also a timekeeper.

The referee is responsible for the direct supervision of the competitors on the mat. He wears a blue sleeve on his right arm and a red sleeve on his left, so that by raising the appropriate arm he can indicate which competitor has scored points.

He starts and ends bouts by blowing a whistle, and may interrupt play where necessary. He declares the winner after the officials have finished their deliberations.

The judge keeps and signs the score sheet and also keeps a scoreboard that is visible to competitors and spectators. He watches play closely and participates in the evaluation of actions or holds. If he notices something that the referee has missed he draws attention to it by raising a red or blue bat, according to the color worn by the competitor who has scored or infringed the rules.

If the judge and referee are in agreement, their decision is valid even without reference to the mat chairman.

The mat chairman must carefully observe competitors, referee, and judge in order to evaluate the conduct of his subordinate officials and make a decision if they disagree. He may interrupt a bout to question the referee or judge on their reasons for making a decision.

Medical service Competition organizers provide a staff of doctors who check the contestants at the weigh-in with especial reference to contagious diseases.

The medical service may require the mat chairman to halt a bout if a competitor is in danger, and may declare a competitor unfit to continue.

PROCEDURE

Preliminary rounds At the weigh-in before the competition, competitors are divided into two groups (A and B) within each weight category, by the drawing of lots. They then draw lots a second time to determine the pairing-off within each group for the first round. Competitors are eliminated on suffering two defeats, and rounds continue until only three competitors remain within each group.

Finals The three leaders from group A now wrestle against their opposite numbers in group B to determine the first six places in their weight category. The competitor placed first in group A fights the one placed first in group B to determine first and second places overall. Those placed second in each group fight for third and fourth places overall, and those placed third, for fifth and sixth places.

©DIAGRAM

WRESTLING 2

Conduct of the bout On being called to the mat by name the competitors go to the appropriate corner according to the color of costume they were ordered to wear.
The referee then calls them to the inner circle and checks their dress, skin, and nails.
The contestants greet each other, shake hands, and are sent back to their corners.
The referee blows a whistle as the signal for them to approach each other and begin wrestling.
The bout is divided into two periods of three minutes each, with a one-minute rest break between. During the break a competitor may be attended and advised by his coach and masseur and must be wiped dry of sweat.
The second period also begins at the blast of the whistle.
The bout may be interrupted by the referee for a total of not more than three minutes on behalf of each competitor in each bout.
The bout may end before the expiry of the time limit in the event of one competitor achieving a victory by a "fall" or "technical superiority" (see below), or of injury or disqualification.
If however the bout runs to the full time limit, the end is signaled by the timekeeper striking a gong and the referee blowing his whistle at the conclusion of any action or hold then in progress.

SCORING

Types of points There are two types of points:
technical or activity points are awarded for the achievement of correct actions or holds during a bout, and may be used to decide the winner of that bout;
classification or positive points are awarded after the bout, according to the manner in which the bout was decided, and are used to determine a wrestler's placing in his group.

One technical point is awarded to a competitor:
a) who passes behind his opponent and brings him to the ground so that three parts of the opponent's body (for example one arm and both knees) touch the ground, and controls him there;
b) who applies a correct hold but without putting his opponent in danger of a "fall" (see below);
c) who by passing behind his opponent, holds and controls him on the mat;
d) who blocks his opponent with both arms outstretched;
e) who is prevented from completing a hold by his opponent using an illegal hold;
f) whose opponent flees from the central wrestling surface.

Two technical points are awarded to a competitor:
a) who applies a correct hold and puts his opponent in danger of a "fall";
b) who places his opponent in an "instantaneous fall" (ie causes him to roll across his shoulders on the mat);
c) whose opponent throws himself off the mat, in a position of danger, while escaping from a hold;
d) whose opponent rolls across his shoulders while applying a hold;
e) who blocks his opponent's hold despite already being in imminent danger of a "fall";
f) who almost executes a "major technical" hold (see below) but fails to bring his opponent directly into a position of danger of a "fall";
g) whose application of a hold is blocked by an illegal hold.

Four technical points are awarded for a "major technical" hold (**1**), which is defined as any hold by which the opponent is placed under tight control, loses all contact with the ground, is made to describe a broadly sweeping curve through the air, and is brought to the ground directly into a position of immediate danger of a "fall."

Victory by "technical superiority" A bout will be ended before the expiry of the time limit if and when one competitor is 12 technical points ahead of the other. The leader is then declared the winner.

Victory by a "fall" A bout will end immediately in victory for the competitor who imposes a "fall" (**2**) on his opponent. This is done by pinning him down, both shoulders in contact with the mat, for as long as it takes the referee to say silently to himself the word "tomber" (French for "fall") and strike the mat with his hand.

Withdrawal or disqualification A bout will end before the expiry of the time limit in the event of one competitor withdrawing or being disqualified, so leaving his opponent the winner.

Classification points or positive points are awarded to both competitors after the bout according to the following scale:

a) if the bout was decided by technical superiority, a "fall," injury, withdrawal, default, or disqualification (but see f, g, h below), the winner is awarded 4 points and the loser 0;

b) if the bout ended with a difference of 8 to 11 technical points between the competitors, the winner gains 3.5 classification points and the loser 0.5;

c) if the winner had a total of 8 to 11 technical points and the loser had 0, the winner gains 3.5 classification points and the loser 0;

d) If the bout ended with a difference of 1 to 7 technical points between the competitors, the winner gains 3 classification points and the loser 1;

e) if the winner had a total of 1 to 7 technical points and the loser had 0, the winner gains 3 classification points and the loser 0;

f) if the bout ended in a disqualification for passivity (failure to wrestle actively) and there was a difference of 8 technical points or more between the competitors, the winner is awarded 3.5 classification points and the loser 0.5;

g) if the bout ended in a disqualification for passivity and the winner had been awarded technical points, he gains 3 classification points and the loser 0;

h) if the bout ended in a disqualification for passivity and the winner had not earned any technical points, he gains 2 classification points and the loser 0.

No classification points are awarded to a competitor who is given a bye.

PROHIBITIONS AND PENALTIES

In Greco-Roman style wrestling a competitor may not grasp his opponent below the hips, or use his own legs to push, press, squeeze, or lift his opponent.

General prohibitions The following prohibitions apply to both Greco-Roman and Freestyle wrestling.

Illegal actions and holds Among the chief prohibitions, it is forbidden to do any of the following to an opponent:

a) bite;
b) pinch the skin;
c) twist the fingers or toes, or twist the arm through more than 90°;
d) pull the ears, genitals, or hair;
e) kick;
f) butt with the head (**3**);
g) strangle;
h) knee or elbow the stomach (**4**);
i) touch the face between the eyebrows and the mouth;
j) seize the foot other than at the upper part of the heel;
k) stretch the spinal column;
l) drop him on his head.

Penalties for illegal actions and holds For an illegal action or hold that does not prevent the completion of an action, one technical point is awarded to the offender's opponent.

For an illegal action or hold that is deliberate and prevents the completion of an action, two technical points are awarded to the offender's opponent.

If the offense amounts to a serious act of brutality the offender may be disqualified from the bout or from the whole competition.

Passivity Failure to wrestle in an active manner is forbidden.

Offenders will first be warned. If the offense amounts to fleeing the mat or fleeing a hold, the offender's opponent may be awarded one or two technical points.

On the second offense the offender will be placed in the "par terre" position (**5**). The opponent places his hands on the offender's back, and wrestling recommences at a blast of the referee's whistle.

YACHT RACING

HISTORY
The first recorded yacht race took place in England in 1661, between King Charles II and his brother, the Duke of York. The yachts were attended by the royal barge and kitchen-boat, and the King won the wager of £100.

Organized regattas and small boat sailing races are first recorded in the late nineteenth century; earlier yacht races had been private matches, arranged between the owners of large sea-going yachts. Inshore yacht racing has been included in the Olympic program since the first games of the modern series. The international governing body, the International Yacht Racing Union (IYRU) was founded in 1907.

SYNOPSIS
Using sail power only, competitors aim to complete a prescribed course in the shortest time. Rules described here are for inshore races sailed in daylight over a triangular course.

COMPETITORS AND OFFICIALS
Competitors The crew carried by a yacht is specified in her class rules. Crews for classes raced in Olympic Games are as listed.

Officials Races are controlled by a race committee, who are responsible for setting the course, and for supervising the starting and finishing lines. The control point may be a good vantage point ashore, or a committee boat anchored near the starting line.

Because no referee or umpires accompany the racing yachts, competitors are expected to acknowledge their own rule infringements and enter protests about those of other yachts. Protests are heard by a jury after the conclusion of the race, and may affect the result.

YACHTS AND EQUIPMENT
Yacht classes All yachts are either keel boats, dinghies, or catamarans. Keel boats and dinghies are further divided into classes. Class rules govern the measurements, shape, weight, buoyancy, and equipment of member yachts, and every yacht must have official certificates of conformity to class rules. There are many internationally recognized classes, but all are one of three kinds:

a) one design classes, in which all boats must be identical;

b) development class, which allows stated variations on the design;

c) formula class (for keel boats only), in which a number of measurements, such as length, draft, and sail area, are inserted into a complex formula to give a result that does not exceed a given limit.

A yacht must be maintained in accordance with her class rules, and alterations that would invalidate her certificate are prohibited.

A yacht may not eject or release from a container any substance (such as polymer) that might reduce the frictional resistance of her hull to the water.

Olympic classes The seven international classes currently eligible for the Olympic Games are as illustrated.

Equipment Required equipment for yachts is prescribed in class rules and in sailing instructions for a specific event. Usual equipment may include an anchor, racing and protest flags, sails with specified identifying inscriptions, and lifesaving equipment.

Ballast carried must conform with class rules, and must be in place the day before the race. Unless prescribed in the class rules, a yacht may not use any device, such as a trapeze or plank, to project a crewman's weight outboard.

Only manual power may be used unless class rules permit a power winch or windlass for weighing anchor after running aground or fouling an obstruction, or a power pump in an auxiliary yacht.

Dress The total weight of clothing or equipment worn by a competitor should not exceed 15kg when soaked with water, unless class rules specify a lesser or greater weight which may not exceed 20kg.

Soling (A)
Keel yacht
Length: 8.16m
Beam: 1.91m
Sail area: 23.22sq.m
(spinnaker carried)
Weight: 998kg
Construction: fiberglass
Crew: 3

Star (B)
Keel yacht
Length: 6.9m
Beam: 1.73m
Sail area: 26.47sq.m
Weight: 671.3kg
Construction: fiberglass
Crew: 2

Tornado (C)
Catamaran
Length: 6.096m
Beam: 3.048m
Sail area: 21.83sq.m
Minimum weight: 133.8kg
Construction: plywood or
fiberglass
Crew: 2

Flying Dutchman (D)
Centerboard dinghy
Length: 6.04m
Beam: 1.79m
Sail area: 18.76sq.m
Minimum weight: 174kg
Construction: molded
plywood or fiberglass
Crew: 2

470 (E)
Centerboard dinghy
Length: 4.70m
Beam: 1.27m
Sail area: 13.48sq.m
(spinnaker carried)
Weight: 118kg
Construction: fiberglass
Crew: 2

Finn (F)
Centerboard dinghy
Length: 4.50m
Beam: 1.51m
Sail area: 9.94sq.m
Minimum weight: 145kg
Construction: molded
plywood or fiberglass
Crew: 1

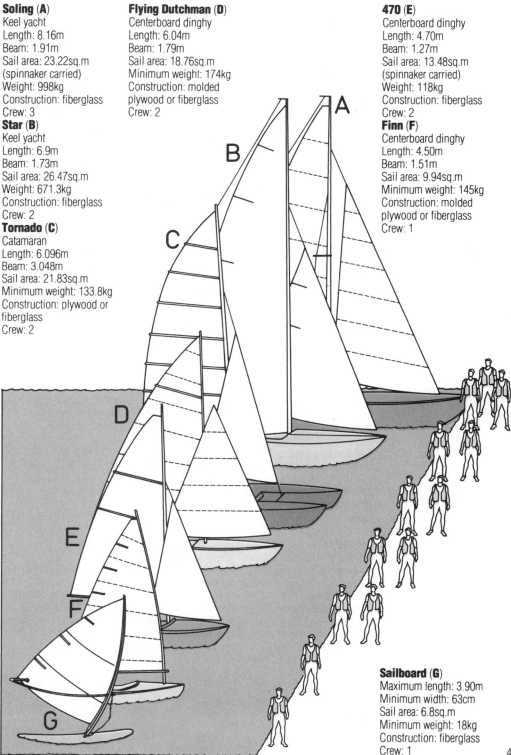

Sailboard (G)
Maximum length: 3.90m
Minimum width: 63cm
Sail area: 6.8sq.m
Minimum weight: 18kg
Construction: fiberglass
Crew: 1

©DIAGRAM

YACHT RACING 2

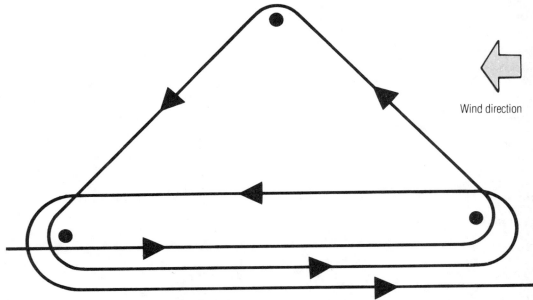

Wind direction

COURSE LAYOUT

Course There are no restrictions on the size or layout of the course. The course length and direction are determined by the race committee, who take into account local tide and weather conditions, the prevailing wind direction, and the class and numbers of the yachts taking part.

Most courses are triangular; a standard Olympic triangular course is illustrated. Turning points on a course are defined by marks (usually buoys) which must be rounded or passed in the correct order and on the required side.

If necessary, because of foul weather or insufficient wind, the race committee may use flag signals to indicate that the course is shortened or reversed, or that the race is canceled, postponed, or abandoned.

The starting line may be between two marks, a mark and a sighting post, or an extension from two starting posts. Race instructions may also define a starting area, which should be indicated by buoys.

The finishing line should be marked in the same way as the starting line.

DEFINITIONS

Leeward The leeward side of a yacht is that on which she is or, when head to wind, was carrying her mainsail.

Windward The windward side is the opposite side to the leeward side.

Luffing is altering course toward the wind until head to wind (**a**).

Gybing A yacht begins to gybe when, with the wind behind her, her mainsail crosses her center line. The gybe ends when the mainsail has filled on the other tack.

Bearing away is altering course away from the wind until the yacht begins to gybe (**b**).

Tacking is altering course from port (left) (**c**) to starboard (right) (**d**) tack, or vice versa, with the wind ahead. A yacht is tacking from the moment she is beyond head to wind until she has borne away to her course on the new tack.

On a tack A yacht is on a tack except when she is tacking or gybing. She is on the tack (port or starboard) corresponding to her windward side.

Wind direction

a    b 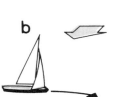   c   d

RACE PROCEDURE

Sailing the yacht A yacht may be propelled only by the natural action of wind on the sails and spars, and of water on the hull and underwater surfaces.

When suitable weather conditions exist, a competitor is permitted to surf or plane a yacht by means of a sudden movement of his body backward or forward ("ooching") or by not more than three rapidly repeated trims and releases of any sail ("pumping").

Sailing actions that are prohibited are:

a) repeated forceful movements of the helm ("sculling");

b) repeated pumping;

c) repeated ooching;

d) persistently rolling the yacht from side to side ("rocking");

e) persistent or rapidly repeated vertical or side-to-side body movements;

f) repeated gybing or roll-tacking in calm or near calm conditions.

Starting procedure Yachts maneuver in the starting area to be in a position to cross the line at the starting signal.

The starting signal is given by three flag signals, usually at five-minute intervals. The flag signals are:

a) the warning signal, when the flag indicating the class to race is hoisted;

b) the preparatory signal, when the code flag "P" (the "Blue Peter") is hoisted, or another distinctive signal is displayed;

c) the starting signal, when both flags are lowered.

Sound signals drawing attention to the flag signals are given with a gun or hooter, but the flag signals are always used for timing purposes.

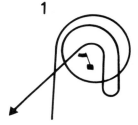

Starting prematurely Any yacht over the starting line at the starting signal must recross the line.

Where yachts have been allotted recall numbers, an individual premature start is signaled by displaying the offending yacht's recall number. Where no recall number has been allotted, the offending yacht may be recalled by lowering the class flag to half-mast, or by hailing her sail number. A general recall, if several unidentified yachts are over the line, is signaled by a special flag. All flag recall signals are accompanied by sound signals.

Failure of a yacht to see or hear her recall signal does not relieve her of the obligation to cross the starting line correctly.

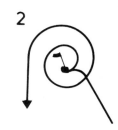

Rounding a mark A yacht must sail the course so that she rounds or passes each mark on the required side and in the correct sequence.

If a yacht passes a mark on the wrong side, she must return by that side and then round or pass the mark on the correct side (**1**).

If a yacht touches a mark, or causes a mark to move to avoid touching it, she must:

a) retire from the race at once; or

b) protest against another yacht for causing her offense; or

c) when the mark is surrounded by navigable water, absolve herself by completing her rounding of the mark and then re-rounding the same mark without touching it (**2**); or

d) when the mark is not surrounded by navigable water, absolve herself by completing her rounding, and then making a 360° turn at the first reasonable opportunity (**3**).

A yacht that touches a starting mark before she has officially started in the race must comply with one of the above alternatives after she has started racing.

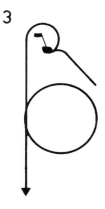

If a yacht touches a finishing mark, she is not considered to have completed the race until she has completed the rounding of the mark and crossed the finishing line again.

Giving room at a mark Providing that an overlap exists between the yachts when they are at least two boat lengths from a mark or obstruction, the yacht on the outside course must give room where possible to:

a) overlapping yachts on the same tack;

b) overlapping yachts on the same or opposite tacks going downwind.

This includes giving room for the inside yacht to tack or gybe if this is an integral part of the maneuver; the inside yacht must tack or gybe at the first opportunity.

Modified rules apply to yachts approaching the starting line before the starting signal has been given.

YACHT RACING 3

Overtaking A yacht is overtaking if she establishes an overlap from clear astern and is within two lengths' distance.

If the overtaking yacht tries to pass to leeward (**A**), the yacht ahead must keep clear and the overtaking yacht must give her room to do so. The overtaking yacht may not luff toward the windward yacht until she has gone clear past.

If the overtaking yacht tries to pass to windward (**B**), the overtaking yacht must keep clear. The yacht ahead may luff the overtaking yacht, and may even touch her provided that no serious damage results (the one exception to the "no collision" rule). The yacht ahead may carry the overtaking yacht to the wrong side of a sailing mark, provided that she also sails the wrong side.

A yacht may luff another only if she has the right to luff all the yachts that might be affected by her action – in which case they can all respond, even if an intervening yacht would not otherwise have had the right to luff.

All these rights cease as soon as the overtaking yacht's helmsman is ahead of the other yacht's mast (**C**).

Modified rules apply to yachts approaching the starting line before the starting signal has been given.

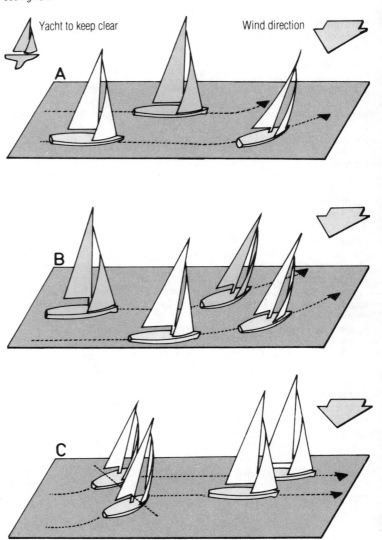

Yacht to keep clear   Wind direction

A

B

C

Right of way Several basic rules apply.

1) When yachts are on opposite tacks, the port tack yacht keeps clear.

2) When yachts are on the same tack, the windward yacht keeps clear.

3) When yachts are on the same tack and one is overtaking, the overtaking yacht keeps clear.

4) When one yacht is changing tack, that yacht keeps clear.

5) When both yachts are changing tack, the yacht on the other's port side keeps clear.

6) When one yacht is anchored, aground, or capsized, the yacht under way keeps clear.

If a yacht touches a mark and has to re-round it, or if a yacht is on the wrong side of the starting line at the starting signal, the yacht that is sailing incorrectly must keep clear of all yachts sailing correctly.

A yacht is permitted to hail a yacht on the same tack for room to tack to clear an obstruction.

Collisions If two yachts are on collision courses, the one that does not have the right of way must keep clear; if that yacht fails to take avoiding action the other yacht must also try to avoid collision. A right-of-way yacht that fails to make a reasonable attempt to avoid a collision may be disqualified as well as the other yacht.

A yacht with the right-of-way does not have complete freedom of maneuver; she must not alter course so that she prevents another yacht from keeping clear, nor obstruct a yacht that is keeping clear.

Where there is contact between the hulls, equipment, or crews of two yachts, both yachts are disqualified unless one of the yachts:

a) retires in acknowledgment of the infringement; or

b) absolves herself by accepting an alternative penalty;

c) registers a protest against another yacht for causing her offense.

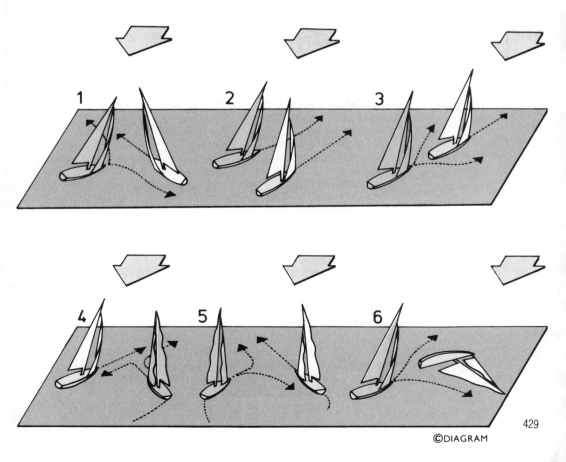

©DIAGRAM

YACHT RACING 4

PENALTIES AND SCORING

Infringements and protests When a yacht infringes rules or instructions, or causes another yacht to do so, she should retire immediately or observe such other penalty as may be imposed in the sailing instructions. If she fails to do either, then other yachts must still observe racing rules toward her.

The crew member in charge of any yacht finishing must sign a declaration that all rules have been observed and, within a time limit, enter any protests against other yachts. Before making a protest he must usually have flown a "protest flag" during the race and hailed the offending yacht that a protest would be made.

In national events, protests are heard by the race committee or a subcommittee; appeal is to the national authority. In international events, protests are heard by an IYRU jury; there is no appeal. Committees and juries may also instigate hearings where no protest has been made. The outcome of a hearing may penalize a different yacht, or invoke a different rule, from those in the original protest.

If the finishing position of a yacht is materially prejudiced by rendering assistance, being disabled when having the right of way, or by act or omission of the race committee, the race may be canceled or abandoned, or other arrangements made. In the Olympics, a yacht so prejudiced receives points equal to her average points (to the nearest one-tenth) for the other five races.

Penalties for acknowledged infringements During the race the penalty may be two full turns through 360°, clear of other yachts, and on the same leg of the course as the infringement.

Causing a collision always requires retirement.

After the race the penalty may be to score for finishing in a place worse than the actual finishing place by 20% of the number of starters (minimum of three places lower; maximum of one place less than the number of starters).

Penalties after a hearing for unacknowledged infringements include:

a) for an infringement of the sailing instructions, to score for finishing in a place worse than the actual finishing place by 30% of the number of starters;

b) disqualification from the race;

c) exclusion from the series;

d) for a gross infringement, the owner or helmsman or crewman in change may be disqualified from racing for a period of time.

Scoring In the Olympic Games and most major competitions, points are awarded as follows:

first place, 0 points;
second place, 3 points;
third place, 5.7 points;
fourth place, 8 points;
fifth place, 10 points;
sixth place, 11.7 points;
seventh place and below, place plus 6 points.

Yachts that do not finish, that sail the course incorrectly, or that retire after infringing the rules score the points for a last place finish.

Yachts disqualified, or infringing the rules and not retiring, score as for a last place finish plus points equal to 10% of the number of yachts starting.

Races are usually held in series. In the Olympic Games, there are seven races for each class, and each yacht counts her best six results for her total score. The yacht with the lowest points score is the winner.

BOARDSAILING

Triangle racing Sailboard races over a triangular course will be included in the 1984 Olympic Games. Sailboards raced must comply with the measurements given (see p. 425). Triangle races are sailed under IYRU rules, with some minor amendments. Races may be sailed in heats if so stipulated in the sailing instructions.

Competitors may be divided into groups depending on their bodyweight. Competitors weighing under 72kg in their first event of a racing season compete in the lightweight group; competitors weighing over 72kg compete in the heavyweight group. If, in subsequent events, the weight of a competitor in the lightweight group is found to exceed 75kg, he is transferred to the heavyweight group. If the weight of a competitor in the heavyweight group falls below 70kg, he is transferred to the lightweight group.

Other events are not, as yet, governed by an international body, but by individual class rules or by sailing instructions issued for a particular competition. Examples of different events are described below.

Slalom races are run on a knock-out basis over three laps of a course marked by six buoys. Two sailboards compete in each heat, with the winner going forward to the next round.

Ins and outs combine elements of slalom and triangle racing courses, and are laid out close to the shore, so that competitors must sail ''in and out'' through surf. Races are run as a series, with points awarded for positions.

Marathon races are long distance massed start races sailed in varying wind and water conditions.

Freestyle events are contested over two rounds. Competitors in the elimination round must perform a set series of tricks on their sailboards. The highest scoring competitors go forward to the second round, and perform a series of tricks of their own choice. Competitors are judged on the technical difficulty of their tricks, and the artistic merit of their performance.

©DIAGRAM